Communication Researchers and Policy-making

The MIT Press Sourcebooks

Communication Researchers and Policy-making

Edited by Sandra Braman

MIT Press Sourcebooks

The MIT Press
Cambridge, Massachusetts
London, England

This book was set in Sabon by SNP Best-set Typesetter Ltd., Hong Kong

Printed and bound in the United States of America.

Library of Congress Cataloging-in-Publication Data

Communication researchers and policy-making / edited by Sandra Braman.
    p. cm—(An MIT Press sourcebook)
  Includes bibliographical references and index.
  ISBN 0-262-52340-X (pbk. : alk. paper)
  1. Communication—Research—United States—History.
2. Communication policy—United States—History. I. Braman, Sandra.
II. Series.
P91.5.U5 C66 2003
302.2′0973′—dc21   2002043157

10   9   8   7   6   5   4   3   2   1

Contents

Acknowledgments

Professor John Brandl of the Humphrey Institute of Public Affairs at the University of Minnesota, with whom I studied during my doctoral work, provided an inspiration and served as a role model by combining significant service to both federal and state governments as well as teaching and research in academia. Thanks also go to the participants in the May 2001 workshop on the subject matter of this book: Pat Aufderheide, Andrew Blau, Carl Botan, Linda Garcia, Brian Kahin, Hans Klein, Katherine Montgomery, Eli Noam, Bryant Paul, Stuart Robbins, Hon. James Rosenbaum, Jorge Schement, Christopher Simpson, Ellen Wartella, Rolf Wigand, and Jonathan Zittrain. Brain Kahin and Eli Noam in particular have taken up the ball and run—Eli with panels on the topic at the Telecommunications Policy Research Conference and Brian with an NSF-funded workshop. Thanks also go to the Ford Foundation and Gigi Sohn for supporting the workshop in part, and to Becky Lentz of the Ford Foundation for partial support of follow-up efforts on my part. And of course both finally and first, it was the interest of Katherine Innis and Robert Prior in the project at the MIT Press that brought the book to life.

I thank the publishers listed below for their permission to reprint.

1   The Long View
Sandra Braman
Prepared for this volume.

2   Policy as a Research Context
Sandra Braman
Prepared for this volume.

3   The Study of Public Administration
Woodrow Wilson
From *Public Administration in the United States: A Reader*, John C.
Koritansky. Focus Publishing/R. Pullins Company, Inc. Reprinted with
permission. Originally published in the *Political Science Quarterly*, Vol.
II, June 1887.

4   The Policy Orientation
Harold Lasswell
From *The Policy Sciences*, Daniel Lerner and Harold Lasswell, editors,
pp. 3–15. Copyright © 1951 by the Board of Trustees of the Leland
Stanford Jr. University, renewed 1979. With the permission of Stanford
University Press, ⟨www.sup.org⟩.

5   National Information Policy
Donald Lamberton
Originally published in *The Annals of the American Academy of
Political and Social Science*, 412, pp. 145–151, 1974. Reprinted with
permission.

6   The Symbolic Uses of Effects: Notes on the Television Violence
Inquiries and the Legitimation of Mass Communications Research
Willard D. Rowland, Jr.
Reprinted by permission of Transaction Publishers. "The Symbolic Uses
of Effects," *Communication Yearbook 5*, edited by Michael Burgoon,
1981, 395–404. Copyright © 1981 by Transaction Publishers.

7   Pornography Research and Public Policy
Dolf Zillmann
Published in *Pornography: Research Advances and Policy
Considerations*, edited by Dolf Zillman and Jennings Bryant. Lawrence
Erlbaum Associates, 1989, 387–405. Reprinted with permission of
Lawrence Erlbaum Associates and the author.

8   Transforming Principles into Policy
Don R. LeDuc
Don R. LeDuc, "Transforming Principles into Policy," Journal of
Communication, 30(2), pages 196–202, 1980, by permission of Oxford
University Press and the author.

9   Government Regulation of "Adult" Businesses through Zoning and Anti-Nudity Ordinances: Debunking the Legal Myth of Negative Secondary Effects
Bryant Paul, Daniel Linz, and Bradley J. Shafer
Published in *Communication Law and Policy* 6, 2001, 355–392, Reprinted with permission of Lawrence Erlbaum Associates and the authors.

10   Facing Out: Researchers and Policy-makers
Sandra Braman
Prepared for this volume.

11   Obituary of an Agency
Fred W. Weingarten
Published in *Communication of the ACM*, V. 38:9, 1995, 29–33. Copyright © 1995 Association for Computing Machinery, Inc. Reprinted with permission.

12   U.S. Mass Communication Research, Counterinsurgency, and Scientific "Reality"
Christopher Simpson
In William S. Solomon and Robert M. McChesney (Eds.), *Ruthless Criticism: New Perspectives in U.S. Communication History*, 313–348. Minneapolis: University of Minnesota Press, 1993. Copyright © Christopher Simpson. Reprinted with permission.

13   From Radio Research to Communications Intelligence: Rockefeller Philanthropy, Communications Specialists, and the American Policy Community
William Buxton
Originally published in *Political Influence of Ideas: Policy Communities and Social Sciences*, edited by Stephen Brooks and Alain-G. Gagnon. Praeger: Westport, CT. 187–209. Copyright © 1994. Reproduced with permission of Greenwood Publishing Group, Inc., Westport CT.

14   A Novel Conference: The Origins of TPRC
Bruce M. Owen
Published in *Telephony, the Internet and the Media: Selected Papers from the 1997 TPRC*, edited by Jeffrey MacKie-Mason and David Waterman. Lawrence Erlbaum Associates, 1998, 1–11. Reprinted with permission of Lawrence Erlbaum Associates and the author.

Originally published in The University of Chicago Legal Forum, pp. 61–82, 1993. Reprinted with permission.

22 Social Science and Social Control
John Dewey
Originally published in *The New Republic*, July 31, 1931, pp. 276–277.

23 Remarks on Administrative and Critical Communications Research
Paul Felix Lazarsfeld
Originally published in *Studies in Philosophy and Social Sciences*, 9, 2–16, 1941.

24 Researchers at the Federal Trade Commission: Peril and Promise
Ivan L. Preston
In James H. Leigh and Claude R. Martin, Jr. (Eds.), *Current Issues of Research in Advertising*, 1–15. Ann Arbor: University of Michigan Press, 1980. Copyright 1980 by The University of Michigan. Reprinted with permission.

25 "Fraught with Such Great Possibilities": The Historical Relationship of Communication Research to Mass Media Regulation
Byron Reeves and James L. Baughman
Originally published in *Proceedings from the Tenth Annual TPRC*, edited by Oscar Gandy, Jr.. Ablex Publishing Corp, Norwood, NJ, 1983. 20–52. Copyright © 1983. Reproduced with permission of Greenwood Publishing Group, Inc., Westport CT.

26 Enduring Tensions and Lessons Learned
Sandra Braman
Prepared for this volume.

Communication Researchers and Policy-making

Introduction

Sandra Braman
2002

By the early 1980s it was widely recognized that medium-specific legal and economic categories for communications policy analysis were inadequate for an environment that had qualitatively changed as a result of technological innovation. Pool's influential book *Technologies of Freedom*[1] spelled the problem out as it manifested itself within the United States, and Bruce, Cunard, and Director[2] did the same for the international arena. For years, however, the policy—and research—response was to try to put the round peg in the square hole, as in the debate over whether cable should be considered more like television or more like telephony. The result was confusion, endless litigation, and ultimately exhaustion.

An alternative approach is to reconceptualize the telecommunications network as a critical form of infrastructure for all other social, economic, cultural, and political activity. Seminal video artist Nam June Paik first conceptualized the network as a superhighway in 1974,[3] and U.S. Senator Mark Hatfield introduced that notion into the policy setting in 1989, but it was only when Vice President Gore took up the language of an information superhighway in the early 1990s that attention began to turn away from the world defined by legacy law and towards the information environment as it was actually developing. Despite the many obvious problems in thinking of the national and global information infrastructure as a "highway," the rhetorical lift provided by the phrase brought about a sea change in both public and policy-making perceptions of what needed to be done. By the late 1990s, as a result, it had come to be understood that communications needed to be reconceptualized as a whole—across media, uses, and effects—to adequately develop policy for contemporary and future conditions. Today, a century after communication began to articulate itself as a distinct field among the social sciences, the task of thinking about just what communication is has essentially begun anew.

Despite the fact that the need to adapt the research agenda of the field of communication in response to technological change was similarly pointed out decades ago,[4] however, communication scholars have largely stood on the sidelines while the nature of the infrastructure has changed radically and transformations in regulatory stance have taken place. Research programs aimed at specific traditional types of communication policy issues—such as the effects of media violence on children—continued, but there has been relatively little attention to the more fundamental changes. As Eli Noam put it, "At the time communications was on the table of national policy . . . communications scholars absented themselves. . . ."[5]

The need for new conceptualizations of the communications environment to serve as a foundation for policy-making was the stimulus for recognition of communication policy as a distinct subfield in the 1970s.[6] As the final pieces of the global information infrastructure fall into place, there is now a hunger for new ways of thinking and the research to back them up. Thus this may be a unique opportunity for the community of researchers dealing with information, communication, and culture to reconnect with the policy community with significant and enduring effect. As the National Communication Association (NCA)[7] argued to the Supreme Court in its *amicus curiae* brief regarding the constitutionality of the Communications Decency Act, communication scholars are particularly well qualified to provide the kind of perspective on electronically mediated communication needed to resolve pressing policy problems.

Doing so would serve the field of communication as well. James Carey[8] joins economic historian Mark Blaug[9] in describing the 1930s as a "happy moment" for economics because the failure of economic thought to fully explain the Depression forced the field to advance theoretically, conceptually, and methodologically. The political hunger for a reconsideration of just what is meant by communication, what its effects are, how those effects differ by medium and content, and why those effects matter similarly makes this a happy moment for the field of communication: The pressing need should thus also be seen as an opportunity.

There was a time early in the twentieth century when communication was a foundational concept in sociology. That focus was lost by the 1940s as institutional justifications for the existence of communication as a distinct field came to dominate over theoretical justifications, and as absorption in broadcasting turned attention away from society and towards technology.[10] Peter Elliott[11] remarked in 1982 that despite endless discussion of the "information society" that conversation had not yet yielded a comprehensive theory of just how information, communication, and culture function in society—the same critique could be levied today. The failure is not only theoretical: as the salience of information infrastructure policy issues has gone up, the percentage of materials dealing with that infrastructure available to scholars has actually gone down.[12]

The century of communication research started with the policy-driven question of how best to persuade those who are citizens and those who are not to take the government's point of view. Since that time the number of policy questions that have been the subject of communication research has multiplied. The vast terrain of the field, however, has made it difficult to keep all such work simultaneously in view. Thus while the ability of the mass media to generate "nervousness" was the subject of study in the nineteenth century, and propaganda studies notoriously launched the twentieth, Bruce Owen[13] says that communications research input into policy-making began only in the 1950s with Ronald Coase's[14] paper on the economics of spectrum allocation.

Communication research intersects with—and is used by[15]—policy-making in multiple ways. Policy-making and governance can be studied as communicative processes in themselves, communication research can serve as inputs into policy-making about other types of policy issues, communication research can provide policy tools (as in communication campaigns) or be the very stuff of them (as in the funding of research to further the use of particular technologies), and communication research can be valuable as input into decision-making about the building, maintenance, regulation, and use of the information infrastructure itself. The emphasis here, though not exclusive, is on the last of these.

Work on this collection began with the expectation that perhaps a dozen or so items could be located that directly bear on the relationship between communication research and policy. At the point at which the search was stopped, hundreds of items had been found published between 1887 and 2001, and it was clear the list could have been expanded yet further. This body of literature is marked by three things:

1. It is self-reflexive. While scholars often try to remove themselves from their reports, these discussions of what happens when researchers try to bring the results of their work to the attention of policy-makers are driven by frustrations and, upon occasion, successes. For this reason they are also revelatory of the lives and working conditions of communication scholars, providing an almost unique autobiographical record that usefully complements the small amount of biographical work that has been undertaken in the field.[16]

2. The most influential communication scholars all felt compelled to contribute to this literature. A list of the authors who have written about the experience of trying to bring their work into the policy world comprises a "who's who" of the field. For graduate students who are wondering what it is (other than a job) that would make their work meaningful, or for junior scholars wondering just what they have gotten themselves into, this should be some inspiration. At one point or another in their careers, almost everyone whose work has endured has not only tried to see the results of his or her work operationalized through the mechanisms of policy—but considered the effort so fundamental to their identities as social scientists that they believed their evaluations of why those efforts succeeded or failed were worth sharing with others.

3. The range of policy issues in which communication scholars have become involved is vast. Certainly some issues (e.g., the effects on children of television violence) have received more attention than others (e.g., uses of telecommunications for purposes of community development). Those that have received a great deal of attention are usually a part of any introduction to the field offered in a graduate program and the work is therefore at least passingly familiar irrespective of individual specialization. In many more areas, however, awareness of relationships between researchers and policy-makers has been limited to those with a specialized interest. Despite the massive amount of funding devoted to health campaigns, for example—about the only type of social science research to receive significant national funding in the early twenty-first century—it is rarely included within discussions of policy-related communication research. We are familiar with the fact that the Federal Trade Commission (FTC) keeps an eye on fraudulent advertising, but few besides historians of advertising regulation are aware of the battles that took place to get the regulatory agency to actually look at research on people's reactions to advertising in making its determinations. One of the lessons of the literature introduced in this book, therefore, is that policy is not a specialized subfield but, rather, the context, and often ultimate motivation, for all of the work within the field whether expressed or not. For this reason, readings in the relationship between the communication research and policy communities would be a valuable accompaniment to graduate proseminar introductions to the field.

Out of the vast literature in this area, a collection of fifty pieces,[17] each introduced by an essay contextualizing the item relative to the policy issues under discussion, the research agenda and personal biography of the scholar involved, and the focal discussion of the book, was presented to a workshop on the relationship between communication research and policy at the International Communication Association (ICA) conference in Washington, DC, in May 2001 with support from the Ford Foundation. Further culling was necessary, however, to fit within a single volume. The items included here should thus be treated as exemplars chosen for the way in which they highlight fundamental issues; extensive references offer those interested a path deeper into the literature, and the essays introducing each section provide pointers to what may be of interest from particular perspectives.

Of course, history is not "merely" about the past; the historical problems discussed here are all pertinent to those who do research on communication, information, and culture today. But neither is the story of the past necessarily that of the future: By placing Homeland Security as an umbrella over many communication policy issues, a situation has been created in the United States and Europe in which the political nature of policy work may today provide an allure rather than a barrier. The story is not even necessarily linear; as Wilke[18] notes, even the history of social science research includes disruptions and detours.

Formal policy mechanisms are only one element within a broader legal field as understood in the Bourdieian sense. Privatization of many formerly public activities, the importance of policy networks that link public and private sector actors, informal aspects of decision-making processes, and the growing importance of other types of structural forces such as computer programming mark important limits to traditional policy analysis. Thus enabling research inputs into policy-making is also of value because it can help policy-makers trained in the formal apparatuses of government to grasp the other factors affecting the ways in which their decisions actually hit the ground.

While there was a great deal of effort on the part of the public interest advocacy community to affect the shape of the Telecommunications Act of 1996,[19] in the end there was very little influence on this rewrite of the Communications Act of 1934 from stakeholders other than large corporations and next to no research input. Just why this is so is a story that still desperately needs to be told. The analytical vacuum here highlights the importance of trying to understand what the barriers are between the research and policy communities. This is not just a question of the personal satisfaction of the researchers involved. Rather, it is a matter of national capacity, the resources available for use in resolving problems of societywide concern. When the knowledge represented by researchers is not used there are consequences at the national, community, and individual levels, for it is often only through research that the policy needs and the effects of policies in place can be brought into view—the only way, that is, to ensure that a genuine diversity of voices and the entire range of values of concern appear in the policy-making discourse. Research also plays a critically important role in developing alternative policy formulations, a matter of ever-increasing importance as the rate of innovation makes the nature of the information environment less and less familiar and the utility of traditional policy tools less and less clear.

Three stories unfold over the course of this collection, one via presence and two via absence. The story of the perceptions communication researchers have of their experiences in the course of efforts to find policy uses for the results of their work is directly observable. There is also the dramatic story of what is not there: although many academics have an influence on public policy through their work as consultants to corporations, I have not been able to find any published reports on the effects of that experience on the way in which they conduct research, the types of research questions chosen, the kinds of theories they find compelling, or their sense of responsibility to either academia or society at large. These are important questions, for the economic allure of corporate consulting draws many of the best minds away from participation in public policy discourse. Indeed, as Joseph Bailey noted when he invited researchers to submit their analyses to his then-employer, the Federal Communications Commission (FCC), in the mid-1990s, despite the request he did not expect a response because anyone capable of providing the kind of input being sought would already be committed to the corporate world via contract. Not only is the data produced and gathered by the private sector proprietary and thus unavailable for scholarly use—but so, apparently, are any thoughts about the implications of such involvement for academics despite the utility of such insights for younger scholars considering alternative career paths and for administrators trying to understand what has happened to their faculties. A third story is not told but is suggested here, and that is what might be learned by secondary analysis of those evaluations of communication policies and reports by the researchers involved in their formation and implementation that are available.

The collection begins by looking at trends in the relationship between the communication research and policy communities over the century plus during which it has itself been a subject of analysis, and goes on to look at the effects of policy as a context for research. Because an interest in the policy implications of research places one between two worlds, the book looks at the issues raised when the same individual faces in each direction, out (to policy) and in (to academia). After a look at problematics of the relationship that appear to be unresolvable, the book concludes by identifying those elements of the situation that can be successfully dealt with if today's researchers are willing to learn from those who have walked this road in the past. It is a sourcebook in three senses: it provides a catalogue of ways in which the communication research and policy communities can interact and the issues that arise when they do so; it offers a collection of primary material in the form of reports on efforts to form such relationships that spans time periods, subject matter, and policy venues; and it provides a running bibliography on pertinent literatures.

Notes

1. Ithiel de Sola Pool, *Technologies of Freedom*, Cambridge, MIT Press, 1983.
2. Robert R. Bruce, Jeffrey P. Cunard, and Mark D. Director, *From Telecommunications to Electronic Services: A Global Spectrum of Definitions, Boundary Lines and Structures*, Butterworth & Co., London, 1985.
3. Peter Weibel, The world as interface: Toward the construction of context-controlled event worlds, in Timothy Druckrey, ed, *Electronic Culture: Technology and Visual Representation*, Aperture, New York, 1996, pp. 338–51.
4. See, e.g., George Gerbner, Larry P. Gross, and William H. Melody, eds, *Communication Technology and Social Policy: Understanding the New "Cultural Revolution,"* Wiley, New York, 1973.
5. Eli M. Noam, Reconnecting communication studies with communications policy, *Journal of Communication*, 43(3) (1993): 199–206.
6. Ithiel de Sola Pool, The rise of communications policy research, *Journal of Communication*, 24: 2 (1974): 31–42.
7. National Communication Association, Brief *amicus curiae* of the Speech Communication Association in support of appellees-plaintiffs, *Janet Reno, et al., v. American Civil Liberties Union, et al.*, #96-511, 1996.
8. James W. Carey, The ambiguity of policy research: Social research on broadcasting, *Journal of Communication*, 28: 2 (1978): 114–19.
9. Mark Blaug, *Economic Theory in Retrospect*, 5th ed, Cambridge University Press, Cambridge, 1997.
10. John Durham Peters, Institutional sources of intellectual poverty in communication research, *Communication Research*, 13: 4 (1986): 527–59.
11. Peter Elliott, Intellectuals, the 'information society' and the disappearance of the public sphere, *Media, Culture & Society*, 4: 2 (1982): 243–53.
12. Bram Dov Abramson, personal communication, 2001; Dan Schiller, Information bypass: Research library access to U.S. telecommunications periodicals, *Journal of Communication*, 39: 3 (1989): 104–9.

13. Bruce M. Owen, A novel conference: The origins of TPRC, in Jeffrey K. MacKie-Mason and David Waterman, eds, *Telephony, the Internet, and the Media: Selected Papers from the 1997 Telecommunications Policy Research Conference*, Lawrence Erlbaum Associates, Mahwah, NJ, 1998, pp. 1–11.

14. Ronald H. Coase, The FCC, *Journal of Law and Economics*, 2 (1959): 1–40.

15. Carol Weiss, The many meanings of research utilisation, in *Social Science and Social Policy*, Allen and Unwin, London, 1994, pp. 31–40.

16. For biographical work on the field of communication, see Everette E. Dennis and Ellen Wartella, *American Communication Research: The Remembered History*, Lawrence Erlbaum Associates, Mahwah, NJ, 1996; Everett M. Rogers, *History of Communication Study*, Simon & Schuster, New York, 1997. There are a few pieces of directly autobiographical work, such as: Theodor W. Adorno, Scientific experiences of a European scholar in America, trans. Donald Fleming, in Donald Fleming and Bernard Bailyn, eds, *Perspectives in American History*, Vol. II, *The Intellectual Migration: Europe and America, 1930–1960*, Harvard University Press, Cambridge, MA, pp. 338–70; Paul F. Lazarsfeld, An episode in the history of social research: A memoir, in Fleming and Bailyn, *op cit.*, pp. 270–337; Samuel F. Stouffer, How these volumes came to be produced, in *The American Soldier: Adjustment During Army Life*, Princeton University Press, Princeton, NJ, 1949, pp. 3–53.

17. Sandra Braman (ed), *Communication Research and Policy: A Critical View*, Vol. I: 1887–1991 and Vol. II: 1991–2001. University of Alabama, Tuscaloosa, Ala., 2001.

18. Jürgen Wilke, Cinematography as a medium of communication: The promotion of research by the League of Nations and the role of Rudolf Arnheim, *European Journal of Communication*, 6(3) (1991): 337–53.

19. Patricia Aufderheide, *Communications policy and the public interest: The Telecommunications Act of 1996*, Guilford, New York, 1998.

1

The Long View

Sandra Braman

The relationship between communication research and policy has seen a number of changes over the past one hundred and thirty plus years from the first theoretical suggestion that such research might be useful to policy-makers, to a flush of infatuation with the possibilities of data as an input into policy-making, to the systematic efforts to include communication research in policy-making of the mid-twentieth century, to the de facto division of responsibilities between the facts offered by social scientists and the strategy offered by policy-makers of the 1970s, to the 1980s' erosion of faith in policy science.[1] By today, the pendulum has swung to the other extreme, with a distrust of social science on the part of policy-makers that can almost be characterized as know-nothingism.

Over time, often in waves of attention, there has been research on questions pertinent to policy issues as diverse as the effects of violence in the media, pornography, deceptive advertising, and universal access to the telecommunications network. Other types of questions have received relatively little attention, such as the impact of structural constraints on content diversity, social effects of governmental information collection and dissemination procedures, bandwidth limits as an entry barrier to content production, the tension between private and public control over privately owned interfaces with the public communications network, and mass media programming as socialization in governance. Across this broad terrain certain trends can be identified:

- the politics of the empirical;
- expansion of the domain;
- theory as a barrier;

- the value of comparison;
- the depoliticization effect of politics;
- the detachment of effects from social processes of originary concern; and
- the emergence of a "post-law" society.

The Politics of the Empirical

The methodological debates that have riven the social sciences over recent decades start from the critique that analyses of actual social conditions and what people do with them are "merely" empirical. Across the longer history of the nation-state, however, gathering such information has been among the most radical of all possible acts. When Lazarsfeld[2] introduced the distinction between critical and administrative research, empirical work was assumed to be a part of both. Such data remain valuable for those doing communication policy research from a critical perspective. Indeed, the growing disinclination on the part of policy-makers to rely upon social science research suggests the use of empirical data may be particularly important—and political—today.

The very word *statistics* is linguistic testimony to the birth of empirical research methods with the modern state and their development in the service of power. Shortly after the French Revolution leaders became aware that if they were to govern on behalf of the people they had to know about those people, and so statistical techniques and related research methods were developed at their behest.[3] Just what those techniques and methods were varied from state to state,[4] as did the way in which information collected was actually used for decision-making.[5] Such differences go far toward explaining differences among nation-states, even within Western Europe.[6]

Long after the modern nation-state appeared, the collection of empirical data retained its politically radical character. Marx relied upon it, Italian Fascists quashed it—and Lazarsfeld himself got his start working with a Viennese team that saw the results of its research into the social impact of unemployment literally burned in 1933 because of what it revealed about the conditions that enabled Hitler to come into power.[7]

Empirical data are often not welcome because the story they tell is not the story being put forward by those in power—data can put the lie to official claims, identify social issues the existence of which is otherwise denied, and bring to light entire populations whose needs have not been taken into account.

In the "post" condition, meaning post–9-11 as well as the post-modern, an additional political dimension of empirical work has appeared as a result of the increasing skew between the amounts and kinds of information the government can obtain about citizens as opposed to the amounts and kinds of information citizens can know about and offer to government. While Jeremy Bentham's concept of the panopticon characterized well information collection in the service of power under modernity, it is De Landa's[8] notion of the panspectron that better captures the situation under postmodernity. The panoptic condition opens with identification of a subject about which knowledge is desired and then arrays the tools of information collection about it. The panspectral condition, however, is one in which information is collected about everything all the time, with individual subjects becoming visible only when specific questions are asked.[9]

De Landa came up with his ideas about the panspectron in the course of looking at the National Security Agency (NSA). For years the NSA and related entities have sought the ability to surveil at will. Technological innovation had made that possible, but organizational inertia and political resistance kept that goal from being achieved. Now, new leadership within the security community has removed the first roadblock and the shock of 9-11 has, at least for the moment, removed the second. Other post–9-11 changes in policy, such as a reinterpretation of the Freedom of Information Act (FOIA) that broadened the national security exemption and dropped the requirement that agencies demonstrate possible harm from release of exemptible information to legally justify a refusal to release it, have made it more difficult for citizens to acquire information about their government. The same types of changes are under discussion within the European Union.

Other shifts in policy demonstrate the growing suspicion of the results of scholarly research among policy-makers and, therefore, a reluctance to accept the stories told by data. The Government Accounting Office

(GAO)—in effect the government's office manager—has told the National Science Foundation (NSF) to intervene in the scholarly review process to rationalize what the GAO sees as too messy. The Office of Management and Budget (OMB), which has had the mandate to develop rules for the information practices of federal agencies since the move toward "paperwork reduction" and the downsizing of government began in the late 1970s, told agencies in September 2001 that they may no longer rely upon any research results unless they have demonstrated their replicability internally. Preferably agencies should undertake that replication themselves before making any data-based policy decisions, a process so costly in resources and time and so difficult logistically that the requirement is likely to completely stop the making of policy in many areas altogether. Congress has voiced its desire that raw data should be interpreted "democratically," rather than by trained scholars with subject-specific as well as methodological expertise—a position to be distinguished from that of post-normal scientific attention to the values served by policy decisions about science and technology. Some empirical data that suggests reasons to question policies proposed by the White House, such as United States Geological Service (USGS) information regarding the impact of endangered species should drilling for oil take place in the Arctic, is being removed from government Web sites in an effort to keep policy-makers from using even the data that is already in their hands. Again, similar moves are taking place in Europe.

The combined effects of these trends are two: While the government can know more about citizens, citizens know less about the government. And the data produced by citizen-researchers is less and less welcome as an input into governmental decision-making processes. Empirical data remain highly political.

Expansion of the Domain

The domain of information and communication policy itself has expanded over time as a consequence of the increasing commodification of forms of information and culture, growing awareness that governance and governmentality as well as government should be the subjects of policy analysis, and through a perceptual shift in the range of activities of interest. The consequence is that the range of types of research questions and methodologies pertinent to policy analysis keeps growing as well.

Three different ways of conceptualizing the information economy have appeared, each adding to our understanding of the subject of information policy by focusing on a different dimension.[10] The earliest, from the 1960s, identifies this as an information economy because the percentage of informational goods and services relative to other kinds of *products* is growing. In the 1970s political economists began to describe this as an information economy because of changes in the way the economic *domain* is bound, having expanded through commodification of types of information never before commodified. And by the 1990s, network economists turned to a focus on shifts in the nature of economic *processes* as an explanation for why this should be understood as an information economy.[11] Each turn of this conceptual wheel brings into view additional types of policy issues that must be addressed even by those with a policy interest that is narrowly bound by economic concerns.

The history of communication research on policy-related issues has tracked shifts in the locus of structural activities that have affected the nature of the nation-state itself. Briefly stated, in the nineteenth century the assumption was that all policy questions were those of *government—* of the governments of nation-states as geopolitical entities that had complete domestic sovereignty and that entered into treaties with other nation-states to govern external relations. By the second half of the twentieth century, the loci of policy issues had expanded to include international organizations with significant structural power; and by the early 1980s, Rosenau[12] was able to describe relationships among the policy-making of nation-states as those of "cascading interdependence." As non-state actors such as non-governmental organizations (NGOs) and transnational corporations (TNCs) also came to play ever-larger roles in decision making with structural effects, it became clear that policy issues also arose out of *governance* practices that are government-like but are often carried out by non-state entities. With globalization came acknowledgment that culture itself is also a site of political struggle the outcomes of which provide a third set of structural loci;[13] Foucault[14] uses the term *governmentality* to refer to the cultural practices out of which policies arise. For those doing research on policy for information, communication, and culture all three are now subjects of study, with the result that formal policy-making processes and the policies that result from them comprise only a portion of the terrain of communication policy needing analysis and research.

There has been a long-standing habit of assuming that communication policy involved First Amendment interpretation and regulation of the mass media only. With the awareness of the transformation to an information society that marked the third stage of the informatization process beginning in the 1960s,[15] however, the vision began to broaden. Just as diverse, historically distinct strands in economics dealing with information have come together into the subfield of the economics of information,[16] so diverse strands of the law have come together into a comprehensive field to which the umbrella term *information policy* is coming into use. This broader domain, defined as including all policy dealing with information creation, processing, flows, and use,[17] includes such additional policy questions as treatment of innovation, education, language, the arts, cultural aspects of international trade, and the formation of a national memory (governmental records retention).[18] Some of that policy explicitly deals with information, communication, and culture and may, in a borrowing from sociologist Robert Merton, thus be described as manifest. Some, however, does so indirectly as a by-product of policy directed at other subjects, or as a consequence of interactions of other types of policies, and may be described as latent.[19]

Theory as a Barrier

The question of whether or not a policy orientation in research impedes or stimulates policy development is discussed in the section of the book dealing with the relationship of policy researchers to academia. A separate problem, however, is the way certain theoretical positions can in themselves serve as barriers to effective use of related research by policymakers. Bunker,[20] for example, presents the contentious suggestion that lawyers will not attend to the analysis of social trends if those undertaking such work fail to remain focused on fundamental constitutional issues.[21] Communication researchers often oversimplify the complexities of the negotiations in which policy-makers are involved[22] or other variables that affect the policy process[23] to such a degree that their suggestions are impracticable. Issue-oriented analysis often fails because it does not include attention to the institutions in which issues are embedded and about which they revolve.[24] It can be difficult for policy-makers to see the relevance of ideas that are presented as abstractions,[25] but failure to consider the wider intellectual frames within which specific policy issues are cast[26] can also void analyses of utility. Because it is necessary to translate the implications of theory into the language of politics[27] if the results of research are to be used effectively, mid-level theory is thus particularly important in the design of policy-related research and its presentation to the public.

Increasingly nuanced understandings of the ways in which those who receive messages actively construct meaning rather than being merely passive receptors have decreased the confidence with which predictions can be made about what the effects of any specific communication will be. This growing appreciation of the complexity of communication processes, the individuality of effects, and the multiplicity of variables involved has led many to simply throw up their hands when faced with the need to offer concrete policy suggestions.[28] Within the larger world of the social sciences, too, growing acknowledgment of the always-unique circumstances in which specific social processes unfold has had similar consequences. Theoretical pluralism has been one response, but like the interdisciplinary work with which it is often associated such a position vastly multiplies the intellectual problem faced by researchers. Chaos and related theories such as complex adaptive systems theory offer another way of thinking about the multiplicity of interactions among systems at the same, supra-, and infra- levels of analysis and expand the world of possible explanations to include nonlinear causal relations as well as those that are linear.[29] However, we are only beginning to master the analytical tools necessary to apply such ideas to social systems, and such theories explain only a small portion of what has historically appeared to be chaotic and uninterpretable.

The Value of Comparison

Many of the problems researchers face in effectively bringing the results of their work to policy-makers' attention are shared across national contexts. Personal issues the researcher must address to undertake the change of role from academic to policy advocate discussed by Hawkins[30] in Australian detail, for example, will be familiar to researchers everywhere. Similarly, the difficulties of translating policy ideals produced by theory into the messiness of the operationally real faced by Finnish broadcasters in the 1960s[31] will be found in every national context.

Other problems may appear to be nationally specific but still provide insights of value in other contexts. Indeed, looking across national borders may make it possible to see issues that internal blinders otherwise keep opaque. In the central planning environments of the Warsaw Pact countries under Soviet control, most types of communication research were actively discouraged[32] until and unless there was governmental purpose assigned.[33] While the United States still does not do classical centralized planning, recent management shifts within the government that include Office of Management and Budget (OMB) use of cost-benefit analysis to determine which regulatory activities are acceptable (including those involving information collection, processing, and access to that information) and the requirement that all agency activities develop and follow five-year plans with clearly defined objectives measurable by quantitative indicators are movements enough in the direction of central planning that they provide at least part of the explanation for the decline in interest in research inputs into policy-making. Jakubowicz's[34] report that the shift to market conditions in Poland in the 1990s was not enough to change long-standing habits regarding a reluctance by policy-makers to consider research inputs provides additional evidence that empirical data is not always the desideratum in environments in which the market is a key regulator.

Those in developing circumstances do face additional problems from the need to try to shape policy discourses unaccustomed to research inputs so that they are more welcoming,[35] the relative recency of national identity as an overweening variable in policy-making,[36] and the lack of experience with democracy itself quite aside from the desire to pursue certain policies within it.[37] It often takes a while for formerly colonial nations to realize they do not need to follow in the regulatory steps of those who had ruled them and thus to undertake the research necessary to develop approaches more appropriate to their own situations.[38] Such problems are even further exacerbated under conditions of conflict: As Tamari[39] explains, for example, the political need to emphasize the uniqueness of Palestinians has made it next to impossible to conduct sociological research that acknowledges features that society shares with others. The relatively small size of the communication research community in many countries means individuals may be called upon for insights outside their realm of expertise.[40] The very difficulty of gaining access to communication theory and research done elsewhere can be crippling for those in peripheral situations.[41] These features are also found to various degrees within North America and Western Europe as well at the subnational level as manifestations of internal center-periphery dependency relations and of the impact of culture on information policy. The paucity of expertise and access to information within marginalized communities makes it difficult even within the United States for communities to use communication policy for purposes of self-determination, for example, and the emphasis upon cultural difference in places such as the southern United States, for example, has more than once led to divergence from national practice in communications.[42]

There are also success stories from around the world from which much can be learned. Communication research has been usefully turned to the ends of political reform in France,[43] in Latin America,[44,45] and South Africa.[46] Advocacy communities in North America and Europe interested in protecting the public interest in communications policy may find it useful to study these examples for translation into their own circumstances, particularly as the self-help methodologies of South-South development assistance mature. Attention to policy as a tool of power[47] is turning attention in this direction again.

The question of the impact of communication research on international policy issues raises additional problems because the relationship of the researchers to power centers is so different[48] and because of the intercultural problems involved.[49] A review of these issues would be particularly valuable at this point in history because governance of the

Internet is increasingly moving to the global level via the Internet Corporation for Assigned Names and Numbers (ICANN) and other entities, but is beyond the scope of this book because of the uniqueness of the problems presented.

The Depoliticization Effect of Politics

Paradoxically, conducting research in a politicized environment can result in a depoliticization of research in the sense that debate turns away from policy-related questions and from policy-makers as a key audience. One of the most devastating forces detracting from the ability of communication researchers in the United States to influence policy has been the absorption in politics internal to the field to the exclusion of those in society at large. This has been to a large extent fueled by tensions along the lines of preference for quantitative versus qualitative research methodologies. As discussed before there is no necessary relationship between a research methodology and either theoretical or ideological position. In recent decades such a linkage has developed for sociological reasons, intertwining such issues with the question of whether one was for or agin' Marxism and, if for, the version to which one pledged allegiance.[50] The impact of Marxism and the Cold War (two related but distinct factors), academic versus social politics, and a lack of recognition that policies and policy tools can serve political ends have all manifested themselves in the relationship between communication research and policy.

Early in the twentieth century communication research was driven by moral concerns raised by the horrors of World War I, the need to incorporate immigrants into society, and issues raised for community survival under the pressures of industrialization. Just as the field was seeking legitimacy as a "science," however, the diffusion of Marxist ideas heightened sensitivity to the politics of researchers and the values promoted by or embedded within their work. Faced with the choice of becoming identified as political or as scientific and irrespective of choices made by particular individuals, the field as a whole went for the latter. In modeling itself on the natural sciences, communication turned away from acknowledgment of the way in which values inevitably color both how communication technologies are used and how they are studied. As Dewey[51] pointed out, however, this was a self-defeating move because for the natural sciences a "fact" is what is left after the human is removed, while the very point of the social sciences is to understand the human.

This dynamic was renewed in the 1970s as energies were diverted away from politics writ large (as a social matter) and towards politics writ small (as a matter internal to academic institutions). One vivid example: Early in the Clinton Administration a White House staffer trained in cultural studies and with the assignment of developing a position on cultural policy for the White House turned to the cultural studies faculty at the University of Illinois for advice about just what that policy should be. The group, then under the intellectual leadership of Larry Grossberg and the administrative leadership of Peter Garrett, refused to respond at all to the invitation to directly tell a sympathetic decision-maker inside the White House what policies the U.S. government ought to put in place on the basis of the theories they were promoting—and this despite the fact that the invitation came at a time when the topic of the Illinois group's ongoing faculty seminar was the intersection between cultural studies and policy—a willingness to make internal political moves, but not to belly up to the public bar, even when invited.

The role that the Cold War played in shaping the relationship between communication research and policy in the second half of the twentieth century is stunningly evident. Though most current members of the International Association of Media and Communication Research (IAMCR)[52] are unaware of it, the very existence of that association—for a long time the only genuinely international association in the field—is due to the decision by an intergovernmental organization (the United Nations Education, Science, and Cultural Organization, or UNESCO) to promote communication research as a policy tool in pursuit of the goal of bringing East and West closer together. The entire field of development communication, too, was motivated by Cold War concerns that led to the belief that certain types of communication campaigns would serve political as well as socioeconomic and cultural ends. Domestically, too, the Cold War drove much of the research agenda, though again not always in ways that were visible to or understood by most of those within the field.

The Detachment of Effects from Social Processes of Originary Concern

Beginning in the nineteenth century, research into the effects of communication was originally driven by concern about social processes and phenomena understood to be at least partially caused by the media. A familiar example is the effects of the media on children, motivated by the growth in violence among teenagers. Once launched, however, effects studies take on lives of their own. This happens whether or not the trigger problems are the only, or the most, important problems on the table and whether or not answers to the research questions are known. International news flow studies, for example, have an independent life even though the original question of the early 1970s—whether or not there was an imbalance in global news flow that requires redress to achieve political and economic equity—has long been answered. In addition, news flow research results are usually quite predictable, and the relative importance of traditional forms of news in political decision-making and action has declined relative to information gained from other media such as the internet.

The reasons for this are understandable—students follow in their professors' research traditions, and it is easier to work with well-developed concepts and methodologies than to struggle to develop one's own. They are not acceptable, however, because this detachment of effects studies from the social issues of originary concern has two effects of its own. First, it can stand in the way of refinement and adaptation of effects studies to reflect changes in the social context of ostensible concern; violence in America in the early twenty-first century, for example, takes different forms and many times is a response to different stimuli than in earlier periods. As Pool[53] notes, overgeneralization of effects manifested in specific historical and cultural conjunctures as if they reflected static and stable effects that endure across time and cultural settings is an endemic problem affecting the utility of effects studies for policy-makers.

Even more seriously, the fixation particular effects of long-standing research popularity inhibits the capacity to respond to new problems as they emerge. While behavioral violence on television remains a legitimate research concern, for example, another kind of violence has also appeared that will have serious political effect. The modeling of mob rule that has become so wildly popular on *Survivor*-type shows in which individuals are excluded from communities by vote on the basis of personality traits or specific unpopular actions is an extremely danger-ous intervention into society at a time when participatory democracy is already threatened. Yet this significant problem is not as yet receiving research attention. Issues raised by individual violence remain important, but habituation to their presence should not blind researchers to addi-tional social problems. The degradation of democratic process currently being modeled on television is of at least equal contemporary concern— perhaps greater, for should the very possibility of democratic process be lost, it will be even more difficult to deal with individual-level violence issues.

The Emergence of a Post-Law Society

There are a number of reasons why the contemporary environment might be described as "post-law," if by that one does not mean that the law disappears but rather that its relationships with other structural forces (e.g., computer programming) are undergoing change, as is the very rela-tionship of law and policy to the state. Factors contributing to the shift to a post-law society include the privatization of formerly public func-tions, the movement of the constitutional locus from the national to the international level, and the transfer of decision-making power from humans to machines.[54]

This does not mean that the time for policy-making, and thus for com-munication policy research, is past. New social forms do not replace but, rather, become layered over those that have come before.[55] The legal system of the nation-state will retain its logistical importance as a struc-tural force and its normative importance as the only venue in which general social concerns rather than those of special interests retain their importance in the value hierarchy. It does mean, however, that the rela-tionship between the legal system and the nation-state is undergoing a change, requiring those engaged in policy analysis to reconsider the subject of their studies as well as methodological invention to facilitate investigations that must cross levels of analysis and types of causal forces.

One of the effects of this transformation is that very often the most important decision making is the least democratic of all. The details of legal deals resolved by contract or in the course of private arbitration—the type of law that increasingly is the only law applicable to information sector arrangements among major corporations[56]—are not a matter of public record, nor is there any opportunity to provide public input or the results of communication research. When structural decisions are made via computer programming or hardware design they are also unavailable for any form of democratic input, despite the fact that those with technical skills making such decisions have no training in how to think about the social impact of what they do. Popular concern about this lack of access to social decision making that has moved to technical venues is in turn one of the reasons that there is a move toward what is called post-normal science that emphasizes the risks of science and therefore its political nature.[57]

This situation presents a threefold challenge to the communication researcher interested in policy-related questions:

1. There is a need to understand how structural decisions are actually being made irrespective of formal descriptions from legacy law. Lessig's[58] work provides an example of this.

2. Points of entry for policy analysis under conditions in which the most important structural decisions are not necessarily made by legal systems or by entities identifiable in traditional geopolitical terms must be identified. Political activists struggling with the World Trade Organization (WTO) and globalization processes provide examples of efforts to struggle with this problem though types of intervention that will actually successfully influence policy (other than the geographic locations in which decisions are made and the amount that must be spent on security for decision makers) have not yet been developed.

3. There is a need for those concerned about the social impact of information technologies to learn more about the technologies themselves so that they can enter conversations in the venues in which many of the most important decisions are being made. Robin Mansell[59] has provided

a role model for social scientists interested in communications policy issues by adding an engineering degree to her training in economics, political economy, and social theory and sitting at the table with engineers.

Discussion

While individual items in the literature on the relationship between communication research and policy report on specific cases of interactions, across the literature it is possible to see the relationship as a key element in the sociology of knowledge and in the evolution of the nature of the nation-state. There is an odd contradiction in the fact that precisely at the moment when the notion that "knowledge is power" has become so widely voiced that it is cliché, there are efforts from both sides—policy-makers as well as academics—to distance researchers from participation in policy-making processes. The institutional consequences of this are familiar—academic departments torn by schisms, a diversion of policy energies into art, and the sketchiest of contacts between the policy and research communities, often ephemeral. The cure, as is discussed throughout this book, is harder to locate than the problem. It includes but goes beyond institutional adaptations to the design of research agendas, reconsiderations of personal stance, sustained attention to interactions between theory and the gathering of empirical data, and the use of genre as a political tool.

Notes

1. A description of the role of social science at the launch of the bureaucratic welfare state is provided in Bjorn Wittrock and Peter Wagner, Social science and state developments: The structuration of discourse in the social sciences, in Stephen Brooks and Alain-G. Gagnon, eds, *Social Scientists, Policy, and the State*, Praeger, New York, 1990, pp. 113–138. Irving Louis Horowitz and James Everett Katz provide an analysis of the beginnings of the move away from optimism regarding the role that social science research can play in the formation of public policy in *Social Science and Public Policy in the United States*, Praeger, New York, 1976.

2. Paul F. Lazarsfeld, Remarks on administrative and critical communications research, *Studies in Philosophy and Social Sciences* 9 (1941): 2–16.

3. Peter Wagner, Carol H. Weiss, Bjorn Wittrock, and Hellmut Wollmann, eds, *Social Sciences and Modern States: National Experiences and Theoretical Crossroads*, Cambridge University Press, Cambridge, 1991; Wittrock and Wagner, *op cit*, Ref. 1.

4. Alain Desrosieres, *The Politics of Large Numbers: A History of Statistical Reasoning*, trans. by Camille Naish, Harvard University Press, Cambridge, 1998.

5. Yasheng Huang, Information, bureaucracy, and economic reforms in China and the Soviet Union, *World Politics* 47 (1994): 102–134; Bernard S. Silberman, *Cages of Reason: The Rise of the Rational State in France, Japan, the United States, and Great Britain*, University of Chicago Press, Chicago, 1993.

6. Liah Greenfeld, *Nationalism: Five Roads to Modernity*, Harvard University Press, Cambridge, 1992.

7. Helga Nowotny, Marienthal and after: Local historicity and the road to policy relevance, *Knowledge* 5 (1983): 169–192.

8. Manuel de Landa, *War in the Age of Intelligent Machines*, Zone, New York, 1991.

9. Brandon Hookway, *Pandemonium: The Rise of Predatory Locales in the Postwar World*, Princeton Architectural Press, Princeton, 1999.

10. Sandra Braman, The information economy: An evolution of approaches, in S. Macdonald and J. Nightingale, eds, *Information and Organisation*, Elsevier Science B. V., Amsterdam, 1999, pp. 109–125.

11. Sandra Braman, The right to create: Cultural policy in the fourth stage of the information society, *Gazette* 60, no. 1 (1998): 77–91.

12. James Rosenau, A pre-theory revisited? World politics in an era of cascading interdependence, *International Studies Quarterly* 28, no. 3 (1984): 245–306.

13. Immanuel Wallerstein, Culture as the ideological battleground of the modern world-system, in Mike Featherstone, ed, *Global Culture: Nationalism, Globalization and Modernity*, Sage, London, 1990, pp. 31–55.

14. Graham Burchell, Colin Gordon, and Peter Miller, eds, *The Foucault Effect: Studies in Governmentality*, University of Chicago Press, Chicago, 1991; Alan Hunt and Gary Wickham, *Foucault and Law: Towards a Sociology of Law as Governance*, Pluto Press, Boulder, CO, 1994.

15. Sandra Braman, Harmonization of systems: The third stage of the information society, *Journal of Communication* 43, no. 3 (1993): 133–140.

16. Donald M. Lamberton, ed, *The Economics of Communication & Information*, 2d ed, Edward Elgar Publishing, Northampton, MA, 1996; Donald M. Lamberton, Information economics research: Points of departure, *Information Economics and Policy* 10, no. 3 (1998): 325–331.

17. Sandra Braman, Defining information: An approach for policy-makers, *Telecommunications Policy* 13, no. 3 (1989): 233–242.

18. Sandra Braman, *Change of State: An Introduction to Information Policy*, The MIT Press, Cambridge, forthcoming.

19. Sandra Braman, The unique characteristics of information policy and their US consequences, in Virgil Blake and Renee Tjoumas, eds, *Information Literacies for the Twenty-first Century*, G. K. Hall, Boston, Mass., 1990, pp. 47–77.

20. Matthew Bunker, Imperial paradigms, First Amendment theory, legal interdisciplinarity and reductionism, *Communication Law & Policy* 3 (1998): 515–562.

21. "Contentious" because it could be a devastating critique, but "contendable" because it may well be that Bunker has not accurately read the work he critiques in this way simply because it does not present its policy assumptions in forms with which he is familiar.

22. William H. Dutton, The ecology of games in telecommunications policy, in Harvey M. Sapolsky, Rhonda J. Crane, W. Russell Neuman, and Eli M. Noam, eds, *The Telecommunications Revolution: Past, Present, and Future*, Routledge, London, 1992, pp. 65–88.

23. David L. Altheide, The impact of television formats on social policy, *Journal of Broadcasting & Electronic Media* 35: 1 (1991): 3–21; Bruce K. Berger, Private issues and public policy: Locating the corporate agenda in agenda-setting, *Journal of Public Relations Research* 13, no. 2 (2001): 91–126.

24. Robin E. Mansell, Is policy research an irrelevant exercise? The case of Canadian DBS planning, *Journal of Communication* 35, no. 2 (1985): 154–166.

25. See Shalini Venturelli, *Liberalizing European Telecommunications: Politics, Regulation, and the Public Sphere*, Oxford University Press, Oxford, 1999.

26. Thomas Streeter, Beyond freedom of speech and the public interest: The relevance of Critical Legal Studies to communications policy, *Journal of Communication* 40, no. 2 (1990): 43–63.

27. Timothy J. Brennan, Integrating communication theory into media policy: An economic perspective, *Telecommunications Policy* 16 (1992): 460–474.

28. Jostein Gripsrud, Cultural studies and intervention in television policy, *European Journal of Cultural Studies* 1: 1 (1998): 83–95.

29. Sandra Braman, The autopoietic state: Communication and democratic potential in the Net, *Journal of the American Society of Information Science* 45: 6 (1994): 358–368; Kenyon DeGreene, *The Adaptive Organization: Anticipation and Management of Crises*, Wiley Interscience, New York, 1982.

30. Gay Hawkins, Writing on the edge of history: Documenting cultural institutions, *Media Information Australia* 73 (August, 1994): 35–44.

31. Taisto Hujanen, Political versus cultural in critical broadcasting research and policy: A reevaluation of the Finnish radical experiment in broadcasting in the late 1960s, in John A. Lent, ed, *A Different Road Taken: Profiles in Critical Communication*, Westview Press, Boulder, Colo., 1995, pp. 257–268.

32. Karol Jakubowicz, Polish broadcasting studies in search of a raison d'être, *European Journal of Communication* 4, no. 3 (1989): 267–285. In Hungary, however, communication research became an explicit tool before the collapse of the Cold War, however, because of differences in institutional conditions; see Támas Szecskö, Communication research and policy in Hungary: Partners in planning, *Journal of Communication* 33, no. 3 (1983): 96–102. James Halloran describes the kind of collaboration seen in Hungary between communication researchers and policy-makers as one of the key points of difference between the East and the West during the Cold War period; see James D. Halloran, The context of mass communication research, in Emile McAnany, J. Schnitman, and N. Janus, eds, *Communication and Social Change*, Praeger, New York, 1981, pp. 21–57.

33. Ellen Mickiewicz, Policy applications of public opinion research in the Soviet Union, *The Public Opinion Quarterly* 36, no. 4 (1972–73): 566–578. Mickiewicz revisited the question of the use of public opinion research following the collapse of the Soviet Union and found less had changed than might have been predicted because of the allure of the marketplace on those who might have turned their research skills to public service ends; see Ellen Mickiewicz, The commercialization of scholarship in the former Soviet Union, *Slavic Review* 52, no. 1 (1993): 90–95.

34. Jakubowicz's findings paralleled those found by Mickiewicz in the early 1990s; see Karol Jakubowicz, Media development in central and eastern Europe: Challenges for research, Presented to the Joint Meeting of the Advisory Council and the College of Fellows, The European Institute for the Media, Düsseldorf, Germany, September 1995. Both communication scholars find support for their analyses in the broader picture presented by William M. Reisinger, Arthur H. Miller, and Vicki L. Hesli, Public behavior and political change in post-Soviet states, *The Journal of Politics* 57: 4 (1995): 941–971.

35. Cornelis B. Pratt and Jarol D. Manheim, Communication research and development policy: Agenda dynamics in an African setting, *Journal of Communication* 38, no. 3 (1988): 199–206.

36. Elijah F. Akhahenda, The imperative of national unity and the concept of press freedom: The case of East Africa, *Gazette* 31: 2 (1983): 89–98.

37. Cecil Blake, Democratization: The dominant imperative for national communication policies in Africa in the 21st century, *Gazette* 59, nos. 4/5 (1997): 253–269; Campbell Lyons and Tanya Lyons, Challenges posed by information and communication technologies for parliamentary democracy in South Africa, *Parliamentary Affairs* 52, no. 3 (1999): 442–450; Chris W. Ogbondah, Communication and democratization in Africa: Constitutional changes, prospects and persistent problems for the media, *Gazette* 59, nos. 4/5 (1997): 271–294; Frank Okwu Ogboajah, Drawing the curtain: Policy issues and communication research in West Africa, in Frank Okwu Ogboajah, ed, *Mass Communication, Culture and Society in West Africa*, Hans Zell Publishers, London, 1985, pp. 309–320.

38. Paul S. N. Lee, Policy process in the broadcasting services in Hong Kong, Presented to the International Communication Association, Chicago, May, 1991.

39. Salim Tamari, Problems of social science research in Palestine: An overview, *Current Sociology* 42, no. 2 (1994): 69–86.

40. Joseph Man Chan, Communication research in Hong Kong: Problematics, discoveries and directions, *Asian Journal of Communication* 2, no. 2 (1992): 134–167.

41. Slavko Splichal, Indigenization versus ideologization: Communication science on the periphery, *European Journal of Communication* 4, no. 3 (1989): 329–359.

42. Kenneth Lipartito, Systems in conflict: Bell confronts the American South, Presented to the International Communications Association, Chicago, May, 1991.

43. Armand Mattelart, Technology, culture, and communication: Research and policy priorities in France, *Journal of Communication* 33, no. 3 (1983): 59–73; Armand Mattelart and Jean-Marie Piemme, New means of communication: New questions for the left, *Media, Culture and Society* 2, no. 4 (1980): 321–338.

44. Elizabeth Fox, Communication research and media reform in South America, *Critical Studies in Mass Communication* 3, no. 2 (1986): 236–245; Elizabeth Fox, Communication media in Latin America, *Journal of Communication* 44: 4 (1994): 4–8; James Lull, Hybrids, fronts, borders: The challenge of cultural analysis in Mexico, *Cultural Studies* 1, no. 3 (1997): 405–418; Jesus Martin-Barbero, Latin America: Cultures in the communication media, *Journal of Communication* 43: 2 (1993): 18–30; Fernando Reyes Matta, The Latin American concept of news, *Journal of Communication* 29, no. 2 (1979): 164–171; Emile G. McAnany, Seminal ideas in Latin American critical communication research: An agenda for the North, in Rita Atwood and Emile G. McAnany, eds, *Communication and Latin American Society*, University of Wisconsin Press, Madison, 1986, pp. 28–47; Robert A. White, Cultural analysis in communication for development: The role of cultural dramaturgy in the creation of a public sphere, *Development* (April, 1990).

45. Elizabeth Fox, Communication research and media reform in South America, *Critical Studies in Mass Communication* 3: 2 (1986): 236–245; James Lull, Hybrids, fronts, borders: The challenge of cultural analysis in Mexico, *Cultural Studies* 1, no. 3 (1997): 405–418; Jesus Martin-Barbero, *Communication, Culture and Hegemony: From the Media to Mediations*, Sage Publications, Thousand Oaks, Calif., 1993.

46. Robert Horwitz, *Communication and Democratic Reform in South Africa*, Cambridge University Press, Cambridge, 2001.

47. See Stuart Cunningham, *Framing Culture: Criticism and Policy in Australia*, Allen & Unwin, Sydney, 1992; Stephen McDowell, The decline of the license raj:

Indian software export policies, *Journal of Communication* 45, no. 4 (1995): 25–50; Gerald Sussman, Transnational communications and the dependent-integrated state, *Journal of Communication* 45, no. 4 (1995): 90–105.

48. Alan Hancock, Communication policies, planning, and research in UNESCO: From the seventies to the nineties, in Cees J. Hamelink and Olga Linné, eds, *Mass Communication Research: On Problems and Policies*, Ablex Publishing Co., Norwood, N.J., 1994, pp. 21–37; Kaarle Nordenstreng, The UNESCO expert panel with the benefit of hindsight, in Hamelink and Linné, *op cit*, pp. 3–19; Ranjan Borra, Communication through television: UNESCO adult education experiments in France, Japan and India, *Journal of Communication* 20, no. 1 (1970): 65–83; Symphonie Experiment Study Group, A UNESCO experiment, *Journal of Communication* 28, no. 3 (1978): 149–156; Birgitta Ulvhammar, Consultation on collaborative research into the impact of new communication technologies in the perspective of the Medium Term Plan of UNESCO, *Nordicom Review* 1 (1986): 7–8; Tapio Varis, UNESCO research project on international flow of television programmes and news, *Nordicom Review* 2 (1982): 4–14.

49. Eric Michaels, Ask a foolish question: On the methodologies of cross cultural media research, *Australian Journal of Cultural Studies* 3, no. 2 (1985): 45–59.

50. John Durham Peters, Institutional Sources of Intellectual Poverty in Communication Research, *Communication Research* 13, no. 4 (1986): 527–559; Ellen Wartella, Communication research on children and public policy, in Philip Gaunt, ed, *Beyond Agendas: New Directions in Communication Research*, Greenwood Press, Westport, Conn., 1993, pp. 137–148.

51. John Dewey, Social science and social control, *The New Republic* July 28 (1931): 276–277.

52. This organization was known for many decades as the International Association for Mass Communication Research.

53. Ithiel de Sola Pool, The rise of communication policy research, *Journal of Communication* 24, no. 2 (1974): 31–42.

54. The impact of the transformation to a postlaw society on the making and effects of information policy is discussed in Braman, *Change of State, op cit*, Ref. 18.

55. Judith Goldstein, Ideas, institutions, and American trade policy, *International Organization* 42, no. 1 (1988): 179–217.

56. Yves Dezalay, The BIG BANG and the law: The internationalization and restructuration of the legal field, *Theory, Culture & Society* 7 (1990): 279–293.

57. Graham Murdock, Popular representation and post-normal science: The struggle over genetically modified foods, in Sandra Braman, ed, *The Metatechnologies of Information: Biotechnology and Digital Information Technologies*, Lawrence Erlbaum Associates, Mahwah, N.J., forthcoming.

58. Lawrence Lessig, *Code and Other Laws of Cyberspace*, Basic Books, New York, 1999.

59. Robin Mansell trained as an industrial economist, added to her intellectual repertoire political economy and sociology, and most recently has received a degree in electrical engineering because of her appreciation of the importance of technical knowledge to social, economic, and political policy concerns. This has enabled her to provide policy input into the premiere engineering society, IEEE, as well as to venues in which social scientists are more familiar.

I

Policy as a Research Context

2

Policy as a Research Context

Sandra Braman
2002

As with every other social practice, the context within which research takes place or towards which the results are directed provide both demands and limits. Policy was defined as a research context for communications even before the field per se existed. Articulations of the policy need for communication research have gone through several iterations in response to changing technological and political conditions. The policy context generates political issues that affect the logistics of how research results are acquired, perceived, and used. At the analytical stage, it must be remembered that data alone cannot provide solutions to normative problems nor determine which among available responses to policy questions would be best under specific circumstances.

The Need: Communication Research as an Input into Policy

In addition to serving as a resource for policy-making on matters dealing with the communication system, the value of communication research to understanding the communicative aspects of governmental decision making has been recognized since at least the late nineteenth century. This need has been articulated in iterations that reflect changes in technologies as well as in the political environment. The two types of research questions—involving the communicative aspects of decision making and the policy issues that arise in the effort to operationalize constitutional communication policy principles—were articulated at the point of the birth of the bureaucratic welfare state in the late nineteenth century. After World War II, the government took a more instrumental interest in communication that went beyond its constitutional role to pursue other ways in which it could serve governmental ends as explored via an expanded "policy science." Once the potential of networked computing began to be widely realized, a sense of the functions of communications as part of a governmental "brain" and of the nation-state as an informational organism led to additional types of policy research questions. Another iteration is needed to define a research agenda adequate for a situation in which much policy-making is the result of networks that bring together private- and public-sector decision-makers, the most important structural decision-making often occurs in arenas other than the formal processes of government, and the management of government itself has become de facto information policy.

Communication and the Birth of the Bureaucratic Welfare State
The study of public administration began in Europe in the eighteenth century but it was not until the late nineteenth century that it became a topic of discussion in the United States. Woodrow Wilson included what would today be called communication research in his original argument for policy studies that was introduced in 1887,[1] elaborated upon in a series of lectures at Johns Hopkins University in the 1890s, and experimented with over the course of his presidency.[2] The modes of thinking and practice launched by Wilson set much of the pattern in the United States for communication research devoted to or flowing from policy matters up until the Second World War.

Writing just as the nation-state in Europe and North America was developing its bureaucratic welfare form[3] and as the practices of professional administration first began to appear in both the public and private sectors,[4] Wilson argued for systematic study of policy-making for several reasons: Since the constitutional question of how to shape decision-making processes had been addressed, the next step for political theory was to turn to more detailed issues. The development of the bureaucratic form of the nation-state raised new types of regulatory problems, with the telegraph and postal systems serving as premiere examples. And while there was already a European tradition of the study of public administration, the problem must be taken up anew in the United States because the nature of the system was so different. Wilson outlined three roles for communication research in the world of policy-making: Polls of public opinion enable citizens to play the important function of critiquing government; data about social processes and phenomena could serve as informational bases for policy-making; and the study of communications among policy-makers should make it possible to improve decision-making processes. Enriching the education of policy-makers, he believed, was important so that they could take better advantage of the information with which they were presented.

Wilson experimented with these ideas during his presidency. He institutionalized the use of press conferences—despite his distaste for news—in pursuit of open government, and for the same reason called for "open covenants openly arrived at" during treaty negotiations at the close of World War I (it did not happen).[5] During the war, Wilson inaugurated the use of information policy in the service of foreign relations with his Committee for Public Information. Though that committee was headed by George Creel and included the U.S. secretaries of war, navy, and state, Wilson remained involved in a detailed way, reviewing proposals for operations and revising galley proofs of propaganda pamphlets prior to distribution.[6] It was also under Wilson that the War Department established the psychological warfare operations that became so important as a funding source for the new field of communication research as it developed after the war. He brought scholars to Washington to develop content for propaganda campaigns and ultimately distributed over 75 million pieces of printed material, most of it written by academics. (Even before the war many scholars had supported the notion of using propaganda in support of foreign policy, with intellectuals such as John Dewey, Thorstein Veblen, and Charles A. Beard among those volunteering to be "information specialists.") Following the war, Wilson further influenced information policy by promoting the international free flow of information so aggressively that Blanchard[7] called it "exporting the First Amendment." Doing so served both political and economic ends: While the concept of free flow provided a democratic mask for the United States as it ended its period of isolationism and entered world affairs, the notion also served to cut a path for activities of U.S.-based media and telecommunication corporations as they began to expand internationally. Domestically, Wilson began the process of centralization of government information[8] and upgrading the government's statistical capacity.[9]

Wilson's legacy contoured the ways in which research and information policy were to be intertwined for several decades. It was during his tenure that many universities established the centers for war propaganda that turned into the communication departments that launched the field, including those at the University of Illinois, the University of North Carolina, and the University of Chicago.[10] The practice of heavy government funding—not always made public—for learning how to communicate persuasively to domestic and foreign populations in pursuit of government goals was established. Meanwhile the habit of developing new communication policies for broadcasting and telecommunications *without* the input of researchers was also put into place, creating a situation in which it was later deemed acceptable for President Hoover to rely upon experts for input in many other areas of policymaking, but not to do so when it came to the Communications Act of 1934 and the formation of the Federal Communications Commission (FCC).[11]

Communication and the Expansion of Policy Science after World War II

The period following World War II saw an upsurge of interest in "policy science," driven by wartime experience in the management of complex and multifaceted enterprises, a moment of optimism by the war's victors that difficult problems could be solved, and the pragmatic needs associated with policy ambitions motivated positively by the desire to build a coherent global economy and negatively by the Cold War. Additional university departments and graduate programs were put into place and foundation support for communication research that had begun before the war expanded significantly.[12] The RAND Corporation, which today contributes to analyses of information warfare and the political effects of the Internet, became the first in what has now become a multitude of think tanks that provide another venue within which communication policy research takes place.[13] Several individuals claimed by the field of communication played important roles in the policy world during this period, including notably Paul Lazarsfeld, Daniel Lerner, and Harold Lasswell.

Lasswell earned the title of the "founder" of policy science with his 1951 definition of the subject as "the disciplines concerned with explaining the policy-making and policy-executing process, and with locating data and providing interpretations which are relevant to the policy problems of a given period."[14] Lasswell saw research as a way of maximizing the use of national resources, and of lengthening the gaze of often shortsighted policy-makers.[15] Like Wilson, he believed public opinion was a critical input into policy-making, and that the study of communications among decision makers was critical to understanding the nature of decision-making processes.[16] He added one more role for communication researchers that is of particular importance in the twenty-first century—expanding the range of possibilities contemplated by policy-makers.[17] Undertaking these responsibilities would serve the individuals involved as well as society in general, he argued, because doing so would enhance their professional status.

Lasswell was quite specific about the ways in which communication research can be useful at each stage of the policy-making process: (1) In the *intelligence* phase, public opinion research should be at the center of efforts to develop alternative policy concepts and tools. (2) During the *promotional* phase, communication research would be valuable in the dissemination of information. (3) Policy-makers seek relatively little help from researchers during the *prescriptive* phase, when they are crystallizing the norms that will be applied to a given situation. (4) There is also relatively little reliance upon research during the *invoking* phase, when a program is operationalized for a concrete situation, but Lasswell believed social science research could play a much larger role here. (5) Social science data is needed again during the *application* stage as administrators seek details about empirical circumstances with which they must deal. (6) Research may play a role in bringing about the *termination* phase. (7) The *appraisal* phase is heavily dependent upon social science research.[18] Contemporary researchers would expand on this by noting the value of the study of decision making during the prescriptive phase and the study of organizational communication during the invoking phase, and by adding the use of informational practices as policy tools in themselves.[19]

Lasswell was aware of the problems social scientists face in effectively influencing policy-making, including conflicts within society and within individuals over values.[20] There are conceptual confusions regarding the difference between specific historical events and general trends. "Index instability" is the lack of operational indexes that enable analytical terms to clearly refer to identifiable and stable referents, sometimes resulting from the failure of researchers to fully develop their concepts, and sometimes from the qualitative nature of concepts for which quantitative indicators are desired. And there are political issues—once researchers turn their work to the service of power (or it is turned for them), they in turn become political targets themselves. In response to these problems, Lasswell's mandates to those doing communication research included focusing on contemporary social issues, using interdisciplinary approaches, treating policy-makers themselves as subjects of research and sources of information, studying decision-making processes themselves, creating new institutional forms to bring academics and policy-makers together, and using models to communicate research results to policy-makers.[21] The model of the communication process that dominated for decades—Who says what in which channel to whom with what effect?—was developed to provide a structure for communication research devoted to policy ends.[22]

The communications research that received by far the greatest amount of research funding after World War II was the development of computing hardware, software, and networking technologies in projects remarkable for their consistent lack of input from the social sciences. Of subjects typically included in histories of the field of communication, the topic that received the most government funding for research was media campaigns for the purpose of diffusion of innovations. While work on persuasion after World War I focused on responding to an enemy, following World War II the emphasis was on educating populations in the developing world about agricultural and medical matters in the hopes of promoting the U.S.-style democracy with which these innovations were associated.

Communication and Policy in the Information Society

Early theorists of the information society outlined research agendas that often had direct policy implications. Machlup,[23] for example, attempted an exhaustive economic analysis of a dozen information industries, beginning with education (only five were complete by the time of his death). In the early 1980s Pool[24] examined the constitutional implications of the convergence of technologies that are the crux of the most important policy debates today. Numerous authors in the famous 1983 "ferment of the field" issue of *Journal of Communication*, at the time clearly the central journal of the field, used their space to talk about adapting existing research agendas to incorporate or respond to new technologies. Porat,[25] whose SIC code-based definition of the information economy was taken up by the U.S. Department of Commerce and subsequently by the rest of the world, also pointed out that the shift to an information economy meant those studying communication policy had to expand their purview to include attention to industries and activities relations previously not defined within the domain.

The research agenda put forward by Donald Lamberton[26] stands out as an exemplar because of the role he has played in bringing together disparate strands of work on informational issues within economics into the subfield of the economics of information.[27] Focusing on one among the functions of communication research noted by Wilson and Lasswell—that of providing informational inputs to decision makers— Lamberton's perspective is also valuable for its relatively grounded articulation of a vision that holds great power today. In its most extreme form, the notion of a "national information policy" appears as a "world brain"[28] or "artificial social intelligence"[29] that is science fiction–like in its utopian versions—and dystopian for those who fear the negative impacts on the quality of decision making that results from undue speed first noted with the telegraph.[30] What Lamberton more realistically suggests is in essence a management information system for the government that simply makes the statistical and data collection practices associated with the nation-state from its beginnings more comprehensive and systematic. Computerization began to draw attention to this possibility,[31] the advent of parallel processing renewed interest,[32] and it is of focal concern in the Homeland Security environment of the early twenty-first century.

Other elements of a research agenda stimulated by the development of the information society include attention to organizational questions such as the nature of computer-supported cooperative work (CSCW), the effects of what has come to be known as the "digital divide," and a transfer of some of the familiar types of effects studies from television to the Net. The problem of government research funds going to the making of technologies but not to understanding the ways in which they are used and their effects remains. Even when large-scale projects have included the study of social aspects in their proposals, once funding is received social scientists have tended to be pushed aside in favor of devoting all resources to engineering and software development.[33]

Communication Research for the Informational State

The role of communication research in policy-making of course changes with evolution of the nature of the state. Discussion of the role of communication research and policy began with the late nineteenth century emergence of the bureaucratic state. In the 1970s, commentators began to note that this form of the state had begun to wane, to be replaced by the early twenty-first century with the informational state.[34] This type of political organization is characterized by its information intensity and by its use of informational power; that is, the exercise of power through control over the informational bases of the material tools and weapons, the rules and institutions, and the symbols and discourse through which other forms of power are manifested. Decision-making in the informational state is characterized—as is the information economy—by network forms that link multiple types of entities in ways that blur institutional boundaries.[35]

There are implications of this change not only for the communication policy research agenda, but also for relationships between communication researchers and policy-makers. The privatization of many public sector activities, the growing importance of policy networks that include members of both the private and public sectors, and the importance of nongovernmental forms of structural decision-making such as those that take place in technical standard-setting discussions and in the very design of the information infrastructure and the computer code that runs it all point to the need to build relationships with private decision-makers as well as public. While historically the term "policy" was reserved for public sector decision-making and the term "strategy" for private, today that distinction no longer holds. These modes of decision-making will be even more difficult to access with the results of social science research, however, for they are not democratic in nature. A few of the decision-making venues, such as those for standard-setting, are still formal, but many of the arenas in which these types of policies are being made are informal and thus are problematic from the outside to even identify, let alone enter.

The increasing information-intensity of government raises another parallel between governance and economics. For economists, "primary," or "final" products are those goods and services that are available to consumers in commodity form; books, films, and software for personal computers are final goods in the information sector. "Secondary" products, on the other hand, are those goods and services that are used in the course of the production of final goods; statistical data and computer programs that run production equipment are examples from the information sector. The distinction has been important in economics because efforts to evaluate the proportion of the economy that is informational began by identifying only those industries that produced final informational products; only recently has the field begun to grapple with the need to include secondary informational goods and services as well. As society becomes increasingly information-intensive, the relative proportion of economic activity devoted to informational secondary goods is growing, though few are aware of the software embedded in many everyday objects such as refrigerators and automobiles.

The same distinction is important to identifying sites of information policy-making within government. Historically, analytical attention has been devoted to what can be described as "final" communication policies—those that are available for public "consumption" in the form of laws, regulations, and court decisions. The increasing information-intensity of government combined with the growing tendency to manage government according to principles used in management of profit-oriented corporations, however, has made what can be described as "secondary" communication policies increasingly important as the frame within which primary, or final, communication policies take their effect. These secondary information and communication policies are inputs into—and structural constraints upon—final policies and the way in which they are implemented.

These secondary communication policies can sometimes have profound effect. The Office of Management and Budget (OMB) provides a dramatic case, for the requirement that all federal agencies comply with its mandates regarding the cost-effectiveness of all information collection, processing, and access provides that agency with the opportunity to rewrite the informational elements of all other federal agencies. Should the OMB, for example, decide that it is not cost-effective to collect information on the health and educational circumstances of the children of migrant farm workers, that information will not be collected, with the policy effect of erasing that population from the view of policy-makers altogether. Once such a decision has been made, the "communication policy" issue of the access to government information mandated by the Freedom of Information Act (FOIA) becomes moot. The contracting out of a variety of information-related services from the government to the private sector[36] similarly transforms the criteria by which fundamental communication policy issues are made. The domain of secondary information and communication policy has not historically been within the purview of other than communication researchers with very specialized tastes. A redefinition of the policy domain to include these matters, however, points to an additional broadening of the problem necessary for those communication researchers who hope that their work will have some influence on policy decisions.

The Politics: Policy Uses of Communication Research

Whatever it is that communication researchers would *like* to see happen to their work once it comes onto the policy screen, politicians will use research processes and results to serve their own ends. Political dynamics can enter into the research process at multiple points: determining where funding will go, designing the ways in which research is incorporated into decision-making processes, and in interpretation of the results.

The general population has become keenly aware of the politics of policy use of research as part of the growing awareness that technological change often increases risk rather than improving conditions. The question was first raised during the Vietnam War when the devotion of some university-based researchers to military ends was questioned. More recently, environmental problems exacerbated by fears of the effects of the genetically modified organisms produced by biotechnology have made arguments for post-normal science a matter of public debate. The impacts of policies put into place on the basis of scientific research are often difficult to assess because of the complexity of the systems into which they are introduced, the length of the causal chains involved, and the imperceptibility of effects when those causal chains extend over long periods of time or across the perceptual borders of the statistical mechanisms of nation-states.[37] As a consequence, nonscientists increasingly argue that the uncertainty and provisionality of scientific claims severely weakens their credibility and leads to the conclusion that any choice by policy-makers to rely upon a particular set of research results must be due to political choices and value orientations rather than the evidentiary value of the data. Some suggest that under such conditions interpretation of research data and decisions about how it should be used should be a democratic matter rather than being reserved for experts, while others use this problem as an opportunity to reject research altogether in favor of a return to decision-making based exclusively on religious thought.

Dysfunctional effects of the use of new information technologies, including the loss in productivity many organizations experience when they take up innovations, the deskilling experienced by both adults and children, and exacerbation of socioeconomic, cultural, linguistic, and geographic class lines as a result of differential access have the potential of bringing post-normal science debates into the communication policy conversation but have not yet done so other than in occasional references to what is popularly referred to as the "digital divide" and concern about protecting children from Net-enabled forms of abuse. The politics of the use of research results by policy-makers and the ways in which attention to research can be designed into policy-making processes to serve political ends, however, have received some attention.

The Politics of Policy Use of Research Results
While within academia disagreements regarding research questions, methodologies, and interpretation of research results are considered healthy evidence of lively and appropriate intellectual debate, policy-

makers often take the same phenomena as proof that social scientists really do not know anything at all. Unwelcome results may be ridiculed, the replicability of results questioned, and counterstudies commissioned. If access to documents not publicly available was a part of the research process, the response to unwelcome findings may be a refusal to allow results to be published. If research that is conducted by entities within government produces results that are politically unwelcome, the agencies responsible may lose their funding altogether.[38] In the first years of the twenty-first century, conflicts over environmental policy have led to accusations that even Cabinet-level officials will actually ignore or completely misrepresent the results of research in order to serve White House policy goals; government employees who have posted research findings that run counter to the Bush Administration's interests have lost their jobs and found their Web sites shut down.

The most detailed study of these politics as applied to communication research has been offered by Rowland,[39] who examined the policy response to disagreements among researchers studying the effects of TV violence in depth. He reports that research undertaken by parents and scholars tended to find negative effects of TV violence on children, while research funded by media corporations tended to find positive effects. Looking at this, congressional leaders fearful of offending the media out of concern over the nature of coverage during election campaigns took the position that it was as a result impossible to know what the effects were and therefore chose to do next to nothing at all. Rowland also points out that the nature and extent of political uses of communication research are completely beyond the control of the researchers themselves. On this others agree; irrespective of a researcher's purpose, all results will be used by policy-makers for their own purposes, and in their own ways.[40]

The Politics of the Policy Process

Research can be a political tool in the course of policy-making processes when it is used to:

- slow down or delay decision making altogether,
- legitimate a decision already made, or

• provide a surrogate for public opinion or consent regarding a contested issue.

An early twenty-first-century example of this problem of great concern is the use of public opinion survey results that illustrate the continuing diffusion of access to the Internet to justify abandonment of policies designed to support experimentation with new information technologies for purposes of community development and other efforts to erase what is popularly referred to as the "digital divide." (Such diffusion does not provide the argument needed for this policy shift because there are multiple points along the diffusion curve during which policy inputs are valuable or even necessary in accordance with certain policy goals.) Awareness of this problem, however, has been expressed only anecdotally; there is as yet no research that details such misuses and abuses of the work of communication researchers.

Zillmann's[41] description of the problems that arose during policy-making on pornography thus stands out as an exemplar of the utility of analysis of the very incorporation of research into the policy process itself. Though original research and syntheses of existing work were commissioned by a group with responsibility for generating recommendations for policy responses to pornography, the results of the commissioned work did not reach policy-makers until *after* a decision had been made. In addition, many critiqued the research panels as having been comprised on political rather than intellectual grounds. The fact that researchers did not agree in their findings made it easier for politicians to dismiss results with implications they did not like. On the basis of this experience, Zillmann offers the useful, if not always practicable, suggestion that identifying policy problems, evaluating research, and making policy recommendations should be separated out as functions to be handled by different committees rather than being comingled in the tasks assigned to one.

The Ideas: Policy-Makers and Scholarship

The attempt to relate the results of communication research to policy adds a series of intellectual problems as well. The need to translate theories and research results into lay terms is not only a genre issue, for to do successful translation the researcher must also have a clear conceptual grasp of the landscapes of both popular and policy-making discourses. Policy discourse is defined by Rein and Schon as "the interactions of individuals, interest groups, social movements, and institutions through which problematic situations are converted to policy problems, agendas are set, decisions are made, and actions are taken."[42] Its analysis is growing in popularity: There are theories of policy networks as discourse coalitions,[43] arguments for improving planning processes by treating them as discursive environments,[44] and the suggestion that the real impact of research results on policy-making is discourse structuration.[45] Despite all this talk, however, there is a disjuncture between analysis of policy discourse by scholars and the use of what is learned from such analyses in the design of presentation of research results to policy-makers or in advocacy work.

Contributing to the education of policy-makers so that they can better appreciate and use the results of social science research demands that those in communication learn to link their work to the disciplines in which policy-makers are trained, largely political science, the law, and economics. To be effective communication researchers entering the world of public decision making must also have a clear sense of policy-making processes in themselves.[46] Meanwhile the demands of rigorous research remain in place—just as bad cases make bad law, so bad research makes bad policy.

Translating Ideas into Policy

Academic researchers thinking about policy matters live in a world very different from the one in which policy operates. There can be many a slip between the abstractions of academia and the realities of daily political life. Even when evaluations of the effects of communication policies are undertaken, they rarely explore the paths by which effects reported had derived from specific policies.

Hujanen[47] thus provides a rare detailed case study of the difficulties faced during efforts to translate theoretically based policies into operationally messy practice by Finnish broadcasters in the 1960s. This work provides a model of the kind of analysis that might be done because it is multidimensional, examining conceptual, political, financial, and logistical factors that led to the failure of what was considered at the time to be a radical experiment in broadcasting—an effort to reverse what was perceived as an audience that was increasingly alienated from politics by providing more information. When Hujanen looked back in the 1990s, there were additional lessons to be learned from this experiment about the dangers of paternalistic policy-making, treatment of the audience as passive rather than active, and the need to consider form as well as content in media regulation.

Many communication researchers fail in efforts to influence policy because they do not understand that policy-making is informal as well as formal and that the questions are different at various stages of the policy process. Researchers often do not appropriately match the level of abstraction of their results with the level of activity towards which those arguments are directed—regulators concerned about regulation of telecommunications pricing simply are not thinking in terms of the Kantian categorical imperative. The structures of the law itself, too, can provide barriers to the translation of theories into policy principles, as does the medium-driven orientation of legacy communication law and regulation.

Finally, researchers may step on their own feet by mixing normative with objective claims in the presentation of their work. In the years leading up to Zillman's engagement with the policy world discussed before, he and his coauthor Jennings Bryant took part in an extended dispute with critics of their work made public in a series of articles in the *Journal of Communication* marked by its vituperative nature. Ritchie's[48] rhetorical analysis of this debate suggests it was launched by the replacement of factual with moral claims and by open advocacy of specific policy positions in the original Zillmann and Bryant[49] piece. Ritchie uses the debate as a case study to illustrate his larger point that the value of social science research publications—to policy-makers as well as scholars—would be increased if there were more attention to their rhetorical nature. In the debate over pornography research, he argues, the implicit taboo against discussion of rhetorical choices in social science literature made it difficult to clarify rhetorical and methodological issues in either critiques or the responses to them.

Translating Ideas into Policy-related Research

Often the hard part is figuring out just what research might be useful. Telecommunications service providers regularly measure "quality of service" by looking at a standard set of indicators, but Mueller and Schement[50] found that completely different kinds of questions needed to be asked to understand the social processes and concerns behind the usage behaviors observed. Some problems derive from the need to respond to criteria put into place by the policy audience itself. There is the frustration that has been voiced since the earliest periods of experimentation with the systematic analysis of social processes[51] that the most important matters, such as the nature of democracy and the quality of life, are next to impossible to capture in the form of the quantitative indicators most familiar to policy-makers and most easy for them to use. Provision of the information demanded by the government may be dysfunctional for an organization because it requires maintaining two distinct information collection and reporting systems to also acquire the data needed internally.[52] Some agencies, such as the Federal Communications Commission, drastically reduce the pool of researchers from whom it can commission input by demanding scholars undertake the laborious and costly steps required to become designated federal contractors.

The use of communication research in the courtroom, where the problem is meeting evidentiary standards, provides a complex example that reveals a variety of the kinds of problems that can be faced in trying to translate academic ideas into policy-relevant research. It is not often that courts rely explicitly on social science research in cases involving communications.[53] When entertainer Wayne Newton used public opinion research to demonstrate damage to his reputation during a libel suit, he was able to persuade the jury but not the judge.[54] Often, pertinent research is not taken up by courts at all.[55] Though the judicial system has been the element of the American political system most open to institutional reform and explicitly welcomes the input of experts, those in communications have lagged far behind those in other social sciences in exploring questions the answers to which would be of use in the courtroom.[56] The questions of how various types of arguments and means of presenting evidence affect juries and of the impact of cameras in the courtroom did start receiving attention in the 1970s, but the courtroom itself was quickly declared off-limits to researchers.[57] Today, however, there appears to be an upsurge of work on issues of interest to the judiciary.[58] The courtroom has become one of the primary means available to attempt to affect the extreme communication policies put in place as part of the Homeland Security package, so this is one venue in which empirical research results can have great political value. Survey evidence suggests that a combination of qualitative and quantitative research is likely to be the most successful in the courtroom.[59]

Criticisms of the use of social science research as courtroom evidence include its contribution to the transformation of the role of the jury from primary to secondary determiners of fact[60] and the possibility that variations in the ability of judges to evaluate social science evidence can lead to inequities in the resolution of cases from court to court.[61] Inevitably, the use of data in the courtroom reflects the relative authority of social science relative to other types of knowledge[62] as well as the tension between objectivity and advocacy.[63] Since journalists can, under certain conditions, protect their sources and/or information obtained under the umbrella of confidentiality from revelation in the courtroom, some social scientists also try to claim confidentiality for their research data in this context.[64] The law and society movement, launched in the early 1960s under instigation by a number of foundations, was an effort both to turn scholarly attention to the social effects of legal decision making and to the kinds of research that might be taken into account by courts and legislators as law is made.[65]

The bad news is that even poor research can have a lot of impact. The good news is that if higher quality research becomes available courts prefer it, as Paul, Linz, and Shafer[66] demonstrate in their analysis of the use of social science research by courts seeking to determine whether or not adult businesses have a negative impact on their geographic surrounds. These scholars model some of the ways communication researchers can have an impact on policy-making by going beyond scholarly journal publication, for they submit *amicus curiae* briefs (one was cited by the Supreme Court), and conduct research for communities seeking to determine the effects of adult businesses on specific neighborhoods in the course of development of municipal zoning laws.

Discussion

There is widespread recognition that our understanding of the effects of the use of new information technologies lags behind development of the technologies themselves, but it is less widely acknowledged that this delay has been a matter of deliberate design. The result of such decisions is that it is very difficult for researchers to get the fundamental support needed to undertake the kinds of research desperately needed by policy-makers. This, too, presents a contradiction in the approach of policy-makers to digital technologies, for a situation has been created in which they must respond to policy problems raised by innovation but have crippled themselves regarding the intellectual tools they need to fulfill that responsibility.

The political uses of communication policy research results and the ways in which attention to those results is incorporated into decision-making processes has not received enough research attention in itself. Too often, academics involved in policy work appear Candide-like in the earnestness with which they believe that simply presenting data will be all it takes to make something happen, and in the confidence they have that what happens as a result will be in accordance with their own policy preferences. This situation might be improved if those who design arguments for alternative policies learned from their colleagues who conduct analysis of the policy and public discourses around issues of concern.

Among the phases of policy-making identified by Lasswell, most communication research efforts have been directed at the prescriptive phase, precisely where they are least likely to be of use. Evaluation of the effects of policies once implemented is invaluable in determining which to keep, which to let go, and what types of adaptations may be necessary but communication researchers almost never take part in such evaluations, abandoning the field to reliance upon cost-benefit analysis as taught in schools of policy and public administration. The fact that rigorously conducting such evaluations is difficult methodologically should be taken as an important challenge, not a reason to avoid the subject.

Developing alternative policy approaches and tools during what Lasswell described as "the intelligence phase" may be the most important function communication researchers can fill in today's environment, given the fundamental nature of change in the subject of communication law and regulation. The need for such thinking has been expressed by policy-makers throughout government; in the United States, beginning in the 1970s, explicit admission of the inability to understand new information technologies and their social effects were an important factor in the argument for deregulation. The scholarship and contemplation required to reconceptualize the policy environment are simply not possible for working policy-makers who must deal simultaneously with a multitude of issues, all on an immediate basis—but they are the daily practices and life commitment of those in academia. The participation of researchers in the contemporary movement for an information commons—whether or not the ideal is practicable in all of its details—is an example of an effort to fulfill such a role.

Notes

1. Woodrow Wilson, The study of public administration, *Political Science Quarterly* 2, no. 2 (1887): 197–222.

2. Kendrick A. Clements, Woodrow Wilson and administrative reform, *Presidential Studies Quarterly* 28, no. 2 (1998): 320–337.

3. David Held, *Political Theory and the Modern State: Essays on State, Power, and Democracy*, Stanford University Press, Stanford, 1989.

4. Alfred D. Chandler and James W. Cortada, eds, *A Nation Transformed by Information: How Information has Shaped the United States from Colonial Times to the Present*, Oxford University Press, Oxford, 2000.

5. David Michael Ryfe, "Betwixt and between": Woodrow Wilson's press conferences and the transition toward the modern rhetorical presidency, *Political Communication* 16, no. 1 (1999): 77–93.

6. Marion K. Pinsdorf, Woodrow Wilson's PR: Wag the Hun, *Public Relations Review* 25: 3 (1999): 309–330; Christopher Simpson, *Science of Coercion: Communication Research and Psychological Warfare, 1945–1960*, Oxford University Press, New York, 1994.

7. Margaret A. Blanchard, *Exporting the First Amendment*, Longman, New York, 1986.

8. Stephen Ponder, Presidential publicity and executive power: Woodrow Wilson and the centralizing of government information, *American Journalism* 11, no. 3 (1994) 257–269.

9. Margo J. Anderson, *The American Census: A Social History*, Yale University Press, New Haven, Conn., 1988.

10. Willis Rudy, *Total War and Twentieth-century Higher Learning: Universities of the Western World in the First and Second World Wars*, Fairleigh Dickinson University Press, Cranbury, NJ, 1991.

11. B. D. Karl, Presidential planning and social science research: Mr. Hoover's experts, *Perspectives in American History* 3 (1969): 347–409.

12. William Buxton, From radio research to communications intelligence: Rockefeller philanthropy, communications specialists, and the American policy community, in Stephen Brooks and Alain-G. Gagnon, eds, *Political Influence of Ideas: Policy Communities and the Social Sciences*, Praeger, Westport, Conn., 1994; Brett Gary, Communication research, the Rockefeller Foundation, and mobilization for the war on words, 1938–1944, *Journal of Communication* 46, no. 3 (1996): 124–148; Marilyn A. Lashner, The role of foundations in public broadcasting, Part I: Development and trends, *Journal of Broadcasting* 20, no. 4 (1976): 529–547; Marilyn A. Lashner, The role of foundations in public broadcasting, Part II: The Ford Foundation, *Journal of Broadcasting* 21, no. 2 (1977): 235–254.

13. Frank Fischer, Policy discourse and the politics of Washington think tanks, in Frank Fischer and John Forester, eds, *The Argumentative Turn in Policy Analysis and Planning*, Duke University Press, Durham, N.C., 1993, pp. 21–42; Stephen McDowell, Policy research institutes and liberalized international services exchange, in Stephen Brooks and Alain-G. Gagnon, eds, *The Political Influence of Ideas: Policy Communities and the Social Sciences*, Praeger, Westport, Conn., 1994, pp. 107–133.

14. Willard D. Rowland, Jr., American telecommunications policy research: Its contradictory origins and influences, *Media, Culture and Society* 8, no. 2 (1986): 159–182.

15. Thomas Conway, The crisis of policy sciences, in Stephen Brooks and Alain-G. Gagnon, eds, *Social Scientists, Policy, and the State*, Praeger, New York, 1990, pp. 169–176.

16. Harold D. Lasswell, *A Pre-view of Policy Sciences*, Elsevier, New York, 1971; Harold D. Lasswell, Communications research and public policy, *Public Opinion Quarterly* 36, no. 3 (1972): 301–310.

17. Robert Hoppe, Political judgment and the policy cycle: The case of ethnicity policy arguments in The Netherlands, in Frank Fischer and John Forester, eds, *The Argumentative Turn in Policy Analysis and Planning*, Duke University Press, Durham, N.C., 1993, pp. 77–100.

18. Harold D. Lasswell, Communications research and public policy.

19. Wesley A. Magat and W. Kip Viscusi, *Informational Approaches to Regulation*, MIT Press, Cambridge, 1992; A. McAlister, A. Ramirez, C. Galavotti, and K. Gallion, Anti-smoking campaigns: Progress in the application of social learning theory, in Ron E. Rice and Charles Atkins, eds, *Public Communication Strategies*, 2d ed., Sage Publications, Newbury Park, Calif., 1989, pp. 291–308; G. J. Nowak and M. J. Siska, Using research to inform campaign

development and message design: Examples from the "America responds to AIDS campaign," in E. Maibach and R. L. Parrott, eds, *Designing Health Messages: Approaches from Communication Theory and Public Health Practice*, Sage Publications, Thousand Oaks, Calif., 1995, pp. 169–185; Charles Salmon, Bridging theory "of" and theory "for" communication campaigns: An essay on ideology and public policy, *Communication Yearbook* 15 (1992): 346–358.

20. Harold D. Lasswell, Some perplexities of policy theory, *Social Research* 41 (1974): 176–189.

21. Harold D. Lasswell, The policy orientation, in Daniel Lerner and Harold D. Lasswell, eds, *The Policy Sciences*, Stanford University Press, Stanford, 1951, pp. 3–15.

22. This model is commonly attributed to Lasswell. However, historical research in the past decades suggests that Rockefeller Foundation staffer John Marshall actually originated the notion during the course of a consultative process involving Lasswell. William Buxton, From radio research to communications intelligence; Brett Gary, Communication research, the Rockefeller Foundation, and mobilization for the war on words, 1938–1944.

23. Fritz Machlup, The economics of information: A new classification, *InterMedia* 1, no. 2 (1983): 28–37.

24. Ithiel de Sola Pool, Thee rise of communication policy research, *Journal of Communication* 24, no. 2 (1974): 31–42.

25. Marc Uri Porat, Global implications of the information society, *Journal of Communication* 28, no. 1 (1978): 70–80.

26. Donald M. Lamberton, National information policy, *The Annals of the American Academy of Political and Social Science* 412 (1974): 145–151.

27. Donald M. Lamberton, *Beyond Competition: The Future of Telecommunications*, Elsevier Science, New York, 1995; Donald M. Lamberton, ed, *The Economics of Communication and Information*, Edward Elgar Publishing, Northampton, Mass., 1996; Donald M. Lamberton, Information economics research: Points of departure, *Information Economics and Policy* 10, no. 3 (1998): 325–331.

28. Gottfried Mayer-Kress, Global information systems and nonlinear methodologies in crisis management, presented to the Santa Fe Institute Complex Systems Summer School, 1992.

29. William Sims Bainbridge, Edward E. Brent, Kathleen M. Carley, David R. Heise, Michael W. Macy, Barry Markovsky, and John Skvoretz, Artificial social intelligence, *Annual Review of Sociology* 20 (1994): 407–437.

30. Daniel J. Headrick, *The Invisible Weapon: Telecommunications and International Relations, 1851–1945*, Oxford University Press, New York, 1990.

31. William H. Dutton, Decision making in the information age: Computer models and public policy, in Brenda Dervin and Melvin J. Voigt, eds, *Progress in Communication Sciences* 5, Ablex Publishing Corporation, Norwood, N.J., 1984, pp. 111–144.

32. John H. Holland, Complex adaptive systems, in N. Metropolis and Gian-Carlo Rota, eds, *A New Era in Computation*, MIT Press, Cambridge, 1993, pp. 17–30.

33. Donald W. Schön and Martin Rein, *Frame Reflection: Toward the Resolution of Intractable Policy Controversies*, Basic Books, New York, 1994.

34. Sandra Braman, *Change of State: An Introduction to Information Policy*, MIT Press, Cambridge, forthcoming.

35. The general theoretical frameworks regarding the nature of the information economy, the information society, and information policy relied upon here are presented in full in Sandra Braman, *Change of State: An Introduction to Information Policy*, MIT Press, Cambridge, forthcoming.

36. Brian Kahin, Making policy by solicitation: The outsourcing of .us, <cip.umd.edu/solicitation.html>, 2001; Eli Noam, Reconnecting communications studies with communications policy.

37. Ulrich Beck, *Risk Society: Towards a New Modernity*, Sage Publications, London, 1993.

38. Bruce Bimber, The death of an agency: OTA and trophy hunting in US budget policy, *Policy Studies Review* 15, nos. 2–3 (1998): 202–226; Bruce Bimber, *The Politics of Expertise in Congress: The Rise and Fall of the Office of Technology Assessment*, State University of New York Press, Albany, 1996; Fred W. Weingarten, The politicizing of science policy, *Communications of the ACM* 37, no. 6 (1994): 13–16; Fred W. Weingarten, Obituary for an agency, *Communications of the ACM* 38, no. 9 (1995): 29–33.

39. Willard D. Rowland, Jr., *The Politics of TV Violence: Policy Uses of Communication Research*, Sage Publications, Thousand Oaks, Calif., 1983.

40. Armand Mattelart and Yves Stourdze Cesta, *Technology, Culture & Communication: A Report to the French Minister of Research and Industry*, Elsevier Science, New York, 1985; Pool, 1974, *op cit*, Ref. 24.

41. Dolf Zillmann, Pornography research and public policy, in Dolf Zillmann and Jennings Bryant, eds, *Pornography: Research Advances and Policy Considerations*, Lawrence Erlbaum Associates, Hillsdale, N.J., 1989.

42. Donald A. Schön and Martin Rein, *Frame Reflection: Toward the Resolution of Intractable Policy Controversies*.

43. Maarten A. Hajer, Discourse coalitions and the institutionalization of practice: The case of acid rain in Great Britain, in Fischer and Forester, *op cit.*, pp. 43–76.

44. Patsy Healey, Planning through debate: The communicative turn in planning theory, in Frank Fischer and John Forester, eds., *The Argumentative Turn in Policy Analysis and Planning*, Durham, N.C., Duke University Press, pp. 233–253.

45. Alain-G. Gagnon, The influence of social scientists on public policy, in Stephen Brooks and Alain-G. Gagnon, eds., *Social Scientists, Policy, and the State*, Praeger, New York, 1990, pp. 1–18.

46. Don R. LeDuc, Transforming principles into policy, *Journal of Communication* 30, no. 2, (1980): 196–202.

47. Taisto Hujanen, Political versus cultural in critical broadcasting research and policy: A reevaluation of the Finnish radical experiment in broadcasting in the late 1960s, in John A. Lent, ed., *A Different Road Taken: Profiles in Critical Communication*, Westview Press, Boulder, Colo., 1995, pp. 257–268.

48. David Ritchie, Forbidden fruit: Rhetoric, science, and pornography effects, Unpublished ms., 2000.

49. Dolf Zillmann and Jennings Bryant, Pornography, sexual callousness, and trivialization of rape, *Journal of Communication* 32, no. 4 (1982): 10–21.

50. Milton L. Mueller and Jorge Reina Schement, Universal service from the bottom up: A study of telephone penetration in Camden, New Jersey, *The Information Society* 12 (1996): 273–292.

51. Alain Desrosières, *The Politics of Large Numbers: A History of Statistical Reasoning*, Harvard University Press, Cambridge, 1998.

52. E. Sam Overman and Anthony G. Cahill, Information, market government, and health policy: A study of health data organizations in the states, *Journal of Policy Analysis and Management* 13, no. 1 (1994): 435–453; E. Sam Overman and Donna T. Loraine, Information for control: Another management proverb? *Public Administration Review* 54, no. 2 (1994): 193–196.

53. Jeremy Cohen and Timothy Gleason, *Social Research in Communication & Law*, Sage Publications, Thousand Oaks, Calif., 1990.

54. Jeremy Cohen and Sara Spears, Newtonian communication: Shaking the libel tree for empirical damages, *Journalism and Mass Communication Quarterly* 67, no. 1 (1990): 51–59.

55. See, e.g., National Communication Association (NCA), Brief amicus curiae of the Speech Communication Association in Support of appellees–plaintiffs, *Janet Reno et al., v. American Civil Liberties Union et al.*, 1996, 96–511; Wayne M. Towers, Empirical research and some major Supreme Court decisions on free press/fair trial conflicts, in Gregg Phifer, ed, *Free Speech Yearbook*, Speech Communication Association, Falls Church, Va., 1978, pp. 60–67.

56. James R. Acker, Thirty years of social science in Supreme Court criminal cases, *Law & Policy* 12, no. 1 (1990): 1–23.

57. Dan Slater and Valerie P. Hans, Methodological issues in the evaluation of "experiments" with cameras in the courts, *Communication Quarterly* 30, no. 4 (1982) 376–380.

58. See, e.g., L. Leets and H. Giles, Words as weapons—When do they wound? Investigations of harmful speech, *Human Communication Research* 24: 2 (1997): 260–301.

59. Lyombe Eko, Trademark parody and the mass media: Going beyond survey evidence in the determination of a "likelihood of confusion," *Communication Law and Policy* 3, no. 4 (1998): 589–608.

60. Marianne Constable, The modern American jury: Fact and law in law and society, *Journal of American Culture* 15, no. 1 (1992) 37–43.

61. Jeremy Buchman, "Thou shalt not sit with statisticians, nor commit a social science": How trial courts address social science evidence in redistricting cases, *American Journal of Political Science* 42, no. 2 (1998): 702–705.

62. John Monahan and Laurens Walker, Social authority: Obtaining, evaluating, and establishing social science in law, *University of Pennsylvania Law Review* 134, no. 3 (1986): 477–517.

63. John P. Jackson, Jr., Creating a consensus: Psychologists, the Supreme Court, and school desegregation, 1952–1955, *Journal of Social Issues* 54, no. 1 (1998): 143–178.

64. Jacques Feuillan, Every man's evidence versus a testimonial privilege for survey researchers, *Public Opinion Quarterly* 40, no. 1 (1976): 39–50.

65. Bryant G. Garth and Joyce Sterling, From legal realism to law and society: Reshaping law for the last stages of the social activist state, *Law & Society Review* 32, no. 2 (1998): 409–471.

66. Bryant Paul, Daniel Linz, and Bradley J. Shafer, Government regulation of "adult" businesses through zoning and anti-nudity ordinances: Debunking the legal myth of negative secondary effects, *Communication Law and Policy* 6 (2001): 355–392.

The Need: Communication Research as an Input into Policy

3

The Study of Public Administration

Woodrow Wilson
1887

I suppose that no practical science is ever studied where there is no need to know it. The very fact, therefore, that the eminently practical science of administration is finding its way into college courses in this country would prove that this country needs to know more about administration, were such proof of the fact required to make out a case. It need not be said, however, that we do not look into college programmes for proof of this fact. It is a thing almost taken for granted among us, that the present movement called civil service reform must, after the accomplishment of its first purpose, expand into efforts to improve, not the *personnel* only, but also the organization and methods of our government offices: because it is plain that their organization and methods need improvement only less than their *personnel*. It is the object of administrative study to discover, first, what government can properly and successfully do, and secondly, how it can do these proper things with the utmost possible efficiency and at the least possible cost either of money or of energy. On both these points there is obviously much need of light among us; and only careful study can supply that light.

Before entering on that study, however, it is needful:

1. To take some account of what others have done in the same line; that is to say, of the history of the study.

2. To ascertain just what is its subject matter.

3. To determine just what are the best methods by which to develop it, and the most clarifying political conceptions to carry with us into it.

Unless we know and settle these things, we shall set out without chart or compass.

I

The science of administration is the latest fruit of that study of the science of politics which was begun some twenty-two hundred years ago. It is a birth of our own century, almost of our own generation.

Why was it so late in coming? Why did it wait till this too busy century of ours to demand attention for itself? Administration is the most obvious part of government; it is government in action; it is the executive, the operative, the most visible side of government, and is of course as old as government itself. It is government in action, and one might very naturally expect to find that government in action had arrested the attention and provoked the scrutiny of writers of politics very early in the history of systematic thought.

But such was not the case. No one wrote systematically of administration as a branch of the science of government until the present century had passed its first youth and had begun to put forth its characteristic flower of systematic knowledge. Up to our own day all the political writers whom we now read had thought, argued, dogmatized only about the *constitution* of government; about the nature of the state, the essence and seat of sovereignty, popular power and kingly prerogative; about the greatest meanings lying at the heart of government, and the high ends set before the purpose of government by man's nature and man's aims. The central field of controversy was that great field of theory in which monarchy rode tilt against democracy, in which oligarchy would have built for itself strongholds of privilege, and in which tyranny sought opportunity to make good its claim to receive submission from all competitors. Amidst this high warfare of principles, administration could command no pause for its own consideration. The question was always: Who shall make law, and what shall that law be? The other question, how law should be administered with enlightenment, with equity, with speed, and without friction, was put aside as "practical detail" which clerks could arrange after doctors had agreed upon principles.

That political philosophy took this direction was of course no accident, no chance preference of perverse whim of political philosophers. The philosophy of any time is, as Hegel says, "nothing but the spirit of that time expressed in abstract thought"; and political philosophy, like philosophy of every other kind, had only held up the mirror to contemporary affairs. The trouble in early times was almost altogether about the constitution of government; and consequently that was what engrossed men's thoughts. There was little or no trouble about administration—at least little that was heeded by administrators. The functions of government were simple, because life itself was simple. Government went about imperatively and compelled men, without thought of consulting their wishes. There was no complex system of public revenues and public debts to puzzle financiers; there were, consequently, no financiers to be puzzled. No one who possessed power was long at a loss how to use it. The great and only question was: Who shall possess it? Populations were of manageable numbers; property was of simple sorts. There were plenty of farms, but no stocks and bonds: more cattle than vested interests.

I have said that all this was true of "early times"; but it was substantially true also of comparatively late times. One does not have to look back of the last century for the beginnings of the present complexities of trade and perplexities of commercial speculation, nor for the portentous birth of national debts. Good Queen Bess, doubtless, thought that the monopolies of the sixteenth century were hard enough to handle without burning her hands; but they are not remembered in the presence of the giant monopolies of the nineteenth century. When Blackstone lamented that corporations had no bodies to be kicked and no souls to be damned, he was anticipating the proper time for such regrets by full a century. The perennial discords between master and workmen which now so often disturb industrial society began before the Black Death and the Statute of Laborers; but never before our own day did they assume such ominous proportions as they wear now. In brief, if difficulties of governmental action are to be seen gathering in other centuries, they are to be seen culminating in our own.

This is the reason why administrative tasks have nowadays to be so studiously and systematically adjusted to carefully tested standards of policy, the reason why we are having now what we never had before, a science of administration. The weightier debates of constitutional principle are even yet by no means concluded; but they are no longer of more immediate practical moment than questions of administration. It is getting to be harder to *run* a constitution than to frame one.

Here is Mr. Bagehot's graphic, whimsical way of depicting the difference between the old and the new in administration:

"In early times, when a despot wishes to govern a distant province, he sends down a satrap on a grand horse, and other people on little horses; and very little is heard of the satrap again unless he sends back some of the little people to tell what he has been doing. No great labour of superintendence is possible. Common rumour and casual report are the sources of intelligence. If it seems certain that the province is in a bad state, satrap No. 1 is recalled, and satrap No. 2 sent out in his stead. In civilized countries the process is different. You erect a bureau in the province you want to govern; you make it write letters and copy letters; it sends home eight reports per diem to the head bureau in St. Petersburg. Nobody does a sum in the province without some one doing the same sum in the capital, to 'check' him, and see that he does it correctly. The consequence of this is, to throw on the heads of departments an amount of reading and labour which can only be accomplished by the greatest natural aptitude, the most efficient training, the most firm and regular industry."

There is scarcely a single duty of government which was once simple which is not now complex; government once had but a few masters; it now has scores of masters. Majorities formerly only underwent government; they now conduct government. Where government once might follow the whims of a court, it must now follow the views of a nation.

And those views are steadily widening to new conceptions of state duty; so that, at the same time that the functions of government are every day becoming more complex and difficult, they are also vastly multiplying in number. Administration is everywhere putting its hands to new undertakings. The utility, cheapness, and success of the government's postal service, for instance, point towards the early establishment of governmental control of the telegraph system. Or, even if our government is not to follow the lead of the governments of Europe in buying or building both telegraph and railroad lines, no one can doubt that in some way it must make itself master of masterful corporations. The creation of national commissioners of railroads, in addition to the older state commissions, involves a very important and delicate extension of administrative functions. Whatever hold of authority state or federal governments are to take upon corporations, there must follow cares and responsibilities which will require not a little wisdom, knowledge, and experience. Such things must be studied in order to be well done. And these, as I have said, are only a few of the doors which are being opened to offices of government. The idea of the state and the consequent ideal of its duty are undergoing noteworthy change; and "the idea of the state is the conscience of administration." Seeing every day new things which the state ought to do, the next thing is to see clearly how it ought to do them.

This is why there should be a science of administrative which shall seek to straighten the paths of government, to make its business less unbusinesslike, to strengthen and purify its organization, and to crown its duties with dutifulness. This is one reason why there is such a science.

But where has this science grown up? Surely not on this side of the sea. Not much impartial scientific method is to be discerned in our administrative practices. The poisonous atmosphere of city government, the crooked secrets of state administration, the confusion, sinecurism, and corruption ever and again discovered in the bureaux at Washington forbid us to believe that any clear conceptions of what constitutes good administration are as yet very widely current in the United States. No; American writers have hitherto taken no very important part in the advancement of this science. It has found its doctors in Europe. It is not of our making; it is a foreign science, speaking very little of the language of English or American principle. It employs only foreign tongues; it utters none but what are to our minds alien ideas. Its aims, its examples, its conditions, are almost exclusively grounded in the histories of foreign races, in the precedents of foreign systems, in the lessons of foreign revolutions. It has been developed by French and German professors, and is consequently in all parts adapted to the needs of a compact state, and made to fit highly centralized forms of government; whereas, to answer our purposes, it must be adapted, not to a simple and compact, but to a complex and multiform state, and made to fit highly decentralized forms of government. If we would employ it, we must Americanize it, and that not formally, in language merely, but radically, in thought, principle, and aim as well. It must learn our constitutions by heart; must get the bureaucratic fever out of its veins; must inhale much free American air.

If an explanation be sought why a science manifestly so susceptible of being made useful to all governments alike should have received attention first in Europe, where government has long been a monopoly, rather than in England or the United States, where government has long been a common franchise, the reason will doubtless be found to be twofold: first, that in Europe, just because government was independent of popular assent, there was more governing to be done; and, second, that the desire to keep government a monopoly made the monopolists interested in discovering the least irritating means of governing. They were, besides, few enough to adopt means promptly.

It will be instructive to look into this matter a little more closely. In speaking of European governments I do not, of course, include England. She has not refused to change with the times. She has simply tempered the severity of the transition from a polity of aristocratic privilege to a system of democratic power by slow measures of constitutional reform which, without preventing revolution, has confined it to paths of peace. But the countries of the continent for a long time desperately struggled against all change, and would have diverted revolution by softening the asperities of absolute government. They sought so to perfect their machinery as to destroy all wearing friction, so to sweeten their methods with consideration for the interests of the governed as to placate all hindering hatred, and so assiduously and opportunely to offer their aid to all classes of undertakings as to render themselves indispensable to the industrious. They did at last give the people constitutions and the franchise; but even after that they obtained leave to continue despotic by becoming paternal. They made themselves too efficient to be dispensed with, too smoothly operative to be noticed, too enlightened to be inconsiderately questioned, too benevolent to be suspected, too powerful to be coped with. All this has required study; and they have closely studied it.

On this side the sea we, the while, had known no great difficulties of government. With a new country, in which there was room and remunerative employment for everybody, with liberal principles of government and unlimited skill in practical politics, we were long exempted from the need of being anxiously careful about plans and methods of administration. We have naturally been slow to see the use or significance of those many volumes of learned research and painstaking examination into the ways and means of conducting government which the presses of Europe have been sending to our libraries. Like a lusty child, government with us has expanded in nature and grown great in stature, but has also become awkward in movement. The vigor and increase of its life has been altogether out of proportion to its skill in living. It has gained strength, but it has not acquired deportment. Great, therefore, as has been our advantage over the countries of Europe in point of ease and health of constitutional development, now that the time for more careful administrative adjustments and larger administrative knowledge has come to us, we are at a signal disadvantage as compared with the transatlantic nations; and this for reasons which I shall try to make clear.

Judging by the constitutional histories of the chief nations of the modern world, there may be said to be three periods of growth through which government has passed in all the most highly developed of existing systems, and through which it promises to pass in all the rest. The first of these periods is that of absolute rulers, and of an administrative system adapted to absolute rule; the second is that in which constitutions are framed to do away with absolute rulers and substitute popular control, and in which administration is neglected for these higher concerns; and the third is that in which the sovereign people undertake to develop administration under this new Constitution which has brought them into power.

Those governments are now in the lead in administrative practice which had rulers still absolute but also enlightened when those modern days of political illumination came in which it was made evident to all but the blind that governors are properly only the servants of the governed. In such government administration has been organized to subserve the general weal with the simplicity and effectiveness vouchsafed only to the undertakings of a single will.

Such was the case in Prussia, for instance, where administration has been most studied and most nearly perfected. Frederic the Great, stern and masterful as was his rule, still sincerely professed to regard himself as only the chief servant of the state, to consider his great office a public trust; and it was he who, building upon the foundations laid by his father, began to organize the public service of Prussia as in very earnest a service of the public. His no less absolute successor, Frederic William III, under the inspiration of Stein, again, in his turn, advanced the work still further, planning many of the broader structural features which give firmness and form to Prussian administration today. Almost the whole of the admirable system has been developed by kingly initiative.

Of similar origin was the practice, if not the plan, of modern French administration, with its symmetrical divisions of territory and its orderly gradations of office. The days of the Revolution—of the Constituent Assembly—were days of constitution-*writing*, but they can hardly be called days of constitution-*making*. The Revolution heralded a period of constitutional development—the entrance of France upon the second of those periods which I have enumerated—but it did not itself inaugurate such a period. It interrupted and unsettled absolutism, but did not destroy it. Napoleon succeeded the monarchs of France, to exercise a power as unrestricted as they had ever possessed.

The recasting of French administration by Napoleon is, therefore, my second example of the perfecting of civil machinery by the single will of an absolute ruler before the dawn of a constitutional era. No corporate, popular will could ever have effected arrangements such as those which Napoleon commanded. Arrangements so simple at the expense of local prejudice, so logical in their indifference to popular choice, might be decreed by a Constituent Assembly, but could be established only by the unlimited authority of a despot. The system of the year VIII was ruthlessly thorough and heartlessly perfect. It was, besides, in large part, a return to the despotism that had been overthrown.

Among those nations, on the other hand, which entered upon a season of constitution-making and popular reform before administration had received the impress of liberal principle, administrative improvement has been tardy and half-done. Once a nation has embarked in the business of manufacturing constitutions, it finds it exceedingly difficult to close out that business and open for the public a bureau of skilled, economical administration. There seems to be no end to the tinkering of constitutions. Your ordinary constitution will last you hardly ten years without repairs or additions; and the time for administrative detail comes late.

Here, of course, our examples are England and our own country. In the days of the Angevin kings, before constitutional life had taken root in the Great Charter, legal and administrative reforms began to proceed with sense and vigor under the impulse of Henry II's shrewd, busy, pushing, indomitable spirit and purpose; and kingly initiative seemed destined in England, as elsewhere, to shape governmental growth at its will. But impulsive, errant Richard and weak, despicable John were not the men to carry out such schemes as their father's. Administrative development gave place in their reigns to constitutional struggles; and Parliament became king before any English monarch had had the practical genius or the enlightened conscience to devise just and lasting forms for the civil service of the state.

The English race, consequently, has long and successfully studied the art of curbing executive power to the constant neglect of the art of perfecting executive methods. It has exercised itself much more in controlling than in energizing government. It has been more concerned to render government just and moderate than to make it facile, well-ordered, and effective. English and American political history has been a history, not of administrative development, but of legislative oversight—not of progress in governmental organization, but of advance in law-making and political criticism. Consequently we have reached a time when administrative study and creation are imperatively necessary to the well-being of our governments saddled with the habits of a long period of constitution-making. That period has practically closed, so far as the establishment of essential principles is concerned, but we cannot shake off its atmosphere. We go on criticizing when we ought to be creating. We have reached the third of the periods I have mentioned—the period, namely, when the people have to develop administration in accordance with the constitutions they won for themselves in a previous period of struggle with absolute power; but we are not prepared for the tasks of the new period.

Such an explanation seems to afford the only escape from blank astonishment at the fact that, in spite of our vast advantages in point of political liberty, and above all in point of practical political skill and sagacity, so many nations are ahead of us in administrative organization and administrative skill. Why, for instance, have we but just begun purifying a civil service which was rotten full fifty years ago? To say that slavery diverted us is but to repeat what I have said—that flaws in our constitution delayed us.

Of course all reasonable preference would declare for his English and American course of politics rather than for that of any European country. We should not like to have had Prussia's history for the sake of having Prussia's administrative skill; and Prussia's particular system of administration would quite suffocate us. It is better to be untrained and free than to be servile and systematic. Still there is no denying that it would be better yet to be both free in spirit and proficient in practice. It is this even more reasonable preference which impels us to discover what there may be to hinder or delay us in naturalizing this much-to-be-desired science of administration.

What, then, is there to prevent?

Well, principally, popular sovereignty. It is harder for democracy to organize administration than for monarchy. The very completeness of our most cherished political successes in the past embarrasses us. We have enthroned public opinion; and it's forbidden us to hope during its reign for any quick schooling of the sovereign in executive expertness or in the conditions of perfect functional balance in government. The very fact that we have realized popular rule in its fullness has made the task of *organizing* that rule just so much the more difficult. In order to make any advance at all we must instruct and persuade a multitudinous monarch called public opinion—a much less feasible undertaking than to influence a single monarch called a king. An individual sovereign will adopt a simple plan and carry it out directly; he will have but one opinion, and he will embody that one opinion in one command. But this other sovereign, the people, will have a score of differing opinions. They can agree upon nothing simple; advance must be made through compromise, by a compounding of differences, by a trimming of plans and a suppression of too straightforward principles. There will be a succession of resolves running through a course of years, a dropping fire of commands running through a whole gamut of modifications.

In government, as in virtue, the hardest of hard things is to make progress. Formerly the reason for this was that the single person who was sovereign was generally selfish, ignorant, timid, or a fool—albeit there was now and again one who was wise. Nowadays the reason is that the many, the people, who are sovereign have no single ear which one can approach, and are selfish, ignorant, timid, stubborn, or foolish with the selfishnesses, the ignorances, the stubbornesses, the timidities, or the follies of several thousand persons—albeit there are hundreds who are wise. Once the advantage of the reformer was that the sovereign's mind had a definite locality, that it was contained in one man's head, and that consequently it could be gotten at; though it was his disadvantage that that mind learned only reluctantly or only in small quantities, or was under the influence of someone who let it learn only the wrong things. Now, on the contrary, the reformer is bewildered by the fact that the sovereign's mind has no definite locality, but is contained in a voting majority of several million heads; and embarrassed by the fact that the mind of his sovereign also is under the influence of favorites, who are none the less favorites in a good old-fashioned sense of the word because they are not persons but preconceived opinions; i.e., prejudices which are not to be reasoned with because they are not the children of reason.

Wherever regard for public opinion is a first principle of government, practical reform must be slow and all reform must be full of compromises. For wherever public opinion exists it must rule. This is now an axiom half the world over, and will presently come to be believed even in Russia. Whoever would effect a change in a modern constitutional government must first educate his fellow-citizens to want *some* change. That done, he must persuade them to want the particular change he wants. He must first make public opinion willing to listen and then see to it that it listens to the right things. He must stir it up to search for an opinion, and then manage to put the right opinion in its way.

The first step is not less difficult than the second. With opinions, possession is more than nine points of the law. It is next to impossible to dislodge them. Institutions which one generation regards as only a makeshift approximation to the realization of a principle, the next generation honors as the nearest possible approximation to that principle, and the next worships as the principle itself. It takes scarcely three generations for the apotheosis. The grandson accepts his grandfather's hesitating experiment as an integral part of the fixed constitution of nature.

Even if we had clear insight into all the political past, and could form out of perfectly instructed heads a few steady, infallible, placidly wise maxims of government into which all sound political doctrine would be ultimately resolvable, *would the country act on them?* That is the question. The bulk of mankind is rigidly unphilosophical, and nowadays the bulk of mankind votes. A truth must become not only plain but also commonplace before it will be seen by the people who go to their work very early in the morning; and not to act upon it must involve great and pinching inconveniences before these same people will make up their minds to act upon it.

And where is this unphilosophical bulk of mankind more multifarious in its composition than in the United States? To know the public mind of this country, one must know the mind, not of Americans of the older stocks only, but also of Irishmen, of Germans, of Negroes. In order to get a footing for new doctrine, one must influence minds cast in every mould of race, minds inhabiting every bias of environment, warped by the histories of a score of different nations, warmed or chilled, closed or expanded by almost every climate of the globe.

So much, then, for the history of the study of administration, and the peculiarly difficult conditions under which, entering upon it when we do, we must undertake it. What, now, is the subject-matter of this study, and what are its characteristic objects?

II

The field of administration is a field of business. It is removed from the hurry and strife of politics; it at most points stands apart even from the debatable ground of constitutional study. It is a part of political life only as the methods of the counting-house are a part of the life of society; only as machinery is part of the manufactured product. But it is, at the same time, raised very far above the dull level of mere technical detail by the fact that through its greater principles it is directly connected with the lasting maxims of political wisdom, the permanent truths of political progress.

The object of administrative study is to rescue executive methods from the confusion and costliness of empirical experiment and set them upon foundations laid deep in stable principle.

It is for this reason that we must regard civil-service reform in its present stages as but a prelude to a fuller administrative reform. We are now rectifying methods of appointment; we must go on to adjust executive functions more fitly and to prescribe better methods of executive organization and action. Civil-service reform is thus but a moral preparation for what is to follow. It is clearing the moral atmosphere of official life by establishing the sanctity of public office as a public trust, and, by making the service unpartisan, it is opening the way for making it businesslike. By sweetening its motives it is rendering it capable of improving its methods of work.

Let me expand a little what I have said of the province of administration. Most important to be observed is the truth already so much and so fortunately insisted upon by our civil-service reformers; namely, that administration lies outside the proper sphere of *politics*. Administrative questions are not political questions. Although politics sets the tasks for administration, it should not be suffered to manipulate its offices.

This is distinction of high authority; eminent German writers insist upon it as of course. Bluntschli, for instance, bids us separate administration alike from politics and from law. Politics, he says, is state activity "in things great and universal," while "administration, on the other hand," is "the activity of the state in individual and small things. Politics is thus the special province of the statesman, administration of the technical official." "Policy does nothing without the aid of administration"; but administration is not therefore politics. But we do not require German authority for this position; this discrimination between administration and politics is now, happily, too obvious to need further discussion.

There is another distinction which must be worked into all our conclusions, which, though but another side of that between administration and politics, is not quite so easy to keep sight of: I mean the distinction between *constitutional* and administrative questions, between those governmental adjustments which are essential to constitutional principle and those which are merely instrumental to the possibly changing purposes of a wisely adapting convenience.

One cannot easily make clear to everyone just where administration resides in the various departments of any practicable government without entering upon particulars so numerous as to confuse and distinctions so minute as to distract. No lines of demarcation, setting apart administrative from nonadministrative functions, can be run between this and that department of government without being run up hill and down dale, over dizzy heights of distinction and through dense jungles of statutory enactment, hither and thither around "ifs" and "buts," "whens" and "howevers," until they become altogether lost to the common eye not accustomed to this sort of surveying, and consequently not acquainted with the use of the theodolite of logical discernment. A great deal of administration goes about *incognito* to most of the world, being confounded now with political "management," and again with constitutional principle.

Perhaps this ease of confusion may explain such utterances as that of Niebuhr's: "Liberty," he says, "depends incomparably more upon administration than upon constitution." At first sight this appears to be largely true. Apparently facility in the actual exercise of liberty does depend more upon administrative arrangements than upon constitutional guarantees; although constitutional guarantees alone secure the existence of liberty. But—upon second thought—is even so much as this true? Liberty no more consists in easy functional movement than intelligence consists in the ease and vigor with which the limbs of a strong man move. The principles that rule within the man, or the constitution, are the vital springs of liberty or servitude. Because dependence and subjection are without chains, are lightened by every easy-working device of considerate, paternal government, they are not thereby transformed into liberty. Liberty cannot live apart from constitutional principle; and no administration, however perfect and liberal its methods, can give men more than a poor counterfeit of liberty if it rest upon illiberal principles of government.

A clear view of the difference between the province of constitutional law and the province of administrative function ought to leave no room for misconception; and it is possible to name some roughly definite criteria upon which such a view can be built. Public administration is detailed and systematic execution of public law. Every particular application of general law is an act of administration. The assessment and raising of taxes, for instance, the hanging of a criminal, the transportation and delivery of the mails, the equipment and recruiting of the army and navy, etc., are all obviously acts of administration; but the general laws which direct these things to be done are as obviously outside of and above administration. The broad plans of governmental action are not administrative; the detailed execution of such plans is administrative. Constitutions, therefore, properly concern themselves only with those instrumentalities of government which are to control general law. Our federal constitution observes this principle in saying nothing of even the greatest of the purely executive offices, and speaking only of that President of the Union who was to share the legislative and policy-making functions of government, only of those judges of highest jurisdiction who were to interpret and guard its principles, and not of those who were merely to give utterance to them.

This is not quite the distinction between Will and answering Deed, because the administrator should have and does have a will of his own in the choice of means for accomplishing his work. He is not and ought not to be a mere passive instrument. The distinction is between general plans and special means.

There is, indeed, one point at which administrative studies trench on constitutional ground—or at least upon what seems constitutional ground. The study of administration, philosophically viewed, is closely connected with the study of the proper distribution of constitutional authority. To be efficient it must discover the simplest arrangements by which responsibility can be unmistakably fixed upon officials; the best way of dividing authority without hampering it, and responsibility without obscuring it. And this question of the distribution of authority, when taken into the sphere of the higher, the originating functions of government, is obviously a central constitutional question. If administrative study can discover the best principles upon which to base such distribution, it will have done constitutional study an invaluable service. Montesquieu did not, I am convinced, say the last word on this head.

To discover the best principle for the distribution of authority is of greater importance, possibly, under a democratic system, where officials serve many masters, than under others where they serve but a few. All sovereigns are suspicious of their servants, and the sovereign people is no exception to the rule; but how is its suspicion to be allayed by *knowledge*? If that suspicion could but be clarified into wise vigilance, it would be altogether salutary; if that vigilance could be aided by the unmistakable placing of responsibility, it would be altogether beneficient. Suspicion in itself is never healthful either in the private or in the public mind. *Trust is strength* in all relations of life; and, as it is the office of the constitutional reformer to create conditions of trustfulness, so it is the office of the administrative organizer to fit administration with conditions of clear-cut responsibility which shall insure trustworthiness.

And let me say that large powers and unhampered discretion seem to me the indispensable conditions of responsibility. Public attention must be easily directed, in each case of good or bad administration, to just the man deserving of praise or blame. There is no danger in power, if only it be not irresponsible. If it be divided, dealt out in shares to many, it is obscured; and if it be obscured, it is made irresponsible. But if it be centered in heads of the service and in heads of branches of the service, it is easily watched and brought to book. If to keep his office a man must achieve open and honest success, and if at the same time he feels himself intrusted with large freedom of discretion, the greater his power the less likely is he to abuse it, the more is he nerved and sobered and elevated by it. The less his power, the more safely obscure and unnoticed does he feel his position to be, and the more readily does he relapse into remissness.

Just here we manifestly emerge upon the field of that still larger question—the proper relations between public opinion and administration.

To whom is official trustworthiness to be disclosed, and by whom is it to be rewarded? Is the official to look to the public for his meed of praise and his push of promotion, or only to his superior in office? Are the people to be called in to settle administrative discipline as they are called in to settle constitutional principles? These questions evidently find their root in what is undoubtedly the fundamental problem of this whole study. That problem is: What part shall public opinion take in the conduct of administration?

The right answer seems to be, that public opinion shall play the part of authoritative critic.

But the *method* by which its authority shall be made to tell? Our peculiar American difficulty in organizing administration is not the danger of losing liberty, but the danger of not being able or willing to separate its essentials from its accidents. Our success is made doubtful by that besetting error of ours, the error of trying to do too much by vote. Self-government does not consist in having a hand in everything, any more than housekeeping consists necessarily in cooking dinner with one's own hands. The cook must be trusted with a large discretion as to the management of the fires and the ovens.

In those countries in which public opinion has yet to be instructed in its privileges, yet to be accustomed to having its own way, this question as to the province of public opinion is much more readily soluble than in this country, where public opinion is wide awake and quite intent upon having its own way anyhow. It is pathetic to see a whole book written by a German professor of political science for the purpose of saying to his countrymen, "Please try to have an opinion about national affairs"; but a public which is so modest may at least be expected to be very docile and acquiescent in learning what things it has *not* a right to think and speak about imperatively. It may be sluggish, but it will not be meddlesome. It will submit to be instructed before it tries to instruct. Its political education will come before its political activity. In trying to instruct our own public opinion, we are dealing with a pupil apt to think itself quite sufficiently instructed beforehand.

The problem is to make public opinion efficient without suffering it to be meddlesome. Directly exercised, in the oversight of the daily details and in the choice of the daily means of government, public criticism is of course a clumsy nuisance, a rustic handling delicate machinery. But as superintending the greater forces of formative policy alike in politics and administration, public criticism is altogether safe and beneficent, altogether indispensable. Let administrative study find the best means for giving public criticism this control and for shutting it out from all other interference.

But is the whole duty of administrative study done when it has taught the people what sort of administration to desire and demand, and how to get what they demand? Ought it not to go on to drill candidates for the public service?

There is an admirable movement towards universal political education now afoot in this country. The time will soon come when no college of respectability can afford to do without a well-filled chair of political science. But the education thus imparted will go but a certain length. It will multiply the number of intelligent critics of government, but it will create no competent body of administrators. It will prepare the way for the development of a sure-footed understanding of the general principles of government, but it will not necessarily foster skill in conducting government. It is an education which will equip legislators, perhaps, but not executive officials. If we are to improve public opinion, which is the motive power of government, we must prepared better officials as the *apparatus* of government. If we are to put in new boilers and to mend the fires which drive our governmental machinery, we must not leave the old wheels and joints and valves and bands to creak and buzz and clatter on as best they may at bidding of the new forces. We must put in new runing parts wherever there is the least lack of strength or adjustment. It will be necessary to organize democracy by sending up to the competitive examinations for the civil service men definitely prepared for standing liberal tests as to technical knowledge. A technically schooled civil service will presently have become indispensable. .

I know that a corps of civil servants prepared by a special schooling and drilled, after appointment, into a perfected organization, with appropriate hierarchy and characteristic discipline, seems to a great many very thoughtful persons to contain elements which might combine to make an offensive official class—a distinct, semi-corporate body with sympathies divorced from those of a progressive, free-spirited people, and with hearts narrowed to the meanness of a bigoted officialism. Certainly such a class would be altogether hateful and harmful in the United States. Any measures calculated to produce it would for us be measures of reaction and of folly.

But to fear the creation of a domineering illiberal officialism as a result of the studies I am here proposing is to miss altogether the principle upon which I wish most to insist. That principle is, that administration in the United States must be at all points sensitive to public opinion. A body of thoroughly trained officials serving during good behavior we must have in any case: that is a plain business necessity. But the apprehension that such a body will be anything un-American clears away the moment it is asked, What is to constitute good behavior? For that question obviously carries its own answer on its face. Steady, hearty allegiance to the policy of the government they serve will constitute good behavior. That *policy* will have no taint of officialdom about it. It will not be the creation of permanent officials, but of statesmen whose responsibility to public opinion will be direct and inevitable. Bureaucracy can exist only where the whole service of the state is removed from the common political life of the people, its chiefs as well as its rank and file. Its motives, its objects, its policy, its standards, must be bureacuratic. It would be difficult to point out any examples of impudent exclusiveness and arbitrariness on the part of officials doing service under a chief of department who really served the people, as all our chiefs of departments must be made to do. It would be easy, on the other hand, to adduce other instances like that of the influence of Stein in Prussia, where the leadership of one statesman imbued with true public spirit transformed arrogant and perfunctory bureaux into public-spirited instruments of just government.

The ideal for us is a civil service cultured and self-sufficient enough to act with sense and vigor, and yet so intimately connected with the popular thought, by means of elections and constant public counsel, as to find arbitrariness or class spirit quite out of the question.

III

Having thus viewed in some sort the subject-matter and the objects of this study of administration, what are we to conclude as to the methods best suited to it—the points of view most advantageous for it?

Government is so near us, so much a thing of our daily familiar handling, that we can with difficulty see the need of any philosophical study of it, or the exact point of such study, should it be undertaken. We have been on our feet too long to study now the art of walking. We are a

practical people, made so apt, so adept in self-government by centuries
of experimental drill that we are scarcely any longer capable of perceiving the awkwardness of the particular system we may be using, just
because it is so easy for us to use any system. We do not study the art
of governing: we govern. But mere unschooled genius for affairs will not
save us from sad blunders in administration. Though democrats by long
inheritance and repeated choice, we are still rather crude democrats. Old
as democracy is, its organization on a basis of modern ideas and conditions is still an unaccomplished work. The democratic state has yet to
be equipped for carrying those enormous burdens of administration
which the needs of this industrial and trading age are so fast accumulating. Without comparative studies in government we cannot rid ourselves of the misconception that administration stands upon an
essentially different basis in a democratic state from that on which it
stands in a non-democratic state.

After such study we could grant democracy the sufficient honor of ultimately determining by debate all essential questions affecting the public
weal, of basing all structures of policy upon the major will; but we would
have found but one rule of good administration for all governments
alike. So far as administrative functions are concerned, all governments
have a strong structural likeness; more than that, if they are to be uniformly useful and efficient, they *must* have a strong structural likeness.
A free man has the same bodily organs, the same executive parts, as the
slave, however different may be his motives, his services, his energies.
Monarchies and democracies, radically different as they are in other
respects, have in reality much the same business to look to.

It is abundantly safe nowadays to insist upon this actual likeness of
all governments, because these are days when abuses of power are easily
exposed and arrested, in countries like our own, by a bold, alert, inquisi-
tive, detective public thought and a sturdy popular self-dependence such
as never existed before. We are slow to appreciate this; but it is easy to
appreciate it. Try to imagine personal government in the United States.
It is like trying to imagine a national worship of Zeus. Our imaginations
are too modern for the feat.

But, besides, being safe, it is necessary to see that for all governments
alike the legitimate ends of administration are the same, in order not to

be frightened at the idea of looking into foreign systems of administration for instruction and suggestion; in order to get rid of the apprehension that we might perchance blindly borrow something incompatible with our principles. That man is blindly astray who denounces attempts to transplant foreign systems into this country. It is impossible: they simply would not grow here. But why should we not use such parts of foreign contrivances as we want, if they be in any way serviceable? We are in no danger of using them in a foreign way. We borrowed rice, but we do not eat it with chopsticks. We borrowed our whole political language from England, but we leave the words "king" and "lords" out of it. What did we ever originate, except the action of the federal government upon individuals and some of the functions of the federal supreme court?

We can borrow the science of administration with safety and profit if only we read all fundamental differences of condition into its essential tenets. We have only to filter it through our constitutions, only to put it over a slow fire of criticism and distil away its foreign gases.

I know that there is a sneaking fear in some conscientiously patriotic minds that studies of European systems might signalize some foreign methods as better than some American methods; and the fear is easily to be understood. But it would scarcely be avowed in just any company.

It is the more necessary to insist upon thus putting away all prejudices against looking anywhere in the world but at home for suggestions in this study, because nowhere else in the whole field of politics, it would seem, can we make use of the historical, comparative method more safely than in this province of administration. Perhaps the more novel the forms we study the better. We shall the sooner learn the peculiarities of our own methods. We can never learn either our own weaknesses or our own virtues by comparing ourselves with ourselves. We are too used to the appearance and procedure of our own system to see its true significance. Perhaps even the English system is too much like our own to be used to the most profit in illustration. It is best on the whole to get entirely away from our own atmosphere and to be most careful in examining such systems as those of France and Germany. Seeing our own institutions through such *media*, we see ourselves as foreigners might see us were they to look at us without preconceptions. Of ourselves, so long as we know only ourselves, we know nothing.

Let it be noted that it is the distinction, already drawn, between administration and politics which makes the comparative method so safe in the field of administration. When we study the administrative systems of France and Germany, knowing that we are not in search of *political* principles, we need not care a peppercorn for the constitutional or political reasons which Frenchmen or Germans give for their practices when explaining them to us. If I see a murderous fellow sharpening a knife cleverly, I can borrow his way of sharpening the knife without borrowing his probable intention to commit murder with it; and so, if I see a monarchist dyed in the wool managing a public bureau well, I can learn his business methods without changing one of my republican spots. He may serve his king; I will continue to serve the people; but I should like to serve my sovereign as well as he serves his. By keeping this distinction in view—that is, by studying administration as a means of putting our own politics into convenient practice, as a means of making what is democratically politic towards all administratively possible towards each—we are on perfectly safe ground, and can learn without error what foreign systems have to teach us. We thus devise an adjusting weight for our comparative method of study. We can thus scrutinize the anatomy of foreign governments without fear of getting any of their diseases into our veins; dissect alien systems without apprehension of blood-poisoning.

Our own politics must be the touchstone for all theories. The principles on which to base a science of administration for America must be principles which have democratic policy very much at heart. And, to suit American habit, all general theories must, as theories, keep modestly in the background, not in open argument only, but even in our own minds—lest opinions satisfactory only to the standards of the library should be dogmatically used, as if they must be quite as satisfactory to the standards of practical politics as well. Doctrinaire devices must be postponed to tested practices. Arrangements not only sanctioned by conclusive experience elsewhere but also congenial to American habit must be preferred without hesitation to theoretical perfection. In a word, steady, practical statesmanship must come first, closet doctrine second.

The cosmopolitan what-to-do must always be commanded by the American how-to-do-it.

Our duty is, to supply the best possible life to a *federal* organization, to systems within systems; to make town, city, county, state, and federal governments live with a like strength and an equally assured healthfulness, keeping each unquestionably its own master and yet making all interdependent and cooperative, combining independence with mutual helpfulness. The task is great and important enough to attract the best minds.

This interlacing of local self-government with federal self-government is quite a modern conception. It is not like the arrangements of imperial federation in Germany. There local government is not yet, fully, local *self*-government. The bureaucrat is everywhere busy. His efficiency springs out of *esprit de corps*, out of care to make ingratiating obeisance to the authority of a superior, or, at best, out of the soil of a sensitive conscience. He serves, not the public, but an irresponsible minister. The question for us is, how shall our series of governments within governments be so administered that it shall always be to the interest of the public officer to serve, not his superior alone but the community also, with the best efforts of his talents and the soberest service of his conscience? How shall such service be made to his commonest interest by contributing abundantly to his sustenance, to his dearest interest by furthering his ambition, and to his highest interest by advancing his honor and establishing his character? And how shall this be done alike for the local part and for the national whole?

If we solve this problem we shall again pilot the world. There is a tendency—is there not?—a tendency as yet dim, but already steadily impulsive and clearly destined to prevail, towards, first the confederation of parts of empires like the British, and finally of great states themselves. Instead of centralization of power, there is to be wide union with tolerated divisions of prerogative. This is a tendency towards the American type—of governments joined with governments for the pursuit of common purpose, in honorary equality and honorable subordination. Like principles of civil liberty are everywhere fostering like methods of government; and if comparative studies of the ways and means of government should enable us to offer suggestions which will practically combine openness and vigor in the administration of such governments with ready docility to all serious, well-sustained public criticism, they will have approved themselves worthy to be ranked among the highest and most fruitful of the great departments of political study. That they will issue in such suggestions I confidently hope.

4

The Policy Orientation

Harold D. Lasswell
1951

The continuing crisis of national security in which we live calls for the most efficient use of the manpower, facilities, and resources of the American people. Highly trained talent is always scarce and costly. Hence the crisis poses the problem of utilizing our intellectual resources with the wisest economy. If our policy needs are to be served, what topics of research are most worthy of pursuit? What manpower and facilities should be allocated to official agencies and to private institutions for the prosecution of research? What are the most promising methods of gathering facts and interpreting their significance for policy? How can facts and interpretations be made effective in the decision-making process itself?

Although the importance of these questions is emphasized by the urgency of national defense, they are in no sense new. For years there has been a lively concern in intellectual circles for the problem of overcoming the divisive tendencies of modern life and of bringing into existence a more thorough integration of the goals and methods of public and private action. The pace of specialization in philosophy, natural science, biology, and the social sciences has been so rapid that colleagues on the faculty of a single university, or even members of a single department, often complain that they cannot understand one another. The unity of the intellectual life and the harmonizing of science and practice have been undermined by these "centrifugal" forces.

For several years new trends toward integration have been gaining strength in America. In liberal arts colleges the elective system has been giving way to a more rigid curriculum, and survey courses have been devised to introduce the student to broad fields of knowledge and to prepare the way for a vision of the whole. At the level of research, mixed teams of specialists have been assembled to work on common problems in the hope of counteracting the deleterious effects of an excessive atomization of knowledge. In the realm of policy, more attention has been given to planning, and to improving the information on which staff and operational decisions are based. We have become more aware of the policy process as a suitable object of study in its own right, primarily in the hope of improving the rationality of the flow of decision.

A policy orientation has been developing that cuts across the existing specializations. The orientation is twofold. In part it is directed toward the policy process, and in part toward the intelligence needs of policy. The first task, which is the development of a science of policy forming and execution, uses the methods of social and psychological inquiry. The second task, which is the improving of the concrete content of the information and the interpretations available to policy-makers, typically goes outside the boundaries of social science and psychology.

In so far, therefore, as the policy orientation is focused upon the scientific study of policy, it is narrower than the psychological and social sciences, which have many other objects of investigation. However, where the needs of policy intelligence are uppermost, any item of knowledge, within or without the limits of the social disciplines, may be relevant. We may need to know the harbor installations at Casablanca, or the attitudes of a population of Pacific islanders to the Japanese, or the maximum range of a fixed artillery piece.

We may use the term "policy sciences" for the purpose of designating the content of the policy orientation during any given period. The policy sciences includes (1) the methods by which the policy process is investigated, (2) the results of the study of policy, and (3) the findings of the disciplines making the most important contributions to the intelligence needs of the time. If we are to advance in our scientific grasp of the policy formation and execution process as a whole, it is obviously essential to apply and improve the methods by which psychological and social-scientific investigations are made. [It is useful, therefore, to emphasize] developments in research which are of unusual importance for the understanding of human choice. If the rationality of the policy process is to be improved, we must single out the intelligence function for special study. To some extent the task of improving the intelligence function depends upon more effective techniques of communication, among research workers, policy advisers, and the makers of final decisions. Therefore the policy sciences are advanced whenever the methods are sharpened by which authentic information and responsible interpretations can be integrated with judgment. To some extent the quality of the intelligence function at any given time depends upon the successful anticipation of policy needs before they have been generally recognized. Successful prediction depends upon the cultivation of certain patterns of thinking. For instance, it is important to consider the entire context of events which may have an impact upon the future problems of policy. Hence the world as a whole needs to be kept at the focus of attention. It is also essential to cultivate the practice of thinking of the past and the future as parts of one context, and to make use of "developmental constructs" as tools for exploring the flow of events in time. An example of developmental thinking on a global scale is exemplified [by work which deals] with the potentialities of the "garrison state."

The expression "policy sciences" is not in general use in the United States, although it is occurring more frequently now than before. Perhaps it should be pointed out that the term is not to be taken as a synonym for any expression now in current use among scholars. It is not another way of talking about the "social sciences" as a whole, nor of the "social and psychological sciences." Nor are the "policy sciences" identical with "applied social science" or "applied social and psychological science." As explained before, the policy orientation stresses but one of the many problems which come within the proper scope of the social sciences, and includes the results of the social, psychological, and natural sciences insofar as they have a bearing on the policy needs of a given period for adequate intelligence.

Nor are the "policy sciences" to be thought of as largely identical with what is studied by the "political scientists"—the term in common use for academic teachers and writers about government. It is true that one group of academic political scientists would identify the field with the study of power (in the sense of decision-making). But at present this is a minority viewpoint. Many of the most valuable contributions to a general theory of choice (including "decisions," defined as sanctioned choices) have been made by persons who are not political scientists (in the academic division of labor). Examples are abundant, and include the "rational theory of choice" (called the "theory of games") developed by the mathematician von Neumann and the economist Morgenstern. . . . [E]conomists Arrow and Katona are particularly concerned with the theory of choice. And it would not be difficult to name psychologists, anthropologists, and others who have specialized to a fruitful degree upon the understanding of choice.

The word "policy" is commonly used to designate the most important choices made either in organized or in private life. We speak of "government policy," "business policy," or "my own policy" regarding investments and other matters. Hence "policy" is free of many of the undesirable connotations clustered about the word *political*, which is often believed to imply "partisanship" or "corruption."

When I speak of the "policy orientation" in the United States I am emphasizing what appears to be a dominant current among many scholars and scientists, notably in the social sciences. The conception of the policy sciences is arising to give insight into these recent trends and to aid in clarifying their full possibilities. The movement is not only toward a policy orientation, with a resulting growth in the policy sciences, but more specifically toward the policy sciences of democracy.

The Emphasis on Method

The meaning of current developments will be more apparent if we review the trends between World War I and World War II. The first of these wars was a turning point in the history of the social and psychological sciences in the United States. Some of these disciplines made conspicuous contributions to the prosecution of the war. Others did not. The problem immediately arose of accounting for the difference. The interwar evolution of the social sciences in the United States is largely to be explained in terms of the answers to this question.

The most influential answer was this: the disciplines which possessed quantitative methods were the ones that rose most rapidly in influence. Consider from this point of view the case of economics. Economists were extensively utilized to estimate the facilities, manpower, and resources necessary to produce the munitions required by the armed forces and to supply men and matériel where needed. The economic scientists who made the greatest direct contribution employed mathematics and statistics. They had method. And they were quantitative. They could manipulate data in the light of a system of general postulates, laws, and hypotheses.

Consider the psychologists. The most successful group used "intelligence tests" as a quick means of selecting personnel for various operations. Immediately after World War I, the results gained enormous publicity when articles appeared in which the remarkable assertion was made that most of the American army was "below average intelligence." It took many years to straighten out the misconceptions in the sensational reports originally made. Obviously the word "average" had entirely different meanings for the reading public and for the psychometricians who created and applied the tests. However, the publicity given to testing and psychology greatly increased scientific and lay interest in the subject. Once again the success of the discipline appeared to depend upon the use of quantitative methods. Intelligence tests were evolved and applied with the aid of statistical procedures.

The rise of economists and psychometricians seemed to indicate that the closer the social scientist came to the methods of physical science the more certain his methods could be of acceptance. This point of view was emphasized by the scholar who took the most important part in remolding the social disciplines, Charles E. Merriam, professor of political science at the University of Chicago. Professor Merriam took the initiative in organizing the Social Science Research Council, which is a delegate body of scholarly associations in political science, economics, sociology, psychology, and other social sciences. Merriam stressed the importance of breaking down the barriers that separate scholars from one another, and of leveling-up methodological competence everywhere. In a typical statement, made in 1925, he wrote in the preface to his *New Aspects of Politics*: "It is . . . the purpose of this study . . . to suggest certain possibilities of approach to a method, in the hope that others may take up the task and through reflection and experiment eventually introduce more intelligent and scientific technique into the study and practice of government, and into popular attitudes toward the governing process."[1]

At the same time that steps were being taken at the national level to organize the Social Science Research Council, leading universities were working out agencies for interdisciplinary research. At the University of Chicago, for example, field studies of the city of Chicago were made by the Local Community Research Committee (later called the Social Science Research Committee). Joint programs were developed at Columbia University and Harvard University. An Institute of Human Relations was established at Yale.

The programs just referred to were financed in large part by the Rockefeller Foundation and the Laura Spelman Rockefeller Memorial Fund, another Rockefeller benefaction. One of the most imaginative and aggressive factors in the program was Beardsley Ruml, who at various times was administratively active on both foundations. Ruml, it is worth noting, was a Ph.D. in psychology, well-versed in statistics, who had a share during World War I in the testing program of the Army.

The outlook of Merriam and his fellow leaders of the postwar generation is made explicit in many publications which appeared during the 1920s. The interdisciplinary theme is prominent in *A History of Political Theories: Recent Times*, a volume edited by Merriam and Professor Harry Elmer Barnes, published in New York in 1924. In addition to the political scientists who contributed to the symposium there were lawyers (E. M. Borchard and Caleb Perry Patterson), an economist (Paul H. Douglas), a historian (Carlton J. H. Hayes), a philosopher (Herbert W. Schneider), sociologists (Barnes, and Frank H. Hankins), a social psychologist (Charles Elmer Gehlke), an anthropologist (Alexander A. Goldenweiser), and a social geographer (Franklin Thomas).

An evidence of the stress on method was the Committee on Scientific Method which was appointed by the Social Science Research Council and in 1931 brought out *Methods in Social Science: A Casebook*, edited by Stuart A. Rice. The book was composed of fifty-two methodological analyses of contributions to the social sciences. The analysts included such authorities from many fields as Robert E. Park and William F. Ogburn (sociology); A. L. Kroeber and Edward Sapir (anthropology); John Maurice Clark and Frank H. Knight (economics); W. Y. Elliott and

George E. G. Gatlin (political science); Heinrich Klüver and Robert S. Woodworth (psychology); Floyd Allport and Kimball Young (social psychology); Philip Klein (social work); Raoul Blanchard and K. C. McMurry (social geography); and Henri Pirenne and Sidney B. Fay (history).

Another means of stimulating interest in method was the post-doctoral fellowship program of the Social Science Research Council. The program was designed to encourage young scholars to improve their scientific equipment by adding a new technique to their primary specialization.

The Consequences of Depression and War

It is against the background of stress on improving the sciences of man by sharpening the tools of research that subsequent developments need to be set. No one seriously doubts that the level of technical excellence of American social science rose between World War I and World War II despite the Depression. When the second of the wars came, new disciplines were well enough evolved to join the older specialties in making themselves felt.

Economics continued to make great contributions in the mobilization of the American economy for World War II. It is generally agreed that the courageous forecasts and plans of a key group of economists on the War Production Board had a decisive impact on the tempo of effective participation by this country. I refer particularly to the work of Stacy May, Simon Kuznets, Robert Nathan, and their associates. (Kuznets was one of Professor Wesley C. Mitchell's most productive associates in the study of business cycles at the National Bureau of Economic Research.)

Psychologists were far more numerous and effective in World War II than in the previous one. Besides developments in intelligence testing, there had been between the wars great advances in measuring aptitudes and personality structure. Sociologists and social psychologists came more prominently into the picture than in the first war. Professor Samuel A. Stouffer and his associates made continuous and systematic studies of the attitudes prevailing among military personnel, utilizing and developing the quantitative procedures evolved between the wars by Professor L. L. Thurstone and others.

In the light of the successes achieved, there is no reason to doubt that the stress put upon quantitative method is amply vindicated. It will continue to inspire ambitious young scholars in the field of human relations. There are, however, grounds for forecasting a somewhat different emphasis among social scientists in the coming years. The battle for method is won. It is likely that social and psychological scientists will be sufficiently sure of themselves to take method for granted and to put the emphasis on the choice of significant problems on which to apply and evolve method. This is the point at which considerations of policy come into the picture.

Knowledge for What?

Although the importance of quantitative method was the dominant theme in interwar social science, there were many indications of rising preoccupation with policy. A vigorous and early exponent of the policy approach was Professor Robert S. Lynd of Columbia University, joint author of certain classical community studies and long the secretary of the Social Science Research Council. Professor Lynd gave a series of lectures at Princeton University in 1939 under the title "Knowledge for What?" in which he insisted upon the importance of utilizing all available means of acquiring knowledge in order to cope with the gigantic crises of our time.

The policy approach is not to be confounded with the superficial idea that social scientists ought to desert science and engage full time in practical politics. Nor should it be confused with the suggestion that social scientists ought to spend most of their time advising policy-makers on immediate questions. Although it may be wise for scholars to devote more time to active affairs, the most fruitful policy science idea is different. The point is that all the resources of our expanding social science need to be directed toward the basic conflicts in our civilization which are so vividly disclosed by the application of scientific method to the study of personality and culture. A fundamental picture of American culture and personality has been drawn by the accumulating results of modern research—by sociologists, anthropologists, psychiatrists, and psychologists.

Choosing Fundamental Problems

The basic emphasis of· the policy approach, therefore, is upon the fundamental problems of man in society, rather than upon the topical issues of the moment. The combined efforts of modern research workers have disclosed roots of tension within our civilization of which we were previously unaware. The difficulties which we face in operating economic and political institutions are obvious to all. What has eluded scientific and policy attention is a large number of the human factors which prevent the resolution of these difficulties by rational means. Building on the work of Freud and other psychopathologists, Harry Stack Sullivan and other psychiatrists traced in detail the fundamental importance of self-esteem for the healthy evolution of human personality. Unless the infant and the child are able to love themselves, they are incapable of loving others. Interferences with the growth of a healthy conception of the self lead to the warping of personality into destructiveness. Sullivan and his associates discovered that the true field of the psychiatrist is not the isolated individual organism but the context of interpersonal relations in which the individual lives. By studying the psychotic, neurotic, and psychopathic manifestations of distorted development, these psychiatrists discovered the way in which specific patterns of culture warp the growth of congenial and productive interpersonal relations. Once discovered and exposed, these sources of human destructiveness can be changed. The basis is laid for a profound reconstruction of culture by continual study and emendation, and not by (or certainly not alone by) the traditional methods of political agitaton.

At an early date in his work, Dr. Sullivan and certain colleagues reached out for cooperation with social scientists. The interplay of psychiatrists, child psychologists, anthropologists, and other social scientists has cast a brilliant light on the impact of culture on personality formation. Among anthropologists, for example, the contributions of Ruth Benedict, Margaret Mead, Ralph Linton, and Clyde Kluckhohn are representative of the best.[2]

The Use of Models

There is scarcely a corner of human society that has not been seen in new perspective as a result of modern psychiatry. One significant feature of this development is that while use is made of careful observation, measurement, and record making, quantification is relegated to a relatively secondary position. The richness of the context in the study of interpersonal relations is such that it can be expressed only in part in quantitative terms. Convincing results can be obtained by studies which are but partially summarized in numbers. An excellent example of this type of contribution to science and policy is the report by Alexander Leighton on human relations in a relocation camp for "Japanese" operated by the United States government during the last war.[3]

The problem of dealing with complex relationships has given to many social scientists more insight into the creative use of models in scientific work. The models may be in prose, and they can be long or short. The models may be in mathematical notation and, if so, they may be related to magnitudes which can or cannot be measured. (Professor Arrow deals with the function of scientific models in his chapter in the present book.) Social scientists and psychiatrists have always derived their most fruitful hypotheses from rather complicated models. Good examples are the conceptions put forward by Freud of the oral, anal, and genital types of personality; or the types of leaders and power relations described by Max Weber, who wrote at some length on the methodological role of "ideal types." When one thinks in basic policy terms, it is essential to operate with models whose elaboration is sufficient to enable the investigator to deal with complex institutional situations.

The significance that revised models have for science and policy was strikingly exemplified in the 1930s. The New Deal of Franklin D. Roosevelt was a brilliant success in the sense that a far-reaching economic crisis was met by policies which were far short of the authoritarian measures of a Fascist or Communist state. This result was achieved, in part, because of the aid which the government received from economists, many of whom had been liberated from the cramping doctrines of classical economic analysis by the ideas of Alvin Hansen in the United States and of John Maynard Keynes in England. There was nothing new about the general idea that the government ought to do something if a mass unemployment crisis developed. But the idea had no rational roots in the prevailing conception among economists of how the free market system operated. Recurring depressions were thought of simply as "frictions" within the system, and government action was grudgingly justified—when it was accepted at all—as a means of dealing with miscellaneous "frictions." The Keynes-Hansen approach was very different. Instead of dismissing prolonged mass unemployment as a result of frictions, Keynes and Hansen showed that unemployment could result from the structure of the free economy itself. If left to themselves, private economic choices might perpetuate the underuse of labor instead of initiating new enterprises to absorb labor. The implications for public policy were obvious: Government intervention is essential in order to eliminate unemployment and to set in motion once more the forces of the free market.

This was a remarkable example of the creative results which may follow, not when new quantifications are made, but when new models of institutional processes are devised, models which can unify quantitative and nonquantitative observations and point the way to new empirical, theoretical, and policy activities.[4]

The Clarification of Goals

The policy-science approach not only puts the emphasis upon basic problems and complex models, but also calls forth a very considerable clarification of the value goals involved in policy. After all, in what sense is a problem "basic"? Evaluations depend upon postulates about the human relations to be called desirable. For purposes of analysis the term "value" is taken to mean "a category of preferred events," such as peace rather than war, high levels of productive employment rather than mass unemployment, democracy rather than despotism, and congenial and productive personalities rather than destructive ones.

When the scientist is reminded to take note of value objectives, he quickly discovers conflicts within culture and within his own personality. His personality has been shaped in a culture of sharp contradictions at the levels of theory and fact. On the doctrinal level, there is the demand to achieve a world community in which the dignity of man is realized in theory and fact. There is also the contradictory demand to make the world safe for "Aryan" or white supremacy. In a word, there are legacies from the world of caste which prevailed before the French and American revolutions gave impetus to the idea of social mobility on the basis of individual merit.

The Policy Sciences of Democracy

It is, I think, safe to forecast that the policy-science approach will bring about a series of "special" sciences within the general field of the social sciences, much as the desire to cure has developed a science of medicine which is distinct from, though connected with, the general science of biology. In the United States the nature of such special sciences can already be discerned. The dominant American tradition affirms the dignity of man, not the superiority of one set of men. Hence it is to be foreseen that the emphasis will be upon the development of knowledge pertinent to the fuller realization of human dignity. Let us for convenience call this the evolution of the "policy sciences of democracy." Abundant indications are at hand to lend weight to this suggestion.

A glaring discrepancy between doctrine and practice in the United States is the mistreatment of Negroes and other colored peoples. The Carnegie Foundation supported a comprehensive survey of trends in ethnic relations in the United States. The purpose was to disclose the true state of affairs, to discover the conditioning factors, and to stimulate policies against discrimination. *An American Dilemma: The Negro Problem and Modern Democracy*, edited by Gunnar Myrdal in 1944, was the outcome.

The initiative for problem-oriented inquiries has been taken not only by private foundations but also by private associations of businessmen. Perhaps the most successful example is the Committee for Economic Development which was organized early in World War II in order to develop policies which would avoid or mitigate a postwar depression in the United States. The research program was carried out by a staff of eminent economists headed by Professor Theodore O. Yntema of the University of Chicago. On the basis of staff studies which were published, the businessmen made policy suggestions to the government and to private organizations and individuals. Since the war the Committee for Economic Development has been continued for the purpose of developing long-range researches and recommendations for the maintenance of a free-market economy. (The figure most prominently associated with the Committee is its initiator and first head, Paul G. Hoffman.)

The Awareness of Time

The policy orientation carries with it a sharpened sense of time. *An American Dilemma* is a good illustration. The project resulting in that book was chosen because ethnic relations in the United States were recognized to be of great importance to the future security of the country, as well as to the realization of democratic aspirations. As a scientist becomes value-orientated, he accepts or rejects opportunities for research according to their relevance to *all* of his goal values, or he initiates research which contributes to these goals.

It is not necessary for the scientist to sacrifice objectivity in the execution of a project. The place for nonobjectivity is in deciding what ultimate goals are to be implemented. Once this choice is made, the scholar proceeds with maximum objectivity and uses all available methods. Further, it is unnecessary to give up the idea of improving method. All of the foregoing points are exemplified in the Myrdal inquiry, since the data were gathered and interpreted in a critical spirit, and methods were improved during the investigation. For example, the methodological appendix which was prepared by Myrdal has been useful in spreading certain important patterns of thinking among American social scientists.

Emphasis on time is not exhausted in the selection of a policy-oriented project. No sooner do you become interested in future goals than you look sharply into the present and the past in order to discover the degree in which trends approximate values. Trends are extrapolated into the future, and the plausibility of the extrapolation is estimated in the light of all available knowledge of trends and factors. Alternative lines of policy are estimated in the same way.

Space Includes the Globe

The perspective of a policy-oriented science is world-wide, since the peoples of the world constitute a community. They affect one another's destiny. Hence the future of basic objectives depends upon world developments as a whole.

It is possible to examine world affairs from the point of view of the invention, diffusion, and restriction of social institutions. In this perspective, Moscow is the eruptive center of the world revolutionary pattern of our time, and one of the tasks of political analysis and management is to assist or to restrict the diffusion of this pattern. More specifically, a major problem of our epoch is to bring to completion the revolutionary processes of our historical period with the smallest human cost. At least this is a problem of all who believe in the dignity of man and therefore hope to keep coercion at a minimum.

Developmental Constructs: The World Revolution of Our Time

The policy sciences of democracy, concerned as they are with events on a global scale in our historical period, must proceed by creating world-encompassing hypotheses. Speculative models of the principal social changes in our epoch can be called "developmental constructs." They specify the institutional pattern *from* which we are moving and the pattern *toward* which we are going.

Strictly speaking, developmental constructs are not scientific hypotheses, since they do not formulate propositions about interdependence of factors. A developmental construct refers only to the succession of events, future as well as past. It should be noted that many hypotheses about the future purport to have scientific validity, such as the Marxist conception that the classless society is emerging. But no claim of "inevitability" can be accepted. Events in the future are not knowable with absolute certainty in advance: they are partly probable and partly chance. Developmental constructs are aids in the total task of clarifying goals, noting trends, and estimating future possibilities.

It is not within the scope of this chapter to present in detail developmental hypotheses about the world revolution of our time. In passing, however, it is tempting to remark that a distinction needs to be drawn between the pattern of the *eruptive center of a world revolutionary movement* and the pattern of the *world revolution of an epoch*. Those who seized power in Paris in 1789 (and immediately thereafter) were unmistakably the elite of the eruptive center of that period. But the pattern which prevailed at that time and place was not identical with the revolutionary pattern of the historical epoch as a whole, although common elements were present. It is apparent that the elite of 1917 in Moscow can be called the elite of the eruptive center of our *time*, but it is very doubtful whether the pattern then prevailing in Moscow has many elements identical with the world revolutionary pattern of our *epoch*. Indeed, one of the major tasks of the policy sciences today is to follow in detail the processes of social invention, diffusion, and restriction throughout the globe for the sake of estimating the significance of specific events.[5]

The Problem Attitude

An additional feature of the policy orientation is the importance attached to the act of creative imagination that introduces into the historical process a new and successful policy. Successful ideas cannot be guaranteed in advance. But the problem attitude can be cultivated, which increases the probability that the thinker will act as a maternity hospital for the delivery of a historically viable policy proposal. Today the perpetual crisis stemming from the expectation of violence (whether war or revolution) calls for the greatest ingenuity in devising policies capable of reducing the cost of bringing to fruition the aims of a democratically oriented policy science. This is not only a matter of improving the organization of the United Nations and other official agencies. It is also a question of introducing a current of salutary transformations wherever policy is made.

The Building of Institutions

The policy scientist is far more interested in evaluating and reconstructing the practices of society than in his private ratiocination about the higher abstractions from which his values are derived. This choice carries with it the de-emphasizing of much of the traditional baggage of metaphysics and theology. An example of what may be expected is the work of John Dewey and other American philosophers of pragmatism who quickly moved to the consideration of social institutions. (Dewey, for instance, launched an experimental school movement.) This inclination of the policy scientist has been expedited by the logical positivism of Rudolf Carnap and his associates, although Carnap has not personally drawn the implications. However, some implications are reasonably evident. If terms are intended to designate events, they do not have stable reference until "operational indexes" are specified. Indexes are operational when they can be applied by an observer with descriptive intentions, competence, and equipment, who occupies an observational standpoint in relation to a field of events to be described. The observational standpoint is the procedure used in entering the situation for data-gathering ("protocol-making") purposes.[6]

The key terms which are used in the policy sciences refer to meanings, and contexts of meaning are changeable. The significance of this is that operational indexes chosen for key words in the social sciences are less stable than the indexes usually employed by physical scientists to describe the events with which they are concerned. Hence we speak of the "index instability" of terms in the policy sciences.

Since operational indexes are unstable, it is necessary to provide for continuous surveys in order to keep operational indexes properly calibrated. The observable characteristics of certain class groups shift through time, for example, and it is therefore necessary to respecify the characteristics which are essential to the identification for descriptive purposes of a given class member.

The technical considerations which have just been outlined reinforce other incentives which induce social and psychological scientists to improve institutions for the self-observation of man in society. One of the most creative suggestions which has been made by and to UNESCO, for instance, is the setting up of a continuing survey of international tension. Activities of this kind are essential if we are to clarify the goals, trends, factors, and alternatives appropriate to the policy sciences of democracy.

The international polling operations which are now in existence are important steps toward providing more significant information than we have had in the past about the thoughts and feelings of mankind.

Closely connected with the setting-up of comprehensive institutions of self-observation is the use of pretesting procedures to assist in the evaluation of policy alternatives. In the world of business, pretesting has been carried to a high level of technical perfection. Minor variations in the ingredients of new products or changes in packaging are tested in a few places which provide samples (in the statistical sense) of potential consumer reactions. Personnel policies are sometimes pretested in a few plants before they are extended to all the plants controlled by a corporation. Systematic pretesting can be extended from the market to many other situations in society.

Social Scientists Are Not the Sole Contributors to the Policy Sciences

One outcome of the policy science conception which has begun to manifest itself in the United States is a more explicit awareness of the fact that social scientists are not the only contributors to the policy sciences. It is true that specialists in social and psychological theory will improve the basic analysis of the policy-forming process itself. But there is some recognition of the fact that men of experience in active policy-making can make greater contributions to basic analysis than the academic experts have admitted. Men of affairs often watch themselves and others in business, government, and similar institutions with great intellectual curiosity and objectivity. Some of these active participants evolve theories of the process that deserve careful criticism in the light not only of expert opinion but also of factual inquiry. Usually the men of action lack the incentives to write technical books or articles in which their theories are systematized and confronted by available data.[7] But it is enormously fruitful for the academic specialist to take some of these ideas and give them the necessary systematization and evaluation.

In order to bring the academician and the active policy-maker into fruitful association, new institutions are needed (or rather, modifications are needed in existing institutions). The seminar is already utilized for this purpose in many institutions of higher learning, as in the Graduate

School of Business and the Littauer School (devoted to government) at Harvard. Many national organizations of public administrators maintain headquarters close to the University of Chicago, an arrangement that fosters contact between the faculty of the University and the staff members of the organizations. Because of the rapid growth of public administration as a learned profession in the United States, the interplay of university-trained intellectuals and public officials (and leaders) is made easy. Until recently the law schools of the United States were wholly given over to the narrowest imaginable conception of professional training. The curriculum consisted in the memorizing and discussion of the decisions (and supporting opinions) of the appellate courts. In recent times there has been a broadening of the curriculum to include factual information about the social consequences of legal doctrines and procedures. The Yale Law School has been a pioneer in this change, even to the extent of appointing social scientists to the faculty.

The policy-science approach has the further implication that is includes, in addition to knowledge about the policy-making process itself, the assembling and evaluating of knowledge—from whatever source—which appears to have an important bearing upon the major policy problems of the time. Today, for example, the knowledge of atomic and other forms of energy which is in the possession of the physicists and other natural scientists has great and obvious relevance to world security. Creative interchange is needed between the physicists, the social scientists, and the men of action.[8] The cultivation of the technique of bringing about easy co-operation among "interdisciplinary teams" is one of the principal tasks of an evolving policy science.

Summary

Between the two world wars, American social and psychological sciences emphasized the improvement of method, especially quantitative method. There resulted a general raising of the level of competence in the making of primary observations and in the processing of data. Recently there is a tendency to take method more for granted and to put the accent upon applying method to problems that promise to make a contribution to policy. We can think of the policy sciences as the disciplines concerned with explaining the policy-making and policy-executing process, and with locating data and providing interpretations which are relevant to the policy problems of a given period. The policy approach does not imply that energy is to be dissipated on a miscellany of merely topical issues, but rather that fundamental and often neglected problems which arise in the adjustment of man in society are to be dealt with. The policy approach does not mean that the scientist abandons objectivity in gathering or interpreting data, or ceases to perfect his tools of inquiry. The policy emphasis calls for the choice of problems which will contribute to the goal values of the scientist, and the use of scrupulous objectivity and maximum technical ingenuity in executing the projects undertaken. The policy frame of reference makes it necessary to take into account the entire context of significant events (past, present, and prospective) in which the scientist is living. This calls for the use of speculative models of the world revolutionary process of the epoch, and puts the techniques of quantification in a respected though subordinate place. Because of the instability of meaning of the indexes available to give operational definition to key terms, it is particularly important to develop specialized institutions to observe and report world developments. This permits the pretesting of possible changes in social practice before they are introduced on a vast scale. It is probable that the policy-science orientation in the United States will be directed toward providing the knowledge needed to improve the practice of democracy. In a word, the special emphasis is upon the policy sciences of democracy, in which the ultimate goal is the realization of human dignity in theory and fact.

Notes

1. Charles E. Merriam, *New Aspects of Politics* (1925), p. xiii.
2. Dr. Sullivan's work is best read in the pages of *Psychiatry*, the journal published by the William Alanson White Psychiatric Foundation, Washington, D.C., with which Sullivan was connected before his death in 1949. Ruth Benedict was professor of anthropology at Columbia at the time of her death in 1948. Her most influential book was *Patterns of Culture* (1934). Margaret Mead and Clyde Kluckhohn are contributors to [*The Policy Sciences*]. For an introduction to Linton, see Linton (ed.), *The Science of Man in the World Crisis* (1945).
3. *The Governing of Men* (1945).

4. Note the following title: E. Ronald Walker, *From Economic Theory to Policy* (1943).

5. I may be permitted to refer to my own writings in which certain of these distinctions have been developed. The earliest exposition is in *World Politics and Personal Insecurity* (1935). More accessible is *The Analysis of Political Behaviour: An Empirical Approach*, published in 1948 in the "International Library of Sociology and Social Reconstruction" edited by Karl Mannheim. See particularly Part II. My 1941 developmental construct of "the garrison state" is reprinted in *The Analysis of Political Behaviour*.

6. Besides Carnap and his school, Alfred Korzybski has been widely read. See his *Science and Sanity* (1933).

7. Chester Barnard is an exception to this statement. While an active business executive he published the well-received *The Functions of the Executive* (1938). Barnard is now president of the Rockefeller Foundation. The Committee of Public Administration Cases (Social Science Research Council) has built up case studies of policy formation by examining written records, and also by interviewing the participants.

8. Successes and failures along this line are often noted in *The Bulletin of Atomic Scientists*, published in Chicago.

5

National Information Policy

Donald M. Lamberton
1974

National information policy can be viewed as embracing efforts to put into practice the basic notion that the social and economic system will function more efficiently if improved information-flows to the decision-making centers can be ensured. This notion underlies much of the effort directed to such seemingly diverse activities as mass education, market research, financial analysis, research and development (R and D) and social management techniques, such as national income accounting and input-output analysis. Each reflects a belief in the efficacy of expenditure on better information; in each case a variety of problems emerges.

Introduction

How can we ensure that the information-flows are tailored to the needs of the moment of decision? How accurate must the information be? How quickly must the information be made available? How much should we rely upon the utilization of existing information, as opposed to the pro-duction of new information? Who should have control over the existing stock and the new flows of information? Who should make the decisions about which information should be preserved and produced? Implicit in these questions is acceptance of the fact that information, as other resources, is not a free good. The passage of time does yield a flow of information to the observer, and this may seem to involve negligible cost. In contrast, the production, storage, dissemination and utilization of society's stock of information resources is an expensive business, as indi-cated by the huge allocation of resources to formal education, R and D, communications, consumer education, market research and the like. The essence of national information policy, then, emerges as a problem of resource allocation to achieve national objectives. Clearly, national information policy decisions must be coordinated with a very wide range of other policy actions; furthermore, equally clearly, information is a precondition for identifying objectives.

To emphasize the allocation of resources might seem to imply that the problems of national information policy are purely economic. However, the point and purpose of the last several centuries of economic thought can be viewed as a search for an answer to the question whether pursuit of private gain can lead to coherence rather than chaos. This question has been basic to economic analysis since 1776, when Adam Smith's *The Wealth of Nations* was published. Smith, sensing the emergent form of industrialized society, assigned a key role to the division of labor. In doing so, he eulogized the free market system, but overlooked the fact that changing technology permitted both division of labor and economy of labor; those who could not adapt suffered unemployment. More perceptive writers who followed him were to provide the nineteenth-century accounts of future shock.

In an updated, computerized society version of Smith's doctrine, Rawls and Arrow have recently interpreted the role of information in society as a cohesive force.[1] If, as they argue, the harmony of social union stems in large part from a natural complementarity among the limited and different information possessed by individuals and groups of individuals, this is clearly the concern of those involved in the process of national information policy formation. Rights in the use of information can give rise to conflicts of interest, the resolution of which must be a policy objective.

It is helpful to look at the role of information from another vantage point. A recent study of the decline of empires[2] gave great importance to growing tensions, lessened cooperation and selfishness. One might argue that group or national identity presupposes a reasonably well-developed information system and that conflict which destroys that identity results from suspension of communication.

Science versus Information Policy

Historically, policy efforts were directed towards one kind of information: scientific knowledge. As early as the 1830s Charles Babbage, inventor of the computer, advocated a national science policy, and early in the present century the English economist Alfred Marshall favored state action to encourage and strengthen British technology in the face of foreign trade competition. The impact of wars, much more than conscious efforts to use science in the solution of social problems, widened the concept of policy to embrace both science and technology. Basic statistics for policy guidance were developed and characteristically related to expenditure on research—pure and applied—and development. In the main a highly simplified, linear conception of the links between science and technology prevailed: scientific advance spawned new technologies which were implemented in the process of industrialization, with a consequential improvement in human welfare.

The last decade has seen widespread efforts to extend the scope of discussion beyond scientific and technological information to a broader concept of information. These efforts have moved along three lines. First, there was the addition of social science. This is illustrated by the developments at the Tavistock Institute in London where it was generally held that to consider any branch of science in isolation could only lead "to a fragmented, unbalanced, and unsatisfying result."[3] Likewise, the Organization for Economic Cooperation and Development (OECD), after playing a major innovatory role in the study and implementation of science policy, came to favor the extension of science and technology policy to include social sciences.[4] Second, a systems approach led naturally to consideration of scientific and technological information in relation to other kinds of information services: to education, including learning-by-doing, mass media, libraries and travel. Third, attention focussed on the new information technologies—for example, computers and satellites—which seemed to symbolize the movement of society into a new industrial revolution: the information revolution.

At this point in time all three strands are intertwined, as is amply demonstrated in the proceedings of the Intergovernmental Bureau of Informatics First World Conference on Informatics in Government held in Florence in 1971 and the World Congress on Human Communication held in Barcelona in 1973 organized by *Asociación de Comunicación Humana y Ecología*. One supposes that it is no accident that this same period has witnessed the emergence of a critique of economic growthmanship which favors the sacrifice of some traditional benefits of economic growth to ensure that diseconomies, or regrettables as Kuznets called them long ago, are minimized.

The Decision Process

As G. L. S. Shackle has made clear . . . decision—decision which is creative—is the human predicament. Available information can never be sufficient to change a decision problem into a matter of routine. The most fundamental case for an information policy rests on this proposition. However, the case is strengthened when one looks more closely at the component activities in the operation of an information system. These activities were classified in the eloquent title of a paper by Marschak: "Economics of Inquiring, Communicating, Deciding."[5]

Each of these activities is indispensable in a technologically and organizationally efficient total information process. A decision-unit's overall efficiency, its responsiveness to change and its innovatory power depend upon the performance of these highly complementary activities. Nevertheless, we should not think of fixed proportions. Trade-offs will be possible. Some units will be better at inquiring than communicating, just as now we recognize that profit differentials are attributable to relative firm skills in, say, production and marketing. An old-fashioned approach would have stopped short with a reference to rents and entrepreneurial skills.

Given the pervasiveness of the information needs among decision makers—that is, their total dependence upon information-flows in a rapidly changing world—it should be no surprise that the only comprehensive study of knowledge production and distribution in an advanced industrial country, the United States, estimated that these activities might account for between 23 to 29 percent of gross national product.[6] Other studies of the input-output type indicate that general inputs into economic activity, such as information and energy costs, have been increasing in relative importance.

An information industry of impressive proportions has developed domestically in industrialized countries and has extended across the world, but even this does not reach the heart of the policy concern today. Economists, Marxist and non-Marxist alike, have long argued that technological change is the primary determinant of growth and structural change. Today this finds expression in the expectation that the multi-faceted information industry may hold the key to the future welfare of industrialized countries. If so, it may be ushering in the next chapter in the continuing story of attempts to bridge the gap between the rich and poor nations. For access to information, which perhaps explains the success of multinational corporations, might have been the means to relative gains for the poor nations. However, the advanced countries, or their business units, seemingly have the advantage and will retain the advantage in the combined function of inquiring, communicating and deciding. This suggests an urgent need both to promote the idea of international information policy and to explore the nature of international information systems.

Information Policy and Its Problems

Policy must be more than a statement of some desired future state of affairs; it must be more than prescription of a method of dealing with a well-defined problem. Policy is, as Shackle says, "the generic name of any formulation, simple or complex, vague or exact, general or special, discretionary or detailed, of guidance for action in the face of circumstances which, lying necessarily in the future, can be approached only by conjecture and imagination."[7]

Applying this concept of policy to information, it becomes apparent that there are fundamental difficulties in relying upon the economist's notion of efficiency as such a guidance for action. For that ambiguous notion is derived in respect of a hypothetical state of affairs called perfectly competitive equilibrium which presupposes perfect knowledge. Many attempts to define perfect knowledge have achieved little; the most useful is Boulding's suggestion that perfect means costless.[8] How, then, can one account for the existence of such a large information industry?

However, this is running ahead of our theme. Consider the question: do we spend too much—or too little—on science and technology? The case for the present levels of expenditure being too low was based on the existence of indivisibilities, inappropriability and uncertainty. A given piece of information was said to be indivisible. Without suitable and effective legal protection, the benefits of information could not be fully appropriated by its possessor. Furthermore, the production of information was well known to be a risky business. It was widely held that these conditions inevitably led to too little being spent on science and technology. Private incentives were inadequate to ensure that what was socially justifiable would be carried out.

This conclusion and its policy implications found favor in industrialized countries regardless of their *ism* classification. Science became the operative ideology. This ideology suited government, industry, the military-industrial complex and professionalized groups. It found favor in less developed countries for a similar set of reasons, as well as for an important additional one: from emulation of the industrialized countries or from a deeper kind of hope, science was seen as the solution to social problems and at times was equated with Marxism.

Yet, there is a flaw in the argument. It takes as given the organization of the decision-making units; furthermore, it ignores the possible, perhaps inevitable, interactions between the information-flows and types of organization. For example, there may be very important economies of scale in the separate activities of inquiring, communicating and deciding and even more important advantages in linking these activities.[9]

The manner in which organization, information, expectation and decision are interconnected was demonstrated in a significant paper by Hirshleifer.[10] He argued most effectively that a too narrow view had been taken of the information process and emphasized the complex effects of technological change upon both anticipated and realized profits. He illustrated the basic point by reference to Eli Whitney's invention of the cotton gin. Whitney battled to protect his patent rights while others made large profits from the consequent price revaluations in cotton, slaves, land, key transport sites and financial assets.

Once the positive incentive of these pecuniary, redistributive changes is taken into account, there is no longer a clear-cut case that there must be too little expenditure on science and technology. The net effect must be known. This cannot be established *a priori*; it will depend upon the nature of the scientific and technological changes, the scope of the decision maker's activities—for example, the extent of integration of materials and machine producing activities with manufacturing and marketing—and the efficiency of the decision maker's information system.

The inconclusiveness of this debate has now been recognized,[11] but some of the implications have not as yet been appreciated. First, policy must give attention to the design of institutions, and it would seem that competence in this would be aided by more effort to study the process of policy formation. In particular, comparative studies of information utilization by individuals, agencies and even countries would be useful.

Second, if current decisions are more a reflection of a science ideology than a reasoned economic analysis of social benefits and costs, it is important to find out what does currently determine the allocation of resources to science, technology and information activities, generally. One suspects that the distribution of economic power—including that of industry, some governmental agencies and established professionalized groups—would prove to be the dominant consideration. Should this be so, it casts doubts on the very notion of a national information policy.

Third, we might say that we should be a little less ambitious. If social evaluation is not yet possible at a national aggregate level, it might nevertheless be possible to make a reasonable evaluation at a less aggregated level. We might then turn to individual research projects. An examination of a list of approvals by an Australian national funding body yielded the following projects: high energy physics; setting up a breeding colony for marsupials; social and economic teachings of the canonists and theologians 1141–1234. Techniques for comparative evaluation of such projects are most certainly lacking, and such approvals must reflect the status quo.

Fourth, models which distinguish the component activities—inquiring, communicating and deciding—and, further, which substitute more complex relationships for the simple linear view of science and technology might pave the way for a better understanding of the processes of change in modern society. They have already suggested research[12] which attempts to classify information inputs into decisions and, in time, may make possible improvement in decision rules for the allocation of resources to these different, but complementary, activities.

Property and Power

Property rights in information may be less well defined and less enforceable than property rights in real assets. However, the growth of the information industry suggests that information, as do other resources, confers both profit and power.

Much thought about income shares derives from a static, timeless economics. Consider the customary categories: wages, profit and rent. These emerged with the early stages of the Industrial Revolution. What was then significant in terms of technology, social classes and political power is no longer appropriate. If in our contemporary world information resources are the most important requirement for economic growth, the analysis of income shares ought to mirror that state of affairs.

No one owns the unexpected, but it seems likely that this resource—as has land, minerals, buildings and machines—has already become the basis of economic and political power. For this reason Alvin Toffler's *Future Shock* adhocracy seems an unlikely development. There has been a secular boom in education, and a new property class has emerged to perform the communication, coordination and control functions needed in the information revolution.

On the domestic scene, as well as the international, the information revolution is bringing structural change. Information is a resource, and control over resources permits the exercise of power and the securing of profit. Insofar as egalitarian principles are put into practice, information policy may prove to be the most important instrument. Those responsible for shaping information policy must determine the appropriate mix of information inputs to achieve social objectives, while at the same time they must have regard for equity considerations.

Notes

1. John Rawls, *A Theory of Justice* (Cambridge, Mass.: Harvard University Press, 1971); K. J. Arrow, "Some Ordinalist-Utilitarian Notes on Rawls's *Theory of Justice*," *Journal of Philosophy*, 70 (9), 10 May 1973, pp. 245–263.

2. C. M. Cipolla, ed., *The Economic Decline of Empires* (London: Methuen, 1970).

3. Tavistock Institute of Human Relations, *Social Research and a National Science Policy* (London: Tavistock pamphlet no. 7, 1964), Preface.

4. Organization for Economic Cooperation and Development, *Information in a Changing Society*.

5. J. Marschak, "Economics of Inquiring, Communicating, Deciding," *American Economic Review*, 58 (2), 1968, pp. 1–18; reprinted in *Economics of Information and Knowledge*, ed. D. M. Lamberton (New York: Penguin Books, 1971).

6. Fritz Machlup, *The Production and Distribution of Knowledge* (Princeton, N.J.: Princeton University Press, 1962).

7. G. L. S. Shackle, *Decision, Order and Time in Human Affairs*, 2nd ed. (Cambridge: Cambridge University Press, 1969), p. ix.

8. Kenneth E. Boulding, "The Economics of Knowledge and the Knowledge of economics, "*American Economic Review*, 56 (2), 1966, 1–13; reprinted in *Economics of Information and Knowledge*, ed. D. M. Lamberton (New York: Penguin Books, 1971).

9. See D. M. Lamberton, "Design Aids: Documentation," Le Conseil international du Batiment pour la recherche, l'etude et le documentation, 53 congres: *De la recherche a la pratique: le defi de l'application* (Versailles, 1971).

10. J. Hirshleifer, "The Private and Social Value of Information and the Reward to Inventive Activity," *American Economic Review*, 61 (4), 1971: 561–574.

11. P. Nelson, "Discussion," *American Economic Review*, 63 (2), 50.

12. For example, R. D. Johnston, "The National Research System—Towards an Economic Assessment." (Paper presented at the Forty-Fifth Congress of the Australian and New Zealand Association for the Advancement of Science, Perth, Australia, August 1973.)

The Politics: Policy Uses of Communication Research

6

The Symbolic Uses of Effects: Notes on the Television Violence Inquiries and the Legitimation of Mass Communications Research

Willard D. Rowland, Jr.
1981

Introduction: Focus and Method

Even without the reminders by historians such as Daniel Boorstin (1974) and David Noble (1958), it has been all too apparent that the experience of 20th century American life has been increasingly ambiguous and that fundamental paradoxes persist. The strengths and meanings of many of our principal institutions and values have been widely called into question, we never seem able to break cleanly with the mistakes of the past, and expressions of the attendant uncertainties may be found in various cultural and political forums.

Public policy concerns about the role of mass communication in American life and related questions about human social behavior represent two such expressions. This chapter summarizes a much more comprehensive study of a major aspect of those two concerns—the issue of research into the effects of violence on television and how it has been used in the policy-making process for broadcasting (Rowland, 1981). The history and institutional interactions reviewed here constitute an examination of the public attempts through the vehicle of legislative oversight and the language of social science to comprehend and interpret the significance of mass communication and its content.

This approach rises out of the developing tradition of critical cultural studies with its emphasis on history and symbolic analysis. To paraphrase the political scientist Murray Edelman (1964), this is a study of the symbolic uses of communications effects research. Edelman strives to call "attention to wide gulfs between our solemnly taught, common sense assumptions about what political institutions do and what they actually do" (p. 2). He asks us "to look searchingly at every unquestioned or widely taught assumption about how government works, for it is a key characteristic of myth that it is generally unquestioned, widely taught and believed, and that the myth has consequences, though not the ones it literally proclaims" (p. 4).

The general subject matter of the research reported here is the interaction among the federal, political process of communications policy-making, the broadcasting industry, the public or citizens' interest groups and the communications effects research community. The specific focus is upon the terms of this interaction as it bears on the question of the effects of violence on television, and in keeping with Edelman's charge, the study examines the beliefs implicit in these relationships and the consequences that derive therefrom. Thus, the research treats the concerns with violence and with television as essentially symbolic issues, as problems bespeaking the uncertainties of the modern era.

The major institutions and figures in this study are the congressmen, commissions, staffs and bureaucracies that have provided the forum for debate of the television effects issue; the prominent spokesmen for communications research who have become principal actors on that stage; the reformers who have tried to carve out a larger role in the policy drama; and the management and research figures in the broadcasting industry who have sought to influence the form and substance of the play. In focusing on these leading actors the research is informed by that approach to intellectual history that Hugh Duncan, building on Kenneth Burke's notion of historiography as parable, calls a "dramatic reconstruction" (Burke, 1965, p. 274; Duncan, 1970, p. 50). It responds to and tries to capture the flavor of the emerging set of linkages among the institutions and patterns of thought in 20th century industry, politics, reform, communications and the academy.

The full study is organized in three parts. Part I traces the early history of mass communications research in the context of the rise of American social science research, giving particular emphasis to the association of science with industrial and political needs in public policy-making. Part II presents the history of violence effects research in interaction with the almost continuous political inquiry into the impact of television, examining the relationships among the principal interested institutional parties. Finally, Part III reviews some of the academic and political implications of this history, stressing the symbolic uses of the violence effects research efforts and their role in shaping popular imagery and public policy toward television. The remainder of this paper summarizes the findings and argument of all three parts of the complete report.

Effects Research as a Mediator of Television

A comprehensive social history of mass communications effects research remains unwritten. Summaries of the literature abound, and popular textbooks now present standard descriptive chronologies. Typical oft-cited reviews have been those contained in Klapper (1960), Weiss (1969), DeFleur and Ball-Rokeach (1975), Katz (1977), and Comstock et al. (1978). But most such accounts mainly attempt to provide legitimation for mainstream empirical trends in mass communication theory and research methodology. Occasionally this effort fosters some attention to intellectual roots and the processes by which the several theories and approaches have emerged, competed and variously failed or prevailed. But, as part of a longstanding American tradition of pragmatism in the social and behavioral sciences, the effects research reviews tend to cast themselves in light of the applied research needs or trends of the moment.

There is little inclination in these accounts to perceive developments in communications and in communications research as part of the broader American social and political history nor to see the research developments as expressions of a social science which has also emerged in interaction with that complex web of changing events and ideas. That is, the standard chronologies of mass communications effects research have a relatively shallow historical consciousness. They are published and faithfully regurgitated in communications curricula with virtually no recognition of the impact upon such research of general ideological and sociopolitical developments nor of the cultural significance of the emergence of effects research in association with the rise of science as a pre-eminent institution in American life.

The Received History of Effects Research

The standard accounts of effects research appear in several sources, but may be summarized as follows: During the two decades following

World War I there emerged widespread concern about the power of the developing forms of mass communication. There was disturbing evidence of the effective deceptions visited upon public opinion through the press and motion pictures by wartime propaganda. Public attendance at motion pictures increased during the 1920s and then leaped ahead again with the arrival of sound, pausing only slightly at the outset of the Depression. Meanwhile the rapid development of a commercial radio industry added further impetus to the redeployment of leisure time and to the emergence of a national entertainment and information culture. Responding to widespread anxiety about the moral and social implications of these developments the sciences of psychology and sociology, newly emergent themselves, sought to measure the impact of these startling, somewhat awesome media. Special studies of such matters as the effects on children of violence depicted on film, of the consequences of the radio broadcast of a science fiction play, of the causes of changes in voting decisions, and of the effects of official campaigns of persuasion during World War II began with the assumption that the mass media have widespread, direct, and powerful effects on attitude and behavior. Heavily influenced by general learning theory and conditioning models in behavioristic psychology these studies grew out of a "hypodermic needle" concept of communications effects.

The received history goes on to argue that, in light of unexpected discoveries in these studies and of ever more sophisticated models, methods and findings in sociology and social psychology, researchers became increasingly suspicious of the earlier assumptions about direct effects. They claimed to have found mounting evidence of important intervening variables and defenses—factors such as the demographic background of the audience, group dynamics, selective perception and other social and mental states that could be taken as mitigating the direct impact of the media or as accounting for considerable portions of the changes occurring during political and commercial campaigns. The consequent "limited effects" models tended to exonerate the media, suggesting that their impact could largely be explained as a function of the social environment in which they operate, that at most their effect is to activate and reinforce preexisting dispositions and that their impact is diffused through the interpretative agencies of "opinion leaders" and a "two-step flow" of communications.

Such histories contend that because of these findings the effects research program turned away from an examination of "what the media do to people" toward the study of "what people do with the media." In one direction, guided increasingly by diffusion models from rural sociology, communications researchers attempted to trace patterns of innovation and information dissemination and the role of the media therein. In another direction, due to the failure of causal models, with their unfulfilled promises of empirical generalization and predictability, and due to the rise in social and organizational sciences of gestalt, systems and other holistic theories, communications researchers adopted functional models from general sociology, hoping to find an explanatory framework of "uses and gratifications" through which audience preferences and reactions are presumably shaped. Later elaborations included attempts to determine the "agenda setting" functions and, under the influence of symmetry and balance theories, the "coorientation" uses of communications media. Here the communications research models respond even more fully to modern social science concepts of the individual and the communications process as being well seated in a nexus of social contexts and structure. Down another yet somewhat parallel path, responding to the rise of cognitive development perspectives in psychology, there has been increased emphasis on "information processing" and applied formative and critical skills research.

While the emphasis varies from version to version, the essential elements of the standard history are here. They represent the received view of an increasingly self-confident, legitimized effects research enterprise. Such an account does not, however, represent the only way of relating the story. To better understand the specific history of the violence effects research tradition it is necessary to recast somewhat the general effects developments.

An Alternative View of Effects: The Problem of Television Violence

As the received version suggests communications inquiries during the past two generations have been informed for the most part by the predominant perspectives of the social and behavioral sciences. In many instances developments in communications research have lagged a decade or so behind the "parent" sciences, but even in those cases where the association has been closer in time the trend has been one of imitation and following. A fundamental, yet seldom asked question in this regard is, why should communication studies in the United States be captured so thoroughly and so early by the empirical sciences?

After World War I, with the rapid spread of film and radio, the economic and social impact of mass communication did become a more serious public issue. Building on earlier important changes in popular culture these more universally visible, national, economically significant media became closely associated in the public mind with cultural and political dislocations that defied easy analysis or acceptance. The growing complexities and ambiguities of modern life, and the role in them of new communications technologies and cultural forms, cried out for explanation.

A normal channel for such interpretation rested in the process of political debate over proper legislative options. But the rise of radio placed the political leadership in a particularly uncomfortable position. The physical properties of broadcast transmission and fears of monopoly control led to an unprecedented degree of communications regulation by government. Limited access to the spectrum dictated a general public interest mandate that offered licenses under a fiduciary principle. Beyond requiring an acceptable standard of technical service, that mandate provided that broadcasters be evaluated on the basis of their programming performance. Having set such criteria, Congress and its agents, first the Federal Radio Commission (FRC), later the Federal Communications Commission (FCC), were faced with establishing and reviewing them. However, in view of constitutional protections for the freedoms of speech and press, closely associated with a liberal mythology that accepted the dangers of governmental censorship, but had difficulty recognizing its existence in the private, corporate imperatives of competitive commercial communications, regulatory power over broadcasting was severely constrained. Moreover the *Radio Act of 1927* and the *Communications Act of 1934* had been written largely to the specifications of the principal industry forces so as to preserve the fundamental system of commercial private enterprise control and network programming dominance that had been developing prior to their passage. The terms of public interest broadcasting implied as a major element the preservation of conditions for a stable, profit-making broadcasting business, and no subsequent congressional review could ignore the general political economic environment dictating that that basic system be allowed to proceed unhampered.

All of these conditions were established before the rise of television, which of all the ambiguities of modern life was among the most troubling. As Boorstin observes (1974, pp. 390–397), television conquered America with dizzying speed, extending, segregating and democratizing experience so as to make everyday life yet more vague and befogged. It reenergized the debate about the impact of modern communications and ever changing technology.

In simple structural terms television's growth during the 1950s greatly changed patterns of leisure time use and commercial and political practices. At the outset major consequences included the decline of attendance at movie theaters, the relegation of radio to background music and news, and the perceived waning of the authority of newspapers. As well, the consumer goods industries discovered in television a powerful new marketing tool, and political figures quickly found it necessary to adjust the style and substance of their campaigns and performances in office in order to attract and exploit the particular projective characteristics of the new medium. These developments combined with other changes in the economy and the political process to enhance the position of national forms of marketing and distribution and to undermine the power of local forms of party organization.

In more general terms, the conflicting reactions generated by television included the extreme poles of evoluation, taking it as both messianic and demonic. As the newest, most spectacular piece of communications technology, television was cast by the American progressive tradition as the repository of hope for a revived democratic process, a stronger set of social bonds, a richer cultural life and a vastly improved educational system. On the other hand it was perceived by established institutions and brokers of morality and values as the latest and most dangerous in a series of technological and social inroads on their authority and status. It represented yet another assault on the family, interpersonal relationships and small-scale, local forms of community by large, bureaucratic, impersonal and nationally oriented forms of organization. From this perspective the political, social and cultural orders were in serous jeopardy. There were several examples of the mixture of love and fear expressed by many observers not just of television, but also of the entire developing universe of popular culture.[1]

This sort of conflict increasingly forced on television the role of lightning rod for the storms of public controversy about the nature of contemporary life, and it became ever more important to find better ways to interpret the significance of this latest development in communications. The public debate required means and terms to mediate the medium, but the customary interpretative institutions seemed no longer to be suited for the task. Traditional criticism approached the problem as a matter of aesthetics, reducing the debate about this pervasive new experience to the class-struggle terms of high and low culture, more appropriate in European than American contexts of social and political commentary. This approach was epitomized in the critiques of "masscult" by Dwight MacDonald (1962). Religious and educational institutions could only fulminate moralistically against television's content values and its presumed impact on family and social structures. Such an attack seemed to become increasingly moot as it became apparent that it was at least in part motivated by the discoveries of the intellectual, sacred and instructional domains that once again, as during the earlier struggles with the film industry (Jowett, 1976), their authority was in the process of being bypassed by yet another form of popular communication. Political, educational and religious institutions were all paralyzed by the conflict between their apprehensions about television and their various interests in harnessing and exploiting it for themselves and their definitions of the public interest.

Some have observed that toward the end of television's first quarter-century there was an expansion among the active parties-at-interest in broadcast policy-making. For instance, several sources show how during the late 1960s and early 1970s the original triumvirate of major policy setters—the Congress, the FCC, and the broadcast industry—were joined in new and significant ways by the White House, the courts and the various groups in the public interest or citizens' action movement (see

Krasnow & Longley, 1978; Branscomb & Savage, 1978; Guimary, 1975; Grundfest, 1976; Cole & Oettinger, 1978). Yet the growing role of the research community goes generally unacknowledged. Standard textbook histories take note of the research issues, but such accounts are largely attempts to relate the trends in the theories of effects (e.g., Head, 1976; DeFleur & Ball-Rokeach, 1975). In virtually no cases have the principal sources on broadcasting and public policy-making for it recognized the institution of research—and more importantly the ideas associated with its particular language, assumptions and methods—as of at least equal importance with the other institutions in the changing terms of reference for debate at all levels about the significance of and the necessary response to television.

Since the normal channels of interpretation had proved unequal to the mediating task, and since it had become accustomed to doing so in other areas of public policy, the political and popular imagination seized on the investigative promise of science to an increasingly significant degree for the television policy debate. For over a century science had steadily grown to undergird a widening range of advances in industrial and commercial enterprise. For nearly as long, certain aspects of science had also been finding their way into prominence in governmental policy-making (Lyons, 1969).[2] Beginning with engineering and the natural sciences in matters of defense, agriculture, and public works and then with statistics and economics in matters of social planning. The political process and its attendant bureaucracies later became adept at employing the increasingly self-confident forms of applied sociology and psychology. During the second quarter of the 20th century the social and behavioral sciences began to make themselves indispensible elements in public planning for a variety of programs in social reform and welfare. With the ground well prepared by this experience in the applied use of social science, the dilemmas encountered in the rise of electronic mass communication could be seen as perhaps equally susceptible to social scientific investigation and analysis.

That the record of social science in public policy-making was far from clearly successful and appropriate was irrelevant. American corporate and government affairs were seen as a series of problems to be solved. Public policy involved less debate over ends and more over means; the issues were those of technique and engineering, not values and morals. The comfortable association of industrial and political objectives dictated a science that was long on technical sophistication and short on epistemological reflection. With goals unspecified, only implicit in the overall structure of commercial and political enterprise, the primary criteria for evaluation were validity, reliability, efficiency and objectivity. From a more removed perspective, particularly that of the philosophy of science and hermeneutics (e.g., Habermas, 1971), the existence of such attributes in social science has come to be highly debatable. Nevertheless the image of their certainty and irrefutability was well entrenched. Their acceptance meshed neatly into the interaction of industrial, political, communications and academic interests.

Moreover the tradition of applied research in American science began to develop an institutional form in the social and behavioral sciences that had considerable significance for the focus of the emerging studies of communication. That is, as reflected in the creation of the Bureau of Applied Social Research at Columbia university, a product largely of cooperation among Frank Stanton of CBS, Paul Lazarsfeld, Hadley Cantril, and the Rockefeller Foundation, there emerged a structure for the pursuit of audience research in the United States rooted firmly in a combination of fascination with empirical social science methodology, practical marketing research experience and broadcast industry commercial and political needs (see Bartos, 1977; Lazarsfeld, 1969). The early efforts of the Bureau involved two important problems faced by the broadcasting industry. One was the vital need to develop a better ratings research capacity that would demonstrate radio's ability to compete with the print media as an effective advertising tool. The second problem was to show that, in spite of all the then current criticism by some in Congress and the FCC, this privately-held, commercially-motivated, and network-dominated medium was in fact exercising its public trust obligations under the law and was providing a socially responsible service.

The legacy of the Bureau was at least two-fold. One, developing on the margins of the academy during the 1930s and World War II, it served as a vehicle for contract research underwritten by both industry and government, often jointly, and as such it became a model for the development during the post-war arrival of television for a host of centers, institutes and schools of communication research that also depended heavily on commercial and governmental grant funding. Two, the work of the Bureau, represented by the long string of research anthologies edited by Stanton and Lazarsfeld (Lazarsfeld, 1940; Lazarsfeld & Stanton, 1941, 1944, 1949), the series of "People Look at . . ." audience reports begun by Lazarsfeld and since carried on in different guises by Steiner, Bower and Roper (Lazarsfeld & Field, 1946; Lazarsfeld & Kendall, 1948; Steiner, 1963; Bower, 1973; Roper, 1979), the seminal campaign studies of Lazarsfeld, Berelson, and Gaudet (1944) and Lazarsfeld and Katz (1955), and the limited effects work of Klapper (1960), helped set the agenda for much of a whole generation of American mass communications scholarship growing up in those new applied research centers. Yet the origins of all that work in the Bureau—its commercial and political purposes—remain obscure in the contemporary communications research consciousness.

Another contributing thread to the genesis of American communications research during the War years was the interaction through the Office of War Information, the Army's Information and Education Division and other aspects of the Allied propaganda and behavioral research efforts of communications industry and government officials with a substantial body of behaviorial and social scientists who were turning their attention increasingly to communications problems. In addition to Lazarsfeld, Stanton, Cantril, and Berelson, this nexus of contacts and projects included such students of communications as Robert Merton, Samuel Stouffer, George Gallup, Elmo Roper, Wilbur Schramm, Carl Hovland, Irving Janis and Nathan Maccoby. Their various efforts led to continued support for the Bureau, the development of the "American Soldier" series (Osborn et al., 1949), its subsequent line of social psychological studies of media effects at Yale (Hovland, Janis, & Kelley, 1953), and a broader set of personal and professional relationships that were to be reflected in the postwar development of communications research in universities around the world and in various other series of basic readers and texts on effects by Schramm (1948, 1949, 1954, 1960, 1971), Berelson and Janowitz (1950, 1953, 1963), Charles Wright (1959, 1975), and Melvin DeFleur (1966, 1972, 1975).

As television became an increasingly significant factor in postwar society and culture, the pressure to explain it became more intense. An important aspect of the response to that pressure is revealed in the history of political inquiry into the effects of media violence. In the violence effects issue and the political concern about television's social impact the mass communications research community found the vehicle necessary for it to begin to obtain identity and ultimately to achieve legitimacy in the academy. The struggles therein for supremacy among competing social sciences had carried over into the effort to interpret the new medium.

A liberal, optimistic and newly retooled American social psychology, increasingly a part of the growing, commercially and federally sponsored research enterprise, proved to be a highly attractive competitor for research funds and public recognition. As noted above, during and shortly after the War studies of interpersonal behavior and communications began to propose more complicated theoretical models and methodological approaches. In light of such work the original behavioral models of communications appeared to be breaking down. As result of the work at the Bureau, much of which began to appear in the postwar research anthologies now edited by Schramm, attention turned increasingly from the outcome of communications to the networks of interpersonal relationships and the demographic characteristics that were perceived to intervene in and guide the process of mass communication.

This newer approach, more comfortable with the technology and complexities of contemporary life, and more secure in its perceptions of emerging social and political stability, was less pessimistic and fearful. It was also closely associated with a long tradition of liberal, progressive reform which in spite of anxieties about large corporate enterprise has always remained hopeful for the long-promised ameliorative, educative, social and political impact of each new technology of communication (see Rowland, forthcoming). Now its review of the previous research seemed to conclude that the proof of deleterious effects claimed under the original models could no longer be sustained. Coming at the end of television's first decade and on the heels of a host of seemingly confirming research, Klapper's analysis (1960) seemed to settle the matter. His work attempted to exculpate television, arguing that it did not have demonstrable negative effects. That such findings were the result of research funded by the industry and conducted long before, as part of Klapper's doctoral work in the Bureau in the 1940s, and that Klapper was by now Director of Research at Stanton's CBS appeared to lead to few questions within the communications research community.

In view of the collection of findings in the various Lazarsfeld-Katz campaign studies, the continuing "People Look at . . ." surveys of the Bureau, and the Klapper work, Bernard Berelson and others, for many of whom communications had never been the primary interest, felt that this field of research had exhausted the possibilities and that the time had come to move on to matters of more pressing concern in social and public welfare. However, many observers retained the view that communications issues remained serious and substantial, and they therefore resisted the pressure to turn away from the study of media impact. These differences led to a communications research equivalent of the "God is Dead" debate which took place in the pages of the *Public Opinion Quarterly* during the late 1950s (see Berelson, 1959; Schramm, Riesman, & Bauer, 1959).

But the new generation, trained during the postwar period with a primary emphasis on methodology and technique, was not encouraged to reflect from a critical, philosophical perspective upon the assumptions and the consequent implications of the contending scientific models. As a result there was among many proponents of the expanding study of mass communications a rush to embrace the new approaches and to redefine communications research in terms of the new sociology and social psychology. That this remodelling had been fostered by and tended to serve the interests of the television industry, now increasingly on the defensive before congressional committees, and that the shift of emphasis was not in the end any real departure from behavioristic views, went largely ignored, or at least little acknowledged. In academic forums the critique of the media turned toward the rationalizations of functionalism and uses and gratifications; in popular debate it turned toward the McLuhanesque embrace of technology and the celebration of an electronic nirvana. The role of the effects research community had ascended from the prophetic to the priestly.

However, the complaints about television content never completely abated. Common sense argued that television was having an obvious major impact on attitudes and behavior, and the evidence of daily observation during the 1960s was unsettling. On the street violence appeared to be increasing. At one level violence became the focus of concern over the rapidity of change and the threat to traditional mainstream values represented by urban and racial conflict. At another level it stunned the popular psyche by injecting itself into domestic and foreign politics. Assassination and war, and their attendant dislocations, were no longer problems of previous, presumably less-settled eras. Intertwined with these developments were the inroads of television into the national consciousness. In whatever forms of fiction—news or drama—it served at least as a messenger of the behavior of force and its related confusion. High levels of television violence persisted, becoming an inescapable part of the evening viewing diet. To many the association of medium content and the social experience of violence was no longer coincidental, nor was it explicable any longer merely as a mirroring phenomenon. The issue of effects still could not be ignored.

In particular the legislative review machinery, that element of the political process responsible for overseeing and representing the public interest in broadcasting, found itself increasingly embroiled in the controversy over the impact of television. As separate issues, both violence and television became matters of greater symbolic import in the general social commentary. Soon they became inextricably intertwined as a single issue at the heart of the debate over the character and directions of an increasingly complex, ambiguous society.

Congressional investigations of television have been almost continuous since 1952. In nearly every Congress one or more House or Senate committees have found occasion to hold hearings on some aspect or another of television performance. While seldom the only focus, the concerns about violence have served as a constant, major theme during most of this period. In association with those concerns the political process has come increasingly to endorse and use approaches laid out by the social and communications research community.

During the initial House hearings on television (Harris Subcommittee) the issue of violence and the use of formal research to investigate its impact were not central. On the whole this first sparring match between Congress and the television industry was a congenial, gingerly handled exercise. The major interest there lay elsewhere, guided by the more consuming contemporary McCarthyite fears about communism in all communications media (U.S. House, 1952).

But by the mid-1950s the social and behavioral sciences had managed to climb into the ring. The Senate juvenile delinquency investigation, beginning with the work of Hendrickson-Kefauver Subcommittee (U.S. Senate, 1954, 1955a, 1955b) and continuing with the Dodd Subcommittee (U.S. Senate, 1961–1962, 1964), became an ever larger promoter of the emerging forms of communications effects research. Nearly all the theoretical and methodological debates about effects within the academy were aired in the various hearings testimony and staff reports of those portions of the investigation bearing on television. While always careful to place caveats on the extent of the ability of communications research to resolve the issues being examined by Congress, leaders in the field such as Lazarsfeld, Schramm, Albert Bandura and Leonard Berkowitz, nonetheless came to be regular participants in the public debates, substantially advancing the interests of their science through their growing political status as expert authorities and their pleas for more federal funds for communications research.

Meanwhile the television industry, increasingly under attack not only about violent content in its programming, but also about such matters as the quiz show and ratings scandals (Barnouw, 1975; Head, 1976), began to respond to the growing political use of communications research, not by direct opposition, but through the continuing, more subtle process of cooption and diversion. Building on the prior relationships with university based research and joint governmental funding, the industry continued to support and promote selected research efforts, while overlooking or avoiding others. Largely under Stanton's careful guidance, CBS, the NAB and other industry organizations collaborated in such efforts as promising in 1954 to develop a long-range investigation into the impact of television programs on children and adults, dusting off Klapper's dissertation and publishing it in 1960, and in 1962 forming a Joint Committee for Research on Television and Children

(JCRTC), with representatives from the industry, foundations, universities and government.

By the late 1960s the purposes and results of these projects were clear. The 1954 NAB "pilot study" for the larger investigation was never commissioned, and it was replaced instead by the CBS-sponsored Steiner report on public attitudes about television—a continuation of the old Lazarsfeld "People Look at . . ." research in the Bureau, which again tended to portray a largely positive image of the industry and which in any case was hardly an effects study. Over a six-and-a-half year period the JCRTC, which had ostensibly been formed to promote, fund and coordinate serious academic effects research and training, managed to underwrite one "catharsis theory" research project by Seymour Feshback, with results that did not disappoint the networks, and it published only one report, a critical review of the effects research literature which turned out to be merely an extension of Klapper's work (see Baker et al., 1969, pp. 593–599; Briand, 1969, p. 347).

In light of this pattern of industry-academic interaction and the subsequent confusion shown in Congress about the extent of the research findings, it is not surprising that the juvenile delinquency investigations led to no significant changes in federal policy toward television. It is unclear whether the congressional leaders were aware at this point that the complexities of the research findings would confound the ability of critics to draw firm conclusions about the impact of television and about the extent of necessary changes. However Barnouw (1975, pp. 304–306) does suggest that, particularly during the period of the Dodd Subcommittee investigation, congressional punches were deliberately pulled.

For a brief period in the late-1960s Congress lost its direct control of the investigation of television violence. In 1968, in the wake of several summers of racial violence in cities all around the country, the mounting, massed public demonstrations against the Vietnam War and the assassinations of Martin Luther King, Jr. and Robert F. Kennedy, President Johnson appointed a National Commission on the Causes and Prevention of Violence (NCCPV). The charge to the Commission was writ broadly enough to incorporate concerns about the role of the media, and in most of its facets the NCCPV became a heavy user of social and behavioral research of all sorts (Graham & Gurr, 1969; Baker & Ball,

1969). During its hearings on the media the Commission therefore heard testimony from many in the communications and industrial research community, including several who had appeared in prior congressional hearings as well as some younger members of this growing field (Briand, 1969). As with those prior hearings, the array of perspectives represented here ranged from classic behavioristic conclusions about the direct causal relationship between televised violence and social aggression to strong, functionalist limited effects views about the existence of prior tendencies, mitigating factors and the reinforcing aspects of media influence.

The one new piece of research enterprise engendered by the Commission was the funding of the first in what was to become an annual series of content analyses of commercial television programming and the incidence of violence therein—a project which represented a considerable further increase in the status of communications research in public affairs. One notes that of all the major research projects related to the violence issue developed during the late 1960s, this has been the most successful in continuing to garner public and private support (Gerbner & Gross, 1976; Gerbner et al., 1980). However, one also observes that it has been the most applied, monitoring aspects of the research—the "violence profile" (the counting of violent acts) and not the "cultural indicators" portion—that has guaranteed that support (for a clear example of the quid pro quo problem here, see U.S. Senate, 1974, pp. 40–41, 48–49, 57).[3]

The final NCCPV report traffics in the scientific evidence put before it, but it carefully avoids reaching any firm conclusions about the effects of media violence (National Commission, 1970). The role of the Commission thus turned out to be similar to that of the prior congressional investigations. It was a ritualistic political response to a matter of apparently increasing public concern that came to don the mantle of science in its process and to adopt the stern demeanor of public authority disappointed in the performance of an industry licensed under a mandate of sacred public trust. The Commission seems to be building a damning case against the commercial television industry, yet in the end it stops short of all but the weakest, least controversial recommendations.

In light of the political needs at least to appear to be taking a close, hard look at the television industry and its possible contributions to the apparent American culture of violence in the late 1960s, Congress could not long defer renewed investigation of its own. Therefore, in 1969 well before the NCCPV had finished its work, Senator John O. Pastore, Chairman of the Senate Subcommittee on Communications, announced his own plans for a further, even more extensive investigation into television and social behavior, to be coordinated under the auspices of the Surgeon General in HEW's National Institute of Mental Health and to be guided by a Scientific Advisory Council of academic and industry research representatives (U.S. Senate, 1969). Established in this manner the project was to be a formal, widespread study of effects that would be rooted extensively in the social and behavioral sciences. Far from having any longer to beg for support and to claim legitimacy for itself, communications research was now going to be annointed at the highest levels of public policy and called upon for a command performance. The study was modeled on the recently concluded Surgeon General's research effort that had seemed to have convincingly established a link between smoking and cancer. Senator Pastore's public announcements seemed to imply his belief that it would be feasible to pursue a parallel process of exploration for a causal link between violence on television and antisocial behavior, and his project now made available to the communications research community an unprecedented amount of funding (over $1.0 million) concentrated in a relatively short period of time.

While many of the studies for the project were in fact merely extensions or reincarnations of previous grants, the scope was large enough to involve several dozen principal investigators and countless additional research colleagues and graduate students from universities all around the country, and it resulted in a seven-volume report, five of which were massive collections of the technical research studies (see the various volumes titled, *Television and Social Behavior*, 1972). In an important sense the project was a monument to those who had built the communications research enterprise over the preceding generation. It was just the sort of organized, large-scale applied research effort involving cooperation among the government, industry and academy that had been the basis for the formation of the Bureau and so many subsequent institutes and schools of communications research. Further, many of the principals in the project, whether on the Advisory Committee, the NIMH coordinating staff or among the contract researchers, had been students of senior scholars such as Lazarsfeld and Schramm or their colleagues, and in no small part due to their ability to participate in the continuing communications violence research investigations represented by this project, many of these younger scholars were becoming heirs to the mantle of leadership for the next generation of communications research.

The findings of the Advisory Committee's summary report were embroiled in controversy even before they were published, and they represent a debate that has never really been settled since. The cautious, caveat-filled language of the summary report (Surgeon General's Scientific Advisory Committee, 1972) outraged many of the academics involved in the project and an even broader collection of like-minded reform proponents who generally felt that much of the technical research pointed to a more convincing case for causality than the report would acknowledge. Initially Senator Pastore appeared to share that outrage, and in a series of hearings before his Subcommittee in 1971 and 1972 he managed to evoke stronger, seemingly more definitive judgments about the causality issue from the Surgeon General, members of the Advisory Committee and other participants in the project (U.S. Senate, 1971, 1972). Many of the published and unpublished sources dealing with the project in the heat of its immediate aftermath also concluded that the evidence was stronger than the summary report allowed (see Bogart, 1972–73; Cater & Strickland, 1975; Comstock, 1975; Meyer and Anderson, 1973; Paisley, 1972).

The critics have typically cited at least two major problems with the report and the process that led to it. One was the extent of industry influence on the Advisory Committee, wherein the broadcasters not only were able to place their own representatives on the Committee, such as Klapper and his counterpart at NBC, Thomas Coffin, but also were permitted to veto the appointment of other research figures, some of whom might well have been more sympathetic to the direct causal findings. Two, many critics have questioned the extent of Senator Pastore's commitment to letting the causal evidence come through and his willingness to act on those findings. In spite of his seemingly hardline approach to the networks in his post-report hearings, the critics have noticed other activities by the Subcommittee during the period of the Surgeon General's report, such as the S. 2004 five-year license renewal bill proposal, that suggest that the Subcommittee and the Congress in general had probably never been willing to permit the Surgeon General's report to lead to any firm changes in federal policy toward the television industry.

It remains questionable how accurate the critics are on the implications of the first count. Surely the composition of the Advisory Committee had an important influence on the cautious tone of the report. But careful, disinterested review of the corpus of the research from the distance of several years does not now lead as easily as the critics would have it to any overwhelming conclusion that the causal link is established or even strongly suggested. Without being an apologist for the industry one can observe that the theoretical assumptions of much of the research and the various methodological and statistical techniques employed leave considerable reason for doubt about the conclusiveness of the findings. On the second matter the implications of the criticism may be somewhat more accurate. While the period of the late 1960s and early 1970s witnessed a substantial increase in the activity of reform groups and in their influence in Congress and at the FCC, current policy research suggests that their impact on the real terms of broadcast industry purpose, structure and control has been negligible and that, indeed, the congressional communications subcommittees have played an important role in deflecting that influence (Rowland, 1982; Haight, 1979).

Thus, whether right or wrong on either of these counts or on the myriad other matters pertaining to the details of the Surgeon General's report, critics and defenders alike all tend to overlook what from the perspective of this paper remains the significance of the project. For, as before, it turns out that this investigation was yet another act in the continuing ritual of public debate and policy avoidance about television, and its history reveals even more thoroughly the problems associated with the increasing role of communications research in that drama. The importance of the way the project was administered and of the argument over its results lies not in the composition of the Advisory Committee nor in the relative strength of the causal evidence, but in realizing how the entire issue of television in society and the means for publicly discussing it came to be captured so thoroughly by the empirical social and behavioral scientific imagination and that none of the difficulties implied by the terms of that form of discourse were ever seriously examined.

Summary

The Surgeon General's report and the continuing aspects of the investigation of television and social behavior since must be seen against the backdrop of the history of the development of public policy for broadcasting and of the simultaneous, inextricably intertwined rise and legitimation of the mass communications research enterprise. In building the case for its approach, the communications science research community found itself tapping popular anxieties about television—the newest, most intrusive medium of mass communication—and associating itself with the highly technical, quantitative social and behavioral research methodologies of other disciplines that had already achieved considerable popular and political acceptance in public policy debate. Throughout this process of development the broadcasting industry alternately supported and opposed the research enterprise, carefully cultivating, and thereby shaping, certain of its aspects and allowing others to wither. Whether or not the product of a conscious choice, the communications research leaders managed to ignore the industrial and political terms of their origins and the closely related problematic issues of epistemology wrapped up in their approaches. As a result, the public controversy over television's effects was allowed to proceed in virtual ignorance of the particular institutional accommodations and sociocultural conceptualizaions upon which it was based. To the extent debate emerged, it centered on issues of methodology and narrow aspects of theory. In the process of legitimation there was little willingness or ability to transcend discussions of research technique to consider the linkages of the entire research enterprise to the general pattern of commercial and political expectations for social science research.

For their part the politicians may be depicted as having found in the effects research efforts a vehicle useful for them to project an image of concerned inquiry, while yet insuring that that inquiry would force them into little, if any, legislative action. Investing in the rise of mass communications research, the federal communications policy-making process associated itself with the popularly acceptable terms of scientific research. All the while, however, the officials involved in this process were discovering that, due to a combination of fundamental constitutional and political economic commitments and the actual inconclusiveness of the research efforts, the research approach not only failed accurately to address the underlying problems of control and purpose of commercial communications, but also served to mask and divert attention from such issues. In all this, for similarly diversionary purposes, the broadcasting industry avoided outright opposition to the trend toward greater governmental attention to the research tool, choosing instead to infiltrate the process of decision-making about appropriate and inappropriate lines of inquiry.

As for the reform groups, the research agenda was well structured by the time they became a more organized part of the policy debate. Yet, as has been the case throughout the history of progressive reform in general, the goals of the newer groups were susceptible to severe compromise due to a continuing pattern of paradox between the ideals of reform and the changing practical conditions under which it has always had to work. As with many of the liberal research community critics with whom they were often affiliated, the media reformers had little ability to recognize the symbolic nature of the debate and the ways in which it might actually be working against the changes they hoped it would foster. A further irony was that the reformers' attacks on television and their calls for more intensive research and policy investigation tended to overstate the significance of the medium, lending it more authority and power than perhaps it otherwise might have commanded.

In the period since the Surgeon General's report many of the earlier policy difficulties have persisted. The problems are apparent in such matters as the arrival and fate of the "family viewing hour," the continuing congressional violence and obscenity hearings throughout the 1970s, the industry response, the research interests reflected in the Reston, NSF/RANN, and "prosocial" effects projects, the debate over the validity of the "cultivation analysis" extension of the violence profile, the shift of some of the reform and research focus away from violence toward advertising and its effects on children, the associated backlash against the Federal Trade Commission (FTC), the increased pressure on the FCC to deregulate the broadcasting and cable industries and the emergence of the efforts to "rewrite" the Communications Act. These developments reveal much about the enduring problems for communication research of the political and reform demands for applicability, of industrial participation in setting the research agenda and of the research community's presumptions about its value-freeness and independence.

Thus there remains for effects research of all kinds and for communication science generally the prodigious, difficult task of reexamining its origins and coming thereby to be able to think more critically about the assumptions guiding its definition of important problems in the relationships between television and society. Under the current frame of reference the basic images of television, of communications in general, and of their social import remain those of the peculiar, and particularly American, tradition of positivistic science that, as it is reflected in the mass communications research community, continues to be largely unaware of the significance of the industrial and political influences upon it.

Notes

1. One of the most vivid examples was reflected in the major swings of opinion during the career of Gilbert Seldes, with first his praise of popular entertainment (1924), then his ominous warning about the use and effect of the popular arts (1951), and finally his struggle for a middle ground (1956).

2. One observes, however, that Lyon's normative account of this history is at least a celebration of the relationship and must be critically read for its argument that closer cooperation between science and government is desirable.

3. After the Eisenhower Commission and Surgeon General's projects there were attempts to broaden the focus of the "profile" to account for the wide variety of cultural themes played out in television programming. But from 1973 on the funding arrangements permitted the work to expand only into the realm of "cultivation analysis," to study aspects of social factors and viewer perceptions in relationship to the profile. By the late 1970s that approach, and particularly its "scary world" hypothesis, had come under substantial attack on both theoretical and methodological grounds (Newcomb, 1978 and Hirsch, 1980, 1981). Whatever the merits of such critiques, there remains little attention to the issue of how the content analysis effort, as with other aspects of the violence research, has been shaped by the practical political needs reflected in the government-industry policy debate.

References

Baker, R. K. et al. The views, standards and practices of the television industry. Appendix III-K in R. K. Baker & S. J. Ball. *Violence and the media: Mass media and violence.* Washington: Government Printing Office, 1969.

Barnouw, E. *Tube of plenty.* New York: Oxford University Press, 1975.

Bartos, R. Frank Stanton: Our first CEO (Interview). *Journal of Advertising Research*, June 1977, 17:6, 26–29.

Berelson, B. The state of communications research. *Public Opinion Quarterly.* Spring 1959, 23:1, 1–6.

Berelson, B. & Janowitz, M. (Eds.) *Reader in Public Opinion and Communication.* Glencoe: Free Press, 1950, 1953, 1963.

Bogart, L. Warning: The Surgeon General has determined that TV violence is moderately dangerous to your child's mental health. *Public Opinion Quarterly*, Winter 1972–1973, 36:4, 491–516.

Boorstin, D. J. *The Americans: The democratic experience.* New York: Vintage Books, 1974.

Bower, R. T. *Television and the public.* New York: Holt, Rinehart and Winston, 1973.

Branscomb, A. W. & Savage, M. The broadcast reform movement: At the cross-roads. *Journal of Communication.* 1978, 28:4, 25–34.

Briand, P. L., Jr. (Ed.), *Violence and the media: Mass media hearings.* Staff Report to the National Commission on the Causes and Prevention of Violence, Vol. 9. Washington: U.S. Government Printing Office, 1969.

Burke, K. *Permanence and change* (2nd Ed.). Indianapolis: Bobbs-Merrill, 1965.

Cater, D. & Strickland, S. *TV violence and the child: The evolution and fate of the Surgeon General's report.* New York: Russell Sage Foundation, 1975.

Cole, B. & Oettinger, M. *Reluctant regulators.* Reading, Mass.: Addison-Wesley, 1978.

Comstock, G. A. *Television and human behavior: The key studies.* Santa Monica: Rand, 1975. R-1747-CF.

Comstock, G. A., Chaffee, S., Katzman, N., McCombs, M., & Roberts, D. *Television and human behavior.* New York: Columbia University Press, 1978.

Comstock, G. A. & Rubinstein, E. A. (Eds.). *Television and social behavior. Reports and papers, Volume I: Media content and control.* Washington: U.S. Government Printing Office, 1972a.

Comstock, G. A. & Rubinstein, E. A. (Eds.). *Television and social behavior. Reports and papers, Volume III: Television and adolescent aggressiveness.* Washington: U.S. Government Printing Office, 1972b.

Comstock, G. A., Rubinstein, E. A., & Murray, J. P. (Eds.). *Television and social behavior. Reports and papers, Volume V: Television effects: Further explorations.* Washington: U.S. Government Printing Office, 1972.

Defleur, M. L. *Theories of mass communications.* New York: David McKay, 1966, 1972.

Defleur, M. & Ball-Rokeach, S. *Theories of mass communication* (3rd Ed.). New York: David McKay, 1975.

Duncan, H. D. *Communication and social order.* New York: Oxford University Press, 1970.

Edelman, M. *The symbolic uses of politics.* Urbana: University of Illinois Press, 1964.

Gerbner, G. & Gross, L. Living with television: The violence profile. *Journal of Communication.* Spring 1976, 26:2, 173–199.

Gerbner, G. et al. The "mainstreaming" of America: Violence profile No. 11. *Journal of Communication,* Summer 1980, 30:3, 10–29.

Gerbner, G. et al. A curious journey into the scary world of Paul Hirsch. *Communications Research.* January 1981, 8:1, 39–72.

Guimary, D. L. *Citizens' groups and broadcasting.* New York: Praeger, 1975.

Graham, H. D. & Gurr, T. R. *Violence in America.* New York: New American Library, 1969.

Grundfest, J. A. *Citizen participation in broadcast licensing before the FCC.* Santa Monica: Rand, 1976. R-1896-MF.

Habermas, J. *Knowledge and human interests.* Boston: Beacon Press, 1971.

Haight, T. R. (Ed.). *Telecommunications policy and the citizen.* New York: Praeger, 1979.

Head, S. W. *Broadcasting in America,* (3rd Ed.). New York: Houghton Mifflin, 1976.

Hirsch, P. M. The "Scary World" of the nonviewer and other anomalies: A reanalysis of Gerbner et al.'s findings on cultivation analysis, Part I. *Communications Research.* October 1980, 7:4, 403–456.

Hirsch, P. M. On not learning from one's own mistakes: A reanalysis of Gerbner et al.'s findings on cultivation analysis, Part II. *Communications Research.* January 1981a, 8:1, 3–37.

Hirsch, P. M. Distinguishing good speculation from bad theory: Rejoinder to Gerbner et al. *Communications Research.* January 1981b, 8:1, 73–95.

Hovland, C. I., Janis, I. L. & Kelley, H. H. *Communication and persuasion: Psychological studies of opinion change.* New Haven: Yale University Press, 1953.

Jowett, G. *Film: The democratic art.* Boston: Little Brown, 1976.

Katz, E. *Social research in broadcasting.* London: British Broadcasting Corporation, 1997.

Klapper, J. *The effects of mass communication.* New York: The Free Press, 1960.

Krasnow, E. & Longley, L. D. (2nd Ed.). *The politics of broadcast regulation.* New York: St. Martin's Press, 1978.

Lazarsfeld, P. F. *Radio and the printed page.* New York: Duell, Sloan and Pearce, 1940.

Lazarsfeld, P. F. An episode in the history of social research: A memoir. In D. Fleming and B. Bailyn (Eds.) *The intellectual migration: Europe and America, 1930–1960.* Cambridge: Harvard University Press, 1969, 270–337.

Lazarsfeld, P. F., Berelson, B., & Gaudet, H. *The people's choice.* New York: Duell, Sloan and Pearce, 1944.

Lazarsfeld, P. F. & Field, H. *The people look at radio.* Chapel Hill: University of North Carolina Press, 1946.

Lazarsfeld, P. F. & Katz, E. *Personal influence.* Glencoe: Free Press, 1955.

Lazarsfeld, P. F. & Kendall, P. *Radio listening in America: The people look at radio—again.* New York: Prentice-Hall, 1948.

Lazarsfeld, P. F. & Stanton, F. N. (Eds.). *Radio research,* 1941. New York: Duell, Sloan and Pearce, 1941.

Lazarsfeld, P. F. & Stanton, F. N. (Eds.). *Radio research,* 1942–1943. New York: Duell, Sloan and Pearce, 1944.

Lazarsfeld, P. F. & Stanton, F. N. (Eds.). *Communications research,* 1948–1949. New York: Harper and Brothers, 1949.

Lyons, G. M. *The uneasy partnership.* New York: Russell Sage Foundation, 1969.

MacDonald, D. *Against the American grain.* New York: Vintage, 1962.

Meyer, T. B. & Anderson, J. A. Media violence research: Interpreting the findings. *Journal of Broadcasting.* Fall 1973, 17:4, 447–458.

Murray, J. P., Rubinstein, E. A. & Comstock, G. A. (Eds.). *Television and social behavior. Reports and papers, Volume II: Television and social learning.* Washington: U.S. Government Printing Office, 1972.

National Commission on the Causes and Prevention of Violence. *To establish justice, to insure domestic tranquility.* New York: Praeger, 1970.

Newcomb, H. Assessing the violence profile of Gerbner and Gross: A humanistic critique and suggestion. *Communications Research.* July 1978, 5:3, 264–283.

Noble, D. W. *The paradox of progressive thought.* Minneapolis: University of Minnesota Press, 1958.

Osborn, F. et al. (Eds.). *Studies in social psychology in World War II.* Princeton: Princeton University Press, 1949.

Paisley, M. B. Social policy research and the realities of the system: Violence done to TV research. Unpublished paper, Stanford University, Institute for Communications Research, ERIC Reports, ED 062 764. 1972.

Roper Organization. *Public perceptions of television and other mass media, a twenty-year review, 1959–1978.* New York: television Information Office, 1973.

Rowland, W. D., Jr. The political and symbolic uses of effects: A social history of inquiries into violence on television and the political legitimation of mass communications research. Manuscript in progress. Institute of Communications Research, University of Illinois, 1981 (revision of Ph.D. dissertation, 1978).

Rowland. W. D., Jr. The illusion of fulfillment: Problems in the broadcast reform movement and notes on the progressive past. *Journalism Monographs,* 1982, 79, 1–49.

Rubinstein, E. A., Comstock, G. A., & Murray, J. P. (Eds.). *Television and social behavior. Reports and papers, Volume IV: Television in day-to-day life: Patterns of use.* Washington: U.S. Government Printing Office, 1972.

Schramm, W. (Ed.). *Communications in modern society.* Urbana: University of Illinois Press, 1948.

Schramm, W. (Ed.). *Mass communications.* Urbana: University of Illinois Press, 1949, 1960.

Schramm, W. (Ed.). *The process and effects of mass communication.* Urbana: University of Illinois Press, 1954.

Schramm, W., Riesman, D., & Bauer, R. Comments on "The State of Communications Research." *Public Opinion Quarterly,* Spring 1959, 23:1, 6–17.

Schramm, W. & Roberts, D. F. (Eds.). *The process and effects of mass communication.* Urbana: University of Illinois Press, 1971.

Seldes, G. *The 7 lively arts.* New York: Sagamore Press, 1952; first published, 1924.

Seldes, G. *The great audience.* New York: Viking Press, 1951.

Seldes, G. *The public arts.* New York: Simon & Schuster, 1956.

Steiner, G. A. *The people look at television: A study of audience attitudes.* New York: Knopf, 1963.

Surgeon General's Scientific Advisory Committee on Television and Social Behavior. *Television and growing up: The impact of televised violence.* Washington: U.S. Government Printing Office, 1972.

U.S. House. Committee on Interstate and Foreign Commerce, Federal Communications Commission Subcommittee. *Investigation of radio and television programming.* Hearings (82,2). June, September, December 1952.

U.S. Senate. Committee on the Judiciary, Subcommittee to Investigate Juvenile Delinquency. *Juvenile delinquency (television programs).* Hearings (83,2). June, October 1954.

U.S. Senate. Committee on the Judiciary, Subcommittee to Investigate Juvenile Delinquency. *Television programs.* Hearings (84,1). April 1955. (a)

U.S. Senate. Committee on the Judiciary, Subcommittee to Investigate Juvenile Delinquency. *Television and juvenile delinquency.* Interim Report (84,1). 1955. (b)

U.S. Senate. Committee on the Judiciary, Subcommittee to Investigate Juvenile Delinquency. *Investigation of juvenile delinquency in the United States, Part 10, Effects on young people of violence and crime portrayed on television.* Hearings (87; 1, 2). June, July 1961; January, May 1962.

U.S. Senate. Subcommittee of Investigate Juvenile Delinquency. *Television and juvenile delinquency,* Interim Report (88,2). 1964.

U.S. Senate. Committee on Commerce, Subcommittee on Communications. *Federal Communications Commission policy matters and television programming.* Hearings, Pts. 1–2, (91,1). March 1969.

U.S. Senate. Committee on Commerce. Subcommittee on Communications. *Scientific advisory committee on TV and social behavior.* Hearings. (92,1). September 28, 1971.

U.S. Senate. Committee on Commerce, Subcommittee on Communications. *Surgeon General's report by the scientific advisory committee on television and social behavior.* Hearings. (92,2). March 21–24, 1972.

U.S. Senate. Committee on Commerce, Subcommittee on Communications. *Violence on television.* Hearings. (93,2). April 3–5, 1974.

Weiss, W. Effects of mass media of communications. In G. Lindzey and E. Aronson (Eds.). *The handbook of social psychology (2nd Ed.), Vol. V. Applied social psychology.* Reading, Mass.: Addison-Wesley, 1969.

Wright, C. *Mass communications: A sociological perspective.* New York: Random House, 1959, 1975.

7

Pornography Research and Public Policy

Dolf Zillmann
1989

In this chapter, we briefly examine how, in recent years, psychological research has been used to derive guidelines for public policy concerning pornography, and to what extent the research may have influenced adopted policies and legislation. We concentrate on procedures that were used to integrate and summarize available research findings for those recommending and/or deciding on policy, as well as on these agents' apparent partialities in extracting information in the necessary process of data reduction. Points of general discontent with these procedures are highlighted, and the ramifications of the discontent of some parties are considered. Finally, we present alternative, potentially superior procedures and discuss their advantages.

Policy Formation in Practice

Generally speaking, a policy issue is created by citizens who deem particular happenings undesirable for society and who seek their curtailment or elimination. The pornography issue is no exception. A great many citizens took offense at what readily available pornography presents and were concerned about effects on sexual behavior, especially on violent sexual behavior, that might result from exposure. Influential and politically connected persons from this subpopulation brought their concerns to the attention of policy- and law makers who, in the case of the pornography issue, decided to consider the merits of the pleas. In accord with common practice, committees were formed to ascertain the facts and, under the assumption that the findings bear out the citizen's concerns, to recommend remedial actions for consideration by law makers. The ascertainment of the facts involves, of course, inspection of the scientific evidence—in this instance, inspection of the sociological and psychological research findings concerning the uses and effects of pornography.

A first Commission on Obscenity and Pornography had been formed in 1970. It was composed of 18 commissioners, and it was supported by 22 staff members and a budget of $2 million. In addition to conducting hearings, this commission supported original empirical research as well as reviews of the pertinent literature by social scientists and legal scholars. The committee was given 2 years to produce recommendations. At the end of this period it fulfilled its mandate by concluding that there was insufficient evidence to consider pornography implicated in the causation of asocial effects and by refraining from recommending more stringent regulation of pornography (Report of the Commission on Obscenity and Pornography, 1970).

The issue did not go away, however. Pressures to regulate pornography continued to be applied, and deficiencies in the 1970 report became apparent. In particular, it became clear that the commission had based its verdict of "no ill effects" on few and tentative findings, many of which had been generated in haste for the commission. There were also the usual charges of partiality in composing the commission, culminating in allegations that "potentially difficult" leading scholars had been ostracized (Cline, 1974). However, in all probability it was the availability of new research findings that gave impetus to the formation of a new commission with the mandate to re-examine the scientific evidence and to recommend regulatory policy. Psychological investigations figured prominently among the new evidence (e.g., Donnerstein, 1980, 1983; Malamuth, 1981, 1984; Zillmann & Bryant, 1982) because their findings seemed to challenge the assessment of the 1970 commission and to warrant different recommendations.

The new commission, the Attorney General's Commission on Pornography, was formed in 1985. Eleven commissioners were appointed. They were supported by a budget of $400,000, assisted by a staff of 9, and given 12 months to complete their mandate. Because of budget and time limitations, empirical research could not be commissioned, nor could extensive reviews of the literature. The 1986 commission was thus restricted to conducting hearings. One of the hearings primarily served the presentation and discussion of social-science research on the effects of pornography.

This hearing was held on September 11, 1985, in Houston, Texas. Numerous psychologists were invited to testify. Many of those who had conducted empirical research on the uses or effects of pornography presented summaries of their findings, and many of those with relevant clinical experience reported their observations. In addition, "pornography addicts" and victims of pornography-related sexual abuse described their agony, torment, anguish, and grief.

The Attorney General's Commission on Pornography was to be assisted by a committee of the Surgeon General. This committee was to ascertain the state of the art in pornography research and report to the Commission on Pornography. Because of complications in the budget appropriation, as well as a host of other trivial reasons, the Surgeon General's committee failed to be formed in time. Eventually it came into being on a budget that barely covered the commission of 5 reviews of the pertinent research literature and the travel costs of about 15 invited participants. The committee was referred to as the Surgeon General's Workshop on Pornography and Public Health. It met for just 3 days, June 22–24, 1986, in Arlington, Virginia.

The Surgeon General's workshop was not attended by members of the Attorney General's commission. However, the chairman of the Attorney General's commission took part in the proceedings by informing the workshop participants of happenings in the Attorney General's commission. The release of final reports is of interest because it shows that, counter to intentions, the efforts of the Surgeon General's workshop were without consequence for the conclusions and recommendations of the Attorney General's Commission on Pornography. Release of the final report of the commission (Attorney General's Commission on Pornography: Final report, 1986) predated that of the workshop's report (Mulvey & Haugaard, 1986) by about 1 month.

Predictable Criticism

From its inception, the 1986 commission was under attack. Those representing the pornography industry considered the very formation of a commission an indictment of pornography (Nobile & Nadler, 1986). Those aligned with the American Civil Liberties Union took a similar stand (Hertzberg, 1986; Linsley, 1989). Most of the immediate criticism concerned the composition of the commission, however. It was deemed intolerable that six commissioners had made public statements to the effect that some restrictions of pornography might be desirable; and the commission's chair was considered unacceptable because he had been a successful prosecutor in a campaign against pornography in theatres and bookstores (Hertzberg, 1986; Paletz, 1988). Others found it objectionable that only three commissioners—a psychologist, a psychiatrist, and a legal scholar—could document professional expertise with pornography (Wilcox, 1987). Yet others saw problems in the way in which the commission conducted its deliberations (Gouran, 1988; Paletz, 1988).

Politically speaking, most of the immediate criticism came from liberal quarters. The conservative side was surprisingly uninquisitive and quiet about the committee, its composition, and its deliberations. It went unnoticed, for example, that one of the expert committee members co-sponsored the proposal that for some sex offenders exposure to pornography would "transiently decrease the likelihood to commit sex crimes" (Abel, Becker, & Mittelman, 1985). Nonetheless, considerable discontent with the committee and the proceedings has been expressed as well (Scott, 1985).

Perhaps somewhat less predictable was the instant criticism of the committee's conclusions and recommendations on the part of psychologists. Minority reports and critical appraisals had been published before—in connection with the 1970 commission (Cline, 1970, 1974). The new report, however, prompted accusations of deliberate misrepresentation of critical findings. In particular, investigators whose own findings and views on policy differed from the committee's conclusions and recommendations published detailed accounts of how, in their view, the data at hand should have been interpreted and what policy should have been recommended (Donnerstein & Linz, 1986; Donnerstein, Linz, & Penrod, 1987; Linz, Donnerstein, & Penrod, 1987).

Moreover, from within the social sciences came assaults on investigations that had generated findings that some apparently viewed as supportive of policies deemed unacceptable, if not abhorrent (Brannigan & Goldenberg, 1987; Christensen, 1986). The criticism produced several published colloquia that are laden with false accusations and marked by a degree of hostility rarely found in the social-science literature (Brannigan, 1987; Christensen, 1987; Linz & Donnerstein, 1988). For the most part, this criticism focused on research methods. It often transcended methodological considerations, however, and became innuendo of the investigators' political motives, if not their religious beliefs (Christensen, 1987).

Some rather unexpected criticism of pornography research, finally, came in the form of a thorough analysis of methodology. Byrne and Kelley (1986, 1989) examined all facets of research procedures that had been employed, and they concluded that all findings on the effects of pornography are exceedingly tentative and unacceptable as a basis of policy recommendations. The fact is that the criteria that were applied in this analysis are so stringent that, if used to judge psychological research at large, they would reduce psychology from a science to an art form. Such humbling self-criticism reveals a decided unwillingness to influence regulatory policy for pornography—an unwillingness that seems to be prevalent among psychologists with a research interest in sexual behaviors.

Reluctance to influence policy is also evident in the evaluation of the work of the Surgeon General's Workshop on Pornography and Public Health. The committee refrained from making policy recommendations and qualified conclusions about effects so as to make them meaningless. For instance, violent pornography was said to affect laboratory aggression. Statements about effects outside the laboratory were conspicuously absent (Linz & Donnerstein, 1988). Additionally, the report (Mulvey & Haugaard, 1986) cautioned that pornography would constitute only one of numerous potential influences on behavior, and it suggested that conceivable interactions among the potential influences would have to be investigated before general statements about the behavioral effects of pornography would be warranted. Presumably because of such caution, the committee's work has been hailed as excellent (Wilcox, 1987). All this is not to deny the usefulness of more and superior research data, nor is it to call the merits of caution into question. The objective, instead, is to point out that caution is not without political implications. Caution, especially in extreme forms, is not by necessity prudent procedure. One should be cognizant of the fact that it can be a strategy favoring the status quo. In short, the call for more inclusive, more decisive, and "absolutely definitive" research may be an effective strategy in support of a policy of inaction.

Principal Difficulties

If nothing else, the debate over pornography research and the possible regulation of pornographic material has made it clear that most of those who gather policy-relevant information, especially psychologists who seek to delineate the causal conditions of behavioral consequences of exposure, find it difficult, if not impossible, to separate presumed facts about effects from personal views on desirable societal policy concerning these effects. The problem is a fundamental one for the social sciences that are to serve the welfare of citizens. There is, after all, no legitimacy in deriving societal precepts from so-called facts about the real world. Imperatives do not follow from declaratives. And what ought to be done about particular circumstances cannot be inferred from knowledge about them, irrespective of how penetrating and veridical that knowledge might be. The endorsement of a precept or the acceptance of a policy, then, simply does not follow from social-science data—no matter how "obvious" the connection might seem to some. If, for instance, it were established that drunk driving kills or maims one-tenth of the population, it would not follow that efforts be made to change the situation. Or if it were established that fictional violence on U.S. television inspires acts of brutality, on average per year, in only seven youngsters, it would not follow that nothing be done about it. And more to the point, if it were compellingly and irrefutably established that pornography promotes rape, that in the United States it leads to the traumatization of 80,000 women each year, it would not follow that we ought to curtail its distribution. In terms of science, the connection between knowledge of causal circumstances and policy is a *strictly arbitrary* one. The justification of social policy is necessarily outside science proper. It is moral for the individual and political at the societal level.

It appears that, in dealing with the pornography issue, policy-makers and social scientists, as well as their critics from various camps, have been rather confused about the relationship between facts and policy. Had they not been, the results of the proceedings and the criticism thereof should have been different.

Committee Composition and Policy
If it is recognized that the mandate of the Attorney General's recent committee was to recommend policy, partly in light of social-science information, any citizen capable of comprehending such and other pertinent information should qualify for membership. Expertise in the area of pornography is of no consequence for the value-based endorsement of a policy. Hence, it should have been treated as immaterial.

Concerns about policy-related convictions of individual committee members, and about the distribution of these convictions in the committee, are probably well founded. If committees are dominated by persons already committed to particular policies, impartial deliberation of policy options is unlikely, and policy recommendations may be foregone conclusions.

This assessment implies, of course, that initial positions tend to be maintained, and that exposure to potentially large amounts of pertinent information tends to be without appreciable effect on committee members. Exposure to pertinent social-science information is similarly viewed as being of little or no consequence, mainly because committee members are likely to attend selectively to information and extract items seemingly supportive of their initial positions. Granted that committee members on occasion do change their positions as the result of exposure to pertinent information, it is difficult to argue that, as a rule, partialities do not exist or are unlikely.

In principal terms, the fair-trial paradigm of criminal justice cannot be applied to policy deliberations, and no one should pretend that it can. The informational conditions are strikingly different. Jurors may be kept uninformed prior to court proceedings about the specifics of cases. They thus may enter these proceedings without having prejudged innocence or guilt of defendants. In contrast, public-policy issues are *public issues* by definition. The circumstances creating these issues are common knowledge, and potential members of policy committees cannot be kept in the dark about them. It must be assumed that, as a rule, members are cognizant of the circumstances in question; furthermore, that members, if they are involved citizens at all, have contemplated and judged the societal desirability or undesirability of these circumstances. Citizens who can be recruited for policy committees are therefore neither ignorant of the issue, nor unlikely to have appraised it and adopted a stand amounting to a willingness to support some policies more than others.

This precondition creates considerable problems. Because a committee composed of issue-ignorant and, hence, initially impartial members cannot be constituted, and because any member imbalance that might favor particular policies ahs been deemed intolerable by many critics, the *balanced committee* is implicitly suggested as a solution. But is it a solution? Quite obviously, if a committee were composed such that half its members favors a particular policy and the other half opposes it, the committee is bound to be deadlocked on every issue. This likely result of balancing is by no means a neutral outcome, however. It should be recognized that any stalemate in policy-recommending committees favors the status quo. It favors a policy of inaction. The insistence on balanced committees can thus be construed as a strategy for inaction.

All this is not to say that *imbalance* in policy committees is desirable. The argument is that the insistence on balance is not, as often implied, a clarion call for fairness and neutrality; it can be, and often is, a policy strategy.

Because there is no apparent solution concerning the composition of policy committees, the best that can be hoped for is that, counter to the perhaps somewhat cynical statements about the rigidity of initial beliefs of committee members, these persons are open to pertinent information and do adjust their policy-relevant convictions in accord with that information—not just occasionally, but regularly.

Expert Testimony and Policy

The composition of expert groups for so-called testimony before policy committees is not without problems either. It is often inconceivable to invite all who, according to some criteria for expertise, might qualify. The necessary exclusion of some then opens the doors for criticism. The Attorney General's recent commission was promptly criticized for limiting expert testimony (Wilcox, 1987).

The opposite stand seems more meaningful. The commission may have been exposed to far too much social-science testimony—in too short a period of time, anyway. At the Houston hearings, almost all psychologists who had done empirical work on pornography uses and effects, along with a large number of clinicians with experience in these matters, had their say. In a string of academic presentations, interrupted only by the occasional testimony of victims of sexual abuse seemingly related to pornography, they compressed their knowledge into brief summaries of their research or experience. Many left no doubt about which policies they favored.

The commission must have been overwhelmed. Absorption of all the evidence presented, and the thorough critical appraisal of this evidence, seems to exceed human capabilities. Moreover, only a small minority of commissioners, at best, had the training to judge the merits of research findings. The likely result of such conditions—that is, of conditions of information overload and inability to separate compelling research findings from dubious ones and from expert opinion—is that "overall impressions" were formed, and that they were formed on the basis of obtrusive assertions and vivid displays. Media coverage of the hearings is telling in this regard. It focused on victim testimony (e.g., the TV cameras were rolling when victims, anonymous behind screens, revealed their fascinating ordeals, not when experts talked research). The commissioners may similarly have focused their attention on images and highly dramatic, yet probably nonrepresentative, clinical cases rather than on the comparatively abstract, general information. This, at least, is what one would expect on the basis of the heuristic principles and shortcuts in information processing that have been explored in cognitive psychology (Fiske & Taylor, 1984; Zanna, Olson, & Herman, 1987).

The relative neglect of particular research findings in proceedings of this kind seems unavoidable. The fact that this circumstance gives almost all investigators who testified cause for complaints and thus explains the frequent allegations of under- or misrepresentation of their stands (Donnerstein, Linz, & Penrod, 1987) may be interesting, but considering the policy process at large, it is rather unimportant. The significant, principal dilemma in the relationship between research evidence and public policy is the enormous loss of social-science information in hearings of policy committees that (a) do not give sufficient time for the evaluation of findings and (b) are composed of members with little, if any, qualifications to evaluate presented findings.

It should be mentioned in this connection that in the Surgeon General's committee a panel of experts was given 3 hours to generate recommendations and reach consensus on the recommendations. The panel decided to refrain from making policy recommendations and sought to reach agreement on statements summarizing the pertinent research evidence. The stipulation that consensus be reached gave every member veto power and resulted in the panel's failure to agree on any generalization of relevance.

The panel's decision to refrain from making policy recommendations, in opposition to its mandate, contrasts sharply with the behavior of the social scientists who testified before the Attorney General's commission. Most were eager to urge particular policies. Few were deliberate in avoiding policy statements and adhered to their mandate of presenting whatever findings they had aggregated. The behavior of most, then, shows that social scientists are often confused about the conceptual boundaries between science and public policy. They have little difficulty in combining the two and, given a chance to testify, want to speak as both scientists and citizens.

Effects of Presumptions about Policy

The fact that at the Houston hearings so many social scientists felt compelled to urge the commission to adopt or reject certain policies concerning the availability of pornography in society would seem to indicate how strongly they personally felt about the issue. In violation of their limited assignment to enlighten the commission about uses and effects of pornography, as known from research or clinical experience, they expressed their views on what ought to be done. In so doing, they essentially voted their erotic preference. Whatever evidence of uses and effects they may have presented, it cannot have justified recommendations concerning the regulation or deregulation of pornography.

Most of those social scientists who pleaded for particular policies behaved as if the Attorney General's commission were set up to determine whether or not the research evidence warrants a total ban on pornography of any kind. Under this presumption, some urged that something be finally done about pornography, and others pleaded for leaving things alone. Such apparent eagerness to influence policy proved highly divisive. It produced factions of censorship supporters, censorship opponents, and indifferent investigators. Additionally, the latter group was suspected of favoring censorship if their findings showed consequences deemed undesirable, and of opposing it if their findings showed consequences that could not be deemed undesirable or if they failed to show relevant consequences altogether. Considerable hostility could be observed between the factions. It eventually clouded scientific judgments. It led, for instance, to recommendations not to publish research that demonstrated certain effects of pornography consumption—not because deficiencies of research procedures could be detected, but because the valid findings might be used by politicians attempting to influence public policy. Such unfortunate dominance of political conviction over scientific judgment would be less likely if social scientists realized that expert testimony before policy-recommending committees does not call for their citizen views on desirable policy, if only because they so obviously do not represent the population at large.

Research Limitations and Policy

As indicated earlier, research on the consequences of exposure to pornography has been subjected to extreme scrutiny and devastating criticism (Brannigan & Goldenberg, 1987; Byrne & Kelley, 1986). Quite obviously, descriptive research, qualitative or quantitative, may help define the societal phenomenon of pornography usage, but is uninformative as far as behavioral effects are concerned. Case studies may be illustrative, but their incidental and arbitrary aggregation does not allow the generalization of findings, including accounts of stimulus-response connections, to populations of interest. Surveys of opinions and beliefs about effects of pornography exposure can inform us about distributions of opinions and beliefs, but not about the etiology of behavioral contingencies. Actually, they do not reliably inform us about opinion distributions either, nor about the distribution of pornography-related habits (e.g., frequency, circumstances, and purpose of usage). Surveys of erotic and sexual preferences are patently unreliable (Eysenck, 1976), mostly because a good portion of the surveyed population is unwilling to reveal its inclinations and habits in the sexual realm. The exploration of "natural" (i.e., uninfluenced, unmanipulated) relationships between pornography consumption and possible behavioral consequences, whether by way of naturalistic inquiry or in quantitative terms, again cannot prove anything definitively about the causation of behavior. It is suggestive at best. The devastating remark that it is "only correlational" is liberally applied to regression studies that seek to determine which aspects of pornography exposure might influence particular behaviors. Similar studies on other, less controversial policy issues are often treated with considerable compassion. The statistical relationship between drunk driving and car accidents is a case in point. It does not provide causal proof. But nobody seems to want to argue that drivers who drink are reckless people; and that reckless people cause accidents, whether or not they are intoxicated. In contrast, the fact that rapists tend to be heavy consumers of pornography and often use it as a turn-on prior to committing rape (Marshall, 1989) is deemed immaterial because it can be argued that exposure to pornography is incidental and rapists, being reckless people, would commit rape independent of exposure.

The burden of proof of behavioral consequences of pornography exposure is thus squarely placed on experimental methodology. Causal relationships are accepted only if exposure to pornography is consistently followed by particular policy-relevant behaviors and if no such exposure is not—all other things being equal.

The usefulness of this paradigm for the determination of the behavioral consequences of exposure to pornography is severely limited. Ethical considerations simply rule out the experiments that could provide definitive proof and resolve the issue. Most obvious is that any form of sexual violence cannot be used as a dependent variable. For instance, men cannot be placed at risk of developing sexually violent inclinations by extensive exposure to violent or nonviolent pornography, and women cannot be placed at risk of becoming victims of such inclinations. Because anything short of demonstrating behavioral changes in these terms has been found wanting (Byrne & Kelley, 1986), one has to accept that compelling proof of a causal connection between the consumption of different types of pornography and sexually violent behaviors, should such a connection exist, is not forthcoming.

Ethical considerations not only prevent experimentation on sexually violent behaviors, but also apply to the study of sexual callousness manifest in social dispositions or attitudes. Early studies have shown, for instance, that repeated exposure to pornography trivializes rape as a criminal offense (Zillmann & Bryant, 1982) or relaxes inhibitions in the contemplation of coercive acts in the pursuit of sexual access (Check, 1985). The experimental subject thus had been placed at risk; and now that such consequences are known, it would be irresponsible to conduct similar investigations to further our understanding of the dynamics of the observed dispositional changes.

Furthermore, ethical considerations prevent any experimental work with children and precollege adolescents. This may seem unimportant, but actually it has significant implications. It turned out that most men, prior to entering college (or prior to reaching college age), already had substantial exposure to various forms of pornography (Bryant & Brown, 1989). If such exposure influences sexual callousness or particular erotic orientations, these influences may have taken hold before these men could become experimental subjects. The result is that experimental manipulations of exposure are ineffective. Conditions of no exposure cannot be created, and no-exposure versus exposure comparisons in experiments would be comparisons between two heavily exposed groups. These conditions are bound to produce null findings in future research, null findings that are likely to be used as evidence for "no effects" (Linz & Donnerstein, 1988).

Experimentation on pornography effects faces numerous other difficulties. Most notably, the apparent temporal separation between cause and effect creates problems (i.e., exposure may have a delayed impact, and numerous exposures may be required to bring it about), and the relationship between measures that can be used and what they are to measure (i.e., measurement validity) tends to be poor.

The bottom line is that research on pornography effects cannot be definitive. It cannot satisfy the demands for rigor and compellingness that have been placed on it. Not now—and in a free society, not ever. The research leaves us with considerable uncertainty about exposure consequences at the societal level. On the other hand, it provides us with a good deal of understanding of some of the issues involved. Limited as the various uses and effects demonstrations may be, they constitute information that is far superior to hearsay, guessing, and unchecked common sense. In these terms, the research findings do offer the best basis for the contemplation and formation of public policy.

Research Eclecticism and Policy

If left to its own devices, social-science research is likely to produce highly eclectic evidence for policy considerations. Investigators select and address research issues for a variety of rather personal reasons. They may, for instance, pick something that intrigues them, that they feel would impress their peers, that promises an easy publication, that might bring fame, or that relates to a deeply felt concern of theirs. Whatever the particular criteria for their choices, the resulting body of knowledge does not necessarily serve the public interest and cannot possibly be considered an optimal basis for policy decisions.

Regarding pornography uses and effects, the available research has failed to address many issues of potential significance for public policy. Issues likely to incite intense controversy have not been touched, and topics deemed safe in these terms have attracted a disproportionate amount of attention. For instance, social-scientists elected to ignore possible effects of pornography on the formation of erotic orientation and sexual preference in adolescents. The possible creation of unrealistic, unfulfillable sexual expectations and temptations, along with their implications for coping, has been neglected. Only one published study deals with such matters as sexual satisfaction or dissatisfaction resulting from prolonged pornography consumption (Zillmann & Bryant, 1988). Effects of early exposure (i.e., during childhood) remain largely unknown. The involvement of pornography in sexual child abuse has been ascertained in descriptive terms only (Lanning & Burgess, 1989). Effects of pornography consumption on values cocerning family and marriage, as well as on the desire for progeny, also have received little attention (Zillmann & Bryant, 1988). In contrast, the least objectionable research item, the effect of "the worst kind" of pornography (i.e., sexually violent material) on "the worst kind" of sexual behavior (i.e., rape), has been explored in numerous studies (Check, 1985; Donnerstein, 1980; Malamuth, 1986).

Oddly enough, this obtrusive eclecticism in the research on pornography uses and effects has been overlooked in the otherwise thorough and seemingly exhaustive aforementioned academic self-criticism. Setting one's own research agenda is apparently considered an essential part of academic freedom that is not to be questioned. From a policy perspective, however, the yield of sporadic research without a defined agenda is of limited value.

Committees that pondered the pornography issue, with a mandate to recommend regulatory policy, were thus confronted with eclectic evidence whose validity has been severely questioned by those who generated this evidence. Given such a dilemma, how can anybody be surprised that committees in the United States, in Canada, and in Britain decided to give little credence to the so-called expert testimony by social-scientists and based their decisions on alternative sources of information (Einsiedel, 1988)?

A Research Policy for Policy Research

As indicated earlier, recent efforts toward the formation of policy regulating or deregulating pornography have gone wrong on many counts. One of them is social-science input, which simply proved inconsequential for policy recommendations and, hence, legislation. The Attorney General's commission was ill-equipped to review social-science evidence; and the Surgeon General's committee, composed of social-scientists and potentially able to assist in a meaningful way, reported only after recommendations had been made.

The process could have been more productive if (a) the Surgeon General's committee would have summarized "the state-of-the-art" research on the uses and effects of pornography more exhaustively and without pressures toward consensus (also without engaging in self-destructive methodological criticism that was apparently motivated by fears of regulatory consequences); and (b) the Attorney General's commission would have worked from this summary rather than from assorted testimony by experts and victims and their personal views on regulatory policy.

Such procedure would still have been far from satisfactory, however, mainly because policy objectives would have remained unclear, and the research evidence would have remained eclectic. To remedy this situation, it would seem to be necessary to proceed in three stages:

1. A *policy-exploring committee* should be formed and charged with (a) the assessment of citizen's grievances pertaining to the issue under consideration, (b) the specification of perceived problems in all their manifestations, and (c) the projection of possible regulatory policy. From a social-science perspective, the second part of this charge is crucial. The assignment calls for an exhaustive listing of presumed effects and ill effects. Research could obviously assist the search for presumed consequences of pornography consumption (surveys of beliefs and reviews of the available research literature). But most importantly, the listing would serve as a *research agenda*. Because this agenda would be comprehensive and exhaustive, as well as focused, the problem of eclectic and unfocused research could be overcome. However, it can be overcome only if funds are provided to conduct the necessary nonexistent investigations.

It should be noticed that such an agenda in no way limits the freedom of investigators to conduct whatever studies they deem important—studies extraneous to the agenda. Research extraneous to the agenda would, in fact, complement agenda research in a most positive fashion, potentially serving as a corrective for incomplete agendas.

2. After a period of time allowing for the execution of needed investigations, a *social-science committee* should be constituted. Its mandate should be the assessment of all pertinent research findings, *irrespective*

of what policy implications they might have. This committee should be composed of social scientists capable of judging the technical merits of the available research. The committee's principal task would be to critically evaluate and integrate all pertinent research findings and to present a summary of findings in terms intelligible to lay persons.

3. A *policy-recommending committee* should be formed and given the mandate to propose policies that, in full view of the research evidence at hand, would best serve the public at large. The formulation of such policies necessarily entails value judgments and thus is best left to those experienced in anticipating reactions of constituencies and in caring for the welfare of these constituencies.

Surely, the evidence at hand will not be "definitive" in the sense that none of its aspects could be questioned by someone. And just as surely, any set of recommended policies cannot satisfy all the people—at least not when the issue is as charged and controversial as pornography, with some feeling their erotic birthright threatened (Money, 1985) and others fearing the decay of morality and the decline of culture (Scott, 1985). Uncertainty will remain, and controversy is assured. The outlined procedure would generate results, however, that should be superior to recommending public policy on the basis of fickle public opinion or the views of a handful of politicians and lawyers.

Acknowledgments

This chapter is an edited version of a same-titled one written for Peter Suedfeld and Philip Tetlock (Eds.), *Psychology and Social Advocacy.* It is reprinted with permission.

References

Abel, G. G., Becker, J. V., & Mittelman, M. S. (1985, September 18). *Use of pornography and erotica by sex offenders.* Paper presented at the eleventh annual meeting of The International Academy of Sex Research. Seattle, WA.

Attorney General's Commission on Pornography: Final report. (1986, July). Washington, DC: U.S. Department of Justice.

Brannigan, A. (1987). Pornography and behavior: Alternative explanations. *Journal of Communication, 37*(3), 185–192.

Brannigan, A., & Goldenberg, S. (1987). The study of aggressive pornography: The vicissitudes of relevance. *Critical Studies in Mass Communication, 4,* 262–283.

Bryant, J., & Brown, D. (1989). Uses of pornography. In D. Zillman and J. Bryant (Eds.), *Pornography: Research Advances and Policy Considerations.* Hillsdale, NJ: Lawrence Erlbaum Associates.

Byrne, D., & Kelley, K. (1986). Psychological research and public policy: Taking a long, hard look before we leap. In E. P. Mulvey & J. L. Haugaard (Eds.), *Report of the Surgeon General's Workshop on Pornography and Public Health* (pp. 67–96). Washington, DC: U.S. Department of Health and Human Services, Office of the Surgeon General.

Check, J. V. P. (1985). *The effects of violent and nonviolent pornography.* Ottawa: Department of Justice for Canada.

Christensen, F. (1986). Sexual callousness re-examined. *Journal of Communication, 36*(1), 174–188.

Christensen, F. (1987). Effects of pornography: The debate continues. *Journal of Communication, 37*(1), 186–188.

Cline, V. B. (1970). *Minority report of the U.S. Commission on Obscenity and Pornography.* New York: Bantam.

Cline, V. B. (Ed.). (1974). *Where do you draw the line?* Salt Lake City: Brigham Young University Press.

Donnerstein, E. (1980). Pornography and violence against women: Experimental studies. *Annals of the New York Academy of Sciences, 347,* 277–288.

Donnerstein, E. (1983). Erotica and human aggression. In R. G. Geen & E. I. Donnerstein (Eds.), *Aggression: Theoretical and empirical reviews. Vol. 2. Issues in research* (pp. 127–154). New York.

Donnerstein, E., & Linz, D. (1986, December). The question of pornography. *Psychology Today,* pp. 56–59.

Donnerstein, E., Linz, D., & Penrod, S. (1987). *The question of pornography: Research findings and policy implications.* New York: Free Press.

Einsiedel, E. F. (1988). The British, Canadian, and U.S. pornography commissions and their use of social science research. *Journal of Communication, 38*(2), 108–121.

Eysenck, H. J. (1976). *Sex and personality.* Austin: University of Texas Press.

Fiske, S. T., & Taylor, S. E. (1984). *Social cognition.* New York: Random House.

Gouran, D. S. (1988). *Questionable inferences in the Attorney General's Commission on Pornography: A case study of unwarranted collective judgment and faulty group decision making.* Unpublished manuscript, Penn State University, University Park, PA.

Hertzberg, H. (1986, July 14 & 21). Big books: Ed Meese and his pornography commission. *The New Republic*, pp. 21–24.

Lanning, K.V., & Burgess, A.W. (1989). The effects of counter-information on the acceptance of rape myths. In D. Zillman & J. Bryant (Eds.), *Pornography: Research Advances and Policy Considerations* (pp. 235–255). Hillsdale, NJ: Lawrence Erlbaum Associates.

Linsley, W. A. (1989). Basing legislative action on research data: Prejudice, prudence and empirical limitations. In D. Zillman & J. Bryant (Eds.), *Pornography: Research Advances and Policy Considerations* (pp. 343–359). Hillsdale, NJ: Lawrence Erlbaum Associates.

Linz, D., & Donnerstein, E. (1988). The methods and merits of pornography research. *Journal of Communication*, 38(2), 180–192.

Linz, D., Donnerstein, E., & Penrod, S. (1987). The findings and recommendations of the Attorney General's Commission on Pornography: Do the psychological "facts" fit the political fury? *American Psychologist*, 42, 946–953.

Malamuth, N. M. (1981). Rape proclivity among males. *Journal of Social Issues*, 37(4), 138–157.

Malamuth, N. M. (1984). Aggression against women: Cultural and individual causes. In N. M. Malamuth & E. Donnerstein (Eds.), *Pornography and sexual aggression* (pp. 19–52). Orlando, FL: Academic Press.

Malamuth, N. M. (1986). Do sexually violent media indirectly contribute to antisocial behavior? In E. P. Mulvey & J. L. Haugaard (Eds.), *Report of the Surgeon General's Workshop on Pornography and Public Health* (pp. 136–163). Washington, DC: U.S. Department of Health and Human Services, Office of the Surgeon General.

Marshall, W. (1989). Pornography and sex offenders. In D. Zillman and J. Bryant (Eds.), *Pornography: Research Advances and Policy Considerations*. Hillsdale, NJ: Lawrence Erlbaum Associates.

Money, J. (1985, December 30). *Statement on pornography.* Unpublished manuscript, Johns Hopkins University, Baltimore, MD.

Mulvey, E. P., & Haugaard, J. L. (1986). *Report of the Surgeon General's Workshop on Pornography and Public Health.* Washington, DC: U.S. Department of Health and Human Services, Office of the Surgeon General.

Nobile, P., & Nadler, E. (1986). *United States of America vs. Sex.* New York: Minotaur.

Paletz, D. L. (1988). Pornography, politics, and the press: The U.S. Attorney General's Commission on Pornography. *Journal of Communication*, 38(2), 122–137.

Report of the Commission on Obscenity and Pornography. (1970). Washington, DC: U.S. Government Printing Office.

Scott, D. (1985, March). Pornography and its effects on family, community and culture. *Family Policy and Insights*, 4(2). Washington, DC: Free Congress Foundation.

Wilcox, B. L. (1987). Pornography, social science, and politics: When research and ideology collide. *American Psychologist*, 42, 941–943.

Zanna, M. P., Olson, J. M., & Herman, C. P. (Eds.). (1987). *Social influence: The Ontario Symposium* (Vol. 5.). Hillsdale, NJ: Lawrence Erlbaum Associates.

Zillmann, D., & Bryant, J. (1982). Pornography, sexual callousness, and the trivialization of rape. *Journal of Communication*, 32(4), 10–21.

Zillmann, D., & Bryant, J. (1988). Pornography's impact on sexual satisfaction. *Journal of Applied Social Psychology*, 18, 438–453.

Zillmann, D., & Bryant, J. (1988). Effects of prolonged consumption of pornography on family values. *Journal of Family Issues*, 9(4), 518–544.

The Ideas: Policy-makers and Scholarship

8

Transforming Principles into Policy

Don R. LeDuc
1980

The crucial distinction between "regulation" and "policy" suggests a role for policy research beyond analysis—making recommendations for the effective realization and regulation of the social objectives which it identifies.

The newest in a line of ever more advanced telecommunications delivery systems, the direct broadcast satellite (DBS), is in the final stages of development and should be in operation over at least three continents by the end of this decade. Competition among industrial nations to be among the first to launch and operate DBS systems is already intense, even if specific communication uses for the broad spectrum of new channels each system will offer remain rather vaguely defined.[1] With progress towards this objective still being measured primarily in terms of technological advances, the "capacity" of each DBS system refers only to the number of channels its satellites are capable of delivering, not the number or variety of communication services a particular society may be capable of receiving and assimilating.

Soon each system will be operating in an efficient and cost-effective fashion, its information services consolidated to avoid disruptive competition, and its mass media channels controlled by those with the experience necessary to produce polished, popular programming.[2] If we have higher aspirations than this for functions to be performed by that expanded spectrum of channels offered through the telecommunications technology, it would seem essential that we expand as well that range of principles that will shape the evolution of these channels. This, of course, suggests the need for further communications policy research. But is there any reason to hope that such research will have a more substantial influence upon the evolution of telecommunications services in the future than it has had in the past (see 6)?

The mass of research publications seems to yield far less in the way of precise policy-related analysis than its bulk might initially suggest (see 5). One explanation for this lack of precision in recent communications policy literature might be that the word "policy", as the word "communications" before it, has become so popular and useful that it is now employed to serve a rather wide variety of undifferentiated purposes. A well-timed plea for further "policy" studies will often succeed in justifying, delaying, or even eventually circumventing a politically sensitive communications issue while continuing to convey a clear sense of commitment to its solution. Similarly, research proposals with the word "policy" in their title seem to have better prospects for federal funding than projects with more mundane communications-oriented designations.

The word "policy" also seems inappropriate as a description for the day-to-day bureaucratic behavior of the typical telecommunications regulatory agency. "Policy" suggests a degree of broad deductive analysis and consistent adherence to primary communication precepts seldom found within actual administrative process. What is often mistaken for "policy" is in reality nothing more than a recurring set of instinctive regulatory responses to parallel patterns of institutional change. In terms of technological challenge, this allows technical and marketing considerations to establish operating standards to which a telecommunications agency can only respond, lacking the capacity once these systems begin operation to do anything but authorize or suppress what they have been unable to guide (2).

What should be the meaning of the word "policy" as it applies to this field of investigation?

Perhaps the most effective way to provide such a definition would be to examine the way in which "policy" relates to "regulation." In its most basic sense, regulation is that form of government that compels those entities over which it has legal jurisdiction to act or refrain from acting in the manner in which they would otherwise tend to act. For example, regulation requiring a telecommunications entity to maximize its profit would seem absurdly redundant, for this would be its natural tendency in the absence of this requirement. However, a regulation requiring each DBS system to dedicate one channel for "public access" messages would probably be essential in order to achieve this end, for it is highly unlikely that there would be sufficient economic incentive for DBS systems to select this course of action on their own.[3]

In this context, "policy" represents one particularized aspect of such regulation. While "regulation" is essentially restrictive, simply reducing the operational options available to telecommunications operators, a "policy" orients this broad general power of control toward the achievement of one specific societal objective. Thus while a regulation forcing DBS system dedication of a "public access" channel might represent the first stage in the development of a "policy" encouraging broader public participation in DBS channel programming functions, pursuance of this objective through law would require far more than the enactment of this single statutory or code provision. The next step in furtherance of this policy might be to establish procedures for obtaining such access, or to create sources of funding for access efforts, or some similar sequence of ever more precise legislative definitions of the social objective. In this sense "policy" can be distinguished quite clearly from routine regulation, because it is not a single, somewhat instinctive response to a particular problem, but a long-term and continual process of legal guidance towards a clearly defined communication goal.

In practice, of course, this ideal type of policy direction seldom occurs anywhere within the regulatory process, and has certainly been conspicuously absent from the field of telecommunications in all areas and at all levels of control. The DBS "public access" concept provides an excellent example of how such research might be presented to a policy-making body.

In its presentation, research by industries begins with a number of tactical advantages over research offered by scholars. Industry research is based upon established engineering and economic principles, while social scientists must argue from broad, unproven assumptions or narrow, empirically derived projections. At the time, the industry evidence will form a seamless pattern of documentation covering all aspects of the issue, while each scholarly research project will tend to focus on only one aspect of the issue, leaving large gaps in the line of argument. Finally, and perhaps most damaging to the scholars' case, telecommunication advocates can argue from experience, while scholars must base their arguments upon speculation, however precisely developed and documented.

Yet, even if the policy-making body should be influenced to support the policy objective described in the communication research proposal, the absence in most reports of any practical recommendations for translating this objective into day-to-day communication practices may either discourage such support or limit its effectiveness in achieving this objective. For example, perhaps the only resolution of the DBS "public access" channel policy debate more damaging than its rejection would be its adoption without the supporting legislation essential for the attainment of that objective. In some cases, in fact, a poorly designed social interest proposal that was adopted and then failed could be far more beneficial in the long run for industry members opposed to the policy than would its prevention in the first place. While the typical scholarly research project cannot propose the specific legislative language necessary to effectuate the policy it supports, it would not seem unreasonable to hope for some discussion of tactics that might be useful to enhance its ultimate benefits for society.

Most proposals fail at the first stage of consideration, unable, if challenged by more experienced and effectively organized industry opponents, to sustain that burden of proof always resting with those advocating change. Even those proposals that survive may find that policy-maker support for the principle they advocate does not always reflect a commitment to support the regulatory program necessary for its realization. However, even if we assume that this particular DBS-delivered "public access" channel policy has been adopted by a governmental body with authority in its own right to enact those regulations necessary to enforce its requirements upon all DBS systems under its jurisdiction, this still does not guarantee in any way that the social objective reflected in that policy will ever be fully realized.[4]

The sole attribute of DBS dissemination that would result in it being specified for the delivery of public access services would be its status as the only type of system with unallocated channel space available for this service. Similarly, in the absence of regulatory distinctions, there would be no logical basis for a researcher to insist on one class of telecommunication system over another in terms of social effects.

At law, however, it is the particular communications *medium* offering a service that determines nearly all rights relating to that service. This occurs in all major industrial nations of the world because statute or code provisions are designed to apply uniformly to all entities possessing the same legally relevant characteristics. This classic principle of legal organization is effective in most instances because it allows legislation to avoid the redundancy that would otherwise occur if statutory or code provisions had to be repeated to encompass each new entity that emerged within a class of entities already defined by law. In addition, it is also equitable in most instances because it accords the same rights and requires the same obligations of similar competing nations.

The crucial flaw for telecommunications law in this system of organization is that the characteristic selected in the past as the definitive one—mode of delivery—is no longer relevant to a determination of most rights in communication.

Thus, regulatory agencies, confined by media-oriented jurisdictional restraints, must approach each communication issue on the basis of the "medium" involved, as if distinguishing between "railroad" and "truck" shipments would somehow reveal the social or economic dimensions of the cargo being carried. This is also the reason, for instance, that the FCC has been compelled to squander its own limited research resources in recent times on such seemingly irrelevant questions as whether a "common carrier" satellite entity can offer subscription broadcast service, whether a broadcaster can provide a specialized point-to-point sideband channel for certain customers, or whether a telephone common carrier should be allowed to operate a broadband communication system.

In the case of DBS-delivered public access service, this irrelevant "medium"-oriented legal classification system could operate to prevent the realization of its public participation objectives at both the international and national levels. In terms of the International Telecommunications Union (ITU) categorization, DBS frequency assignments must be classified as either Fixed Satellite Services (FSS) or Broadcast Satellite Services (BSS). Thus each satellite in a DBS system, limited to either one or the other of these services by those frequencies it has been assigned by the ITU, would not be capable of disseminating public access programming to a general audience if any portion of its remaining services were FSS in nature. In many instances national law would impose a second barrier to implementation of DBS public access service, because satellite entities are at present considered to be communication "common carriers," and common carriers are not accorded the right by their traditional point-to-point classification to disseminate messages of any kind to the general public.

Thus, even if the DBS public access proposal would be successful in gaining policy-maker support, its prospects for survival within a "medium"-bound communications law definitional and jurisdictional system would appear to be extremely dim. In essence, this system, whether Common Law or Civil Law, operates to discourage innovation in communication services at every stage of the policy process because of an orientation requiring that it assess every proposed function in terms of its degree of conformance with those traditional services it already administers(3).

The structure of the policy-making body, its ability to enact necessary legislation, and even the attitude of that agency responsible for its enforcement, all may have a substantial influence upon the ultimate form of telecommunications principles.

So much attention is generally devoted to the isolation of those areas of telecommunication law requiring policy revision that none seems to remain for selecting the proper organization to formulate it. Yet the choice of a particular type of policy-making structure to resolve those questions raised by an initial inquiry is likely to have a profound and generally predictable effect upon this process. For example, if policy is to be formulated by the telecommunications agency that is currently regulating the dominant form of communication service within that society, the natural tendency will be for it to "regularize" or consolidate services as a primary principle, adopting policies relegating new services to a secondary or auxiliary status in order to attain this objective. In contrast, if policy-formulation responsibility is delegated to a newly emerging governmental body charged with an obligation to encourage technological advances in the field of telecommunications, the result will likely be recommendations supporting all functions proposed that would challenge the dominant position of the traditional medium in that field, and that will also incidentally tend to expand its own base of authority.

In an effort to avoid these obvious types of structural biases, some nations have turned to new organizations or commissions specially created to formulate telecommunication policies. Unfortunately, however, the impartial nature of such bodies cannot be maintained for long, since they must be staffed with experienced telecommunication administrators, whose experiences have probably created those preconceptions that the commission was crested to avoid.

Once these deliberations have ended, in most cases any policy pronouncements issued must be referred to a legislative or administrative body for action. Here again, the same type of influences within the committee of the legislature or the bureau of the agency may operate to alter or ignore those communication principles which the policy statement may reflect.

Yet even if legislative or code provisions are drafted that incorporate each aspect of the telecommunications principle supported by the policy statement, one last crucial stage remains—the administrative agency charged with its enforcement must develop those procedures essential for its supervision. It is here that the crucial distinction between "regulation" and "policy" becomes most apparent. If any agency simply acquiesces to an enactment it opposes, its refusal to provide those detailed regulatory guidelines essential to direct its function will usually succeed in effectively frustrating its objectives. A slightly more subtle but equally effective bureaucratic technique for vitiating a policy it opposes might be to enact dutifully the proper policy guidelines required but at the same time to let it be known that it has no strong commitment to their enforcement. These examples illustrate an administrative agency's substantial if generally unrecognized influence over the nature of those principles that will shape telecommunication services in each nation.

*In addition to expanding the capacity to adapt to and influence future
telecommunications policy formulation, communications policy
research can analyze the process itself as a system of communication
and as a framework for evaluations of telecommunications functions.*

For example, scholars involved in investigations of telecommunications evolution might point out the inappropriateness of the present "medium"-based jurisdictional and legal definition system in communications regulation. Other researchers might challenge the continued relevance of terms such as "common carrier" or "broadcaster" in telecommunication policy deliberations. Where, for example, can we now draw a line between those supposedly mutually exclusive terms to distinguish a first-come, first-served public access service now classified as a broadcast function, from the traditional "open to the public without distinction" characteristic of the common carrier? When does a common carrier, through its development of a general public data or information program such as "teletext" or "mass informatics," become transformed by its mass audience content creation and dissemination into a broadcaster?

The telecommunications regulator is too deeply enmeshed in current administrative controversies to attempt such reform, and the legislator, policy-maker, and communications attorney are too preoccupied with the operation of the existing process to consider, much less undertake, the responsibility for its improvement.

Communications policy research traditionally has been confined to an analysis of the communication process, delegating to others responsibility for realizing its principles through law. Although greater knowledge of the policy process itself will give the research no greater authority over its operation, it could in many instances suggest the most effective tactics for developing particular principles in terms of legal implementation and directing them for consideration to the proper policy-making forum. A more comprehensive knowledge of the policy-making process should also encourage communication researchers to propose improvements in that accretion of historical accidents that now defines the scope of most telecommunications services. With an awareness of the nature and function of regulation, perhaps social research or communications policy will be able to make more studied, more practical, and more far-reaching recommendations for the emerging DBS systems. If not, then the vigil for a messianic medium somehow capable of its own redemption must begin anew.

Notes

1. The race has reached the point where some nations are already beginning to declare themselves the winner. Japan is the acknowledged leader at the moment, but Canada claimed one small victory by announcing in September 1979 that it was the first nation in the world offering direct satellite to home television service on a regular basis, even though this service was available only to one small, isolated segment of its population (1). West Germany, France, and Italy have announced intentions to launch domestic DBS systems of their own in the near future if the European Broadcasting Union-sponsored direct broadcast satellite program fails to progress. The great pressure to excel of course has economic implications as well, for those domestic industries that gain the initial experience in developing and launching such systems will be in the best competitive position for contracts from other nations to develop their systems in the future.

2. This pattern of granting channels only to those entities that are already involved in telecommunications or broadcasting is already apparent in Japan and West Germany, for example, where only "establishment" common carrier or broadcast organizations are being considered for channel allocations.

3. This statement may appear "culture bound" at first glance, for it may seem to apply only to private commercial telecommunication organizations. Yet criticisms of PTT tariffs for broadcast service in Western Europe, as just one example, indicate that even non-profit, quasi-governmental organizations are sensitive to attacks upon their allocation of budget resources that may induce the same concern for economic constraints experienced by their "profit-minded" counterparts (see ref. 4).

4. This, of course, is a giant assumption. Governmental task forces in the United States, Canada, Australia, Great Britain, New Zealand, and others have each issued massive communication policy formulations during the past decade that have never been enacted into law.

References

1. Canada, Department of Communications. Mimeo, September 25, 1979.

2. LeDuc, Don. "The FCC v. CATV et al.: A Theory of Regulatory Reflex Action." *Federal Communications Bar Journal* 23(2), Winter 1969, pp. 93–109.

3. LeDuc, Don. *Cable Television and the FCC*. Philadelphia: Temple University Press, 1974, chapters 3–4.

4. LeDuc, Don. "Direct Broadcast Satellite Services for Western Europe: The Hidden Barrier." *Satellite Communication*, February 1978, pp. 34–41.

5. Ploman, Edward. "Proposal: A Media Policy." *Intermedia*, September 1979, pp. 26–29.

6. Pool, Ithiel de Sola. "The Rise of Communications Policy Research." *Journal of Communication* 24(2), Spring 1974, pp. 31–42.

9

Government Regulation of "Adult" Businesses Through Zoning and Anti-Nudity Ordinances: Debunking the Legal Myth of Negative Secondary Effects

Bryant Paul, Daniel Linz, and Bradley J. Shafer
2001

Since 1976, the United States Supreme Court has decided a series of cases focusing on whether the free speech clause of the First Amendment allows cities and states to enact legislation controlling the location of "adult" businesses.[1] These "zoning" regulations, which may prevent a sex-related business from operating, for example, within a certain number of feet from residences, schools and houses of worship or a given distance from one-another, have been predicated on the notion that cities and other municipalities have a substantial interest in combating so-called "negative secondary effects" on the neighborhoods surrounding adult businesses. These secondary effects have most often included alleged increases in crime, decreases in property values, and other indicators of neighborhood deterioration in the area surrounding the adult business. Typically, communities have either conducted their own investigations of potential secondary effects or have relied on studies conducted by other cities or localities.

In more recent years, the Court has considered the constitutionality of anti-nudity legislation passed by municipalities or states that have relied on the negative secondary effects doctrine as justification.[2] The Court in *Barnes v. Glen Theatre, Inc.* held that the State of Indiana could regulate nudity; with a plurality of the Court concluding that the government could undertake such regulation to protect the public order and morality.[3] In a concurring opinion, however, Justice Souter argued that the State had justified the ban on the basis of the *presumed* negative secondary effects on the surrounding community.[4]

Most recently, in *City of Erie v. Pap's A.M.*, the Court again held that municipalities have the right under appropriate circumstances to pass anti-nudity ordinances.[5] Again, however, the Court was fractured. Three justices agreed with Justice O'Connor's opinion that combating negative secondary effects supposedly associated with adult businesses was a legitimate basis for the imposition of an anti-nudity regulation.[6] Most notable for the purposes of this article was, however, Justice Souter's partial concurrence and partial dissent, in which he significantly revised the position he took regarding secondary effects in *Barnes*. In *Pap's*, Justice Souter admitted that the evidence of a relationship between adult businesses and negative secondary effects is at best inconclusive.[7] He called into question the reliability of past studies that purported to demonstrate these effects and suggested that municipalities wishing to ban nudity must show evidence of an actual relationship between adult businesses and negative effects.[8]

The recent expansion of the secondary effects "doctrine" to include not only the zoning of adult businesses but now the regulation of the content of expression within these establishments, raises the question: How reliable and valid are the so called "studies" conducted by individual municipalities and shared nationwide with other municipalities attempting to regulate the location of, and most recently, erotic expression within, adult businesses? Examined in this article is the scientific validity of the research considered by municipalities across the country as a justification for the regulation of adult businesses.

The Supreme Court on Obscenity

Early attempts to regulate adult businesses involved enforcement of obscenity laws. The United States Supreme Court rendered its first authoritative decision on obscenity in *Roth v. United States*.[9] The Court ruled that obscene material was not protected by the First Amendment to the Constitution. It defined obscene materials as those that "appeal to a prurient interest" in sex (defined as a shameful, morbid and unhealthy interest in sex) and are presented in a "patently offensive way."[10]

Through the 1960s, the *Roth* test was refined to reflect objections to the suppression of erotica. In *Kingsley International Pictures Corp. v. Regents*, the Court found that a film based on the erotic novel, *Lady*

Chatterly's Lover, was not obscene under the *Roth* test.[11] The Court greatly expanded the scope of permissible sexual portrayals with its decision in *Memoirs v. Massachusetts*.[12] At issue was the literary work, *Memoirs of a Woman of Pleasure*, commonly known as *Fanny Hill*, by John Cleland. The Court ruled that the prosecution must prove to the jury's satisfaction that the work in question is "utterly without socially redeeming value." In the Court's view the First Amendment protection given to "socially redeeming ideas" was sufficient to override the accompanying portrayals of sexual activity.[13] Later, the Court further broadened its notion of permissibility by striking down another obscenity conviction in *Stanley v. Georgia*.[14] In this case, the defendant had been found guilty of possessing obscene materials in his home. The Supreme Court ruled that the First Amendment provides protection for the individual's right to receive information and ideas about sex.[15]

The body of social science research sponsored by the 1970 Presidential Commission on Obscenity and Pornography in the United States was the first systematic academic foray into the study of exposure to sexually explicit materials.[16] Consistent with the more liberal Supreme Court rulings in the 1960s, the Commission concluded that there were no scientifically demonstrated harmful effects from pornography and recommended legalization of all forms of sexually explicit communication.

A more politically conservative Court ruled, in *Miller v. California*, that "contemporary community standards" must be used to resolve the underlying questions of fact regarding "prurient interest" and "patent offensiveness."[17] By the late 1980s and early 1990s empirical studies estimating community standards for sexually explicit materials suggested that even in politically conservative communities, the majority of citizens actually found such materials non-obscene.[18]

Recently, some feminists have argued that the traditional obscenity perspective, with its emphasis on sexual explicitness and its notion of offensiveness, moral corruption and shame, is misguided.[19] In their view, the regulation of pornography should not be a means for the government to preserve public morals. Instead, regulation should prevent harms to women, including sexual harassment, discrimination and sexual assault.

Efforts to change the legal system to allow women to address pornography's supposed harms were undertaken in the 1980s. The purpose of these laws was to permit women to address the harms claimed to have been done to them by pornography, both as individuals and as a class of persons. In the early 1980s, a model ordinance was introduced in Minneapolis, where it was rejected, and in Indianapolis, where it passed and became law for a time. The ordinance defined pornography as the "graphic sexually explicit subordination of women." Immediately after its passage, the Indianapolis ordinance was challenged. A federal district court declared the Indianapolis ordinance unconstitutional in *American Booksellers Association v. Hudnut*, arguing that an ordinance that makes injuries of pornography actionable is unconstitutional under the First Amendment because the law prohibits expression of a point of view.[20] Social science research testing feminist sociolegal theory has examined pornography's effect on attitudes that justify violence towards women, undermine viewer sensitivity to female victims of rape and violence and increase discriminatory and sexually explicit behavior.[21]

Most recently, governments have shifted away from obscenity prosecutions and are attempting to regulate live performances in adult nightclubs across the United States. These regulations have often been based on the notion that government is permitted to ban behavior, such as nude dancing, if such laws can be shown to be "content neutral" and directed at curbing the so-called adverse secondary effects allegedly associated with adult businesses.[22] Lawmakers across the country have referred to a number of secondary effects studies undertaken by municipalities interested in "zoning" adult businesses as justification for regulating nudity in the business. The scientific validity of this research is the subject of this study.

The Zoning of Adult Entertainment Businesses and the First Amendment

Beginning with the 1976 case, *Young v. American Mini Theatres, Inc.,*[23] several United States Supreme Court decisions have provided guidance as to what constitutes permissible government regulation of the location of adult entertainment establishments, given the protection provided by the Free Speech Clause of the First Amendment.[24] The Court has normally subjected ordinances that restrict the location of adult businesses to an evaluation under the framework for content restrictions on symbolic speech set forth in the four-part test in *United States v. O'Brien*.[25]

Justice Powell applied the four-part *O'Brien* test in his plurality opinion in *Young*.[26] In that case, the Court upheld a Detroit zoning ordinance that regulated the location of adult theaters. The ordinance mandated that adult theaters not locate within 1,000 feet of any two other "regulated uses" or within 500 feet of a residential area. The Detroit ordinance did not attempt to eliminate adult entertainment; rather its aim was to disperse such businesses in an effort to minimize so-called negative secondary effects. In upholding this ordinance, the plurality opinion of the Court reaffirmed the doctrine that a government regulation must have a real and substantial deterrent effect on legitimate expression before it will be invalidated.[27] The Court said the ordinance was not an invalid prior restraint on protected expression because it had neither the intent nor the effect of suppressing speech but was aimed at controlling the secondary effects caused by adult businesses on surrounding uses.[28]

In another landmark decision regarding a municipality's attempt to control secondary effects allegedly caused by adult businesses, *City of Renton v. Playtime Theatres, Inc.*, the Court upheld a Renton, Washington, zoning ordinance that, although not banning adult businesses altogether, did prohibit them from locating within 1,000 feet of any residential zone, church, park or school.[29] The Court held that the Renton ordinance did not restrict First Amendment rights, as the purposes of the ordinance were unrelated to the suppression of speech and the restrictions were the least intrusive means by which to further the government's interests.[30] Part of the precedent set by *Renton* is a three-prong test stipulating that an ordinance must: (1) Be content neutral and aimed only at curbing secondary effects, (2) provide alternate avenues of communication and (3) further a substantial governmental interest.[31]

Further, the Court stated for the first time that a city interested in restricting the operation of adult businesses was not required to show adverse impact from the operation of adult theaters in its own community, if no such experience existed, but could instead rely on the experiences of other cities as a rationale for supporting the passage of an ordinance.[32] The court of appeals had found that "because the Renton ordinance was enacted without be benefit of studies specifically relating to 'the particular problems or needs of Renton,' the city's justifications for the ordinance were 'conclusory.' The Supreme Court maintained that the court of appeals had placed an unnecessary burden of proof on the city, ruling that Renton—which had no adult businesses—could rely primarily on experiences of and studies produced by the nearby city of Seattle as evidence of a relationship between adult uses and negative secondary effects.[34] Thus, the Court ruled that the First Amendment does not require a city to conduct new studies or produce new evidence before enacting an ordinance, so long as the evidence relied upon is reasonably believed to be relevant to the problem the city faces.[35]

Since *Renton*, a number of cities, counties and states have undertaken investigations intended to establish the presence of such secondary effects and their connection to adult facilities. These studies have, in turn, been shared with other municipalities and generally serve as the basis for claims that adult entertainment establishments are causally related to harmful secondary side effects, such as increased crime and decreases in property values. Many local governments across the United States have relied on this body of shared information as evidence of the secondary effects of adult businesses. Further, in most cases, cities and other governmental agencies have used the findings of a core set of studies from other locales as a rationale for instituting regulation of such businesses in their own communities.

Recent Applications of the Secondary Effects Doctrine

In 1991, the U.S. Supreme Court began down the road to expanding the "secondary effects" doctrine as a justification for a total ban on nude dancing. In *Barnes v. Glen Theatre, Inc.*,[36] the enforcement of Indiana's public indecency law, which prevented totally nude dancing by indirectly requiring a dancer to perform in no less than pasties and a G-string, did not violate the First Amendment's guarantee of freedom of expression.[37] Led by Chief Justice Rehnquist, a plurality found the anti-nudity ordinance in question was constitutional because it was aimed at protecting societal order and morality.[38] The Court had held in previous cases that such an objective represented a sufficient government interest.[39] Couching the decision as simply supporting a constitutionally protected time, place and manner restriction of expression, the plurality argued that the Indiana statute did not proscribe erotic dancing. Instead, the Chief Justice argued, it simply ensured that any such performance would include the wearing of scant clothing.[40]

Justice Souter's concurring opinion gave particular attention to the notion of a state's substantial interest in combating the secondary effects of adult entertainment establishments.[41] Justice Souter stated that the type of entertainment the Indiana statute was aimed at regulating was clearly of the same character as that at issue in a number of past decisions by both the Supreme Court[42] as well as lower courts.[43] He went on to suggest that it was therefore no leap to say that live nude dancing of the sort at issue in *Barnes* was ". . . likely to produce the same pernicious secondary effects as the adult films displaying 'specified anatomical areas' at issue in *Renton*."[44] Souter then applied the precedent set forth in *Renton*, stating:

In light of Renton's recognition that legislation seeking to combat the secondary effects of adult entertainment need not await localized proof of those effects, the State of Indiana could reasonably conclude that forbidding nude entertainment of the type offered at . . . the Glen Theatre's "bookstore" furthers its interest in preventing prostitution, sexual assault and associated crimes.[45]

Thus, Justice Souter wrote that municipalities could *assume* that negative secondary effects result from nude dancing establishments when justifying regulation of such expression.

The Supreme Court most recently addressed the constitutionality of regulating adult entertainment in *City of Erie v. Pap's A.M.* A fractured majority upheld an Erie, Pennsylvania, ordinance that, like the statute considered in *Barnes*, required a dancer to wear at least pasties and a G-string during a performance.[46] A majority of five Justices agreed that the case called for the application of the *O'Brien* test. Further, a majority held that the Erie ordinance was aimed at the important government interest of combating the harmful secondary effects associated with nude dancing.[47] A plurality of four justices—*not* a majority of the Court—held that Erie had met this burden by relying on the evidentiary foundation[48] set forth in both *Renton* and *Young*.[49]

Justice Souter's Partial Dissent in *Pap's*

Only a plurality of justices agreed that the city of Erie had demonstrated *evidence* of a compelling government interest. Justice Souter disagreed.[50] In *Barnes*, he opined that the government could assume that "pernicious secondary effects" would result from the presence of nude dancing estab-lishments.[51] In *Pap's*, however, Justice Souter demanded that cities such as Erie, interested in regulating nude dancing on the basis of adverse sec-ondary effects, should be required to provide germane evidence of a rela-tionship between nude dancing and these secondary effects.[52] Ruefully, Justice Souter stated:

> Careful readers . . . will of course realize that my partial dissent rests on a demand for an evidentiary basis that I failed to make when I concurred in *Barnes*. . . . I should have demanded the evidence then, too, and my mistake calls to mind Justice Jackson's foolproof explanation of a lapse of his own, when he quoted Samuel Johnson, "Ignorance, sir, ignorance." McGrath v. Kristensen, 340 U.S. 162, 178 (1950) (concurring opinion). I may not be less ignorant of nude dancing than I was nine years ago, but after many subsequent occasions to think further about the needs of the First Amendment, I have come to believe that a govern-ment must toe the mark more carefully than I first insisted. I hope it is enlight-enment on my part, and acceptable even if a little late.[53]

In his opinion, Justice Souter questions the evidence used by munici-palities of a relationship between adult businesses and negative sec-ondary effects, concluding that such a relationship can no longer be presumed from past studies.[54] In support of his position, Justice Souter cited an amici brief that contained a condensed summary of the critique of existing secondary effects studies reported below.[55]

Evaluating the Validity of Secondary Effects Studies

Since the secondary effects doctrine appears to be expanding, it is imper-ative that it be based on solid evidence that the operation of an adult entertainment business has a deleterious effect on the surrounding com-munity. Unfortunately, when municipalities have conducted studies in the past, there has not been a set of methodological criteria or minimum standards, to which the cities were required to adhere. Without such standards, cities may be relying on flawed databases. This problem is further compounded when courts allow previous studies, conducted in other cities, to supplant data collected in the city where the ordinance is being proposed. A flawed study replicates errors across localities. It makes little sense to generalize to the experiences of other cities on the basis of what may be an invalid investigation in the first place.

The basic requirements for the acceptance of scientific evidence, such as secondary effects studies, were prescribed by the Supreme Court in the 1993 case of *Daubert v. Merrell Dow Pharmaceuticals, Inc.*[56] In *Daubert*, the Court held that there are limits on the admissibility of scientific evidence offered by "expert witnesses" in federal courts. The Court noted that scientific knowledge must be grounded in the methods and procedures of science and must be based on more than subjective belief or unsupported speculation.[57] Offering observations as to how this connection can be made, the Court provided a list of factors that federal judges could consider in ruling on a proffer of expert scientific testimony, including the notion of falsifiability, peer review and publication, error rate and adherence to professional standards in using the technique in question.[58]

Since a core set of studies has been and continues to be relied upon by hundreds of local municipalities as evidence of negative secondary effects, a central concern must be the methodological rigor, and therefore trustworthiness, of these studies. This is particularly true when the Supreme Court requires that a municipality establish that such regulations are necessary to further the governmental interest of ameliorating secondary effects and that such regulations are no broader than is essential to the furtherance of such interest.[59]

To evaluate the validity of the secondary effects studies cited by communities across the country, this article will abstract and analyze the methods and major empirical findings in the relevant research. With few exceptions, the methods most frequently used in these studies are seriously and often fatally flawed. Specifically, these studies do not adhere to professional standards of scientific inquiry and nearly all universally fail to meet the basic assumptions necessary to calculate an error rate—a test of the reliability of findings in science. More importantly, those studies that are scientifically credible demonstrate either no negative secondary effects associated with adult businesses or a reversal of the presumed negative effect.

The Core Set of Frequently Cited Scientific Studies of Secondary Effects

Amassed for this study were a large body of laws enacted for the regulation of adult entertainment businesses and as many as possible of the empirical and non-empirical reports examining potential secondary effects of such businesses produced or purportedly relied upon by municipalities considering the issue. Often, the laws—usually municipal ordinances—contain "preambles" that specifically set forth which of the various "secondary effects studies" the municipality is relying on as justification for enacting the particular regulation. Presumably, these studies are listed in order to comply with the *Renton* requirement that a municipality rely upon evidence "reasonably believed to be relevant to the problem that the city addresses."[60]

The interest is in examining the methodological legitimacy of every "study" cited by municipalities as containing evidence of the relationship between adult entertainment businesses and negative secondary effects. Several steps were taken to obtain as many such studies as possible. First, several attorneys known for their experience and expertise in the arena of adult business regulation were contacted and asked to provide lists and, when possible, printed copies of studies that they were aware had been cited in municipal and state zoning ordinances. Second, the citations found in each of the obtained studies and zoning ordinances were scanned for additional studies on secondary effects. Finally, several additional individuals that have expert knowledge in the area of adult business regulation were asked to supplement the list of "studies."[61] In all, a total of 107 reports were eventually obtained. To be included in the analysis, each report must have been cited by at least one municipality as evidence of a relationship between adult entertainment businesses and negative secondary effects. Although it is more than likely that not every single "secondary effects study" is included in this review, the extensive literature search nevertheless resulted in a large and, more importantly, a representative number of such reports. This study has located, collected and analyzed the vast majority of "studies" that communities purport to rely upon when enacting regulations of adult businesses.[62]

First considered in detail are the four most frequently cited (and relied upon) studies of secondary effects: Indianapolis, Indiana (1984),[63] Phoenix, Arizona (1979),[64] Los Angeles, California (1977),[65] and St. Paul, Minnesota (1978).[66] As can be seen in table 9.1, these studies have been cited as evidence of the relationship between adult entertainment businesses and negative secondary effects by no less than twenty-seven different municipalities. The problems that have been found in these four reports in regard to misunderstandings of their "findings" and methodological failings (discussed in detail below) pertain as well to the next six most frequently relied-upon reports. Discussed next are these six studies, in brief, at the end of the review of the four most frequently cited studies. Accordingly, the concerns that are outlined below apply to all of the "top ten" relied upon "secondary effects studies." And, virtually all of the reports that have been analyzed have these same failings, often because they themselves relied upon earlier "studies" that contained the same flaws discussed below.

The Basic Requirements for the Acceptance of Scientific Evidence

In an attempt to prevent the proliferation in courtrooms of "junk science," the United States Supreme Court in *Daubert* held that there are limits on the admissibility of scientific evidence offered by "expert witnesses" in federal courts.[67] The Court opined that scientific knowledge must be grounded "in the methods and procedures of science" and must be based on more than "subjective belief or unsupported speculation."[68] Thus, the Court said, "the requirement that an expert's testimony pertain to 'scientific knowledge' establishes a standard of evidentiary reliability."[69] In a footnote, the Court observes that "[i]n a case involving scientific evidence, *evidentiary reliability* will be based upon *scientific validity*."[70] Offering "some general observations" as to how this connection can be made, the Court provided a list of factors that federal judges could consider in ruling on a proffer of expert scientific testimony: (1) The "key question" is whether the theory or technique under scrutiny is testable, borrowing Karl Popper's notion of falsifiability.[71] (2) Although publication was not an absolute essential, the Court noted that peer review and publication increased "the likelihood that substantive flaws in methodology will be detected."[72] (3) Error rate.[73] (4) Adherence

Table 9.1
Ten Most Frequently Referenced Studies and Municipalities That Referenced
Them in Drafting Legislation Regulating Adult Businesses

---

1. Indianapolis, Ind. (1984): Dallas (1986), The Bronx (1995), Ramsey
(1990), Manchester, N.H., Brooklyn, Minn., Beaumont (1982), St. Paul, Minn.
(1987/1988), Times Square, N.Y. (1993), Newport News, Va. (1996), Kansas
City, Mo. (1998), Falcon Heights, Minn. (1994), Fridley, Minn., Brooklyn
Park, Minn., Manatee County, Fla., Lynnwood, Wash. (1990), Oklahoma City
(1986), New Hanover County (1989), Rochester/Olmsted (1988), Seattle
(1989), St. Cloud, Minn. (1982), St. Croix (1993), St. Paul (1994)

2. Phoenix, Ariz. (1979): Dallas (1986), The Bronx (1995), St. Paul (1994),
Ramsey (1990), Manchester, N.H., Brooklyn, Minn., St. Paul, Minn.
(1987/1988), Times Square, N.Y. (1993), Newport News, Va. (1996),
Minnesota (1989), Kansas City, Mo. (1998), Falcon Heights, Minn. (1994),
Fridley, Minn., Brooklyn Park, Minn., Manatee County, Fla., New Hanover
County (1989), Rochester/Olmsted (1988), St. Cloud, Minn. (1982)

3. Los Angeles, Calif. (1977): Dallas (1986), The Bronx (1995), Broward
County, Fla., Times Square, N.Y. (1993), Newport News, Va. (1996), Garden
Grove (1991), Bellevue, Wash. (1987) Manhattan (1994), Seattle (1989), St.
Cloud, Minn. (1982), St. Paul, Minn. (1994), St. Croix (1993), Brooklyn Park,
Minn.

4. St. Paul, Minn. (1987): Dallas (1986), Ramsey (1990), St. Paul, Minn.
(1987/1988), Times Square, N.Y. (1993), Minnesota (1989), Bellevue, Wash.
(1987), Brooklyn, Minn., Falcon Heights, Minn. (1994), Brooklyn Park,
Minn., Manatee County, Fla., Lynnwood, Wash. (1989), Rochester/Olmsted
(1988)

5. Austin, Tex. (1986): Dallas (1986), The Bronx (1995), Manchester, N.H.,
Broward County, Fla., Kansas City, Mo. (1998), Manatee County, Fla.,
Manhattan (1994), Seattle (1989), St. Cloud, Minn. (1982), St. Paul, Minn.
(1994)

6. St. Paul, Minn. (1987/1988): Brooklyn, Minn., Times Square, N.Y. (1993),
Minnesota (1989), Kansas City, Mo. (1998), Falcon Heights, Minn. (1994),
Fridley, Minn., Rochester/Olmsted (1988), St. Cloud, Minn. (1982), St. Paul,
Minn. (1994)

7. Amarillo, Tex. (1977): Dallas (1986), Beaumont (1982), Newport News,
Va. (1996), Manatee County, Fla., New Hanover County (1989), St. Croix
(1993), St. Paul, Minn. (1994)

8. Detroit, Mich. (1972): Beaumont (1982), Times Square, N.Y., (1993),
Bellevue (1987), New Hanover County (1989), St. Croix (1993)

9. Beaumont, Tex. (1982): Dallas (1986), Newport News, Va. (1996),
Manatee County, Fla., New Hanover County (1989), St. Croix (1993)

10. Kent, Wash. (1982): Des Moines, Wash., Bellevue, Wash. (1987),
Lynnwood, Wash. (1990), Seattle (1989)

---

to professional standards in using the technique in question.[74] (5) Finally, though not the sole or even the primary test, general acceptance could "have a bearing on the inquiry."[75]

While it may not be necessary to hold municipalities to each of these considerations when weighing the validity of evidence substantiating the existence of secondary effects research with adult businesses, at least two factors are indispensable. It is at least a testable proposition that secondary effects may result from adult establishments, or else a study would not have been undertaken in the first place. It can be further presumed that a lengthy peer review and publication process may be unlikely due to the sense of urgency when communities tend to address these issues. In addition, the general acceptance requirement is held to have a bearing but is not an absolute consideration. The third and fourth factors, however, the calculation of an error rate and adherence to professional standards in using techniques or procedures, need to be applied to these studies in order to ensure "evidentiary reliability." Without this reliability, there is no basis to determine whether there is a substantial or important governmental interest involved, whether a specific piece of legislation is "necessary" in order to further that interest, or whether it is "reasonable" for a municipality to rely upon such a study as a basis for enacting legislation.[76]

In a scientific study, the error rate refers to the probability of accepting a result as true, when in fact it is false.[77] The rate is an indication of the reliability of a finding. An error rate is determined by first calculating an estimation of a population characteristic (a statistic) that summarizes the data that have been collected and then asking how likely it is that that statistical value would be obtained by chance alone. The error rate is the degree of chance a scientist will allow. In the social sciences, it is conventional to set the error rate at five percent or less (that is, a researcher will tolerate an error rate of five times out of one hundred that the results may be obtained by chance).[78]

Unless certain assumptions are met, statistical tests cannot be applied to the data, and an error rate cannot be calculated. Most important of these assumptions in regard to, for example, survey research, is that the units of analysis (for example, survey respondents) are randomly selected from the population, or in regard to an experiment, that the units of analysis (for example, subjects) are randomly assigned to experimental and control or comparison groups.[79] The results of properly conducted experiments and surveys are always couched in terms of an error rate.

In many cases, especially in field research, it is not possible to randomly assign units of analysis to an experimental group and a control group.[80] This is universally true of "secondary effects" studies.[81] When this is the case, adherence to a set of professional standards that have been devised by scientists in a particular area of inquiry to insure methodological integrity and thus the validity of a study is all the more necessary. These standards vary somewhat depending on the area of inquiry or social science discipline, but they are generally known as professional standards for conducting "quasi-experiments."[82]

Four Criteria for Insuring a Scientifically Valid Study of Secondary Effects

The majority of the secondary effects studies reviewed in this article generally assume the following form. Researchers assemble crime statistics and calculate average property values and other general measures of neighborhood quality or deterioration (for example, residential turnover rate, local tax revenue, etc.) in the geographical area surrounding adult entertainment businesses. In a few studies these measures are compared to other areas that do not contain adult businesses. Another popular data gathering method is to perform a survey in which residents or business owners are asked for their opinions of the likely impact of adult entertainment businesses on their neighborhoods.

Four criteria are crucial in insuring that a scientifically valid study of secondary effects has been conducted. First, in order to insure accurate and fair comparisons, a control area must be selected that is truly "equivalent" to the area containing the adult entertainment business.[83] Since most studies of secondary effects attempt to uncover increases in crime or neighborhood economic deterioration, professional standards dictate that the control (non-adult) site must be comparable (matched) with the study (adult) site on variables related to crime and deterioration. Of particular importance when studying crime is that the study and control areas are matched for variables such as ethnicity and socioeconomic status of individuals in both areas. Additionally, economic factors, such as median home value and total individuals employed and unemployed, should be comparable in both areas. A concerted effort should also be made to include only comparison areas with similar real estate market characteristics including property values, rental rates and proportion of unused commercial and industrial space in either area. The study and control areas in a crime study should be approximately equal in total population. Finally, because of the effect of businesses that serve alcoholic beverages on increases in crime and neighborhood deterioration, the study and control area should be matched on the presence of alcohol-serving establishments.[84]

Second, a sufficient period of elapsed time, ideally both prior to and following the establishment of an adult entertainment business, is necessary when compiling data in order to ensure that the study is not merely detecting an erratic pattern of social activity. Most methodologically sound, quasi-experimental, time-series analyses rely on at least a one-year period prior to and after the introduction of the event under study to test for significant changes. Generally, the longer the time period before and after the event under consideration, the more stable (and more valid) the estimates of the event's effects tend to be.[85]

Third, the crime rate must be measured according to the same valid source for all areas considered.[86] Studies on secondary effects typically focus on two general types of crime in relation to adult entertainment businesses. These two types of crime are "general criminal activity" (including, but not limited to, robbery, theft, assault, disorderly conduct and breaking and entering) and "crimes of a sexual nature" (including, but not limited to, rape, prostitution, child molestation and indecent public exposure). It is especially important that the measurement of these crimes is based on the same information source for both sites and throughout the entire study period. For example, if the study area measures crime by the number and type of calls made to the police department, the control area must also rely on such a measure when the two areas are compared.

In addition, the crime information source must be factually valid and reliable, such as a daily log kept by police or a compilation of the number of arrests. Many studies claim to measure area crime by asking survey respondents about their estimates of the likelihood of being a victim of crime. Such data are not preferred because of their subjectivity and as such, cannot be trusted as a valid representation of actual criminal activity in a particular area. Social scientists should hesitate to rely upon such "evidence" to establish a causal link between adult businesses and secondary effects. The *Daubert* standard suggests such information may not have sufficient "trustworthiness" to be admissible in a federal court. However, if such subjective opinion research on crime is to be undertaken, it should conform to the standards for conducting reliable and valid survey research.

Researchers must also acknowledge any change in police surveillance techniques once an adult entertainment business has been established in a particular community. Obviously, increased surveillance of an area simply because an adult business is located there will have an impact on the amount of crime detected by the police. If increased police surveillance and the opening of an adult business in a particular area are confounded in this way, it is impossible to tell whether crime has increased due to the presence of the adult entertainment business or increased surveillance police discovering more crime.

Finally, survey research, if relevant to the question at all, must be properly conducted. Most survey research in this area involves asking real estate professionals, local property owners, law enforcement officers and/or community residents to estimate the effect of the presence of an adult entertainment business on a particular community. Less frequently, surveys of citizens' perception of crime and victimization are also undertaken. While subjective surveys may provide a sense of the general opinion of a particular group regarding the impact of adult entertainment businesses on surrounding neighborhood property values or criminal activity, this kind of survey does not provide sound empirical evidence of any true relationship between these businesses and their actual impacts on the surrounding areas. For instance, while the opinions of real estate professionals are legitimate and important in regard to other matters, they have a particularly strong interest in the issue and as such, may produce biased results.

Survey evidence is not comparable to, nor can it replace, the evidence supplied by objective comparisons of, for example, property values and/or crime statistics complied by the police within areas containing adult entertainment businesses, with property values or crime statistics within areas containing no such businesses. Such a comparative analysis is the preferable social scientific means by which to establish a relationship between the presence of adult entertainment businesses and either decreases in property values or increases in crime for the surrounding areas.

Even if some survey research may be relevant to the issue at hand—although we doubt whether it truly is—it must be properly conducted in order for the researcher to calculate an error rate. Professional standards do exist for performing methodologically valid social scientific survey research so that it possesses some degree of reliability and trustworthiness. Adherence to these standards is essential if researchers hope to obtain legitimate unbiased survey results. First, it is important to ensure that a random sample of potential respondents is included in the study.[87] Second, a sufficient response rate must be reached, and those who do respond must not be a biased sub-portion of the sample.[88] Finally, there must be a sufficient number of respondents to provide a stable statistical estimate.[89]

The Four Most Frequently Cited Studies

The four most frequently cited studies and the degree to which they are scientifically valid according to the criteria laid out above are summarized in table 9.2. The studies are described below, including their findings and conclusions as well as their methodological strengths and weaknesses, in reverse order of how often they have been cited by municipalities.

St. Paul, Minnesota (1978)[90]

This study represents the most methodologically sound of all of the empirical research reviewed. Ironically, the St. Paul study does not claim to have found any support for the existence of a relationship between sexually oriented adult entertainment businesses and negative secondary effects.

The study was methodologically stronger than most others for at least two reasons. First, the researchers examined all seventy-six census tracts

Table 9.2
How the Four Most Frequently Referenced Studies Fulfill the Criteria
Necessary for Valid Research Concerning Secondary Effects

Criteria Study	Study and Control Areas Properly Matched	Valid Measures of Crime Statistics	Sufficient Time Lag
Indianapolis, Ind. (1986)	Significant differences in population size, zoning mix, and property value. (−)	Measures appear valid. (+)	Used only a three- year average for crime rates and property values. No measures taken prior to existence of adult businesses. (−)
Phoenix, Ariz. (1979)	Significant differences in average income and age of housing stock. (−)	Measures appear valid. (+)	No significant time series data considered. No measures taken prior to existence of adult businesses. (−)
Los Angeles, Calif. (1977)	Areas were comparable. (+)	Measures appear valid. (+)	Data from over a six-year period were considered. During that time a number of businesses both opened and closed. (+)
St. Paul, Minn. (1978)	Areas were comparable. (+)	Did not consider crime as a variable. (NA)	Data from over a six-year period were considered. During that time a number of businesses both opened and closed. (+)

Change in Police Surveillance	Correct Survey Methodology	Evidence of Negative Secondary Effects
No change in police surveillance mentioned. (+)	Used random sample of real estate appraisers. Though only asked for reaction to a hypothetical scenario. (+)	Contains evidence both for and against a relationship.
No change in police surveillance mentioned. (NA)	No survey data collected. (NA)	Contains some equivocal evidence of a relationship.
Admit to "stepped up" police surveillance. (−)	Used completely biased, nonrandom sample of local residents and real estate professionals who lived or worked within 500 feet of an adult business. (−)	Contains absolutely no objective evidence of a relationship.
Did not consider crime as a variable. (NA)	No survey data collected. (NA)	Contains absolutely no evidence of a relationship.

within the St. Paul region. The authors compared all tracts containing
adult entertainment establishments with all of those that did not. As
such, the study examined the entire geographical "study universe,"
negating the need for random assignment of control areas or the appropriate matching of selected control areas to the study area. Second, the
study, which compared levels of neighborhood deterioration for study
and control areas, maintained a substantial time lag between the first
measures of deterioration and the second. Deterioration was determined
by examining crime counts, housing values and market and legal influences over the study period. Therefore, changes in neighborhood climate
between the first and second measures are more likely representative of
reliable neighborhood changes rather than erratic fluctuations in social
activity.

The most important aspect of this study is that it found absolutely no
relationship between sexually oriented businesses and neighborhood
deterioration. In fact, the study found that the only factor that was predictive of neighborhood deterioration was whether an alcohol-serving
establishment was operating within the area. No relationship was found,
however, between neighborhood deterioration and the presence of establishments that both served alcoholic beverages and offered live nude
entertainment.

Los Angeles, California (1977)[91]

This study is perhaps the most often incorrectly referenced of any empirical research investigating the effects of adult-oriented businesses on
surrounding areas. In fact, although it is the third most relied-upon piece
of research that was found supposedly establishing the relationship
between adult-oriented businesses and negative social repercussions,
the researchers actually never claim any significant support for such a
connection.

The study report consists of four parts. In the first part of the study,
the researchers openly admit that they found no evidence of a relationship between the operation of adult entertainment businesses and potential negative effects. These conclusions were based on the results of a
comparison of the average property value changes for five study areas
and four control areas. Each of the five study areas was chosen because

it contained a known cluster of adult entertainment businesses. The four control areas were chosen because of their proximity and supposed similarity to at least one of the study areas and because they did not have an adult entertainment business operating within their borders. All of the study and control areas were in Hollywood, North Hollywood or Studio City.

The researchers reported that it was difficult to find any consistent increase or decrease in property values associated with adult businesses. Results of the comparisons found that for some study and control area comparisons, there was a far larger decrease in the control (non-adult) area. Such a result is contrary to the assumption underlying the secondary effects doctrine (that adult establishments themselves cause a decrease in property values). Similarly, at least one study (adult) areas increased in value by more than 400% over their comparable control (non-adult) area. Again, this result is directly opposite to what one would expect to see by assuming a connection between adult businesses and secondary effects. Given these objective findings, the researchers stated that there is ". . . insufficient evidence to support the contention that concentrations of sex oriented businesses have been the primary cause of these patterns of change in assessed valuations between 1970 and 1976."[92] It seems that those who have incorrectly referenced this study as supporting the relationship between adult entertainment businesses and lower property rates have simply disregarded the preceding statement by the study's authors.

The second part of the Los Angeles study claimed that survey results suggest that public opinion is strongly opposed to the operation of adult businesses. Such a "study" does nothing more than attempt to gauge subjective opinions and does not then serve to answer the more relevant question of whether adult businesses actually cause secondary effects. In addition, even in this subjective endeavor, the researchers failed to adhere to minimum professional standards by failing to conduct the research in accordance with proper survey techniques—most importantly, they failed to obtain a random sample of respondents. Without adherence to the requirement that a random sample of respondents be obtained, the study authors cannot calculate an error rate, and the reliability of the results cannot be determined. Instead, the Los Angeles study authors are left with a non-random survey of the opinions of potentially biased property owners and real estate professionals who each lived and/or worked within 500 feet of an adult entertainment business. Such a "survey" offers no insight as to whether adult establishments engender secondary effects and is not even representative of the broader public opinion on the issue.

In the third part of the Los Angeles study, the researchers openly acknowledge that they found no significant differences in crime rates between the census tracts encompassing the areas containing adult entertainment businesses and areas containing no such establishments. This part of the study consisted of an examination of the crime and population statistics for each of the census tracts containing clusters of adult entertainment businesses. Only tracts containing the clusters of adult businesses considered within the study areas for the first part of the study (discussed above) were considered. These data were when compared to those obtained from the census tracts containing each of the comparison control (non-adult) areas used in the first part of the study. Both sets of data were analyzed and compared over time in order to determine any significant differences concerning crime rates. The study authors concluded that in general there were no significant differences in crime rates between the census tracts encompassing the study (adult) and control (non-adult) areas and that no firm conclusions relevant to the study could be developed.

The fourth and final part of the Los Angeles study involved a "special" police study of the areas of Hollywood containing clusters of adult entertainment businesses. However, the researchers failed to adhere to even the most basic and rudimentary professional standards by failing to attempt to make a comparison of crime statistics in these areas with those in comparable control (non-adult) areas. The researchers failed to compare the areas surrounding adult businesses with comparable control (non-adult) areas. In addition, the researchers admitted to a substantial change in police surveillance of the area under study, which renders any results at least suspect and most likely meaningless. Although the findings of this study suggested high levels of criminal activity within these clusters, any implication that this is connected to the presence of adult businesses is invalidated by the fact that the researchers admitted to "stepped up" surveillance within these areas. Put simply, the police most likely found greater amounts of crime in the adult establishment areas because they were trying harder to find it. These failings and problems take this portion of the study outside of the reliability criteria of *Daubert* discussed above.

Phoenix, Arizona (1979)[93]

This report presents the findings of a study performed in Phoenix that attempted to examine the relationship between adult entertainment businesses and local crime rates. This study claimed to find higher overall crime rates in study areas containing adult-oriented businesses compared to control areas containing no such businesses. However, the evidence of negative secondary effects was equivocal at best. In addition, the study fails to adhere to professional standards because the control sites are not sufficiently comparable with the study site and there was not a sufficient period of time for the collection of data, both prior to and following the establishment of an adult entertainment business. The time control is necessary to ensure that the study is not merely detecting an erratic pattern of social activity.

The researchers selected three geographically diverse study areas, each comprised of one census tract in which at least one adult entertainment business was in operation. They further selected three control (non-adult) tracts located directly adjacent to the study tract. An attempt was made to match each of the three control areas with the study areas on several dimensions, including the number of buildings built since 1950, the median family income, median population age, percentage of acreage used residentially and percentage of population that was non-white.

It is essential that the selected study and control areas be accurately matched, but the matching of study and control census tracts for this study was unacceptable. The median income for study area 1 was 30% lower than that in the matching control, control area 1 had a substantially greater number of buildings built since 1950 than the corresponding study area, and study areas 2 and 3 each had significantly lower median income levels than did their matching control areas. Since income and crime levels are generally inversely related one might expect to see higher crime rates with lower income irrespective of the presence of adult businesses. These failures to sufficiently match the study and control areas suggest that this study does not adhere to acceptable professional standards for scientific research.

In addition, there was an insufficient period of time, both prior to and following the establishment of an adult entertainment business for reliable measures of crime or economic deterioration to be obtained. The study was limited to crime rates for a one-year period. Because of the extremely short period of time, one cannot be sure that the study was not merely detecting an erratic pattern of social activity.

Finally, although the study findings suggested that overall crime rates were higher in each of the study areas than those for each matching control area, a composite index of "violent crimes," which included murder, robbery, assault and rape, was also constructed. Each study (adult) area showed a lower rate of violent crime (including rape) than the matched control (non-adult) area. In addition, the rate of child molestation was higher in the control (non-adult) areas than in the matched study (adult) areas. The results of the study offered, at best, equivocal evidence of the relationship between crime rates and the operation of adult entertainment businesses.

Indianapolis, Indiana (1984)[94]

This study appeared to be the report most widely cited and relied upon by municipalities as evidence of negative secondary effects. Regardless of the problems with this report as outlined in this summary, the overall study offered equivocal findings regarding the supposed relationship between adult businesses and negative secondary effects. More importantly, in a subarea analysis most relevant to the question of the relationship between adult businesses and secondary effects, lower rather than higher crime rates were found in all study (adult business) areas when compared to control (no adult business) areas. In addition, the overall study failed to adhere to rudimentary professional standards of scientific evidence, and an error rate could not be calculated due to a failure to meet basic statistical assumptions.

The methodological problems with this study can be summarized as follows: (1) The control sites were not sufficiently comparable (properly matched) with the study sites. (2) No measurements were taken prior to the establishment of an adult entertainment business to ensure that the study was not merely picking up an already established crime pattern that is independent of the adult businesses in the area. (3) There was a potential confounding effect caused by adult entertainment businesses that supplied both sexually oriented entertainment and alcoholic beverages. (4) The researchers did not adhere to minimum professional standards by failing to conduct a survey study of real estate professionals in accordance with proper survey techniques. Beyond being purely subjective, the most striking limitations of this survey study were that it asked a national sample of real estate appraisers who were not from Indianapolis to consider only a hypothetical scenario concerning adult businesses in an unspecified community. Thus, the survey results are not applicable to the question of whether an adult business would have a negative (even subjective) effect upon property values in the Indianapolis area.

The Indianapolis study contained reports of four separate analyses. Each had significant methodological problems that undercut its reliability.

While the first set of analyses purported to show that higher crime rates were associated with adult entertainment businesses, the researchers failed to adhere to minimum professional standards by not properly matching study and control areas and by not including a sufficient period of time prior to the establishment of an adult entertainment business for collection and analysis of data. In this portion of the report, the researchers compared crime rates for six study areas containing at least one adult entertainment business with crime rates for six control areas containing no adult entertainment businesses. The study authors attempted but failed properly to match control and study areas on a number of criteria, including zoning mix, population size and age of housing stock. Significant differences existed in reference to the zoning mix within the majority of study versus control sites. In addition, the control sites were 37% more heavily populated than the study sites. Since population density and zoning mix are often associated with higher crime rates, any differences found between the study and control areas could very well have been due to these factors rather than the presence of adult businesses.

Another problem with the study was that it did not include a sufficient period of time prior to the establishment of an adult entertainment business for the collection and analysis of data. This lack of a measurement some time before the adult business located in the area made it impossible to determine whether findings of higher or lower crime rates in either area were associated with the operation of adult entertainment businesses or whether the study was simply detecting an already established pattern of criminal activity.

Finally, also problematic was the fact that at least one establishment that served alcoholic beverages was included within each of the study areas, while this was not the case for each of the control areas. As at least one study has found evidence that the presence of alcohol-serving establishments are associated with higher rates of criminal activity,[95] this must be viewed as a potentially serious flaw (confound) to the study's validity. One would expect to see higher crime rates in areas that contained establishments that served alcoholic beverages, regardless of the presence or absence of any sexually oriented businesses.

Particularly interesting was the fact that the Indianapolis report included a sub-area analysis that found lower rather than higher crime rates in all areas where adult businesses were located compared to control (non-adult) areas. This analysis involved a comparison of crime statistics for a smaller sub-area of the larger areas considered in the first analysis described above. The researchers examined crime rates in a 1,000-foot radius around the adult businesses in the study areas. They compared these crime rates to those within a 1,000-foot radius around a random centroid located within the control areas used in the first analysis. This portion of the study would then appear to be the most relevant of all to the question of whether adult businesses create or cause secondary effects in the areas immediately surrounding them. However, this sub-area analysis found lower crime rates in all study areas compared to control areas.

The Indianapolis report authors also claimed to have found a substantially smaller increase in property values for the study areas than for the control areas. However, the researchers failed to adhere to minimum professional standards by not properly matching study and control areas for this analysis. This portion of the study was therefore unreliable from a scientific standpoint.

The analysis compared the average home mortgage value and average number of homes sold for the control and study areas discussed in the first study, as well as those for the center township area. Since the data came from the same study and control areas discussed in the first analysis, these data are fraught with the same methodological problems associated with that data set (that is, the study and control areas were not properly matched). The average mortgage values in the study areas were initially 49% higher than those in either the control areas or the central township area. As such, the finding that the average mortgage value for the control areas and central township area increased by 77% and 56%, respectively, while the study areas saw only an average increase of 26%, can be explained as the result of what is known as a ceiling effect. The study area values may have initially been far more inflated than the two comparison areas. Thus, it would come as no surprise that the study areas saw a smaller increase in property value than the comparison areas. The vast differences in initial mortgage values associated with the failure to properly match control and study areas rendered the two areas far too dissimilar to consider as suitable comparison groups. Finally, it should also be noted that despite the greater increase in mortgage values for the control and center township areas in comparison to the study (adult) areas, the study area still maintained a higher average mortgage value when the final measures were taken.

The fourth analysis described in the Indianapolis report included the results of a national survey of members of the American Institute of Real Estate Appraisers. The data collection for this analysis was flawed in three ways. First, survey research on perceived likely deterioration effects is completely subjective and does not answer the question as to whether there are secondary effects associated with adult establishments in terms of actual property values, such as average home prices or other economic indicators. Second, even in this subjective analysis, the researchers failed to adhere to minimum professional standards by failing to conduct the study in accordance with proper survey techniques. Although a random sample of real estate professionals was obtained, the response rate was unacceptably low (only one third of the respondents returned the questionnaire). Further, no error rate was calculated for the percentages reported in the study. Without the calculation of an error rate, the researchers cannot establish a "confidence interval" around the percentages calculated in the study. This is especially troublesome given the fact many of the findings hovered around the fifty percent mark. Without some indication of the confidence one can place in these estimates, it is unclear if the majority or a minority of respondents projected a negative impact if adult businesses were to locate in a community.

Third, and even more problematic, the sampled appraisers were asked only to consider a brief hypothetical situation concerning a middle-class family that lived in an area in which an adult bookstore would soon be opening in a nearby building. The respondents were asked five questions concerning the potential effects on the value of the family's home. A fatal flaw in this study is that it asks a nationally selected group of appraisers—none of whom were from Indianapolis—to consider only a hypothetical scenario. Thus, it has little to say about how an Indianapolis community appraiser might actually view the value of a home in Indianapolis (if such a question was even truly relevant to the secondary effects doctrine).

Summary of the Six Other Most Frequently Referenced Reports

Table 9.3 provides a brief description of the methodological features of each of the remaining studies in the "top ten," and illustrates the degree to which the studies are scientifically valid. The remaining six most frequently referenced studies in descending order were reports produced by Austin, Texas (1986),[96] St. Paul, Minnesota (1987, 1988),[97] Amarillo, Texas (1977),[98] Detroit, Michigan (1972),[99] Beaumont, Texas (1982)[100] and Kent, Washington (1982).[101] Two of these, the reports by Beaumont and Detroit, are not empirical studies. The Beaumont "study", for example, is merely a report prepared by the planning department of that municipality, suggesting a need for regulation of adult businesses. The remaining four reports did not adhere to minimum professional standards of valid scientific research by failing to meet one or more of the four necessary criteria discussed above.

Table 9.3
How Well the Top Ten Referenced Studies Meet the Necessary Criteria for Good Social Scientific Research

Criteria Study	Matched Control	Valid Measure of Crime Statistics	Sufficient Time Lag	Change in Police Surveillance	Correct Survey Methods	Additional Serious Flaws
Indianapolis (1984)	No (−)	Yes (+)	No (−)	No (+)	Yes (+)	Yes (−)
Phoenix (1979)	No (−)	Yes (+)	No (−)	No (+)	NA	No (+)
Los Angeles (1977)	Yes (+)	Yes (+)	Yes (+)	Yes (−)	No (−)	Yes (−)
St. Paul (1978)	Yes (+)	NA	Yes (+)	NA	NA	No (+)
Austin (1986)	No (−)	Yes (+)	No (−)	No (+)	Yes (+)	No (+)
St. Paul (1987), (1988)	No (−)	Yes (+)	No (−)	No (+)	NA	Yes (−)
Amarillo (1977)	No (−)	Yes (+)	No (−)	No (+)	NA	No (+)
Detroit (1972)†	NA	NA	NA	NA	NA	NA
Beaumont (1982)†	NA	NA	NA	NA	NA	NA
Kent (1982)	NA	NA	NA	NA	No (−)	Yes (−)

† = not an empirical study.

The studies produced by Austin, St. Paul and Amarillo all failed to compare neighborhood characteristics (crime rates or property values) for areas containing adult entertainment businesses with control areas containing no such businesses. In addition, these three studies failed to include measures of neighborhood characteristics over a sufficient period of time, both prior to and following the establishment of adult entertainment businesses. Further, the Kent study, which contained a report of an attempt to query neighbors of adult business establishments, failed to adhere to even the most minimal professional standards for proper survey research.

Conclusions

This article has abstracted and analyzed the methodology and major empirical findings of studies purporting to detect secondary effects of adult businesses. It has demonstrated, with few exceptions, that the scientific validity of the most frequently used studies is questionable and the methods are seriously and often fatally flawed. These studies, relied on by communities throughout the country, do not adhere to professional standards of scientific inquiry and nearly all fail to meet the basic assumptions necessary to calculate an error rate. Those studies that are scientifically credible demonstrate either no negative secondary effects associated with adult businesses or a reversal of the presumed negative effects.

Specifically, this article applied four criteria for methodological validity and found that the majority of studies failed to meet at least one, and often all, of these criteria. First, a number of studies attempting to compare areas containing adult businesses to areas containing no such businesses failed to include comparison (control) areas that were sufficiently matched regarding important characteristics, such as age of housing stock or racial make-up. This lack of comparability between study and control areas prevents researchers from determining whether neighborhood deterioration is related to the operation of adult businesses in an area or that some other confounding variable is responsible for the outcome. Second, a number of the studies using neighborhood crime measures have collected these statistics improperly. Although many studies gathered legitimate and consistent measures of crime statistics, such as police arrest reports over a sufficient period of time, a number of others used less scientifically acceptable measures, such as cross-sectional survey results of residents' opinions of levels of crime. Third, the majority of studies failed to include a sufficient period of elapsed time, both prior to and following the establishment of an adult entertainment business, when measuring the relationship between the presence of adult businesses and a number of negative outcomes, such as higher crime rates and lower property values. Without a sufficient study period, it is difficult to determine whether a relationship exists between adult entertainment businesses and negative secondary effects, or whether the data are simply a reflection of an erratic pattern of local activity. Finally, most of the studies that included survey results utilized non-random and therefore biased samples of residents and/or business owners, rendering them scientifically invalid. Even if methodologically valid, such studies offer only subjective opinions concerning the impact of adult businesses and provide little, if any, evidence of actual negative secondary effects.

The studies reviewed here have been (and continue to be) shared across communities. As such, the methodological flaws found in these studies prevent them from being used to establish a sufficient government interest in the regulation of adult businesses within a particular community. However, these unsound studies have been repeatedly misused as evidence across a large number of other municipalities. For example, the Indianapolis study is cited by no fewer than 22 communities as evidence of a relationship between adult businesses and negative secondary effects. This study contained several substantial methodological flaws and found evidence both supporting as well as rejecting negative secondary effects. Thus, the potential exists that as many as twenty-two zoning ordinances have been founded on a false premise about the substantial government interest in regulating the location of these businesses.

Although not specifically mandating such, the United States Supreme Court in *Pap's* may be perceived by some municipalities as permitting the extension of use of these flawed studies to the regulation of expressive conduct *within* an adult business as a basis for upholding an ordinance to regulate nudity on the ground that such a restriction would serve to eliminate negative secondary effects of such expression. Such regulation would be based on the same false premise as the zoning regulations addressed in *Young* and *Renton*—that there is valid evidence of a substantial government interest at stake, and that these types of laws further those interests (if they indeed exist).[102]

Even if the studies undertaken to justify zoning were not scientifically flawed, there are a number of other reasons why it may be inappropriate to extend the secondary effects doctrine to the regulation of nudity. First, and perhaps most obvious, there have been no studies that have been specifically designed to measure the impact of nudity per se on adverse secondary effects. Of most use would be studies wherein rates of adverse secondary effects for areas surrounding nude dancing establishments are compared to those surrounding establishments where pasties and a g-string are required. In the absence of such a direct test, it cannot and should not be assumed that the studies reviewed here, even if methodologically sound, would generalize to the regulation of nudity.

In fact, from a social psychological standpoint there are several factors that may prevent the generalization of the evidence collected to justify the application of zoning regulations to the regulation of nude dancing. For example, there may be substantial differences in the characteristics of the patrons who frequented the adult establishments studied to justify zoning compared to those who now visit establishments offering live nude dancing. Further, the earlier secondary effects studies were conducted to address the problem of adult businesses that purveyed explicit depiction of sexual intercourse and other sexual acts, whereas nude dancing does not involve such explicit performances. In addition, live entertainment may produce substantially different effects than filmed or videotaped acts. Finally, the interpersonal element of live nude dance establishments must be considered. Viewing a live dancer and later perhaps interacting with that dancer may produce significantly different outcomes than viewing erotic movies or the other fare usually purveyed in businesses considered in earlier secondary effects studies. Until these questions are addressed through scientifically valid empirical research, the applicability of the secondary effects doctrine to yet another area of speech regulation is highly questionable.[103]

The Application of Social Science Evidence to the Regulation of Nude Dancing

Because the antinudity ordinance under scrutiny in *Pap's* was so similar to that considered in *Barnes*, it seems likely that with its *Pap's* decision, the Supreme Court had hoped to replace the fractured decision in *Barnes* with a clear majority ruling. Such a ruling may have offered the lower courts, lawmakers, adult business owners, and First Amendment scholars a coherent precedent towards which to look when considering the constitutionality of anti-nudity regulations based on the secondary effects rationale. Yet, while the Court's decision in *Pap's* appears to be another fractured decision, there may be more coherence to the ruling than is at first apparent.

Five justices and thus a majority embraced the secondary effects doctrine in *Pap's*. Justice Souter, who dissented in part, not only agreed with the plurality's application of the *O'Brien* test to nude dancing as a form of symbolic speech, but, in theory, he also supported the secondary effects doctrine. Justice Souter merely disavowed his assertion in *Barnes* that secondary effects may be *presumed*. In *Pap's*, he questioned whether such a relationship has been empirically demonstrated in previous studies. It appears that Justice Souter is willing to accept application of the secondary effects doctrine to regulation of nudity in a particular community, if empirical evidence of a relationship between nude dancing and negative secondary effects can be obtained and, since his concurrence is necessary to obtain a majority that the O'Brien secondary efforts doctrine applies, this opinion may in fact be the Constitutional holding of *Pap's*.

Neverless, in *Pap's*, the plurality provides room for challenges, based on the collection of empirical evidence, to the assertions made by municipalities regarding a relationship between adverse secondary effects and nude dancing. The plurality noted that the adult business in question in *Pap's* could have challenged the City of Erie's assertion that nudity led to ill effects but that it did not do so. This leaves room for the introduction of secondary effects evidence collected by adult businesses both in city council hearings and as a basis for court litigation.

It is likely, based on the plurality's decision in *Pap's*, (that is, that the secondary effects doctrine pertains to nudity regulations), coupled with Justice Souter's admonition that secondary effects must be demonstrated convincingly (that is, empirically), that future court rulings concerning the constitutionality of regulations of nudity within adult businesses will continue to involve an application of some form of the *O'Brien* test. In considering the compelling government interest prong of the *O'Brien* test, lower courts intending to remain consistent with the Supreme Court's holding in *Pap's* may be forced to consider the methodological legitimacy of any evidence of a relationship between negative secondary effects and adult businesses collected by municipalities and by business owners who attempt to challenge governmental regulations predicated upon the allegation of such a connection.

In evaluating the admissibility of this evidence, the courts may be best served by turning to standards laid out in *Daubert* for the admissibility of scientific evidence. The application of such standards, bolstered by Justice Souter's opinion in *Pap's*, may force the courts to reject the studies previously relied upon as evidence of negative secondary effects, and require new, more methodologically sound, studies to demonstrate a compelling government interest in regulating nudity.

The courts should be mindful of the criteria designated above for collecting empirical evidence in a methodologically sound manner. Specifically, only evidence obtained using relatively closely matched control and experimental comparison areas should be acceptable. Further, where possible, a time-series analysis should be undertaken. All indicators of neighborhood quality (for example, crime rate and property values) must also be consistently measured across the study conditions. Courts may then accept any evidence (or lack thereof) that met all of the above criteria as definitive. Only such evidence of a relationship between adult entertainment businesses and negative secondary effects should be acceptable, both social scientifically as well as legally.

In this article, it has been demonstrated that there is sufficient room for a serious challenge to the assumption made by communities across the United States that past studies of secondary effects show an empirical relationship between adult businesses and negative effects. Further, there is presently no legitimate basis for extending the secondary effects doctrine to the regulation of expression within adult businesses based on these studies. City councils, municipalities, and the courts are best served by the collection of new evidence based on sound scientific standards.

Notes

1. See, e.g., City of Renton v. Playtime Theatres, Inc., 475 U.S. 41 (1986); Young v. Am. Mini Theatres, Inc., 427 U.S. 50 (1976).

2. See, e.g., Barnes v. Glen Theatre, Inc., 501 U.S. 560 (1991); City of Erie v. Pap's A.M., 120 S. Ct. 1382 (2000).

3. 501 U.S. at 567–68.

4. Id. at 582–84 (Souter, J., concurring).

5. 120 S. Ct. 1382.

6. Id. at 1393 (O'Connor, J., concurring).

7. Id. at 1404–05 (Souter, J., concurring in part and dissenting in part).

8. Id. at 1402–03 n.3.

9. 54 U.S. 476 (1957).

10. Id. at 488.

11. 360 U.S. 684, 689–90 (1959).

12. 383 U.S. 413 (1966).

13. Id. at 418.

14. 394 U.S. 557 (1969).

15. Id. at 567–68.

16. Presidential Comm'n on Obscenity and Pornography, Technical Reports of the Presidential Comm'n on Obscenity and Pornography (1970).

17. 413 U.S. 15, 24–25 (1973).

18. See Daniel Linz et al., *Estimating Community Tolerance for Obscenity: The Use of Social Science Evidence*, 55 Pub. Opinion Q. 80 (1991); Daniel E. Linz et al., *Measuring Community Standards for Sex and Violence: An Empirical Challenge to Assumptions in Obscenity Law*, 29 L. & Soc'y Rev. 127 (1995). Social science research suggests that communities may tolerate and/or accept for others, sexually explicit material involving consenting adults. However, sexual violence, the use of children in pornography and extreme forms of nonsexual violence are not tolerated. See id.

19. See In Harm's Way: The Pornography Civil Rights Hearings (Andrea Dworkin & Catherine A. MacKinnon eds., 1988); Catherine MacKinnon, *Not a Moral Issue*, 2 Yale L. & Pol'y Rev. 321 (1984).

20. Am. Booksellers Ass'n v. Hudnut, 598 F. Supp 1316, 1320 (S.D. Ind. 1984), *aff'd*, 771 F.2d 323 (7th Cir. 1985), *aff'd*, 475 U.S. 1001 (1986).

21. See EDWARD DONNERSTEIN ET AL., THE QUESTION OF PORNOGRAPHY (1987).

22. See Daniel Linz et al., *Testing Legal Assumptions Regarding the Effects of Dancer Nudity and Proximity to Patron on Erotic Expression*, 24 L. & HUM. BEHAV. 507 (2000). This social science investigation demonstrated that contrary to the assumption made by Chief Justice Rehnquist in *Barnes*, 501 U.S. 560 (1991), laws that prescribe putting pasties and G-string on exotic dancers are, in fact, not seen as content neutral. Results of a field experiment in which dancer nudity (nude vs. partial clothing and dancer proximity significantly altered the message of erotic performances. See Linz et al., *supra* note 22.

23. 427 U.S. 50 (1976).

24. See id.; City of Renton v. Playtime Theatres, Inc., 475 U.S. 41 (1986); Barnes v. Glen Theatre, Inc., 501 U.S. 560 (1991); City of Erie v. Pap's A.M., 120 S. Ct. 1382 (2000).

25. 391 U.S. 367, 376–77 (1968). The landmark decision sets forth a series of criteria courts must consider when determining the constitutionality of government suppression of speech. For a restriction to pass the *O'Brien* test, the courts must consider (1) whether the regulation is within the constitutional power of government, (2) whether it furthers an important or substantial governmental interest, (3) whether that interest is unrelated to suppression of free expression and (4) whether the restriction on First Amendment freedoms is no greater than is essential to the furtherance of that interest. Id.

26. *Young*, 427 U.S. at 79–82 (Powell, J., concurring). Most important for present purposes, the Court suggested that the Detroit ordinance passed the second prong of the *O'Brien* test because it was aimed at preserving the stability of the city's residential and commercial neighborhoods. Id. at 73. The Court noted that a city's interest in protecting the quality of urban life is one that must be accorded high respect. Id.

27. Id. at 60.

28. Id. at 73 n. 34 (plurality opinion). The Court remarked that the city of Detroit had offered evidence that a concentration of "adult" movie theaters causes the area to deteriorate and become a focus of crime. Further, no such relationship was found for theaters showing other types of films. Id. This marks the first time the Court explicitly mentions the term "secondary effects." The Court suggests that "[i]t is this secondary effect which these zoning ordinances attempt to avoid, not the dissemination of 'offensive' speech" that allows the Court to find the Detroit ordinances constitutionally sound. Id.

29. 475 U.S. 41 (1986).

30. Id. at 83.

31. Id.

32. Id. at 50–53.

33. City of Renton v. Playtime Theatres, Inc., 748 F. 2d 527, 537 (9th Cir. 1984), *rev'd*, 475 U.S. 41 (1986).

34. Id. at 50–51. See Northend Cinema, Inc. v. Seattle, 585 P.2d 1153 (1978). In *Northend*, the Washington State Supreme Court held that the city of Seattle had provided sufficient evidence of a need for a zoning code amendment aimed at preventing the secondary effects on the neighborhoods surrounding adult theaters. This evidence came in the form of "a long period of study and discussion of the problems of adult movie theaters in residential areas of the City." Id. at 1154–55. The city offered the Washington court a report, among other things, analyzing the City's zoning scheme and describing land uses around existing adult motion picture theaters. In addition, the trial court heard "expert testimony on the adverse effects of adult motion picture theaters on neighborhood children and community improvement projects." Id. at 1156. In *Renton*, the United States Supreme Court found that the city in question was entitled to rely on the evidence summarized in the Washington court's opinion. 475 U.S. at 50–53.

35. *Renton*, 475 U.S. at 51–52.

36. 501 U.S. 560 (1991).

37. Id. at 561.

38. Id. at 569.

39. See, e.g., Paris Adult Theatre I v. Slaton, 413 U.S. 49, 61 (1973).

40. *Barnes*, 501 U.S. at 587.

41. Id. at 582 (Souter, J., concurring).

42. See, e.g., California v. LaRue, 409 U.S. 109, 111 (1972); Renton v. Playtime Theaters, Inc., 475 U.S. 41 (1986); Young v. Am. Mini Theatres, Inc., 501 U.S. 560 (1991).

43. See, e.g., United States v. Marren, 890 F.2d 924, 926 (7th Cir. 1989) (arguing that prostitution is associated with nude dancing establishments); United States v. Doerr, 886 F.2d 944, 949 (7th Cir. 1989) (same).

44. *Barnes*, 501 U.S. at 584.

45. Id.

46. 120 S. Ct. 1382, 1384 (2000). In *Barnes*, Justice Souter used the secondary effects doctrine as a justification of the anti-nudity ordinance. 501 U.S. at 584 (Souter, J., concurring). In *Pap's*, the city adopted Justice Souter's reasoning and argued that the same devaluation of the surrounding areas attributed to adult businesses can be attributed to establishments featuring live nude entertainment. See 120 S. Ct. at 1394. The city argued that the government's vital interest in protecting and preserving the desirability of residential neighborhoods and business districts is a sufficient justification for the ordinance's incidental encroachment on protected expression. See id. at 1394.

47. Id. at 1394. The Court cited the *Renton* precedent allowing municipalities to rely on secondary effects evidence produced by other, similar municipalities to fulfill the evidentiary burden. Id. None of the justices in the fractured majority explained, however, how the requirement of wearing pasties and a G-string would in fact reduce prostitution, sexual assaults or other problems associated with places where dancers appear nude.

48. Id. Justice Scalia, joined by Justice Thomas, concurred with the Court's majority opinion, but for different reasons. The justices held that the Erie ordinance prohibits not merely nude dancing but the act of going nude at all—irrespective of whether it is engaged in for expressive purposes. Id. at 1398 (Scalia, J., concurring). He found the statute constitutionally permissible because it was a general law regulating conduct and not specifically directed at expression. Id. at 1401. As such, the ordinance was not subject to First Amendment scrutiny at all. See id. at 1401–02. Justice Scalia suggested that there was no need to consider the presence or absence of "secondary effects" because the government was well within its rights in regulating non-expressive behavior. Id. The opinion of Justice Scalia, when combing with that of Justice O'Connor, with whom Chief Justice Rehnquist, Justice Kennedy and Justice Breyer joined, left the Court with a 6–3 majority that the law was consititutional. Yet, there was no controlling opinion. In other words, the Court agreed that Erie can regulate nudity, but could not agree on why.

49. *Renton*, 475 U.S. at 83; *Young*, 501 U.S. at 564.

50. Id. at 1402 (Souter, J., concurring in part and dissenting in part).

51. *Barnes*, 501 U.S. at 584 (Souter, J., concurring).

52. 120 S. Ct. 1382 at 1403–04 (Souter, J., concurring in part and dissenting in part).

53. Id. at 1405–06.

54. Id.

55. Brief for First Amendment Lawyers Association at 16–23, id. (No. 98–1161). Justice Souter stated:

The proposition that the presence of nude dancing establishments increases the incidence of prostitution and violence is amenable to empirical treatment, and the city councilors who enacted Erie's ordinance are in a position to look to the facts of their own community's experience as well as to experiences elsewhere. Their failure to do so councilors who enacted Erie's ordinance are in a position to look to the facts of their own community's experience as well as to experiences elsewhere. Their failure to do so is made all the clearer by one of the *amicus* briefs, largely devoted to the argument that scientifically sound studies show no such correlation.

Id. (Souter, J., dissenting).

56. 509 U.S. 579 (1993).

57. Id. at 590.

58. Id. at 593–95.

59. See Renton v. Playtime Theater, Inc., 475 U.S. 41 (1986); Young v. Am. Mini Theatres, Inc., 427 U.S. 50 (1976); United States v. O'Brien, 391 U.S. 367 (1968).

60. *Renton.* 475 U.S. at 51–52 n.26.

61. All of the reports included in the analysis were obtained by contacting the specific communities and municipalities that originally sponsored or produced them.

62. It should be noted that although the study began with 107 municipal reports addressing the relationship between adult entertainment businesses and negative secondary effects, and although a large percentage of these claim to report "scientific" evidence of such a relationship, this analysis found only 29 of these studies to contain empirical data. A number of the remaining 78 reports simply contained the minutes of city planning committee meetings during which options for the regulation of adult businesses were discussed. Others simply contained samples of arrest reports from inside adult entertainment businesses. Needless to say, such information did not meet even the most basic criteria for empirical evidence. However, such studies have been used (often consistently) as representing empirical evidence of the relationship between adult entertainment businesses and negative secondary effects.

63. City of Indianapolis, Indiana, Adult Entertainment Businesses in Indianapolis—An Analysis (1984).

64. City of Phoenix, Arizona, Relation of Criminal Activity and Adult Businesses (1979).

65. City of Los Angeles, California, Study of the Effects of the Concentration of Adult Entertainment Establishments in the City of Los Angeles (1977).

66. City of St. Paul, Minnesota, Neighborhood Deterioration and the Location of Adult Entertainment Establishments in St. Paul (1978).

67. Daubert v. Merrell Dow Pharm., Inc., 509 U.S. 579, 590 (1993).

68. Id. at 599.

69. Id. at 590.

70. Id. n.9.

71. See id. at 593 (citing Karl Popper, Conjectures and Refutations 37 [5th ed. 1989]).

72. Id.

73. See id. at 594.

74. See id.

75. Id. at 593–94.

76. This is perhaps the most important notion underlying this research. Results suggesting no reliable and/or valid evidence of a relationship between negative secondary effects and adult entertainment businesses would mean that the courts

would need seriously to reconsider whether municipalities indeed have a substantial interest in regulating such uses. At the very least, it would suggest that most, if not all, municipalities with codified restrictions on adult uses have based their justification of such restrictions (according to the requirements set forth in *Young* and *Renton*) on inaccurate data.

77. See JACOB COHEN & PATRICIA COHEN, APPLIED MULTIPLE REGRESSION/CORRELATION ANALYSIS FOR THE BEHAVIORAL SCIENCES 166–76 (2d ed. 1983); DAVID C. HOWELL, STATISTICAL METHODS FOR PSYCHOLOGY 394–50 (4th ed. 1997); GEOFFREY KEPPEL, DESIGN AND ANALYSIS: A RESEARCHER'S HANDBOOK 164–65 (3d ed. 1991); ROBERT R. PAGANO, UNDERSTANDING STATISTICS IN THE BEHAVIORAL SCIENCES 215–16, 384 (5th ed. 1998).

78. See COHEN & COHEN, *supra* note 77, at 21.

79. See EARL BABBIE, THE PRACTICE OF SOCIAL RESEARCH 202–10 (8th ed. 1998); ROYCE A. SINGLETON, JR. ET AL., APPROACHES TO SOCIAL RESEARCH 136–51 (2d ed. 1993).

80. See DONALD T. CAMPBELL & JULIAN C. STANLEY, EXPERIMENTAL and QUASI-EXPERIMENTAL DESIGNS FOR RESEARCH 34 (1963).

81. Obviously, it is not possible randomly to assign adult businesses to some neighborhoods and hold other neighborhoods as controls.

82. See CAMPBELL & STANLEY, *supra* note 80, at 34–71.

83. See BABBIE, *supra* note 79, at 213–14.

84. See, e.g., CITY OF ST. PAUL, MINNESOTA, *supra* note 66.

85. See SINGLETON ET AL., *supra* note 79, at 213–41.

86. See CAMPBELL & STANLEY, *supra* note 80, at 5, 9.

87. See BABBIE, *supra* note 79, at 176–82.

88. See id. at 240.

89. See id.

90. See CITY OF ST. PAUL, *supra* note 66.

91. See CITY OF LOS ANGELES, *supra* note 65.

92. Id. at 25.

93. See CITY OF PHOENIX, *supra* note 64.

94. See CITY OF INDIANAPOLIS, *supra* note 63.

95. CITY OF ST. PAUL, *supra* note 66.

96. CITY OF AUSTIN, TEXAS, REPORT ON ADULT ORIENTED BUSINESSES IN AUSTIN (1986).

97. CITY OF ST. PAUL, MINNESOTA, ADULT ENTERTAINMENT—A 40-ACRE STUDY (1987); CITY OF ST. PAUL, MINNESOTA, ADULT ENTERTAINMENT—SUPPLEMENT TO THE 1987 ZONING STUDY (1988).

98. CITY OF AMARILLO, TEXAS, REPORT ON ZONING AND OTHER METHODS OF REGULATING ADULT ENTERTAINMENT IN AMARILLO (1977).

99. City of Detroit, Michigan, Detroit's Approach to Regulating "Adult" Uses (1972).

100. City of Beaumont, Texas, Regulation of Adult Uses (1982).

101. City of Kent. Washington. City of Kent Adult Use Zoning Study (1982).

102. In his dissent in *Pap's*, joined by Justice Ginsburg, Justice Stevens argued that no rationale existed for an extension of the secondary effects doctrine as a justification for censoring nude dancing. City of Erie v. Pap's A.M., 120 S. Ct. 1382, 1406 (2000) (Stevens, J., dissenting). This doctrine was originally developed in *O'Brien* and extended to the regulation of adult businesses as a justification for zoning in *Young*. Stevens wrote that, although two fractured majorities of the Supreme Court have found such an application of the secondary effects rationale acceptable, the assumption that these secondary effects studies, even if they were not methodologically flawed, could be applied to justify regulation of forms of expression such as nude dancing may be unfounded. Id. at 1408–09. He suggested that the secondary effects doctrine, as it had previously been applied to adult businesses, was tailored towards zoning, that there existed no clear rationale for extending this doctrine as a justification for the regulation of expressive content, and that doing so represented a dangerous extension of censorship. Id. Stevens wrote:

Until now the "secondary effects" of commercial enterprises featuring indecent entertainment have justified only the regulation of their location. For the first time, the Court has now held that such effects may justify the total suppression of protected speech. Indeed, the plurality opinion concludes that admittedly trivial advancements of a State's interests may provide the basis for censorship. The Court's commendable attempt to replace the fractured decision in *Barnes* . . . with a single coherent rationale is strikingly unsuccessful; it is supported neither by precedent nor by persuasive reasoning.

Id. at 1406. Justice Stevens also stated:

To believe that the mandatory addition of pasties and a G-string will have *any* kind of noticeable impact on secondary effects requires nothing short of a titanic surrender to the implausible. It would be more accurate to acknowledge, as JUSTICE SCALIA does, that there is no reason to believe that such a requirement "will at all reduce the tendency of establishments . . . to attract crime and prostitution, and hence to foster sexually transmitted disease."

Id. at 1409 [citing id. at 1402 (Scalia, J., concurring)]. Justice Stevens, therefore, viewed Erie's anti-nudity ordinance as an unwarranted and ineffective restriction on expression. Justice Souter noted that there had been an adult business zoning ordinance on the books in Erie for 23 years before the anti-nudity ordinance in question had been used to censor nude dancing. However, the city had not enforced this ordinance. Justice Souter indicated that the anti-nudity ordinance did not represent the least restrictive means for curtailing secondary effects because the city had not enforced its less restrictive zoning ordinance and had instead chosen to apply a total ban on nude dancing. As such, the anti-nudity ordinance failed the fourth prong of the *O'Brien* test. Id. at 1405 (Souter, J., dissenting).

103. See Alameda Books, Inc. v. Los Angeles, 222 F.3d 719 (9th Cir. 2000). The Ninth Circuit has addressed the applicability of studies conducted on adverse secondary effects for a particular purpose to another, arguably unrelated concern. Id. at 724–28. The appeals court affirmed a lower court's decision to strike down a Los Angeles ordinance prohibiting the operation of adult businesses that both sell adult products and contain facilities for the viewing of adult movies or videos. Id. at 728. The court rejected Los Angeles's attempt to use a study conducted in 1977 (reviewed here), which examined the relationship of adverse secondary effects and the concentration of adult businesses as evidence of a compelling government interest to regulate single business with combined uses. The court reasoned that the 1977 study offered no information on the effects of the combination of product-video booth within a single business. Id. at 724. "For the purposes of the secondary effects identified in the Los Angeles study, a solitary bookstore/arcade combination is hardly of the 'same character' as a grouping of multiple adult business establishments in a given geographical area." Id. at 726 n.7. As such, the court refused to allow a leap in logic similar to that of the plurality in *Pap's*.

II
Relationships with Policy-makers

10

Facing Out: Researchers and Policy-makers

Sandra Braman
2002

Relationships between social scientists and the state are affected by three things: prevailing paradigms of the relationship between social science knowledge and public policy, the career activities of social scientists as they try to create a market for their work, and changes in the functions and needs of the state that create the demand for social science research in the policy process.[1] Though scholarly writing has never been considered an official source of law in the western legal tradition, it has played a decisive role in framing legal rules, disseminating legal knowledge throughout the world, and training those who become policy-makers.[2] Beyond the world of scholarship, researchers may have a variety of relationships with government, including the roles researchers may play as staffers, consultants, advocates, or facilitators both within and outside of government who bring the two sides together. Teaching is also a path to policy influence, for some of the most valuable facilitators are active politicians whose education engrained in them a habit of relying upon research and the skills to critically evaluate it.[3]

The only systematic research into academic participation in communication policy-making was a 1973 study[4] that looked only at individuals from the Association for Education in Journalism and Mass Communication (AEJMC) who were involved with teaching broadcasting which found only a very small percentage of faculty members had made any attempt at all to offer input to policy-makers. Those who had done so were more likely to have advanced degrees from elite institutions, and to have spent more years in teaching and research than those who had not. The greatest successes occurred at the local level, where personal relationships of trust reinforced the impact of any scholarly expertise. Because input was generally offered via letters never read by the politicians to whom they were sent, most information offered by academics never reached those to whom it had been sent. While the population examined in this study was small, a broader study that looked across the social sciences similarly found that researchers involved were largely working at the "handicraft, informal, self-help level"[5] on borrowed or contributed time.

Formal relationships with the government may be direct and publicized, as when research organizations such as the Congressional Research Service (CRS) or the Office of Technology Assessment (OTA) are set up specifically for the purpose of providing input into policymaking, or they may not be public, as when researchers become involved in classified defense-related work or work at the level of "invitation only" communications. Informal but direct relationships develop via conferences, through the influence of foundations, via lobbying, and as a result of ad hoc interactions. Influence can also be indirect, whether intended (as through the work of public intellectuals) or unintended (as when the results of research reported upon by the mass media have an impact on the thinking of decision-makers).

Formal Relationships: Working for the Government

The degree to which the relationship between researchers and policymakers is formalized is among the important ways in which the policymaking processes of nation-states differ. In France, for example, an elite educational institution prepares researchers specifically for permanent government service, while in the United States relationships form via multiple routes and may be sporadic. In the abstract formal and enduring positions within government might seem ideal, but in practice—at least in the U.S. context—the experience has been so fraught with political complications that it has lead to a great deal of frustration on at least the part of many researchers. Schools of policy and public administration in the United States do provide training for government service, largely preparing those who go into middle management rather than leadership positions, and most often for individuals who will go into service at the state rather than the federal level. Research grants are another way scholars can work directly for the government. Such grants are usually, but not always, provided quite publicly, most often today from the National Science Foundation (NSF) but also from the Department of Commerce (in communication, often via the National Telecommunications and Information Administration, or NTIA), the National Institute of Health (NIH), and other sources.

Public Relationships

There have been several attempts to institutionalize the incorporation of research into communication policy-making processes, though it is striking that even presidents who depend heavily upon research in other contexts have often failed to do so when it came to information technologies and their uses. President Hoover, on whose watch the FCC was formed, is a premiere example—while he relied heavily upon research in other areas of policy-making, when it came to the communications industry he turned almost exclusively to the corporate world.[6] The Congressional Research Service regularly issues reports on communication policy matters, but these are often merely compilations of proposed legislation or of the range of policy alternatives on the table.[7] The Federal Communications Commission (FCC) conducts research on its own[8] and solicits input from scholars regarding policy options, but too often relies almost exclusively upon data provided by corporations in the industries being regulated in a form of industry capture through control over information and upon economics for the analytical tools to be used.[9]

There was a short period during which a communication policy function was brought within the White House via the Office of Telecommunications Policy (OTP),[10] but this group often actually tried to reduce the impact of research on policy-making. In 1971, for example, then-director of the OTP Clay Whitehead attacked the use of audience research by those in public broadcasting as inappropriately giving in to commercialism during the Administration's general campaign against the media.[11] The fact that research undertaken within the OTP produced outcomes that did not always agree with what the White House wanted[12] may have also had an influence on the entity's ultimate abandonment, though policy analysis that cannot be critical is much diminished in value. Overall, the researchers who held positions in the OTP had to balance their expertise with service to the president's political needs.[13] Ultimately, the OTP morphed into the National Telecommunications and Information Administration (NTIA), which for a number of years continued to commission research on the use of new information technologies, particularly via evaluations of experimental uses of such technologies for purposes of community developoment. The Clinton White House paid a great deal of attention to information technology through advisors to the president, but while the shell for this type of input remains in place, it is hollow under George W. Bush.

The Office of Technology Assessment (OTA), established in 1972 to respond to congressional requests for background reports on science and technology problems,[14] lead the way for a number of years in identifying emergent policy issues raised by the use of new information technologies. The relationship between the OTA and Congress went through a series of stages,[15] falling apart completely just at the point that making policy for the information infrastructure had risen to the top of the national agenda. A variety of factors accounted for this failure, including perceptions of staff overpoliticization, the need to serve multiple constituencies simultaneously, and the lack of a direct link with an outside client in whose interests it was to ensure OTA's survival. Many believe that the tension between the short-term interests of legislators and the long-term nature of policy problems examined by the OTA was another factor that may have undermined its support.[16] Legislators' lack of familiarity with the processes of technology assessment combined with the importance of the choices to be made also contributed to discomfort with the OTA for its reports brought into public view congressional inadequacies. All of these factors combined to make the agency an easy target for those looking for items to cut out of the federal budget.[17] The OTA remains on the books, however, and if funds are appropriated could be brought back to life. Suggestions to do so have reappeared in the first years of the twenty-first century though they do not yet seem politically likely to succeed.

While the federal government has spent huge sums of money on research grants dealing with new information technologies, very little of it has gone to social scientists. The vast majority of funding in the area of communications by the NSF has gone to support the development of hardware and software, not research into the uses and effects of the technologies. Even when social science research questions are designed into a research proposal, they are often sidelined once funds arrive at an institution.[18] Only in the late 1990s did the NSF launch some research programs seeking analysis of digital technologies by those in the social sciences. Access to these funds, however, is limited to those social scientists who can design their projects into a collaboration with colleagues involved in the most advanced and large-scale of hardware and software projects. In addition, many of those funds have been redirected since 9–11 to development of new surveillance technologies or to cover non-research activities otherwise being cut from the federal budget. Support for the Smithsonian Institution, for example, is now supposed to be an NSF matter rather than a separate line item, drawing further funds away from research. Massive sums are also directed to R&D in the area of information technologies by the Department of Defense, but again the goal is to develop technologies rather than to evaluate them. While there was an assumption for a long time that innovations generated in response to defense needs would "trickle down" into society-wise use, historical analysis shows that this actually is very rarely the case.[19] Those competing for the research funds available are most likely to succeed if they can demonstrate the kind of sustained and in-depth focus that builds genuine expertise in a specific substantive area.[20]

Becoming involved with lobbying is another public way in which researchers can attempt to bring the results of their work into the policy-making process. Individuals may choose to become lobbyists themselves—which in the United States requires registering with the government and reporting annually on income and expenses, the general and specific issues issues upon which one lobbies and the specific bill numbers involved, and the names of clients (though *not* the names of legislators of executive branch officials individually lobbied). A significant percentage of those who work full-time for advocacy groups promoting the public interest in the area of information and communication policy have advanced degrees, including among the leadership. These nonprofit organizations—which must also register as lobbyists with the government—often undertake and publish research of their own, sometimes presenting their work within scholarly contexts as well as via the mass media and in genres aimed directly at policy-makers. Many also use their websites to provide portals to pertinent academic research of which they are aware. Even more academics provide support functions to lobbyists and lobbying groups in areas on issues about which they particularly care, helping to create analytical materials, providing background information, and participating in public events.

Non-public Relationships

The military has been an important influence on communication regulation since the beginning.[21] Secret relationships between researchers and the government develop when social scientists are commissioned in support of national security goals, whether during wartime or peace. Christopher Simpson,[22] an investigative journalist turned scholar with a penchant for archival research, has examined such secret relationships in the field of communication. Much of the information on which his history of communication research is based was classified and only became accessible once declassified and made available through use of the Freedom of Information Act (FOIA). The work has been controversial; many institutions about whom he reports, such as the Institute of Communications Research at the University of Illinois, prefer not to acknowledge the relationships uncovered in their own versions of their histories. There is of course the possibility that unacknowledged support may bias the work that results, as Rowland[23] suggests was the case with Ithiel de Sola Pool's analyses of international communication that were secretly funded by the NSF.

Informal Relationships: Working with the Government

Informal relationships between communication researchers, though they may be ad hoc, may have more enduring impact than those that are formal. This can happen when they shape the perceptions and modes of thought of policy-makers in addition to or instead of providing specific policy suggestions; such impact derives from personal relationships of trust between decision makers and researchers. Informal relationships can also have widespread impact when those involved play leadership roles in the field, for their activities and ideas will provide direction and structure for what many other researchers do and how the field of communications is taught. Think tanks, foundations, and conferences provide informal means through which such relationships can be built.

Think Tanks and Foundations

Foundations and think tanks, a U.S. policy innovation that has by now been exported for use in both the developed and developing worlds,[24] have been among the most successful institutional responses to the problem of systematically bringing the results of research into policy-making processes. They play important roles in the development of communications policy by directing both researchers and policy-makers to specific questions and by funding research and institutional and technological experimentation useful for the examination of policy alternatives. The Rockefeller Foundation led the way, concerned with communication issues first because of the United States' need to integrate immigrants into society in the 1930s and then because of the need to build support for American entry into World War II.

Shaping public and governmental discourses on policy matters has been a key function of think tanks and foundations.[25] The Ford Foundation gets credit, for example, for bringing the phrase "behavioral sciences" into play to describe what many social scientists do, having chosen the term for its own purposes at a time when there was debate within Congress over how to describe the activities of the National Science Foundation at its creation.[26] In communication, the "Lasswellian formula" for modeling the process of communication—who says what to whom in what channel with what effect—developed in the course of Rockefeller Foundation conversations that intended to and succeeded in establishing a research agenda for the field of communication.[27]

Examples of foundation influence upon the field of communication are rife: The Ford Foundation's support for diffusion research in the 1940s was key to the emergence of development communications and, later, to the establishment of public television in the United States.[28] Rand's work with operations research and the application of game theory to problems of warfare provided a model for the type of projects appropriate for the

National Science Foundation (NSF) once it was established. In a more recent example, Ford supported experimentation with information technologies for peace-making and peace-keeping purposes via incorporation of their use into arms control agreements.[29] Think tanks such as the American Enterprise Institute, Heritage Foundation, and the Hoover Institution promoted deregulation of communications, as well as the incorporation of trade in services (international information flows) within international trade agreements.[30] One of the extremely powerful but indirect means by which foundations influence policy is in serving as agenda-setters for government funding agencies such as the NSF.

Up until the late 1960s, foundations could devote their resources directly to the promotion of specific policies—Ford support for public television was a particularly successful example of such efforts. A change in the law, however, now makes it illegal for foundations to directly engage in advocacy work if they want to retain their nonprofit status. It is still possible, however, for such organizations to fund the research necessary for development of policy alternatives or that can provide evaluations of existing policies. They can also still support venues in which multiple voices both within and outside of government can be brought into a common discourse on policy problems.

Policy historian Frank Fischer[31] believes that without access to foundations as a medium of discourse, no interest group can today effectively participate in the policy process. At the time of writing, a number of think tanks and foundations are active in the area of communication policy. The Markle and Benton foundations support efforts to represent the public interest in communication policy-making. Each is involved in several issue areas, but as examples of their foci the Benton Foundation is devoting much of its resources in the early twenty-first century to problems raised by the digital divide, and the Markle Foundation has taken the lead in providing support for public debate over the civil liberties implications of the often radical changes in pertinent policy put in place since the attack on the World Trade Center. The Ford Foundation is promoting closer relationships between researchers and policy-makers, trying to broaden the community of communication researchers involved in the policy process, and building an evidentiary record to strengthen the ability of those concerned about the public interest in communication policy to build strong arguments. The Rockefeller Foundation is interested in the Internet as both a site of political activity and of community development, and in the relationship of the arts to both of those. The Carnegie Endowment for International Peace is pursuing questions that arise out of the impact of new information technologies on foreign policy.

While much of the work that think tanks and foundations undertake is publicly announced, many of their most influential forms of influence my are not a matter of public knowledge because they are conducted in "invitation only" settings. One of the most powerful ways in which a group such as the Rockefeller Foundation can assert influence is through shaping the research agenda for a governmental entity such as the National Science Foundation, a form of power that occurs not only via published reports but also through interpersonal connections based on long-standing institutional and personal relationships. The Social Science Research Council (SSRC) is another example of an entity that is described as "independent" and "not for profit" that plays a powerful role in shaping government policy in the area of communication, information, and culture through a combination of commissioned reports the importance of which is communicated in private settings to government officials who expect to have an open ear to this particular source of input. These are highly influential ways of bringing the results of communication research to the attention of policy-makers—but they are available only to those who have achieved entry into an "inner circle" of scholars whose work has been deemed acceptable, most often scholars from a small number of elite institutions.[32]

Conferences

Conferences are a means through which policy-makers, policy analysts who serve as consultants, and academics can come to get to know each other both through formal presentations of relevant work and through informal networking. General conferences in the field, such as those of the International Communication Association (ICA) and the International Association for Media and Communication Research (IAMCR), are often attended by those involved in policy analysis just for this purpose. One annual conference specific to this purpose was set up in the early 1970s as an offshoot of the OTP, the Telecommunications Policy Research Conference (TPRC). Owen,[33] long an insider, reports on TPRC at the 25-year mark. One of the functions since the beginning has been serving as a venue for explicit examination of problems that have been arising from the convergence of broadcasting and telecommunications technologies. Park's analysis of the impact of cable research at the first TPRC in 1972, for example, was one of the first to appear. Part of TPRC's impact has come from publication of a series of volumes of a small proportion of the papers presented each year.

While TPRC has remained at arm's-length from the government, under the leadership of former government employee Brian Kahin, the Department of Commerce and other governmental agencies have organized a conference on a new type of issue, the policy implications of the outsourcing of governmental functions, in the fall of 2002. Kahin, who previously ran a successful and important series of conferences out of the JFK School at Harvard and is now on the faculty of the University of Maryland, provides a model of the value of the broker function between academic research and policy-making.

Another model of the utility of convening policy-makers and academics for focused attention on specific issues is provided by Eli Noam's Columbia Institute for Tele-Information (CITI). For years Noam has run a series of day-long seminars on a wide range of issues raised by telecommunications policy. Not as full-blown as conferences, these seminars have the advantage that it is much easier to attract a high-powered set of participants to an event that requires only a day rather than a longer time period. Noam's events often present the first public conversation about cutting edge issues and ideas; early twenty-first-century seminars have looked, for example, at the topics of nano-regulation of the global information infrastructure and at the effect of the stock market and innovative investment instruments on the impact of the implementation of telecommunications policy. CITI serves an additional discourse-shaping function by running longer training seminars, often with attendees from around the world, in technical matters such as the accounting systems used by telecommunications regulatory agencies.

One of the ways that the organizers of conferences effectively extend their impact to audiences far larger than those of attendees is through publication of books that result from conference presentations and discussion. TPRC has not done this every year, but has produced some volumes of this kind. Kahin's series of conferences that constituted the Harvard Information Infrastructure Project produced a number of highly influential books.[34] Many of Noam's seminars also have produced books for wider dissemination of the ideas presented.[35]

Indirect Relationships: Serving the Polity

In a democracy, everyone participates in the policy process to the extent that they take part in discourse in the public sphere, express opinion, and vote. Thus ways in which communication researchers can attempt to influence decisions by policy-makers include those efforts directed at the polity as a whole and at discourse within the public sphere. It is for this reason that Habermasian notions are increasingly important to policy analysts.[36] Some of this activity takes place when researchers deliberately take on the role of public intellectual in an effort to shape policy-related discourse, some comes about in the course of research on how to design content that contributes to that discourse, and some occurs simply as a by-product of reports on the results of research in the mass media. There are genre implications for researchers who seek to communicate with lay audiences; the effectiveness of policy arguments can be vastly increased when the results of research and their implications are translated into terms accessible to the press.[37]

The Public Intellectual

During the 1990s, a number of those within the field began to call for a larger presence of communication researchers among public intellectuals—that is, as individuals who present their scholarly ideas in public forums such as the mass media with the intention of contributing to policy-related public discourse. This is a particularly important time for those who know something about the effects of the use of information and communication technologies to step forward.[38]

Ellen Wartella[39] points to the failure of academics to enter public conversations as among the reasons that research into the effects of media violence on children has had so little impact in the policy world.[40] Each new medium has stimulated research into its effects on children; with television, this became one of the most-researched topics in the field.[41] Though the word "policy" is not usually attached to decision making in the private sector, research on children and television is also pertinent to content producers as part of their self-regulatory efforts to improve the quality of television, as in the formative work that led to the prosocial children's programming of *Sesame Street*.[42] Since such private sector decision making is not susceptible to the types of formal input opportunities found in public sector decision making, the role of public intellectuals is even more important as one of the few ways of reaching the decision-making audience. The broader implication is that with the growing privatization of formerly public government functions, therefore, public intellectuals become even more important.

Research for the Polity

Questions such as universal access to the Internet, the degree to which voices heard through the mass media express diverse viewpoints, and programming choices by government-supported media all raise research questions regarding the nature of the public sphere on behalf of the polity itself.[43] The relationship between the shaping of funding sources through regulation and content diversity has received some research attention,[44] but other topics involving the polity have not. With a few notable exceptions,[45] research on the actual experience of attempts at universal service, for example, have been driven by telephone company concerns about quantitatively measurable service levels and penetration rather than the needs and desires of individual users.

In a dramatic manifestation of the disappearance of the individual and the household from consideration in analysis of telecommunications policy, the term "users" now actually refers to large corporations such as Citibank and American Express rather than human beings. Just as in the late 1970s and early 1980s the naivete of policy-makers regarding the concept of "standards" when applied to technical matters made it possible for AT&T to gain a certain amount of policy-making support for what was believed to be its standards for quality of service rather than specific technological features, so the shift in the definition of "user" enabled policy-makers to misread some portions of the Telecommunications Act of 1996: The universal access provisions of the Act are actually references to mandated forms of interconnection among corporations that are service providers, not another facet of universal access to service by individuals and households.

Stavitsky[46] has explored the reluctance of those involved with public radio to use research to determine the actual needs, interests, and responses of the audience. (Public broadcasting is a policy issue both because of the public support involved and because of the purposes it is intended to serve in society.) It is a revealing analysis: Much of the resistance to the use of audience ratings in public broadcasting stems from the fear that analyzing the audience would in itself transform nonprofit content into something driven by the profit motive. Though ratings data and related types of quantitative analysis have been used by the British public radio service, the BBC, since the 1930s and began to receive attention in the United States in the 1970s,[47] it was long resisted in the United States because it was perceived to be only of commercial rather than public interest concern. This yielded one more contradiction—denial of the importance of the public in programming for the public.[48] Communication research and policy can interact in many ways in the area of public broadcasting: as in any type of organization, research can be used both to justify a budgetary commitment and to destroy a budget; or to identify a community as defined through its preferences and to destroy a community as defined by a shared commitment to public radio production.[49] Still, resistance to its use has remained so great that as part of its public interest advocacy program the Benton Foundation commissioned a report encouraging more independent research devoted to improving the quality of public broadcasting.[50]

Research on the Public Sphere

Research reports need not be directly aimed at policy-makers in order to have an impact. Mass media reports of research results of interest to journalists also provide inputs into policy-making. It is for this reason that the National Communications Association (NCA) has inserted itself into the gatekeeping process for journalists seeking sources on communication-related matters, trying to direct queries to scholars whose expertise the association deems pertinent. Increasing numbers of individual scholars, too, have realized that keeping their campus media relations people informed about their research can lead to public exposure to their work that in turn can reach the ears and eyes of policymakers. General publication of the results of public opinion surveys can also fill this function. Gaziano[51] analyzed the correlation between shifts in public opinion on First Amendment-related issues and Supreme Court decisions in the same area as one example of how this can happen; while the relationship she describes is only correlational, not causal, it makes clear the role that survey results can play as decision-making support.

The impact of public opinion research on other types of decision-makers has been more thoroughly studied.[52] The political impact of public opinion suggests that another important topic of study for researchers is the construction of surveys themselves. It is well known that differences in wording can significantly affect survey results; a study of all public opinion surveys on First Amendment-type issues through the mid-1980s at the national and State of Minnesota levels (over three hundred fifty surveys), for example, found that support for free speech was much higher when questions were phrased in the abstract rather than including details of specific problem situations.[53] Shifts in wording in surveys dealing with political matters over time serve as indicators of changes in public discourse.[54] Both substantive information and environmental cues may affect responses to policy-relevant survey questions.[55] The results of survey research will be more easily accepted if the questions asked are in terms comprehensible to the audience intended for the results.[56] As sociologist David Riesman[57] commented in a notable piece that today reads poignantly for what it tells us about our loss of research innocence, the mode of presentation of surveys and the identity of those conducting surveys, too, can influence whether or not respondents will in fact reveal their policy preferences.

Discussion

There is a wide range of roles that researchers can play if they want the results of their work to be taken into account in the course of policy-making. At the most common end of the spectrum, individuals within academia produce work for publication in typical scholarly venues that they then distribute to pertinent policy-makers in hopes the work—despite the peculiarities of the peer-reviewed journal article genre, the length and density of the texts that result, and the opacity of academic jargon—will be both read and its implications understood. At the other extreme, researchers can of course enter public office themselves, though the personality traits that characterize researchers means that they are rarely tempted by the lifestyle of politicians. In between come roles such as contract researcher, government employee, advocate, and public intellectual. Other roles less typically viewed as policy relevant, such as that of the teacher, also have significant potential for influence in the long run. The more enduring impacts of social scientists specializing in communications on government have not always come from those relationships that are public and/or direct. This is at least in part due to the fact that such efforts are often piecemeal, while less public and/or indirect relationships may underlie massive ongoing programs that have field-shaping consequences.

Academic socialization does not always prepare individuals for success in the policy world. Intellectual life is highly competitive and often combative, while the work of policy-makers is most successful when it builds strong personal relationships and trust. Academics make their careers by promoting ideas that differ from those of others, but policy-makers seek consensus. While the slow rhythms of academic life are precisely what is needed to do the research and thinking needed to come up with new policy ideas and substantive critiques, they also leave many researchers unprepared or unable to respond in a sufficiently timely way to the deadline-oriented needs of policy-makers. The need to cope with these tensions leads to the kinds of negotiations discussed in the section of this book on relationships with academia. They leave behind the messages, though, that developing a focused research agenda and building personal relationships with policy-makers are key. The sustained and focused efforts by Eli Noam and Brian Kahin provide models of the value of combining individual research with activities that bring policy-makers and academics together in the course of building a discourse and epistemic community around cutting-edge issues.

Notes

1. Alain-G. Gagnon, The influence of social scientists on public policy, in Brooks & Gagnon, 1990, *op cit.*, pp. 1–18.

2. Ugo Mattei, *Comparative Law and Economics*, University of Michigan Press, Ann Arbor, 1998.

3. Thomas J. Martin, Information and communication policy research in the United States: The researcher as advocate, facilitator, and staff member, in Brenda Dervin and Melvin J. Voigt, eds, *Progress in Communication Sciences, Vol. IV*, Ablex, Norwood, N.J., 1984, pp. 23–41.

4. Donald P. Mullally and Gerald M. Gillmore, Academic participation in communication policy-making, *Journalism Quarterly* 50, no. 2 (1973): 353–357.

5. Alex Inkeles, Intellectual consequences of federal support, in Samuel Z. Klausner and Victor M. Lidz, eds, *The Nationalization of the Social Sciences*, University of Pennsylvania Press, Philadelphia, 1986, pp. 237–246.

6. Karl, 1969, *op cit.*

7. Recent examples of Congressional Research Service reports on communication policy issues include Bernard Gelb, *Telecommunications Services Trade and the WTO Agreement*, Congressional Research Service, Washington, D.C., RS20319, 2001, which discusses the fact that there was no legislation currently on the table to express congressional concern over contemporary international trade law as it affects the telecommunications network; Angele Gilroy, *The Telecommunications Discounts for Schools and Libraries*, Congressional Research Service, Washington, D.C., IB98040, 2000, which describes FCC efforts to implement the Telecommunications Act of 1996 mandate to ensure access to the internet in schools and libraries; Charles Doyle, *Wireless Communication and Public Safety Act of 1999*, Congressional Research Service, Washington, D.C., RS20359, 1999, which compares House and Senate versions of a bill dealing with wireless communications; and Leonard G. Kruger & Angele A. Gilroy, *Broadband Internet Access: Background and Issues*, Congressional Research Service, Washington, D.C., IB10045, 2001, which provides details of one proposal dealing with broadband access to the Internet. All of these studies, produced by government employees, merely summarize existing or proposed legislation.

8. Recent publications by the FCC's Office of Plans and Policy (OPP) include: Jay M. Atkinson and Christopher C. Barnekov, *A Competitively Neutral Approach to Network Interconnection*, FCC, OPP Working Paper no. 34, Washington, D.C., 2000, which describes an approach to network interconnection that is allegedly competitively neutral; Patricia DeGraba, *Bill and Keep at the Central Office as the Efficient Interconnection Regime*, FCC, Washington, D.C., OPP Working Paper no. 33, 2000, which details the pricing scheme associated with the approach to interconnection described in the previous paper; and Michael Kende, *The Digital Handshake: Connecting Internet Backbones*, FCC,

Washington, D.C., OPP Working Paper no. 32, 2000, which provides an explanation of the context within which Internet backbone interconnection decisions must be made. All of these rely upon economic analysis alone to justify FCC policy positions and none explore alternative approaches, even within the realm of economic explanation.

9. No one has yet systematically analyzed the informational inputs the FCC uses to make its decisions.

10. James Miller, Policy planning and technocratic power: The significance of OTP, *Journal of Communication*, 32, no. 1 (1982): 53–60; James Miller, The president's advocate: OTP and broadcast issues, *Journal of Broadcasting*, 26, no. 3 (1982): 625–639.

11. Alan G. Stavitsky, Counting the house in public television: A history of ratings use, 1953–1980, *Journal of Broadcasting & Electronic Media*, 42, no. 4 (1998): 520–534.

12. Political economist Vincent Mosco, one of the most articulate critics of U.S. and Canadian communication policy, was working in the OTP as a postdoctoral fellow when he encountered the outspoken work of Herbert Schiller. Vincent Mosco, Living on in the number one country: The legacy of Herbert I. Schiller, *Journal of Broadcasting & Electronic Media*, 45, no. 1 (2001): 191–198.

13. Francis E. Rourke and Roger E. Brown, Presidents, professionals, and telecommunications policy making in the White House, *Presidential Studies Quarterly*, 26, no. 2 (1996): 539–550.

14. Rhoda Walters, The Office of Technology Assessment of the United States Congress: A model for the future? *Government and Opposition*, 27, no. 1 (1992): 89–109.

15. Fred M. Weingarten, Obituary for an agency, *Communications of the ACM*, 38, no. 9 (1995): 29–33.

16. Linda Garcia, Presentation to Pre-Conference Workshop on Communication Research and Policy, International Communication Association, Washington, D.C., May, 2001; Fred Weingarten, The politicizing of science policy, *Communications of the ACM*, 37, no. 6 (1994): 13–16.

17. Bruce Bimber, *The Politics of Expertise in Congress: The Rise and Fall of the Office of Technology Assessment*, State University of New York Press, Albany, 1996; Bruce Bimber, The death of an agency: OTA and trophy hunting in US budget policy, *Policy Studies Review*, 15, nos. 2–3 (1998): 202–226.

18. Schön & Rein, 1994, *op cit.*

19. Arthur L. Norberger, with Judy E. O'Neill and Kerry J. Freedman, *Transforming Computer Technology: Information Processing for the Pentagon, 1962–1986*, Johns Hopkins University Press Baltimore.

20. Ellen Wartella, Presentation to the Workshop on Communication Research and Policy, International Communication Association, Washington, D.C., May, 2001.

21. e.g., Susan J. Douglas, *Inventing American Broadcasting, 1899–1922*, The Johns Hopkins University Press, Baltimore, 1987; Gertrude J. Robinson, "Here be dragons": Problems in charting the U.S. history of communication studies, *Communication*, 10, no. 2 (1988): 97–119; Bruce Lannes Smith, Trends in research on international communication and opinion, 1945–55, 20, no. 1 (1956): 182–195.

22. Simpson, 1994, *op cit.*

23. Rowland, 1986, *op cit.*

24. For a discussion of the influence of such organizations on television programming in Brazil, for example, see Michele Mattelart & Armand Mattelart, *Carnival of Images*, Bergin & Garvey, New York, 1990. In a second example, foundations and think tanks helped develop audiovisual policy for Europe; see Philip Schlesinger, From cultural defence to political culture: Media, politics and collective identity in the European Union, *Media, Culture & Society*, 19, no. 3 (1997): 369–391.

25. Frank Fischer, Policy discourse and the politics of Washington think tanks, in Fischer and Forester, *op cit.*, pp. 21–42.

26. David Easton, *A Framework for Political Analysis*, University of Chicago Press, Chicago, 1979.

27. William Buxton, From radio research to communications intelligence: Rockefeller philanthropy, communications specialists, and the American policy community, in Stephen Brooks & Alain-G. Gagnon, eds, *Political Influence of Ideas: Policy Communities and the Social Sciences*, Praeger, Westport, Conn., 1994, pp. 187–209. 1994; Brett Gary, Communication research, the Rockefeller Foundation, and mobilization for the war on words, 1938–1944, *Journal of Communication*, 46, no. 3 (1966): 124–148.

28. Marilyn A. Lashner, The role of foundations in public broadcasting, Part I: Development and trends, *Journal of Broadcasting*, 20, no. 4 (1976): 529–547; Marilyn A. Lashner, The role of foundations in public broadcasting, Part II: The Ford Foundation, *Journal of Broadcasting*, 21, no. 2 (1977): 235–254.

29. Lewis A. Dunn, *On-site Inspection for Arms Control Verification: Pitfalls and Promise*, Center for National Security Negotiations, McLean, Va., 1989.

30. Stephen McDowell, Policy research institutes and liberalized international services exchange, in Brooks and Gagnon, 1994, *op cit.*, pp. 107–134.

31. Fischer, 1993, *op cit.*

32. The Social Science Research Council currently has programs in the areas of culture, information technology, and globalization that are producing numerous reports pertinent to information policy.

33. Owen, 1998, *op cit.*

34. A partial listing of the work this research agenda has produced includes: Erik Brynjolfsson and Brian Kahin, eds, *Understanding the Digital Economy: Data, Tools & Research*, The MIT Press, Cambridge, 2000; Brian Kahin and

Janet Abbate, eds, *Standards Policy for Information Infrastructure*, Harvard Information Infrastructure Project, Cambridge, 1995; Brian Kahin and James Keller, eds, *Coordinating the Internet*, The MIT Press, Cambridge, 1997; Brian Kahin and Charles Nesson, *Borders in Cyberspace: Information Policy and the Global Information Infrastructure*, The MIT Press, Cambridge, 1996; Brian Kahin and Hal Varian, eds, *Internet Publishing and Beyond: The Economics of Digital Information and Intellectual Property*, The MIT Press, Cambridge, 2000; Brian Kahin and Ernest Wilson, eds, *National Information Infrastructure Initiatives: Vision and Policy Design*, The MIT Press, Cambridge, 1996.

35. A partial listing of these books includes Eli M. Noam and James Alleman, eds, *The New Investment Theory of Real Options and its Implication for Telecommunication Economics*, Kluwer Academic Publishers, Amsterdam, 1999; Eli M. Noam and Aine Nishuilleabhain, eds, *Private Networks, Public Objectives*, Elsevier Science, Amsterdam, 1996; Eli M. Noam and Gerard Pogorel, eds, *Asymmetric Deregulation: The Dynamics of Telecommunications Policy in Europe*, Greenwood Publishing Group, Boulder, Colo., 1994; Eli M. Noam and Alex J. Wolfson, eds, *Globalism and Localism in Telecommunications*, Elsevier Science, Amsterdam, 1997.

36. See, e.g., John Forester, Toward a critical sociology of public policy: Probing policy-shaped contradictions in the communicative infrastructure of society, in *Critical Theory, Public Policy, and Planning Practice: Toward a Critical Pragmatism*, SUNY Press, Albany, 1993, pp. 135–178.

37. Katherine Montgomery, Presentation to Pre-Conference Workshop on Communication Research and Policy, International Communication Association, Washington, D.C., May, 2001.

38. David Docherty, David Morrison, and Michael Tracey, Scholarship as silence, *Journal of Communication*, 43, no. 3 (1993): 230–238; Jay Rosen, Making things more public: On the political responsibility of the media intellectual, *Critical Studies in Mass Communication*, 11, no. 4 (1994): 363–388.

39. Ellen Wartella, Communication research on children and public policy, in Philip Gaunt, ed, *Beyond Agendas: New Directions in Communication Research*, Greenwood Press, Westport, Conn., 1993, pp. 137–148; Ellen Wartella, Presentation to Pre-Conference Workshop on Communication Research and Policy, International Communication Association, Washington, D.C., May, 2001.

40. See, e.g., George Gerbner, Science or ritual dance? A revisionist view of television violence effects research, *Journal of Communication*, 34, no. 3 (1984): 164–173; Dale Kunkel, The role of research in the regulation of U.S. children's television advertising, *Knowledge: Creation, Diffusion, Utilization*, 12, no. 1 (1990): 101–109; Michael A. McGregor, Assessing FCC response to report of Children's Television Task Force, *Journalism Quarterly*, 63, no. 3 (1986): 481–487, 502.

41. Ellen Wartella and Byron Reeves, Historical trends in research on children and the media: 1900–1960, *Journal of Communication*, 35, no. 2 (1985): 118–133.

42. George Comstock, The role of social and behavioral science in policy-making for television, *Journal of Social Issues*, 32, no. 4 (1976): 157–178.

43. Warren Bareiss, Public space, private face: Audience construction at a non-commercial radio station, *Critical Studies in Mass Communication*, 15, no. 4 (1998): 405–422; John F. Long and Paul J. Traudt, Discriminating audience donor factors for public radio: A tale of two cities, *Journal of Media Economics*, 12, no. 1 (1999): 51–66.

44. Petros Iositides, Diversity vs. concentration in the deregulated mass media domain, *Journalism and Mass Communication Quarterly*, 76, no. 1 (1999): 152–162; Dominic L. Lasorsa, Effects of newspaper competition on public opinion diversity, *Journalism Quarterly*, 68, nos. 1–2 (1991): 38–47; Maxwell McCombs, effect of monopoly in Cleveland on diversity of newspaper content, *Journalism Quarterly* 64, no. 4 (1987): 740–744, 792; Michael H. McGregor, Importance of diversity in controversy over financial interest and syndication, *Journalism Quarterly*, 61, no. 4 (1984): 831–834; Susan Dente Ross, Doors to diversity: The First Amendment implications of telephone video options under the Telecommunications Act of 1996, *Journal of Broadcasting and Electronic Media*, 43, no. 2 (1999): 254–270.

45. e.g., Kenneth Lipartito, Systems in conflict: Bell confronts the American South, Presented to the International Communications Association, Chicago, May, 1991; Milton Mueller and Jorge Reina Schement, Universal service from the bottom up: A study of telephone penetration in Camden, New Jersey, *The Information Society*, 12 (1996): 273–292; Lana F. Rakow, Technology and social change: The telephone in the history of a community, Presented to the International Communications Association, Chicago, May, 1991.

46. Alan G. Stavitsky, "Guys in suits with charts": Audience research in U.S. public radio, *Journal of Broadcasting and Electronic Media*, 39, no. 2 (1995): 177–189.

47. Wenmouth Williams, Jr., Two approaches to the identification and measurement of public radio audiences, *Journal of Broadcasting*, 25, no. 1 (1977): 61–69; Wenmouth Williams and David L. LeRoy, Alternate methods of measuring public radio audiences: A pilot project, *Journalism Quarterly*, 53, no. 3 (1976): 516–521.

48. Stavitsky, 1995, *op cit.*; Alan G. Stavitsky, Counting the house in public television: A history of ratings use, 1953–1980, *Journal of Broadcasting & Electronic Media*, 42, no. 4 (1998): 520–534.

49. Alan G. Stavitsky, Theory into practice: By the numbers—The use of ratings data in academic research, *Journal of Broadcasting & Electronic Media*, 44: 3 (2000): 535–539.

50. S. C. Ivers, *How Independent Research Can Strengthen Public Broadcasting* Benton Foundation, Washington, D.C.: 1993.

51. Cecilie Gaziano, Relationship between public opinion and Supreme Court decisions: Was Mr. Dooley right? *Communication Research*, 5, no. 2 (1978): 131–149.

52. See, e.g., Philip J. Powlick, The sources of public opinion for American foreign policy officials, *International Studies Quarterly*, 39, no. 4 (1995): 427–452.

53. Sandra Braman, *Public Opinion Surveys on First Amendment Issues, 1936–1985*, Report to the Minneapolis Star & Tribune Company, Minneapolis, Minnesota, 1986.

54. Jacob Shamir, Neta Ziskind, and Shoshana Blum-Kulka, What's in a question? A content analysis of survey questions, *Communication Review*, 3, no. 4 (1999): 1–25.

55. Jeffrey Mondak, Question wording and mass policy preferences: The comparative impact of substantive information and peripheral cues, *Political Communication*, 11, no. 2 (1994): 165–183.

56. Carl Botan, Presentation to Pre-Conference Workshop on Communication Research and Policy, International Communication Association, Washington, D.C., May, 2001.

57. David Riesman, Orbits of tolerance, interviewers, and elites, *Public Opinion Quarterly*, 20, no. 1 (1956): 49–73.

Formal Relationships: Working for the Government

11

Obituary for an Agency

Fred W. Weingarten
1995

These days, it is not considered particularly seemly to feel friendly toward government of any kind or level. An attitude ranging somewhere between contempt and downright hatred seems to prevail. Nevertheless, I have great affection and respect for the Office of Technology Assessment (OTA) and was deeply saddened when congressional budget cutters, not only in search of every dime but looking to exhibit symbolic examples of self-sacrifice to the voters, decided to eliminate the OTA.

(Admittedly, my affection is partly personal. I spent 10 years at the OTA, managing the program on Communication and Information Technologies. But, I also believe firmly in the OTA's mission, and was proud of participating in its unique experiment in fusing politics, technology, and policy.)

It's instructive to explore why the agency was so vulnerable to political attack. It certainly did not suffer from old age. Formed in 1972, it was barely 23 years old. But that brief time span might as well have been a century long in light of the tremendous swing in political attitudes the nation experienced.

The OTA was formed in an era of political optimism, when the prevailing attitude [was] that with sufficient forethought and the right analytical processes, we could foresee potential problems and issues with new technology. Armed with this foresight, we would be able to logically frame and analyze possible policy options, choose the best one, and carry it out with competence. It was an optimistic and rationalist view of public policy.

Today, political attitudes seem to be marked by pessimism about government competence, and a view of public policy as arising mainly from nothing more than conflicting self-interests.

What happened? Who knows? But, whatever the cause, the OTA, created at one end of the pendulum swing, fell at the other.

In 1972, the public and the political leaders had begun to see that many of the pressing policy problems the country faced were either the result of technology or involved technology in their resolution. The environmental movement was in full swing; a debate had broken out over investing in a new supersonic transport plane. Atomic power, long touted as a source of cheap, plentiful energy, seemed beset with concerns over reactor safety and disposal of spent fuel.

A new field of study, called "technology assessment" had begun to spring up in the U.S. and European universities (In Europe, technology assessment seemed to take a more negative rhetorical tone, antagonistic to technology. In the United States it developed as a more pragmatic, analytical field, identifying threats, to be sure, but also looking at opportunities and how to capture them.) NSF had even established a program of research support in technology assessment focused on building methodology for very long-term assessment. This program was eliminated several years ago.

It was against this background the OTA was created to study the social, economic, and political impacts of technology. The introduction to the Technology Assessment Act of 1972 sets forth quite clearly the assumptions and high expectations for the new agency:

1. "As technology continues to change and expand rapidly, its applications are—(1) large and growing in scale; and (2) increasingly extensive, pervasive, and critical in their impact, beneficial and adverse, on the natural and social environment.

2. "Therefore, it is essential that, to the fullest extent possible, the consequences of technological applications be anticipated, understood, and considered in determination of public policy on existing and emerging national problems.

3. "Accordingly, it is necessary for the Congress to—(1) equip itself with new and effective means for securing competent, unbiased information

concerning the physical, biological, economic, social, and political effects of such applications; and (2) utilize this information, whenever appropriate, as one factor in the legislative assessment of matters pending before the Congress, particularly in those instances where called upon to consider support for, or management or regulation of, technological applications."

It still sounds like a pretty persuasive argument to many of us! But bringing this charge to reality was never easy for a new, tiny agency operating in a highly politicized environment, while trying to invent a whole new field of analysis. It quickly became apparent, for instance, that the developing academic field of technology assessment had little guidance to offer on the very pragmatic question of how to give Congress useful and objective advice and survive.

In its brief history, the OTA went through three phases of development, under three directors.

Politicized Staff.   The first stage, which lasted only a couple of years, was under the direction of Emilio Daddario, a retired member of Congress who had helped shepherd the OTA Act through Congress. Under Daddario, the agency was highly politicized, essentially run like a congressional committee. Members of the legislatively created Technology Assessment Board (TAB), representatives and senators from both parties, appointed the staff and involved themselves closely in the studies. That operating style was nearly the death knell for an agency that was intended to be nonpartisan and analytical in its studies. After a firestorm of complaints that the OTA was behaving like a "Shadow Cabinet" for the Democrats (in particular for Ted Kennedy, chair of TAB), Daddario resigned and Russell Peterson, a director with no congressional background, was hired.

Big Picture.   Peterson conceived of the OTA as a highly independent "think tank," conducting its studies without fear or favor, and with no congressional meddling. The studies were to be "big picture," broadly sweeping in their scope, looking far into the future. Unfortunately, if politicizing the agency was dangerous, removing it from the daily reality of politics and ignoring the needs of its congressional clients was even worse. Congress did not form the OTA to be charitable or to be an independent force; it formed the agency to help do its work – look again at the words in the charter. Peterson barely lasted the year. He resigned after the agency published a long-range strategic plan that seemed to be carving out its own—rather than Congress's—policy agenda.

Client Centered.   This time, several members of Congress were ready to close the agency, but its supporters wanted to give it one more chance. They hired as director John Gibbons, a physicist who specialized in energy and environmental policy at the University of Tennessee, and who also had roots at the Federal Energy Administration and with Oak Ridge National Laboratory. Gibbons was well aware he represented the last chance for the agency. He brought a much more pragmatic perspective to the OTA, stressing smaller, shorter-term studies that directly focused on the needs of congressional committees. Gibbons insisted the studies have bipartisan support and be clearly tied to the legislative agenda of Congress. In a sense, he wanted the agency to walk a narrow line: the studies were to be conducted by professional staff, free from political interference; but if done well, they were to feed into the immediate political debate on urgent issues. In other words, the OTA was to serve the needs of Congress, as the Act, itself, stated. And he succeeded, In the eyes of most observers, the next 12 years under Gibbons was a "Golden Age" for the OTA. Although there was the occasional fuss over a study that stepped on some political toe or other, the OTA produced a steady stream of excellent, well-received reports that made constructive contributions to the legislative process.

Nonetheless, there were enduring problems. Among them were the following:

1. *Whom did it serve?* The OTA found itself in the middle of a dangerous paradox. In order to survive politically, it clearly had to be seen to serve everyone, not within each and every study, of course, but taken across the body of work produced over the years. The OTA reports had to be useful to all parties to the conflict. (One assistant director used to say he considered the most successful reports to be those that were quoted during a floor debate by all opposing parties.) The problem: in serving everybody, one serves nobody in the sense that, although lots of

members respected the OTA and generally supported its work, few real champions stepped forward and shed blood for it when the attacks came.

2. *Rationality versus conflict.* Once I was describing a possible study on satellite communications to the senior communications staff member of a key Senator. "The Senator has already made up his mind on that issue," she said.

"Wouldn't he like to know whether it was technologically feasible?" I asked.

"Of course not!" she snapped. "Why would he?"

One view of policy-making by Congress is it simply acts as a referee in fights between opposing constituencies. The opposing view is it senses problems and tries to find optimal ways to solve them. In truth, either description can apply, depending on the particular debate, the parties involved, the temperature of public rhetoric, and the level of attention of powerful interests. But, the OTA is inherently predicated on adding rationality to the debate. This means that almost never can an OTA report fully determine a legislative outcome, and the most carefully reasoned analysis can be trampled in a political stampede.

Many of the newer members of Congress believe they came to revolutionize the size and role of government. Technology policy analysis has little to do with this form of raw ideological struggle. Asked if they want an OTA, the revolutionaries snap, "Of course not! Why would we?"

3. *Partisan suspicion.* In the minds of some of the older members, the OTA never really overcame the early suspicion that it was really a hotbed of out-of-work Democrats, feeding information and studies to the opposition with which to embarrass and sometimes block the usually Republican White House. It is rumored among congressional staff that, when Gibbons went to the White House as Science Advisor, taking several senior OTA staff members with him, those suspicions hardened into certainty.

4. *Outside supporters.* Legally, the OTA worked for Congress, no one else. It had no other clients and served no other constituencies. In reality, many studies were most effective when stakeholder groups used them to frame their arguments, At hearings, they would wave OTA reports at the members and say, "Your own agency says . . . " While some members

thought such use was just fine—a successful case of the OTA enriching the political debate—many were less than thrilled at seeing a congressional agency's analysis thrown back in their faces.

The academic and nonprofit research community have also been big supporters of the OTA, but at times their rhetoric suggested they viewed the office as their own personal, but publicly funded, window into the policy process. This attitude also led to resentment and partisan concerns on the part of Congress, since the research community is largely viewed, rightly or wrongly, as predominantly liberal and Democrat.

5. *Inward looking.* Finally, and this is my only real criticism of the agency, the OTA seemed in recent years to have retreated into a shell. As mentioned, the conservative approach of Gibbons rescued the agency in its early years, but over the last decade, it also narrowed the focus and shortened the time horizon of most studies. As a result, the OTA seemed to become more inward-looking at the cost of its ability to anticipate and respond to new technological issues. Furthermore, this inertia seemed to make it hard for the agency to find new ground and redefine itself as the political climate changed.

Speaking from the admittedly parochial view of information systems, for example, it was surprising that, just as the information infrastructure was becoming one of the major technology policy stories of the decade, the OTA closed down its information technology program. It relocated (buried?) some of the staff and studies in a program called "Industry, Telecommunications, and Commerce," in a directorate titled "Industry, Commerce, and International Security." At a time when issues such as privacy, intellectual property, and first amendment rights are cropping up and major telecommunications legislation is moving through Congress, the decision does not signal that the broader societal issues of information and communication policy are going to be given much attention. And, indeed, in the NII debate, the OTA has been conspicuous by its absence. A similar charge of irrelevance was leveled in the Senate Appropriation hearings about the role it played in the health care debate last year.

Given all of these forces against it, one might ask, "How did it survive at all?" A good question. The answer seems to be that over the years enough men and women of good will on both sides of the aisle were convinced that, for all its faults and conflicts, it was the right agency at the right time. And, they kept that conviction when the OTA stumbled, or even when a report seemed to go against their own political benefit. It seems a reasonable enough proposition. None of the factors listed are overwhelming problems that can't be managed or corrected, nor do they negate the solid rationale for the OTA put forth by those who created it in the first place.

Technology is surely not the cause of all the problems of our society, nor is it the panacea for everything that ails us. But, as technological change weaves its way through our society, it is surely a critical piece of the puzzle, and it confronts us with complicated choices. Few can argue with the proposition that, in the words of the legislation cited, technological applications are "increasingly extensive, pervasive, and critical in their impact, beneficial and adverse on the natural and social environment."

Our large and complex society is both shaped by and shapes technology, for good and bad. Technology assessment may not be able to give us as precise a view into the future as we might like. Who knows how to do that but it can help us think more clearly about the outcomes of choices we have to make. Congress has thrown a wrench through the view screen of one of the few navigational instruments we have available to us, cloudy as it is. This can only be good news if you think our ship of state should be rudderless.

12

U.S. Mass Communication Research, Counterinsurgency, and Scientific "Reality"

Christopher Simpson
1993

Many people remember the CIA's Phoenix program in Vietnam as an assassination and political murder operation. Phoenix operatives killed about 20,000 Vietnamese rebels, according to CIA Director William Colby—about twice that many according to Vietnamese estimates.[1] Figure 12.1 shows a Phoenix "wanted" poster; most of the men illustrated in it were murdered. Colby says that an "imaginative U.S. Information Agency officer" came up with the poster design.

But reducing Phoenix to simply assassinations underestimates the program's sophistication and the CIA's ambitions for it. Colby insists that Phoenix would be better understood as a means of "establishing democratic legitimacy in the villages," and that it was primarily an intelligence project to "provide a non-communist structure to counter the claims of the [Vietnamese] Liberation Committees."[2] The posters were an "antiterrorist" device, he says in his memoirs.

Colby's explanation is in part simply euphemism, but its importance goes beyond that. For the CIA, Phoenix was really an experiment in the state of the art of the social psychology of controlling unrest in U.S. client states—an experiment that Colby considers to have been a "great success."[3] Most simply, the CIA's idea was to encourage the cooperation of the Vietnamese population through a combination of terror, careful redefinition of Viet Cong rebels as the "real" terrorists, and orchestrated offers of purported democracy and progress to encourage compliance with the U.S.-sponsored regime.

Phoenix became a key aspect of the CIA's overall vision for "developing" Vietnamese society. It sought to coordinate the regime's police and military efforts to uproot the Viet Cong and replace it with a U.S.-

Phụng - Hoàng

ĐÂY, NHỮNG CÁN BỘ CỘNG SẢN MÀ
CHIẾN DỊCH PHỤNG HOÀNG ĐANG TRUY NÃ

PHAN VĂN MÂM tự MƯỜI THÀNH	TRẦN VĂN DŨNG tự HÙNG	NGUYỄN VĂN MINH tự CÂY MINH	MAI VĂN TỐC
sanh năm 1908	sanh năm 1930	sanh năm 1937	sanh năm 1931
Phó Ban Binh Vận	Trưởng Ban Nông Hội	Trưởng Ban Quân Sự	Cán sự Nông Hội
Xã An Thái Trung	Xã An Thái Trung	Xã An Thái Trung	Ấp An Nhơn
Quận Giáo Đức	Quận Giáo Đức	Quận Giáo Đức	Xã An Hữu
			Quận Giáo Đức

Đồng bào thân mến,

Nếu đồng bào biết nơi ẩn trốn của các cán bộ Cộng Sản trên đây. yêu cầu thông báo cho nhân viên Cảnh Sát Quốc Gia hoặc Chánh quyền và Quân đội VNCH gần nhất. Đồng bào sẽ được tưởng thưởng và tên tuổi đồng bào sẽ được giữ kín.

Cùng các bạn cán bộ Cộng-Sản

Các bạn không thể lẩn trốn mãi được vì mọi người đã nhận diện các bạn.

Các bạn hãy ra hồi chánh để hưởng sự khoan hồng của Chánh Phủ. Các bạn sẽ được tiếp đón niềm nở và đối xử tử tế.

ỦY BAN PHỤNG HOÀNG
TỈNH ĐỊNH TƯỜNG

CC 703-70

Figure 12.1
A Phoenix "wanted" poster identifying suspected Vietnamese rebels.

sponsored alternative. Colby viewed the 20,000 killings carried out during the first phases of Phoenix as a scientific, rational, and even "humane"—his word—means of executing the war, at least compared with conventional military action. This did not work in Vietnam, and perhaps it cannot work in any fundamental sense. Nonetheless, these tactics did prolong the agony of colonized peoples and they continue to be used for that purpose today.

The CIA's strategy was based in large part on sociological methods and theories on communication and society popularized by Daniel Lerner, Ithiel de Sola Pool, and other specialists at the Massachusetts Institute of Technology's Center for International Studies (CENIS), which during the 1950s and 1960s was one of the most important centers of communication research in the United States. It applied the most advanced sociological techniques to the challenge of controlling human attitudes and behavior on a mass scale. Various professors at the center had their own interests, but taken as a whole the CENIS project began with consideration of the impact of mass media on social devel-opment in the Third World, extended into research for Phoenix-type programs that combined media with various forms of coercion, then con-tinued into devising strategy and tactics for nuclear was as a means of literally "sending messages" to the USSR during some final crisis for humanity.[4]

This essay deals with the evolution of the preconceptions and preju-dices in one of the fields in which CENIS specialized, mass communica-tion research. This is a small field in the social sciences, but an intriguing one. Communication research today provides the framework for the college- and graduate-level training of journalists, public relations and advertising personnel, and the related craftspeople who might be called the "ideological workers" of contemporary U.S. society. A rela-tively new specialty, it crystallized into a distinct discipline with colleges, curricula, the authority to grant doctorates, and so on, between about 1950 and 1955.[5] These characteristics permit researchers to make a clear study of the field's history and—more to the point here—to document the role of U.S. government psychological warfare and counterinsur-gency programs in the creation of what are known as the dominant par-adigms of U.S. mass communication research.

During the decades since World War II, the U.S. government's national security interests usually overlapped with the commercial ambitions of major advertisers and media companies, and with the aspirations of a particularly enterprising stratum of U.S. university administrators and professors. U.S. military, intelligence, and propaganda agencies helped bankroll substantially all of a generation's research into techniques of persuasion, advertising, interrogation, public opinion polling, political and military mobilization, propagation of ideology, and related questions. The persuasion studies, in particular, provided much of the scientific underpinning for modern advertising and motivational techniques. The government conducted security-related communication research on a scale that went well beyond what would have been possible with private sector money alone, often exploiting its unique access to pools of military recruits useful as test subjects.[6]

At least six of the most important U.S. centers of postwar communication research grew up as de facto adjuncts of government psychological warfare programs. For years, government money—although it was not always publicly acknowledged as such—made up more than seventy-five percent of the annual budgets of institutions such as Paul Lazarsfeld's Bureau of Applied Social Research at Columbia University, Hadley Cantril's Institute for International Social Research at Princeton, Ithiel de Sola Pool's CENIS Program at MIT, and others.[7] In one case, the U.S. State Department secretly (and illegally) financed the National Opinion Research Center's studies of U.S. popular opinion as part of the department's Cold War lobbying campaigns on Capitol Hill—thus making NORC's ostensibly private, independent surveys financially viable for the first time.[8] In another case, the CIA clandestinely underwrote American University's Bureau of Social Science Research studies of torture—there is no other word for it—of prisoners of war.[9] In sum, it is unlikely that mass communication research could have emerged in anything like its present form without constant transfusions of money for the leading lights in the field from U.S. military, intelligence, and propaganda agencies.

Government psychological warfare programs helped form mass communications research into a distinct scholarly field. The state usually did not directly determine what scientists could or could not say, but it did strongly influence the selection of who would do the "authoritative" talking in the field, who would be recognized as leaders, and which one of several competing scientific paradigms concerning communication would be funded, elaborated, and encouraged to prosper.

This essay is organized in two basic parts. First, I will look at how the concept "communication" came to be defined in U.S. social science circles. Next, I will examine psychological warfare and counterinsurgency programs sponsored by U.S. military, propaganda, and intelligence agencies since 1945, focusing on how these agencies applied social science research and analysis techniques to tasks of social control, covert operations, and intelligence missions. In both sections I will deal with how paradigms in the social sciences are constructed.

Before World War II

Two seminal works in modern U.S. communication research that remain in wide use in graduate programs today are Walter Lippmann's *Public Opinion* (1922) and Harold Lasswell's *Propaganda Technique in the World War* (1926).[10] Both were the product of the prototypical psychological warfare operations of World War I. Both investigated the impact of the then-new phenomenon of genuinely mass communication on Western, industrial society, and both were distinctly hostile to the professed values of democracy. They argued that new technologies for communication and transportation had awakened millions of disenfranchised people to a world outside their factories and villages, but that the traditional economic and political structures that had shaped Europe during the nineteenth century remained in place. This would lead to explosive situations, as Lippmann and Lasswell saw things, including the Bolshevik revolution of 1917 and the wave of labor rebellions that swept through Europe and the United States in the wake of World War I.

Lippmann concluded that "representative government . . . cannot be worked successfully, no matter what the basis of election, unless there is an independent, expert organization for making the unseen facts [of the new world] intelligible to those who have to make the decisions."[11] Lasswell developed a similar idea, emphasizing selective use of assassinations, violence, and other coercion, as well as propaganda, as a means of "communicating" with and managing people.[12]

Lippmann and Lasswell articulated a narrow paradigm that substituted, for communication as such, one particular manifestation of communication that is pronounced in hierarchical industrial states. They contended, in short, that communication's essence is its use as an instrument for imposing one's will on others, and often on masses of others. Their articulation of communication-as-domination permitted a rapid application of a positivist scientific method to the study of communication for the first time.

For Lasswell, the study of all communication could be reduced to "/who/ says /what/ to /whom/ with /what effect/"—a motto that is practically inscribed in stone over the portals of today's colleges of communication. It is a seemingly simple, logical approach, but it carries with it sweeping implications. With the Lasswellian method, it became possible to isolate and measure systematically those aspects of communications that were of greatest relevance to powerful groups in U.S. society. In the United States, consumer capitalism is based to an important degree on privately owned media's sales of the attention of mass audiences to advertisers. To market this commodity, media companies must have some means for measuring it. Thus, the field of mass communication research—its techniques, body of knowledge, institutional structure, and so on—evolved symbiotically with the evolution of the modern capitalist state generally, and particularly with the media industry and those segments of the economy most dependent on mass markets.[13]

World War and Early-Modern Communication Research

Through the end of the 1930s, the work of Lasswell, Lippmann, and other mass communication theorists and researchers remained mainly scholastic or commercial. There were a variety of intellectual currents in the field, ranging from Lasswell's self-consciously Machiavellian analysis to the radical reformism of Robert Lynd, Harry Field, and others. The sociologists and social psychologists of the day (from which the nascent field of communication research was gradually being born) seemed to many outside observers to call for progressive, even fundamental, changes in society.

World War II changed all that: the construction of a paradigm of communication-as-domination and the institutionalization of communication research took decisive steps forward during the conflict. Nazi intellectuals pioneered many of the strictly political uses of modern communication analysis and technologies. Josef Goebbels's work in social manipulation and in some forms of public communication is well known. On a more academic plane, a bright young Nazi security service agent, Otto Ohlendorf, established a German research center known as the Deutsche Lebensgebiete in 1939 to apply new tools such as opinion surveys to the problem of determining /who/ said /what/ to /whom/ with /what effect/ inside Germany. He was successful, on the whole, and his performance at the Deutsche Lebensgebiete laid the foundation for his later career as commandant of SS Einsatzgruppe D in the Caucasus, and as the senior manager of post-war economic planning for the SS. He had truly a remarkable career, in some ways, until he was convicted and hanged for organizing the murder of 90,000 people, most of them women and children.[14] Ohlendorf's principal sponsor and mentor was a leading SS intellectual, Dr. Reinhard Hoehn of the Institute for State Research at the University of Berlin. Hoehn managed to escape his pupil's fate and emerged after the war as one of German's most prominent experts on questions of public opinion and the state.[15] Several other leading German mass communication and public opinion specialists contributed their skills to Nazi publicity and opinion-monitoring projects. Notable among them was Elisabeth Noelle-Neumann, who began her career at the Goebbels intellectual journal *Das Reich* and eventually emerged as one of Europe's most celebrated communication theorists.[16]

The war spurred the emergence of psychological warfare as a particularly promising new form of applied communication research. The phrase *psychological warfare* first entered English in 1941 as a translated mutation of the Nazi concept *Weltanschauungkreig* (literally, "world-view warfare"), meaning the purportedly scientific application of propaganda, terror, and state pressure as a means of securing an ideological victory over one's enemies.[17] William "Wild Bill" Donovan, the director of the recently established U.S. intelligence agency OSS, viewed an understanding of Nazi psychological tactics as a vital source of ideas for "Americanized" versions of many of the same strategems. Use of the new term quickly became widespread throughout the U.S. intelligence community. For Donovan, psychological warfare was a full fourth arm of the U.S. military, equal in status to the army, navy, and air force.[18]

The personal, social, and scientific networks established in U.S. social sciences during World War II, particularly among communication researchers, later played a central role in the evolution (or "social construction") of U.S. sociology after the war.[19] There were six main U.S. centers of psychological warfare research during the conflict. Several of them went through name changes and reorganizations in the course of the war, but they can be summarized as follows: (1) Samuel Stouffer's Research Branch of the U.S. Army's Division of Morale; (2) the Office of War Information (OWI), led by Elmer Davis; (3) the Psychological Warfare Division of the U.S. Army, led by Brigadier General Robert McClure; (4) the Office of Strategic Services, led by William Donovan; (5) Rensis Likert's Division of Program Surveys at the Department of Agriculture, which provided field research personnel inside the United States for the Army, OWI, and other government agencies; and (6) Harold Lasswell's War Communications Division at the Library of Congress.

Dozens of prominent social scientists particpated in the war through these organizations. The Office of War Information included Elmo Roper (of the Roper survey organization), Elmo Wilson (also of Roper), Leonard Doob (Yale), Wilbur Schramm (University of Illinois and later Stanford), Alexander Leighton (Cornell), Leo Lowenthal (Institut für Sozialforschung, USIA, and University of California), Hans Speier (RAND Corporation), Nathan Leites (RAND), Edward Barrett (Columbia journalism school dean and *Columbia Journalism Review* founder), and Clyde Kluckhohn (Harvard), among others. (The institutions in parentheses simply indicate the affiliations for which these scholars may be best known.) OWI simultaneously extended contracts for communication research and consulting to Paul Lazarsfeld, Hadley

Cantril, Frank Stanton, and George Gallup, and to Rensis Likert's team at the Agriculture Department.[20]

In addition to his OWI work, Nathan Lietes served as Lasswell's senior research assistant at the Library of Congress project, as did Heinz Eulau (Stanford). Other prominent contributors to the Lasswell project included Irving Janis (Yale) and the young Ithiel de Sola Pool (MIT), who, with Lietes, already had begun systematic content analysis of communist publications long before the war was over. Lasswell's Library of Congress project is remembered today as the foundation of content analysis in the United States.[21] The list presented in table 12.1 summarizes some basic data about the work of prominent U.S. social scientists in World War II psychological warfare programs. The names here are simply a selection of those who have since played important roles in mass communication research; the list is not intended to be complete.

The day-to-day significance of these networks has been explored by social psychologist John Clausen, a veteran of Samuel Stouffer's Research Branch. Clausen made a systematic study during the early 1980s of the postwar careers of his former colleagues who had gone into mass communication research, sociology, or psychology. Twenty-five of twenty-seven veterans who could be located responded to his questionnaire; of these, twenty-four reported that their wartime work had had "lasting implications" and had been "a major influence on [their] subsequent career." Clausen quotes the reply of psychologist Nathan Maccoby (Stanford): "The Research Branch not only established one of the best old-boy (or old-girl) networks ever, but an alumnus of the Branch had an open door to most relevant jobs and career lines. We were a lucky bunch." Nearly three-fifths of the respondents indicated that the Research Branch experience "had a major influence on the direction or character of their work in the decade after the war," Clausen continues, "and all but three of the remainder indicated a substantial influence . . . fully three fourths reported the Branch experience to have been a very important influence on their careers as a whole."[22] To jump ahead for just a moment, figure 12.2 shows a 1952 document from the U.S. Psychological Strategy Board, which was an interagency coordinating committee for U.S. psychological warfare efforts during the Korean

Table 12.1
Communication research scholars in World War II U.S. psychological warfare programs

---

Office of War Information

Staff

Elmo Roper (Roper Surveys)

Elmo Wilson (Roper Surveys)

Leonard Doob (Yale)

Wilbur Schramm (U. Illinois, Stanford)

Alexander Leighton (Cornell)

Leo Lowenthal (Frankfurt School, USIA, U. California)

Hans Speier (RAND Corporation)

Nathan Leites (RAND Corporation)

Edward Barrett (State Department, Columbia)

Clyde Kluckhohn (Harvard)

Consulting contracts

Paul Lazarsfeld (Bureau of Applied Social Research)

Hadley Cantril (Princeton)

Frank Stanton (CBS)

George Gallup (Gallup Polls)

Rensis Likert (Institute for Social Research)

National Opinion Research Center

War Communications Division (Library of Congress)

Staff

Harold Lasswell (Yale)

Nathan Leites (RAND Corporation)

Heinz Eulau (Stanford)

Irving Janis (Yale)

Ithiel de Sola Pool (MIT)

Psychological Warfare Division (U.S. Army)

Staff

William Paley (CBS)

C. D. Jackson (Time/Life, *Fortune*)

W. Phillips Davison (Columbia, RAND Corporation)

Saul Padover (New School for Social Research)

Morris Janowitz (Frankfurt School, U. Michigan)

John W. Riley (Rutgers)

Daniel Lerner (MIT, Stanford)

Edward Shils (U. Chicago)

Office of Strategic Services

Staff

W. Phillips Davison (Columbia, RAND Corporation)

Saul Padover (New School for Social Research)

Morris Janowitz (Frankfurt School, U. Michigan)

Howard Becker (U. Wisconsin)

DeWitt Poole (State Department, Public Opinion Quarterly)

Alex Inkeles (Harvard)

Walter Langer (U. Wisconsin)

Douglas Cater (Aspen Institute)

Herbert Marcuse (Frankfurt School, U. California)

Consulting contracts

Stanford University

University of California (Berkeley)

Columbia University

Princeton University

Institute of Human Relations (Yale)

National Opinion Research Center

RECORDS OF THE
PSYCHOLOGICAL STRATEGY
BOARD

PROPOSED CONSULTANT PANELS

1. Panel of top evaluation officers actually engaged in evaluating
   Government operations, particularly the activities of the departments represented on PSB. This would include such persons
   as
           Ben Gedalecia, State Department (PRS)
   and   Dr. Leo Lowenthal, Evaluation Chief,(State Dept.) OIB.

2. Policy Panel, consisting of individuals in Government who are
   working on plans and policy at a fairly high level. This would
   include such persons as

           Paul H. Nitze, Director, Policy Planning Staff (S/P),
               State Department,
           Howland H. Sargeant, Assistant Secretary for Public
               Affairs (State Dept.), or
           Joseph B. Phillips, Deputy Asst. Secy. for P (State),
           and others.

3. An Operational Panel - a group of individuals actually responsible for the operation of the various aspects of our psychological
   strategy, including, for example,

           Dr. Wilson S. Compton, Chief, International Information
               Administration, State Department,
           Frank Wisner, of CIA,
           George W. Perkins, Assistant Secretary for European Affairs,
               State Department, or
           (the head of whatever geographical area seems most appro-
               priate).

In certain cases, it might be desirable for all three of these panels
to meet together; in other circumstances it might be preferable to
meet with each of them separately.

4. Panel of Social Science research experts outside Government. This
   should include such persons as

           Dr. Hadley Cantril of Princeton,
           Dr. Daniel Lerner of Stanford,
           Victor Hunt (or Dr. Hans Speier) of Rand Corporation,
           Dr. Harold Lasswell of Yale,
           and others.

                                                  5. A Panel

Figure 12.2

Psychological Strategy Board memo illustrates the durability of networks of
state sponsors and communication scholars.

RECORDS OF THE
PSYCHOLOGICAL STRATEGY
BOARD

5. A Panel of Foreign Affairs experts outside Government. This
   should include such persons as

James Burnham	James Perkins
Erwin O. Canham	George Franklin
Hadley Cantril	Paul Hoffman
J. Wallace Carroll	John Foster Dulles
John Sherman Cooper	
Gardner Cowles	
Mark Foster Ethridge	
George H. Gallup	
Ben Hibbs	
John D. Rockefeller, III	
Nelson A. Rockefeller	
Bertram D. Wolfe	
and others.	

6. A Panel of names of individuals to whom PSB could turn for advice
   and assistance on appropriate occasion. This list should cover a
   broad field, and might include such persons as

   Dr. Hans Speier and
   Philip Davidson - of Rand Corporation
   Dr. Daniel Lerner of Stanford
   Kingsley Davis of Columbia
   Jerome Brunner of Harvard
   Maurice Janowitz of the University of Michigan
   Rensis Likert, University of Michigan
   Wilbur Schramm, University of Illinois
   John Riley, Rutgers
   Gabriel Almond, Princeton
   Elmo C. Wilson, President, International Public Opinion
        Research (IPR), New York
   Clyde Kluckohn, Harvard
   Willmoore Kendall, Operations Research Office, Johns Hopkins
   Philip Selznick, UCLA
   Alexander Leighton, Cornell

   and Area Specialists, such as

   David Rowe, Yale (China)
   David Mandelbaum, UCLA (India)
   Philip Moseley, Cornell (Soviet Union)
   George Homans, Harvard

   These persons (5. and 6.) are in addition to those already included in
   the panels above - and who might be consulted individually.

Figure 12.2 continued

War. It also clearly illustrates the durability of the social networks among these academics.[23]

Thus, the World War II experience of psychological warfare operations and research contributed substantially to the construction of a remarkably tight circle of men and women who shared important conceptions about mass communication research. They regarded mass communication as a tool for social management and as a weapon in social conflict. They expressed common assumptions concerning the usefulness of quantitative research—particularly experimental and quasi-experimental effects research, opinion surveys, and quantitative content analysis—as a means of illuminating what communication "is" and improving its application to social management. They also demonstrated common attitudes toward at least some of the ethical questions intrinsic to performing applied social research on behalf of a government.

These men and women were not obscure college professors. They were much of the central command of mainstream U.S. sociology, and the names discussed here were particularly prominent in various stages of communication studies. To a very large degree, it was they who wrote the textbooks, enjoyed the heavy government contracts that often are necessary for professional prominence in the United States, served on the editorial boards of the key journals, and became the deans and emeritus professors of the most influential schools of communication and journalism in this country. What can be seen here, in sum, is the construction of social networks whose specialty was claimed to be "knowledge" about a particular topic—in this case, communication.

The Search for "Magic Keys"

In the first decade after the war, many social scientists and some government agencies believed that sociology, social psychology, and related fields were on the brink of decisive breakthroughs in engineering human affairs. The so-called hard sciences had employed the positivist scientific method to bring society radar, penicillin, and atomic energy. Now the social sciences would use the same methods to usher in a new era of reason, security, and social peace under the umbrella of the United States.

The rising U.S. intelligence community—the OSS at first, and later the CIA and the various military intelligence groups—placed itself at the forefront of this effort. Here is how Brigadier General John Magruder of the OSS put it in testimony at a U.S Senate hearing in late 1945:

In all of the intelligence that enters into waging war soundly and waging peace soundly, it is the social scientists who make a huge contribution. The government of the United States would be well advised to do all in its power to promote the development of knowledge in the field of the social sciences. . . . Were we to develop a dearth of social scientists, all national intelligence agencies servicing policy makers in peace or war would be directly handicapped . . . research of social scientists [is] indispensable to the sound development of national intelligence in peace and war.[24]

Magruder introduced a chart into the Senate record to illustrate the OSS's perspective (see figure 12.3). It is revealing on two counts.[25] First, in the OSS view, there was a seamless continuum between wartime and peacetime operations. While different tactics could be employed as situations changed, the intelligence community's fundamental perspective remained that U.S. interests would best be achieved by dominating rival powers, regardless of whether the United States was technically at peace or at war at any given time. Magruder saw relatively peaceful engineering of consent for U.S. aims as desirable, but the option of using violence remained essential. Second, as the chart illustrates, the OSS believed that virtually every aspect of postwar intelligence operations should make use of sociology or social psychology, or both.

This opened the era of what has been called the "search for magic keys" to communication.[26] Leo Lowenthal, who was formerly of the Frankfurt School and who during the Korean War became chief of research for the Voice of America, said in 1951—only half jokingly—that the Voice was seeking "the ultimate miracle . . . the push button millennium in the use of opinion research in psychological warfare. On that distant day," he said, "the warrior would tell the research technician the elements of content, audience, medium and effect desired. The researcher would simply work out the mathematics and solve the algebraic formula," and the war would be won.[27]

Germany became a major testing ground for studies in social engineering, as the United States took as its mission the reeducation of Germans in the wake of the Nazi years. This helped open the door for

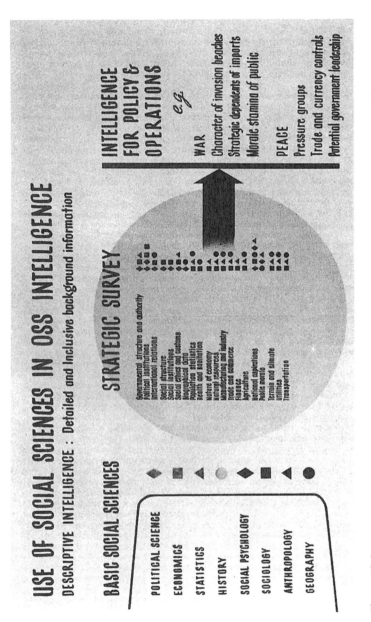

Figure 12.3
Intelligence application of the social sciences, as viewed by the OSS, 1945.

reformist, liberal social scientists to undertake purportedly objective research studies that they might earlier have rejected as immoral or politically suspect.[28]

Figure 12.4 presents survey results from a widely disseminated U.S. textbook on communication of the period. It describes the impact of mass bombing on German civilian populations, with the bombs literally taken as a form of "communication" with their targets.[29] Note that the

TABLE 2

PERCENT WILLING TO SURRENDER

	Heavy bombing	Medium bombing	Light bombing	Un-bombed
Nazi party members.......	43	49	38	37
Nonmembers	60	57	50	53
Difference	17	8	12	16
Ideological Nazis	20	30	12	14
Non-Nazis	65	53	57	65
Difference	45	33	45	51

In the tables of this chapter the base of the percentages is the number of people falling in each cell. For example, in table 2, 43 percent of *Nazi Party members who were heavily bombed* said they were willing to surrender. Sixty percent of *nonmembers heavily bombed* were willing to surrender, etc.

TABLE 3

PERCENT REPORTING WAR WEARINESS

	Heavy bombing	Medium bombing	Light bombing
Nazi party members	73	76	53
Nonmembers	73	73	63
Difference *	0	(3)-	10
Ideological Nazis	42	42	37
Non-Nazis	76	79	65
Difference	34	37	28

* Difference in parentheses is in direction opposite from expectation.

Figure 12.4
Bombing of civilians depicted as a form of communication, in Cold War era communication textbook.

TABLE 13

PERCENT WILLING TO SURRENDER

	Heavy bombing	Medium bombing	Light bombing	Un-bombed
High status	55	59	38	33
Middle status	58	53	51	48
Low status	63	62	61	61

TABLE 14

PERCENT WILLING TO SURRENDER

	Heavy bombing	Medium bombing	Light bombing	Un-bombed
Catholic	66	63	73	57
Protestant	54	51	48	52

Figure 12.4 continued

medium-strength bombing proved to be marginally more cost-effective, in many cases, in inducing the desire to surrender. That insight permitted more efficient targeting of U.S. atomic weapons, which at the time seemed to be in short supply, at least as the Air Force saw things.

How is it that liberal, social-democratic, and reform-minded social scientists become enmeshed in psychological warfare, counterinsurgency, and even preparations for nuclear war? One part of the answer lies in many scientists' ability to create self-contradictory conceptual structures that permit them to isolate themselves from the consequences of their acts. Here is one example. In late 1947, the U.S. National Security Council took two actions to provide the first bureaucratic-administrative structure for U.S. clandestine warfare during peacetime. These decisions illustrate the extent to which U.S. psychological warfare has had from its inception multiple, overlapping layers of cover stories, deceits, and euphemistic explanations. In this case, the NSC created two such layers simultaneously, each contradictory to the other.

First, the NSC approved a relatively innocuous policy document known as "NSC 4: Coordination of Foreign Information Measures."[30]

It assigned the assistant secretary of state for public affairs responsibility to lead "the immediate strengthening and coordination of all foreign information measures of the U.S. government . . . to counteract effects of anti-U.S. propaganda." Importantly, NSC 4 was classified as "confidential," the lowest category of government secret. As a practical matter, this meant that word of this confidential action would likely be publicized in the news media as an NSC "secret decision' within days, perhaps within hours.

That is precisely what took place. In time, a series of public decisions grew up around NSC 4 involving policy directives and funding for the U.S. Information Agency, scholarly exchange programs, operation of America House cultural centers abroad, and similar overt information programs. Officially, the position of the U.S. government on such matters was that "truth is our weapon," as Edward Barrett—who was soon to be put in charge of the program—put it. This widely announced policy held that the United States openly presented its views on international controversies, and frankly discussed the flaws and advantages of U.S. society in a bid to win credibility for its point of view. This was not "propaganda" (in the negative sense of that word), Barrett insisted, it was "truth."[31]

In reality, only minutes after completing action on NSC 4, the NSC took up a second measure: NSC 4-A. This was classified "top secret," a considerably stricter security rating. This status bars the disclosure of even the existence of the decision to any person outside an authorized circle. In NSC 4-A, the NSC directed that "the foreign information activities of the U.S. Government," now supposedly led by the assistant secretary of state, "must be supplemented by covert psychological operations." The CIA was to organize and administer these officially nonexistent programs, in part under cover provided by the "confidential" program—that is, the public program—authorized under NSC 4.[32]

The NSC's action removed the U.S. Congress and public from any meaningful debate over whether or not to undertake clandestine psychological warfare abroad. More than that, the "deniability" of the psychological operations themselves ensured that the public would remain effectively excluded from decision making on this form of war for decades—a legacy that remains to this day.[33]

The scientists, operatives, and government administrators active in these programs created a euphemistic sublanguage of terms that permitted those who had been initiated into the arcana of national security to discuss psychological warfare and clandestine operations in varying degrees of specificity (depending upon the audience) while simultaneously denying the very existence of such programs when it was politically convenient to do so. In an added confusing twist, NSC 4 had established an officially confidential (but in reality public) program of bland "Foreign Information Measures" that sometimes also were referred to as "psychological measures" or "psychological warfare" in public discussions. Although officially confidential, these highly public activities became decoys to divert public and congressional attention away from more deadly affairs. These seemingly contradictory conceptual structures helped preserve the myth that the United States was dealing with the world in a straightforward manner consistent with its professed ideals, while the Soviets were waging a different sort of Cold War, one that relied upon deceit, "propaganda," and clandestine violence.

Building an Institutional Identity for Communication Research

For the first decade after 1945—which is to say, the decade in which communication research crystallized into a distinct scholarly field, complete with colleges, graduate degrees, and so on—U.S. military, propaganda, and intelligence agencies provided the overwhelming majority of all project funding for the field. The earliest cumulative data concerning government funding of social science is provided by the National Science Foundation in 1952: it shows that more than ninety-six percent of all reported federal funding for social science at that time was draw from the U.S. military. The remaining four percent of government funding was divided about equally between conventional civilian agencies (Department of Labor, Department of the Interior) and civilian agencies with clear national security missions (such as the Federal Civil Defense Administration). Social science funding rooted in national security missions totaled $12.27 million that year, the NSF reported, while comparable civilian funding totaled only $0.28 million.[34]

This extreme skew in favor of research to support military, intelligence, and propaganda missions was particularly pronounced in mass communication studies. A close review of *Public Opinion Quarterly* and other scholarly mass communication literature during the decade after 1945, for example, reveals several dozen medium- to large-scale communication research projects funded by the Office of Naval Research, the U.S. Air force, CIA, and U.S. Information Agency. The only comparable "civilian" study appears to have been a 1950 Department of Agriculture survey of the effects of television on dressmakers—one of the earliest such studies of television effects—that apparently was never written up for scholarly mass communication journals.[35]

At least a half dozen of the most important centers of U.S. communication research were dependent for their survival on funding from a handful of national security agencies, although the limits of space here permit discussion of only three. Their reliance on psychological warfare money was so exclusive as to suggest clearly that the crystallization of mass communication research into a distinct scholarly field would not have come about during the 1950s without substantial military, CIA, and USIA intervention.

The Survey Research Center (SRC) at the University of Michigan (today known as the Institute for Social Research, or ISR), for example, was established by Rensis Likert in the summer of 1946 using a number of the personnel who had served under Likert during the war. The "SRC functioned during its first year as something of an outpost of the federal government," writes Jean Converse in *Survey Research in the United States*.[36] Major early contracts included a ten-year grant from the Office of Naval Research for studies of the psychological aspects of morale, leadership, and control of large organizations, and a series of contracts for surveys of Americans' attitudes on economics for the Federal Reserve Board, which in those years was deeply concerned about the potential for a renewed 1930s-style depression and social upheaval as veterans returned to the civilian work force. Early SRC/ISR research with strategic intelligence applications included U.S. Air Force-funded interview studies of Soviet defectors and refugees. The point of that enterprise was twofold: first, to identify social psychological attributes of the Soviet population that could be exploited in U.S. propaganda, and second, collection of intelligence on military and economic centers inside the USSR that would be targeted for atomic or conventional attacks in the event of war.[37]

SRC/ISR archival records show that federal contracts contributed fully 99 percent of the institution's revenues during its first full year in 1947, and well over 50 percent of SRC/ISR revenues during its first five years of operation.[38]

At the National Opinion Research Center (NORC), perhaps the most liberal and reform-minded of the early centers of communication research, about 90 percent of the organization's work during the war years was made up of contracts from the Office of War Information, the U.S. government's principal monitor of civilian morale. This backing was "probably critical in making [NORC's] national capacity [for conducting surveys] viable," Converse writes. In 1944, Congress canceled the OWI project, but the NORC field studies of U.S. civilian morale and attitudes continued under secret "emergency' contracts with the Department of State. This arrangement became institutionalized and provided a survey vehicle onto which NORC later could market "piggyback" survey questions for commercial customers.[39]

A second noteworthy NORC contract during the center's first decade was a series of inquiries, for the U.S. Army Chemical Corps, into individual and group responses to community disasters. NORC used natural disasters such as earthquakes and tornados as analogues to model responses to an attack with chemical weapons. In time, NORC undertook a related series of disaster studies that became the U.S. government's main data base for evaluating the psychological effects of nuclear war.[40]

Funding for the Bureau of Applied Social Research (BASR) at Columbia University appears to have been more diversified. BASR records prior to 1950 are sketchy, but Converse concludes that approximately 50 percent of BASR's budget from 1941 through 1946 stemmed from commercial work such as readership studies for *Time* and *Life* magazines. But by 1949, the BASR was deeply in debt to Columbia University and lacked a cushion of operating funds with which to cover project expenses while waiting for clients to make payments. The cash-flow problem was so severe that Paul Lazarsfeld speculated in fund-raising appeals that BASR would be forced to close if help were not forthcoming.

By the end of that year, however, BASR's Kingley Davis won new military and intelligence contracts that substantially improved BASR's financial situation. By fiscal year 1950–51, BASR's annual budget had reached a new high, 75 percent of which consisted of contracts with U.S. military and propaganda agencies.[41] Major federally funded BASR projects of the period included two Air Force studies for intelligence gathering on urban social dynamics abroad, a large project for the Office of Naval Research, and a multiyear contract for the Voice of America for public opinion surveys in the Middle East.[42]

The Voice of America project began in September 1950. Extensive, methodologically ambitious surveys were conducted in Iran, Turkey, Egypt, and four other countries, each of which was a major target of U.S. psychological warfare efforts of the period. (Two of the countries, Iran and Egypt, underwent CIA-supported coups d'état while the study was under way.) Lazarsfeld helped compose the survey questions, which eventually were asked by native-language researchers in the field.[43] BASR designed the survey to elicit specific guidance for U.S. propaganda and intelligence operations in the region.

Still another important BASR contract focused on engineering public opinion in the Philippines, and particularly on measuring the effectiveness of psychological warfare and counterinsurgency operations against the Huk guerrillas. These programs helped generate several basic building blocks of today's communication theory, including understanding of the key role of opinion leaders in shaping mass public sentiment and the well-known "personal influence" and "two-step" models of communications behavior.[44] The Philippines project simultaneously became the proving ground for techniques designed to monitor the impact on Filipino public opinion of U.S.-backed search-and-destroy counterinsurgency squads, counterguerrilla "hunter-killer teams," the "pacification" of peasant villages, and other tactics that later became well known in Vietnam, El Salvador, and similar conflicts.[45]

The public opinion studies and the hunter-killer teams developed as interlocking characteristics of a single theory for managing insurgencies in U.S. client states such as the Philippines. MIT's Center for International Studies played a particularly important role in the elaboration of these tactics during the second half of the 1950s. CENIS was funded largely by the CIA and the Air Force, often using the Ford Foundation as a cover.

CENIS might be called the second generation of postwar U.S. communications research. By the mid-1950s, both academics and policymakers gradually realized that the earlier search for "magic keys" and the "push-button millennium" in social engineering had largely failed. Audiences proved to be far more resilient and resistant than theorists first had thought.

CENIS articulated a new group of tactics for managing international conflicts, and these became quite popular with government funders. CENIS scholars such as Ithiel de Sola Pool, Daniel Lerner, and Max Millikan (who had been the CIA's assistant director for intelligence prior to becoming CENIS director) argued that propaganda could be more effectively blended with controlled economic developments, arms transfers, police and military training, and counterinsurgency support for U.S.-backed regimes. These multifaceted tactics had developed more or less informally during U.S. interventions on Greece and the Philippines. Part of CENIS's job for the government was to articulate fully and systematize those insights into packages that included background data on various contested countries, plus tactics and systems for counterinsurgency that supposedly could be applied virtually anywhere in the world.[46] Among sociologists, these tactics took the name "development theory"; among military planners the same approach came to be called "limited warfare."[47] Figure 12.5 is a reproduction of a slide from a social science seminar organized for the U.S. Army in the spring of 1962, as counterinsurgency warfare in Asia was beginning to reach full velocity. Note the integrated tactics—and the B-52s.[48]

The CIA spent tens of millions of dollars on communication research projects throughout the 1950s. It typically passed money through a front organization such as the Human Ecology Fund, the RAND Corporation, or one of several foundations.[49] This sponsorship, and the ostensibly civilian cover it enjoyed, encouraged what many people would consider to be criminal enterprises to enter the intellectual mainstream in the United States. At the Bureau of Social Science Research (BSSR) at

Figure 12.5
Sociology integrated into counterinsurgency: illustration from a 1962 U.S. Army symposium on "limited war."

American University in Washington, D.C., for example, researchers under contract to the CIA systematically documented the use of drugs, electroshock, and other forms of torture in interrogation of prisoners. A related project traced the steps leading to the psychological collapse of prisoners of war. In time, BSSR social scientists wrote up such projects for mainstream journals such as *Sociometry*, where they were received with some critical acclaim.[50] Another major CIA-funded communication research project provided a $1 million research grant to Hadley Cantril, a major figure in U.S. public opinion studies and a founder of the transactional analysis school of psychology.[51]

U.S. military projects also became central to the evolution of the discipline of communication research, including its *Zeitgeist* or overall perspective on communication itself. One example of U.S. Air Force programs will illustrate this. During the 1950s, the Air Force paid about a third of a million dollars to Stuart Dodd of the University of Washington to study the effects of propaganda leaflets dropped from airplanes. This became known as Project Revere, and it was one of the largest series of communication studies of its day. It since has been recognized as the foundation of what is known as diffusion research, the study of how messages move through a population.[52]

The project was both a study of propaganda and a propaganda project in its own right. Dodd's experiment consisted of dropping millions of leaflets (such as that shown in figure 12.6) on rural communities and small towns in Washington State, Alabama, and the far West. Using survey research, his team then tracked the dispersal of this message—*Communist bombers might attack your neighborhood*—through the population.[53] In fact, many of the communities targeted by Dodd's study were inaccessible to American commercial airliners, much less Soviet bombers. Among the more interesting results: children, in particular, were inclined to pick up pretty, fluttery papers dropped from airplanes. One may wonder how much Dodd or the Air Force remembered of these results when the Air Force went about designing the pretty, fluttery, air-dropped antipersonnel mines that took such a devastating toll on Vietnamese children a few years later.

The Dodd project simultaneously became a major source of overt and tacit promotion for psychological warfare within the academic community. Figure 12.7 presents Dodd's own list of what he termed "Revere-connected papers" published in the scholarly literature as of 1958.[54] The list includes substantial representation of Revere papers in virtually every major U.S. sociological publication of the day. Note particularly the titles. There is something interesting happening in the rhetoric of the field of communication research. The presentation of this work has taken on a strong aroma of "science," "objectivity," and "professionalism." The values and many of the political preconceptions of the psychological warfare projects are being absorbed into new, "scientificized" presentations of communication theory that tended to conceal the prejudices of the early 1950s programs under a new coat of "objective" rhetoric. Basic terms in the field began to change. Terms such as *propaganda* and *psychological warfare* fell out of favor; they became instead *international*

Figure 12.6
U.S. Air Force-sponsored communication research as propaganda. University of Washington scientists dropped millions of leaflets like this one on towns in the northwestern United States at the height of the "bomber gap" crisis.

communications, development, and *public diplomacy.* This was a refinement of the contradictory conceptual structures concerning communication discussed earlier.

This professionalization of the discipline brought with it a new rhetoric that downplayed the relatively blatant role of psychological warfare in mainstream mass communication research that had characterized the first decade after 1945. Scientists increasingly adopted a vocabulary that was self-consciously neutral, but that maintained (and in fact develop) the core conceptions of what communication "is" and what to do with it. This process of changing the labels while preserving the core paradigm can clearly be seen in the projects that were unfortunate enough to be caught on the cusp of the change.

At the Bureau of Social Science Research, for example, Chitra M. Smith prepared an extensive annotated bibliography in late 1952 titled *International Propaganda and Psychological Warfare.*[55] This was clearly an old-style presentation. It is useful from a historical point of view, because as an annotated bibliography, Smith's work provides a good indication of the scope of the concept of psychological warfare in 1952.

By 1956, however, the rhetorical tide had begun to turn. That year, the RAND Corporation published virtually the same bibliography with only two substantive changes: the title became *International Communication and Political Opinion* and two authors were credited—Bruce Lannes Smith and Chitra M. Smith.[56] The earlier acknowledgement of psychological warfare as the unifying theme of the collection—in fact, as its raison d'être—completely disappeared, *without* any change to the actual content of the work. This is one example of a broader process by which the "psychological warfare" of one generation became the "international communication" of the next.

A similar incident took place at Harvard's Russian Research Center. In 1954, Clyde Kluckhohn, Alex Inkeles, and Raymond Bauer prepared a psychological warfare study for the U.S. Air Force titled *Strategic Psychological and Sociological Strengths and Vulnerabilities of the Soviet Social System.*[57] Much of this work concerned the USSR's national communication system, which was Inkeles's specialty. In 1956, the authors deleted about a dozen pages of recommendations concerning psychological operations during nuclear war and published the remaining

Chart Two.

DR. STUART DODD'S LIST OF

'REVERE CONNECTED PAPERS' (1958)

BIBLIOGRAPHY OF REVERE-CONNECTED PAPERS

1. Bowerman, Charles, with Stuart C. Dodd and Otto N. Larsen, "Testing Message Diffusion—Verbal vs. Graphic Symbols," *International Social Science Bulletin*, UNESCO, Vol. 5, September 1953.
2. Catton, William R., Jr., "Exploring Techniques for Measuring Human Values," *American Sociological Review*, Vol. 19, 1954, pp. 49-55.
3. ———, and Melvin L. DeFleur, "The Limits of Determinacy in Attitude Measurement," *Social Forces*, Vol. 35, 1957, pp. 295-300.
4. ———, and Stuart C. Dodd, "Symbolizing the Values of Others," in *Symbols and Values: An Initial Study*, Thirteenth Symposium of the Conference on Science, Philosophy, and Religion, New York, Harper, 1954, Chap. 34, pp. 485-496.
5. ———, and Richard J. Hill, "Predicting the Relative Effectiveness of Leaflets: A Study in Selective Perception with Some Implications for Sampling," *Research Studies of the State College of Washington*, Proceedings of the Pacific Coast Sociological Society, 1953, Vol. 21, pp. 247-251.
6. DeFleur, Melvin L., and Ørjar Øyen, "The Spatial Diffusion of an Airborne Leaflet Message," *American Journal of Sociology*, Vol. 59, 1953, pp. 144-149.
7. Dodd, Stuart C., "The Interactance Hypothesis—A Gravity Model Fitting Physical Masses and Human Groups," *American Sociological Review*, Vol. 15, 1950, pp. 245-256.
8. ———, "Sociomatrices and Levels of Interaction—for Dealing with Plurels, Groups, and Organizations," *Sociometry*, Vol. 14, 1951, pp. 237-248.
9. ———, "On Classifying Human Values—a Step in the Prediction of Human Valuing," *American Sociological Review*, Vol. 16, 1951, pp. 645-653.
10. ———, "On All-or-None Elements and Mathematical Models for Sociologists," *American Sociological Review*, Vol. 17, 1952, pp. 167-177.
11. ——— and staff, "Testing Message Diffusing in C-Ville," *Research Studies of the State College of Washington*, Proceedings of the Pacific Coast Sociological Society, 1952, Vol. 20, 1952, pp. 83-91.
12. ———, "Testing Message Diffusion from Person to Person," *Public Opinion Quarterly*, Vol. 16, 1952, pp. 247-262.
13. ———, "Controlled Experiments on Interacting—Testing the Interactance Hypothesis Factor by Factor," read at the Sociological Research Association Conference, Atlantic City, N. J., September 1952.
14. ———, "Human Dimensions—a Re-search for Concepts to Integrate Thinking," *Main Currents in Modern Thought*, Vol. 9, 1953, pp. 106-113.
15. ———, "Testing Message Diffusion in Controlled Experiments: Charting the Distance and Time Factors in the Interactance Hypothesis," *American Sociological Review*, Vol. 18, 1953, pp. 410-416.
16. ———, "Can the Social Scientist Serve Two Masters—An Answer through Experimental Sociology," *Research Studies of the State College of Washington*, Proceedings of the Pacific Sociological Society, Vol. 21, 1953, pp. 195-213.
17. ———, "Formulas for Spreading Opinion—a Report of Controlled Experiments on Leaflet Messages in Project Revere," read at A.A.P.O.R. meetings, Madison, Wis., Apr. 14, 1955.
18. ———, "Diffusion Is Predictable: Testing Probability Models for Laws of Interaction," *American Sociological Review*, Vol. 20, 1955, pp. 392-401.
19. ———, "Testing Message Diffusion by Chain Tags," *American Journal of Sociology*, Vol. 61, 1956, pp. 425-432.

20. ———, "Testing Message Diffusion in Harmonic Logistic Curves," *Psychometrika*, Vol. 21, 1956, pp. 192-205.
21. ———, "A Predictive Theory of Public Opinion—Using Nine 'Mode' and 'Tense' Factors," *Public Opinion Quarterly*, Vol. 20, 1956, pp. 571-585.
22. ———, "Conditions for Motivating Men—the Valuance Theory for Motivating Behaviors in Any Culture," *Journal of Personality*, Vol. 25, 1957, pp. 489-504.
23. ———, "The Counteractance Model," *American Journal of Sociology*, Vol. 63, 1957, pp. 273-284.
24. ———, "A Power of Town Size Predicts Its Internal Interacting—a Controlled Experiment Relating the Amount of an Interaction to the Number of Potential Interactors," *Social Forces*, Vol. 36, 1957, pp. 132-137.
25. ———, with Edith D. Rainboth and Jiri Nehnevajsa, "Revere Studies on Interaction" (Volume ready for press).
26. Hill, Richard J., "A Note on Inconsistency in Paired Comparison Judgments," *American Sociological Review*, Vol. 18, 1953, pp. 564-566.
27. ———, "An Experimental Investigation of the Logistic Model of Message Diffusion," read at AAAS meeting, San Francisco, Calif., Dec. 27, 1954.
28. ———, with Stuart C. Dodd and Susan Huffaker, "Testing Message Diffusion—the Logistic Growth Curve in a School Population," read at the Biometrics Conference, Eugene, Ore., June 1952.
29. Larsen, Otto N., "The Comparative Validity of Telephone and Face-to-Face Interviews in the Measurement of Message Diffusion from Leaflets," *American Sociological Review*, Vol. 17, 1952, pp. 471-476.
30. ———, "Rumors in a Disaster," accepted for publication in *Journal of Communication*.
31. ———, and Melvin L. DeFleur, "The Comparative Role of Children and Adults in Propaganda Diffusion," *American Sociological Review*, Vol. 19, 1954, pp. 593-602.
32. ———, and Richard J. Hill, "Mass Media and Interpersonal Communication," *American Sociological Review*, Vol. 19, 1954, pp. 426-434.
33. Nehnevajsa, Jiri, and Stuart C. Dodd, "Physical Dimensions of Social Distance," *Sociology and Social Research*, Vol. 38, 1954, pp. 287-292.
34. Pence, Orville, and Dominic LaRusso, "A Study of Testimony: Content Distortion in Oral Person-to-Person Communication," submitted for publication.
35. Rainboth, Edith Dyer, and Melvin L. DeFleur, "Testing Message Diffusion in Four Communities: Some Factors in the Use of Airborne Leaflets as a Communication Medium," *American Sociological Review*, Vol. 17, 1952, pp. 734-737.
36. Rapoport, Anatol, "Nets with Distance Bias," *Bulletin of Mathematical Biophysics*, Vol. 13, 1951, pp. 85-91.
37. ———, "Connectivity of Random Nets," *Bulletin of Mathematical Biophysics*, Vol. 13, 1951, pp. 107-117.
38. ———, "The Probability Distribution of Distinct Hits on Closely Packed Targets," *Bulletin of Mathematical Biophysics*, Vol. 13, 1951, pp. 133-138.
39. ———, "'Ignition' Phenomena in Random Nets," *Bulletin of Mathematical Biophysics*, Vol. 14, 1952, pp. 35-44.
40. ———, "Contribution to the Mathematical Theory of Mass Behavior: I. The Propagation of Single Acts," *Bulletin of Mathematical Biophysics*, Vol. 14, 1952, pp. 159-169.
41. ———, "Response Time and Threshold of a Random Net," *Bulletin of Mathematical Biophysics*, Vol. 14, 1952, pp. 351-363.
42. ———, and Lionel I. Rebhun, "On the Mathematical Theory of Rumor Spread," *Bulletin of Mathematical Biophysics*, Vol. 14, 1952, pp. 375-383.
43. ———, "Contribution to the Mathematical Theory of Contagion and Spread of Information: I. Spread through a Thoroughly Mixed Population," *Bulletin of Mathematical Biophysics*, Vol. 15, 1953, pp. 173-183.

Figure 12.7
Stuart Dodd's list of "Revere-connected" papers (1958).

44. ——, "Spread of Information through a Population with Socio-structural Bias: I. Assumption of Transitivity," *Bulletin of Mathematical Biophysics*, Vol. 15, 1953, pp. 523-533.

45. ——, "Spread of Information through a Population with Socio-structural Bias: II. Various Models with Partial Transitivity," *Bulletin of Mathematical Biophysics*, Vol. 15, 1953, pp. 535-546.

46. ——, "Spread of Information through a Population with Socio-structural Bias: III. Suggested Experimental Procedures," *Bulletin of Mathematical Biophysics*, Vol. 16, 1954, pp. 75-81.

47. Shaw, John G., "Testing Message Diffusion in Relation to Demographic Variables: an Analysis of Respondents to an Airborne Leaflet Message," submitted for publication.

48. Turabian, Chahin, and Stuart C. Dodd, "A Dimensional System of Human Values," Transactions Second World Congress of Sociology, International Sociology Association, 1954, pp. 100-105.

49. Winthrop, Henry, and Stuart C. Dodd, "A Dimensional Theory of Social Diffusion—an Analysis, Modeling and Partial Testing of One-way Interacting," *Sociometry*, Vol. 16, 1953, pp. 180-202.

Theses

50. M.A. Catton, William R., Jr., "The Sociological Study of Human Values," 1952.

51. M.A. Øyen, Ørjar, "The Relationship between Distances and Social Interaction—the Case of Message Diffusion," 1953.

52. Ph.D. Catton, William R., Jr., "Propaganda Effectiveness as a Function of Human Values," 1954.

53. Ph.D. DeFleur, Melvin Lawrence, "Experimental Studies of Stimulus Response Relationships in Leaflet Communication," 1954.

54. Ph.D. Hill, Richard J., "Temporal Aspects of Message Diffusion," 1955.

55. Ph.D. Larsen, Otto N., "Interpersonal Relations in the Social Diffusion of Messages," 1955.

56. Ph.D. Shaw, John G., Jr., "The Relationship of Selected Ecological Variables to Leaflet Message Response," 1954.

57. M.A. West, S. S., "Variation of Compliance to Airborne Leaflet Messages with Age and with Terminal Level of Education," 1956.

Monographs Published

58. DeFleur, Melvin L., and Otto N. Larsen, *The Flow of Information*, New York, Harper, 1958.

Figure 12.7
(continued)

400-page text under the title *How the Soviet System Works*. That book, in turn, became a standard graduate reader in U.S. studies of the USSR throughout the 1960s. The Kluckhohn, Inkeles, and Bauer text thus moved from its original incarnation as a relatively naïve how-to manual for the exploitation of a rival system to make a much more sweeping— yet paradoxically more seemingly objective and scientific—claim concerning how Soviet reality "works."[58]

Conclusion

In conclusion, then, the following pattern becomes apparent. First, a prototypical paradigm of communication-as-domination and the research techniques for applying it emerged from the war, class conflict, and the early organization of mass markets via newspapers and radio during the first decades of this century. Lasswell's and Lazarsfeld's insights and methodologies, for example, permitted forms of audience measurement without which the structure of modern radio and television probably could not exist. In this way, early communication research often became one instrument in a broader campaign of suppression of discourse other than the messages and values promulgated by monopoly enterprises and central governments.

Second, World War II encouraged the construction of a network of scientists and state sponsors for psychological warfare. That is what the Clausen study showed.

Third, this network played a pivotal role in creating a new branch of social science, euphemistically termed "communication research," which in turn further developed and institutionalized a highly influential framework for how "communication" itself was to be regarded. That work helped enforce the preconceptions and worldview of mainstream U.S. social science and, in an indirect and more complex manner, of U.S. society as a whole. As James Carey has put it, "We first produce the world by symbolic work, and then take up residence in the world we have produced. Alas," he continues, "there is magic in our self deceptions."[59] By the 1970s, the institutions created during the evolution of communication research—graduate schools, social science think tanks, professional societies, and the like—had won considerable public and commercial sector funding and emerged as the main centers for advanced training in the United States of men and women who might well be called professional ideological workers.

Finally, this essay has discussed briefly the conceptual structures used for thinking about communication and social order, and euphemism's important role in providing cover for scientific enterprises that many people might otherwise regard as criminal. Such euphemisms seem to be essential in maintaining the otherwise obvious split between society's professed values—the reasons it claims for doing things—and its actual behavior.

Notes

1. William Colby, with James McCargar, *Lost Victory* (Chicago: Contemporary Books, 1989), 281, 331–33. Colby's figures, it should be noted, cover the period 1968–71 only, although the program continued in various forms until at least 1975. Colby's version seeks to distance the CIA from responsibility for murders, and stresses the political and sociological aspects of Phoenix. For a detailed discussion from a more critical point of view of the evolution and tactics of Phoenix, see Douglas Valentine, *The Phoenix Program* (New York: William Morrow, 1990).

2. Colby, *Lost Victory*, 253.

3. Ibid., 259.

4. Massachusetts Institute of Technology, Center for International Studies, "The Center for International Studies: A Description," MIT, Cambridge, July 1955. See also U.S. Department of State, Foreign Service Institute, "Problems of Development and Internal Defense," Country Team Seminar, June 11, 1962.

5. In order to maintain a tight focus, this essay exclusively tracks the role of U.S. government psychological warfare, propaganda, and intelligence programs in U.S. mass communication research. It is not intended to be a complete history of the field or of the forces that shaped it. Commercial research and strictly academic developments have also been important, of course. The latter is a comfortable topic that continues to be discussed exhaustively in mainstream mass communication historiography, often without serious consideration of the social and economic context in which the academic work was performed. The former often has been ignored (with a few noteworthy exceptions), as has the government's psychological warfare effort.

Some of the best overviews of the professionalization of communication research during the first half of the 1950s, the emergence of doctorate-granting institutions, and so on include Jean M. Converse, *Survey Research in the United States* (Berkeley: University of California Press, 1987); Daniel Czitrom, *Media and the*

American Mind (Chapel Hill: University of North Carolina Press, 1982); Jesse Delia, "Communication Research: A History," in *Handbook of Communication Science*, ed. Charles Berger and Steven Chaffee (Newbury Park, Calif.: Sage, 1987), 20–98.

On ideological workers: today a substantial majority of employers of entry-level television and radio reporters, newspaper and magazine editors and writers, many types of advertising specialists, and public relations personnel (or, to use the currently preferred term, "public communication" experts) require new hires to arrive with advanced degrees in one of several varieties of mass communication study. See W. W. Schwed, "Hiring, Promotion, Salary, Longevity Trends Charted at Dailies," *Newspaper Research Journal* (October 1981); Lee Becker, J. W. Fruit, and S. L. Caudill, *The Training and Hiring of Journalists* (Norwood, N.J.: Ablex, 1987); Lee Becker and Thomas Engleman, "Class of '87 Describes Salaries, Satisfaction Found in Jobs," *Journalism Educator*, Spring 1989.

6. Albert Biderman and Elizabeth Crawford, *The political Economy of Social Research: The Case of Sociology* (Springfield, Va.: Clearinghouse for Federal Scientific and Technological Information, 1968).

7. On BASR, see Converse, *Survey Research*, 269, 275–76, 506–7, fn. 37, fn. 42. On Cantril's IISR, see John Crewdson and Joseph Treaster, "The CIA's 3-Decade Effort to Mold the World's Views," *New York Times*, December 25, 26, 27, 1977, with discussion of Cantril and the IISR on December 26. For Cantril's version, which conceals the true source of his funds, see Hadley Cantril, *The Human Dimension: Experiences in Policy Research* (New Brunswick, N.J.: Rutgers University Press, 1967). On CENIS, see Christopher Simpson, *Psychological Warfare and Communication Research: Science, Power, and Sociology in the Cold War* (New York: Oxford University Press, forthcoming); Ithiel de Sola Pool, "The Necessity for Social Scientists Doing Research for Governments," *Background*, August 1966. Other major communication research projects that depended heavily on funding from U.S. government psychological warfare agencies included the National Opinion Research Center, the Survey Research Center (now the Institute for Social Research), and the Bureau of Social Science Research, among others. The text that follows discusses these in more detail.

8. For details on the Department of State contracts, which produced a scandal when they were uncovered in 1957, see U.S. Congress, House, Committee on Government Operations, *State Department Opinion Polls*, 85th Cong., 1st Sess., June–July 1957 (Washington, D.C.: U.S. Government Printing Office, 1957).

9. Albert Biderman, "Social-Psychological Needs and 'Involuntary' Behavior as Illustrated by Compliance in Interrogation," Sociometry (June 1960); Louis Gottschalk, *The Use of Drugs in Information-Seeking Interviews*, Bureau of Social Science Research Report No. 322 (December 1958), BSSR Archives, series II, box 11, University of Maryland Libraries Special Collections, College Park, Md.; Albert Biderman, Barbara Heller, and Paula Epstein, A *Selected Bibliography on Captivity Behavior*, Bureau of Social Science Research Report No. 339-1 (February 1961), BSSR Archives, Series II, box 14, University of Maryland

Libraries Special Collection, College Park, Md. Biderman acknowledges the Human Ecology Fund—a well-known CIA conduit—and U.S. Air Force Contract No. AF 49 (638)727 as the source of his funding for this work. For more on the CIA's use of the Human Ecology Fund and the related Society for the Investigation of Human Ecology, see John Marks, *The Search for the Manchurian Candidate* (New York: Times Books, 1979), 147–63.

10. Walter Lippmann, *Public Opinion* (New York: Harcourt Brace, 1922); Harold Lasswell, *Propaganda Technique in the World War* (Cambridge: MIT Press, 1971 [1926]).

11. Lippmann, *Public Opinion*, 31, 32. John Dewey wrote that Lippmann's writing style was so accomplished that "one finishes the book almost without realizing that it is perhaps the most effective indictment of democracy as currently conceived ever penned"; *New Republic*, May 3, 1922. W. S. Myers commented that Lippmann "is essentially a propagandist, and his work is influenced by this characteristic attitude of approach toward any subject"; *Bookmark*, June 1922. Lippmann was a publicist for U.S. expeditionary forces during World War I, and later executive secretary of the Inquiry, an early U.S. intelligence agency set up to support U.S. negotiators at the Versailles peace talks.

12. Lasswell advocated what he viewed as a scientific application of persuasion and precise violence, in contrast to bludgeon tactics, to achieve more effective social control. "Successful social and political management often depends on proper coordination of propaganda with coercion, violent or nonviolent; economic inducement (including bribery); diplomatic negotiation; and other techniques," he wrote. Harold Lasswell, Ralph Casey, and Bruce Lannes Smith, *Propaganda and Promotional Activities: An Annotated Bibliography*, (Chicago: University of Chicago Press, 1969 [1935]), 43. See also Harold Lasswell, "Propaganda," in *Encyclopedia of the Social Sciences*, vol. 11 (New York: Macmillan, 1937), 524–25. Although Lasswell's importance as a theoretician of social control has long been recognized, it has been brought to renewed public attention in the United States in recent years largely through Noam Chomsky's media studies. See Noam Chomsky, *Intellectuals and the State* (Netherlands: Johan Huizinga-lezing, 1977), 9 ff.; Noam Chomsky, "Democracy and the Media," in *Necessary Illusions: Thought Control in Democratic Societies* (Boston: South End, 1989).

13. To carry this point further, the elaboration of the Lippmann-Lasswell model of what communication "is" permitted communication research to become in part a method for the *suppression* of indigenous, rival approaches to communication.

As noted in the text, the evolution of pervasive consumer capitalism is interlocked with development of techniques to measure the extent and responses of mass audiences to various forms of communication. The sales of products and services in a mass society, in turn, depend to an important degree on the advertiser's success in substituting its values and preconceptions for those previously held by its audience. Automobile marketers, for example, do not tout their products simply for their usefulness as transportation; they seek to define their customers' self-esteem in terms of owning or using the product to the greatest degree possible. Thus, people do not simply purchase commodities, they become them—both literally and figuratively—and that transformation can take place only at the expense of rival systems of human society and consciousness.

My thinking on this point was spurred by Oskar Negt's discussion of Horkheimer and Adorno in "Mass Media: Tools of Domination or Instruments of Liberation? Aspects of the Frankfurt School's Communication Analysis," *New German Critique* (Spring 1978): 61 ff.

14. Arthur Smith, Jr., "Life in Wartime Germany: Colonel Ohlendorf's Opinion Service," *Public Opinion Quarterly* (Spring 1972): 72; Lawrence Stokes, "The Sicherheitsdienst (SD) of the Reichsfuhrer SS and German Public Opinion," doctoral dissertation, Johns Hopkins University, 1972.

15. Ibid.; Carsten Klingemann, "Angewandate Soziologie im Nationalsozialismus," *1999, Zeitschrift fur Sozialgeschichte des 20 und 21 Jahrhunderts* (January 1989), 25; Christoph Cobet (Hrsg.) *Einfuhrung in Fragen an die Soziologie in Deutschland nach Hilter 1945–1950* (Frankfurt am Main: Verlag Christoph Cobet, 1988). For an examination of interlocking problems concerning German geographical studies of the same period, which overlapped in certain respects with communication studies, see Mechtild Roessler, *Wissenschaft und Lebensraum: Geographische Ostforschung im Nationalsozialismus* (Berlin: Dietrich Reimer Verlag, 1990).

16. Chris Raymond, "Professor Is Accused of Promulgating Anti-Semitic Views as Journalist in Germany and U.S. in World War II, "*Chronicle of Higher Education*, December 11, 1991.

17. Ladislas Farago, *German Psychological Warfare* (New York: Putnam, 1941). For history of the origin of the term, see William Daugherty, "Changing Concepts," in *Psychological Warfare Casebook*, ed. William Daugherty and Morris Janowitz (Baltimore: Operations Research Office, Johns Hopkins University Press, 1958), 12.

18. Alfred Paddock, *U.S. Army Special Warfare: Its Origins* (Washington, D.C.: National Defense University Press, 1982, 5–8, 23–37.

19. John Clausen, "Research on the American Soldier as a Career Contingency," *Social Psychology Quarterly* 47 (1987), 207 ff.; Simpson, *Psychological Warfare and Communication Research*.

20. On Roper and Wilson, see Converse, Survey Research, 171–72. On Doob and Lietes, see Daniel Lerner, *Propaganda in War and Crisis* (New York: George Stewart, 1951), vii–viii. On Kluckhohn, Leighton, Lowenthal, and Schramm, see William Daugherty and Morris Janowitz, eds., *Psychological Warfare Casebook* (Baltimore: Operations Research Office, Johns Hopkins University Press, 1958), xiii–xiv. On Speier, see Christine Nasso, ed., *Contemporary Authors* (1st rev.), vol. 21–24 (Detroit: Gale Research, 1969), 829. On Barrett, see Edward Barrett, *Truth Is Our Weapon* (New York: Funk & Wagnalls, 1953), 31–32. After Barrett's death, the Associated Press identified him as a former member of the

the OSS; see "Edward Barrett Dies; Started Columbia Journalism Review," *Washington Post*, October 26, 1989. On contracts with Lazarsfeld, Stanton, et al., see Converse, *Survey Research*, 163, 172, 309.

21. On Leites and Eulau, see Wilbur Schramm, "Beginnings of Communications Study," in *The Media Revolution in America and Western Europe*, ed. Everett Rogers and Francis Balle (Norwood, N.J.: Ablex, 1985), 205; Harold Lasswell and Nathan Lietes, *The Language of Politics* (New York: George Stewart, 1949), 298. On Ithiel de Sola Pool, see Lasswell and Lietes also, pp. 153, 334 ff.

22. Clause, "Research on the American Soldier."

23. Mallory Brown, "Evaluation of the National Psychological Effort of [the] U.S." with attachment "Proposed Consultant Panels," April 8, 1952, in records of the Psychological Strategy Board, File PSB 091.412, No. 2, Harry S. Truman Presidential Library, Independence, Mo.

24. U.S. Congress, Senate, Committee on Military Affairs, *Hearings on Science Legislation (5.1297)*, 79th Cong., 1st Sess., October–November 1945, part 4, 899–902.

25. Ibid., chart follows 900.

26. Shearon Lowery and Melvin De Fleur, *Milestones in Mass Communication Research* (New York: Longman, 1983).

27. American Association for Public Opinion Research Conference Proceedings, "Contributions of Opinion Research to Psychological Warfare," *Public Opinion Quarterly* (Winter 1951–52): 802.

28. Biderman and Crawford, the Political Economy of Social Research, 40–44.

29. Lerner, Propaganda in War, 355–66. The data in Lerner are draw from U.S. Strategic Bombing Survey, Morale Division, *The Effects of Strategic Bombing on German Morale*, vol. 1, 33–37.

30. U.S. National Security Council, *NSC 4: Coordination of Foreign Information Measures*, December 9, 1947, RG 273, U.S. National Archives, Washington, D.C.

31. Barrett, *Truth Is Our Weapon*.

32. U.S. National Security Council, *NSC 4-A: Psychological Operations*, December 9, 1947, RG 273, U.S. National Archives, Washington, D.C.

33. U.S. National Security Council, *NSC 10/2: Office of Special Projects*, June 15, 1948, RG 273, U.S. National Archives, Washington, D.C. For a good overview of modern U.S. clandestine warfare, see John Prados, *The President's Secret Wars* (New York: Morrow, 1986).

34. National Science Foundation, *Federal Funds for Science* (Washington, D.C.: U.S. Government Printing Office, 1953), 39–40. The major private foundations cooperated closely with federal psychological warfare programs and became closely intertwined with them, despite frequent claims to the contrary. "Perhaps most intriguing" in this regard, Clausen writes in the same study cited earlier, "was the number of our members who became foundation executives. Charles

Dollard became president of Carnegie. Donald Young shifted from the Presidency of SSRC [Social Science Research Council] to that of Russell Sage [a major funder and publisher of U.S. sociological studies], where he ultimately recruited Leonard Cottrell. Leland Devinney went from Harvard to the Rockefeller Foundation. William McPeak . . . helped set up the Ford Foundation and became its vice president." Clausen also offers a list of further examples.

Some foundations provided cover for intelligence agency funds passed to scholars, and often provided seed money for psychological warfare and mass persuasion research projects considered too hot to handle by public propaganda agencies such as the Voice of America. Carl Hovland's now-classic studies at Yale, for example, tested the effects of various types of propaganda appeals on audiences, including use of threats, fear, atrocity stories, and neutral education. Hovland's work technically was funded by Carnegie, but remained closely coordinated with, and dependent upon, Department of Defense projects throughout its existence. Hovland's work remains widely recognized as the scientific foundation of much of modern advertising. See Carl Hovland, Arthur Lumsdaine, and Fred Sheffield, *Experiments on Mass Communication*, vol. 3 of the *American Soldier* series (Princeton, N.J.: Princeton University Press, 1949); Carl Hovland, Irving Janis, and H. H. Kelley, *Communication and Persuasion* (New Haven, Conn.: Yale University Press, 1953). For an overview of the Hovland work and its impact, see Werner Severin and James Tankard, *Communication Theories*, 2d ed. New York: Longman, 1988), 159–77; for Hovland's role in psychological warfare research and operations, see Simpson, *Psychological Warfare and Communication Research*.

35. Harry Alpert, "Opinion and Attitude Surveys in the U.S. Government," *Public Opinion Quarterly* (Spring 1952). Alpert states in the introduction of this article that virtually all military-, intelligence-, and foreign propaganda-related studies have seen excluded from the scope of his article.

36. Converse, *Survey Research*, 340–41, 353, 357.

37. Clyde Kluckhohn, Alex Inkeles, and Raymond Bauer, *Strategic Psychological and Sociological Strengths and Vulnerabilities of the Soviet Social System* (USAF Contract No. 33[038]-12909) (Cambridge: Russian Research Center, Harvard University, 1954), 20–22 and Annex 1 (on ISR role) and 360–68 (on use in strategic air offensive against the USSR).

38. Converse, *Survey Research*, 353, 531, fn. 17.

39. Converse, *Survey Research*, 309, 321–22, 327. See also House Committee on Government Operations, *State Department Opinion Polls*.

40. Charles Fritz and Eli Marks, "The NORC Studies of Human Behavior in Disasters," *Journal of Social Issues* 10, no. 3 (1954): 26–41.

41. Converse, *Survey Research*, 269, 275–76, 506–7, fn. 37, fn. 42.

42. On Air Force and Office of Naval Research studies, see ibid., 290, 506, fn. 37. On the Voice of American study, see Daniel Lerner, with Lucille Pevsner, *Passing of Traditional Society: Modernizing the Middle East* (Glencoe, Ill.: Free Press, 1958), 79–80. The Lerner study, which was conducted by CENIS using

BASR data, is widely regarded as the foundation of the U.S. school of "development theory," which specializes in U.S. tactics in developing countries. For more detailed work on the origins of development theory, see Rohan Samarajiva and Peter Shields, "Integration, Telecommunication, and Development: Power in the Paradigms," *Journal of Communication* (Summer 1990), 84 ff.; Rohan Samarajiva, "The Murky Beginnings of the Communication and Development Field," in *Rethinking Development Communication*, ed. N. Jayaweera and S. Amunugama (Singapore, Asian Mass Communication and Development Centre, 1987).

43. Lerner, *Passing of Traditional Society*, 79–80.

44. Simpson, *Psychological Warfare and Communication Research*. See also Bruce Lannes Smith, "Trends in Research in International Communication and Opinion, 1945–1955," *Public Opinion Quarterly* (Spring 1956).

45. For the role of Philippines counterinsurgency in the evolution of U.S. limited war strategy, see D. Michael Shafer, *Deadly Paradigms: The Failure of U.S. Counterinsurgency Policy* (Princeton, N.J.: Princeton University Press, 1988), 205–39.

46. MIT. CIS, "The Center for International Studies"; U.S. Department of State, FSI, "Problems of Development and Internal Defense."

47. William Lybrand, ed., *The U.S. Army's Limited-War Mission and Social Science Research*, symposium proceedings. (Washington, D.C.: Special Operation Research Office, 1962).

48. Ibid., chart follows 28.

49. For *New York Times* and Lloyd Free's acknowledgment of the CIA's $1 million grant to Cantril, see note 7. On the CIA's use of the Human Ecology Fund and the related Society for the Investigation of Human Ecology as a conduit for clandestine funding of social science research, see Marks, *The Search for the Manchurian Candidate*, 147–63. On CIA contracting with the RAND Corporation, see Bruce L.R. Smith, *The RAND Corporation* (Cambridge: Harvard University Press, 1966); RAND Corporation, *RAND 25th Anniversary Volume* (Santa Monica, Calif.: RAND Corporation, c. 1974).

50. For examples of CIA-funded studies of torture of prisoners, see note 9. For secret U.S. government research into use of LSD, electroshock, insulin shock, and related "interrogation" techniques, see Marks, *The Search for the Manchurian Candidate*; Martin Lee and Bruce Shlain, *Acid Dreams* (New York: Grove, 1985).

51. On funding for Cantril, see note 7. Cantril's first target became a study of protest voters in France, whom the CIA regarded as hostile to U.S. foreign policy. Cantril followed the French study with a tour of the USSR under private scholarly cover and public opinion and mass media analyses of a series of countries that might serve as a checklist for CIA interventions of the period: Cuba, Brazil, the Dominican Republic, Egypt, India, Nigeria, the Philippines, Poland, and so on. On Cantril's studies in France, see Hadley Cantril, *The Politics of Despair*

(New York: Basic Books, 1958). On Cantril's studies in the USSR and the Third World, see Cantril, *The Human Dimension*, 1–5, 131–44.

U.S. public opinion about foreign affairs, particularly about the Vietnam War and other controversial issues, became a major preoccupation of the research institute that Cantril founded with CIA funds. In those surveys, Cantril introduced an important methodological innovation by breaking out Americans' political opinions by their demographic characteristics and their place on an ideological spectrum he had devised—a forerunner of the political opinion analysis techniques that have revolutionized U.S. election campaigns during the past decade. See Lloyd Free and Hadley Cantril, *The Political Beliefs of Americans* (New Brunswick, N.J.: Rutgers University Press, 1967). For an example of modern usage of a similar technique, see "Redefining the American Electorate," *Washington Post*, October 1, 1987, A-12, with data provided by the Times Mirror-Gallup organization.

52. Lowery and De Fleur, *Milestones*, 205–31. See also Stuart Dodd, "Testing Message Diffusion from Person to Person," *Public Opinion Quarterly* (Summer 1952), 247 ff. Air Force contract No. AF 13(038)-27522 underwrote much of the Project Revere enterprise.

53. Copies of some Revere leaflets are available via the University Archives at the University of Washington Libraries and in the papers of the Marks *Manchurian Candidate* study, which are now held by the National Security Archive, Washington, D.C. On the key role of children in diffusing air-dropped messages, see Otto Larsen and Melvin De Fleur, "The Comparative Role of Children and Adults in Propaganda Diffusion," *American Sociological Review* 19 (1954): 593–602.

54. Stuart Dodd, "Formulas for Spreading Opinions," *Public Opinion Quarterly* (Winter 1958): 537.

55. Chitra M. Smith, *International Propaganda and Psychological Warfare: An Annotated Bibliography*, BSSR Archives, Series II, Box 7, Project 819, university of Maryland Libraries Special Collections, College Park, Md.

56. Bruce Lannes Smith and Chitra M. Smith, *International Communication and Public Opinion* (Princeton, N.J.: RAND Corporation and Princeton University Press, 1956).

57. Kluckhohn, Inkeles, and Bauer, *Strategic Psychological and Sociological Strengths*.

58. Raymond Bauer, Alex Inkeles, and Clyde Kluckhohn, *How the Soviet System Works: Cultural, Psychological and Social Themes* (New York: Vintage, 1961 [1956]).

59. James Carey, *Communication as Culture* (Boston: Unwin Hyman, 1989), 30.

Informal Relationships: Working with the Government

13

From Radio Research to Communications Intelligence: Rockefeller Philanthropy, Communications Specialists, and the American Policy Community

William Buxton
1994

Lasswell's Formula and Marshall's Chart

Who
Says What
In Which Channel
To Whom
With What Effect?

These words of Harold Lasswell, introducing an article that he wrote in 1948 (Lasswell, 1948: 37), have come to enjoy a mantra-like status within the field of communication studies. For mainstream thinkers, Lasswell's formula has been recurrently used as a framework for discussing research findings in the discipline (DeFleur and Ball-Rokeach, 1975: 208). Even scholars of a more critical disposition have found Lasswell's prophetic statement to be of value in orienting research in the field. William Leiss devoted the 1990 Southam lecture (given each year at the annual meetings of the Canadian Communication Association) to an exploration of how the "message transmission" theory, as developed by Lasswell and elaborated a year later by Shannon and Weaver (1949), could serve as the basis for integrating research results in the area of public policy communications (Leiss, 1991: 2).

In deploying the message transmission theory to codify research initiatives in communications, writers like DeFleur, Ball-Rokeach, and Leiss have assumed that understanding its meaning is unproblematic. As a matter of course, they have treated Lasswell's formula as nothing more than a set of abstract categories that could serve as a template for imparting coherence to research in communications. They have, in effect, largely begged the questions of where the words originated, why they were selected by Lasswell, what they had come to mean at the time they were written, through which channels they had been directed, and to whom they had been addressed. In what follows, I use an exploration of the origins of Lasswell's formula as a point of departure for critically examining how the field of communications emerged in the United States during the decade prior to the end of World War II. In doing so, I give particular attention to how the Rockefeller Foundation was able to shape and direct the course of communication studies in accordance with its views on how the production of social scientific knowledge could be brought to bear on matters of public concern. It is hoped that an analysis of this kind might help communication studies learn from the lessons of its past in order to confront the nature and meaning of current intellectual practices in the field.

As Morrison (1978) has pointed out, Lasswell's formula can be traced to a series of seminars held in 1939–1940, sponsored and organized by the Rockefeller Foundation. A number of leading figures doing research in communications took part with the intent of "conceptualizing and organizing the field." It was during these meetings, Morrison claims, "that Lasswell first developed his now celebrated model of the communication process—who says what to whom in what channel with what effect—a conceptual model which had tremendous importance for the field's future history" (Morrison, 1978: 358).

Morrison is correct in attributing the origins of Lasswell's formula to the seminars. But a closer reading of the relevant documentation reveals not only that the concept had a different authorship but that it had a much different meaning and purpose within its original context. To a large extent, the authorship and purpose were closely related. Although undoubtedly all the members of the seminar contributed to the genesis of the communications schema,[1] it was John Marshall, associate director of the Humanities Division of the Rockefeller Foundation, who appears to have provided its initial formulation. And this formulation, as we will now examine, was inherently linked to Marshall's practical vision of the role in public life to be played by the emergent field of communications.

The formula first emerged at a meeting of the seminar held on May 8, 1940 (Rockefeller Archive Center, 1940c). In order to conclude the seminar with a coherent account of the year's work, Marshall suggested the need to systematize what had been discussed:

He hoped that a "chart" of research in the communications field might be developed, clarifying the need for such research, outlining the research itself, showing the interpretations that might develop from it and their significance, and suggesting the outcomes which might be expected. Such a chart is needed to lay the basis for the co-ordination and supplementation of parallel studies in the three fields of communication. (Rockefeller Archive Center, 1940c: 1)[2]

After considerable discussion of the issues raised by his initial comments, Marshall summarized what had been said in the following manner:

General answers of a valid character are not to be expected. Valid answers can be found only when specific problems are framed. The field of communications research lacks basic data on how people's experiences are being modified by communications. A "chart" is necessary, applicable in any study, which would remind those carrying it of the context which must be taken into account; a "chart" fixing the context within which studies, to be adequate, must be undertaken. In addition to defining the context, it should list the resources for implementing that context. If studies were structured in this way, it would furnish an integrating mechanism. (Rockefeller Archive Center, 1940c: 5)

The members of the seminar agreed that the process of charting would be attempted at the next meeting, to be held in June 1940. This was to involve the listing of a series of questions, along with the sources that were available to answer them. A number of the seminar members were assigned particular parts of the chart to complete (Rockefeller Archive Center, 1940c: 5).

Although no record of the subsequent—and possibly final—session of the seminar could be found, a number of the "parts" of the chart, as prepared by seminar members, have been preserved. Taken together, they reveal that Lasswell's formula not only originated in the seminar but had begun to serve as a framework for ordering and systematizing research. Marshall (1940a) wrote the introduction to the chart, which now took the form of a draft memorandum. He drew particular attention to "mass communication" and how it might be analyzed.[3] The analysis of mass communications was of "value to those who direct their use—particularly those who are conscientious in meeting the responsibilities that entails" (Marshall, 1940a: 2). Overall, the thesis of the memorandum was "that study of what mass communications are today doing in American society can yield knowledge which will be of practical value both to those who direct the use of the media of mass communication and to those concerned with their control in the public interest—not only governmental agencies, but industrial and civic groups as well (Marshall, 1940a: 4). The memorandum could be considered a success if "it will lead others to agree that the time has come to undertake systematic observation and reporting on the current flow of mass communications, its trends through time, and its effect through time" (Marshall, 1940a: 5). Research of this kind was of practical value to those in control of mass media because it would provide "knowledge of what effect can be expected for a given type of communication, at a given time, and under given circumstances." Knowledge of this kind would be built up from the results of specific studies. These, in turn, could be of immediate practical value "if they are made to deal with communications bearing on questions of evident social importance." As Marshall emphasized, special studies must have a "general view of mass communications" as their context, if they are to realize their full value:

Analysis of the effect of any given communication . . . involves answering the basic question, *to whom was it said*. To generalize any specific finding on effect, the investigator . . . must be able to relate *what was said* to *what was being said* through the various media at the time in question and at earlier times. Finally, he must be able to relate *what is said to who said it*, and if possible, to the intention that the communicator had. (Marshall, 1940a: 6; emphasis added)

The remainder of the "parts," written by other members of the seminar, fleshed out the schema. Lasswell (1940) addressed the question of who communicates. Gorer (1940) discussed how content could be classified. Waples (1940) wrote a short account of how effects might be examined. Finally, Lazarsfeld (1940a) wrote on audience research, in effect addressing the "whom" to which mass communication is directed.

Mass communications was not simply chosen for study because of its inherent fascination; it was of interest because it was so closely bound up with problems of generating public consent for the policy measures undertaken during the "emergency" period of World War II. The draft document arising from the seminar can best be viewed as a strategic vehicle for institutionalizing communications research along particular lines. It represented an effort by communications researchers to make their emergent field relevant to the problems faced by policy-makers with the onset of a period of emergency. What remains to be better understood is how and why this institutionalization occurred, and the role of the Rockefeller Foundation in the process. We will now examine more in detail how a "communications group" developed to the point of being poised to make its presence felt in the wartime effort. This will involve an examination of the background to the group's formation with particular reference to how Rockefeller philanthropy became involved in communications through its sponsorship of the Princeton Radio Research Project and related initiatives. I will conclude by briefly considering how the Rockefeller Foundation was instrumental in mediating between communications researchers and governmental officials after the conclusion of the communications seminar of 1939–1940.

The Princeton Radio Research Project

In May 1937, the Rockefeller trustees approved a grant to Hadley Cantril of $67,000 over two years to be administered by the School of Public and International Affairs at Princeton University (Rockefeller Archive Center, 1937a). The main concern of the study was to examine "the essential value of radio to all types of listeners." Cantril maintained that "if radio is to serve the best interests of the people, it is essential that an objective analysis be made of what these interests are, and how the unique psychological and social characteristics of radio may be devoted to them." Moreover, the study sought to develop methodological techniques appropriate to the analysis of the radio audience (Cantril, 1937).

Cantril's study was part of a broader program of research administered by the Federal Radio Educational Committee (FREC). The body had been formed by the Federal Communications Commission in 1935 to "formulate plans for furthering cooperation between broadcasters and various non-profit groups."[4] Composed of representatives from both broadcasters and educators, FREC had as one of its major goals the undertaking of "a thoroughgoing study of how educational broadcasting is to be financed, or more particularly how the expense involved is to be shared by the broadcasters, educational agencies, the foundations, and possibly the government" (Marshall, 1935: May 15–16). To this end, it formed numerous research committees whose collective goal was to produce findings that would help to reconcile differences between educators and broadcasters. As it became increasingly evident that the projects proposed by the research committees were potentially far too costly and badly in need of streamlining, a "Committee of Six" was formed, consisting of three broadcasters and three educators.[5] It was given the task of combining some of the studies in order to reduce its costs (Studebaker, 1937). Ultimately, the Committee of Six evolved into FREC's executive committee, charged with the responsibility of overseeing the projects and generating funding for them from the broadcasting industry and other private sources.

John Marshall, working on behalf of the Humanities Division of the Rockefeller Foundation, adeptly worked through FREC to advance his agenda for communications research. The Committee of Six, in this sense, served a dual purpose. On the one hand, through his contacts on the committee (particularly Willis, Tyson, and Cantril), he was able to have some influence on the committee's choice of research projects. Working closely with the committee, the Foundation was able to generate funding from a variety of sources for a focused set of research initiatives. In effect, by virtue of its own prestige and influence the Rockefeller Foundation had been able to give FREC credibility in the eyes of industry, so much so that they were willing to provide funding for some of its projected studies. Having thus established the credibility of this committee, John Marshall was able to argue to the Rockefeller Foundation trustees that any funding allocated to FREC-sponsored studies would be subject to review by a group who had "the public interest" of radio broadcasting in mind.

This argument appeared to be crucial for generating support for Cantril's research proposal. In making the case to the trustees for support of the study, Marshall stressed that the project was part of a broader program of research within FREC, which had been supported by the radio industry. As he noted, not only had the industry's representatives supported the Committee of Six as a coordinating agency, but they had agreed to underwrite some of the projects at considerable cost (Marshall, 1937). Evidently swayed by the case Marshall had made, the trustees attached a good deal of weight to the fact that Cantril's study would be vetted by the Committee of Six:

As findings are to be released only through this Executive Committee, they will automatically carry the approval of three representatives of the industry whose authority cannot be questioned. At the same time, the presence on the Executive of three prominent educators assures due protection for educational and cultural interests. (Rockefeller Archive Center, 1937a)

Hence, they viewed the proposal as potentially significant because work of this kind was "fundamental for the success of the co-operative efforts of the radio industry and non-commercial agencies that are directed towards broadening radio's range of public service" (Rockefeller Archive Center, 1937a).

The Princeton Radio Research Project was initially supported because Rockefeller officials felt that it potentially could yield important insights into how commercial broadcasting could incorporate more educational material into its programming. It was believed that if the tastes and interests of the listening audience were better understood (assumed to be the desire for a greater diversity of non-commercial fare), commercial broadcasters would begin to offer more programs of an educational, artistic, and public interest nature. This would mean, in turn, that the tastes and standards of the listening audience would be elevated. Although such a goal might now seem naive and unrealistic, it was fully consistent with the Humanities Division's notion that radio could be used as a vehicle for enhancing the cultural levels of the mass public.

Once the Princeton Radio Research got under way, however, it began to move inexorably away from its original purpose of "broadening radio's range of public service" through encouraging cooperation between educational and commercial broadcasters. Undoubtedly, the rapid decline of advocacy for educational radio after the Communications Act of 1934 made the issue of mediating between the two interest groups appear less pressing. However, much of the change in the orientation of the Project could be attributed to the selection of Paul Lazarsfeld as its first director in the summer of 1937, after neither Cantril nor Frank Stanton was willing to assume the position. Even as Lazarsfeld worked within the guiding framework of the Princeton Project, namely that of "studying the meaning of radio to all types of listeners" (Lazarsfeld, 1938b: 1), he sought to place it on a much more rigorous methodological footing. As he noted, the study of "who listens to what, why, and with what effect" is "a rather large order and one of our primary problems is to restrict the scope of our activities." This meant that "the *theoretical and conceptual analysis* of the listener problems confronting radio today is, therefore, one definite part of our activities" (Lazarsfeld, 1938b: 1–2). Lazarsfeld shifted the project away from its original goal of reconciling the differences between educators and broadcasters; it became much more oriented toward methodological questions and the study of a broad range of issues related to radio broadcasting and its effects.[6]

Nevertheless, given that the Project was still part of the research program coordinated by the FREC, an effort was made to give the appearance that its results would be of direct or at least indirect benefit to educational broadcasting. This presentation of the Project was evident in a report submitted to the Committee of Six in November 1938 (Rockefeller Archive Center, 1938b). The report contained accounts of the principles by which the research was guided, the plans for publication, and the kinds of research that were slated for the next phase of the Project's activities. It also included a statement on the general purpose of the Project as it had been summarized in the 1937 Annual Report of the Rockefeller Foundation. Following from its mandate to examine "the use of radio for educational or cultural purposes," the report emphasized how the Project sought to meet the needs of educational broadcasters. This included the development of "short-cut methods" to help undertake listener research, the stimulation of interest by "universities and other research agencies" in listener research, setting an example for educational researchers of how cooperative ventures with private agencies could be developed, and collecting the results of studies done by "commercial research agencies" and making them available to educators (Rockefeller Archive Center, 1938b: 4–5). More generally, the Project was guided by the concern to develop a "theoretical framework" that would "guide us in empirical research and in our interpretation of the findings." This would involve "the systematic study of actual efforts made currently with educational programs." Along the same lines, the Project sought to survey the "main fields in which radio obviously has its greatest social effects" (such as music, news broadcasting, and politics), and to determine the "social, regional and other differences" in the radio audience.

These principles, however, were not particularly in evidence in the list of eleven publications that had been planned; most were only marginally related to the needs and concerns of educational broadcasters. Indeed, only one projected volume (on studies in educational broadcasting) had any direct bearing on their concerns. The rest were either narrowly methodological in orientation[7] or discussions of various aspects of contemporary radio.[8] The only publication resulting from the Project at that point was a "radio issue" of the *Journal of Applied Psychology*, which was due to appear in February 1939. Clearly, the Project had strayed significantly from its goal of furthering the cause of educational and cultural broadcasting through research. It had embarked on a bewildering range of studies whose state of development was unclear and ill-defined.

Nevertheless, in its repot on the Project, the Committee of Six of the Federal Radio Education Commission found that it was "being conducted in full accordance with the original plans" and recommended that "funds for its completion over an additional three years . . . be provided by the Rockefeller Foundation." Overall, the Committee commended "the progress of the work thus far" (Tyson, 1938).

Despite the positive recommendation of the Committee of Six, Marshall believed that "the disinterested opinion of a group of qualified specialists" should be solicited before the Foundation Board of Directors could consider a renewal of the Project's grant (Rockefeller Archive Center, 1938b). That the Foundation found it necessary to enlist the services of an additional reviewing committee was an indication of the degree to which the Committee of Six, as the executive body of FREC, had failed to live up to its expectations as an agency to direct and validate studies in radio research. There were other signs that the Project had not been as successful as its directors and the Committee of Six had claimed. Judging by the response of publishers to the Project's proposed series, it was unlikely that the proposed volumes would ever appear in print. As D.C. Poole (the Princeton University official responsible for the Project) noted to Stevens, the three publishers that had been approached[9] unanimously agreed that "the studies are of value but that their publication in the ordinary commercial way is not feasible" (Poole, 1938).

The reviewing committee for the Princeton Radio Survey met with its three directors in January 1939.[10] It was the Committee's view that although the Project had done "an excellent and intelligent job of exploration," it should "be focused in a general way upon certain important problem areas" (Rockefeller Archive Center, 1939a: 1). Members of the Committee then went on to indicate what some of these areas might be. The issue also came up of the relationship of the Project to educational concerns. Gilbert Seldes felt that the Project had an "educational bias" and that "the commercial and entertainment aspects of broadcasting should not be neglected." Cantril responded:

the Princeton Project is one of a series set up by the Committee of Six of the Federal Education Commission; . . . the Committee of Six feels that the Project should have an educational slant and expects to review all of the material collected by the Project before publication; . . . the Project finds itself in a situation involving conflicting allegiances and responsibilities; . . . the Directors would like to see the Project divorced entirely from the Committee of Six. (Rockefeller Archive Center, 1939a: 5)

Replying to a question posed by Robert Lynd about "whether the Directors were bound to confine themselves to a study of educational broadcasting," Marshall stated "that they were not; that the word 'educational' was not mentioned in the Foundation's grant to the project; and that the field was wide open, at least as far as this Reviewing Committee is concerned" (Rockefeller Archive Center, 1939a: 5).[11] Taking its lead, the Committee agreed that "the Project should be free to study all kinds of programs, including commercial and entertainment programs" (Rockefeller Archive Center, 1939a: 5).

Although the ostensible purpose of the Committee was to evaluate the Project, its actual function appears to have been to set it on a particular course. This was evident in its suggestions for future research. Rather than continuing to concern itself with questions of relevance to educational broadcasting, the Project was to devote itself to such matters as "the effects of radio listening" and the determination of "whether radio can accomplish certain effects independently or only as part of a more general process or situation" (Rockefeller Archive Center, 1939a: 9). Under the general categories of "attitudes toward authority" and "levels of anxiety," it was suggested that the Project give attention to how well radio was able to accomplish the following social objectives:

1. to supply listeners information not otherwise available

2. to restore the spontaneity and freshness of local viewpoints

3. to assist in decreasing the social lag incident to technological change

4. to increase the selective response of groups to the radio

5. to increase tolerance toward experts and expert knowledge in social affairs (Rockefeller Archive Center, 1939a: 10).

The directors responded enthusiastically to the suggestions. Stanton indicated that "a good deal of the groundwork for carrying out the Committee's suggestions had already been done." Along the same lines, Lazarsfeld "accepted that the work already begun points in the direction suggested by the Committee and can be pointed still more; and that a real attempt had been made during the first year and a half of the Project's work to decide problems on just such bases as those the Committee had in mind" (Rockefeller Archive Center, 1939a: 10).

That the directors of the Project took the Committee's suggestion to heart is evident in the proposal they submitted during the next month for a renewal of their grant. A number of the suggestions of the Committee were reiterated almost verbatim, followed by a statement that "the present proposal seems to the officers to give adequate consideration to most if not all these recommendations of the Reviewing Committee" (Rockefeller Archive Center, 1939c).

Despite the Committee's conviction that the Project was promising, it recommended that "the evidence accumulated be fully formulated before proceeding with any additional research" (Rockefeller Archive Center, 1941). Such an assessment only served to fuel the growing impatience of Foundation officials with the Project. As Marshall noted in an internal memorandum,

There has been a good deal of scepticism as to what the Project could accomplish. J.M. [John Marshall] naturally believed with Lazarsfeld that the Project can and does offer much information of significance for better broadcasting; but others do not share his belief. The burden of proof is now Lazarsfeld's. More generally there is a scepticism about what the methods of social psychology can accomplish. . . . Finally J.M. said quite candidly, that in some quarters Lazarsfeld himself suffered from the reputation of being a starter and not a finisher. (Marshall, quoted in Morrison, 1978: 356)

Marshall communicated the Foundation's concerns to Lazarsfeld in a telegram:

Discussions in office indicate reluctance to invest in new research pending formulation of present findings stop feeling here that need is for breathing spell to save project from being victim of its own success stop no recommendation to trustees now stop ready to review situation in June if formulation is sufficiently advanced by then to proved basis. (Marshall, quoted in Morrison, 1978: 355)

The situation was indeed reviewed in June, but a final decision on the renewal was not reached. Rather, following the suggestion of the review committee, the Foundation "appropriated $17,500 in 1939 in addition to the amount available from the 1937 grant" for the formulation of the evidence that had been accumulated (Rockefeller Archive Center, 1941). In effect, the Foundation made the renewal of the grant contingent on publication in an acceptable form of the material that the Project had conducted until that point.

This pressure by the Foundation appears to have galvanized the directors of the Project into action. Lazarsfeld submitted a draft of *Radio and the Printed Word* (1940b),[12] which was then sent by Marshall to a number of consultants for comments.[13] Stanton sent Marshall an outline of a book to be entitled *Listener Research Techniques*.[14] Indicating some impatience with its formulation, Marshall posed these questions to Stanton: "Is this book or the project elsewhere to suggest not only the ways of getting information but also the information it seems desirable to get? . . . Has the project formulated any notion of what an educational station needs to know about its audience?" (Marshall, 1939b). Cantril requested a subsidy for the publication of his study of the Orson Welles broadcast "The War of the Worlds," which had originally been supported by a grant-in-aid from the General Education Board (Cantril, 1940). Marshall explained to Cantril that " the interest which promoted this grant-in-aid . . . goes no further than having the study made and available for general education" (Marshall, 1939d: July 25).

By the end of August 1939, Lazarsfeld was able to provide for the first time a clear indication that the works in progress would be forthcoming as publications.

The monograph [Lazarsfeld, 1940b] will appear jointly with Dr. Stanton's text on the measurement of radio audiences and Dr. Cantril's text on the mass hysteria study [Cantril, 1940]. We feel that these three publications, together, will give a very good start, and will enable the public to get a picture of what the radio project of Princeton University is doing. (Lazarsfeld, 1939)

The flurry of activity by the directors over the summer apparently convinced Marshall that the Project was finally on track. He noted the following to Herbert Brucker, who was in the process of preparing a report on the Project:

It [the Princeton Project] has now been whipped into pretty good shape. But, as that implies, some whipping was necessary. With some reason, the Directors of the Project had let their work range pretty widely—so widely in fact that it seemed fairly clear that steps would have to be taken to pull the various leads together. As a result, the terms of the grant made last spring were such as to insist on the formulation of data already in hand. . . . that job is now progressing to a satisfactory conclusion. But "complete satisfaction" would neglect an earlier feeling that the Project had got a bit out of hand and was, as we put it last spring, in danger of becoming the victim of its own success. Certainly an enterprise of this kind needs firm administration, and I am not satisfied that this particular enterprise has always had it. (Marshall, 1939c)

Marshall's earlier lack of confidence in the administration of the Project had led him to consult with Robert Lynd, professor of sociology at Columbia University, who had been closely involved with the Project since its inception. Lynd noted to Marshall:

I think what he needs is a stronger hand (you, a committee on?) holding him to a *defined* program. I don't believe he had a clear-cut set of definitions and of criteria as to priority in undertaking the job. . . . the Foundation did not know what it wanted but wanted a field of alternative possibilities opened up. This played into Paul's overwide field of interest and aided and abetted him in following his curiosity rather than narrowing a program.

He is so darned able that there is no point in throwing out baby and bath. Every researcher has an Achilles heel. His is his intellectual curiosity about everything interesting. He can be channelled. . . . The need, therefore, is to use his great strength but to see that his sailing orders are more explicit. (Lynd, quoted in Morrison, 1978: 356)

The Communications Group

The "sailing orders" materialized in the form of a series of seminars, which began in September 1939 and continued until June 1940.[15] The purpose of the seminars was to channel Lazarsfeld's research along more systematic lines. Marshall recalled:

We felt that Lazarsfeld's research for the first period was admirable, but that it was scattered and unfocused. With Lazarsfeld's agreement we therefore subjected him to a day's examination. We had a group of people and we sort of cross-examined Lazarsfeld all that day, trying to get him to define some focus for his work in the next period of his work. While we did get Lazarsfeld to agree to certain foresight to what he would go on to do, the work was still in a conceptual muddle. There was no sharpness to it whatsoever. So we came to agree in the spring of 1939 that we should hold this series of meetings at monthly intervals throughout the coming academic year. (quoted in Morrison, 1978: 357)

The first meetings of the committee took place on September 20 and 23, 1939. Dubbed the "communications group," it would subsequently meet on a regular basis throughout the academic year. These meetings led to the production of numerous memoranda, commentaries, and working papers, culminating in two summary documents, "Research in Mass Communications" (Rockefeller Archive Center, 1940d) and "Needed Research in Communications" (Rockefeller Archive Center, 1940e).

Although the initial plan for the seminar was to embark on a theoretical discussion of mass communication, the "war situation" changed its orientation. As Marshall stated, "it now seemed advisable that instead it consider what research studies might be undertaken at once . . . studies that would be of immediate significance and would furnish immediate returns through current reporting of results" (Rockefeller Archive Center, 1939b: 1). After indicating the trends that would likely occur during this period of "emergency psychology," the members of the committee "made various suggestions for research which might be undertaken at this time" (Rockefeller Archive Center, 1939b: 2). The subsequent discussion addressed the issue of how informed public opinion could be cultivated during the emergency, with particular reference to the role of communications in this process. It was felt that "the committee should attempt to make the public more keenly aware of trends resulting in America from the war situation, so that the people would know what was going on and would not be swamped by these trends but could cope with them, combat them, or adjust to them more readily and intelligently" (Rockefeller Archive Center, 1939b: 1–2). In order to address the issues raised by the committee's concerns, it was decided that documents would be prepared and would serve as the basis for seminar discussions. The preparation of the documents, at least initially, was primarily the responsibility of two subcommittees, namely research (consisting of Lasswell, Gorer, and Marshall) and government (consisting of May and Slesinger). In addition, other members of the seminar were to occasionally prepare reports on particular topics.

From the outset, it was evident that Harold Lasswell and John Marshall both played a particularly crucial role in the development of the seminar. Both worked from a broad vision of how systematic research in communications could have a practical bearing on the changing political circumstances. Marshall acted as a guiding force, ensuring that the group kept to its focus of defining the field of communications. To a large extent his views coincided with those of Lasswell, who consistently spoke in favor of "the creation of a body of social scientists and experienced public characters which would construct probable outcomes of trends and policies, then measure the flow of communications regarding them in terms of standards of communication it would develop, with particular emphasis upon clear reporting" (Rockefeller Archive Center, 1939c: 2). Lasswell and Marshall undoubtedly bore most of the responsibility for the production of the major document considered by the seminar in its early meetings, judging by its orientation and emphasis. The final section of the memorandum (pp. 53–55) discussed the "Role of the Central Coordinating Agency," maintaining that it would be necessary to have a coordinating body to "stimulate concurrent researches, to perform continuously approximate coordinations, and to provide a channel for intercommunication and interstimulation between the separate studies" (Rockefeller Archive Center, 1939c: 53).

Evidently both Marshall and Lasswell believed that the seminar itself should serve as a coordinator of research. In response to the suggestion of Bryson that it begin to map out the field of communications, Lasswell suggested that "the seminar might discuss going and proposed research."

When Marshall pointed out that the seminar was to act as a coordinating agency for specific research projects, Lasswell stated that "it was this problem of coordination and integration that interested him especially. He suggested that the seminar might be able to effect such integration after it became a coordinating agency." To this end, he "felt that a secretariat for the seminar should be created, which would be useful in coordinating activities and also in connection with preparation for the meetings of the seminar." Building on Lasswell's suggestions, "Slesinger moved that the seminar become a body to discuss going and prospective research projects, with a view toward later developing a more general theory of communications" (Rockefeller Archive Center, 1939d: 6). This view gained assent from the other seminar members.

From this point on, the texture of the seminar changed. A number of sessions were given to the discussion of particular research projects and working papers.[16] The work of the communications group culminated in a draft document framed by the communications formula. It was on the basis of this schema that the field of communications was to develop. The practical impulse of the communications group's work is evident in the two memoranda they produced after the seminar's completion (Rockefeller Archive Center, 1940d, 1940e). To a large extent, they drew on the earlier discussion as articulated in the draft memorandum produced for the June 1940 meeting.

The purpose of the communications group, according to the first of these memoranda, was to "throw light upon the ways and means by which, given the necessity for change, the public mind can most effectively be helped to adapt itself in time to necessary change" (Rockefeller Archive Center, 1940d: 1). To this end, with its interest in "the relevance of research to public policy," the group was concerned with what Walter Lippmann (and Noam Chomsky) would have considered to be "the manufacture of consent":

Government which rests upon consent rests also upon knowledge of how best to secure consent. Policies which there are no real grounds to question risk defeat unless account is taken of public predisposition and of public need, unless the interpretation of purpose and probable result is actively communicated. Research in the field of mass communication is a new and sure weapon to achieve that end. (Rockefeller Archive Center, 1940d: 2)

It was in this sense that the "vast, existing resources of mass communication can influence profoundly the speed and success of adaptation in the human mind" (Rockefeller Archive Center, 1940d: 4). To illustrate how such ideals might be realized in practice, the memorandum discussed at length how communications research could intervene to deal with the hypothetical case of how an address on a radio program "dealing with the dangers of subversive activities on the part of the aliens" led to "outbreaks of feelings against alien groups" (Rockefeller Archive Center, 1940d: 8). The memorandum then went into some detail about how the resources of communications research could be effectively mobilized to address a problem of this kind (Rockefeller Archive Center, 1940d: 8–17). It was concluded that "the critical situation of our fable . . . rather than exaggerating, perhaps only puts into perspective the consequences of mistaken use of mass communications and the help which research can give in avoiding such mistaken use" (Rockefeller Archive Center, 1940d: 16). Indeed, the point of the fable was to "[make] clear what the job of research in mass communications is . . . that job is to learn what mass communications do in our society." This involved "getting evidence with which to answer four basic questions":

What they do became a question of *what effects* do mass communications as a whole, or any single communication, have. What effects they have likewise inescapably involved discovering *to whom what was said*. How these effects occurred necessitated analysis of *what was said*. And that analysis . . . required answers to a fourth and final question—*who said it and with what intention*. In brief, then, the job of research in mass communications is to determine who, and with what intention, said what, to whom, and with what effects. (Rockefeller Archive Center, 1940d: 17; emphasis added)

The second memorandum, which appeared in October 1940, was much more sharply focused on the direct practical relevance of communication research to the affairs of state (Rockefeller Archive Center, 1940e). As it had become increasingly evident that the "emergency period" was going to be of long duration and that the United States could very likely be drawn into the conflict, the communications group began to reflect more seriously on how their initiative could gain public and governmental support. It was on the basis of support of this kind that their vision of an institutionalized agency coordinating communication could become a reality. These considerations likely account for the shift away from technical and academic discourse toward a much more direct and accessible form of expression. Originally, the group had planned to assemble several documents from the seminar and circulate them to a wider audience. However, "the problems of national defense have become so urgent that it was agreed that a briefer statement would be of interest." Nevertheless, the group pointed out that the "general remarks" of the memorandum "are fortified at all points by the more technical material that was considered by the conferees" (Rockefeller Archive Center, 1940e: 1).

The opening paragraph of the document made its intent clear:

> Facts, not now available, are urgently needed to provide a basis for more effective communication. Second, that the means of getting the needed facts are ready at hand. Third, that getting them must be closely geared to making communication more effective. It recommends that the work of getting them be begun at once. (Rockefeller Archive Center, 1940e: 1)

The communication in question was that which took place between the government and the people. It was through new forms of research, the group stated repeatedly, that communication between government and the people could be developed as a genuine two-way process. At face value, the memorandum appears to advocate a dialogical model of communication, as based on new research initiatives and findings. However, when it is examined more closely, a much different conception of the relation between government and the public seems to have formed the basis for the group's proposals for the development of the field of communications. The memorandum took its point of departure from the "wider and wider responsibility for the welfare of the people" that events imposed on "our central government" (Rockefeller Archive Center, 1940e: 3). This involved the making of decisions "with a maximum of speed." These decisions, in turn, were communicated to the people along with proposals and explanations. In response, "from the people comes an answering stream of counter-proposal, explanation, and consent." The government then takes these into account "in final decision and administration." However, the memorandum stresses, "if this two-way process of communication does not function, democracy *is* endangered" (Rockefeller Archive Center, 1940e: 3).

As the group appeared to suggest, the course of recent events had caused strains in this process of communication, thereby imperiling democracy. It noted that "the pace of governmental decision in this country, particularly in foreign affairs and national defense, is outstripping that of explanation." This meant not only that "adequate explanation" did not reach the people affected by the decisions," but that "the gap between the government and the people is widening." Hence, there was a need to create more effective ways of communicating. The government required better ways of explaining its decisions and proposals to the people, and the people needed "better ways of explaining to the government how they feel themselves affected by its proposals or decisions" (Rockefeller Archive Center, 1940e: 4).

It was the group's contention that research was essential if this "two-way process" of communication was to be restored:

[F]irst, to supply facts needed to make explanation both prompt and adequate; and, second, to bring back from the people an equally prompt and adequate response. With such research, the present gap between the government and the people can be closed. The government can then exercise its wider responsibility without risking loss of confidence and impaired morale. The people then can sanction changes in their lives with the assurance that their government has taken their responses into account. (Rockefeller Archive Center, 1940e: 5)

According to the group, democracy depended on a two-way process of this kind. For if explanation by the government was to be effective, it "needed to get behind the opinions of the moment, and enable the people intelligently to consent or dissent" (Rockefeller Archive Center, 1940e: 8). However, the democratic process "has been endangered in times of increased tension more by ignorance than by intention. Those responsible have lacked the knowledge that they needed to make democracy strong enough to meet new stress and strain. One means to strengthen it lies in such research as it is here described which gives them a factual basis for distinguishing between consent or dissent of the moment, and genuine agreement or justified objection" (Rockefeller Archive Center, 1940e: 15–16).

In this sense, "the widening gap between the government and the people will close only when that flow removes the feeling of being governed by remote control, and substitutes a feeling of belonging to something that is worth belonging to." Research, then, "can ensure the flow of communication that is vital to the democratic process." This gives it "an urgency which seems to justify any risk or possible misuse" (Rockefeller Archive Center, 1940e: 15).

Even as the memorandum concentrated on the domestic aspects of communication, it was already looking ahead to the role that communications could play if the United States were to enter the fray.

If . . . events force this country into a belligerent part in world politics, communications will have still other tasks, particularly that of conveying to the enemy countries information calculated to be effective in the winning of the war. Again, research will be essential, both for the process of communicating effectively with the people of the enemy countries, and for gauging their response. (Rockefeller Archive Center, 1940e: 16)

The memorandum concluded by examining how an initiative of communications research of this kind could be institutionalized. It stressed that "research can make its contributions promptly enough to be of practical use, if [it] is properly organized and coordinated. The next step is to mobilize existing facilities and personnel so that they may be ready and available." This would involve the following course of action:

The need is first, to mobilize research workers already competent to apply known and tested methods of research, and to recruit and train others who are qualified for training; second, to put into usable form the facts which earlier research has already made available; and third, to agree on assignment of responsibility for further research, in ways that assure the coordination of inquiry and continual pooling of results. (Rockefeller Archive Center, 1940e: 18)

As the memorandum stressed, work in communications justified planning in terms of these three steps. As it indicated through a concise inventory, considerable work was being done in various research centers.[17] It was emphasized that those who wrote the memorandum were prepared "at once to take these first two steps, if they are able to secure the help they need—cooperation from those concerned, and funds to meet the costs" (Rockefeller Archive Center, 1940e: 20).

In the view of the group, the research in question "can probably best be undertaken within the government." Nevertheless, research would take place outside the government as well. What was needed was the "definite assignment of responsibility." This called for the formation of a central authority or agency charged with organizing and monitoring research initiatives in communications.

> The ideal organization and coordination would be through some central agency, perhaps an institute of research in communication, within the government or outside it, similar to the national institutes for research in economics, which would, in assigning responsibility, ensure the comparability of findings, and their pooling in some central formulation and reporting. (Rockefeller Archive Center, 1940e: 21)

This suggested a "central institute or council for research, with local or regional offices across the country, so placed as to have ready access to representative samples of the population" (Rockefeller Archive Center, 1940e: 22). In conclusion, the signers of the memorandum appealed to its readers "to consider in severely practical terms what organization of the research it outlines will be most advantageous." They emphasized that they and other communications researchers would be "quick to do what they know they can, when others who recognize the need for their contribution are ready to help in making it of use" (Rockefeller Archive Center, 1940e: 22).

Toward Communication Intelligence

Of those who signed the memorandum, it was Lasswell and Marshall who took the initiative in seeking support for the development of an agency responsible for coordinating research in communications. They met on October 2, 1940, to discuss the next steps that could be taken. It was decided that Lasswell and Cantril would organize a conference on research in communications "based probably on the memorandum in communications" that had been produced by the seminar of the previous year. The purpose of the conference followed closely from the proposals developed in the final two memoranda. A list of people qualified to direct communications research would be compiled. A plan for putting the "available knowledge of communications" in a form that would be "useable for present purposes" was to be developed. Finally, an effort would be made to reach agreement on "how responsibility for various phases of research can be assigned." Marshall told Lasswell that the Rockefeller Foundation would be able to support the meeting through its conference funds (Marshall, 1940b: October 2).

The Conference on Communication Research took place on January 18, 1941, at the Princeton Club. It brought together "specialists in communication research"[18] with "representatives of various government agencies with a present or potential interest in the results of such research."[19] After providing an overview of the various types of research in communication, Lasswell claimed that its results might be called "communication intelligence," analogous to "military intelligence." A number of the communications specialists then summed up their ongoing research and indicated the procedures that were used.

The representatives of government agencies made it clear that they were in need of the findings that communications researchers could offer. James McCamy noted that he had been "soaking up" the data reported because it was precisely what "he and his associates sorely needed." He added that there was almost a "'dangerous lack of facts' of this kind which are needed as a basis for policy formation." Saul Padower supported McCamy's remarks, stating that "with no means of predicting public response, decisions have to be made by guess and b'gorry." James Allen discussed the resistance in Washington by executive agencies to studies of public opinion. Luther Evans remarked that the Library of Congress had sought to make members of Congress aware of their inadequate information on the state of public opinion. Kenneth Kane described how the Department of Justice had begun to study current communication in order to determine when foreign government agents had not been registered with the State Department (Marshall, 1941: January 18).

Overall, it was felt that there was a need to "find some way of making available to government agencies findings arrived at by agencies outside the government." Evans reported that the Library of Congress had begun to move more in this direction with an expanded information service. It was also considering how it could help to pool research findings. Marshall raised the issue of the need to avoid duplication in research between the government and external agencies, but he was not able to get a clear answer from the government officials who were present. During informal exchanges following the conference, "more was said about the desirability for organizing and coordinating communication research and for pooling findings in a way that would make them promptly available. One possibility was that a government committee be set up which would operate much as do the other research committees of the National Defense Council" (Marshall, 1941: January 18). A few days later, Lasswell told Marshall that the government representatives at the conference all believed there was a need for "the development of research under government auspices" and that the duplication of effort would be avoided as a result of the conference (Marshall, 1941: January 20).

A valuable outcome of the conference, Marshall noted in his diary, was that it had given him access to numerous people working in government agencies who believed that research in communications was needed. In a visit to Washington to attend a conference on "Morale and Communication Research" on January 29, 1941, he met with some of these officials again. In talks with the Federal Communications Commission and the Department of Justice, particularly, he explained the kind of communications research that the Foundation would consider supporting, and he "expressed his hope that his contacts in these agencies would help him in avoiding any duplication with government activities." He also discussed the possibility that an agency coordinating research could be established. There was some agreement that this function might best be served by the Library of Congress, possibly through Lasswell's newly created office there (Marshall, 1941: January 29).

Over the next months, strategies for cooperation between government agencies began to take shape. Both the Neutrality Bureau of the Department of Justice and the Federal Communications Commission had made plans for the study of wartime communications. These provided for "advisors, drawn from private research," who would not only take part in governmental research but "relate to it the findings of nongovernmental investigation." Marshall noted:

Eventually these advisors might become an advisory committee which among other things would assure the articulation and full exploitation of the findings of the two agencies—the Department of Justice dealing with print and film, and the FCC with radio. It was further agreed that the RF could serve a useful function by enabling qualified alien investigators ... who cannot be directly employed by the government, to continue in related research. Finally, it was pointed out that the government is not yet able to undertake studies of the effects of communications analyzed, and that accordingly, the Foundation might well wish to consider support for such work to complement what the government can do. (Marshall, 1941: March 20)

This complementary function accurately describes the role that the Humanities Division of the Rockefeller Foundation had came to assume, largely through the initiatives of John Marshall, in relation to the linkage between communications research and the policy process. Initially, through its support and sponsorship of radio research, it sought to address a critical policy issue arising from the 1934 Communications Act, namely the reconciliation of educational and commercial broadcasting (see Buxton, 1993b). When this problem was no longer a matter of concern, it turned its attention more generally toward helping build the foundations for research in mass communications, largely through the vehicle of the Princeton Radio Research Project. This initiative, in turn, provided the basis for addressing the broader question of how research could help facilitate better communications between policymakers and the public. To this end, it was instrumental in the consolidation of a "communications group" sharing a common concern to generate research of practical relevance to building public consent to new lines of policy made necessary by the "emergency period." This was carried out not only through the provision of financial support and organizational resources but also through sustained and focused intellectual guidance.

Once the network of communications specialists had been consolidated, the Rockefeller Foundation turned its attention to the problem of how the equivalent of this body—taking the form of a coordinator of communications—could be institutionalized. In the same way that it had earlier brought educators together with commercial broadcasters, it now sought to bring together communication researchers and members of the policy community. At the same time, it continued to support projects directed toward "process research," with a view to generating more effective communication intelligence. At all stages of the process, the guiding direction of John Marshall was in evidence. In this sense, Marshall's chart provides us with a much richer and more compelling understanding of the origins of communications studies than does Lasswell's better-known formula.

Acknowledgments

I wish to thank the Rockefeller Archive Center for giving me permission to quote from material in its collection. This chapter has been written with the support of a research grant from the Social Science and Humanities Research Council of Canada. I am grateful to Charles Ackland for his comments on a draft of this chapter.

Notes

Editor's note: An extensive bibliography is included with this piece as a useful addition to the chapter's content.

1. Lazarsfeld had used the phrase "who listens to what, why, and with what effect" the previous year in describing the tasks of radio research. He claims to have come across it in an unspecified document (Lazarsfeld 1938a: 1).

2. He was referring to film, radio, and print.

3. This may have been the first time that the term "mass communication" was used in an analytical way.

4. This initiative was intended to diffuse the tension between educational broadcasters and commercial broadcasters in the aftermath of the Communications Act of 1934. Prior to the passage of the Act, educators and supporters of noncommercial broadcasting had lobbied to have a fixed portion of the airwaves reserved for educational broadcasting. However, their efforts failed; the 1934 Act supported the principle that broadcasting was to be primarily privately owned and commercial in nature.

5. The three broadcasters chosen were Frederic Willis, assistant to the president, Columbia Broadcasting System; James Baldwin, executive director of the National Association of Broadcasters; and John Royal, vice-president in charge of operations, National Broadcasting System. The three educators were W. W. Charters of Ohio State University; Levering Tyson of Columbia University; and Hadley Cantril.

6. Indeed, Lazarsfeld had little interest in mass communications per se; he apparently saw the Princeton Radio Research Project as a useful vehicle for developing new forms of methodology. As he informed David Morrison in an interview, "Look, you have to understand that I had no interest whatsoever in mass communications. I mean everything in a way is interesting to a methodologist, but I certainly didn't find that in the beginning an important topic at all. It was exclusively that it was rather a spectacular job" (Lazarsfeld, quoted in Morrison, 1978: 349).

7. This group included "The Panel as a Tool in Listener Research," "Statistical Methods as Applied to Radio Research," "Handbook of Listener Research," and "Measurement Techniques" (Rockefeller Archive Center, 1938b: 2).

8. These included "The Art of Asking Why," "Radio Commentators," "Music on the Air," and "Radio and Reading" (Rockefeller Archive Center, 1938b: 2).

9. The publishers were Henry Holt and Company, McGraw-Hill publishing Company, and John Wiley and Sons.

10. The members of the committee were Irvin Stewart, Douglas Waples, Davidson Taylor, Harold Lasswell, R. L. La Piere, Lyman Bryson, Gilbert Seldes, James Angell, and Robert Lynd.

11. Yet in a review of Rockefeller involvement in radio written shortly after the Princeton Project was approved, Marshall included the Project as one of those that was involved in "educational and public service." He noted that the "anticipated outcomes" of projects of this kind included the "development of research procedures that will set new standards in evaluating broadcasting's educational and cultural contributions" and "the development of a more explicit appreciation of broadcasting's opportunities and responsibilities for education and public service on the part of the industry and nonprofit agencies concerned with broadcasting" (Rockefeller Archive Center, 1937c: 3).

12. That the prodding of the Rockefeller Foundation precipitated the writing of the book is evident in Lazarsfeld's foreword to it:

A series of investigations covering a rather wide range of problems was undertaken [by the Office of Radio Research]. One group of studies which seemed of obvious importance related radio to other media of communication such as newspapers and books. In June, 1939, when the first general progress report was due, these studies formed a natural unit for summary. The volume on "Radio and the Printed Page" in its present form grew out of discussion of this first report. (Lazarsfeld, 1940b: vii)

13. D. S. Freeman, editor of the *Richmond News Leader*, gave the work mixed reviews. Although he was pleased with the research it showed and the inclusion of material based on George Gallup's figures, he found the text "infernally verbose" (Freeman, 1939). Marshall agreed with Freeman that the manuscript was "verbose in the extreme," and he added that this problem needed to be remedied, "if the monograph is to get any adequate publication." A. G. Crane, president of the University of Wyoming, evidently found it to be a "valuable job" (Marshall, 1939d).

14. I could find no record of this book's publication.

15. The regular seminar participants were Charles Siepmann, Lyman Bryson, Lloyd Free, Geoffrey Gorer, Harold Lasswell, Robert Lynd, Donald Slesinger, Douglas Waples, Paul Lazarsfeld, and John Marshall. In addition, R. J. Havighurst, Stacy May, I. A. Richards, and David H. Stevens took part in the discussions (Rockefeller Archive Center, 1940d).

16. These included the Cantril, Doob-Zinn-Child, Lazarsfeld, and Lasswell-Gorer research proposals for studies of public opinion (Rockefeller Archive Center, 1939e), Douglas Waples's project on reading (Waples, 1940), I. A. Richards's memorandum on content (Rockefeller Archive Center, 1940b), the

studies of Slesinger and Gorer "on the movies as a medium of mass communication" (Rockefeller Archive Center, 1940c), and, finally, the "lists of social changes" that Lynd and Bryson believed to be desirable (Rockefeller Archive Center, 1940c: 6; see also Lynd, 1940).

17. Many of these were under the umbrella of Rockefeller-sponsored projects. These included the annotated bibliography written in 1935 for the Social Science Research Council (Lasswell, Smith, and Casey, 1935); the development of polling under Gallup and the Institute of Public Opinion; the *Fortune* poll under Elmo Wilson; the *Public Opinion Quarterly*; the work of the Graduate Library School at Chicago and the Columbia University Office of Radio Research; the Public Opinion Research Project at Princeton; and the Princeton Listening Center.

18. A number of the researchers (Lasswell, Cantril, Bryson, Lazarsfeld, Slesinger, Waples, and Harwood Childs of Princeton) who came to the conference had taken part in the seminar of the previous year. The others who took part were Weinberg (Professor of History at Johns Hopkins), Pendleton Herring (Department of Government, Harvard), and Ralph Casey (University of Minnesota School of Journalism).

19. The government representatives present were James McCamy (assistant to the secretary of agriculture), Saul K. Padower (assistant to the secretary of the interior), James Allen (assistant to the attorney general), Kenneth Kane (director of the Neutrality Bureau of the Department of Justice), David Lloyd (Federal Communications Commission), Lieutenant-Commander Galvin of the Navy Department, and Luther Evans (assistant general administrator of the Library of Congress).

References

Adkin, L. E. (1992). "Counter-Hegemony and Environmental Politics in Canada." In W. K. Carroll (ed.), *Organizing Dissent: Contemporary Social Movements in Theory and Practice*, pp. 135–56. Toronto: Garamond Press.

Agh, A. (1990a). "The Emergence of the Science of Democracy in Hungary and Its Impact on the Democratic Transition." Paper presented at the Conference of the International Committee for the Study of the Development of Political Science, Barcelona, May 14–20.

———. (1990b). "Transition to Democracy in Central Europe: A Comparative View." Paper presented at the first meeting of the U.S.-Hungarian Roundtable in Political Science, San Francisco, August 28–29.

Alger, C., and G. Lyons. (1974). "Social Science as a Transnational System: Report of a Seminar." *International Studies Notes* 1, no. 3: 1–13.

Almond, G. A. (1988). "The Return of the State." *American Political Science Review* 82: 853–74.

Althusser, L. (1971). *Lenin and Philosophy*. London: New Left-Books.

Antonio, R. (1980). "Review of Mlynar, Nightfrost in Prague." *Telos* 44: 233–39.

Archibald, Clinton. (1984). "Corporatist Tendencies in Quebec.' In Alain-G. Gagnon (ed.), *Quebec: State and Society*, 1st ed., pp. 353–64. Toronto: Methuen.

Aronowitz, S. (1992). *The Politics of Identity: Class, Culture, Social Movements.* New York: Routledge, Chapman and Hall.

Aronson, Jonathan. (1988). "Negotiating to Launch Negotiations: Getting Trade in Services onto the GATT Agenda." Pittsburgh: Pew Program in Case Teaching and Writing in International Affairs.

Ashley, W. (1970). "Philanthropy and Government: A Study of the Ford Foundation's Overseas Activities." Unpublished Ph.D. dissertation. New York: New York University.

Atkinson, M. M., and W. D. Coleman. (1989a). "Strong States and Weak States: Sectoral Policy Networks in Advanced Industrial Nations." *British Journal of Political Science* 19: 46–67.

———. (1989b). *The State, Business, and Industrial Change.* Toronto: University of Toronto Press.

———. (1992). "Policy Networks, Policy Communities and the Problems of Governance." *Governance* 5, no. 2: 154–80.

Augelli, Enrico, and Craig Murphy. (1988). *America's Quest for Supremacy and the Third World: A Gramscian Analysis.* London: Pinter.

Bashevkin, S. B. (1985). *Toeing the Lines: Women and Party Politics in English Canada.* Toronto: University of Toronto Press.

Bauer, R. A., I. DeSola Pool, and L. A. Dexter. (1972). *American Business and Public Policy*, 2d ed. Chicago: Aldine.

Beard, Charles A. (1960). *An Economic Interpretation of the Constitution of the United States.* New York: MacMillan.

Beer, S. (1974). *The British Political System.* New York: Random House.

Benda, Julien. (1969). *The Treason of the Intellectuals* (translation of La trahison des clercs). New York: W. W. Norton.

Bentley, Arhur. (1908). *The Process of Government.* Chicago: University of Chicago press.

Berelson, Bernard. (1959). "The State of Communication Research." *Public Opinion Quarterly* 23: 1–6.

Berger, S. (ed.). (1981). *Organizing Interests in Western Europe.* New York: Cambridge University Press.

Berlin, Isaiah. (1982). "Montesquieu." In *Against the Current: Essays in the History of Ideas*, pp. 130–61. New York: Penguin Books.

Bibic, A. (1979). "Political Science in Yugoslavia." Paper presented at the Eleventh IPSA World Congress, Moscow, August 12–18.

————. (1982). "Yugoslavia." In W. A. Andrews (ed.), *International Handbook of Political Science*. Westport, CT: Greenwood.

Bina, V. (1983). "Czech Sociology and Marxism-Leninism." *Mens en Maatschappij* 58, no. 1: 53–77.

Block, F. (1987). *Revising State Theory*. Philadelphia: Temple University Press.

Bloom, Allan. (1987). *The Closing of the American Mind*. New York: Simon and Schuster.

Boardman, R. (1992). "The Multilateral Dimension: Canada in the International System." In R. Boardman (ed.), *Canadian Environmental Policy: Ecosystems, Politics, and Process*, pp. 224–45. Toronto: Oxford University Press.

Bourdieu, P. (1984). *Homo academicus*. Paris: Les éditions de Minuit.

Bourne, L. S. (1988). "On the Role of University-Based Research Institutes: Reflections on the Institutional Environment of Research." In *Culture, Development and Regional Policy*. Canadian Issues, Vol. 9, pp. 177–83. Montreal: Association for Canadian Studies.

Bradford, N. (1994). *Creation and Constraint: Economic Ideas and Politics in Canada*. Unpublished dissertation, Carleton University, Ottawa.

Brady, Alexander. (1958). *Democracy in the Dominions: A Comparative Study in Institutions*, 3d ed. Toronto: University of Toronto Press.

Brecher, I. (1957). *Monetary and Fiscal Thought and Policy in Canada, 1919–1939*. Toronto: University of Toronto Press.

Bressand, Albert, and Kalypso Nicolaides (eds.). (1989). *Strategic Trends in Services: An Inquiry into the Global Service Economy*. New York: Harper and Row.

Brock, William E. (1982). "A Simple Plan for Negotiating on Trade in Services." *World Economy* 5, no. 3 (November).

Brodie, J., and J. Jenson (1988). *Crisis, Challenge and Change*. Ottawa: Carleton University Press.

Brooks, S. (1990). "The Market for Social Scientific Knowledge: The Case of Free Trade in Canada." In S. Brooks and A. Gagnon (eds.), *Social Scientists, Policy and the State*. New York: Praeger.

Brooks, S., and A. Gagnon. (1990a). "Politics and the Social Sciences in Canada." In A. Gagnon and J. Bickerton (eds.), *Canadian Politics: An Introduction to the Discipline*. Peterborough: Broadview Press.

————(eds.). (1990b). *Social Scientists, Policy and the State*. New York: Praeger.

Brown, A. (1984). "Political Science in the Soviet Union: A New Stage of Development?" *Soviet Studies* 36, no. 3: 317–44.

————. (1987). "Eastern Europe's Western Connection." In L. Gordon (ed.), *Eroding Empire: Western Relations with Eastern Europe*. Washington, DC: Brookings.

Brym, Robert J. (1987). "The Political Sociology of Intellectuals: A Critique and a Proposal." In Alain-G. Gagnon (ed.), *Intellectuals in Liberal Democracies: Political Influence and Social Involvement*. New York: Praeger.

Brzezinski, Z. (1965). *Alternative to Partition*. New York: McGraw-Hill.

———. (1970). *Between Two Ages*. New York: Viking.

Buchstein, H., and G. Göhler. (1990). "After the Revolution: Political Science in East Germany." *Ps: Political Science and Politics* 23, no. 4: 668–73.

Bueckert, D. (1992). "Four Women's Groups Withdraw Support." *Ottawa Citizen*, August 1, p. A5.

Buxton, William. (1993a). "The Harvard Industrial Hazards Project, 1930–1943." *Rockefeller Archive Center Newsletter*, Spring, pp. 12–15.

———. (1993b). "The Political Economy of Communications Research: The Rockefeller Foundation, the 'Radio Wars' and the Princeton Radio Research Project." In Robert Babe (ed.), *Economy and Communications*. Dordrecht: Kluwer.

Cab 124/572. (n.d.). *Cabinet–Post War Agricultural Policy*. London: Public Records Office.

Cairns, A. (1988). "The Governments and Societies of Canadian Federalism." In D. Williams (ed.), *Constitution, Government, and Society in Canada*. Toronto: McClelland and Stewart.

———. (1990). "Constitutional Minoritarianism in Canada." In R. L. Watts and D. M. Brown (eds.), *Canada: The State of the Federation 1990*, pp. 71–96. Kingston: Institute of Intergovernmental Relations.

———. (1991). *Disruptions* (ed. Douglas Williams). Toronto: McClelland and Stewart.

Cameron, D. (1989). "Political Discourse in the Eighties." In A. Gagnon and B. Tanguay (eds.), *Canadian Parties in Transition: Discourse, Organization, Representation*. Toronto: Nelson.

Cameron, D., and D. Drache (1988). "Outside the Macdonald Commission: Reply to Richard Simeon." *Studies in Political Economy* 26 (Summer).

Campbell, J. C., et al. (1989). "Afterword on Policy Communities: A Framework for Comparative Research." *Governance* 2: 86–94.

Campbell, R. (1987). *Grand Illusions*. Peterborough: Broadview Press.

Campion, F. D. (1984). *The AMA and U.S. Health Policy since 1940*. Chicago: Chicago University Press.

Canadian Advisory Council on the Status of Women. (1989). *Canadian Charter Equality Rights for Women. One Step Forward or Two Steps Back?* Ottawa: Ministry of Supply and Services.

Canadian Forum. (1936). Vol. 16, no. 184 (May).

Cantril, Hadley. (1937). "Project I." RF. RG 1.1 Series 200. Box 271. Folder 3234. Rockefeller Archive Center.

————. (1940). *The Invasion of Mars: A Study in the Psychology of Panic.* Princeton: Princeton University Press.

Carson, Rachel. (1962). *Silent Spring.* Boston: Houghton Mifflin.

Cawson, Alan. (1985). "Varieties of Corporatism: The Importance of the Meso-Level of Interest Intermediation," and "Conclusion: Some Implications for State Theory." In Alan Cawson (ed.), *Organized Interests and the State: Studies in Meso-Corporatism,* pp. 1–21, 221–26. Beverly Hills, CA: Sage.

Chomsky, Noam, and Edward Herman. (1988). *Manufacturing Consent: The Political Economy of the Mass Media.* New York: Pantheon Books.

Clarke, H., et al. (1991). *Absent Mandate.* Toronto: Gage.

Clark-Jones, M. (1987). *A Staples State.* Toronto: University of Toronto Press.

Coates, D. (1989). *The Crises of Labour: Industrial Relations and the State in Contemporary Britain.* Oxford; Phillip Allen.

Cohen, Jean L. (1982). *Class and Civil Society: The Limits of Marxian Critical Theory.* Amherst: University of Massachusetts Press.

————. (1985). "Strategy or Identity: New Theoretical Paradigms and Contemporary Social Movements." *Social Research* 52, no. 4 (Winter): 663–715.

Cohen, S. D. (1988). *The making of United States International Economic Policy,* 3d ed. New York: Praeger.

Coleman, William D., and Grace Skogstad (eds.). (1990). *Policy Communities and Public Policy in Canada: A Structuralist Approach.* Mississauga: Copp Clark Pitman Ltd.

Commoner, B. (1966). *Science and Survival.* New York: Viking.

————. (1972). *The Closing Circle.* New York: Bantam.

Cox, Robert W. (1979). "Ideologies and the New International Economic Order: Reflections on Some Recent Literature." *International Organization* 33, no. 2 (Spring): 257–302.

————. (1983). "Gramsci, Hegemony and International Relations: An Essay in Method." *Millennium: Journal of International Studies* 12, no. 2: 162–75.

————. (1986). "Social Forces, States and World Orders: Beyond International Relations Theory." In Robert O. Keohane (ed.), *NeoRealism and Its Critics.* New York: Columbia University Press.

————. (1987). *Production, Power and World Order: Social Forces in the Making of History.* New York: Columbia University Press.

Critchlow, Donald T. (1984). "Brookings: The Man and the Institution." *Review of Politics* 46, no. 4 (October): 561–81.

Dahl, R. (1961). "The Behavioral Approach in Political Science: Epitaph for a Monument to a Successful Protest." *American Political Science Review* 55, no. 4: 763–72.

Daub, M. (1984–1985). "A History of Canadian Economic Forecasting." *Journal of Business Administration* 15.

DeFleur, Melvin L., and Sandra Ball-Rokeach. (1975). *Theories of Mass Communication*. 4th ed. New York: Longman.

Destler, I. M. (1986). *American Trade Politics: System under Stress*. Washington, DC: Institute for International Economics.

Diani, M. (1992). "The Concept of Social Movement." *Sociological Review* 40, no. 1: 1–25.

Doern, G. B. (1992a). "Johnny-Green-Latelies: The Mulroney Environmental Record." In F. Abele (ed.), *How Ottawa Spends 1992–93: The Politics of Competitiveness*, pp. 353–76. Ottawa: Carleton University Press.

———. (1992b). *The Greening of Canada: Twenty Years of Environmental Policy*. Unpublished report prepared for the Department of Environment, Ottawa.

Dyson, Kenneth. (1980). *The State Tradition in Western Europe: A Study of an Idea and Institution*. Oxford: Martin Robertson.

Easton, David. (1965). *A Systems Analysis of Political Life*. New York: Wiley.

Ehrensaft, P., and W. Armstrong. (1981). "The Formation of Dominion Capitalism." In A. Moscovitch and G. Drover (eds.), *Inequality: Essays on the Political Economy of Social Welfare*. Toronto: University of Toronto Press.

Engelbrekt, K. (1990). "The Waning of Communist Ideology." *Report on Eastern Europe*, July 27, pp. 5–8.

English, H. E. (1991). *Tomorrow the Pacific*. Toronto: C. D. Howe Research Institute.

Esping-Andersen, G. (1985). *Politics against Markets*. Princeton: Princeton University Press.

Evans, Peter B., Dietrich Rueschemeyer, and Theda Skocpol. (1985). "On the Road toward a More Adequate Understanding of the State." In Peter B. Evans, Dietrich Rueschemeyer, and Theda Skocpol (eds.), *Bringing the State Back In*, pp. 347–66. Cambridge: Cambridge University Press.

Eyerman, R., and A. Jamison. (1991). *Social Movements: A Cognitive Approach*. Cambridge: Polity Press.

Faudemay, Marie-Pierre. (1989). "The OECD Testing of the Conceptual Framework." Paper prepared for an information-sharing session organized by the Centre for Applied Studies in International Negotiation (CASIN), 20 October 1989.

Faulkner, J. H. (1982). "Pressing the Executive." *Canadian Public Administration* 25, no. 2: 240–54.

Federation of European Accountants (FEE). (1990). *The Impact of the Uruguay Round Services Negotiations on the Accountancy Profession*. Proceedings from meeting held February 1–2, Vevey, Switzerland. Brussels: FEE.

Feketekuty, Geza. (1988). *International Trade in Services: An Overview and Blueprint for Negotiations.* Washington, DC: American Enterprise Institute/Ballinger.

Feldstein, P. J. (1988). *The Politics of Health Regulation.* Ann Arbor: University of Michigan Press.

Fischer, G. (1964). *Science and Politics: The New Sociology in the Soviet Union.* Ithaca: Cornell University.

Fisher, D. (1980). "American Philanthropy and the Social Sciences: The Reproduction of a Conservative Ideology." In R. Arnove (ed.), *Philanthropy and Cultural Imperialism.* Boston: G.K. Hall.

Ford Foundation. (1990). *Current Interests of the Ford Foundation 1990 and 1991.* New York: Ford Foundation.

Fosdick, R. (1952). *The Story of the Rockefeller Foundation.* New York: Harper & Brothers.

Fowler, R. (1940). "Design for a New Dominion." *Maclean's Magazine*, January 8.

Freeman, D. C. (1939). "Letter to John Marshall, 3 July." RF. RG 1.1. Series 200. Box 272. Folder 3241. Rockefeller Archive Center.

French, R. (1984). *How Ottawa Decides.* Toronto: James Lorimer.

Friedan, B. (1963). *The Feminine Mystique.* New York: Dell.

Furet, François. (1978). *Penser la révolution française.* Paris: Editions Gallimard.

Gagnon, A. (1989). "Social Scientists and Public Policies." In *International Social Sciences Journal* 122, no. 4: 555–67.

Gagnon, Alain (ed.). (1987). *Intellectuals in Liberal Democracies.* New York: Praeger.

Gamson, W. A. (1991). "Commitment and Agency in Social Movements." *Sociological Forum* 6, no. 1: 27–50.

Geertz, Clifford. (1983). *Local Knowledge: Further Essays in Interpretive Anthropology.* New York: Basic Books.

Geiger, R. (1988). "American Foundations and Academic Social Science, 1945–1960." *Minerva* 26, no. 3: 315–41.

General Agreement on Tariffs and Trade, Group of Negotiations on Services. (1989). "Trade in Professional Services: Note by the Secretariat." MTN.GNS/W/67, 25 August 1989.

Genov, N. (1984). "Research Problems in the Area of Social Activity and Social Systems." *Sociologicky Casopis* 20, no. 2: 208–13.

Gerth, H., and C. W. Mills (eds.). (1958). *From Max Weber: Essays in Sociology.* New York: Oxford University Press.

Giarini, Orio (ed.). (1987). *The Emerging Service Economy.* New York: Pergamon.

Giddens, A. (1986). *The Constitution of Society.* Oxford: Polity Press.

Gill, Stephen. (1990). *American Hegemony and the Trilateral Commission.* Cambridge: Cambridge University Press.

Gill, Stephen, and David Law. (1988). *The Global Political Economy: Perspectives, Problems and Policies.* New York: Harvester.

Godber, G. (1988). "Forty Years of the NHS." *British Medical Journal* 297: 37–43.

Goldstein, J. (1988). "Ideas, Institutions and American Trade Policy." In G. J. Ikenberry, D. A. Lake, and M. Mastanduno (eds.), *The State and American Foreign Economic Policy.* Ithaca and London: Cornell University Press.

Goldthorpe, John H. (1984). "The End of Convergence; Corporatism and Dualist Tendencies in Modern Western Societies." In John H. Goldthorpe (ed.), *Order and Conflict in Contemporary Capitalism: Studies in the Political Economy of Western European Nations*, pp. 315–43. Oxford: Oxford University Press.

Goranov, K. (1986). "Political Relations in the Stage of Accomplishment of the Development of Socialism." Sofia: Partizdat.

Gordon, L. (ed.). (1987). *Eroding Empire: Western Relations with Eastern Europe.* Washington, DC: Brookings Institution.

Gorer, Geoffrey. (1940). "Content Classification." RF. RG 1.1. Series 200. Box 224. Folder 2678. Rockefeller Archive Center.

Gouldner, Alvin. (1970). *The Coming Crises of Western Sociology.* New York: Basic Books.

Gourevitch, P. (1986). *Politics in Hard Times.* Ithaca: Cornell University Press.

———. (1989). "Keynesian Politics: The Political Sources of Economic Policy Choices." In P. Hall (ed.), *The Political Power of Economic Ideas.* Princeton: Princeton University Press.

Gourevitch, P., et al. (1984). *Unions and Economic Crisis: Britain, West Germany and Sweden.* London: Allen & Unwin.

Gramsci, A. (1971). *Selections from the Prison Notebooks.* New York: International Publishers.

Granatstein, J. L. (1982). *The Ottawa Men.* Toronto: University of Toronto Press.

Grant, W. P., and S. Wilks. (1983). "British Industrial Policy: Structural Change. Policy Inertia." *Journal of Public Policy* 3: 13–28.

Grant, W. P., W. Paterson, and C. Whitson. (1988). *Government and the Chemical Industry.* Oxford: Clarendon.

Gray, C. (1988). "Why Can't Women Get Their Act Together?" *Chatelaine* 61, no. 11: 82–83, 232–34, 238–40.

Grigorov, K. (1968). "Modern Bourgeois Sociological Theories about the Economic Cycles." Sofia: BAN.

Gruchin, B., and V. Zamochkin. (1972). "Yesterday, Today, and Tomorrow: Remarks about the Seventh World Congress of Sociology." *American Sociologist* 17: 17–20.

Gustafsson, B. (1973). "Review Article—A Perennial of Doctrinal History and the Stockholm School." *Economy and History* 16: 114–28.

Gyorgy, S. (1988). "Theoretical Questions of the Socialist State and the Challenge of Democracy." Paper presented at the IPSA World Congress, Washington, DC, August 28–September 1.

Habermas, J. (1972). *Knowledge and Human Interests.* London: Heinemann.

Habermas, Jurgen. (1991). *The Structural Transformation of the Public Sphere* (trans. Thomas Burger). Cambridge, MA: MIT Press.

Hall, Peter A. (1986). *Governing the Economy: The Politics of State Intervention in Britain and France.* Cambridge: Polity Press.

———(ed.). (1989). *The Political Power of Economic Ideas.* Princeton: Princeton University Press.

———. (1990). "Policy Paradigms, Experts and the State: The Case of Macroeconomic Policy-making in Britain." In Stephen Brooks and Alain-G. Gagnon (eds.), *Social Scientists, Policy and the State,* pp. 53–78. New York: Praeger.

Hamilton, M. (1989). *Democratic Socialism in Britain and Sweden.* Basingstoke: Macmillan Press.

Hansen, W. L. (1990). "The international Trade Commission and the Politics of Protectionism." *American Political Science Review* 84: 21–45.

Hardin, H. (1974). *A Nation Unaware: The Canadian Economic Culture.* Vancouver: J. J. Douglas.

Hartz, L. (1955). *The Liberal Tradition in America.* New York: Harcourt Brace Jovanovich.

Havighurst, C. C., R. B. Helms, C. Bladen, and M. V. Pauly. (1988). *American Health Care.* London: Institute of Economic Affairs.

Heclo, Hugh. (1974). *Modern Social Politics in Britain and Sweden.* New Haven: Yale University Press.

———. (1978). "Issue Networks and the Executive Establishment." In A. King (ed.), *The New American Political System,* pp. 87–124. Washington, DC: American Enterprise Institute for Public Policy Research.

Heclo, H., and H. Madsen. (1987). *Policy and Politics in Sweden.* Philadelphia: Temple University Press.

Hegedus, A. (1980). "Interview." *Telos,* no. 47: 132–37.

———. (1982). "Hungary in 1956." *Telos,* no. 53: 163–71.

Heinrich, E. (1992). "Recession Chills Out Green Groups." *Financial Post.* February 10, p. 8.

Held, D. (1991). "Between State and Civil Society: Citizenship." In G. Andrews (ed.), *Citizenship,* pp. 19–25. London: Lawrence and Wishard.

Hernes, Gudmund, and Arne Selvik. (1981). "Local Corporatism." In Suzanne Berger (ed.), *Organizing Interests in western Europe: Pluralism, Corporatism, and the Transformation of Politics*, pp. 103–19. Cambridge: Cambridge University Press.

Higgins, W. (1985). "Ernst Wigforss: The Renewal of Social Democratic Theory and Practice." *Political Power and Social Theory 5*.

Hoberg, G. (1993). "Environmental Policy: Alternative Styles." In M. Atkinson (ed.), *Governing Canada: Institutions and Public Policy*, pp. 307–42. Toronto: Harcourt, Brace, Jovanovich.

Hodgetts, J. (1968). "Public Power and Ivory Tower." In T. Lloyd and J. McLeod (eds.), *Agenda 1970: Proposals for a Creative Politics*. Toronto: University of Toronto Press.

Hollander, P. (1989). "Social Science and Social Problems in Hungary." *Society* 26, no. 2: 14–21.

Horowitz, G. (1968). *Canadian Labour in Politics*. Toronto: University of Toronto Press.

Horvat, B. (1979). "Some Political Preconditions for a Free Society." In R. Merritt (ed.), *International Political Science Enters the 1980s*, vol. 1. Abstracts of papers presented at the Eleventh World Congress of the International Political Science Association, Moscow, August 12–18, 1979. Oslo, Norway: International Political Science Association.

House of Commons. *Parliamentary Debates*, 5th Series, vol. 397, 25 February 1944.

Howard, R. (1991). "Reproductive Technology Commission Facing Lawsuit." *Globe and Mail*, November 30, p. A1.

Ikenberry, G. J. (1988). "Conclusion: An Institutional Approach to American Foreign Economic Policy." In G. J. Ikenberry, D. A. Lake, and M. Mastanduno (eds.), *The State and American Foreign Economic Policy*. Ithaca and London: Cornell University Press.

Ingham, G. (1974). *Strikes and Industrial Conflict*. London: Macmillan.

International Political Science Association. (n.d.). "Synthesis Report on the I.P.S.A. 20 Years Activities 1949–1969." Oslo, Norway: International Political Science Association.

Iribadjakov, N. (1960). " 'Modern' Critics of Marxism." Sofia: Partizdat.

Jamison, A., R. Eyerman, J. Cramer, and J. Laessoe. (1991). *The Making of the New Environmental Consciousness: A Comparative Study of the Environmental Movement in Sweden, Denmark and the Netherlands*. Edinburgh: Edinburgh University Press.

Jan Hus Educational Foundation. (1990). *Report*. London: Jan Hus Educational Foundation.

Jenkins, J. C. (1983). "Resource Mobilization Theory and the Study of Social Movements." *Annual Review of Sociology* 9: 527–54.

Jenson, J. (1986). "Gender and Reproduction: Or, Babies and the State." *Studies in Political Economy* 20 (Summer).

―――. (1989). "Different' But Not 'Exceptional': Canada's Permeable Fordism." *Canadian Review of Sociology and Anthropology*, Winter.

―――. (1990). "Representations in Crisis: The Roots of Canada's Permeable Fordism." *Canadian Journal of Political Science* 23, no. 4: 653–84.

―――. (1991). "All the World's a Stage: Ideas, Spaces and Times in Canadian Political Economy." *Studies in Political Economy* 36 (Fall): 43–72.

―――. (1992a). "Citizenship Claims: Routes to Representation in a Federal System." Paper presented to the Federalism and the Nation State Conference, University of Toronto.

―――. (1992b). "Naming Nations: Nationalisms in Canadian Public Discourse." Paper presented to the Workshop on Culture and Social Movements, University of California, San Diego.

Jessop, B. (1990). *State Theory.* Oxford: Polity Press.

Jhappan, R. (1992). "A Global Community? Supranational Strategies of Canada's Aboriginal Peoples." Paper presented to the Canadian Political Science Association, University of Prince Edward Island.

Jordan, A. G. (1990). "Sub-Governments, Policy Communities and Networks." *Journal of Theoretical Politics* 2, no. 3: 319–38.

Jordan, A. G., and J. J. Richardson. (1982). "The British Policy Style or the Logic of Negotiation?" In J. J. Richardson (ed.), *Policy Style in Western Europe.* London: George Allen and Unwin.

―――. (1987). *Government and Pressure Groups in Britain.* Oxford: Clarendon.

Jordan, A. G., and K. Schubert. (1992). "A Preliminary Ordering of Policy Network Labels." *European Journal of Political Research* 21: 7–28.

Journal of Applied Psychology. (1939). Vol. 23, no. 1 (February), "Special Issue on Radio Research."

Katzenstein, Peter J. (1978). "Conclusion: Domestic Structures and Strategies of Foreign Economic Policy." In P. Katzenstein (ed.), *Between Power and Plenty: Foreign Economic Policies of Advanced Industrial States*, pp. 295–336. Madison: University of Wisconsin Press.

―――. (1985). *Small States in World Markets: Industrial Policy in Europe.* Ithaca and London: Cornell University Press.

―――. (1987). *Policy and Politics in West Germany: The Growth of a Semi-Sovereign State.* Philadelphia: Temple University Press.

Kaulbars, M. (1992). "The Movement That Never Was." *CEN Bulletin* 2, no. 4. Ottawa: Canadian Environmental Network.

Keane, John. (1988). "Introduction" and "Despotism and Democracy." In John Keane (ed.), *Civil Society and the State*, pp. 1–31, 35–71. London: Verso.

Kent, T. (1958). "The Gordon Commission." *Winnipeg Free Press*, Editorial Series, April–May.

Keohane, R. A. (1984). *After Hegemony: Cooperation and Discord in the World Political Economy*. Princeton: Princeton University Press.

Kingdon, John. (1984). *Agendas, Alternatives, and Public Policies*. Boston: Little Brown.

Kitschelt, H. (1990). "The Medium Is the Message: Democracy and Oligarchy in Belgian Ecology Parties." In W. Rüdig (ed.), *Green Politics One*. Edinburgh: Edinburgh University Press.

Klandermans, B., and S. Tarrow. (1988). "Mobilization into Social Movements: Synthesizing European and American Approaches." *International Social Movement Research* 1: 1–38.

Klingemann, H. D. (1991). "Developing Research Projects in Central and Eastern Europe." *Participation* 15, no. 1: 8–9.

Konrad, G., and I. Szelenyi. (1979). *Intellectuals on the Road to Class Power*. Brighton: Harvester.

Krasner, S. D. (1978). "United States Commercial and Monetary Policy: Unravelling the Paradox of External Strength and Internal Weakness." In P. J. Katzenstein (ed.), *Between Power and Plenty*. Madison: University of Wisconsin Press.

Krauss, Melvyn B. (1984). "'Europeanizing' the U.S. Economy: The Enduring Appeal of the Corporatist State." In Chalmers Johnson (ed.), *The Industrial Policy Debate*, pp. 71–90. San Francisco: Institute for Contemporary Studies Press.

Kriesi, H. (1988). "The Interdependence of Structure and Action: Some Reflections on the State of the Art." *International Social Movement Research* 1: 349–68.

———. (1989). "New Social Movements and the New Class in the Netherlands." *American Journal of Sociology* 94, no. 5: 1078–116.

Krommenacker, Raymond J. (1984). *World-Traded Services: The Challenge for the 1980's*. Dedham, MA: Artech House.

Kuechler, M., and R. J. Dalton. (1991). "New Social Movements and the Political Order." In R. J. Dalton and M. Kuechler (eds.), *The Challenge of New Movements*, pp. 277–99. Oxford: Oxford University Press.

Laclau, E., and C. Mouffe. (1985). *Hegemony and Socialist Strategy*. London: New Left Books.

Lamontagne, M. (1954). "The Role of Government." In G. P. Gilmour (ed.), *Canada's Tomorrow*. Toronto: Macmillan.

Langille, David. (1987). "The Business Council on National Issues and the Canadian State." *Studies in Political Economy* 24 (Autumn): 41–85.

Lapidus, G. (1980). "Patterns of Daily Life." *IREX Occasional Papers* 1, no. 4.

Lash, S., and J. Urry. (1987). *The End of Organized Capitalism*. Cambridge: Polity Press.

Lasswell, Harold. (1940). "Who Communicates." RF. RG 1.1. Box 224. Folder 2678. Rockefeller Archive Center.

———. (1948). "The Structure and Function of Communication in Society." In Lymon Bryson (ed.), *The Communication of Ideas*, pp. 35–51. New York: Harper and Brothers.

Lasswell, Harold, B. Smith, and R. Casey. (1935). *Propaganda and Promotional Activities: An Annotated Bibliography*. Minneapolis: University of Minnesota Press.

Latham, Earl. (1956). "The Group Basis of Politics: Notes for a Theory." In Heinz Eulau, Samuel Eldersveld, and Morris Janowitz (eds.), *Political Behaviour: A Reader in Theory and Research*. Glencoe, IL: Free Press.

Laumann, E. O., and D. Knoke. (1987). *The Organizational State*. Madison: University of Wisconsin Press.

Laxer, G. (1989). *Open for Business*. Toronto: Oxford University Press.

Lazarsfeld, Paul F. (1938a). "Letter to the Committee of Six. 7 November." RF. RG 1.1. Series 200. Box 271. Folder 3236. Rockefeller Archive Center.

———. (1938b). "Princeton Radio Research Project." RF. RG 1.1. Series 200. Box 271. Folder 3236. Rockefeller Archive Center.

———. (1939). "Letter to John Marshall. 29 August." RF. RG 1.1. Series 200. Box 272. Folder 3241. Rockefeller Archive Center.

———. (1940a). "Notes on Audience Research." RF. RG 1.1. Series 200. Box 224. Folder 2678. Rockefeller Archive Center.

———. (1940b). *Radio and the Printed Page*. New York: Duell, Sloan and Pearce.

Lehmbruch, Gerhard. (1979). "Liberal Corporatism and Party Government." In P. Schmitter and G. Lehmbruch (eds.), *Trends toward Corporatist Intermediation*, pp. 147–83. Beverly Hills, CA: Sage.

Leiss, William. (1991). "The 1990 Southam Lecture: On the Vitality of Our Discipline—New Applications of Communications Theory." *Canadian Journal of Communication* 16: 291–305.

Lindblom, Charles. (1977). *Politics and Markets*. New York: Basic Books.

Lindquist, E. A. (1990). "The Third Community, Policy Inquiry, and Social Scientists." In S. Brooks and A.-G. Gagnon (eds.), *Social Scientists, Policy and the State*, pp. 21–51. New York: Praeger.

———. (1991). "Confronting Globalization and Governance Challenges: Canadian Think Tanks and the Asia-Pacific Region." In J. W. Langford and K. L. Brownsey (eds.), *Think Tanks and Governance in the Asia-Pacific Region*, pp. 189–213. Halifax: Institute for Research on Public Policy.

————. (1992). "Public Managers and Policy Communities: Learning to Meet New Challenges." *Canadian Public Administration* 35, no. 2: 127–59.

Lippman, Walter. (1922). *Public Opinion*. London: Allen & Unwin.

Lipset, Seymour Martin. (1968). "Moisei Ostrogorski and the Analytical Approach to the Comparative Study of Political Parties." In *Revolution and Counterrevolution: Change and Persistence in Social Structures*. New York: Basic Books.

————. (1981). *Political Man*, expanded ed. Baltimore, MD: Johns Hopkins University Press.

Lobby Digest. (1990). "Women Power: How Wiener Got Roasted." Vol. 8, p. 5.

Lowery, Shearon, and Melvin L. DeFleur. (1975). *Milestones in Mass Communication*, 4th ed. New York: Longman.

Luers, W. (1987). "The United States and Eastern Europe." *Foreign Affairs* 65, no. 5: 976–94.

Lynd, Robert. (1940). "Desirable Social Changes to Be Researched On." Memorandum to the Communications Group, May 5. RF. RG 1.1. Series 200. Box 224. Folder 2678. Rockefeller Archive Center.

Macdonald, D. (1991). *The Politics of Pollution*. Toronto: McClelland and Stewart.

Mackintosh, W. A. (1948). "Trade and Fiscal Policy." In *Canada Looks Ahead*. Ottawa: Tower Books.

————. (1953). "Federal Finance." *Canadian Tax Journal* 1.

————. (1965). "The White Paper on Employment and Income in Its 1945 Setting." In *Canadian Economic Policy since the War*. Ottawa: Carleton University.

Magnusson, W., and R. Walker. (1988). "De-centring the State: Political Theory and Canadian Political Economy." *Studies in Political Economy* 26 (Summer).

Maheu, Louis. (1983). "Les mouvements de base et la lutte contre l'appropriation étatique du tissu social." *Sociologie et Sociétés* 15, no. 1: 77–92.

Maier, Charles. (1988). *The Unmasterable Past: History, Holocaust and German National Identity*. Cambridge, MA: Harvard University Press.

Mann, M. (1984). "The Autonomous Power of the State: Its Origins, Mechanisms and Results." *Archives Européennes de Sociologie* 25: 185–213.

Marmor, T. (1970). *The Politics of Medicare*. London: Routledge and Kegan Paul.

Marmor, T., J. L. Mashaw, and P. L. Harvey. (1990). *America's Misunderstood Welfare State*. New York: Basic Books.

Marschall, M. (1989). Interview. Keene, NH. July 22–23.

Marsh, D., and R. A. W. Rhodes. (1992). *Policy Networks and British Government*. Oxford: Oxford University Press.

Marshall, John. (1935). Officer's Diary. Rockefeller Foundation Archives. 905 MAR. Rockefeller Archive Center.

———. (1936a). Officer's Diary. Rockefeller Foundation Archives. 905 MAR. Rockefeller Archive Center.

———. (1936b). "Statement on Radio. June." RF. RG 3.1. Series 911. Box 5. Folder 51. Rockefeller Archive Center.

———. (1937). "Memorandum on Cantril's Proposal." RF. RG 1.1. Series 200. Box 271. Folder 3234. Rockefeller Archive Center.

———. (1939a). "Letter to A. G. Crane. 13 July." RF. RG 1.1. Series 200. Box 272. Folder 3241. Rockefeller Archive Center.

———. (1939b). "Letter to Frank Stanton. 12 July." RF. RG 1.1. Series 200. Box 272. Folder 3241. Rockefeller Archive Center.

———. (1939c). "Letter to Herbert Brucker. 21 November." RF. RG. 1.1. Series 200. Box 272. Folder 3242. Rockefeller Archive Center.

———. (1939d). Officer's Diary. Rockefeller Foundation Archives. 905 MAR. Rockefeller Archive Center.

———. (1940a). "Introduction." RF. RG 1.1. Series 200. Box 224. Folder 2678. Rockefeller Archive Center.

———. (1940b). Officer's Diary. Rockefeller Foundation Archives. 905 MAR. Rockefeller Archive Center.

———. (1941). Officer's Diary. Rockefeller Foundation Archives. 905 MAR. Rockefeller Archive Center.

Martin, A. (1984). "Trade Unions in Sweden." In P. Gourevitch et al. (eds.), *Unions and Economic Crisis*. London: Allen & Unwin.

McDowell, Stephen D. (1991). "Gender and the Liberalization of Service Institutions." Paper delivered at the meeting of the International Studies Association, Vancouver, British Columbia, March.

Meadows, Dennis L., et al. (1972). *The Limits to Growth*. New York: New American Library.

Melucci, Alberto. (1985). "The Symbolic Challenge of Contemporary Movements." *Social Research* (Winter), pp. 789–818.

———. (1988). "Social Movements and the Democratization of Everyday Life." In John Keane (ed.), *Civil Society and the State: New European Perspectives*, pp. 245–60. London: Verso.

———. (1989). *Nomads of the Present: Social Movements and Individual Needs in Contemporary Society*. London: Hutchinson Radius.

Mittelstaedt, M. (1991). "Saving the Planet Can Wait." *Globe and Mail*, November 28, p. A1.

Montaigne, Michel Eyquem, Seigneur de. (1958). *Essays* (trans. J. M. Cohen). London: Penguin Books.

Montesquieu, Charles Louis de Secondat, Baron de. (1973). *Persian Letters* (trans. C. J. Betts). Harmondsworth: Penguin Books.

———. (1989). *The Spirit of the Laws* (trans. and eds. Anne M. Cohler, Basia Carolyn Miller, and Harold Samuel Stone). Cambridge: Cambridge University Press.

Morrison, David. (1978). "The Beginning of Modern Mass Communication Research." *Archives of European Sociology* 19: 347–59.

Murray, Charles. (1984). *Losing Ground: American Society Policy, 1950–1980.* New York: Basic Books.

Myer, J. W., and B. Rowan. (1977). "Institutionalized Organizations: Formal Structure as Myth and Ceremony." *American Journal of Sociology* 83: 340–63.

Myles, J. (1989). "Introduction: Understanding Canada: Comparative Political Economy Perspectives." *Canadian Review of Sociology and Anthropology* (Winter).

Myrdal, G. (1973). *Against the Stream.* New York: Pantheon Books.

Nash, R. (ed.). (1968). *The American Environment: Readings in the History of Conservation.* Reading, MA: Addison-Wesley.

———. (1980). "The Separation of Form and Content in Liberal Democratic Politics." *Studies in Political Economy* 3 (Spring): 5–16.

Neatby, H. B. (1976). *William Lyon Mackenzie King, 1932–1939.* Toronto: University of Toronto Press.

Nettl, J. P. (1968). "The State as Conceptual Variable." *World Politics* 20: 559–92.

Neufeld, Mark. (1991). "The Reflexive Turn in International Relations Theory." Working Paper No. 4, Centre for International and Strategic Studies, York University, Toronto, January.

Nikolov, S. (1990). "Is Non-Profit Activity Possible under Socialism?" Paper presented at Research Forum of Independent Sector, Boston, MA, March 15–16.

Nordlinger, E. (1981). *On the Autonomy of the Democratic State.* Cambridge, MA: Harvard University Press.

———. (1988). "The Return to the State: Critique." *American Political Science Review* 82, no. 3: 875–85.

Odell, J. (1982). *U.S. International Monetary Policy.* Princeton: Princeton University Press.

Offe, Claus. (1980). "The Separation of Form and Content in Liberal Democratic Politics." *Studies in Political Economy* 3 (Spring): 5–16.

———. (1981). "The Attribution of Public Status to Interest Groups: Observations on the West German Case." In Suzanne Berger (ed.), *Organizing Interests in Western Europe: Pluralism, Corporatism, and the Transformation of Politics*, pp. 123–58. Cambridge: Cambridge University Press.

———. (1985). *Disorganized Capitalism* (ed. John Keane). Cambridge: Polity Press.

———. (1991). "Reflections on the Institutional Self-Transformation of Movement Politics: A Tentative Stage Model." In R. J. Dalton and M. Kuechler (eds.), *The Challenge of New Movements*, pp. 232–50. Oxford: Oxford University Press.

Olson, Mancur. (1982). *The Rise and Decline of Nations: Economic Growth, Stagflation and Social Rigidities*. New Haven, CT: Yale University Press.

Organization for Economic Cooperation and Development. (1987). "Elements of a Conceptual Framework for Trade in Services." Paris: OECD.

———. (1989a). "Testing the Conceptual Framework for Trade in Services in the Field of Tourism and International Travel." Paris: OECD.

———. (1989b). *Trade in Services and Developing Countries*. Paris: OECD.

———. (1990). *Trade in Information, Computer and Communication Services*. Paris: OECD.

Orlow, Dietrich. (1986). *Weimar Prussia 1918–1925: The Unlikely Rock of Democracy*, Pittsburgh: University of Pittsburgh Press.

Ostrogorski, Moisei. (1902). *Democracy and the Organization of Political Parties*. New York: Macmillan.

Ottawa Citizen. (1991). "Sleeping with the Enemy." *Ottawa Citizen*, October 13, p. A5.

Owram, D. (1986). *The Government Generation: Canadian Intellectuals and the State 1900–1945*. Toronto: University of Toronto Press.

Paltiel, K. Z. (1989). "Political Marketing, Party Finance and the Decline of Canadian Parties." In A.-G. Gagnon and A. B. Tanguay (eds.), *Canadian Parties in Transition*, pp. 332–53. Scarborough: Nelson.

Panitch, Leo. (1979). "Corporatism in Canada?" *Studies in Political Economy* 1: 43–92.

———. (1980). "Recent Theorizations of Corporatism: Reflections on a Growth Industry." *British Journal of Sociology* 31, no. 2 (June): 159–87.

Parsons, Talcott. (1951). *The Social System*. New York: Free Press.

Pekkarinen, J. (1989). "Keynesianism and the Scandinavian Models of Economic Policy." In P. Hall (ed.), *The Political Power of Economic Ideas*. Princeton: Princeton University Press.

Peon, M. M. (1979). *Harry S. Truman versus the Medical Lobby*. Columbia: University of Missouri Press.

Peschek, Joseph G. (1987). *Policy-Planning Organizations: Elite Agendas and America's Rightward Turn*. Philadelphia: Temple University Press.

———. (1989). " 'Free the Fortune 500!' The American Enterprise Institute and the Politics of the Capitalist Class in the 1970s." *Critical Sociology* 16, no. 2–3 (Summer–Fall): pp. 165–80.

Petkov, K. (1989). "The Causes of Alienation." *World Marxist Review*, October, pp. 51–2.

Phillips, S. D. (1991a). "How Ottawa Blends: Shifting Government Relationships with Interest Groups." In F. Abele (ed.), *How Ottawa Spends 1991–92: The Politics of Fragmentation*, pp. 183–228. Ottawa: Carleton University Press.

———. (1991b). "Meaning and Structure in Social Movements: Mapping the Network of National Canadian Women's Organizations." *Canadian Journal of Political Science* 24, no. 4: 755–82.

———. (1992). "Action, Meaning and Structure in Social Movements: A Project Analytic Study of Women's Organizations." Ottawa: School of Public Administration Discussion Paper Series.

Pickersgill, J. (1960). *The Mackenzie King Record*, vol. 1. Toronto: University of Toronto Press.

Pickersgill, J., and D. Forster. (1970). *The Mackenzie King Record*, vol. 3. Toronto: University of Toronto Press.

Plevza, V. (1979). "National Self-Determination and the Change of Political and Social Systems." In R. Merritt (ed.), *International Political Science Enters the 1980s*, vol. 1. Abstracts of papers presented at the Eleventh World Congress of the International Political Science Association, Moscow, August 12–18. Oslo, Norway: International Political Science Association.

Pocock, J. G. A. (1975). *The Machiavellian Moment*. Princeton: Princeton University Press.

Pontusson, J. (1987). "Sweden." In J. Krieger et al. (eds.), *European Politics in Transition*. Lexington, MA: Heath.

———. (1988). "Swedish Social Democracy and British Labour: Essays on the Nature and Condition of Social Democratic Hegemony." Western Societies Program Occasional Paper no. 19. Ithaca: Cornell University.

Poole, D. C. (1938). "Letter to David H. Stevens. 9 December." RF. RG 1.1. Series 200. Box 271. Folder 3236. Rockefeller Archive Center.

Powell, D., and P. Shoup. (1970). "The Emergence of Political Science in Communist countries." *American Political Science Review* 64: 572–88.

"The Power of Advanced Theory." (1982). *World Marxist Review* (September): 29–33.

Precan, V. (1990). "The Crumbling of the Soviet Bloc." *Journal of Democracy* 1, no. 1: 79–85.

Pross, A. P. (1986). *Group Politics and Public Policy*. Toronto: Oxford University Press.

———. (1992). *Group Politics and Public Policy*, 2d ed. Toronto: Oxford University Press.

Razack, S. (1991). *Canadian Feminism and the Law*. Toronto: Second Story Press.

Reich, Robert B. (1983). *The Next American Frontier*. New York: Times Books.

———. (1991). *The Work of Nations*. New York: Vintage Books.

Rhodes, R. A. W. (1981). *Control and Power in Central-Local Relations*. Aldershot: Gower.

———. (1986). *Beyond Westminster and Whitehall*. London: Unwin Hyman.

———. (1990). "Policy Networks: A British Perspective." *Journal of Theoretical Politics* 2, no. 3: 292–316.

Rhodes, R. A. W., and D. Marsh. (1992). "New Directions in the Study of Policy Networks." *European Journal of Political Research* 21: 181–205.

Rice, J. (1985). "Politics of Income Security: Historical Developments and Limits to Future Change." In B. Doern (ed.), *The Politics of Economic Policy*. Toronto: University of Toronto Press.

Richardson, J. J., and A. G. Jordan. (1979). *Governing under Pressure*. Oxford: Martin Robertson.

Richter, Melvin. (1969). "Comparative Analysis in Montesquieu and Tocqueville." *Comparative Politics* 1, no. 2: 129–60.

———. (1970). "The Uses of Theory: Tocqueville's Adaptation of Montesquieu." In Melvin Richter (ed.), *Essays in Theory and History*, pp. 74–102. Cambridge, MA: Harvard University Press.

Rockefeller Archive Center. (1937a). "Hotlist." April 28. Rockefeller Foundation Archives. RF. RG 1.1. Series 200. Box 271. Folder 3234. Princeton Radio Research Project.

———. (1937b). Memorandum of May 21 Approving Grant to School of Public and International Affairs, Princeton University. RF. RG 1.1. Series 200. Box 271. Folder 3233. Princeton Radio Research Project.

———. (1937c). "Radio in RF and GEB Program: Retrospect and Prospect." RF. RG 3.1. Series 911. Box 5. Folder 51. Princeton Radio Research Project.

———. (1937d). Rockefeller Program in Broadcasting. RF. RG 1.1. Series 200. Box 271. Folder 3234. Princeton Radio Research Project.

———. (1938a). Application to Rockefeller Foundation for Renewal of Grant. RF. RG 1.1. Series 200. Box 272. Folder 3239. Princeton Radio Research Project.

———. (1938b). "Report of Activities." RF. RG 1.1. Series 200. Box 271. Folder 3236. Princeton Radio Research Project.

———. (1939a). Memorandum of 25 January, 1939 (allocating $750 for the costs of arranging for a review of the Princeton Radio Research Project by a qualified reviewing committee). RF. RG 1.1. Series 200. Box 271. Folder 3233. Princeton Radio Research Project.

———. (1939b). "Public Opinion and the Emergency." RF. RG 1.1. Series 200 Box 224. Folder 2677. Princeton Radio Research Project.

———. (1939c). Report for the Reviewing Committee, Princeton Radio Survey, 20 February. RF. RG 1.1. Series 200. Box 273. Folder 3245. Princeton Radio Research Project.

———. (1939d). Seminar Memorandum No. 1: Summary of Discussions of Communications Seminar, September 20 and 23, 1939. RF. RG 1.1. Series 200. Box 224. Folder 2678. Princeton Radio Research Project.

———. (1939e). Seminar Memorandum No. 2: Summary of Discussions of Communication Seminar, September 29, 1939. RF. RG 1.1. Series 200. Box 224. Folder 2678. Princeton Radio Research Project.

———. (1939f). Seminar Memorandum No. 4: Summary of Discussions of Communication Seminar, November 24, 1939. RF. RG 1.1. Series 200. Box 224. Folder 2678. Princeton Radio Research Project.

———. (1939g). Seminar Memorandum No. 5: Summary of Discussions of Communications Seminar, December 21, 1939. RF. RG 1.1. Series 200. Box 224. Folder 2678. Princeton radio Research Project.

———. (1940a). "Needed Research in Communication." RF. RG 1.1. Series 200. Box 224. Folder 2677. Princeton Radio Research Project.

———. (1940b). "Research in Mass Communications." Rockefeller Foundation Archives. RF. RG 1.1. Series 200. Box 224. Folder 2677. Princeton Radio Research Project.

———. (1940c). Seminar Memorandum No. 6: Summary of Discussions of Communications Seminar, February 16, 1940. RF. RG 1.1. Series 200. Box 224. Folder 2678. Princeton radio Research Project.

———. (1940d). Seminar Memorandum No. 7. March 15, 1940. RF. RG 1.1. Series 200. Box 224. Folder 2678. Princeton Radio Research Project.

———. (1940e). Seminar Memorandum No. 9. April 12, 1940. RF. RG 1.1. Series 200. Box 224. Folder 2678. Princeton Radio Research Project.

———. (1940f). Seminar Memorandum No. 10. May 8, 1940. RF. RG 1.1. Series 200. Box 224. Folder 2678. Princeton Radio Research Project.

———. (1941). Memorandum on the Princeton Radio Research Project. RF. RG 1.1. Series 200. Box 272. Folder 3243. Princeton Radio Research Project.

Roelofs, J. (1990). "Foundations and Political Science." Paper presented at the Workshop of the IPSA Research Committee on the Study of Political Science as a Discipline, Paris, May 21–22.

Ross, G. (1987). "Adieu Vieilles Idées." In G. Ross (ed.), *Contemporary France*. London: Routledge.

———. (1991). "French Intellectuals from Sartre to Soft Ideology." In Charles Lemert (ed.), *Intellectuals and Politics*. Newbury Park, CA: Sage.

Rothstein, B. (1985). "Managing the Welfare State: Lessons from Gustav Moller." *Scandinavian Political Studies* 13.

Rucht, D. (1988). "Themes, Logics, and Arenas of Social Movements: A Structural Approach." *International Social Movement Research* 1: 305–28.

———. (1991). "The Strategies and Action Repertoires of New Movements." In R. J. Dalton and M. Kuechler (eds.), *The Challenge of New Movements*, pp. 156–75. Oxford: Oxford University Press.

Sabatier, P. A. (1987). "Knowledge, Policy Oriented Learning, and Policy Change: An Advocacy Coalition Framework." *Knowledge* 8, no. 4: 649–92.

Salter, L. (1988). *Mandated Science: Science and Scientists in the Making of Standards*. Norwell, MA: Kluwer Academic Publishers.

Sampson, Gary P. (n.d.). "Developing Countries and the Liberalization of Trade in Services." Washington, DC: Ford Foundation Project.

Sandel, Michael (1984). "The Procedural Republic and the Unencumbered Self." *Political Theory* 12 (February): 81–96.

Saunders, P. (1975). "They Make the Rules." *Policy and Politics* 4: 31–58.

Schattschneider, E. E. (1960). *The Semi-Sovereign People*. Hinsdale, IL: Dryden Press.

Schmitter, Philippe. (1974). "Still the Century of Corporatism." *Review of Politics* 36, no. 1 (January): 85–131.

———. (1981). "Interest Intermediation and Regime Governability in Contemporary Western Europe and North America." In Suzanne O. Berger (ed.), *Organizing Interests in Western Europe*, pp. 285–327. Cambridge: Cambridge University Press.

Schmitter, Philippe, and Gerhard Lehmbruch. (1982). *Patterns of Corporatist Policy-Making*. Beverly Hills: Sage.

Schrecker, T. (1984). *The Political Economy of Environmental Hazards*. Ottawa: Law Reform Commission.

———. (1992). "Of Invisible Beasts and the Public Interest: Environmental Cases and the Judicial System." In R. Boardman (ed.), *Canadian Environmental Policy: Ecosystems, Politics, and Process*, pp. 83–108. Toronto: Oxford University Press.

Schumpeter, Joseph. (1962). *Capitalism, Socialism and Democracy*. New York: Harper Torchbooks.

Scott, F. R. (1937–1938). "The Royal Commission on Dominion-Provincial Relations." *University of Toronto Quarterly* 7.

Seybold, P. (1982). "The Ford Foundation and Social Control." *Science for the People* 14, no. 3: 28–31.

Shannon, Claude E., and Warren Weaver. (1949). *The Mathematical Theory of Communication*. Urbana, IL: University of Illinois Press.

Shelp, Ronald K. (1981). *Beyond Industrialization: Ascendancy of the Global Service Economy*. New York: Praeger.

————. (1986–1987). "Trade in Services." *Foreign Policy* 65 (Winter): 64–84.

Simeon, R. (1987). "Inside the Macdonald Commission." *Studies in Political Economy* 22 (Spring).

Simeon, R., and I. Robinson. (1990). *State, Society and the Development of Canadian Federalism.* Toronto: University of Toronto Press.

Skocpol, Theda. (1985). "Bring the State Back In: Strategies of Analysis in Current Research." In Peter B. Evans, Dietrich Rueschemeyer, and Theda Skocpol (eds.), *Bringing the State Back In*, pp. 3–43. Cambridge: Cambridge University Press.

Smiley, D. (1962). "The Rowell Sirois Report, Provincial Autonomy, and Post-War Canadian Federalism." *Canadian Journal of Economics and Political Science* 28, no. 1: 54–69.

Smith, Bruce Lannes, Harold D. Lasswell, and Ralph D. Casey. (1946). *Propaganda, Communication, and Public Opinion: A Comprehensive Reference Guide.* Princeton: Princeton University Press.

Smith, M. J. (1989). "The Annual Review: The Emergence of a Corporatist Institution?" *Political Studies* 37: 81–96.

————. (1990a). "Pluralism, Reformed Pluralism and Neo-Pluralism." *Political Studies* 38: 302–22.

————. (1990b). *The Politics of Agricultural Support in Britain.* Aldershot: Gower.

————. (1991). "From Policy Community to Issue Network: Salmonella in Eggs and the New Politics of Food." *Public Administration* 69: 235–55.

————. (1993). *Pressure Power and Policy: State Autonomy and Policy Networks in Britain and the United States.* Hemel Hempstead: Harvester Wheatsheaf.

Social Science Federation of Canada. (1987). *University Research Centres in the Social Sciences and Humanities.* Proceedings of a national conference held in Ottawa, March 1987. Ottawa: University of Ottawa Press.

Social Science Research Council. (1987–1988). *Annual Report.* New York: SSRC.

Soros Foundation. (1987). *Annual Report.* Sofia.

————. (1988). *Annual Report.* Sofia.

————. (1990). "Open Society Fund." Sofia.

Stinchcombe, A. L. (1990). *Information and Organizations.* Berkeley: University of California Press.

Stones, R. (1990). "Government-Finance Relations in Britain 1964–67: A Tale of Three Cities." *Economy and Society* 19: 32–55.

Struthers, J. (1983). *No Fault of Their Own.* Toronto: University of Toronto Press.

Studebaker, J. W. (1937). "Report of Progress of Federal Radio Education Committee." Address delivered at Second National Conference on Educational Broadcasting. Chicago, 30 November. General Education Board. GEB Advisory Committee. Series 1, Sub-series 2, Box 359, Folder 3706. Rockefeller Archive Center.

Swenson, P. (1989). *Fair Shares: Unions, pay and Politics in Sweden and West Germany*. Ithaca: Cornell University Press.

Szelenyi, I. (1986–1987). "The Prospects and Limits of the East European New Class Project: An Auto-Critical Reflection of the Intellectuals on the Road to Class Power." *Politics and Society* 15, no. 2: 103–44.

Tarkowski, J. (1987). "Political Science and Sociology: Different Responses to the Polish Crisis." Paper presented at the Conference on the Comparative Study of the Development of Political Science, Cortona, September 21–6.

Tarkowski, J., and R. Siemienska. (1979). "Local Leaders in the Socialist Countries of Eastern Europe." In R. Merritt (ed.), *International Political Science Enters the 1980s*, vol. 1. Abstracts of papers presented at the Eleventh World Congress of the International Political Science Association, Moscow, August 12–18. Oslo, Norway: International Political Science Association.

Tarrow, S. (1983). *Struggling to Reform: Social Movements and Policy Change during Cycles of Protest*. Ithaca: Cornell University, Western Societies Program, Paper No. 15.

———. (1989). *Struggle, Politics, and Reform: Collective Action, Social Movements, and Cycles of Protest*. Ithaca: Center for International Studies, Cornell University.

Taylor, Charles. (1975). *Hegel*. Cambridge: Cambridge University Press.

———. (1991a). "Civil Society in the Western Tradition." In Ethel Groffier and Michel Paradis (eds.), *The Notion of Tolerance and Human Rights: Essays in Honour of Raymond Kiibansky*, pp. 117–36. Ottawa: Carleton University Press.

———. (1991b). "Comprendre la culture politique." In Raymond Hudon and Rejean Pelletier (eds.), *L'engagement intellectuel: Mélanges en l'honneur de Léon Dion*, pp. 193–207. Sainte-Foy, Quebec: Les Presses de l'Université Laval.

Therborn, G. (1989). " 'Pillarization' and 'Popular Movements.' " In F. Castles (ed.), *The Comparative History of Public Policy*. Cambridge: Polity Press.

Thompson, E. P. (1981). *The Making of the English Working Class*. Harmondsworth: Penguin.

Tilton, T. (1990). *The Political Theory of Swedish Social Democracy*. Oxford: Oxford University Press.

Tocqueville, Alexis de. (1945). *Democracy in America*, vols. 1, 2 (trans. Henry Reeve, rev. Francis Bowen). New York: Vintage Books.

———. (1955). *The Old Regime and the French Revolution* (trans. Stuart Gilbert). Garden City, NY: Doubleday Anchor Books.

Toner, G. (1990). "Whence and Whither: ENGOs, Business and the Environment." Ottawa: Carleton University, Department of Political Science (unpublished paper).

———. (1991). "The Canadian Environmental Movement: A Conceptual Map." Ottawa: Carleton University, Department of Political Science (unpublished paper).

Toronto Star. (1985). "Canada Gets Blueprint for Future." September 6.

Trent, J. E. (1988). "Research Institutes in Canada: Underdeveloped, Underappreciated and Underfunded." In *Culture, Development and Regional Policy*, Canadian Issues, vol. 9, pp. 221–29. Montreal: Association for Canadian Studies.

Truman, David B. (1951). *The Governmental Process.* New York: Alfred A. Knopf.

Tuohy, Carolyn. (1990). "Institutions and Interests in the Occupational Health Arena: The Case of Quebec." In W. D. Coleman and G. Skogstad (eds.), *Policy Communities and Public Policy in Canada: A Structuralist Approach*, pp. 238–65. Toronto: Copp Clark Pitman.

Tyson, Levering. (1938). "Letter to David H. Stephens. 19 November." RF. RG 1.1. Series 200. Box 271. Folder 3236. Rockefeller Archive Center.

Underhill, F. (1975). *In Search of Canadian Liberalism.* Toronto: Macmillan.

United States Congress. House. (1986). *List of Organizations Involved in Exchange Programs with the Soviet Union and Eastern Europe.* 99th Congress, 2d. session. Washington, DC: USGPO.

United States Department of State. (1974). *A Human Contribution to the Structure of Peace: International Educational and Cultural Exchange.* Washington, DC: USGPO.

Vacca, Giuseppe. (1982). "Intellectuals and the Marxist Theory of the State." In Anne Showstack Sassoon (ed.), *Approaches to Gramsci.* London: Writers and Readers.

Vasilev, M., et al. (1983). "Sociology in Bulgaria." *International Review of Modern Sociology* 13: 35–77.

Vernon, Raymond. (1988). "Launching the Uruguay Round: Clayton Yeutter and the Two-Track Decision." Pittsburgh: Pew Program in Case Teaching and Writing in International Affairs.

Vickers, J. M. (1988). "Politics as if Women Mattered: The Institutionalization of the Canadian Women's Movement and Its Impact on Federal Politics 1965–1988." Paper presented to the ACSANZ'88 Canadian Studies Conference, Canberra.

Vogel, David. (1989). *Fluctuating Fortunes: The Political Power of Business in America.* New York: Basic Books.

Waarden, F. van (1992). "The Historical Institutionalization of Typical National Patterns in Policy Networks between State and Industry: A Comparison of the USA and the Netherlands." *European Journal of Political Research* 21: 131–62.

Waddock, S. A. (1988). "Building Successful Social Partnerships." *Sloan Management Review* 17 (Summer): 17–23.

Waples, Douglas. (1940). "Some Considerations Involved in Studies to Describe the Effects of Communications." RF. RG 1.1. Series 200. Box 224. Folder 2678. Rockefeller Archive Center.

Weaver, R. Kent. (1989). "The Changing World of Think Tanks." *PS: Political Science and Politics* 22, no. 3 (September): 563–78.

Weber, Max. (1958). "Politics as a Vocation" and "Capitalism and Rural Society in Germany." In H. H. Gerth and C. Wright Mills (eds.), *From Max Weber: Essays in Sociology*, pp. 77–128, 363–85. New York: Oxford University Press.

Weir, M., and T. Skoepol. (1985). "State Structures and the Possibility of 'Keynesian' Responses to the Great Depression in Sweden, Britain and the United States." In P. B. Evans, D. Reuschemeyer, and T. Skocpol (eds.), *Bringing the State Back In*, pp. 107–63. Cambridge: Cambridge University Press.

Wiatr, J. (1990). "The Impact of Democratization on Political Science in Eastern Europe: The Polish Experience." Paper presented at the Conference of the International Committee for the Study of the Development of Political Science, Barcelona, May 14–20.

Wilks, S., and M. Wright. (1987). "Conclusion: Comparing Government-Industry Relations: States, Sectors, and Networks." In S. Wilks and M. Wright (eds.), *Government-Industry Relations*. Oxford: Clarendon Press.

Williams, G. (1985). "Symbols, Economic Logic and Political Conflict in the Canada-U.S.A. Free-Trade Negotiations." *Queen's Quarterly* 92, no. 4 (Winter).

———. (1986). *Not for Export*. Toronto: McClelland and Stewart.

Wilson, D. (1991). "Little Voice Becomes a Roar." *Globe and Mail*, September 16, p. A2.

Wilson, J. (1992). "Green Lobbies: Pressure Groups and Environmental Policy." In R. Boardman (ed.), *Canadian Environmental Policy: Ecosystems, Politics, and Process*, pp. 109–25. Toronto: Oxford University Press.

Wilson, V., and O. P. Dwivedi. (1982). "Introduction." In V. Wilson and O. P. Dwivedi (eds.), *The Administrative State in Canada*. Toronto: University of Toronto Press.

Wilson, William J. (1987). *The Truly Disadvantaged: The Inner City, the Underclass, and Public Policy*. Chicago: University of Chicago Press.

Winham, Gilbert R. (1989). "The Prenegotiation Phase of the Uruguay Round." *International Journal* 44, no. 2 (Spring): 280–303.

Wolfe, A. (1989). *Whose Keeper? Social Science and Moral Obligation*. Berkeley: University of California Press.

Wolfe, D. (1984). "The Rise and Demise of the Keynesian Era in Canada: Economic Policy, 1930–82." In M. Cross and G. Kealey (eds.), *Readings in the Social History of Canada*. Toronto: McClelland and Stewart.

Wolfe, J. (1991). "State and Ideology in Britain: Mrs. Thatcher's Privatization Programme." *Political Studies* 39: 237–52.

Woodrow, R. Brian (ed.). (1990). *Uruguay Round Trade in Services Perspectives*. Proceedings from the First International Forum on Global Services Trade and Trade Liberalization, Geneva, May 16–17. Geneva: Applied Services Economic Centre.

Woods, L. T. (1987). "Comparative National Approaches to Pacific Economic Cooperation: A Post-Fieldwork Report." Sydney: Research School of Pacific Studies, Australian National University, mimeo.

————. (1988). "Diplomacy and International Nongovernmental Organizations: A Study of the Pacific Economic Cooperation Movement." Doctoral dissertation, Australian National University.

World Commission on Environment and Development. (1987). *Our Common Future*. Oxford: Oxford University Press.

Yoffie, David B., and Joseph L. Badaracco, Jr. (1983). "Trade in Services and American Express." Cambridge, MA: Harvard Business School.

Yoffie, David B., and Sigrid Bergenstein. (1985). "Creating Political Advantage: The Rise of the Corporate Political Entrepreneur." *California Management Review* 28, no. 1 (Fall): 124–39.

Zysman, J. (1983). *Government, Markets and Growth*. Ithaca: Cornell University Press.

14

A Novel Conference: The Origins of TPRC

Bruce M. Owen
1998

The twenty-fifth annual Telecommunications Policy Research Conference (TPRC) provides an opportunity to reflect on the origins and achievements of TPRC. An objective of TPRC has been to provide not merely a forum for communication policy researchers to exchange ideas, but also a channel for policy-relevant research to reach regulators and other government officials, and for the latter to convey their research needs to academics. Therefore, any discussion of the history of TPRC should be placed in the context of evolving government policy.

TPRC arose, not coincidentally, at the beginning of an extraordinary period in the history of telecommunications policy and regulation. Before the early 1970s, for example, it was unlawful for anyone but AT&T to offer public long distance service; there was no domestic satellite industry; it was unlawful for cable systems to import any but a limited number of distant signals; it was unlawful for any broadcaster or cable operator to offer pay-TV service consisting of entertainment series, sports events that had been on TV in the last four years, or movies less than two or more than four years old; and it was unlawful for customers to attach a "foreign"—i.e., any—device to the telephone network. More generally, it was the mainstream view that the telephone business was and ought to be a regulated monopoly, and that broadcasters were and ought to be protected from excessive competition in order to promote their ability to offer public service and especially local programming.

Further, and even more generally, the 1970s was a unique period in American economic history: one in which the validity of the notion of natural monopoly and the virtues of regulation came into question. During these years academic skepticism or even cynicism about regulation, emanating especially from the Chicago School, spilled over into public debate. The result was not just communication policy reform but intercity bus, airline, trucking and railroad deregulation, the beginnings of related reforms in the securities and financial services industries, and other deregulation initiatives. A dramatic change illustrative of the growing currency of economics took place at the Department of Justice Antitrust Division, which today employs four or five dozen Ph.D. economists. Before 1974 the Antitrust Division had *no* permanent staff of such economists. Similar changes occurred at the FTC. Many other countries have followed the U.S. intellectual lead in these matters, in some cases showing greater courage in implementing regulatory reform.

TPRC arose also during a period of extraordinary growth and change in telecommunications technology. Remote terminals of mainframe computers, geosynchronous satellites, fiber optic transmission lines, electronic switches, digital transmission and compression, the Internet, and many other advances created pressures for regulatory reform and facilitated reform.

TPRC Beginnings

The institution of TPRC was neither the beginning of academic interest in communications policy nor the first time academics—lawyers, political scientists, engineers, and economists—had a direct impact on communications policy. Modern academic interest in communication policy can be traced to Ronald Coase's (1959, 1962) famous property rights papers on spectrum allocation, and to such theoretical work on utility regulation as the well-known Averch and Johnson (1962) paper.

Those unfamiliar with the field will wonder what is meant by "communication" or "telecommunication" in the present context. What is meant, roughly, is those activities historically subject to the jurisdiction of the Federal Communications Commission. This usage is curious, since telephone regulation has much more in common with electricity or natural gas regulation than with broadcasting. If industry research were focused on firms with basic similarities in their products and technologies, we would have separate conferences on mass media and on public utilities. That the same research community, and even the same individual researchers, focused on the legal jurisdiction rather than the more natural economic classifications illustrates the important influences that government has on policy research.

While important and relevant research existed, the government appeared to remain ignorant of it until the late 1960s, when Lyndon Johnson convened the President's Task Force on Telecommunications Policy, headed by undersecretary of state Eugene V. Rostow (President's Task Force, 1968). The Task Force was established in part to hold back a rising sea of political pressure that had begun to lap at the White House gates. The pressure arose from the desire of potential entrants to arbitrage the growing gap between prices and costs or between actual and best-practice technologies, and from those incumbents who relied on government to protect economic rents. These pressures were manifest chiefly in controversies involving long distance telephone service, domestic communication satellites, and the import of distant TV signals by cable systems.

Rostow assembled a talented staff. For example, Richard A. Posner was seconded from the Justice Department and Walter Hinchman from Commerce. Leland L. Johnson came from RAND. More than thirty academic consultants were retained, including William J. Baumol, William F. Baxter, William Capron, William K. Jones, Charles J. Meyers, Monroe E. Price, and Lester D. Taylor. Government agencies sent representatives, such as Roger G. Noll from the Council of Economic Advisors. The Task Force, its consultants, and its research contractors, well aware of relevant academic research, produced a report that was cautiously progressive, suggesting for example an "open skies" policy for domestic communication satellites, and a greater role for competition in telephony. The staff and contractors also produced several innovative papers on marketable spectrum rights. Finally, the Task Force recommended establishment of an executive branch agency to formulate and coordinate telecommunication policy. More important than the specific recommendations, however, the Task Force implicitly validated the notion that there was such a thing as "telecommunications policy," that it was susceptible to analytical policy research and analysis, and that there existed a newly self-aware community of scholars interested in such research.

Establishment of the Office of Telecommunications Policy

When President Johnson did not run for reelection, his Task Force lost its constituency. Politics notwithstanding, however, the incoming Nixon administration picked up on and sought to implement many of the Task Force recommendations. Clay T. (Tom) Whitehead, a Special Assistant to the President assigned to communication matters, perhaps because he had a Ph.D. from MIT (in political science), pushed to implement both the satellite open skies policy and the establishment of an executive branch policy agency. The resulting Office of Telecommunication Policy (OTP) was created by Executive Order as part of the Executive Office of the President in 1970. Tom Whitehead became the first director of the agency, reporting at least in theory directly to the President.

OTP inherited the frequency management and emergency preparedness roles formerly exercised by the defunct Office of Telecommunications Management (OTM), along with many of OTM's staff. Whitehead added only a small number of new professional staff. Among them were general counsel (now Justice) Antonin Scalia, and legislative and press relations officer Brian Lamb (later to found C-SPAN). I was the first economist at OTP, initially as a Brookings Economic Policy Fellow, and later as chief economist. Other early OTP economists included Stanley M. Besen, Ronald Braeutigam and Gary Bowman.

OTP tended to see itself, not indefensibly, as a beacon of reason adjoining an ocean of bureaucratic backwardness. Lacking significant political power (President Nixon and his senior staff did not accord much priority to telecommunications policy even before Watergate), line authority or political experience, Whitehead was reduced chiefly to issuing position papers, making speeches, and writing policy letters to the FCC chairman, which were mostly ignored. This was of course frustrating to those of us aware of the enormous gap between the implications of academic research and the actual state of communications policy in the United States.

The 1972 Conference

Several influences led to the convening of the first telecommunications policy research conference. First, it seemed that exposing other policy-makers to academic ideas might eventually make them more susceptible to OTP's positions. Second, OTP had a research budget to spend, and a conference appeared to be a sensible use of research funds. Earlier expenditures had sometimes produced embarrassing results, such as studies whose conclusions were at odds with OTP's positions. Third, since academic research appeared to be the major positive factor on OTP's side of most issues, OTP wanted to promote more of it. Giving academics a live audience of policy-makers seemed likely to stimulate interest among policy scientists and their students.

Finally, to those of us with academic backgrounds the Washington telecommunications policy community in the early 1970s was a lonely and inhospitable place. It is not an overstatement to say that ideas like "selling the spectrum" or "breaking up *the* telephone company," or even allowing competition with it, were treated with derision and contempt by responsible officials at all levels. A policy research conference would be good for morale—a booster shot for the OTP staff and the few "enlightened" analysts in other agencies.

The first telecommunications policy research conference was held on November 17–18, 1972 in the New Executive Office Building. The audience consisted of federal government employees from OTP, the FCC, and the Departments of Justice, Commerce, and Defense, among others. Papers were presented and discussed by fifteen academics (thirteen economists and two lawyers). Among the most luminous academics were Ronald Coase and William Baumol. [. . .] The research papers were published by OTP (Owen, 1972).

The topics discussed at the first conference are for the most part still on the policy agenda. There were, for example, papers on cross subsidization, financing public broadcasting, spectrum markets, and cable television regulation. There were also papers on subjects that have not been much addressed in subsequent conferences, such as democracy in the newsroom, and one paper analyzing the effect of policy research on FCC decision-making. The first conference was regarded as a success by most of the participants, and there developed a consensus that it would be useful to have an annual conference.

An Annual Event

Although I conceived and organized the 1972 OTP conference, arguably the true beginning of TPRC was at Airlie House on April 16–19, 1974. (The program of the 1974 conference appears as an Appendix in Owen, 1976.) Although OTP provided partial funding, this was the first independently organized meeting. The 1974 conference was organized by a group of academics (Donald A. Dunn, Stanley M. Besen, Gerald Faulhaber, Leland Johnson, and Ithiel de Sola Pool).

In later years funding came from government agencies such as OTP, the Federal Communications Commission, the National Telecommunications and Information Administration, and the National Science Foundation, as well as from private foundations and programs that either sponsored TPRC directly or funded research that was presented at TPRC. These institutions included the Markle Foundation, the Kettering Foundation, the Sloan Foundation, the Ford Foundation, and the Aspen Institute.

It was the practice of organizing committees in the early years to appoint their successors, with little or no overlap from year to year. Also, it was usual for the organizing committee to include representatives from those few organizations with concentrations of telecommunications policy researchers, such as the RAND Corporation, Bell Labs, and Stanford University. Each organizing committee had to manage funding as well as the program and other administrative arrangements. Because the conference had no permanent home for purposes of funding and administrative services there were frequent difficulties. By the early 1980s many established participants felt that TPRC had drifted away from its original character and goals. Accordingly, in 1985, the conference was reorganized in such a way as to separate program responsibility from fund raising and administrative concerns. Administrative matters were undertaken by a Board of Directors, whose self-perpetuating members have overlapping terms. The Board also has the duty to appoint the annual organizing committee, which has responsibility for the program and local arrangements. Since 1989 Economists Incorporated has provided administrative services to TPRC at cost; in practice this work has been organized by Dawn Higgins.

TPRC is, if not unique, certainly unusual in being a long-running event with no singly individual or organization continuing in charge. Conferences like TPRC are more typically organized by learned societies. TPRC has been fortunate in having attracted such a long string of interested and capable organizing committee members. Continuing interest is no doubt also stimulated by the cataclysmic events that have shaken the communication industries since the early 1970s.

TPRC is unique in another respect: the participation of industry researchers. From the beginning, researchers from organizations such as Bell Labs have been an integral part of TPRC. Nevertheless, in the early years there was much debate, which continues, about the participation of industry "lobbyists."

Influence of TPRC

It is difficult to say what influences TPRC has had on the development on government policy and on academic policy research because we lack a "control" world with no TPRC. Some of what we are inclined to attribute to TPRC may be due simply to the technological changes that led to revisions in telecommunications industry structure and regulation. But in celebrating TPRC's twenty-fifth anniversary, perhaps we should not demand too much analytical rigor on this point.

One obvious and demonstrable change on the input side is the growth in the number of economists and other professionals with similar training now employed by the FCC and other agencies responsible for telecommunication. In 1970 the FCC had no more than three or four Ph.D. economists; today there are many dozen, and an even greater number employed by regulated firms and consulting firms. Any given bureau of the FCC today is likely to employ more economists specialized in communications than there were in the nation in 1970. Further, FCC lawyers and other staffers who are not economists have adopted much of the language and many of the precepts of economics.

On the output side, changes have been revolutionary. No important FCC policy statement issues these days without explicit attention to its economic welfare effects. It is true that similar strides have been made in other areas. One is struck, for example, that at the 1977 Tokyo summit meetings on the environment, one of the United States' principal goals was the establishment of tradable emission right. Nevertheless, communications was undoubtedly the first of the major regulatory fields to be thus reformed, and has progressed the most. TPRC facilitated this in two ways. First, by increasing academic interests in the field, it increased the supply of interested graduate students and relevant dissertations. Second, the private and government lawyers who have always been central participants in the policy process heard at TPRC a whole new set of arguments and principles that transcended the usual motifs of legal argument. Lawyers are always competing to win arguments, and TPRC supplied them with new and more effective ammunition. Further, many academic lawyers became interested in communications policy research, often as part of interdisciplinary teams.

A cynic might say that a great portion of what has changed is that the same old vested interests now feel compelled to make their public interest arguments in terms acceptable to scholars, without necessarily leading to any change in outcomes. But such cynicism cannot explain how the pre-existing industry structure was transformed into entirely new "vested" economic interests, such as IXCs, RBOCs, CLECs, DOMSATs, and PCS licensees. Under the old regime these would all have been departments of AT&T, or would not have existed at all.

TPRC's unique contribution, in the end, was the creation of what Stan Besen calls an "invisible college" or virtual community of communication researchers scattered at different institutions and agencies. However characterized, TPRC promoted both academic collaboration and the delivery of relevant policy analysis to government agencies, phenomena previously unknown in the communication world.

Editor's note: The entire first conference program and a list of members of the TPRC organizing committee for the first ten years were appended to this chapter when it was originally published.

Acknowledgment

I am grateful to many of those mentioned by name herein for reviewing the manuscript and pointing out at least some of the errors.

Bibliography

Averch, Harvey and Leland Johnson. Behavior of the Firm Under Regulatory Constraint. 52 Amer. Econ. Rev. 1052 (1962).

Coase, Ronald. The Federal Communications Commission. 2 J. Law & Econ. 1 (1959).

Coase, Ronald. The Interdepartment Radio Advisory Committee. 5 J. Law & Econ. 17 (1962).

Owen, Bruce M., editor. Papers and Proceedings, Conference on Communication Policy Research. November 17–18, 1972. Executive Office of the President, Office of Telecommunications Policy. (NTIS accession number PB 218 981/9).

Owen, Bruce M., editor. Telecommunication Policy Research: Report on the 1975 Conference Proceedings. Aspen Institute Program on Communications and Society. 1976.

President's Task Force on Communications Policy. Final Report. Established Pursuant to the President's [August 14, 1967] Message on Communication Policy. GPO, December 7, 1968. Staff Papers of the President's Task Force on Telecommunications Policy (1968). (NTIS accession numbers PB 4184413-PB 184424).

Indirect Relationships: Serving the Polity

15

Communication Research on Children and Public Policy

Ellen Wartella
1993

In this chapter I wish to make one argument: Both the historical record and current events demonstrate that communication research and scholarship *can* make a difference in children's media, but that they usually do not. For this situation to change requires no less than a redirection of research and scholarship and a fundamental change in how we envision them, requiring us to put aside our "paradigm debates" and focus instead on the public nature of our enterprise.

To advance this argument, I would like to treat briefly several current issues in children's media and to survey the history of the interplay between communication research and children's media policy and public debate. Consider these three issues: the Children's Television Act of 1990; the case of Whittle Communication's Channel One daily in-school news program; and the 1992 battle over funding for public television.

The passage of the Children's Television Act in 1990 was a milestone: It was the first federal law regarding children and television to gain congressional approval and presidential acquiescence in the history of television; indeed it was the first federal law regarding children and media in this century. While some critics of children's television feel it has little power actually to change the problems of children's television, it does establish a precedent for treating children as a unique audience with special needs who therefore deserve special services. Among its provisions, this law now requires that broadcasters must serve the "educational and information needs of children through programming" and that they may be held accountable for their actions with regard to children when they come up for license review every five years; it limits the amount of advertising time during children's programs to 10.5 minutes per hour on weekends and 12 minutes per hour on weekdays; and it establishes a National Endowment for Children's Educational Television, through which new programming ventures can be funded.

Since passage of the 1990 act, there has been movement on the various proposals within it: local broadcasters seem to be interested in child audiences (for example, the National Association of Broadcasters [NAB] has held at least one national conference on children's television); and *TV Guide* now regularly identifies programming for children that parents might want to know about. Advertising time standards are now in place, although the extent to which they are being enforced is still at issue. The National Endowment for Children's Educational Television has been established as of October 1991, and the first board meeting of the endowment was held in September 1992.

In spring 1989, Whittle Communications began broadcasting its ten-minute news show, "Channel One," to school districts across the nation and providing those districts with the hardware—a satellite dish, VCRs and television monitors—to show the program to all students in a school. Now in over 8,000 districts, "Channel One" is an attempt to combat the deficiencies of American high school students' cultural literacy—their knowledge of current events, political issues, geography and so forth—with a daily student-oriented news program aired in school. The controversy focuses on the two minutes of advertisements for things like jeans, candy bars and Coke that are inserted in each program and that help make the service profitable for Whittle. However, recent research commissioned by Whittle (Johnstone and Brzezinski, 1992) suggests that relatively little learning about the news is actually going on. Nonetheless, this past spring, Chris Whittle announced his plans for the Edison Project, a national network of private schools that will exploit communications technologies such as television and computers to provide exceptional education for school-aged children.

During April and May 1992, conservatives in Congress (and in the public arena) debated a Senate appropriations bill to fund public television. Although funding did pass, the political opposition to the Public Broadcasting Service (PBS) left its future in question and raised new charges against the idea of public stewardship of television. Reiterating the arguments made in the early 1980s regarding the need to deregulate broadcasting, conservative critics of the "liberal tilt" of PBS argued that a federally funded public broadcasting system is no longer necessary or "even worthwhile because cable networks have arisen that offer the same kinds of programs" (*New York Times*, April 1992). Even the highly acclaimed "Sesame Street," one of the few preschool programs available on over-the-air broadcast television, was criticized: the Heritage Foundation's Bradley Resident Scholar, Laurence Jarvik, was quoted in the *Times* as saying " 'Sesame Street' is just another kids' show. No better than 'Underdog' or 'The Flintstones.' What did the taxpayers get for their investment in 'Sesame Street'? A generation of kids who spray graffiti on the walls of New York City. If 'Sesame Street' was so effective, why do we have such a literacy problem?" He went on to argue (falsely) that the Children's Television Workshop (CTW) should not be taking public money for "Sesame Street" when it makes millions of dollars through its licensing agreements. (The fact is that CTW is well off, with an existing endowment of more than $50 million; however, CTW has not taken any money from the Corporation for Public Broadcasting since 1982, and funds "Sesame Street" with its own money, amounting to more than $90 million in the past ten years.)

These are but a few of the current public issues that cry out for reasoned discussion and informed communication scholarship. Yet too often communication research is not mentioned in the discussion, is irrelevant, or uninformative or all three.

These public issues underscore the intense public interest in, attention to and concern about the role of communication in modern life. The issues focus on the effects of television on viewers, and in particular, on children viewers. This chapter will examine the question: How has communication research on children and media informed these discussions or influenced policy-making? By communication research I mean a very wide range of research study, including policy research, historical study, traditional audience effects research and interpretive analyses of various media products.

These are questions about the ability of communication researchers and our research to have a visible public face in the current controversies about the communications media.

As James Carey (1989) has noted, communication and the various types of cultural expression are a site for "social conflict over the real" (p. 87). And so in one sense many of these debates might be regarded as skirmishes in the larger political battles of the conservative right to control the political and cultural agenda of this country; they need to be responded to nonetheless in ways that have both moral power and persuasive appeal. In this sense, the ability of communication researchers to mount appealing arguments in the public arena of debates about media is certainly one way of assessing the state of our discipline beyond the paradigm debates of the past decade.

As I have argued elsewhere (Wartella and Reeves, 1985), the public controversies about the effects of media on children, and in particular the ability of the major mass media of film, radio and television to provide for the educational benefits of children, have been part of the recurring controversies about children and media throughout this century. Scrutiny of the vast literature on children and media in the United States through the century demonstrates that it has been the *public agenda* of concern about media effects on youth that in turn has set the *research agenda* for communication scholars and others who have heavily studied the role of media in children's lives and how children learn and are influenced by media portrayals (Wartella and Reeves, 1985). I believe that by reexamining the current public controversies about children and television—by examining the influence of communication research on public discussions and the development of programming for children—we can come to some tentative conclusions about the influence of communication research in public life.

Furthermore, such an assessment might provide us with prescriptions for future communication research, which as this book suggests will go beyond the current paradigm debates and research agendas to have an impact in the public arena.

While this is not the place for an extended critique of the state of the field of communication study, it could be useful at least to consider the ways in which the body of communication research in the broadest sense of various traditions and methods has enlightened public debates about children and media issues. For this purpose let me consider the three issues outlined earlier. In doing so, I hope to illustrate my point about our field and its public responsibilities.

Communication Research and Public Debates about Children and TV

By one yardstick, 1990 was a banner year for those concerned about children's television and for the influence of communication research in the policy arena. With the 1990 act, two of the most visible public controversies about children's television of at least the past twenty-five years were attended to legislatively; the need for more educational programming for children, and concern over the proliferation of advertising to children (see Kunkel, 1991). These two topics have received considerable research attention since the 1970s (Wartella and Reeves, 1985).

The 1990 law was the last version of a series of congressional bills regarding television broadcasters' responsibilities to children, bills that had been introduced into Congress nearly every year between 1981 and 1989. The new law has not, however, ended the controversy about the appropriate regulation of television for children. For instance, in June 1992, legislation was proposed in Congress under the "Ready to Learn" act that would use public television and cable to become involved in providing educational programming to preschool children as part of an intensive national effort in preschool education and health. Promoted and encouraged by Ernest Boyer of the Carnegie Council on Education, Ready to Learn hopes to utilize television in the service of national preschool preparedness in a manner that extends "Sesame Street" beyond its current confines.

Furthermore, as Kunkel (1991) has noted, the 1990 Children's Television Act will not ameliorate all of the perceived problems of children's television. For instance, it does not address at all the issue of television violence (the number one topic to occupy public discussions about television since its inception). Neither will the law in and of itself resolve the two major issues of educational programming and advertising limits. According to Kunkel (1991), there are considerable battles yet to be fought in the policy arena. For instance, the Federal Communications

Commission (FCC), in implementing the law, has held that thirty- and sixty-second informational "drop-ins" could qualify as educational programming, not just full-length children's programs as children's advocates would prefer.

Nonetheless, as Kunkel (1991) notes, "the most meaningful change accomplished by the Act is that the law now says that children's television matters; it is an essential part of the public interest that broadcasters are licensed to serve" (p. 199). Furthermore, a case can be made that the past twenty years of research on children and television has been influential in bringing about this law. A specific example is the effect that Edward Palmer's 1988 book *Television and America's Children: A Crisis of Neglect* had on the policy debates. It served as a catalyst for the establishment of the National Endowment for Children's Educational Television. The book led to Senate hearings conducted by Senator Daniel Inouye in the summer of 1989 and the inclusion of this proposal in the 1990 law. It should be pointed out that this was not the first time such an endowment had been proposed; Eli Rubinstein, a co-editor of the first surgeon general's study of television and social behavior in 1972, had made just such a proposal in the mid-1970s (see Rubinstein and Brown, 1985).

Moreover, throughout the congressional hearings (and throughout the 1990s in the various hearings over different children and television bills) communication research was central and pertinent to the arguments marshalled for passing such bills. In particular, advocates for better children's television were able to point to research on the paucity of educational programming on commercial television, the ability of television to educate children when produced with an educational goal and with a well-formed curriculum, and the enormous amount of time children spend with television. All of these studies formed a persuasive argument to suggest the failure of the "free marketplace" of deregulated television to accommodate the needs of child audiences with high-quality, educational and informational programs.

This has not always been the case: in the late 1970s and early 1980s, communication researchers and advocates for better children's television were spectacularly unsuccessful in bringing about either Federal Trade Commission (FTC) advertising policy or FCC programming policy (see

McGregor, 1986). The reasons for this are multiple. First, in the early 1980s the Reagan presidency brought an antiregulatory environment to Washington; specifically, both the FTC and FCC set about actively dismantling regulatory apparatus. Second, Entman (1993) argues that unlike other areas of federal regulatory policy, which rely on empirical evidence for shaping policy initiatives, the First Amendment area has been devoid of empirical research in policy-making. Clearly, the political winds were favorable in 1990 as they had not been a decade earlier (Kunkel, 1991).

I think scrutiny of the record regarding the 1990 law would demonstrate that communication research was helpful in the political process of negotiating this bill. The research was germane to the public issues about educational potential and advertising limits, and it was used by advocates in the policy arena—that is, it made it into the policy discussions.

Whittle's "Channel One," however, may be a counterexample. When Whittle announced plans for this news program in 1989, a hue and cry developed over the advisability of using classrooms and the captive audience of teenagers found there for advertising messages. A number of school districts around the country publicly announced they would not accept Whittle's offer, for to do so would lead to the commercialization of children in schools.

The outcry against commercialization of the nation's classrooms was largely from education faculty; communication researchers were most prominent by their absence from the debate. Nowhere in the public discussions have communication scholars, or others, come forth to place this issue in the larger context of media commercialization of youth and the lack of a reasonable treatment of television issues in American public schools.

The mass media have been commercializing youth at least since the 1920s, when they helped to identify and promote the youth culture of America's college students, the flappers. Since then ever younger age groups of youth have been the target of media programming and advertising campaigns: the teenagers of the 1950s with their teen pictures and rock music were succeeded by elementary school children, who became the market for 1960s and 1970s "kidvid" on American television.

During the past decade, the merging of television programming with toy production to develop an overall strategy to market toys to preschool children has left no age group of youth uncommercialized or excluded as a segment of the mass audience (Wartella and Mazzarella, 1990). As any parent of a preschooler can attest, the interrelatedness of television programs featuring a character based on a toy line, such as "Teenage Mutant Ninja Turtles," the toys themselves and the proliferation of products with the character's logo, reaches children still in diapers.

Now marketers have found a new venue for commercialization of youth: the schools. When looked at against the history of commercialization of youth through the mass media, it seems obvious that keeping Whittle out of the schools will not resolve the problems of overcommercialization of young children. That does not mean the line could not or should not be drawn here. For moral or ideological reasons, we could well decide that schools are out of bounds, or that young children are out of bounds as an audience for marketers' messages. But this is a moral argument. The only useful communication research that might be brought to bear on the argument is descriptive research on what commercialization exists and historical evidence of its proliferation.

Whether we do or do not allow Whittle into the schools, it is clear to me that the educational establishment has been neglectful in treating television seriously. For instance, schools might consider utilizing "Channel One" to educate their students about commercialization, to critique the media presentations and to make their students more media literate. It will be interesting to see how the proposed Edison Project, Whittle's foray into for-profit schooling, will utilize television. The educational community has by and large framed television as an out-of-school nuisance and a threat to its domain.

To use television as a positive force in children's education would require that educators take a more serious look at television and not dismiss it quite so easily as a bad influence on children, an influence working at odds with the public school system. It would require that more than the controversy about the effects of TV violence on children's social behavior make its way into the textbooks and coursework of students training to become teachers.[1] Education elites would need to change their views of television; they would need to recognize that not

all television is bad, that some programming can be beneficial and informative and even morally uplifting (as viewers of the public television
series "The Civil War" and "Eyes on the Prize" might agree). To change
educators' and others' views, communication researchers need to consider this larger context of the role of television in children's lives, as well
as the role of television as a cultural forum and popular art form. In
short, we need to reshape the discourse about children and television into
a larger set of considerations. Here, we as communication scholars must
help reshape the public's understanding of the television and children
issue. As a community, communication researchers have failed at this
task.

Lastly, consider the battle over the funding of public television, the
major purveyor of educational television today. As Willard Rowland and
Michael Tracey (1990) have argued, public broadcasting throughout the
major industrialized democracies has been under assault for at least the
past decade. The growth of cable and satellite television, fiscal and political problems, as well as the complicity of public broadcasters, who
define their mission in marketplace terms rather than as a public cultural
forum, are forces all working to dismantle public broadcasting. As
Aufderheide (1991) has argued, public television should provide the
"public space" for cultural and political discussions. This is the promise
of ITVS, the federally funded independent television service, which is
supposed to channel money to independent producers and multicultural
and minority programs. However, there are plenty of examples of public
television actively shying away from broadcasting such minority programming for fear of fanning the fires of conservative attack on the
grounds of being too liberal. The 1991 controversy over "Tongues
Untied," the PBS program on homosexuality, is such an example.

What intrigues me most in this debate is the assault on even the educational benefits of public television. Even the seemingly unassailable
"Sesame Street" was assailed. Conservative critics of public broadcasting challenged the well-documented evidence that "Sesame Street" does
teach viewers its educational curriculum (Palmer, 1988). There is a considerable body of research on the effectiveness of different programming
forms and formats for increasing children's attention to and understanding of television content (Huston and Wright, 1983).

And, more important, the success of "Sesame Street" has set a model for the production of children's educational television. This model involves the use of communication research—on how children of different ages attend to and make sense of programming elements—in the actual production of such shows. It is now standard policy for children's educational television to include what is called formative research (research that is the basis of production decisions) in their production. Moreover, indeed whether and how communication research is used in the production of children's television often helps to distinguish the quality of the programming—and whether or not the programming has educational potential.

There is ample evidence that public television has been the main source of educational programming for children available on over-the-air broadcast television (Wartella et al., 1990). Although cable television does have considerably more educational programming for children than does commercial television, not only is cable not available to all American children (fewer than two-thirds of American homes have cable), but it is unclear what sort of commitment cable television has to the production of new educational programs for children. Any perusal of this year's new programs, and there is a lot of children's programming on cable, suggests that the vast majority of such programs are comparable to the commercial networks. That is, they are produced to deliver the child audience to advertisers and therefore the most important criterion of production is whether or not they attract the children's attention. Indeed, Nickelodeon makes it a point to advertise itself as the kid's channel that's fun for kids (implying it is not one that's educationally good for you).

Indeed, the recurring public controversies over first film, then radio and television programming for children, demonstrate that the commercial media systems of this century have never lived up to their educational promises for children. While public concern about children's use of media echoes wider concerns about the adoption of new technologies into American society, such concern also rests on the fact that commercial media have been unwilling to support educational programming (Wartella, 1990). This is the case even when commercial media interests publicly promote the educational benefits of new technologies. Why? Because such programming is viewed as "uncommercial," unable to attract large enough audiences (there are about 15 million children in a nation of 250 million) to bring in the advertising dollars and profit margins wanted in the industry. I should point out that even when successful educational programs are produced that do attract large numbers of child audiences, such as "Sesame Street," such programs are viewed as unviable for the commercial system—they are too expensive.

How should we assess the impact of communication research in this public arena? It's a mixed response. As far as I have seen, the communication policy arguments about the need for a public space for public broadcasting have not yet entered the wider policy debates about public television. Neither has the historical research demonstrating a failure of the industry to live up to its professed social responsibility to children been used effectively in marshalling arguments for the need of a public broadcasting space. What public discourse there *has* been has been monopolized by a marketplace metaphor and in the service of the political right, which held sway in Washington during the Reagan-Bush years.

More successful has been the use of research on child audiences in the actual production of educational programs for children. Here, studies of how to produce programs for children of different ages that they both like to watch and can learn from have enjoyed some success. Communication researchers and developmental psychologists studying children and television often serve as advisers to such programs. However, without motivation to air such programs, the latter success is illusory

This leads me to my concern for how communication research can be more effective in the public arena: How can we improve the public face of communication?

The Public Face of Communication

As the argument thus far suggests, I think as communication researchers we can and should direct our research and scholarship to addressing the public debates about media in contemporary life. To my mind, one's theoretical or methodological perspective matters far less than the quality of the argument one brings to bear on questions that the public has with full force let us know it believes are important. Further, no one perspective or method has a corner on truth; the debates of the past dozen years should at least have convinced us that each perspective can bring something of interest to enlighten our understanding of a problem area. It is by the quality of the research and its interpretation that we assess the worth of a piece of scholarship. While its political worth may depend on its ideological commitment, its worth as scholarship does not.

I want to argue that irrespective of the theoretical perspective, the methodological tools and the particular paradigmatic commitments of the researcher, the important issue for the future research agenda is to address the public arena. Elsewhere I have argued that communication researchers lack a clear vision about who we are, which is manifested in a fractured set of subfields whose practitioners not only know little about each other but seem more intent on the internal debates of our field than on our public responsibility as scholars of an increasingly important topic. We have little visible presence as public intellectuals. We offer an inchoate curriculum for communication study on the undergraduate level that perpetuates generations of college graduates (including communication majors) who know little about communication scholarship, including what is covered by the term "communication study" (Wartella, 1990).

The nature of communication scholarship, its politics and its impact, is predicated upon how we approach our research and how we relay it in the public arena. Mostly, my fear is that our scholarship never even makes it to the public arena (a lot of bad research in *any* paradigm our field embraces should not, of course). We do have a body of knowledge after eight decades of study of mass communication that I believe we are too timid in sharing. We are, moreover, often ignorant of how to act as public intellectuals and advocates for a particular point of view. Is this a manifestation of what the American academy has been criticized for—an overwhelming commitment to the study of narrow academic subspecialties, thus forsaking the kind of scholarship that makes for public intellectuals (as Jacoby argued in 1987)? Is communication study plagued with the problems besetting other disciplines in the academy?

Clearly, to the extent that the popular media take up intellectual questions about communication, they will seek out scholars to comment and contribute to the public dialogue. If communication faculty are to be those public scholars commenting on communication, then we need not just to promote our research in all of the usual ways—by insuring that it is well written and well situated within public definitions of concerns, and that it is presented in a public forum beyond our academic journals, such as in op-ed pieces, letters to the editor, articles for the elite intellectual magazines and, most important, in book form; we also need to insure that we craft our work to have a pragmatic commitment. One public we cannot ignore is our own students, communications and journalism majors who can and do emerge from university with no real sense of what communication research is, does, knows or what it can contribute to the world. The ruptures between speech communication and mass communication, between journalism education and media studies, must be addressed. Moreover, undergraduate education throughout communication needs to integrate better theory, research, and practice. And once we take up that pragmatic commitment we need to think about which public we are addressing in our research: the public at large, those media audiences we often study, public policy-makers at the federal and state levels, communication practitioners or other cultural elites who write and talk about communication?

Furthermore, to approach communication scholarship today without an understanding of the political commitments inherent in a line of research, in the kind of issues that are taken up for study, and in the potential uses of that research, is incredibly naive. We can no longer claim timidity as public scholars.

The message seems pretty clear to me. Communication scholarship (like all scholarship) needs to be addressing public issues. How we maneuver through the public agenda, select problems and frame research about them in terms of our theoretical understanding is up to each individual scholar. I do not believe that one type of scholar or theoretical position is inherently more attuned to public issues or is more political than another; indeed, just calling oneself a "critical" communications scholar does not insure that one's work will have the political outcome intended, and calling oneself a "communication scientist" or "television researcher" does not imply that one's research is apolitical. The politics of research is not easily read off with reference to question, theory or method.

Rather, we need to understand self-consciously what research questions we take up in our work, how we situate them within the national public and intellectual debates, and how we attempt to convey our work to that segment of the "public arena" we believe we are addressing.

The recent history of public controversies about children and television issues suggest that there is ample opportunity for communication research to have a visible influence in shaping public debates, but this happens far too rarely. My suggestion, then, for going beyond agendas is to renew our commitment to public scholarship and to reinvigorate the public face of our field.

Note

1. In my examination of a dozen experimental psychology and introductory psychology texts, I found that typically fewer than a dozen of the 400 to 500 pages of each text were devoted to questions about media and children. What mention there was tended to be dominated by the violence controversy, with occasional reference to "Sesame Street." Missing, then, were any references to the power of television to influence racial, ethnic and gender attitudes; the range of social and affective development, including identity formation; and the relationship of television to academic achievement.

References

Aufderheide, P. (1991). Public television and the public sphere. *Critical Studies in Mass Communication, 8,* 168–183.

Carey, J. W. (1989). *Communication as culture: Essays on media and society.* Boston: Unwin Hyman.

Entman, R. (1993). Enhancing American democracy through the press: Putting the first amendment in its place. *University of Chicago Legal Forum.*

Huston, A. C., & Wright, J. (1983). Children's processing of television: The informative function of formal features. In J. Bryant & D. Anderson (Eds.), *Children's understanding of television* (pp. 33–54). New York: Academic Press.

Jacoby, R. (1987). *The last intellectuals: American culture in the age of academe.* New York: Academic Press.

Johnstone, J., & Brzezinski, E. (1992, April). Taking the measure of Channel One: The first year. Ann Arbor, MI: Institute for Social Research.

Kunkel, D. (1991). Crafting media policy: The genesis and implications of the Children's Television Act of 1990. *American Behavioral Scientist, 35*(2), 181–202.

McGregor, M. (1986). Reassessing the Children's Television Task Force. *Journalism Quarterly*, *63*(3), 168–183.

Palmer, E. (1988). *Television and America's children: A crisis of neglect.* New York: Basic Books.

Rowland, W. D., & Tracey, M. (1990). Worldwide challenges to public service broadcasting. *Journal of Communication*, *40*(2), 8–27.

Rubinstein, E., & Brown, J. D. (Eds.). (1985). *The media, social science and social policy.* Norwood, NJ: Ablex.

Wartella, E. (1990, November). *The public face of communication.* Sage Anniversary Lecture, Stanford University, Stanford, California.

Wartella, E., Heintz, K. E., Aidman, A., & Mazzarella, S. (1990). Television and beyond: Children's video media in one community. *Communication Research*, *17*(1), 45–64.

Wartella, E., & Mazzarella, S. (1990). An historical comparison of children's use of time with media: 1920's to 1980's. In R. Butsch (Ed.), *For fun and profit* (pp. 173–194). Philadelphia: Temple University Press.

Wartella, E., & Reeves, B. (1985). Historical trends in research on children and the media: 1900–1960. *Journal of Communication*, *35*(2), 118–133.

16

"Guys in Suits with Charts": Audience Research in U.S. Public Radio

Alan G. Stavitsky
1995

A significant change in the practice of U.S. public radio during the 1980s was the acceptance of audience research as an essential management function. In commercial broadcasting the need for audience research has long been evident: to provide the institutional knowledge used by advertisers and broadcasters to buy and sell audiences (Beville, 1988; Buzzard, 1990; Webster & Lichty, 1991). For many years, however, public radio managers widely resisted the conduct and application of audience research as marking the ascendance of market considerations over public broadcasting's social and cultural imperatives. Nonetheless, during the 1980s what has been described as a "research revolution" swept across U.S. public radio (Giovannoni, 1991). Today audience research is extensively utilized by public radio managers, both network and station-based, when making decisions about programming and fundraising, and a cottage industry of consultants has emerged. The degree to which audience research has been embraced by the public radio community became evident when research consultants Tom Church and David Giovannoni were honored with awards for service to public radio during the 1994 Public Radio Conference ("Kudos for audience gurus," 1994).

The rise of audience research in U.S. public radio, however, has become a lightning rod for critics both within and outside the industry, a symbol of the changing nature of public broadcasting. Some critics argue that the increased emphasis upon audience research reflects the transformation of public radio from its educational, service-based origins to an audience-driven orientation, in which public stations target those listeners most likely to support the stations financially (for examples of this line of argument, see Fisher, 1989; Josephson, 1992; Katz, 1989; Lee

& Solomon, 1990; Rauber, 1993; Rowland, 1986; Rowland, 1993). One of public radio's foremost personalities, Garrison Keillor, told an interviewer: "I think there has been an influx of commercial people . . . Guys in suits with charts and pages of numbers. I think that this is a pretty dreadful development," (quoted in "Thoughts from Lake Wobegon," 1994, p. 58). Reacting to the awards given Church and Giovannoni, Larry Bensky, a journalist for the Pacifica chain of public radio stations, argued, "Not since Henry Kissinger won the Nobel Peace Prize has there been a more inappropriate award" (personal communication, May 7, 1994). Still another critic, independent producer Larry Josephson, contends that "Obsession with audience size, revenue and formal have replaced the spiritual underpinnings of public radio, which sought to maximize intellectual and moral growth, passion, variety and pleasure," (personal communication, May 7, 1994).

Lumley, in a seminal book on audience research published in 1934, noted three "important questions" related to audience measurement: "What are the purposes of . . . radio broadcasting in general? How can methods be developed to determine validly whether broadcasting fulfills these purposes? Is it possible to standardize the measurement techniques which have been found to be useful?" (1934/1971, p. 3) This study illuminates anew Lumley's fundamental issues. Debate over audience research in public radio centers on Lumley's first question, which deals with the essence of broadcasting, and researchers have grappled with the latter two questions in seeking to apply research techniques developed for the commercial sector to noncommercial communication. This study also highlights the relationship between research and practice; the availability of research techniques and applications shaped thinking about public radio's mission, and the reverse. Drawing heavily upon personal interviews with public broadcasters, audience researchers and other individuals concerned with the issue, this paper will describe the evolution of audience research in U.S. public radio and its implications.

A definitional issue must be noted. While there are nearly 1,700 U.S. radio stations licensed by the Federal Communications Commission as "noncommercial educational" ("By the numbers," 1994), the stations generally referred to as public radio are those which provide a regular schedule of programming intended to serve the public. Such a categorization would exclude noncommercial religious stations as well as low-powered stations operated by educational institutions, which may not broadcast during school holidays and for which training students is the primary function. A survey funded by the Corporation for Public Broadcasting estimated there are about 750 U.S. stations which would thus be categorized as public radio (Giovannoni, Thomas, & Clifford, 1992).

A "Pre-History" of Audience Research

Prior to their contemporary engagement with audience research, U.S. public radio broadcasters were not as concerned about accountability to their audiences as were Western European public-service broadcasters. Because public-service broadcasters were the first—and, for many years, the only—electronic media in much of Western Europe, they sought to be comprehensive: to educate, inform, and entertain. Their reliance upon listener support through license fees provided justification for audience research as a form of feedback, as well as providing a form of feedback in itself, to ensure that the public was being satisfied. The British Broadcasting Corporation; for example, set up a Listener Research Unit in 1936 (Blumler, 1992; Silvey, 1974).

In contrast, a number of forces militated against either an ethic of comprehensiveness in U.S. educational radio or a perceived need for accountability to audiences. Educational broadcasting in the United States was considered a supplement to the dominant commercial system—"a palliative," in the words of Raymond Williams (1974, p. 37). Popular, mass-appeal programming was considered the domain of the commercial sector (Rowland, 1993. Educational broadcasters, generally based at colleges and universities, saw their industry as an oasis in the desert of commercial programming. Further, financial support for educational broadcasting prior to the Public Broadcasting Act of 1967 was largely institutional or from philanthropic foundations (Blakely, 1979), so the broadcasters did not need to feel beholden to the public.

Accordingly, audience research in U.S. educational radio (as noncommercial radio was known prior to the 1967 act) was sporadic and unsystematic. A study of educational radio stations found that station managers conducted audience research of various kinds as early as the

1920s (Stavitsky, 1993b; see also Charters, 1930). Examples of early research included coverage maps from the 1920s, upon which stations indicated those areas from which they had gotten notice that people had received their signal; and 1930s-era analyses of how many and what kinds of letters had been received from listeners about programs. However, such research was generally limited to stations based at land-grant universities. Further, the methods employed by educational broadcasters lagged in sophistication behind those used when researching commercial radio listening during the 1930s and 1940s. Commercial approaches to audience research in this era included telephone surveys conducted by the Cooperative Analysis of Broadcasting and C.E. Hooper, as well as A.C. Nielsen's Audimeter, a mechanical device which metered the usage of radio sets (see Beville, 1988; Buzzard, 1990).

During the 1950s several prominent faculty members who conducted audience research—notably Harrison Summers of Ohio State, a former NBC vice president—sought to encourage its use through presentations at National Association of Educational Broadcasters (NAEB) conventions and articles in academic journals (Summers, 1950). Interest in audience research spread, albeit gradually (see Wright, 1961, for an annotated bibliography of selected research findings to that time; also see Avery, Burrows, & Pincus, 1980; Becker, 1962). NAEB established a Research Committee, which considered hiring an audience research consultant as early as 1953; lamented the lack of money for such research in 1954; and discussed purchasing Nielsen ratings data in 1955 (NAEB Research Committee, 1953; 1954; 1955). As a former Wisconsin educational radio manager said: "It's not that the interest wasn't there, the money wasn't (Ralph Johnson, former WHA station manager, personal communication, June 30, 1989). However, lack of funds and concern about commercialism kept such research widely scattered and limited to the larger stations (Stavitsky, 1993b).

Enter CPB

The Corporation for Public Broadcasting (CPB) is an independent, non-profit organization, created as a result of the Public Broadcasting Act of 1967, that receives federal funds and allocates them to stations, program producers, and others involved in the industry. CPB was charged by Congress with assisting in the establishment and development of a system of public radio and television stations (Public Broadcasting Act of 1967). In public television, station officials who had been troubled by what they perceived as an "East Coast, liberal bias" of National Educational Television, educational television's program service, were determined to avoid creating a network in the model of U.S. commercial television (Robertson, 1993; Rowland, 1986). The Public Broadcasting Service (PBS) was created by public television station leaders as a distribution entity, forbidden from producing public television programs. Leaders of the lower-profile public radio system, on the other hand, had no such reluctance about a national programming organization; most of educational radio's previous shared programming had been "bicycled" from station to station on a sporadic basis, with the exception of occasional ad hoc wired or wireless networks (Wood & Wylie, 1977). National Public Radio (NPR), therefore, was established to produce as well as distribute programming to a system of stations interconnected for the first time (Avery & Pepper, 1979). NPR began to distribute programs nationwide in 1971—initially classical music concerts and the newsmagazine *All Things Considered* (see Stamberg, 1982; Stavitsky & Gleason, 1994).

While CPB commissioned analyses of Nielsen ratings for the public television system as early as 1969 (Willard D. Rowland, Jr., former PBS research director, personal communication, February 23, 1993), CPB's then-director of research, Jack Lyle, was primarily interested in television, and little attention was paid to public radio research until 1973 (David J. LeRoy, former CPB deputy director of research, personal communication, February 15, 1994). In 1973, with new CPB president Henry Loomis placing an increased emphasis on radio, the corporation made its first purchase of Arbitron ratings data for public radio (Bailey & Church, 1979; leRoy, personal communication, February 15, 1994). The size of public radio audiences was difficult to determine; listenership to public stations was not routinely listed in the ratings books, which were produced for commercial stations, and required customized computer runs by the ratings service and hand-tabulation by CPB staffers.

Though the ratings data were provided to public radio stations, the role and value of audience research on the local level as an audience-building tool was neither initially valued nor emphasized. Jack Mitchell, then an NPR producer, learned to interpret and apply ratings data not from CPB, but rather from a neighbor who happened to work for Arbitron (Mitchell, personal communication, October 25, 1993). CPB officials utilized the audience information primarily for representational purposes: the data were taken to Congress to demonstrate that people were indeed listening to public radio and that the CPB appropriation was justified (Bernadette McGuire, director of planning and research, Association of Public Television Stations, personal communication, March 5, 1993; Rowland, personal communication, February 23, 1993). Even after public radio professionals embraced audience research for programming and marketing purposes, its representational function remained important. For instance, public broadcasters faced charges of elitism—that public broadcasting serves a relatively well-educated and wealthy audience, and that tax-based support therefore unfairly subsidizes upper-class tastes (Rowland, 1993). NPR officials, like their counterparts in public television, have long sought to counter this criticism by presenting audience demographic data to demonstrate that public broadcasting appeals to a broad spectrum of the U.S. citizenry (see Corporation for Public Broadcasting, 1993).

Research and the Station

The notion that audience research could be—and should be—fundamental in station programming became paramount after Tom Church, who had previously worked at Arbitron, joined CPB's research office in 1976. Church sought to merge the non-commercial broadcaster's sense of mission with the commercial concept of serving listeners. As he wrote in a primer on audience research for public radio: "While non-commercial stations may define success in more esoteric terms than profit, the bottom line for all radio stations is that a mission . . . cannot be achieved if there are no listeners" (Radio Research Consortium, 1986, p. 1). Church made a technical, but significant, change in the type of data purchased from the ratings service. Whereas CPB had previously requested a customized tabulation of ratings diaries based upon the stations' signal coverage areas, Church began buying diaries from the station's actual home markets, or Area of Dominant Influence, as defined by Arbitron. The effect was that, for the first time, public radio stations could compare their audiences to those of their commercial competitors (Church, personal communication, March 1, 1993).

In 1977 Church began sending to public radio stations national rankings of stations in terms of cumulative audience (cumes), the size of a station's unduplicated audience during a specified period of time, and he encouraged local stations to make further use of Arbitron data from their home markets; such as extracting demographic data (Church, personal communication, October 22, 1993). This provided an opening for the research consultants who were to have a major impact on the rise of audience research in public radio. The leading consultants, as noted by individuals interviewed for this study, were Lawrence Lichty, who had studied under Harrison Summers at Ohio State and was on leave from a faculty position at Wisconsin; David Giovannoni, who had been Lichty's graduate assistant; and George Bailey, another former student of Lichty's, who was a professor at Wisconsin-Milwaukee and also managed the university radio station, WUWM.

However, while station managers such as Peter Dominowski in Orlando, Wallace Smith in Los Angeles, and Max Wycisk in Denver welcomed audience research during the late 1970s as a form of feedback, others in public radio "greeted the methods, paradigms and proponents of research with open hostility and disdain," according to Giovannoni (1991, p. 3). These critics—who included producers such as Larry Josephson and managers such as Marvin Granger, then in Spokane, both of whom participated in a debate with researchers at a 1978 conference—believed that concern for ratings "collided with the art of programming noncommercial radio" (Marvin Granger, personal communication, May 24, 1994). Anti-research antagonism boiled over at the 1978 Public Radio Conference. After a presentation by Church, E.B. Eiselein, an academic from Arizona and consultant to public radio stations, stood up and proclaimed, "Arbitron is bullshit." Many of the conferees cheered; Church realized more missionary work was needed (Church, personal communication, March 1, 1993).

The Audience Research Road Show

Church convinced CPB then—Research Director Leon Rosenbluth of the need for a series of seminars of station managers on the value and function of audience research. The seminars were modeled after a series of CPB-sponsored meetings on public television programming techniques and NAEB seminars on ascertainment during the mid-1970s (LeRoy, personal communication, February 15, 1994; Thomas A. McCain, Ohio State University professor and participant in NAEB seminars, personal communication, February 25, 1993). CPB's Office of Communication Research funded eight seminars across the United States between 1978 and 1981, entitled "Public Radio and the Ratings," to which managers and program directors were invited (CPB, 1981). To help him conduct the seminars Church enlisted Lichty, Bailey, Giovannoni, and a cast of station managers.

Bailey characterized the attendees in three categories: managers who believed research was irrelevant because they had missions to fulfill; skeptics who doubted the validity of research because their low ratings conflicted with intuition (often from phone or personal contacts) that many people were listening; and, "converts" to research who sought more information about their audiences (George Bailey, personal communication, October 8, 1993). The presenters described the basics of social-scientific research, discussed the applications of ratings data, and sought to dispel some of the mythology surrounding audience research, such as the notion that a station's Friends group or program guide readers were representative of the audience at large. Humor helped. Asked at one seminar about "the best time to schedule radio drama," Bailey replied: "1938" (Bailey, personal communication, October 8, 1993).

More than 220 station managers attended the sessions (CPB, 1981). While the "road show" was but one of a number of factors contributing to the incremental acceptance of audience research during the late 1970s and early 1980s, the seminars served to expose many managers to the techniques and availability of research, as well as providing a forum for research proponents to argue that conducting research did not in itself compromise a public station's mission (Church, personal communication, March 1, 1993; Giovannoni, personal communication,

March 1, 1993; Lichty, personal communication, February 9, 1993). This process was also fostered by similar workshops at NPR meetings, numerous articles in professional publications (see, for example, Bailey & Church, 1979) and industry newsletters, and word of mouth.

The *Morning Edition* Project

Another significant episode in the diffusion of audience research involved the creation of NPR's *Morning Edition*, which was marketed with the help of research and led to the establishment of the network's research unit. The network's first news program, *All Things Considered* (ATC), had been scheduled for late afternoon because some public stations were not even on the air in radio's "morning drive" time and because a morning program would have been more difficult for NPR's small staff to produce (Lichty, personal communication, February 9, 1993). After ATC had established itself, NPR sought to add a morning news program in 1978, but several prominent stations, such as Boston's WGBH and WGUC in Cincinnati, resisted on grounds that another network offering would displace local morning programming (Samuel Holt, personal communication, March 4, 1993). NPR's vice president for programming, Samuel Holt, used research to make the case that a morning news program would increase audience size throughout the day, as well as in the morning.

Holt contracted with Lichty in 1978 to survey morning radio listening. Some stations were dismayed to learn how few listeners they were attracting in the mornings, the time when radio listening in general was highest and when research showed there was high demand for news (Holt, personal communication, March 4, 1993; Lichty, personal communication, February 9, 1993). "If you want to serve listeners, you need to behave like radio," Holt told managers (Holt, personal communication, March 4, 1993). He asked stations whether they could justify rejecting the network's proposed morning program based on the performance of local programming. Holt offered them *Morning Edition* in a modular format, borrowed from his commercial radio experience, in which stations could insert local material between the national segments. Though fewer than half of NPR's member stations carried *Morning Edition* when it debuted in November 1979, the program gradually was picked up by more stations—and even surpassed ATC in cumulative audience by 1989—supporting NPR's research claims about the importance of a morning news program (Piantadosi, 1979; Weinstein, 1989).

Nonetheless, Holt wanted more detailed audience information about national listenership to NPR programs, especially *Morning Edition*, than was currently available by summing up individual station comes (Holt, personal communication, March 4, 1993). Lichty was hired in 1979 as director of audience research and evaluation for NPR and brought on Giovannoni to develop a system to measure the NPR audience. The Public Radio Audience Profile (TRAP) was laboriously constructed by sampling local market listener diaries to compute national cumulative and average-quarter-hour audiences for public radio network programs (Giovannoni, personal communication, March 1, 1993). PRAP yielded its first audience estimates in 1981, the year that Lichty left NPR to work on a PBS documentary, and Giovannoni took over as head of research. That same year Church left CPB to form the Radio Research Consortium, a membership organization that provides stations with audience research data and consulting.

By the mid-1980s discord over the use of audience research in public radio had largely faded. As station manager Marvin Granger noted, "The issue was settled and the researchers won" (personal communication, May 24, 1994). In addition to NPR's active research unit, individual stations were conducting audience studies by the mid-1980s, often with the help of consultants, though occassionally using station staff or university students (see Giovannoni, 1991; Stavitsky, 1990). As an example, the Ohio public radio station for which the author worked hired consultants to conduct a "psychographic analysis" of its listeners in 1985, to assess their preferences regarding the station's programs and personalities.

Several external forces contributed to the ascendance of audience research. With taxbased funding for public broadcasting flat or decreasing during the 1980s, most station managers were forced to depend more on listener and underwriter dollars (Rowland, 1993). Audience research became increasingly valuable as a means of assessing the appeal of programming to listeners, and of pitching audiences to potential underwriters. Further, FM had become radio's dominant band during the 1970s, which exposed more listeners to the public stations clustered between 88 and 92 megahertz, the portion of the spectrum set aside for noncommercial broadcasters. Stations also reaped the benefits of NPR popularity as *All Things Considered* and *Morning Edition* developed audiences; stations that had been run without concern for or awareness of how listeners used radio "lucked into an audience" nonetheless, in Bailey's words (personal communication, October 8, 1993).

Changing Application of NPR Research

Within this environment the applications of audience research broadened in the early 1980s. in 1981 NPR first purchased data on public radio listeners from the Simmons Market Research Bureau, which surveys people nationwide on their media usage, product usage and buying behavior, and demographics (Giovannoni, personal communication, March 1, 1993). This marked a shift from asking simply *how many* were listening to asking *what kinds* of people were tuning to public radio— demographics and psychographics. In this manner audience research became a tool for underwriting in addition to programming. For example, a spring 1991 survey found NPR news listeners were 47 percent more likely than average to own an Acura automobile; public station underwriting salespeople could descend on their local Acura dealerships armed with such data ("Who is listening," 1992).

The focus on underwriting at the national level was driven by NPR's fiscal exigencies of the 1980s. In light of the Reagan Administration's marketplace ideology, even that federal support for public broadcasting was no longer assured. Under NPR President Frank Mankewicz, in 1982 the network attempted to become fiscally independent through a profit-making subsidiary and technology ventures, as well as increased underwriting sales. However, amid a $3 million deficit and charges of fiscal irresponsibility, Mankewicz resigned. With NPR on the verge of bankruptcy, its affiliated stations and CPB bailed the network out with an emergency loan in 1983 (Witherspoon & Kovitz, 1987).

Given NPR's financial straits in a time of uncertain federal support, under new president Douglas Bennet the function of research at the national level shifted further from a focus on building audience to an emphasis on underwriting and listener support (Giovannoni, personal communication, March 1, 1993). The network's audience research operation became analogous to a commercial station's sales department. Research became instrumental in determining who are the people most likely to listen to public radio, and why they do—or don't—support their local stations. Giovannoni left NPR in 1986 to devote full time to consulting. After several interim managers, the network hired a veteran of commercial radio programming and marketing, John Sutton, as its research director in 1990.

Today NPR's Audience Research unit provides information to support the efforts of member stations to generate revenue (John Sutton, personal communication, March 3, 1993). For example, a recent study involved a comparison of fundraising programming, seeking to determine what styles and strategies would yield the best listener response. Among other services, the department also provides stations and program producers with Simmons data on the demographics, and product and media usage of NPR listeners; ZIP code analyses of where pockets of each station's listeners reside; information on what motivates listeners to give money; and customized profiles of station contributors, for purposes of eliciting increased donations and membership renewals (National Public Radio, 1993). For the network itself, the unit provides data to help NPR market its programs to member stations and to attract underwriters. Public radio's contemporary application of research at the network level, therefore, reflects a commercial orientation.

Leading Role of Consultants and Stations

At CPB support for audience research in public radio declined after the corporation's Office of Communication Research was disbanded in 1982 by CPB's new administrators, who were displeased with OCR's line of research (John Fuller, PBS director of research, personal communication, March 2, 1993; LeRoy, personal communication, February 15, 1994). OCR studies had become "very sociological" and were generating "little actionable research," according to another researcher (Fuller, personal communication, March 2, 1993). An audience research unit at CPB was later restored in 1985 on a smaller scale as part of the planning department, by which time consultants and station managers had taken the lead in audience research that stressed programming applications (Ted Coltman, CPB director of plans and policy, personal communication, March 3, 1993)

Giovannoni, for example, produced a series of studies with CPB support. The so-called "Cheap 90" study—named for the roughly 90 percent of public radio listeners who do not support their local stations financially—compared supporters with non-supporters (Giovannoni, 1985). According to "Cheap 90," listeners who said public radio was important in their lives were more likely to support it, and "programming causes audience." "Audience 88" was a study of public radio listeners' demographic, values, and lifestyle characteristics, as well as their uses of radio (Giovannoni, Liebold, Thomas, & Clifford, 1988). "Audience 88" contended that public radio listeners tended to be well educated, professionally employed, fairly well-off financially, 35 to 44 years old, and involved in social causes. Bailey, doing business with Church as Walrus Research, began consulting with CBS Radio's FM stations as well as public radio clients and encouraged public radio managers to apply more sophisticated research methods, such as those utilized by commercial stations (Bailey, personal communication, October 8, 1993). One such application was the Denver Project, supported by CPB between 1988 and 1992, in which commercial research techniques were adapted for use at Denver public radio station KCFR. In addition to standard Arbitron data (e.g., rating and audience share), the Denver Project involved analysis of individual listener Arbitron diaries to determine such characteristics as audience loyalty; recontact of diary keepers to ask about financial support for KCFR and attitudes toward the station; focus groups; a telephone "perceptual" survey, to check the reliability of the focus group information about the image of the station; and, auditorium music testing, in which segments of prospective programs were played for groups of listeners, to assess what types of music appeal to what types of listeners (Giovannoni, 1991).

The Denver Project reflects the second wave of research in public radio: research as a predictive tool. The first phase of audience research in public radio involved technical mastery—developing the ability to compile ratings for public radio—and working to foster broad acceptance and application of audience research on the part of managers.

However, research was largely descriptive of past performance. Now researchers are seeking to use research as a *predictive* tool, a means of determining the preferred program choice from a range of options. This is the idea behind research for the CPB Radio Program Fund, a pool of money available to producers of prospective public radio programs. To help decide which programs will receive funding in their formative years, the fund's director, Richard Madden, uses auditorium testing and a model known as Programming Economics (Giovannoni, Thomas, Clifford, Berky, & Madden, 1989), which seeks to determine how many listeners the funded program delivered per CPB dollar spent (Madden, personal communication, March 4, 1993).

However, in keeping with public radio's long-standing contention over audience research, the debate still roils at individual stations. For instance, public radio listeners in four states organized successful campaigns during the past ten years to restore broadcasts of the Metropolitan Opera. Station officials had attempted to cancel the opera broadcasts, citing low ratings at a prime listening time—Saturday morning and early afternoon (Behrens, 1993; "Opera listeners triumphant," 1993). At this writing, a dispute over Bailey's research for WUSF in Tampa had become an issue of community controversy after the station's news director stated publicly that the research findings would lead to elimination of local news coverage (Conciatore, 1994; Rosen, 1994).

Changing Conceptions of Localism

The rise of audience research in U.S. public radio reflects changing conceptions of localism, as well as the fiscal realities of noncommercial media in a mediascape dominated by private entities. As described in a previous edition of the *Journal of Broadcasting & Electronic Media*, the conception of localism in contemporary U.S. radio broadcasting has shifted to a *socially* derived conception from the traditional *spatial* notion of localism (Stavitsky, 1994). This theory holds that radio broadcasters, both commercial and public, seek to reach audiences defined by shared interests, tastes, and values. Conceiving of audiences in social terms contrasts with a spatial conception, for which the parameters are geographic entities such as cities, counties, and regions. The spatial conception corresponds with the U.S. policy ideal of localism: broadcasting that speaks—often in local voices—to the concerns and needs of residents of a specific geographic entity. Nonetheless, commercial radio stations have sought to construct audiences in social terms since radio adopted niche formats in response to the arrival of television. Few radio stations try to serve *all* of the people in their listening areas some of the time; instead they seek to serve some of the people all of the time with tightly defined formats (e.g., Classic Rock, New Country, Sports Talk).

In public radio, however, consolidation of programming into focused formats, a necessary condition for social localism, was a phenomenon of the 1980s, and is still ongoing for some stations (see Hinman, 1992; Stavitsky, 1993a). According to a 1992 study (Giovannoni, Thomas, & Clifford, 1992), public radio stations have increasingly focused their formats to attract a loyal audience drawn to a consistent type of programming, an audience that would be willing to support the stations financially. This narrowing of programming, for example, may involve eliminating public affairs from jazz formats or opera from classical formats, which some stations have done despite the listener opposition noted earlier (Behrens, 1993). Because audience research informs managers on the construction of a social community of listeners, public radio's engagement with audience research has fostered this changing conception of localism.

Conclusions

Educational broadcasters often viewed their mission from a teacher-student perspective: as educators, they sought to transmit the information they believed their listeners needed to be informed and enlightened. While a number of educational broadcasters were interested in audience feedback (see Stavitsky, 1993b), concerns of audience appeal were generally secondary to concerns about program quality and pedagogical value in educational radio, as determined by the educational broadcaster's sense of the commonweal and audience "needs." However, in contemporary public radio, audience researchers were successful in imbuing managers with the notion that audience size and composition *did* matter, that public radio could not justify itself if few people chose to listen—and could not survive if fewer still chose to contribute. External forces contributed to the diffusion of audience research during the past 15 years: the uncertainty of tax-based funding forced public stations to depend more upon listener and underwriter support, for which audience research was instrumental.

However, while audience research has been successfully diffused into public radio's managerial culture, its application continues to elicit concern at the level of producers. Put another way, the debate seems no longer to revolve around whether or not to conduct research. Instead the contemporary conflict involves the ways in which research is applied in *the service of mission*; the manager or program director's view of mission may clash with the news or music producer's view. From a station manager or program director's standpoint, mission may be measurable in audience and revenue terms, while the producer's currency is often more amorphous—fealty to internalized professional values and standards. Nonetheless, the fiscal realities of contemporary U.S. public radio—indeed of public broadcasting worldwide—dictate that stations must be cognizant of their appeal to listeners who will support them financially, and thus audience research will remain an essential management function.

References

Avery, R. K., & Pepper, R. (1979). Balancing the equation: Public radio comes of age. *Public Telecommunications Review*, 7, 19–30.

Avery, R. K., Burrows, P. E., & Pincus, C. J. (1980). *Research index for NAEB journals, 1957–1979*. Washington, D.C.: National Association of Educational Broadcasters.

Bailey, G., & Church, T. (1979, November/December). Public radio and the ratings. *Public Telecommunications Review*, 7, 47–49.

Becker, S. (1962). New methods for measuring broadcasting effectiveness. *NAEB Journal*, 21, 28–34.

Behrens, S. (1993, September 20). Programmers resent opera's live-only policy. *Current*, pp. 1, 13, 16.

Beville, H. M. (1988). *Audience ratings: Radio, television, cable*. Hillsdale, NJ: Lawrence Erlbaum.

Blakely, R. J. (1979). *To serve the public interest: Educational broadcasting in the United States*. Syracuse, NY: Syracuse University Press.

Blumler, J. (Ed.) (1992). *Television and the public interest: Vulnerable values in West European broadcasting.* London: Sage.

Buzzard, K. S. (1990). *Chains of gold: Marketing the ratings and rating the markets.* Metuchen, NJ: Scarecrow Press.

By the numbers. (1994, August 22). *Broadcasting & Cable*, p. 50.

Charters, W. W. (1930). Research in radio education. In *Education on the air: Yearbook of the Institute for Education by Radio* (pp. 271–275). Columbus, OH: Ohio State University Press.

Conciatore, J. (1994, June 20). Dispute over research sunders Tampa staff. *Current*, pp. 1, 10–11.

Corporation for Public Broadcasting. (1993). *Facts and figures about public broadcasting in America.* Washington, DC: CPB.

Corporation for Public Broadcasting. (1981). *Review of 1980 CPB communication research findings.* Washington, DC: CPB.

Fisher, M. (1989, October 22). The soul of a news machine. *Washington Post Magazine*, pp. 16–23, 37–42.

Giovannoni, D. (1991). *Radio intelligence, 1988–1990.* Washington, DC: CPB.

Giovannoni, D. (1985). *Public radio listeners: Supporters and non-supporters.* Washington, DC: CPB.

Giovannoni, D., Liebold, L. K., Thomas, T., & Clifford, T. (1988). *Audience '88: A comprehensive analysis of public radio listeners.* Washington, DC: CPB.

Giovannoni, D., Thomas, T., & Clifford, T. (1992). *Public radio programming strategies.* Washington, DC: CPB.

Giovannoni, D., Thomas, T., Clifford, T., (with Berky, J., and Madden, R.). (1989, June). *Programming economics.* Washington, DC: CPB.

Hinman, C. (1992, April 26). New public radio strategy: Less variety, more listeners. *Orlando Sentinel*, p. F1.

Josephson, L. (1992, April 27). We're drunk on numbers, boring to our listeners. *Current*, p. 31.

Katz, H. (1989). The future of public broadcasting in the US. *Media, Culture and Society*, 11, 195–205.

Kudos for audience gurus Church and Giovannoni. (1994, April 25). *Current*, p. 13.

Lee, M., & Solomon, M. (1990). *Unreliable sources.* New York: Carol Publishing Group.

Lumley, F. H. (1971). *Measurement in radio.* New York: Amo Press (Original work published 1934).

National Association of Educational Broadcasters, Research Committee. (1953; 1954; 1955). *Report of the NAEB Research Committee.* "Unpublished manuscripts." Madison, WI: State Historical Society of Wisconsin, NAEB papers.

National Public Radio. (1993). *NPR Program support services*. Washington, DC: NPR (brochure).

Opera listeners triumphant at Matthusen's station. (1993, December 13). *Current*, p. 12.

Piantadosi, R. (1979, November 1). Radio. *Washington Post*, p. D12.

Public Broadcasting Act of 1967 Actname, 47 U.S.C. § 396 (1988).

Radio Research Consortium. (1986). *Audience ratings: A primer for non-commercial radio stations*. Silver Spring, MD: Radio Research Consortium.

Rauber, P. (1993, March 5). Off-mike: Mid-life crisis at KPFA. *East Bay Express* (Berkeley, CA), pp. 1, 10–18.

Robertson, J. (1993). *Televisionaries*. Charlotte Harbor, FL: Tabby House Books.

Rosen, M. (1994, July 5). Fight at WUSF is for survival. *St. Petersburg Times*, p. 3B.

Rowland, W. D. (1986). Continuing crisis in public broadcasting: A history of disenfranchisement. *Journal of Broadcasting & Electronic Media*, 30, 251–274.

Rowland, W. D. (1993). Public service broadcasting in the United States: Its mandate, institutions, and conflicts. In R. K. Avery (Ed.), *Public service broadcasting in a multichannel environment: The history and survival of an ideal* (pp. 157–194). White Plains, NY: Longman.

Silvey, R. (1974). *Who's listening? The story of BBC audience research*. London: Allen & Unwin.

Stamberg, S. (1982). *Every night at five: Susan Stamberg's "All Things Considered" book*. New York: Pantheon.

Stavitsky, A. G. (1990). *From pedagogic to public: The development of U.S. public radio's audience-centered strategies—WOSU, WHA, and WNYC, 1930–1987*. Unpublished doctoral dissertation. The Ohio State University, Columbus.

Stavitsky, A. G. (1993a). Ear on America. *Media Studies Journal*, 7, 77–91.

Stavitsky, A. G. (1993b). Listening for listeners: Educational radio and audience research. *Journalism History*, 19, 11–18.

Stavitsky, A. G. (1994). The changing conception of localism in U.S. public radio. *Journal of Broadcasting & Electronic Media*, 38, 19–34.

Stavitsky, A. G., & Gleason, T. W. (1994). Alternative Things Considered: A comparison of National Public Radio and Pacifica Radio news coverage. *Journalism Quarterly*, 71, 775–786.

Summers, H. (1950). University contributions to audience research. In Institute for Education by Radio. *Education on the air* (pp. 407–412). Columbus. OH: Ohio State University Press.

Thoughts from Lake Wobegon on the superhighway. (1994, January 10). *Broadcasting & Cable*, pp. 56–58.

Webster, J. G., & Lichty, L. W. (1991). *Ratings analysis: Theory and practice.* Hillsdale, NJ: Lawrence Erlbaum.

Weinstein, S. (1989, November 2). A decade as NPR's amiable morning man. *Los Angeles Times*, p. F1.

Who is listening to NPR news? (1992, May). Washington, DC: National Public Radio, Audience Research Department.

Williams, R. (1974). *Television: Technology and cultural form.* London: Fontana/Collins.

Witherspoon, J., & Kovitz, R. (1987). *The history of public broadcasting.* Washington, DC: Current Newspaper.

Wood, D. N., & Wylie, D. G. (1977). *Educational telecommunications.* Belmont, CA: Wadsworth.

Wright, C. R. (1961). Television and radio program ratings and measurements: A selected and annotated bibliography. *Journal of Broadcasting, 5,* 165–186.

17

Relationship between Public Opinion and Supreme Court Decisions: Was Mr. Dooley Right?

Cecilie Gaziano
1978

The relationship between public opinion and decisions of the United States Supreme Court has intrigued commentators and scholars for many years. Their findings range from the literary musings of Mr. Dooley, who posited that "th' supreme court follows th' illicition returns" (Dunne, 1962) to the more precise calibrations of social scientists.

The role and function of public sentiment and sanction in democratic theory assumes that there is a relationship between the law as expressed in Supreme Court decisions and public opinion. This [chapter] explores a dimension of that relationship with regard to one type of First Amendment issue, that of freedom of expression for deviant, political groups.

This issue was selected as an indicator of the relationship between the work of the Court and its popular acceptance because it has been a particularly volatile concern over a long period of time and because there is a substantial number of court pronouncements on the subject of freedom of expression and the unpopular or deviant individual or group. Similarly, there are ample public opinion data on the subject, and a correlation between the two is possible.

Although evidence for a correlation between them in the United States is primarily anecdotal (Brown, 1972), Sheldon (1967) provides some more systematic evidence. He compared Supreme Court decisions in 1950–1961 with an analysis of historical events and one Stouffer study question on the jailing of communists, and he concluded that shifts in Court rulings meshed with waves of public tolerance for communists' rights. He also pointed to evidence by Justices Douglas (Scales versus U.S., 1961) and Black (Dennis versus U.S., 1951) that the high court felt intense public pressure during this period.

Some political scientists (Dahl, 1967; Murphy, 1964; Peltason, 1955) believe that public opinion acts as a brake on judicial decision making even if it is felt only indirectly by the justices. However, the relationship does not seem to work in the other direction. In general, the Court seems to have little public visibility, even when controversial issues are involved in cases (Giles, 1973; Dolbeare and Hammond, 1968; Dolbeare, 1967; Murphy and Tanenhaus, 1968).

Brown argues that public opinion does not significantly alter most decisions of either trial or higher courts except under conditions of high public anxiety and high level of media attention. At least two segments of the period examined by Sheldon fulfilled these conditions. A model of judicial behavior predicted by social psychological conceptualization of a court as a task group is: the higher the tension and the greater the uncertainty, the more likely the group is to seek the dominant outside referent—and the more likely that referent is to be public opinion.[1]

The hypothesis of this [chapter] is suggested by the above evidence and the group psychology model. It is: *decisions of the Supreme Court on freedom of expression for deviant, political groups are related to public opinion on this issue.* Legal scholars disagree about whether or not the high court should consider public opinion. The paper does not take a position on this issue.

Method

The primary source of data on public opinion about free speech issues over time is Erskine's (1970) compilation of results reported by eight polling organizations for a 34-year period, 1937–1970. Major subjects were rights of communists, criticism of government, and war dissent. Two secondary sources provide information supplementing the Erskine data (Erskine and Siegel, 1975; Simon, 1974).

All Supreme Court cases involving communists during this period, of which there are 60, apply to this study because freedom of association under the First Amendment was an implicit issue in each one.[2] Thirteen other free speech cases developed during the same time span, and they were related to the following issues: rights of war dissenters and conscientious objectors (9), a "fascist's" rights (1), criticism of government (1), questioning of loyalty of a government employee believed to be associated with communists (1), and the right of labor union "radicals" to meet (1). The types of free speech questions in the polls limited the types of cases included. Those touching on religious objection to war, civil rights, and labor unions were excluded (except for the labor union "radicals" case, which was specifically named in four poll questions; Hague versus C.I.O., 1939) because they involve other variables beyond the scope of this study.

Results

Public Opinion Poll Data

Ninety-seven percent of respondents agreed on abstract freedom of speech the last time (1940) pollsters asked about this in the question, "Do you believe in freedom of speech?" Since then pollsters have concentrated on circumstances in which people would limit freedom of speech.

The poll data taken altogether indicate a relatively low consensus on rights of communists/fascists in 1938 when around 35–40% favored their holding meetings. Amount of consensus on extremists' free speech rights climbed to a high in the mid-1940s, e.g., 50% supported broadcast speeches by communists and 64%, speeches on any topic.

Between the end of World War II and the early 1950s, public support for communists' rights of free expression plummeted to the lowest points observed for the entire period. For example, during these years, which included the Korean War (1950–1953) and the McCarthy hearings,[3] 14%–16% would let communists broadcast over the radio, 27% would allow their making public speeches (Erskine, 1970), and 6% would tolerate communists teaching in public schools (Erskine and Siegel, 1975). Speeches on "any topic" were acceptable to 54% at this time.

Public support for free expression increased perhaps six points for communists' broadcasts and speeches on any topic for a few years after the end of the McCarthy era, but public approval sank again in the later 1950s (e.g., 17% favored communists' views aired over the radio in 1957).

The events of the Vietnam War apparently depressed public support just as opinion began to rise favorably in the early 1960s.[4] A slight gain in regard for communists' First Amendment rights seems to have appeared in the latter part of the decade, but at the same time, public favor for war protesters' rights declined. To illustrate: in 1965, 89% thought communists to be harmful to American life, and 65% believed that "student demonstrators who engage in protest activities" were harmful. Four years later the respective percentages were 85% and 72% (Erskine and Siegel, 1975). After 1965–1967, when 60% approved of "peaceful war demonstrations," toleration for war dissent seems to have waned considerably—perhaps as much as a 35% decline—but this is difficult to assess because the available questions (Erskine, 1970) use somewhat different wordings. For instance, 42% in 1970 agreed to criticism of government, but only 21% would accept organized protest against the government.

It is notable that data for the early 1970s (Erskine and Siegel, 1975) indicate rising support for free speech rights of both war dissenters and communists. In 1973, those finding communists "harmful to American life" totaled 71%; those objecting to the harmful effects of student demonstrators totaled 48% (compared to the percentages given above for 1965 and 1969).

Erskine's data for freedom of speech with any limitations are summarized in averages for different polls for different years, allowing for a rough comparison in the following manner: (1) the maximum percentage believing in freedom of speech with "nonspecific limitations" remained relatively stable at 68%–70% between 1938 and 1960, but the amount of support declined to 61% between 1961–1970. (2) Those favoring freedom of speech for extremists declined in every decade after 1938 from a maximum of 49% before 1950 and 29% between 1950–1960 to 21% after 1960. Explanation for the differences in these two trends may be difference in the subjects of questions. For instance, questions about communists and speeches on any topic predominated until about 1960. After that questions tended to concern criticism of government and demonstrations against the Vietnam war.

[Tables 17.1 and 17.2 and figure 17.1] focus on trends for the only questions in the Erskine data which can be compared over time. First,

Table 17.1

Opinions on Rights of Communist Party Members to Speak on the Radio (1943–1964)

	For complete freedom (%)	Opposed, want limited (%)	No opinion (%)
"In peacetime, do you think members of the Communist party in this country should be allowed to speak on the radio?" (NORC)			
November 1943	48	40	12
November 1945	49	39	12
July 4, 1946	49	39	12
April 1948	36	57	7
"Do you think members of the Communist party in this country should be allowed to speak on the radio?" (NORC)			
November 25, 1953	19	77	4
January 21, 1954	14	81	5
January 26, 1956	16	81	3
December 28, 1956	20	77	3
April 26, 1957	17	80	3
January 1964	18	77	5

Figure 17.1 and table 17.1 present percentages of respondents answering two similar questions about rights of communists to speak on the radio between 1943 and 1964. Between 1946–1954 support for Communist Party members' radio broadcast rights fell 35 points, rising somewhat in the middle 1950s before slumping again. Sheldon's data support this indication of three differentiated periods of public opinion in the 1950s.

Second, table 17.2 shows that support for freedom of speech on any topic was much lower in the early 1940s than in the mid-1940s. The suggestion of a substantial drop between 1938 and 1941 is supported by data from another question, on communists'/fascists' rights to hold meetings and give speeches (decreasing from less than 35% in 1938 to

Table 17.2
Support for Freedom of Speech (1940–1957)

	For complete freedom (%)	Opposed, want limited (%)	No opinion (%)
1a. "Do you think that in America anybody should be allowed to speak on any subject any time he wants to, or do you think there are times when free speech should be prohibited or certain subjects or speakers prohibited?" (Roper for *Fortune*, OPOR)***			
February 1940 (Roper)	49	44	7
January 28, 1941 (NORC)	44	53	3
b. "In peacetime, do you think people in this country should be allowed to say anything they want to in a public speech?" (NORC)***			
November 1943	63	34	3
November 1945	64	32	4
July 4, 1946	64	32	4
May 14, 1953**	53	45	2
November 26, 1954**	56	43	1

2. "In peacetime, do you think the newspapers should be allowed to criticize our form of government?" (NORC)***

	Yes	Qualified Yes**	No	
1943	66		30	4
1944	66		30	4
1946	66		30	4
1948	70		27	3
1953**	57	7	35	4

3a. "In peacetime, do you think the Socialist Party should be allowed to publish newspapers in this country?" (NORC)***

	Yes	Qualified Yes**	No	
November 1943	57		25	18
1944 (no month given)	57		25	18
November 1945†	57		29	14
1946 (no month given)	58		26	16
May 1953**†	45	5	34	16
January 1954**†	41	6	39	14
January 26, 1956**†	41	6	40	13
December 28, 1956**†	47	5	38	10
April 27, 1957**†	43	5	39	13

b. Preceding 1956 question: "now a couple of questions about things in the United States." "In peacetime" omitted in 1956 and 1957.†

c. Preceding 1957 question: "Now here's an interesting question."†

† Additional data obtained from David Cook, Assistant Data Librarian, NORC, by phone 12/15/77.
*** NORC: National Opinion Research Center, University of Chicago. OPOR: Ofice of Public Opinion Research, Princeton, NJ.
** Change in coding methods to allow qualified answers may account for most of the shift after 1952. "Qualified Yes" percentages are in addition to "for complete freedom" percentages.

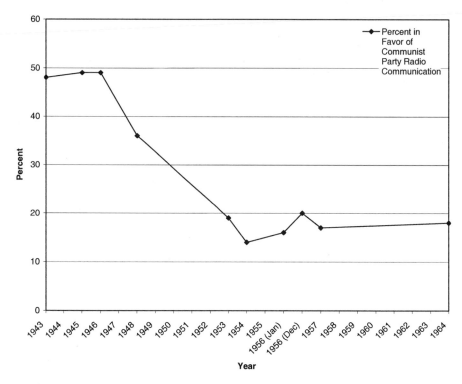

Figure 17.1
Percent in favor of Communist Party radio communication [Source: Erskine (1970: pp. 487–489)].

between 16%–20% in 1941). A decline occurred during the McCarthy era with a slight upswing registered after the hearings ended. Two other questions may be compared with this data. They follow a similar pattern except that a slight upswing in support for publication of socialist newspapers did not appear until somewhat later.

The reader should note that these polls utilize two different types of sampling: (1) quota sampling (prevalent in the 1930s, 1940s, and part of the 1950s), and (2) the more accurate probability sampling used today. Results of the two types of techniques are not directly comparable without compensation for the problems of quota samples (Glenn, 1970). The major problem is underrepresentation of the lower education, income, and occupational groups. The correction has not been made in tables 17.1 and 17.2 (and figures 17.1 and 17.3); however, since the data from Erskine show that lower SES groups are consistently less tolerant of free speech rights than higher SES groups, the actual results may be even less supportive of free speech than shown here.

Supreme Court Decisions

Analysis of the 73 Supreme Court decisions included (1) comparison with lower court rulings, (2) determination of broadness of ruling on freedom of speech, and (3) analysis of degree of consensus on each decision.

First, Supreme Court decisions cannot be predicted from lower court rulings. Sixty-seven percent of Supreme Court decisions upheld freedom of speech, in contrast to only 10% of lower court rulings which upheld it. The high court overturned 66% of lower court decisions limiting free speech, in contrast to 29% of lower court rulings upholding free speech which were overturned. (It cannot be determined from this data if the lower court decisions are representative of lower court positions on free speech issues, or if they are indicators of which cases are appealed.)

Second, Supreme Court decisions restricting freedom of expression are concentrated in the period 1950–1961 when the Court made 22 of its 24 decisions restricting the First Amendment, as table 17.2 shows. The other two adverse decisions occurred in the Vietnam war era.

Third, as figure 17.2 shows also, 14 of the 22 decisions limiting free speech in 1950–1961 were close (5–4 or evenly divided). In contrast, five decisions *for* free speech at this time were close. Two other close pro-free speech decisions occurred in the Vietnam era (involving communism and war protest), one in 1959 (a "fascist's" speech), and one in 1967 (communists' rights). Close decisions tend to be clustered in two periods, between 1949 and 1952 and between 1958 and 1961.

Comparison of Poll Data and Court Decisions

The decisions were grouped into six different periods in order to assess whether or not public opinion and Court decisions varied together. Rulings upholding an absolutist view of free speech characterize

N=47

Year	For	FOE*
37	8-0	5-4
39		5-2
43	6-3	9-0
46	7-0	
49		5-4
50	8-0	
51	5-3	
52	8-0	
55	8-0, 8-0	6-3, 7-2
56		6-3, 5-4
57	7-1, 5-3, 6-2	6-1, 5-2
58	5-4, 7-1, 5-4	6-3, 6-2
59	5-4, 5-4, 6-3	
61	5-4, 9-0	9-0, 5-2
64	6-3, 7-2	
65	5-4, 9-0, 9-0, 5-4, 6-3	5-2, 6-3, 7-2, 9-0, 7-2
68	6-3	
69	9-0, 7-2	
70	9-0, 9-0, 9-0, 5-3	

Limiting

Year	Limiting	FOE*	N=24
50	3-3	6-2, 5-4, 9-0	
51	4-4	6-1, 6-3	
52	5-2	6-3	
53	6-3	7-2	
55	5-4, 5-4	5-4, 6-3	
61	5-4	5-4	5-4, 5-4, 5-4, 5-4
68	7-2, 7-1		

*FOE = Freedom of expression (for political extremists)

Figure 17.2

Supreme Court decisions for and against freedom of expression for political extremists by year, showing number of cases within a year and whether or not vote was split within the decision.

three periods, and rulings restricting free speech typify the other three periods.

In period 1 (1937–1949), when the seven decisions occurring then all favored the First Amendment, public support shifted from the somewhat low levels (35%–40%) of the first six years to the relatively higher levels of 1943–1946 (50%–65%) before dropping again to about the same initial levels.

The Court began to take a much more limited view of free speech in period 2 (1950–1954), upholding such rights in only 21% of the 14 cases received at this time. Public opinion supporting communists' rights of free expression sagged to an all-time low in polling history.

In period 3 (1955–1957) the Court broadened the range of application of the First Amendment in all 11 cases, in striking contrast to the previous period. Public opinion seems to have supported this, although the upward swing depicted in figure 17.1 is small.

The Court again changed direction in period 4 (1958–1961) when only half of the 22 cases decided then favored free expression. Since there are no poll data for this time, it is useful to consult Sheldon's historical analysis. He contends that a number of groups ("Southern racists, states' rightists, lawyers, many members of the business community, local law enforcement agencies, the F.B.I. and anti-Communists") combined forces in opposition unforeseen by the Court, and they worked through Congress to make their feelings known to the Court. He concludes, "Despite the continuing argument for curbing the Court, the retreat of 1958–1961 was fairly successful in removing from the arena of constitutional politics the one issue—communism—upon which all of the Court's opponents could agree."

Period 5 (1962–1966) evidences a shift in direction again. The Court rendered rulings favorable to free speech in all eight cases occurring then. Poll data indicate low support for freedom of speech initially, rising slightly for communists, and relatively high for dissent against war (about 60%).

Period 6 (1967–1970) includes 13 cases, two of which restricted First Amendment rights. Public favor for war protest seems to have declined relatively rapidly from 1965, when the United States entered the war, to about 1970, although amount of U.S. involvement peaked in 1968.

Table 17.3
For Complete Freedom

	College	High School	Grammar School
1953	26	19	17
1954	20	11	13
1956 (Jan.)	26	13	13
1956 (Dec.)	28	19	16
1957	36	16	10
1964	—	—	—

Erskine's data indicate a great decrease in public favor for war protest, although questions are not easily compared.

Discussion

The poll data, taken together with the Court decisions, present a picture of a Supreme Court endeavoring to sustain rights guaranteed by the First Amendment even when only four persons in ten sanction a broad guarantee. When the level of public support dropped below this percentage, the Court did not seem able to sustain an absolutist approach to the First Amendment.

Examination of the degree of consensus within the Court provides further information. There are 23 decisions (almost one-third of the total) in which the Court was closely or evenly divided.[5] Sixty percent of Court decisions greatly restricted the range of the First Amendment during two of the periods of strongest public feeling against extremists (periods 2 and 4). This suggests that the Court felt great strain when handing down these decisions. The greater strain appears in period 4 (1958–1961) when 91% of decisions not reinforcing the First Amendment were close. Period 2 (1950–1954—which contains the events of a major war and the McCarthy hearings) depicts less strain as 36% of the decisions restricting the First Amendment were closely or equally divided. Of all rulings limiting free speech, 58% were made by a closely split Court. This analysis suggests that the Court's holdings limiting the First Amendment were difficult for the Court to make even when public opinion buttressed them.

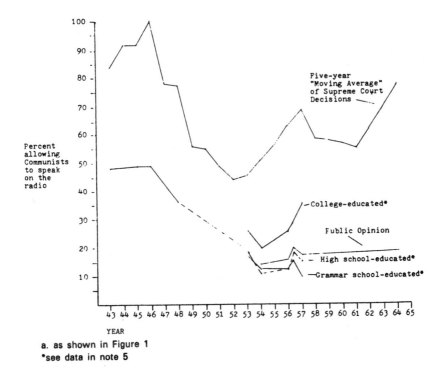

a. as shown in Figure 1
*see data in note 5

Figure 17.3
Average percentages of justices voting for broad guarantee of free speech,
compared with public opinion[a].

Turning to the close decisions upholding the right of free expression,
one can find further support for this contention. There were much fewer
close decisions in this direction—nine. Six of these occurred in a period
of strong public disapproval of communists (four in period 4 and one
each at the beginning and end of period 1). One other took place in a
time of low, but increasing, public favor for extremists' rights, and the
other two took place at a time of relatively high support for war dissenters and low but rising support for communists.

The last evidence to help determine whether or not there is a relationship between public opinion and Supreme Court decisions is in
figure 17.3, which is figure 17.1 compared with a graph of the average
percentages of justices voting to upheld a broad guarantee of free speech
in individual cases. The Court's graph is based on computations of five-

year "moving averages" calculated from the split in decisions shown in table 17.1 (i.e., a 6–3 decision in favor of the First Amendment = 67% of the Court favoring free expression. Then all rulings for a year are averaged together, and this result is averaged with results for five-year spans). Although there is a lack of data for some individual years, the shape of the graph for the Court is very much like the shape of the graph of public opinion. The distance between the Court's and the public's graphs indicates a Court that was more protective of the free speech constitutional guarantee than the public. The shape, however, suggests a Court altering its decisions according to the influence of public opinion. The justices may have known of the published polls as well as have been reacting to other public contacts. It is also likely that both the Court and the public were reacting similarly to some external events such as wars and the McCarthy hearings.

The Court appears to have been more in tune with highly educated persons than with the lesser educated when one looks at poll-data breakdown by education (also shown in figure 17.3).[6] The graphs of those with high school and grammar school educations parallel the average for the public as a whole, although at a lower level. However, the graph for the college-educated parallels the average for the public at a higher level, until 1957 when the Court and the college-educated portion of the public increased support for free speech but lesser-educated segments of the public decreased their support. The Court's apparent congruence with the more highly educated is logical, since members of the Court are more likely to interact with such persons than with the lesser educated, in both their professional and personal lives.

Support for the Hypothesis and Conclusions

Aspects of support for the hypothesis developed in the analysis are the following:

1. when fewer than four in ten members of the public approved of a broad guarantee of free speech, the Court restricted the First Amendment;

2. when fewer than four in ten members of the public supported the First Amendment, the Court's decisions were much more likely to be close

ones in either direction but especially when rulings were adverse to free speech;

3. when a low level of public favor for free speech rights of extremists was rising, the Court was more likely to render decisions upholding the First Amendment even though less than 50% of the public supported free speech for political extremists.

First, all of the Court's decisions restricting the range of application of the First Amendment occurred during times of low public favor for free speech, so that the influence of public opinion appears most strongly in these instances. Sheldon's evidence argues for great influence of public opinion in periods 2 and 4, as does Erskine's data for period 2. It is also likely that the comparatively large number of cases in these two periods was at least partially attributable to intense public hostility to free speech rights of extremists. Public support for free speech rights of war protestors was dropping rapidly at the two times of adverse rulings in period 6. The 1967 case not upholding free speech involved rights of communists, at a time when communists were not well regarded. The 1968 decision restricting the First Amendment had elements of violence in it (draft card burning and incitement of onlookers), so that opinion opposing nonpeaceful dissent sanctioned this ruling.

Second, all of the rulings upholding an absolutist view of the First Amendment occurred either at a time of relatively high public receptiveness to free speech for all (the middle of period 1) or at times of low, but rising, public favorability (periods 3 and 5). In the latter two periods upward shifts in public support, although still at low levels, seemed to provide sufficient backing for decisions upholding free speech rights. It also appears that the Court was more comfortable in handing down these decisions because there were only four close ones during periods 1, 3, and 5. This compares with the large number of close decisions in periods 2 and 4 when public hostility ran high and when many decisions in either direction (restricting the First Amendment or broadening it) were close.

Third, figure 17.3 provides evidence that public opinion and Court decisions were related because the shapes of the graphs for the Court and for public opinion, as measured by polls, were similar. This graph portrays a 22-year span, almost two-thirds of the time period studied.

Therefore, for these three reasons, it is concluded that the hypothesis is supported—that decisions of the Supreme Court involving freedom of speech for deviant, political groups are correlated with public opinion on this issue. It is recognized that facts varied in the cases and that cases arose several years before the Supreme Court decided their final outcome; however, it is argued that the decisive factor on rulings limiting First Amendment rights was the level of public sentiment favoring its broad application.

Notes

1. Model suggested by Phillip J. Tichenor in a conversation on June 1, 1977.

2. The table of cases is available from the author by writing to her c/o 111 Murphy Hall, School of Journalism and Mass Communication, Church Street, University of Minnesota, Minneapolis, MN 55455.

3. The McCarthy era dates are 1953–1954. The Permanent Investigation sub-committee of the Senate Committee on Government Operations (the McCarthy Committee") began investigation of alleged spying at Fort Monmouth, NJ in October 1953. Hearings were televised from April 22 through June 17, 1954 (Source: *Dictionary of American History*).

4. U.S. involvement in the Vietnam war began in 1965 and peaked in 1968, the year of the Tet offensive. In 1975 the last American troops left Vietnam.

5. During 1955–1957 when public heat had lessened, Burton and Harlan tended to divide their support, and Frankfurter consistently favored freedom of expression. During the next period, in which there was intense public opposition, 1958–1961, the same three were most affected, this time withdrawing their support. Three other members of the Court (Reed, Jackson, and Stewart) show different voting patterns depending upon which period is examined, a time of higher public favor for free speech (when they voted for it) or a time of low public support (when they voted against it). Further, Harlan and Stewart changed support again in 1967–1968, voting against free speech. These six (Burton, Harlan, Frankfurter, Reed, Jackson, and Stewart) may be termed "swing men," because they switched their positions in times of strong public sentiment against free speech. Taking consistent positions for a broad guarantee of freedom of expression were Douglas, Black, Warren, and Brennan. Consistently voting to limit it were Clark, Vinson, Minton, and Whittaker. The latter four plus the six "swing men" account for the change in Court voting behavior against freedom of expression for communists.

Truman appointees had strongest impact on Court conservatism toward free speech since none of them proved to be pro-free speech for extremists. The Roosevelt years produced three "swing men" and two who were pro-free speech, and the Eisenhower years contributed two "swing men," one opposed to free speech, and two for it.

6. Data on education breakdown in figure 17.3 (from Erskine 1970):

For Complete Freedom

	College	High School	Grammar School
1953	26	19	17
1954	20	11	13
1956 (Jan.)	26	13	13
1956 (Dec.)	28	19	16
1957	36	16	10
1964	—	—	—

Cases

DENNIS v. United States (1951) 341 U.S. 494.

HAGUE v. C.I.O. (1939) 307 U.S. 496.

SCALES v. United States (1961) 367 U.S. 203.

References

BROWN, D. W. (1972) "Public opinion and judicial decision-making." Presented to the American Political Science Association, Washington, DC.

DAHL, R. A. (1967) Pluralist Democracy in the United States. Chicago: Rand McNally.

DOLBEARE, K. M. (1967) "The public views the Supreme Court," in H. Jacob (ed.) Law, Politics, and the Federal Courts. Boston: Little, Brown.

———and P. E. HAMMOND (1968) "The political party basis of attitudes toward the Supreme Court." Public Opinion Q. 32: 16–30.

DUNNE, F. P. (1962) The World of Mr. Dooley. New York: Collier Books.

ERSKINE, H. (1970) "The Polls:" Freedom of Speech." Public Opinion Q. 34: 483–496.

———and R. L. SIEGEL (1975) "Civil liberties and the American public." J. of Social Issues 31, 2: 13–29.

GILES, M. W. (1973) "Lawyers and the Supreme Court." J. of Politics 35: 480–486.

GLENN, N. D. (1970) "Problems of comparability in trend studies with opinion poll data." Public Opinion Q. 34: 83–91.

MURPHY, W. F. (1964) Elements of Judicial Strategy. Chicago: Univ. of Chicago Press.

—— and J. TANENHAUS (1968) "Public opinion and the Supreme Court: the Goldwater campaign." Public Opinion Q. 32: 31–50.

PELTASON, J. W. (1955) Federal Courts in the Political Process. New York: Random House.

SHELDON, C. H. (1967) "Public opinion and high courts: Communist Party cases in four constitutional systems." Western Pol. Q. 20: 341–360.

SIMON, R. J. (1974) Public Opinion in America: 1936–1970. Chicago: Rand McNally.

III

Relationships with Academia

18

Facing In: Researchers and Academia

Sandra Braman
2002

Any researcher looking at policy questions must undergo several negotiations in the course of her work. In addition to developing relationships with the institutions that are the subject of study and the publics
to whom one communicates the results of one's research, a researcher
must negotiate with him or herself regarding the nature of the object of
study and the motivations for undertaking it, and with one's colleagues
regarding the legitimacy and scholarly value of the work.[1] The very
extensiveness of the scholarly literature discussing problems raised for
communication researchers engaged in policy-related work is testimony
of the power of such issues.

Much of the tension raised by doing policy research from an academic setting is pragmatic. While examining the policy implications of
research results and bringing those insights to the attention of policy-
makers may have great value to society, doing so can impede the career
of an academic by taking time and energy away from the peer-reviewed
publications that are the primary criterion for tenure and promotion.
Even when the scholarly content is rich and irrespective of the rigor of
the research involved, publication in venues accessible to policy-makers
or intended to stimulate and enrich public debate on issues of public-
wide concern usually counts only as "service" at best. The internal contradiction that this presents to universities has recently become a matter
of open debate within academia, for as administrators face growing
budgetary constraints they increasingly question the value of supporting
communication departments if those units are unable to help resolve the
pressing policy issues raised by changes in the nature of the information
environment.

An intriguing suite of three pieces by Australian cultural policy analyst Stuart Cunningham offers a picture of what negotiations with academia can look like when the tensions they produce are expressed to different audiences. Cunningham is operating within a context in which cultural policy is at the top of the national agenda because of Australia's need to define a cultural home for itself within its essentially Asian economic and political region, so the political matters he addresses are widely viewed as pressing. In one piece he translates policy analysis produced for government regulators into the terms of scholarship to make his policy-related work comprehensible to colleagues within academia.[2] In another, he directs an explicit justification for his participation in policy work to his academic colleagues.[3] And in a third he struggles to redefine the scholarly turf in such a way that policy-related work would fall inside rather than outside of it by definition—rather than requiring special justification. Thus he pleads with the global cultural studies community to incorporate the problem of television violence into their research agendas.[4]

There are substantive issues as well. Debates over the impact of the policy context on scholarly work deal both with the question of whether it advances or impedes the development of theory and with the quality and design of research that results. There is a spectrum of possibilities: Carey[5] argues that policy analysis is destructive to the study of communication because it inclines scholars away from the most fundamental questions about the nature of society that should drive any analysis of communication. Cunningham[6] makes the opposite argument, claiming that the need to deal with policy-based problems forces theorists to engage with the full complexities of the world rather than selecting only certain isolated features for attention. Hawkins[7] falls in between, taking the position that since all scholarly research takes place within a political, institutional, social, and economic context that affects the nature of the questions asked and the ways in which they are pursued policy research is no different in this regard. And Katz[8] suggests that a policy orientation has no impact on theory development either way.

Negotiating Theory: Policy Impact on Theory Development

Many believe that the relative marginalization of communication among the social sciences is a result of the fact that it has no theory of its own.

Though early in the twentieth century a number of sociologists believed that communication was key to understanding all other social processes, subsequent work has largely focused either on media as technologies or on trying to figure out how to make something specific happen (sales, or elections, or economic development). Particular policy-related ideas may have such power that in themselves they impede both further theory development and research into the phenomena and processes with which they deal.[9]

Policy Research as a Barrier to Theory Development

For James Carey,[10] the most important problem facing scholars in the field is understanding communication as a fundamental social force, a task that must start from and contribute to theories of society. Doing that, he suggests, is the most useful support that can be provided to policy-makers. The danger in focusing more narrowly on specific policy issues, he believes, is that it draws attention away from the fundamental questions and thus eviscerates the intellectual effort. Policy research as a result eviscerates the ability to draw strong thinkers to the study of communication therefore damages the field as a whole. There is historical support for his argument, for as Peters[11] notes, when the field turned to policy questions in the 1970s doing so merely added items to a list of topics without introducing new ideas or forcing theoretical development.

Carey was moved to consider the problem by Elihu Katz's[12] report to the BBC in response to a request from that public service broadcaster for a research agenda. This event was a turning point for communication policy research, for after long rejecting research input one of the most important broadcasting organizations in the world had a change of heart, a policy matter because the BBC is in essence an entity of the British government. Looking back on the disagreement after almost twenty-five years, Carey[13] comments,

I suppose I have not changed my mind in any essential way, though the issues are more complex than I admitted at the time. In a brief review of a particular monograph and a particular moment in the history of communications I inevitably oversimplified. In retrospect, events in the meantime give some plausibility to what I was trying to say. Beginning not long before I wrote, neo-conservatives began an assault on conventional assumptions governing communications at both the theory and policy levels and they have proven decisive. This was not done by concentrating on the policy questions directly but rather by developing a new understanding of social theory, that is, how it is societies are put together. William Buckley later explained the success of neo-conservatism about as follows, though what is quoted is merely paraphrased. Conservatism was always clear about its views of the economy and state. Indeed, its understanding of these two issues came directly from the Enlightenment itself. However, conservatives had no understanding of social theory and no articulate view of social problems beyond the market and the authority of the state. The bringing of sociologists into the conservative movement (at the moment he was thinking of Moynihan, Glazer, Kristol and Bell, though not all those stayed) taught us we had to develop a powerful theory of society or our policies for reform of the economy and the federal government would fail and be unpersuasive. The analysis they provided was worked out in journals such as *The Public Interest* (founded by the above sociologists) at the interstices between the educated/policy oriented public and the academic community which did the actual work.

The response of the left has been in intellectual terms unavailing and unconvincing. The old left has simply kept repeating the story of industrial concentration. While the story has truth nothing of interest has been added to it in fifty years. I once heard Herb Schiller asked, after a typically blistering condemnation of the "media" the following question: What kind of market in communications do you want anyway? He had no answer. He obviously didn't want a market of any type but how then did he believe the resources of communications should be allocated or what types of intellectual analysis were necessary to justify alternative institutional arrangements. But there was nothing there. The new left—the cultural studies left—had a hundred different analyses of ideology and of the ideological effects of the media but they didn't have an ideology of their own except as negative dialectics. That is, they were against everything but for nothing; they lacked a theoretically informed vocabulary that pointed in policy directions because they were not attacking fundamental intellectual problems.

The neo-conservative views are now tired and producing undesirable side effects but we still lack a viable alternative. So, my original critique largely stands. You get progress when people attack significant intellectual problems which derive from the central issues in social theory and only then do you get significant policy research and applications.

Structural schisms within academia exacerbate the problem. In most cases those in political science will have nothing to do with those in policy fields, and vice versa—political scientists treat the policy folks as "merely" professional, while those regularly involved with the policy world consider political scientists to be working so abstractly that often their work simply does not pertain to the daily world of political decision making. Communication researchers who incorporate ideas about the nature of the political process in their policy work may find that their alignment with one or the other of these disciplines may make their institutional lives more difficult. The consequence is that those in political science committed to development of theory often remain several removes away from the empirical ground of their ultimate subject matter and from the experience of working with it, while those trying to think about how to cope with immediate and pressing policy problems may never be exposed to the very theories they most need.

Policy Research as a Stimulus to Theory Development

Each of the theoretical perspectives identified as a barrier to policy research briefly introduced in chapter 1, "The Long View," however, suggests a way in which attending to policy might in fact move theory forward. The critique that those who analyze the law in terms of its social effects fail to influence policy because they lose sight of fundamental constitutional issues may begin with a misunderstanding of that work but also might be responded to by theoretical efforts to include the constitutional dimension into anaysis of social processes. The claim that policy analysts tend to underestimate the number and range of variables that influence policy-making processes suggests the need to develop theories of the communicative aspects of decision-making and negotiation that incorporate all of the factors encountered empirically. Issue analyses that fail to have any effect because they do not take into account the institutional environments within which those issues—and decision-making about them—unfold provide a positive impetus to work on three types of theoretical problems: developing ways of linking theories at different levels of analysis in general, relating institutional analysis to other types of social theory in particular, and expending more effort on mid-level theories that link abstractions with what happens on the ground.

Though Katz was criticized by Carey for providing recommendations to the BBC, the Katz oeuvre, like Carey's, models the value of the development of communication theory as the necessary foundation for any useful policy work. The fact that Katz was asked to propose a research agenda to the BBC marked a real turn in that governmental organization's attitude towards input from researchers, for only a few years earlier its director-general described using television license fee funds to support academic research as picking people's pockets to peer into their heads. The change of heart may have been due to the fact that Katz had been a broadcaster himself, while the chairman of BBC served as what Martin[14] describes as a "broker" for research, having been an academic himself. There had been fear of official criticism for not paying more attention to what researchers have learned, the need for new decisions to be made in response to social change, and decline in the power of the norms that had traditionally guided public service television programming. Katz suggests that competition—between the BBC and the Independent Broadcasting Authority (IBA)—provided the extra stimulus necessary to drive the BBC to use any resources it could acquire.

Katz responds to Carey's critiques by unpacking what happens once a commissioned report is submitted, an elaborate process in itself involving multiple players, interests, and constraints that are so important that those studying policy processes should include such informal negotiations in their definition of the subject. He closes, however, with perhaps the most astonishing and absolutely the most depressing defense of any ever offered by communication researchers who do policy analysis— Carey should not be critical of the BBC report, Katz says, because his work will have no impact at all.

Theory as a Barrier to Policy Research

Theory itself can actually serve as a barrier to policy research. Work that starts from the assumption that it is individuals in the audience, not the message producer, who create meaning has suggested to many that a corollary is that policy work is meaningless and doomed to be ineffective. Robert Entman[15] makes the stunning argument that reliance upon the First Amendment can itself impede the ability of researchers to influence policy because of its totemic power: Once the First Amendment is raised, all other questioning stops and as a result there is neither development of theory nor research. The consequences are felt throughout communication policy, though all federal agencies are required to meet evidentiary standards to support their regulatory decisions, for example, the FCC has in practice been exempted from this requirement.

This is an extraordinarily important argument. It offers one among the reasons for the reliance of the FCC on microeconomic analysis to the exclusion of systematic examination of the effects of its decisions upon the public sphere, and it provides a challenge to researchers to direct more energy to the effort to examine such effects. Other scholars also point to unexamined assumptions underlying communication policy— see, for example, Streeter's[16] analysis of the role of liberal thought. At times the ideas that serve as blinders to research come from researchers themselves, as when ideological biases prevent academics from analyzing policy positions in their entirety and their complexity.[17]

No theory in itself requires abandonment of the policy enterprise. Work on participatory development, for example, is an explicit attempt to apply a respect for audience production of meaning to the processes by which decisions about the nature and uses of a community's information infrastructure are made. Theorization of the global information infrastructure as produced through local practices[18] provides support for community-based policy efforts.[19] Once the research-stopping effect of the First Amendment is recognized it is possible to go on to serious research with the goal of improving national capacity to act upon the principles the First Amendment embodies.

Negotiating Research: Policy Impact on Research Design and Implementation

The policy context often adds methodological constraints as well. In some cases there has been concern that the deadline and other internal pressures of regulatory agencies may force researchers to drop their standards for rigor.[20] The disjuncture between the research and policy discourses means that researchers often find it difficult to cast their theoretical questions in ways that can get at the empirical matters of concern to the policy world, let alone to present the results of their work in genres accessible to the lay reader with little time.

Administrative versus Critical Research

The shaping of research questions even once an area of shared interest between the research and policy communities is identified may also be affected. Lazarsfeld's[21] distinction between administrative and critical research has provided a focal point for much of the field's debate over the impact on research of a policy orientation, though he was neither the only nor the first to call for critical work.[22] These categories still provide the poles around which debate over ways in which research and policy relate to each other revolves. Lazarsfeld presented the distinction as a contribution to self-reflection within a relatively new area of social science. Briefly, administrative research is that which intends to improve the functioning of a communication system within existing parameters, while critical research is that which strives to provide insights that will lead to parametric change in the communication system.[23] As Lazarsfeld puts it, administrative research looks at messages that exist, while critical work looks at those that do not. The value of critical research, he argues, lies in looking at media in new ways, expanding the range of questions asked, and enlarging the realm of subjects of which those questions are asked.

Though most who have used or written about the distinction since the original piece see the two types of research in opposition, Lazarsfeld believed the two could usefully be combined. Doing so, he believed, would provide intellectual stimulation as well as moral leadership. Less ambitiously, administrative research could answer questions addressed to it by critical research and vice versa.[24] In demonstration of this conviction, Lazarsfeld published books on both qualitative research methods[25] and on quantitative research methods,[26] and both types of researchers pay tribute.[27] Despite this openness to qualitative research methods, most assume that Lazarsfeld's inability to work with Theodor Adorno[28] was due to the latter's interest in qualitative aesthetic issues rather than questions addressable by quantitative survey research.[29] However, Lazarsfeld had no difficulty working with at least one other scholar whose focal interest was aesthetic (Rudolf Arnheim)[30]—suggesting the problem may instead have been personality driven.

In practice, administrative research tends to view the media as neutral in effect while critical research is more suspicious of media-based biases.[31] The structural considerations of critical scholars often lead them to the study of policy itself rather than specific policies. For Slack and Allor,[32] critical research distinguishes itself from administrative in its concern with ways in which the control of knowledge is central to the exercise of social power. While administrative research often works at the micro-level of analysis (focusing on effects of the media on individuals) and critical at the macro-level (focusing on effects of the media on society), often institutionally framed problems can be approached through either perspective.[33] Despite Lazarsfeld's encouragement of collaborative or complementary efforts, however, the divide between those who identify themselves as critical researchers and those who do administrative research has gotten more extreme over time. The former has been described as "emancipatory"[34] or "utopian"[35] and the latter as "repressive."

Proportionately, there has been more critical work at the international level than at the national. It may be easier to conduct critical work in that environment because researchers pursuing international questions may be less linked to specific governing structures. The approach was deliberately taken as the foundation of the UNESCO research program.[36] Blumler[37] claims European communication researchers were far more critical than were Americans through the 1970s, but this claim is based on examination of only one American journal (the traditionally empirical *Journalism Quarterly*). Blumler's view also oversimplifies a history in which key figures—beginning with Robert Park early in the twentieth century—moved back and forth between Europe and the United States.

Critiques of the administrative/critical distinction have been several. Because Lazarsfeld's earliest work was in advertising and he continued to use quantitative techniques, some felt that he did not truly understand the difference between doing research into marketing questions and studying issues dealing with power and politics.[38] Lazarsfeld himself suggested that the extreme sensitivity of the media industry to criticism made analysts in turn so nervous that it reduced the amount of critical work done.[39] The dichotomy is meaningless within a Marxist-Leninist environment (as is the distinction between basic and applied research), for under such conditions generating empirical data of the kind described as administrative in Western Europe and the United States can in itself be deeply critical.[40] Indeed, the question of which approach provides the greater challenge to existing power relations may be the reverse of what has been claimed in recent years in North America and Europe. In Poland, for example, "critical" research based on Marxist principles served to further the government's goals while positivist empirical work produced results that were genuinely critical and often led to the destruction of scholars' careers because it turned up "inconvenient" data.[41] The distinction is also meaningless when applied to research involving living populations because of the Hawthorne effect, the effect of research upon the populations studied. Since the results of all research can and will be used by policy-makers irrespective of the desires of those who undertake it, Michaels[42] would distinguish only between research that is accountable and that which is not.

Many define *all* policy research as critical.[43] Meanwhile, ironically, scholars who positioned themselves as critical in their studies of U.S. communication policy during the 1980s and 1990s actually argued for maintenance of the status quo.[44] Some suggest a third set of alternatives between administrative and critical research. The notion of formative research[45] is prescriptive rather than descriptive or critical. The most successful use of formative research may have been in production of the children's television program, *Sesame Street*. Other approaches include attention to ethical issues on the part of empirical researchers, embedding the study of communications within the study of society, and acknowledging the culture-boundedness of most communication research.

Policy as Research Design

There are times when governments explicitly use social experimentation as a policy tool to determine which among alternative approaches might be most fruitful. This was done in Finland 1960s when Kaarle Nordenstreng's ideas about how to achieve a better informed and more engaged polity were put into practice in public radio.[46] The Japanese launched a wide variety of types of experimentation with new information technologies at the community and organizational levels as soon as the concept of the information society (which appeared there before it did in the United States) emerged in the 1960s.[47] In the United States, Department of Commerce programs such as Telecommunications and Information Infrastructure Assistance Program (TIIAP) and Technology Opportunities Program (TOP)—abandoned by President George W. Bush—encouraged community-level experimentation with the use of networking technologies for a decade or so. Recognition of the value of such experimentation in the United States seems to come and go; while there was an upsurge of appreciation for it in the late 1970s,[48] in the Homeland Security environment of the early twenty-first century it appears to be falling away altogether.

The French minitel experiment is a famous example of social experimentation as a policy tool. Just as the Socialists were voted into power in the early 1980s, the country was shocked by the conclusions of the globally influential report to the French government on the "computerization" of society by Nora and Minc[49] that suggested, among other things, that U.S.-based corporations controlled the European information infrastructure. In response, the Socialists sought to use culture and communication as tools for social change with the goal, as President Mitterand put it in 1981, of democratizing computers rather than computerizing society.[50] In a dramatic move, the government launched the "minitel," a dumb computer terminal that would be cheap enough to produce that they could be distributed by the government to French citizens for free. The intention was to serve multiple policy goals at once: If successful, the minitel program would support a domestic industry that could provide an export niche for France in the global economy; it would encourage the "informatization" of French citizens; and it would stimulate the development of a French information service industry by creating a market for the industry from the point of launch. In the end, however, the difficulties of correctly guessing about trends during periods of rapid innovation and of launching massive programs rather than small experiments were vividly demonstrated: It took far longer than projected to produce enough computers to distribute them as widely as had been intended; while an information service industry did develop, its strongest sector was pornography; and by the time production capacity was sufficient to support exports, the personal computer had come into use and dumb terminals were no longer of interest.

Whether or not specific policies are intended to serve the purposes of experimentation, however, researchers may treat them as such. Thus Dewey reverses the typical relationship between research and policy: While most assume that research comes before policy-making as an input into the process, Dewey believes policies should be considered experimental interventions into social life and the job of researchers is to evaluate the results. For Dewey, the very point of social science is to make a policy difference by opening up new ways of thinking about how to organize society. The position that social scientists can usefully support the development of policies, he argues, is a "complete error,"[51] for the social sciences should be complementary to lay analyses of a "self-guiding society" rather than providing authoritative truths for a "scientific society."[52] Research is a means by which people can come to understand that their individual actions have consequences for others besides themselves and thus understand the need to commit to society as a whole.[53] Social sciences therefore should serve diagnostic and normative roles in addition to prescriptive. Dewey did not convince everyone; Toulmin[54] described this position as "destructive" to the entire project of philosophy.

Research, too, can be a form of social experimentation that can be used as a policy tool. The International Development Research Centre (IDRC), a Canadian nonprofit organization heavily involved in trying to improve access to the Internet and other telecommunications services throughout the developing world, foregrounds the Hawthorne effect in its work. Rather than denying its reality, the IDRC argues that the Hawthorne effect enhances the utility of conducting research in support of policy goals by turning the research itself into another policy tool. The organization has found this to be a particularly valuable argument for persuading host policy-makers in the developing world who would otherwise not see the point to include research as an important element of the process by which policies are developed and evaluated.[55]

Policy Impact on Research Practices

Designing research for policy purposes, especially when undertaken within the government, can have an impact on research practices as well. Preston[56] found the experience of working inside the Federal Trade Commission (FTC) filled with both "peril and promise" after life as a researcher in an academic institution. Though scholars who had earlier had the same experience found their work underutilized, by the time Preston arrived there had been changes in the FTC in terms of its receptivity to research and the types of research it would support. The most important shift in the latter area was a turn away from looking just at the content of advertising in making their determinations about deception to looking at how they were actually perceived. The FTC not only began to pay more attention to research in the course of its internal deliberations but was also more likely to use research as evidence in the courtroom, whether prosecuting or defending themselves. Improvement in the quality of advertising research and interest in corrective advertising were mentioned as possible reasons for these shifts. Unfortunately, however, Preston reports that academics who get involved in research on advertising for use in the courtroom at times are still so swayed by the environment or the money that they may produce interpretations of results that run counter to what those whose audiences are solely academic find. Academics contributed to the rising interest in consumer protection by the FTC during the 1960s by applying what had been learned about communications to advertising issues and urging the regulatory agency to take up the use of survey research as a means of refining and applying their policy tools.[57] After a couple of decades of effort in this area, guidelines for researchers began to develop.[58]

Disjunctures between Policy and Research Discourses

Even the most casual discourse analysis shows that policy-makers and researchers speak in different tongues. Reeves and Baughman[59] read the history of U.S. communications research through the lens of its interactions with the policy world, identifying several factors that may have prevented the results of research from having more impact. Researchers rarely link their work to actual legislation under discussion, for example, and tend to underappreciate the degree to which government interest in the effects of the mass media can actually alter the behavior of media corporations. Policy-makers were also to blame, being much slower to take up research dealing with communication policy than were decision makers in many other areas.

In some cases, however, the impact of communication research on policy-makers has been surprising and perhaps antithetical to that intended: Reeves and Baughman report that it was Newton Minow's reading of the 1961 Schramm study of television that made him realize there were potentially prosocial as well as antisocial effects, with the consequence that his critique of television was blunted. They also suggest that for most of the twentieth century communication researchers and policy-makers were "out of sync" with each other, asking questions of the media so different that the two discourses did not meaningfully link up. The failure of communication researchers to enter the policy conversation regarding digital technologies would be an important contemporary example of this.

Brown[60] argues that more attentive reading of the policy discourse by academics could lead to engaging more fully and productively with policy-makers. When then-FCC Chair Mark Fowler provided an intellectual justification for the shift to a market orientation as the principle that would guide broadcast regulation in a law review article published in 1982,[61] there was enormous outcry from scholars whose theoretical position, ideology, and/or simple reading of the law felt that in doing so the regulatory agency was abandoning its mandate to make decisions in accordance with the public interest. Brown's analysis of the Fowler argument and academic responses to it showed that while Fowler had presented a complex set of ideas that included acknowledgment of the limits beyond which such an approach need not go, scholarly discussion dealt only with the first point of many. In so doing, Brown argues, those opposed to the shift in regulatory stance actually provided support for the move by permitting discussion of the limits of the marketplace approach to drop away rather than forcing Fowler and others to carry through on all dimensions of the position as first articulated.

Discussion

The study of policy analysis itself, what Browne[62] calls the "analysis of analysis," and Dutton[63] refers to as "metapolicy," places a larger frame around the frustrations researchers who would like to see the results of their work inform policy experience on a daily basis. From this perspective, three features of the discussion about the intellectual impact of engagement with policy matters become of interest. In each case it becomes clear that the limitations of policy-oriented research lie not with the subject matter or the endeavor, but with the intellectual equipment brought to bear upon it.

First, both ends of the spectrum of positions in the debate over whether or not a policy orientation impedes or stimulates theoretical development assume that those engaging in policy analysis must limit their intellectual scope in particular—though never discussed—ways. Such oversimplifications fail to map onto the history, let alone the possibilities for future work. Schon and Rein[64] provide a review of several stages in the history of policy analysis, each of which added another layer to the range of analytical tools used. "Policy science" as developed by Lasswell and others following World War II treats the choice among approaches to the resolution of specific problems as the central question, tends to assume the policy-maker is a rational actor, and relies heavily upon techniques such as cost-benefit analysis. In the late 1960s and early 1970s, a tradition of political analyses of policy problems arose in which policy-making came to be seen as a process of contention among multiple interest groups vying for the control over definition of the policy problem and the allocation of resources in their resolution. Viewed in this manner, policy outcomes are the products of a competitive political game such as the "ecology of games" described by Dutton.[65] A third approach began to appear in the late 1970s that flourished in the 1980s, which started from the assumption that policy-making is a game of conflicting interests and powers and developed theories of mediated negotiations for analytical use. Once attention had turned to the negotiation as critical to understanding how policy issues are resolved, discourse analysis became important. Schon and Rein add an additional layer of analysis of the frames within which policy discourses are cast, and Foucault's approach to governmentality adds another layer of cultural analysis as the context for discourse frames. Today the entire range of social theory is being used in the course of policy analysis, with each critique serving to direct attention to what may have been previously unexamined assumptions.

Second, policy analyses are often critiqued as intellectually thin because they often address only one piece of the complex picture that is the stuff of policy-making processes. Salmon[66] notes, for example, that though campaign theory is often turned to policy ends, such as the design of campaigns to achieve health goals like reducing the incidence of AIDS, it most often stands alone in researchers' hands. Pointing out that most analyses of health campaigns treat them as independent variables that might be manipulated to achieve different outcomes (what he calls theory "for" campaigns), Salmon suggests they are also dependent variables that are the outcome of particular configurations of social, political, and ideological forces peculiar to a social system at a given point in time (theory "of" campaigns). Combining these two types of analyses can provide insights regarding just when campaigns are likely to be more or less effective than other types of policy tools and enable policy-makers to evaluate them relative to other options.

Third, oversimple analyses of policy positions are another way in which engagement might impede theoretical development but this, too, is a matter that is in the hands of researchers rather than necessarily determined by the policy environment itself. In an example discussed above, evidence of this can be found fairly early in the conversation about whether or not the market should govern FCC decision making regarding broadcasting. That discourse quickly became polarized, with the loss to the discourse of complexity and nuance.

In sum, policy analysis is not limited in its theoretical richness and at its best grapples as profoundly with fundamental questions about the nature of society as does any other specialization within the social sciences. Critiques of policy analysis that does not reach this level need to be heard; the most useful response to this critique is not to walk away but rather to struggle to bring the best that social theory has to offer to the effort to resolve social problems.

The institutional problems facing researchers who wish to engage with the world of policy are more difficult to resolve because the solutions are not within the hands of individuals. The same technological innovation that has created such a need for the input of communication researchers into policy-making, however, is forcing universities to reconsider their functions and their relations to related institutions such as publishers and libraries. As relations among these information industries are renegotiated and the boundaries redrawn, it is a relatively good time to introduce into the discourse the need to reevaluate treatment of policy work by scholars so that personal career considerations might become less of a barrier.

Notes

1. Gay Hawkins, Writing on the edge of history: Documenting cultural institutions, *Media Information Australia*, 73 (1994): 35–44.

2. Stuart Cunningham, Television and violence: From critique to policy, *Australian Journal of Communication*, 16 (1989): 87–100.

3. Stuart Cunningham, Cultural critique and cultural policy: Handmaiden or no relation? *Media Information Australia*, 54 (1989): 7–12.

4. Stuart Cunningham, Cultural critique and cultural policy.

5. James W. Carey, The ambiguity of policy research.

6. Stuart Cunningham, Cultural critique and cultural policy.

7. Gay Hawkins, Writing on the edge of history.

8. Elihu Katz, Get out of the car: A case study on the organization of policy research, *Gazette*, 25, no. 2 (1978): 75–86.

9. Robert M. Entman, Putting the First Amendment in its place: Enhancing democracy through the press, *The University of Chicago Legal Forum* (1993): 61–82.

10. James Carey, The ambiguity of policy research: Social research on broadcasting, *Journal of Communication*, 28: 2 (1978): 114–119.

11. John Durham Peters, Institutional sources of intellectual poverty in communication research, *Communication Research*, 13: 4 (1986): 527–559.

12. Elihu Katz, *Social Research on Broadcasting: Proposals for the BBC*, British Broadcasting Corporation, London, 1977.

13. James Carey, personal communication, April 2, 2001.

14. Martin, 1984, *op cit.*

15. Entman, 1993, *op cit.*

16. Streeter, 1990, *op cit.*

17. Duncan H. Brown, The academy's response to the call for a marketplace approach to broadcast regulation, *Critical Studies in Mass Communication*, 11: 3 (1994): 267–273.

18. Susan Leigh Star & Karen Ruhleder, Steps toward an ecology of infrastructure: Design and access for large information spaces, *Information Systems Research*, 7: 1 (1996): 111–134.

19. The nonprofit association Computer Professionals for Social Responsibility (CPSR), for example, has organized two workshops in 2002 under the leadership of Andrew Clement of the University of Toronto—one in the United States and one in Europe—to strengthen the capacity for participatory policy work around the information infrastructure.

20. Ivan L. Preston, Researchers at the Federal Trade Commission: Peril and promise, in James H. Leigh and Claude R. Martin, Jr., eds, *Current Issues &*

Research in Advertising, The University of Michigan Press, Ann Arbor, 1980, pp. 1–15.

21. Lazarsfeld, 1941, *op cit.*

22. Hanno Hardt, The return of the "critical" and the challenge of radical dissent: Critical theory, cultural studies, and American mass communications research, *Communication Yearbook*, 12 (1989): 558–600.

23. William H. Melody and Robin E. Mansell, The debate over critical vs. administrative research: Circularity or challenge, *Journal of Communication*, 33, no. 3 (1983): 103–116.

24. Todd Gitlin, Media sociology: The dominant paradigm, *Theory and Society*, 6 (1978): 205–253.

25. Paul F. Lazarsfeld, *Qualitative Analysis* Allyn & Bacon, Boston, 1971.

26. Paul F. Lazarsfeld, *Mathematical Thinking in the Social Sciences* Russell & Russell Publishers, New York, 1969.

27. Robert K. Merton, James S. Coleman, and Peter H. Rossi (Eds.), *Qualitative and Quantitative Social Research: Papers in Honor of Paul F. Lazarsfeld*, Free Press, New York, 1979.

28. Theodor W. Adorno, Scientific experiences of a European scholar in America, trans. Donald Fleming, in Donald Fleming and Bernard Bailyn, eds, *Perspectives in American History, Vol. II, The Intellectual Migration: Europe and America, 1930–1960*, Harvard University Press, Cambridge, 1968, pp. 338–370. Paul F. Lazarsfeld, An episode in the history of social research: A memoir, in Fleming and Bailyn, 1968, *op cit.*, pp. 270–337.

29. See, e.g., Towers, 1977, *op cit.*

30. Wilke, 1991, *op cit.*

31. Jay G. Blumler, Purposes of mass communications research: A transatlantic perspective, *Journalism Quarterly*, 35, no. 1 (1978): 219–230.

32. Jennifer Daryl Slack and Martin Allor, The political and epistemological constituents of critical communication research, *Journal of Communication*, 33, no. 3 (1983): 208–218.

33. Dallas Smythe and Tran Van Dinh, On critical and administrative research: A new critical analysis, *Journal of Communication*, 33, no. 3 (1983): 117–127.

34. Everett M. Rogers, The empirical and the critical schools of communication research, *Communication Yearbook*, 5 (1982): 125–144.

35. Toby Miller, Culture with power: The present moment in cultural policy studies, *Southeast Asian Journal of Social Science*, 22 (1994): 264–283.

36. Nordenstreng, 1994, *op cit.*

37. Blumler, 1978, *op cit.*

38. Ronald A. Fullerton, The art of marketing research: Selections from Paul F. Lazarsfeld's "Show Buying in Zurich" (1933), *Journal of the Academy of Marketing Science* 18, no. 4 (1990): 319–328.

39. Lazarsfeld, 1948, *op cit.*

40. Szecskö, 1986, *op cit.*

41. Jakubowicz, 1989, *op cit.*

42. Michaels, 1985, *op cit.*

43. See, e.g., Dallas Smythe, The political character of science (including communication science), or science is not ecumenical, in Armand Mattelart and Seth Singleaub, eds, *Communication and Class Struggle*, International General/International Mass Media Research Center, New York 1979, pp. 171–176.

44. Gripsrud, 1998, *op cit.*; Noam, 1993, *op cit.*

45. Edward L. Palmer, Formative research in the production of television for children, in Gerbner, *et al.*, *op cit.*, 1973, pp. 229–245; Blumler, 1978, *op cit.*; Katz, 1978, *op cit.*

46. Hujanen, 1995, *op cit.*

47. Youichi Ito, *Johoka* as a driving force of social change, *KEIO Communication Review*, 12 (1991): 33–58.

48. See, e.g., A. M. Shinn, Jr., The utility of social experimentation in policy research, in M. C. J. Elton, W. A. Lucas, and D. W. Conrath, eds, *Evaluating New Telecommunications Services*, Plenum, New York, 1978, pp. 681–700.

49. Simon Nora and Alain Minc, *The Computerization of society*, MIT Press, Cambridge, 1980.

50. Armand Mattelart and Yves Stourdze Cesta, *Technology, Culture and Communication: A Report to the French Minister of Research and Industry*, trans. David Buxton, North-Holland, *Amsterdam*, 1985.

51. Dewey, 1931, *op cit.*, p. 277.

52. Rune Premfors, Knowledge, power, and democracy: Lindblom, critical theory and postmodernism, *Knowledge and Policy*, 5, no. 2 (1991): 77–93.

53. Jay Rosen, *Democracy Overwhelmed: Press and Public in the Nuclear Age* New York University Center for War, Peace, and the News Media, New York, Occasional Paper #4, 1988.

54. Stephen Toulmin, *Cosmopolis: The Hidden Agenda of Modernity*, University of Chicago Press, Chicago, 1990.

55. The impact of the IDRC approach on communities is even further enhanced through the use of research techniques they have developed that enable community members to participate in the research themselves.

56. Preston, 1980, *op cit.*

57. Ernest Gellhorn, Proof of consumer deception before the Federal Trade Commission, *Kansas Law Review*, 1969, pp. 559–572; Richard W. Pollay, Deceptive advertising and consumer behavior: A case for legislative and judicial reform, *Kansas Law Review*, (1969): 625–637.

58. Thomas J. Maronick, Copy tests in FTC deception cases: Guidelines for researchers, *Journal of Advertising Research*, 31, no. 6 (1991): 9–18.

59. Reeves and Baughman, 1983, *op cit.*

60. Duncan H. Brown, The academy's response to the call for a marketplace approach to broadcast regulation, *Critical Studies in Mass Communication*, 11, no. 3 (1994): 257–273.

61. Mark S. Fowler and Daniel L. Brenner, A marketplace approach to broadcast regulation, *Texas Law Review*, 60, no. 207 (1982): 207–257.

62. Mairead Browne, The field of information policy: 2—Redefining the boundaries and methodologies, *Journal of Information Science*, 23, no. 5 (1997): 339–352.

63. Dutton, 1992, *op cit.*

64. Schon and Rein, *op cit.*

65. William H. Dutton describes this approach in The ecology of games in telecommunications policy, in Harvey M. Sapolsky, Rhonda J. Crane, W. Russell Neuman, and Eli M. Noam (Eds.), *The Telecommunications Revolution: Past, Present, and Future*, Routledge, London, 1992, pp. 65–88; he elaborates upon it in response to critiques received in The ecology of games and its enemies, *COmmunication Theory*, 5, no. 4 (1995): 379–392.

66. Charles T. Salmon, Bridging theory "of" and theory "for" communication campaigns: An essay on ideology and public policy, *Communication Yearbook*, 15 (1992): 346–358.

Negotiating Theory: Policy Impact on Theory Development

19

The Ambiguity of Policy Research

James W. Carey
1978

*The oft-felt danger [is] that research itself has become a menace, . . .
a semantic crucifix warding off modern vampires of public and
political pressure.*

The publication of Elihu Katz's report for the BBC on priorities in broadcasting research is an important though ambiguous event. The importance is easy enough to state. First, Katz is among the most distinguished senior scholars in communications and his attempt to shape the contours of the field while advising the BBC merits serious attention. Second, the BBC is perhaps the most distinguished broadcasting organization in the world. Its willingness to support Katz's inquiry and to encourage and support basic research signals a new period of cooperation between broadcasters and researchers: a movement beyond deténte or the partnership in an official estrangement toward active cooperation and mutual support. Third, the report itself proposes a number of important lines of investigation, some of which we have long recognized but delayed because of short funds, the absence of sponsorship, and a failure of nerve and method. Many of the proposals are, however, quite novel and will be mined by students and researchers for years to come and with quite productive results. Finally, the report is peppered, and I can't emphasize this too strongly, with sharp observations concerning broadcasting, communications, and the research process.

Yet there are ambiguities in the argument presented and dangers in the report itself. Rather than concentrate on the individual proposals, I would like to present some reactions to the report as a whole: to the directions it seems to impel the field, to the underlying assumptions in the argument, and to the circumstances of its creation. While I have exceptional respect and admiration for Professor Katz, I think it is necessary to dwell on the problems the report creates rather than on the more obvious opportunities it presents.

There is a danger, first of all, that the report will be taken as definitive rather than merely suggestive, a statement of fact rather than an invitation to argument. Katz clearly states throughout that the proposals represent one man's vision of the needs of the field, albeit a vision shaped by extensive conversation with BBC personnel and British and American researchers. While Katz is an unusually gifted and sympathetic interpreter of the work of others, they remain his interpretations of what was said and his statement of priorities. And, as I hope to show, some of the interpretations are quite arguable.

The danger is that in an intellectual community hungry for ideas, in which an oversupply of researchers chases an undersupply of researchable notions, the Katz proposals are likely to have an impact which, if not definitive, is nonetheless powerful. His own reputation plus the sponsorship of the BBC might shortcut the careful and sustained argument that will be necessary if the research community, like a collective character from a Stephen Leacock poem, is not to leap upon its horse and set off simultaneously in several directions. Of course, this says more about a persistent quality of the field than about the proposals.

The arguable assumptions of the Katz report center on three areas: the nature of policy research and of the BBC assignment, the history of mass communication research implicit in the report which provides the background to the proposals, and the isolation of the proposals from any informing social theory, that is, the decision to make the report theoretically eclectic. Let me take each in turn.

The proposals were developed to meet criteria stated in advance by the BBC: "to take account of past and ongoing work in Britain and elsewhere, and have policy and/or editorial implications for the BBC."

While Katz interpreted this charge as broadly as possible, the necessity of recommending research that had policy implications for the BBC is felt throughout the report in the definition of problems and in the details of the proposals. It was possible for him to accept the charge from the BBC because he assumes that "what the broadcaster would like to know . . . is not so different from what the social scientist would like to know." We need not necessarily agree with that assumption or with the parallel assumption that the active cooperation of professional broadcasters and researchers will benefit both broadcasting and scholarship.

By accepting the policy framework, the Katz report is not an encouragement to "rethink" television or a call for scholarship about it—it is a call for research on it. That call must pretty much assume the existing social structure and political arrangements and the existing role television plays in our personal, political, and cultural life. We are back in the bind of administrative and critical research. Policy research must assume that TV is a policy problem, that we need to know how to get television to operate more effectively and with less danger and abrasion. It cannot, for example, raise, even in fantasy, the question of whether television should be abolished or that the trouble is not in the messages or in the institutions but in the medium itself. Nor can the proposals start from the far less radical notion that, at the very least, the role television plays in social life has to be decisively cut back. Similarly, the specific research proposals developed within a policy framework must pretty much study television directly. However, we have learned that it is often best when studying television to ignore the medium in order to concentrate on the leisure behavior, states of consciousness, social structures, and political phenomena with which television intersects.

Let me be fair. Katz realizes this more than most and his restless imagination and intelligence keep expanding beyond the limits of his assignment. Many of his most important proposals concern the study of ordinary conversation, conventional conceptions of time, and the structure of differentiation in modern societies. But the policy stipulation does lead to a real danger: the policy priorities are not the same as the intellectual priorities and when the actual research is funded, it will be the latter that will be abandoned. Such action, in turn, augments the oft felt danger that research itself has become a menace, that it functions merely as symbol and talisman: not an attempt to get real understanding but a symbol of an organization's rectitude and progressiveness and simultaneously a semantic crucifix warding off modern vampires of public and political pressure.

But the policy framework bespeaks a deeper problem. It is possible, as the report shows, to frame theoretical speculation and empirical inquiry in terms congenial to both professional broadcasters and communications researchers. This is because a silent embrace has been growing up between these two communities. But is this embrace beneficial to scholarship and society? I do not think it produces any necessary or potential benefits for scholarship.

In fact, I think a better case can be made that scholarship, like many of the arts, flourishes when it stands in determined opposition to the established order.

If you are in opposition, you have to work very much harder to get a hearing at all and that extra effort makes the critical difference. But, more importantly, to attract and hold major scholars, the field of communications must formulate puzzles and dilemmas that are intellectually challenging and provocative. While questions of policy research can at times also be intellectually interesting, that is not necessarily the case. In economics there was such a happy moment with the simultaneous failure of classicial theory to account for unemployment and the policy questions surrounding "the great depression." No such happy moment has yet occurred in communications. It is not so much, as Bernard Berelson once charged, that the field has lost its major figures but that it has not attracted enough people of unusual ability. To attract such people major intellectual questions must be on the agenda.

Formulating research priorities in terms of policy research is not likely to improve the situation for the research is grounded in institutional needs, not in the theoretical dispute or persistent intellectual dilemmas. While there are some intellectually interesting proposals in the Katz volume, much of the research called for, even if of value to a broadcasting organization, is intellectually trivial, in the precise sense that it does not address as the first order of business theoretical dispute or intellectual puzzles.

If the embrace of the research and broadcasting community places limitations on scholarship, it may also be socially damaging. There is an often conscious struggle in modern societies over who is to control broadcasting: the state, the public, commercial institutions, professional broadcasters. Social scientists have become one of the status groups in the fray. There are shifting coalitions among these groups depending upon time, place, and circumstance. The status interests of broadcasters and researchers are often in sharp conflict and those interests in turn lead to sharp differences in research priorities and, above all, in the interpretation and application of data. The Katz report tends to fudge those conflicts in order to produce a marriage. But that fudging in turn leads to a devitalizing of research questions. Were Katz successful it would rob society of the one useful role scholars can perform: the statement of problems, issues; and solutions in terms that are outside and opposed to the established center of power and authority. That scholars have been badly corrupted on this matter is no argument to extend the corruption.

The second problem derives from the history of mass communication research that Katz assumes as background and occasionally moves to the center of focus.

The history, which I must strip down to the point of burlesque, goes something like this. Early work on mass communications concentrated on the question of effects and built a model of the powerful influences of the media. Subsequent research, in the forties and fifties, systematically cut this model down to size, hedging in and modifying the claims for powerful effects, with empirical data showing the relative ineffectiveness of the media in producing fundamental changes: in short, building a model of "limited effects." At this point Katz felt the field was, in a well-known phrase, "withering away." Subsequently, attention shifted to the needs of the audience leading to a growth in uses and gratifications research. Then in the sixties the image of the powerful mass media returned because of the impact of McLuhan and other scholars and the rejoining of communication research to the problem of public opinion.

There is nothing startling in this history and it is correct as far as it goes. But it omits two critical elements. The history of mass communication research is more than the history of "findings," the history of the autonomous processes of theoretical and empirical development. The history of mass communication research must include, as a parallel, a history of the changing world of mass communications: of the purposes to which these institutions are put, the audiences that gather to them, the social structures they more or less shape. In terms of this latter history, it can be argued that the basic reason behind the shift in the argument about effects from a powerful to a limited to a more powerful model is that the social world was being transformed over this period, transformed by a series of cycles moving around a linear trend. That is, the basic model for studying communication effects is that of business cycles: the inflation and deflation of effects around a linear historical movement. Powerful effects of communication were sensed in the thirties because the Depression and the political currents surrounding the entrance into war created a fertile bed for the production of certain kinds of effects. Similarly, the normalcy of the fifties and sixties led to a limited effects model. In the late sixties a period of war, political discord and inflation again conspired to expose the social structure in fundamental ways and to make it permeable by the media of communication. These cyclical movements occurred around a fundamental social process, however: the progressively deeper penetration of the media into the social structure and its constituent institutions. One need only look at the role of popular culture and the media in the schools, for example.

The history of communication effects, however, intersects at every point with the history of communication researchers: their interests and implicit ideological position.

When I say the "interests" of researchers, I mean that often maligned word in a dual sense: the problems which interest researchers and the self-interest, particularly the status interests of researchers. I elsewhere argued, with a colleague, Albert Kreiling, that the shift from a powerful effects model to a limited effects model paralleled a shift in the outlook of social scientists from a prophetic to a priestly class: from a group of outsiders hurling barbs at established society to a group of insiders. Researchers were joined to the establishment and research underwent what Kenneth Burke called a "bureaucratization of the imaginative." This incorporation in turn paralleled a depoliticization of the social structure, a declaration of the end of ideology and a convergence of status interests between university researchers and other powerful elements within society. In turn the re-politicalization of the social structure in the late sixties was marked by the decided tension between these groups, a slight but significant radicalization of faculties, a re-attentiveness to propaganda and manipulation, and the growing neces-sity within universities under the force of students (and the drying up of federal funds) of adopting critical and prophetic stances. But researchers retained certain status interests however realigned: look, for example, at the differing tones and conclusions of the commission reports on pornography and violence.

The point is a simple one: the problem of communications effects is a diachronic not a synchronic one. The failure to grasp this leads to a deeper theoretical weakness. Katz continues to press for a natural science of communication, a science wedded to causal and functional models, revealing universal needs of persons and societies, stating invariant laws. That this model has pretty much exhausted its usefulness is, I think, clear. As I tried to briefly exemplify above, we need a model that is throughly historical and reflexive: a model in which the history and intentions of the observer are part of the history and meaning of the observed.

Finally, these weaknesses come down to one overriding consideration: the absence in the volume of any informing relation between communication and social theory.

The proposals themselves can only be described as eclectic, despite Katz's efforts to categorically order them. Eclecticism can be a virtue and it never is the worst of intellectual sins. Yet the decision to draw proposals out of a wide variety of theoretical positions—structuralism, phenomenology, functionalism, organization theory, etc.—inevitably has given the work a sense of inconsistent backgrounds, a gnawing uncer-tainty as to what the program, if rigorously pursued, would add up to, if anything, in intellectual terms. The inconsistency of backgrounds is masked by Katz's rhetorical transformation of proposals into categories. But this also masks the fact that the proposals as a whole contain a social theory, a theory which is never exposed and therefore cannot be critiqued. I suppose we could call it a BBC view of the world, a form of democratic meliorism. But the insinuation rather than the statement of this theory makes an important point: any adequate theory of communication or any set of proposals must derive from an underlying theory of society.

There are only two directions to go in this matter. One can develop a theory of communication and a program of research from a theory of society or one can develop a theory of communications that is explicitly a theory of society. You can start from Marx or Kenneth Burke. But the point is that powerful and fundamental work in this field, as in the other social sciences, will only proceed under the reflexive guidance and criticism of such theory. Without such a theory the proposals in the Katz volume will fragment into so many atomized investigations which never produce an informing vision of the relation of broadcasting to society, to social stratification and group psychology, to, most importantly, the growth of a human culture. And that consequence is itself a theoretically guided political intervention.

Lastly, the proposals as put forward will fail to capture in research the major currents of contemporary life and the involvement of broadcasting in them. In failing to do this they will also fail to meet the minimal demand on scholarship: that it attach the life of the citizen and scholar to the fundamental currents of social change of which broadcasting is such an important part. I do not think this set of proposals, taken as a whole, as an imaginative program, will attach history to biography or produce an informing and reliable knowledge of mass communication.

20

Get Out of the Car: A Case Study on the Organization of Policy Research[1]

Elihu Katz
1979

In 1970, UNESCO joined with the Centre for Mass Communication Research at the University of Leicester in sponsoring a seminar on broadcaster-researcher relationships (Halloran and Gurvitch, 1971). The meeting left no doubt about the suspiciousness, even hostility, with which British broadcasters regard social research, even if one could also observe a degree of mutual recognition—both personal and professional—which is quite uncharacteristic, I thought, of relations in the United States between top network executives and communications researchers. This was the occasion on which Charles Curran, then director general of the BBC, coined the well-remembered metaphor that the use of funds from the license fee (the levy on radio and television sets which supports British Broadcasting) for academic research was tantamount to picking peoples' pockets to peer into their heads.

Five years later, the BBC—still under Charles Curran—asked me to commute to London over an extended period in order to prepare an "agenda for new projects of social research in the field of broadcasting which would (1) take account of past and ongoing work in Britain and elsewhere, and (2) have policy/editorial implications for the BBC." Sir Charles presided at the public lecture I gave upon submission of my report (Katz, 1977). The lecture was entitled "Looking for Trouble." Title notwithstanding, there followed an announcement of the BBC's resolve to explore ways of establishing a Trust (foundation) for the purpose of pursuing the lines of enquiry outlined in the Report.

In what follows, I want to reflect on how—some would prefer whether—this change of heart came over the BBC. I want to repeat what I have said elsewhere about some of the commonalities that I think I discerned in interviewing broadcast policy-makers about their concerns and communications researchers about their projects. I will outline briefly some of the sorts of proposals I put forward and some of the organizational problems implicit in their implementation. I will speak about reactions to the Report, and to the BBC's resolve, as they emerged from various quarters, and will dwell on what has been accomplished so far in the attempt to institutionalize the BBC's decision. I will conclude by reviewing certain problems of the organization of policy research which will emerge, explicitly, as we proceed.

Why the BBC Asked

The Leicester meeting was only another bit of evidence of the strained relations between British broadcasters and researchers. Thus, Tom Burns' new book on the BBC is based on field work done in 1963 with the consent of the BBC which then refused publication (Burns, 1977). Ten years later, in an act of contrition, the BBC invited Burns back to look again and to publish without interference. The industry outcry over Halloran's study of media coverage of the anti-Vietnam demonstration in Grosvenor Square is another example (Halloran, Elliot and Murdock, 1970). A more recent example is the impassioned reaction of broadcasters and even legal action against the Glasgow University Media Group (1976) over publication of their book, *Bad News*, a study of the treatment of industrial relations on British television. I am not here arguing the merits of these particular studies—or indicating where I take issue with them. My object, rather, is to point, first of all, to the critical character of much of British research on broadcasting; secondly to the degree of attention paid by broadcasters to academic research; and thirdly, to what most observers would agree to be a pattern of defensive overreaction, particularly on the part of the BBC. The British take broadcasting seriously, and react to criticism even more negatively than Lazarsfeld (1948) noted to be the case in American media.[2]

Why, then, did the BBC ask me to prepare an agenda for the further development of social research on broadcasting? (Some people would prefer to ask why the BBC asked *me*)[3] before agreeing to the project, and during the rounds I made of both broadcasters and researchers, a number of reasons emerged. I do not wish to give the impression that the eighty or more BBC executives with whom I spoke expressed a desperate need for social research, but what I think I heard is as follows:

1. For the first time, the Chairman of the BBC was (still is) an academic. A distinguished scientist, Sir Michael Swann noted with surprise how little use the BBC had for, and made of, academic research. His support was central to my undertaking. Nevertheless. I might not have been asked anyway if it were not for the coincidence that senior staff members thought I might actually be able to understand them because of the time, however brief, I had spent as a television executive.

2. The Annan Committee—the latest in a series of national commissions on the future of broadcasting—was due to report in 1977. The BBC had reason to expect that it might be criticized in the Report (Committee, 1977) for negligence in its support of social research, apart from the notable work of its own Audience Research Department. While my project could not possibly affect either the BBC's submissions to Annan, or the Annan Report itself, there were brownie points to be gained in the announcement of the BBC's initiative and possible preemptive value in having a program of action ready in anticipation of Annan. As it turns out, the Annan recommendations on research are rather weak, and, ironically, in public discussion, Lord Annan has joined forces with those who see most British communications research as a destructive force.[4]

3. Broadcasting in Britain often finds itself under heavy criticism. I am not now referring to the criticism of researchers, but to that of Parliament or public broadcasters for deprivation, discrimination, disloyalty, and other sins. These are familiar cries, of course, but they resound more loudly, perhaps, with the decline in established authority including the traditional authority of broadcasting itself and the rise of new groups which demand recognition. Thus, broadcasting must take account of the revival of regionalism; of the revolt of the demographic groups—age, sex and class; and of calls for decentralization in public life. There is need for independent examination of allegations of bias, for example. Broadcasters sense an increasing dependence on academic research in these respects, and are trying to overcome their suspicion of the researchers.

4. There is a further irony in the decline not only of the traditional authority of broadcasting but of the very norms to which such authority can appeal, when it has to appeal. I am thinking specifically about the concepts of objectivity. If social science is gradually convincing the world that reality is a social construction, on what base can journalism, including broadcast journalism, rest its theory of itself as mirror of reality? Ultimately the professionalization of journalism depends on grounding in the methods and philosophy of social science, and there is some awareness of this dependence among sensitive broadcasters, in their desire to cope with challenges to receive professional practice.[5]

5. Much more pervasive, however, is the concern over whether British broadcasting is fulfilling its mission in the service of the commonwealth. Although I have been criticized—as will be manifest—for naively assuming that a professional group can be seriously dedicated to the public interest, I insist that I repeatedly heard this expression of concern, even anxiety, over whether the BBC was living up to its mission. Is television news understandable? Is there social danger in the show of violence? Do current affairs programs make political participation more efficacious? Has the displacement of print negatively affected the rational processing of information? These academic-sounding questions were not only put to me explicitly by members of the BBC but were being debated publicly by broadcasters in professional forums and even in the daily press. It was these sorts of expressions of concern which strengthened me in the conviction that researchers and (public) broadcasters are not very far apart. Here again, I think, one can discern something of the seriousness with which British broadcasters treat relevant academic research, even when they scoff.

6. I do not wish in all this high-sounding talk to underestimate the influence of competition on the curious emergence of BBC interest in broadcasting research. The BBC and IBA have become increasingly competitive, and despite all of the legal and moral restraints on this competition, there is a constant striving to beat the other side. At its best, this is competition for excellence—at a level to which popular culture has only rarely been treated. At its worst, or in-between, it is just plain old competition for attention (and associated perquisites of power and glory and cash), using all the tools that both sides can command, including research.

What I Proposed

I am convinced not only that there is interest in the BBC in research for the reasons mentioned, but that research has something to say to these policy/editorial concerns. Unfortunately, I cannot make room here to talk about new developments in communications research—particularly in the conceptualization of effect—which make such an alliance seem promising. Let me say only that the thrust of research, as I see it, is moving toward a definition of the role of the media in the construction of reality; this is a classic concern, of course, but has only recently been given operational form. It is very far from the definition of effect as change of attitude, opinion or action.

In response, I proposed an agenda of studies, which broadcasters and researchers would find mutually interesting. I emphasized that this was a personal selection, and given the audience for my Report, attempted to group the studies together under headings that the broadcasters, rather than the academics, would find congenial. Thus, the studies are grouped under the headings of programming fantasy (entertainment); programming reality (relating to news and current affairs) and programming identity. There are three more general sections which deal with overall problems of media attributes, audience dynamics and creative organizations. I shall not elaborate on these either.

What I would like to emphasize, rather, is my suggestion that the studies proposed fall roughly into three different types, each of which implies a rather different kind of relationship between broadcasters and researchers.

One kind of study—the most familiar—I call evaluation. It answers the question "How are we doing?" In the present context, it would ask, for example, what people remember and understand of this evening's news, whether they see connections among the items, whether they put what they see and hear to use of any sort—in conversations with family and friends, for example. It implies a certain closeness of relations between researchers and broadcasters in the traditional manner of survey research, and in the sense that competition may require a certain husbanding of information, for a time (though not forever). In many cases, such evaluation research will lead to experimental intervention in production such as trying a different format for a news program to see whether recall and understanding can be improved for a particular group.

A second kind of study I call critical. It answers the question, "What are we doing?" Ideally, it requires distance between broadcaster and researcher in the sense that the researcher must be free to define the latent messages and latent functions that broadcasting may have. This is the place for investigation of the allegation that British television presents labor as action—in the process of agitation and troublemaking—and management as surrounded by the furniture of authority and the halo of statistics. It is the rubric which invites inquiry into the hypothesis that the message of the media is that the world is a dangerous place, or alternatively, that the media are spokesman of the status quo, assuring one and all that the world, or at least our side of it, is in good hands. It would address the allegation that the broadcasting of terror supports terror. Stuart Hall of Birmingham University has proposed an empirical study of some of the more famous of these latent messages which have been accumulating since the days of the Frankfurt School (Adorno and Horkheimer, 1973), including his own hypothesis about the latent effect of the television rule that every issue has two sides. This is also the place where the image of woman or of biased treatment of religious, racial, or political groups, would be addressed. We are very short of innovative methods on this front, however, to marry semiology to content analysis and content analysis to viewers' perceptions.

The third type of study is called diagnostic. It answers the question, "What should we be doing?" It implies a constant scanning of the needs of society and a response to the question of whether broadcasting is (or should be) addressing itself to the needs so discovered. Understanding why people like to see violent stories would be an example. The BBC literacy program is another. No attention has been paid by broadcasting to the presence of a distinct group of illiterates in the midst of British society, but having identified such a group, an effort has now been mounted by the BBC's Further Education Department—aided by a grant from the Ford Foundation—to marry volunteer tutors with volunteer tutees by means of a sort of dating service supported by radio programs (for tutors) television programs (for tutees) and textbooks. The rise of regionalism—the desire for regional identity and accent—and what to do about it is yet another example of a newly identified need.

The solution to problems of this kind lie not only in identifying problems and making decisions, but often in making programs about them. Collaboration of the Sesame Street sort (Palmer, 1973), now known as formative research, implies relationships between producers and researchers. Moreover, the final product, typically, is not a report but a program.

Reactions I: The BBC and Broadcasting Industry

Taking my agenda as the programmatic basis for a new Trust (foundation) is the BBC's translation, not mine. I was uncertain—more at first than now—that this was the right answer, i.e., whether the different kinds of work I proposed should have a single patron rather than being decentralized functionally, in the Audience Research Department, in University research centers and in new organizational forms like the Workshop which produced Sesame Street. It may well be, however, that the BBC's idea of a Trust may have some special wisdom. It is an attempt to create a body that will both be close enough to the policy process, but not identical with the policy-makers; one that will be committed to publication, though not always immediately. It is almost as if the BBC had insight into Coleman's (1972) Dilemma.

Discussion of the Report within the BBC was positive, more positive than might have been expected. There were reservations and objections, some acrimonious, and it is interesting to remark that divisions of the BBC which have lesser power—Radio 4, BBC2, Further Education and the like—expressed more interest than the powerful directors of BBC. It is also likely that the higher echelons of the Corporation would be more interested than the rank and file producer who has more anxiety about being studied.

While the official BBC response was very supportive, certain problems began to loom as soon as the statement was published. On the positive side, management and Board of Governors had taken affirmative action, and a very senior staff member was put in charge of the project. On the other hand, the first stories that were given to the press associated the new enterprise with the effects of violence and allied public concerns in a way which satisfied the journalists and moralists but misrepresented the place of such matters in the Report. The official pronouncement also made clear that the BBC wished to ally itself with others in establishing the new organization. By this the BBC was saying that it would contribute only part of the necessary funds, perhaps only a small part, thus making the establishment of the project contingent on the response of others.

Which others? At first there was hope that the IBA would join as a partner. But that does not seem to be happening. Competition is one explanation. The fear of junior-partnership may be lurking here, as a result of the BBC's seeming unwillingness to share its ideas at an earlier stage. There may also be a lesser willingness for research by the very prosperous production companies which are federated and controlled by the IBA; the IBA depends on the companies almost as much as it depends on them and, if I am correct, the companies are less intellectually curious and less concerned with public service than is the BBC. There is likelihood of ad hoc collaboration on particular projects however.

Thought has been given to joining with the public broadcasting organizations of similar structure in other European countries. Indeed, the research situation in a number of countries is quite similar: the broadcasting organization(s) typically has a research division of its own—sometimes two—to conduct ratings and to do other kinds of research. In addition, there is usually some sort of Social Science Research Council which awards ad hoc grants for research on broadcasting to academic institutions which, however, have no continuing relationship—and hardly even dialogue—with the broadcasters. Thus, structurally, the kind of linking function conceived for the Trust might be usefully extended across the borders. Substantively, too, the problems are similar enough to warrant comparative study—or, sometimes, even the delegation of a problem to study in one country for generalization to others. But this kind of internationalism may yet be somewhat cumbersome and premature.

Foundations in Britain and elsewhere are likely partners and indeed a number have expressed interest in joining forces or offering support. This is an important development but requires caution if researchers are not to be alienated, as will be noted below.

Whether the trust will actually happen however, is still uncertain: the next few months will tell whether the right combination of partners and a sufficient amount of cash have been assembled. If it does happen, it will probably take the following form: It will almost certainly start small, and may want to stay small. It will see itself in two roles, as broker or matchmaker, and as chaperone. As a broker, it will seek to link broadcasters' policy problems with those of interested academic researchers and vice versa. In other words, it will attempt to search out and address problems of policy which will interest serious researchers by encouraging both sides—researchers and broadcasters—to make their concerns explicit to each other. Where possible, it will support such work directly; where not, it will seek outside funding for such projects. At the same time, it will act as a kind of chaperone, making certain that the proper distance is kept between the parties to the affair, sometimes insisting on minimal contact to preclude contamination, sometimes encouraging closeness. It will, in all instance, insist on communication between the partners at key points in the joint enterprise.

Some things have already begun. Four preliminary projects have been commissioned by the BBC itself even before the Trust is officially structured and inaugurated. Two of these—one on understanding the news, another of a more formative kind requiring close interaction between producers and researchers—are being directed by visiting scholars. A third project, based at Leeds, has to do with audience dynamics and a fourth project is being conducted by BBC Audience Research. Effort has been made to enlist appropriate counterparts among the broadcasters for each project.

Another possible outcome of the BBC's response so far is the prospective establishment of a second permanent University center of communication research. To date, Leicester is the only major University with an endowed center not exclusively dependent on project financing. To the credit of its director, it must be said that the call from Leicester for additional centers at other Universities has been long, loud, and clear. Now, as a result of the flurry of new interest in research on broadcasting, it appears that such a development is possible, and that the BBC is lending full (moral) support.

There has been surprising attentiveness to all of this in broadcasting and the press in Britain and elsewhere. Partly, of course, this is due to the way in which the BBC finds itself in the role of opinion-leader. More interesting, however, is the apparent similarity of problems in other countries—the sort enumerated at the outset—which makes the Report relevant. Thus, following publication of the Report, and announcement of the BBC response, other broadcasting organizations began to take an interest. The Report has been translated into several languages and discussed in broadcasting organizations, and some of the academic centers, of almost every European country. So have some of the criticisms which follow.

Reactions II: The Academics

While public broadcasters have reacted vigorously—many with genuine interest, others with none at all—the academics have, on the whole, been much more wary. Appreciation, criticism, and much skepticism, were expressed at the symposium held last summer at the Annenberg School at USC (Filep, 1977), and more recently, in the special section of the Spring issue of the Journal of Communication (1978) which is devoted to the Report. I would like to state some of these criticisms and reply to them; curiously, all start with the assumption that the Report is actually in danger of being implemented! They tend to confuse the Report with its translation as a Trust, but no matter.

The arguments are intertwined and therefore worth considering together. They speak, I hope, to some of the central issues of the organization of policy research.

One major argument holds that policy research and critical research are incompatible. Academics should stay away from establishments, goes the familiar part of this; their job is to look in from outside. One can have no quarrel with this position, of course, except to argue that policy research is not the equivalent of Lazarsfeld's (1941) administrative research. Indeed, I would argue that critical research, no less than administrative research, *is* policy research—applied research if you will—and that the issue, rather, is Who is the client? The classical argument for critical research is, as I read it, an argument for treating society as the client. The Frankfurt School was trying to tell society that it was being victimized by the mass media which had become agents of pacification and for the selling of the status quo by a coalition of political and economic interests. They perceived a connection between mass culture and fascism. From then until now, critical research on mass media and popular culture has been sounding this warning, along with a note of despair that there is almost nothing that can be done. This, I suggest, is a kind of policy research aimed at vaguely defined elites—until the student movements of the late '60s (and, lately, certain neo-Marxists) took note. The assumption that such critical research would go unheeded if addressed to the broadcasters has not really been tested. In a sophisticated dialectical argument, Gouldner (1976) discusses the conditions under which media managers will act contrary to their class interests in supplying information to the public. This is not because they are nice guys. Criticism of political or religious or industrial issues has always attracted (and worried) media managers.

This, then, relates to a second issue: whether one conduct of policy research for an establishment in effect dictates the agenda—or the frame of reference—within which research will be done. My critics suggest that the BBC imposed its agenda on me, especially since I took the trouble to inventory their problems. It is said that I was not free to propose research on the benefits that might accrue from the dismemberment of the BBC, for example, or from reduction of the number of hours of television. It is said that I was blinded to the coming integration of print and broadcast technology because I had to take the BBC not only as a given, institutionally speaking, but as desirable. I deny this: I think I was free to speculate as I wished. Coleman (1972) might argue that the policymaker's point of view is a legitimate one, and that my denial is out of order anyway. But it seems to me that as soon as one admits other interested parties—even if they do not have formal decision making power—their presence in the policy arena must be noted by academics who must consider the possibility of serving these other interests. At the same time, it is true that I elected, of my own free choice, to assume that broadcasting technology as presently deployed in Britain would persist for some time, and would constitute the basis of my proposals for research. I speculated, however, on such things as the implications for culture and broadcasting of the displacement of words by pictures, or on the call for a deepening of regional identity. Whether the proposed Trust can or should include research commissioned from the point of view of competing interests, is a question that needs to be debated.

I would be more apologetic about this, perhaps, if I did not believe, as I do, that a case can be made that the professions—among which I shall include public broadcasting, for the moment—are committed to the public service. Blau and Scott (1962) define professions in this way—cui bono? they ask—and the good of the client is the professional's answer. My strongest critics argue, however, that I am not only wrong about (public) broadcasting—Tom Burns (1978) says as much in his book— but about the professions in general: they are organizations for self-defense, guilds for mutual protection and mystification, and far from having their clients' interest uppermost are in fact actively undermining their clients' best interests. This is the kind of neo-Marxism with which Milton Friedman would probably agree.

Even if professional organizations have deviated in this way, it seems to me of consequence, sociologically, to differentiate between organizations and individuals who pronounce such goals and those who don't. The question then becomes under what conditions can one appeal to the legitimacy of such norms. Indeed, the self same question applies to scientists, including social scientists: why is *their* professionalism any more sacred? And if it should prove to be more in conformity to the common weal, one would like to know as a researcher why this is so. If one accepts the argument that the professions are conspiracies to do the public in, obviously policy research in behalf of the public must urgently be solicited, but itself suspect. If there is some overlap of values, however, among public, professionals, and researchers—perhaps the contradiction is more tolerable, though one should not ignore it even then.

The academic criticism of my Report tends to see the BBC acting not as broker and chaperone, but as gatekeeper allowing "safe" projects to get through, diverting money from sources of support that might otherwise go directly to academics, and exerting a nefarious influence on existing foundations as to who and what they should be supporting in broadcasting research. Such a danger exists perhaps: the BBC Trust may yet corner the market, but it is unlikely. My critics feel that I am compromising them, that broadcasters will hold researchers' hands not in cooperation but in restraint, that I have forgotten the Charles Curran of 1970.

Ironically, my problem in writing the Report was almost opposite. I saw critical research as reasonably assured, though underfinanced. I did not give much thought to its place within a Trust, since I did not myself conceive the idea of a monolithic organization dominated by broadcasters. But even if such an organization evolves, it will not—as I see it—be dominated by broadcasters, and will—perhaps despite itself—be supportive of critical research.

My concern was, and is, over the likely fate of what I call diagnostic research, particularly the special case of formative research, in which producers in the studio—unlike some of their bosses—have reason to be squeamish about collaboration of this kind. Sesame Street can be held up as an example. Yet it is this kind of (1) identification of need, and (2) creative solution that I would not like to see forgotten. Everybody except me seems to think that the problem is how to prevent broadcasters from sitting too close to researchers; and I think that the problem is how to get them to sit closer.

Get Out of the Car

To return to a point made earlier, the critics of the report tend to assume, prematurely, that the Report is so much in danger of immediate and total implementation that its possible damage must be immediately proclaimed and thwarted. As Halloran say, alarmedly, "the BBC is already writing and talking in terms of the Katz concepts."[7]

Nobody except me and some friends (in academia and the BBC) is concerned that perhaps none of this will ever happen, and thus that there will be nothing real for anybody to worry about. It reminds me of the story of the man who decided one day that he simply had to arrange a reunion between his family and out-of-town relatives. Contemplating the impending journey, he notified his young son that there was a good chance that the whole family would be going to visit the relatives on

Sunday provided a rental car were available, provided the relatives were prepared to receive them, etc. Reporting the picture in his head, the father said to Jack, "I will drive, mother will sit alongside me, and you and Jill will sit in the back." Jack began to protest. "I want to sit in the front." This so enraged the father that he turned to the boy and commanded, "Jack, get out of the car!"

The moral of the story is that policy research is as much of a problem for the researchers as for the policymaker, even when the researcher is extremely anxious to influence the decision-making process. Some researchers want not only to sit next to the driver; they want to drive themselves, and believe that the "accountability" which is part of the creed of public broadcasters in Britain should find expression in direct underwriting of University research on a sustaining—not a project— basis. Others, who find some use in my proposals and in the BBC's response, think it might be worth seeing whether the car will materialize at all, whether it will move, and whether there is room for some good people inside. Seating arrangements still remain to be worked out.

Notes

1. Paper delivered at the 33rd Annual Conference of the American Association for Public Opinion Research: Roanoke, Virginia, June 1–4, 1978.
2. "If there is any one institutional disease to which the media of mass communication seem particularly subject, it is a nervous reaction to criticism. As a student of mass media I have been continually struck and occasionally puzzled by this reaction, for it is the media themselves which so vigorously defend principles guaranteeing the right to criticize" (Lazarsfeld, 1948, p. 123).
3. At least one answer is that I was an outsider.
4. He has called British researchers "guerrillas."
5. For an interesting elaboration of this problem, see Janowitz (1977).
6. For further discussion of this point, from which I have profited, see Blumler (1977).
7. In the *Journal of Communications* (1978) symposium.

References

Adorno, Theodor, and Max Horkheimer, 1973, "The Culture Industry: Enlightment as Mass Deception," in: Adorno and Horkheimer, *Dialectic of Enlightenment*, London: Allen Lane.

Blau, Peter M., and Richard Scott (1962), *Formal Organizations*, San Francisco: California.

Blumler, Jay G., 1977, "The Social Purposes of Mass Communications Research: A Transatlantic Perspective," Founders' Lecture read at the Annual Conference of the Association for Education in Journalism, Madison, Wisconsin.

Burns, Tom, 1977, The BBC: *Public Institution and Private World*, London: Macmillan.

Coleman, James S., 1972, *Policy Research in the Social Sciences*, Morristown, N.J.: General Learning Press.

Committee on the Future of Broadcasting (Chairman: Lord Annan), 1977, London: Her Majesty's Stationery Office.

Filep, Robert, ed., 1977, *Social Research & Broadcasting: Proceedings of a Symposium*, Los Angeles, California: The Annenberg School of Communications at the University of Southern California.

Glasgow University Media Group, 1976, *Bad News*, London: Routledge.

Gouldner, Alvin W., *Dialectics of Ideology and Technology*, London: Macmillan, 1976.

Halloran, James D., Philip Elliot, and Graham Murdock, *Demonstrations and Communication*, Harmondsworth: Penguin, 1977.

Halloran, James D., and Michael Gurvitch, eds., *Broadcaster-Research Cooperation in Mass Communication Research*, University of Leicester, 1971.

Janowitz, Morris, 1977, "The Journalistic Profession and the Mass Media," in: J. Ben-David and T. Clark, eds., *Culture and Its Creators*, Chicago: University of Chicago Press.

Journal of Communication (1978 Spring), Symposium on the Katz Report.

Katz, Elihu, 1977a, Social Research on Broadcasting: *Proposals for Further Development*, London: BBC.

Katz, Elihu, 1977, "Looking for Trouble: Social Research on Broadcasting," London: BBC Lunchtime Lectures, 11th Series, February 25, 1977.

Lazarsfeld, Paul F., 1941, "Administrative and Critical Communications Research," *Studies in Philosophy and Social Sciences*, Vol. 9.

Lazarsfeld, Paul F., 1948, "The Role of Criticism in the Management of Mass Media," *Journalism Quarterly*, Vol. 25.

Palmer, Edward L., 1973, "Formative Research in the Production of Television for Children," in: Gerbner, Gross and Melody, eds., *Communications Technology and Cultural Policy*, New York: Wiley.

21

Putting the First Amendment in Its Place: Enhancing American Democracy through the Press

Robert M. Entman
1993

Achieving a "system of free expression," as that term is conventionally understood, will not produce healthy democracy. In fact, we have already very nearly attained such a system, insofar as one can be molded and promoted under the regime of the First Amendment. The constraints on the news media that are due to legal action or government regulation are now generally minor. Yet this forbearance has not yielded news media that consistently meet the standards that Professor Sunstein suggests: a sufficient amount of attention to public issues and the expression of diverse views on these issues.[1] If we continue to constrain our discussion within traditional First Amendment parameters, it is difficult to imagine communications law and policy doing much to improve matters.

By the standards of the Hutchins Commission Report,[2] democracy and the press have made little progress since 1947. The Hutchins Commission's description of the press reads much as it would if written today:

The news is twisted by the emphasis on firstness, on the novel and sensational; by the personal interests of owners; and by pressure groups. Too much of the regular output of the press consists of a miscellaneous succession of stories and images which have no relation to the typical lives of real people anywhere. Too often the result is meaninglessness, flatness, distortion, and the perpetuation of misunderstanding among widely scattered groups whose only contact is through these media.[3]

Exactly how accurate this indictment is today can be debated, but the literature supporting similar charges against the current media is voluminous.[4] Many observers consider today's highly competitive media scene a marked improvement over the past, and we have recently seen a significant augmentation in television news outlets with the introduction of CNN and C-SPAN. But research suggests these news sources have had little impact on the democratic process because relatively few Americans consistently watch such programs.[5] Even assuming the quality of the press has improved, it continues to fall short in terms of at least two important measures of the impact that journalism could have on democracy.[6] First, controlling for the increase in education, the American public appears *less* informed now than in the late 1940s.[7] That is, college graduates today are less politically aware than college graduates in the late 1940s. Second, Americans now vote less religiously than they used to. Despite some scholarship to the contrary,[8] these two indices suggest that the American media are not enhancing the democratic process as the Hutchins Commission hoped they would.[9]

In addition, leaving aside the quality of public input, and assessing instead the quality of government's policy outputs, we might also find the government's responses and responsiveness to major problems insufficient.[10] The reasons for these conditions are complex and certainly cannot be traced to the media alone. Although I focus my attention on the press in this article, I do not fail to appreciate that other elements of society, including the public education system, the political party system, campaign financing, and ideological or cultural biases, also contribute to the imperfections of American democracy.

Certainly a case can be made that American democracy is healthy, with the American press a vigorous partner in the process. Is the glass half empty or half full? Of course it is both. By the criteria I weigh most heavily, however, especially the level of the public's knowledgeable voting participation and the government's accountability, honesty, and responsiveness on policy issues vital to the quality and fairness of life in the United States, I judge the emptiness most salient, and that judgment is the basis of my analysis.

I will argue two basic propositions related to Professor Sunstein's four "half-truths":

1. Despite the First Amendment, the government heavily influences or, in many cases, determines the information that most Americans receive via the news media. The First Amendment does not prevent government from shaping most important dimensions of the news media's messages. This relationship is rooted in the seemingly voluntary reliance of news

organizations on public officials and agencies for most of the assumptions and information that frame and suffuse the news.[11] Although government *policy and law* have relatively little direct impact on the information that appears or does not appear in the news, government *officials* have very much to do with media content.

In Professor Sunstein's terms, the government actively discriminates in favor of some viewpoints, greatly controlling which are publicly available. What I add to Professor Sunstein's discussion of his first "half-truth"[12] is that this occurs largely outside of any legal or regulatory compulsion as these are generally understood. My point also amplifies Professor Sunstein's third half-truth, that penalizing and subsidizing speech may be difficult to distinguish in practice.[13]

2. In recent years, the government's use of the First Amendment in policy decisions toward the media has tended to neglect the goals cited by the Hutchins Commission and others, like Professor Sunstein. Instead, the First Amendment ironically has had a chilling effect on public discourse about the legitimate tools and ultimate ends of public policies toward the communications media. Policy-makers and judges should ask themselves how best to achieve the Hutchins Commission's, or some other, democratic vision, rather than uphold an interpretation of the First Amendment that ignores the government's informal influence over media content. These points elaborate on all four of Professor Sunstein's half-truths, especially the problematic assumption that content-based regulation is the gravest threat to media autonomy,[14] and that content neutrality is preferable or even attainable.[15]

Analyzing the "free and responsible press" strictly in First Amendment terms, while natural enough for a law school forum, misses most of the forces that affect how well the press serves democracy in the United States. Taking account of larger social forces and contexts would help connect First Amendment theory more closely with the real-world production, distribution, and consumption of news, and thus with the effects that the press has on democracy. Professor Sunstein writes that we need a "thorough empirical understanding of the free speech 'status quo,' and here there is a distressingly large gap in the free speech literature."[16] But in fact my disciplines of communication studies, journalism, and political science offer an enormous literature—not couched in terms of evaluating the abstract system of free speech, but empirically exploring and normatively evaluating how the news media actually influence the American democratic process.[17]

I am not saying it would be good to have government restrictions on press expression. Less still am I suggesting that government's lack of formal control over the press is irrelevant to the quality of American democracy. But this laudable constraint on government's legal power over the media has tightened since 1964 and *New York Times Co. v Sullivan*[18] without noticeably enhancing democracy. To me, this indicates that conventional First Amendment law and policy may offer few ways to improve the press enough to revitalize the democratic process.

In this article, I first explore institutionalized viewpoint discrimination by the government. Next, I examine the chilling effect of the First Amendment on policy discourse. I conclude by offering recommendations on how to reduce the government's informal power to shape the news.

Institutionalized Viewpoint Discrimination by the Government

Professor Sunstein describes his first half-truth as the notion that the Constitution prohibits viewpoint discrimination.[19] The law says "government may not distort the deliberative process by erasing one side of a debate."[20] Yet functionally, government does precisely this all of the time. Indeed, large staffs in the White House and throughout the Executive Branch exist solely to dominate public perceptions and debate, and empirical research shows that they often succeed.[21] Moreover, if by "government" Professor Sunstein means the entire governmental apparatus, including the legislative and judicial branches, then most of the time government erases not just one, but most, of the potential sides of any debate. The discourse among the elites who run the three branches of the federal government frames the feasible diagnoses and options that achieve wide distribution in the national media, and in this sense government largely determines the viewpoints that reach public consciousness.[22] If, despite the First Amendment, government can exert such extensive control over the distribution of ideas, the press will have a difficult time disseminating information that helps the public hold that very same government accountable.

This informal regulatory relationship is different from and preferable to formal regulatory prohibitions against publicizing particular ideas. But to ignore the informal regulatory power is to lose touch with the media system as it actually operates. Government constantly engages in viewpoint discrimination, and such discrimination is inherent in the First Amendment regime. That is, the press is free to pass along the propaganda of the current administration in Washington, with no obligation to give equal access to the opposition party, let alone to views beyond the two parties' discursive boundaries. If an opposition party disagrees with the administration but fails to play the media spin game effectively, dissenting views may be hard to find in the news. If the Democratic and Republican parties are in accord, the chance that opposing views will receive enough visibility in the mass media to affect public opinion is even more remote.[23] In most cases, only when elites are engaged in energetic public dispute will the content of the news exhibit viewpoint diversity that the public is likely to notice.[24]

It is true that government spokespersons and politicians may take public stands in response to, or in anticipation of, likely public or media reactions, indicating that government itself is not autonomous; there are reciprocal power flows among media, government elites, and public. But research suggests that the greatest source of power in the equation is that of government, and especially that of the executive branch.[25] For our purposes, the key face is that government greatly influences news and commentary. The notion of a large realm of autonomous media production and distribution of ideas fails to square with empirical research.[26]

When officials comment in harmony on an event or issue, the media tend to mirror the dominant line. For example, research comparing the coverage of two quite parallel civilian airliner tragedies, the Korean Airline Flight 007 attack in 1983 and the Iran Air Flight 655 attack in 1988, illustrates this worst-case scenario for media-assisted accountability.[27] For both events, there was virtually no debate among the government elite, and media coverage was thoroughly government scripted at the most overt and the most subtle (yet powerful) levels.[28]

Thus, for example, the covers of both *Time* and *Newsweek* following the Korean Airline tragedy illustrated a Soviet fighter plane within a few hundred feet of the civilian airliner.[28] In an unconscious but effective way, these illustrations supported the American government's claim that the Soviets deliberately murdered 269 innocent men, women and children, as did the cover headlines: "Murder in the Air" and "Shooting to Kill."[30] Journalistic and Congressional research later revealed that the Reagan administration knowingly misled the public and the press on Soviet intentions and actions; in fact, the Soviets were unaware that the Korean plane was a civilian airliner.[31] The important point for our purposes is that a unanimous government elite was able to control virtually every dimension of the information distributed in the mass media—the choice of nouns, adverbs, and adjectives; the visual images; and the Cold War themes and symbols.

After the Iran Air incident, the unified elite was more or less silent. Unlike its reaction to the Korean Airline affair, the press offered little moral analysis or outrage when American forces shot down a civilian airliner. In that case, the press went along with the administration's and the Pentagon's insistence—unchallenged by congressional elites—on total American innocence. Again, more recent revelations suggest a different story.[32] Nevertheless, journalists at the time accepted the government's version of the events, despite the lessons of Vietnam and, more recently, of the Korean Airline story. These lessons suggest the need for deep skepticism of an administration's claims about a confusing event, the interpretation of which the administration would obviously like to control.

While questions about the official American "line" in both cases could be found in the press, public opinion polls suggest this material went unnoticed by most people.[33] Practically speaking, the government controlled the coverage. Furthermore, the failure of the media to question the administration line in both cases had significant policy consequences.[34]

Even where oppositional claims arise and attain some publicity, they often tend to be de-emphasized as compared to official administration views. Despite the implications of much First Amendment scholarship, good or true ideas have no inherent momentum that makes them more salient and believable to the mass public; nor is there any force in the press or the journalistic process that guarantees or even raises the probability that better ideas will get wider and more prominent distribution than weaker ideas.

Research on the debate over American policy toward Iraq after its invasion of Kuwait reveals that even in a best-case scenario in which government elites engage in strong public argument, the administration enjoys a marked preference in the news coverage.[35] During the period immediately after President Bush announced the doubling of the American troop commitment to the Middle East, the most prominent reports in the *New York Times* and on ABC's *World News Tonight* emphasized substantive support of the Bush administration by nearly a three-to-one ratio.[36] Assuming that early coverage of an event is the most important phase of public exposure because it frames audience reactions to all succeeding information, the widespread support of President Bush's policy in the elite paper of record and on the most heavily watched network was an important achievement for the Bush administration. Had oppositional viewpoints achieved a more balanced distribution during this time, when the change to an offensive posture was just becoming known, it is conceivable that media coverage of the ensuing policy debate in Congress would have been more informative.

Instead, the Bush administration dominated coverage of what was arguably the most intense period of elite dissension regarding the use of American military force since the Vietnam War. When administration spokespersons such as President Bush, Vice President Dan Quayle, or Defense Secretary Richard Cheney made public statements, they tended to receive extensive and prominent attention in the press. When opponents, even well-known persons such as two former chairmen of the Joint Chiefs of Staff, criticized President Bush's policy during Senate hearings, they received only brief attention that slighted their substantive arguments. While editorial pages frequently called for vigorous public debate on the looming Gulf War, actual news treatments seemed to discourage the public from grasping and weighing the pro-war and pro-sanctions sides equally. In the policy debate before the Gulf War, the administration engaged in successful *viewpoint discrimination* if not absolute censorship. During the Gulf War, the administration did engage in censorship,[37] and the First Amendment offered little help. Meanwhile, discourse among government elites, including congressional opponents and the administration, effectively prevented the public from hearing of a third alternative to the administration-framed choice of sanctions versus war. Because no major official from either party advocated the option of initiating negotiations with Saddam Hussein, that alternative was virtually invisible in the mass media and to the public.[38]

How should we judge such performances in terms of democracy? First Amendment scholarship focuses mostly on the production of ideas, in the apparent belief that as long as freedom of production is allowed, the free market will take care of distribution. Yet democratic theory emphasizes the distribution and use of information.[39] The public must enjoy easy access to information to have any hope of understanding its own interests and the way in which the government impinges on them. Too many press observers assume that if the information is published once in a single outlet, then it is genuinely visible to the entire public. In fact, however, one story appearing in a single outlet is unlikely to have any impact on the political process.

A free and responsible press should habitually offer the mass citizenry easy access to information that helps them hold government accountable for its actions. A necessary condition for modern American democracy, given the manner in which the political and policymaking systems now operate, is the wide availability of information that contextualizes and challenges the preferred positions and the existing policies or actions of the incumbent administration. The information must be displayed prominently and repeatedly in the media on which most Americans rely: the network news shows, the daily newspapers, and the weekly news magazines. Possession of such information creates the potential for people to influence government in the three primary ways that now exist: by registering opinions in surveys that may pressure government to shape policy in a certain way; by joining political groups or movements that bring organized pressure to bear; or by making more informed choices at the ballot box.

Operationally, to achieve this goal, the news media would have to offer balanced attention to competing views in all coverage, and would have to self-consciously define their primary role to be educating citizens to participate in policy discourse. The latter would yield an increase in information that is easily accessible, attractive, and well organized for consumption. In this vision, anti-administration information would be as simple to find and digest as pro-administration information, and reforms in law, regulation, and media practice would make balanced coverage their central aim. Given the constraints on media practice documented in the literature, this would, in practical terms, provide ideas endorsed by members of Congress and policy experts equal distribution with the ideas of the administration. Such a goal would not prevent the unity of coverage seen during the airliner tragedies, but it would mean that a debate such as that over the Gulf War would receive more even-handed and civically useful treatment.

To some observers, this goal might fall short; it accepts the basic regime of informal government discrimination. While some would argue the largest problem for democracy is the press's failure to transcend boundaries of conventional discourse among "responsible" elites,[40] it is quixotic as a practical matter to expect a media industry itself dominated by establishment elites to go beyond those borders for news and opinion. Such straying by journalists would not only antagonize the most powerful news sources, but would also likely displease mass audiences who are themselves steeped in conventional wisdom. Realistically, the national media cannot widely disperse those views that transcend the ideas of important leaders in the Washington elite. Only in extraordinary circumstances, such as those presented during the war in Vietnam, is there much broadening of the discourse beyond official boundaries.[41] Even during Vietnam, the media were generally hostile to the anti-war cause.[42]

The Chilling Effect of the First Amendment

Flaws in First Amendment analysis, and the absence of an empirical understanding of the relationships just described, have an important real-world impact on public policy towards the communications media, and thus affect how well the media serve democratic values. With government exerting so much informal power over media content, the key question becomes how law and policy might reduce that informal control, or otherwise enhance media performance. Defining the problem in this way illuminates the precise goal that formal government policy intervention might seek: to diminish media dependence on government elites and the concomitant public dependence on information that is heavily shaped by the very officials whom the public needs to hold accountable.

I suggest that the First Amendment has had a chilling effect on discourse regarding communications policy, preventing analysts from identifying this goal. The diversity, depth, and precision of debate has been reduced by the enormous rhetorical power analysts can exercise by simply invoking the First Amendment.[43] The position that has recently dominated deliberations at the Federal Communications Commission ("FCC"), and indeed most analytical discourse, stresses that the primary meaning of the First Amendment, and the best way to promote its values, is maximizing media owners' rights to expression unimpeded by government. The now-dominant view subsumes other interpretations of First Amendment goals in its determination to shield owners from formal government intrusion. It holds that the government should encourage competitive communication markets, because competition will yield the optimum flow of diverse ideas—or at least it is more likely to do so than any other regulatory scheme.

I believe that when government decisionmakers and judges invoke the First Amendment, they largely avoid the kind of careful analysis of costs and benefits that is practiced in virtually every other policy field in government. Leaving aside some important inconsistencies and exceptions, such as national security and indecency, policy and legal analysis has appeared to assume that any policy that might impinge on the autonomy of news organizations has infinite costs for which no benefits can be great enough. The description applies best to the FCC of the Reagan and Bush administrations, quite well to courts, and less well to Congress; calibrating these judgments is a task for future research. I focus here on the FCC under Presidents Reagan and Bush, the locus of the most important communications-policy decisions in recent years. While President Clinton's appointees to the FCC could apply a different or more diverse interpretation of the First Amendment, the view identified here will remain highly influential. It has many adherents among interest groups, scholars, and experts—and in the judicial branch, where the previous administrations' judicial appointees serve for life. The FCC's recent policy and legal discourse has barely hinted at the complexities highlighted by this Symposium and by the writings of many legal scholars.[44]

I formulated two hypotheses in a small pilot study to check for an empirical basis to my suspicion that the First Amendment has chilled analytical discourse in communications policy. The first hypothesis is that when the FCC, between 1981 and 1992, used the rhetoric of the First Amendment, it failed to refer to the many conflicting interpretations of the First Amendment's meaning and goals that are discernible in legal scholarship. Instead, the FCC used the First Amendment narrowly and simplistically. The second hypothesis is that during this period, the FCC ignored scholarly or scientific evidence about how the media and their audiences actually behave. The mere mention of the First Amendment obviated the need for reference to the empirical world and thereby chilled analysis of communications policy.

To test my hypotheses, I conducted a content analysis of three FCC rulings: the Fairness Doctrine,[45] the deregulation of radio,[46] and the consideration of children's television rules.[47] These are among the most far-reaching and controversial media deregulation policies since 1980, and the FCC should therefore have been on its best analytical behavior in justifying them. These rulings should be a hard test for my claim. I counted and categorized all mentions in these rulings of the First Amendment and of freedom of speech, press, or expression, in an attempt to determine how the FCC has employed these notions. Furthermore, I searched for all references in these FCC rulings to scholarly writings.

I found that when the FCC invoked the First Amendment, it almost exclusively referenced just two goals: (1) creating robust debate in a diverse marketplace of ideas; and (2) protecting the freedom of media owners from governmental intrusion into editorial decisionmaking. Table 21.1 demonstrates the results of this analysis.

The above table reveals that the FCC espoused a relatively consistent but narrow idea of the First Amendment's goals. Assuming these rulings comprise a best-case, or at least a reasonable, test, the FCC had in mind only those two goals whenever it mentioned "free expression" or "the First Amendment." Furthermore, in these three rulings, the FCC

Table 21.1

Invocations of "First Amendment" or "Freedom of Expression, Speech, or Press" in FCC Decisions on the Fairness Doctrine, Deregulating Radio, and Children's Television[48]

Decision	Ideas Referenced		
	Diverse Marketplace	Editorial Autonomy	Indefinite[49]
Fairness	14	34	17
Radio	2	4	1
Children's TV	0	8	1
Total	16	46	19

emphasized the goal of editorial autonomy much more than the goal of achieving a diverse marketplace of ideas. Both of these goals are instrumental; that is, the FCC did not reason in terms of final or end goals, a practice that again distinguishes it from other regulatory agencies. Equally important, the more strongly emphasized aim of editorial autonomy is the most clearly instrumental objective of the FCC's dual goals, and is the most distant from the ultimate values protected by the First Amendment.

The FCC's faith in these two instrumental goals, I believe, blinded it to the need for careful analysis of how to reach final ends such as those suggested by Professor Sunstein and the Hutchins Commission.[50] Nor do I think that Congress or the courts have done much better in recent years, although at this point, I must limit my claim to the FCC. The FCC did not demonstrate in any detail how the instrumental goals serve any final aims. Indeed, the FCC did not mention ultimate objectives at all.

This brings me to my second hypothesis. Among the footnotes to the rulings, numbering 328 altogether, just two offer (extremely sketchy) references to scholarship discussing the manner in which media organizations and audiences actually behave in idea production or consumption.[51] To talk about instrumental or ultimate goals in an empirical rather than speculative way would require reliance on the scholarly literature. Instead, the FCC virtually ignore—at least in the published justifications for its decisions—research evidence about behavior and how it might change with a policy alteration.

In failing to look at empirical evidence, the FCC distinguishes itself from other regulatory agencies that follow the Administrative Procedures Act.[52] Under the Administrative Procedures Act, other regulatory agencies must weigh their final goals, or at least are supposed to do so. For example, the EPA cannot implement a pollution regulation without empirically demonstrating a reasonable likelihood that the policy will have a net positive effect on the environment.[53] By contrast, citing to the First Amendment allows the FCC to get away with decisions that might otherwise be labelled arbitrary and capricious.

The problem gets worse: this situation appears to be self-reinforcing. As suggested earlier, in the real commercial market, the media do not create an information supply that resembles the metaphorical vision of a buzzing marketplace of ideas. In its absence, consumers may not be educated to demand a diversity of information that is independent or critical of government policy—the kind of information supply envisioned in the marketplace-of-ideas metaphor and needed to fulfill democratic ideals.

Economists would call this an externality problem. Externalities are the unintended effects of market exchanges. For my purposes here, the most important externality—that is, the most important effect of market transactions in mass communications that are not part of the intended bargain—is the impact of the commercial market on civic interest and knowledge. The commercial market underproduces news that enhances citizens' political interest, knowledge, and sophistication, in large part because the commercial pressure on suppliers is to attract the largest audience possible. The average audience member does not seek complex, sophisticated information, and the mass media must target that average member. Without a more socially useful idea supply in the mass media, consumers remain too uninformed to demand such a supply. The externality reinforces itself.

This again marks communications policy as a unique field. In other areas, such as the environment or consumer safety, the externalities are not self-reinforcing; on the contrary, they tend to call forth strong and sometimes overzealous political demands for correction. In communications, however, the externality has the effect of suppressing both economic demand within the market and political demand outside the market for solutions. Because of this unique quality alone, communications policy-makers ought to be hyperconscious of the connection between and among policy instruments and final goals. Because of the chilling effect of the First Amendment, I believe policy-makers at the FCC have neglected to make these connections. Indeed, the FCC seemed unaware that when it intervened to reinforce the power of the commercial market by deregulating broadcasters, it may have actually reinforced the externality just described. In this sense, the FCC may have acted unwittingly to reduce demand for enhanced civic content in the media.

As a specific example, the failure of the three major broadcast networks to devote much coverage to the presidential nominating conventions in 1992 reflects the deregulatory mood at the FCC. The FCC, having ceased to enforce the public-trustee concept of licensing, could not conceivably threaten license renewal for neglecting to cover the conventions gavel-to-gavel. Yet research has shown that the conventions, when covered heavily, offer important learning opportunities for a public not terribly interested in or informed about politics.[54] Absent that opportunity, their knowledge may deteriorate further. Perhaps more important, the networks' decision to broadcast sitcoms and detective shows rather than political conventions conveys a deeply cynical message about the political process and its relevance to individual citizens' lives. Hence the self-reinforcing phenomenon: the decrease in the public's political interest and knowledge stemming from the failure to cover political conventions might further reduce audience demand and render it even less profitable for the networks to cover the conventions and other important political events fully in the future.

Among other worrisome effects, a less politically aware public is less likely to realize how government policy has allowed, and even encouraged, the major broadcast networks to reduce their convention coverage, thus diminishing their political awareness still further.[55] Communications policy may therefore influence the distribution of preferences in the political process, in this case, for communications policy decisions themselves. Such indirect government effects on the content of the public's demands upon the government appear no more compatible with First Amendment ideals than direct intervention to promote or restrict ideas. These effects lend further support to Professor Sunstein's half-truth analysis of the defects in assuming that government cannot and does not engage in viewpoint discrimination.[56]

The identification of the possibility that communications policy indirectly and inadvertently shapes the distribution of ideas suggests questions about the FCC's second instrumental goal, maximizing the freedom of media owners from government regulation. The problem is that in practice, even when ostensibly acting to free expression from constraints, as it did in *Fairness Doctrine, Deregulating Radio,* and *Children's Television,* government may actually be turning regulatory power over to the commercial market. As another of Professor Sunstein's half-truths suggests,[57] this means that deregulation might well be interventionist in its own way: the policy of deregulation, by exposing media owners to the full force of market competition and consumer demand, greatly affects the ideas that broadcasters can practically choose to produce and distribute if they want to stay in business. The idea of a competitive market is precisely premised on the notion that consumer demand constrains the options of suppliers. In other words, it may be that by deregulating the media, the FCC does not prevent intrusion into the autonomy of the media, but instead merely changes the mix of intruding forces.

Most analysts find it acceptable for the public to "vote" through the economic market, and thus to limit and guide media expression.[58] If the market is efficient, this means minority tastes will be served by marginal outlets. Unpopular ideas will be functionally invisible to most of the public, which will be saturated by the conventional and the popular. This situation is the predictable result of market constraints on the expression of mass communication outlets. In this light, by deregulating broadcasting and substituting market pressures, government may not be acting in a genuinely content-neutral way.[59] Yet most analysts now hold that it is impermissible for the public to vote through representative government institutions to affect media expression and ameliorate these conditions.[60] Is this because government has more resources than the market to pressure and put a medium out of business or to induce a change in management and its practices? Assuming the current First Amendment regime, the answer is surely no; the market can and does achieve that much more effectively.

Forces arising from the private market can pose as great a threat to free expression as government. If energetic and diverse public debate is the goal, then government regulation might be desirable in this context; intervention might even promote expression by protecting the media from the full censorious powers of the market. On the other hand, we will have to deal with the problem cited by Ithiel Pool: in practice, broadcast regulation in the old days never did enhance public debate very much.[61]

If government really wanted to nurture speakers' ability to express diverse ideas and have them heard (that is, widely distributed), it would have to transcend conventional First Amendment approaches. Forcing speakers to find private investment or charity funds, and advertisers or paying customers to support the production and distribution of their ideas, is not genuinely content-neutral, if indeed such a thing is possible. Such a system restricts expressors' freedom to be heard and raises the costs to the disengaged mass audience of finding more diverse and independent views.

To be sure, the constraining force of the audience, its interests, capabilities, and prejudices, exists under any system of free expression and information distribution. Moreover, the dangers of political pressure from government agents are real. Yet analysts should always weigh the risks of a policy against its likely benefits and, in this case, against the market alternative under which economic pressures are guaranteed to constrain the production and distribution of ideas.

Additionally, this critique of the FCC's conventional First Amendment wisdom leaves aside many other issues. For example, the FCC's version of the First Amendment has neglected the role and professional autonomy of journalists. Journalists have no First Amendment expressive rights within their media organizations, and that may have major impacts on the circulation of ideas. Recent research[62] suggests reasons to fear for reporters' and even publishers' autonomy, with advertising revenues stagnating or shrinking and news organizations being forced to become more responsive to advertiser complaints. Indeed, the implication of the FCC's reasoning, which relied almost exclusively on media owners' motivations and decisions to animate the "marketplace of ideas," is precisely that media owners constantly oversee and interfere with the journalists who actually produce or disseminate ideas. Otherwise, the FCC's reasoning would logically have to focus on other parties'—including journalists'—freedom in addition to that of media owners.

This point brings me back to my basic theme. Despite the complexities in the relationships of government policy to the production and consumption of ideas, the main use of the First Amendment in legal and policy analysis has been as an analytical stopper, a chiller of discourse. If a proposed communications law or policy seems to violate the First Amendment, little additional investigation into its actual impact occurs. We need to root debates over the First Amendment in the way that the media and audiences actually behave, not in an abstracted ideal that neglects what scholars and practitioners of journalism know about the real world. Relatedly, we should strip the First Amendment of its sacred status. We should treat it as a malleable embodiment of ideals for the media's role in democracy rather than as a clear guide to policy that has the single meaning of mandating minimal government intervention in communications markets.

Recommendations

The foregoing analysis does not yield a recommendation for traditional government regulation. The social-science understanding of the news process cautions that we cannot compel audience interest and attention to any mandated content. That is the key problem with ignoring market forces. This conundrum is one that those who favor traditional government intervention have not yet dealt with satisfactorily, one that becomes more critical as communications outlets proliferate and grow more competitive. The future will pose more difficulties for intervention, as the audience will be scattered over many more media outlets. Already the cable alternatives have reduced newspaper penetration and the ratings of the network news. Audience fragmentation may limit the practical utility of traditional government regulations like the Fairness Doctrine.

If traditional policies designed to affect content and distribution are less likely to be effective, arguably the most important policies to facilitate First Amendment or Hutchins Commission values will be those that expand the telecommunications infrastructure to ensure that no information gap develops between the rich and poor. This means subsidizing citizens' access to the ever-increasing information stores that are being produced and that will soon be distributed not in traditional mass media form but on telecommunications networks. With the very notion of a "mass medium," in flux, we need to have a vigorous and unfettered discussion about ultimate democratic goals, one unchilled by the First Amendment. Major transformations in the news industry provide all the more reason to be clear on how journalism might contribute to the democratic process.

In practice, we really do not want strict content-neutrality; we want some discrimination in the distribution of information, if only because government resources and, perhaps more important, people's time and attention are scarce. The market is a good mechanism for content discrimination in distribution. Thus, a practical scheme might adapt and expand upon Dean Bollinger's idea of a mixed system[63] and Professor Sunstein's ideas on a new deal for free expression,[64] wherein some media persist as profitmaking entities, some more regulated than others, and other news organizations receive public subsidies.

A mixed system should be keyed to the information media just now emerging—information will probably be delivered by telephone or cable companies accessed via a multimedia personal computer offering a combination of video and text. If this is the information network of the future, some form of "information stamps" or vouchers analogous to food stamps might provide a way of combining the best features of subsidies and markets. Government might fund information production and its availability on the information network; distribution would be determined by consumers themselves using, if necessary, their information vouchers. Clearly, more thought is needed to prevent such a mechanism from simply duplicating the outcomes of the existing market. And other policy mechanisms also worth exploring can be examined once we free ourselves from the First Amendment's chilling effect on analyzing and achieving the ultimate goals of our democracy.

A newly free and diverse debate on how to realize First Amendment goals might yield such other proposals as these:

• Subsidize newspapers so that they drop their politically potent opposition in Congress to the telephone companies' provision of information in new and potentially democracy-enhancing forms. Meanwhile, the subsidy might allow the newspapers to keep their per-household circulation from shrinking.

• Subsidize the broadcast networks' practice of broadcasting the party nominating conventions so that obligations to stockholders, to maximize advertising revenues, will not force them to neglect an important opportunity to educate the public about presidential candidates.

• Forbid the broadcast of short television political advertisements or of poll results within one month of an election, so as to preserve the widest ambit for autonomous public decision making.

Such policies would not directly reduce the government's informal power to shape the news. Nevertheless, they could accomplish a marginal improvement in the political sophistication of the American citizenry. In turn, this heightened political awareness might increase demand for higher quality civic information—and form communications policies that make furthering the health of democracy a higher priority.

Notes

1. Cass R. Sunstein, *Half-truths of the First Amendment*, 1993 U Chi Legal F 25, 33. See also Lee C. Bollinger, *Images of a Free Press* (University of Chicago Press, 1991).

2. Commission on Freedom of the Press, *A Free and Responsible Press* (University of Chicago Press, 1947) ("Hutchins Report").

3. *Id*. at 68.

4. See Kathleen Hall Jamieson, *Dirty Politics: Deception, Distraction, and Democracy* (Oxford University Press, 1992); W. Lance Bennett, *The Governing Crisis: Media, Money, and Marketing in American Elections* (St. martin's Press, 1992); Robert M. Entman, *Democracy Without Citizens: Media and the Decay of American Politics* (Oxford University Press, 1989).

5. Entman, *Democracy Without Citizens* (cited in note 4).

6. I shall use the term "press" to encompass both print and electronic news media.

7. See Michael X. Delli Carpini and Scott Keeter, *Stability and Change in the US Public's Knowledge of Politics*, 55 Pub Op Q 583, 607 (1991). Even without controlling for educational changes, the American public actually appears less

knowledgeable now about certain subjects. See W. Russell Neuman, *The Paradox of Mass Politics: Knowledge and Opinion in the American Electorate* (Harvard University Press, 1986).

8. An emerging literature in political science essentially argues that while the average American voter is little interested and poorly informed, such an orientation to public affairs may be rational. These scholars suggest voters do surprisingly well at matching their likes or preferences to the candidates who fit best. See, for example, Samuel L. Popkin, *The Reasoning Voter: Communication and Persuasion in Presidential Campaigns* (University of Chicago Press, 1991); Paul M. Sniderman, Richard A. Brody, and Philip E. Tetlock, *Reasoning and Choice: Explorations in Political Psychology* (Cambridge University Press, 1991). Among the problems with this conclusion, however, is that it treats likes and preferences as autonomously determined by each individual, and ignores those who do not vote at all.

9. It is possible that due to some unmeasured factors, the American public world have been even less informed and less disposed to vote than they are now were it not for vast improvements in the media's performance. That, however, seems much more speculative than accepting the conventional analysis, which suggests the continued pertinence of the Hutchins critique.

10. See William Greider, *Who Will Tell the People: The Betrayal of American Democracy* (Simon & Schuster, 1992); Bennett, *The Governing Crisis* (cited in note 4).

11 This relationship is not truly voluntary. It is encouraged and cemented by mutually reinforcing commercial incentives, professional norms, and cultural values that make reliance upon government elites the most rational practice for news organizations. See Herbert J. Gans, *Deciding What's News: A Study of CBS Evening News, NBC Nightly News, Newsweek, and Time* (Pantheon Books, 1979); David L. Paletz and Robert M. Entman, *Media Power Politics* (Free Press, 1981).

12. Sunstein, 1993 U Chi Legal F at 26 (cited in note 1).

13. Id at 39–40.

14. Id at 30.

15. Id at 41.

16. Sunstein, 1993 U Ch Legal F at 33 (cited in note 1).

17. See the works cited in notes 4, 7, and 8. See also Doris A. Graber, *Mass Media and American Politics* (CQ Press, 4th ed 1993); Murray Edelman, *Constructing the Political Spectacle* (University of Chicago Press, 1988); Daniel C. Hallin, *The "Uncensored War": The Media and Vietnam* (Oxford University Press, 1986); Thomas E. Patterson, *The Mass Media Election: How Americans Choose Their President* (Praeger Publishers, 1980).

18. 376 US 254 (1964). See Rodney A. Smolla, *Suing the Press* (Oxford University Press, 1986); Anthony Lewis, *Make No Law: The Sullivan and the First Amendment* (Random House, 1991).

19. Sunstein, 1993 U Chi Legal F at 26 (cited in note 1).

20. Id at 27.

21. See Michael B. Grossman and Martha J. Kumar, *Portraying the President: The White House and the News Media* (Johns Hopkins University Press, 1981); Mark Hertsgaard, *On Bended Knee: The Press and the Reagan Presidency* (Farrar, Straus & Giroux, 1988); Samuel Kernell, *Going Public: New Strategies of Presidential Leadership* (CQ Press, 2d ed 1993); John A. Maltese, *Spin Control: The White House Office of Communications and the Management of Presidential News* (University of North Carolina Press, 1992); Entman, *Democracy Without Citizens* (cited in note 4).

22. Reliance on government elites is documented in Leon V. Sigal, *Reporters and Officials: The Organization and Politics of Newsmaking* (D. C. heath & Co., 1973); Gans, *Deciding What's News* (cited in note 11); Paletz & Entman, *Media Power Politics* (cited in note 11); Hallin, *Uncensored War* (cited in note 17); W. Lance Bennett, *Toward a Theory of Press-State Relations in the United States*, 40 J Commun 103 (Spring 1990). See also John Zaller, *The Nature and Origins of Mass Opinion* (Cambridge University Press, 1992); Robert A. Dahl, *Democracy and Its Critics* (Yale University Press, 1989). Problematic exceptions are policy experts outside official government roles, and social movements. Without going into detail, research suggests that neither of these sources gets very far in shaping public discourse unless government officials take up their cause. See Todd Gitlin, *The Whole World is Watching* (University of California Press, 1980); Robert M. Entman and Andrew Rojecki, *Freezing Out the Public: Elite and Media Framing of the U.S. Antinuclear Movement*, 11 Pol Commun 155–73 (1993).

23. See Hallin, *Uncensored War* (cited in note 17); Entman, *Democracy Without Citizens* (cited in note 4); Bennett, *The Governing Crisis* (cited in note 4); W. Lance Bennett, *Marginalizing the Majority: Conditioning Public Opinion to Accept Managerial Democracy*, in Michael Margolis and Gary Mauser, eds, *Manipulating Public Opinion* 321 (Brooks/Cole Publishing Co., 1989).

24. See Hallin, *Uncensored War* (cited in note 17); Zaller, *Mass Opinion* (cited in note 22). See also Richard A. Brody, *Assessing the President: The Media, Elite Opinion, and Public Support* (Stanford University Press, 1991).

25. See Entman, *Democracy Without Citizens* (cited in note 4); Jarol B. Manheim, *All of the People, All the Time: Strategic Communication and American Politics* (M. E. Sharpe, 1991); Maltese, *Spin Control* (cited in note 21); Robert M. Entman and Benjamin I. Page, *The News Before the Storm: The Iraq War Debate and the Limits to Media Independence*, in W. Lance Bennett and David L. Paletz, eds, *Taken by Storm: The Media, Public Opinion, and US Foreign Policy in the Gulf War* (University of Chicago Press, 1994).

26. See Entman, Democracy Without Citizens (cited in note 4).

27. See Robert M. Entman, *Framing US Coverage of International News: Contrasts in Narratives of the KAL and Iran Air Incidents*, 41 J Commun 6 Autumn 1991).

28. Id.

29. Time (Sept 12, 1983); Newsweek (Sept 12, 1983).

30. Time (Sept 12, 1983); Newsweek (Sept 12, 1983).

31. See, for example, Seymour M. Hersh, *"The Target is Destroyed": What Really Happened to Flight 007 and What America Knew About It* (Random House, 1986); *Soviet Error Blamed for KAL Attack*, Chicago Trib 1–3 (Jan 14, 1988).

32. See *Sea of Lies*, Newsweek 28 (July 13, 1992).

33. See Entman, *Framing US Coverage* (cited in note 27).

34. See Hersh, *The Target is Destroyed* (cited in note 31); Entman, *Framing US Coverage* (cited in note 27).

35. See Entman & Page, *The News Before the Storm* (cited in note 25).

36. See id. The *Washington Post* was more critical during this period, but other media, such as *time*, were not. On balance, it seems fair to suppose that the bulk of media coverage was either neutral or supportive of the administration. It would be impossible to list the hundreds of articles on which this statement is based. The conclusion here comes from a quantitative content analysis of all coverage of the Gulf War policy in these outlets from November 8–16 and November 27–December 5, 1990. See id.

37. See John R. MacArthur, *Second Front: Censorship and Propaganda in the Gulf War* (hill & Wang, 1992).

38. The editorial page of the *New York Times* did discuss the negotiation alternative, but it never penetrated the news pages, where a demonization of Hussein and a focus on the sanctions-versus-war options reigned. See Entman & Page, *The News before the Storm* (cited in note 25). This point takes no position on whether negotiation was in fact a wise course. It was not considered an outlandish proposal in much of the European press, but the key point for this article is that the absence of a position in the public utterances of government elites created a vacuum in media content. This may be inevitable, even by some lights desirable, given the limitations on the public's ability to evaluate every conceivable policy solution. The influence of government over media content is much too complicated to probe sufficiently here. See Robert M. Entman, *Projections of Power: Media and American Foreign Policy since Vietnam* (University of Chicago Press, 1994).

39. See John A. Ferejohn and James H. Kuklinski, eds, *Information and Democratic Processes* (University of Illinois Press, 1990); Benjamin I. Page and Robert Y. Shapiro, *The Rational Public: Fifty Years of Trends in Americans' Policy Preferences* (University of Chicago Press, 1992); Zaller, *Mass Opinion* (cited in note 22); Dahl, *Democracy and Its Critics* (cited in note 22); Entman, *Democracy without Citizens* (cited in note 4).

40. See Michael Parenti, *Inventing Reality: The Politics of the Mass Media* (St. Martin's Press, 2d ed 1992); Edward S. Herman and Noam Chomsky, *Manu-*

facturing Consent: The Political Economy of the Mass Media (Pantheon Books, 1988).

41. See Gitlin, *The Whole World* (cited in note 22); Hallin, *Uncensored War* (cited in note 17).

42. Gitlin, *The Whole World* (cited in note 22).

43. See Robert M. Entman and Steven S. Wildman, *Reconciling Economic and Non-Economic Perspectives on Media Policy: Transcending the "Marketplace of Ideas,"* 42 J Commun 5 (Winter 1992). Parts of the current essay extend the argument in this article. See also Frederick Schauer, *The First Amendment as Ideology*, 33 Wm & Mary L Rev 853 (1992).

44. Good sources for this sort of complicated thinking include Cass R. Sunstein, *Democracy and the Problem of Free Speech* (Free Press, 1993); Judith Lichtenberg, ed, *Democracy and the Mass Media* (Cambridge University Press, 1990); Steven H. Shiffrin, *The First Amendment, Democracy, and Romance* (Harvard University Press, 1990); Frederick Schauer, *Free Speech: A Philosophical Enquiry* (Cambridge University Press, 1982); Bollinger, *Images of a Free Press* (cited in note 1). Note that the Clinton-era FCC might engage in reasoning more influenced by such considerations.

45. *Inquiry into Section 73.1910 of the Commission's Rules and Regulations Concerning Alternatives to the General Fairness Doctrine Obligations of Broadcast Licensees*, 2 FCC Rec 17, 5272 (1987).

46. *Deregulation of Radio*, 84 FCC2d 968 (1981).

47. *Children's Television Programming and Advertising Practices*, 96 FCC2d 634 (1984).

48. This analysis includes the text of footnotes but excludes the dissenting statement of Commissioner Rivera in *Children's Television*, 96 FCC2d at 634.

49. In fifteen instances, the words were used without any contextual idea; in four cases, the words referred to other ideas.

50. See Stanley Ingber, *The Marketplace of Ideas: A Legitimizing Myth*, 1984 Duke L J 1.

51. *Children's Television*, 96 FCC2d at 649 n 36, cites a non-scholarly article by the head of an interest group which in turn quotes an unnamed "Michigan State University study." The note also references *Television and Behavior: Ten Years of Scientific Progress and Implications for the Eighties* (National Institute of Mental Health, 1982).

Fairness Doctrine, 2 FCC Rec at 5300 n 86, cites an article by Bruce M. Owen, *The Role of Print in an Electronic Society*, in Glen O. Robison, ed, *Communication for Tomorrow: Policy Perspectives for the 1980's* 229, 230 (Praeger Publishers, 1978). This note quotes three sentences in the Owen article that assert that the role of print news editors is to package ideas and reduce the burden of information processing on readers.

Two other footnotes mention scholarly studies concerning the marketing (not the production or consumption) of ideas: Philip Kotler, *Marketing Management: Analysis, Planning, and Control* (Prentice Hall, 1976); Joseph R. Dominicle [sic, should be Dominick], *The Effects of Commercial Clutter on Radio News*, 20 J of Broadcasting 169 (1976). See also *Deregulation of Radio*, 84 FCC 2d at 1004–05 n 71, n 75.

52. 5 USC sec. 551–559, 701–706 (1988),

53. See, for example, Toxic Substances Control Act, 12 USC sec. 2605 (a)–(c) (1988).

54. See Dean E. Alger, *The Media and Politics* 217 (Prentice Hall, 1989).

55. In 1992, political candidates used other formats for conveying political information, such as talk-show appearances and "infomercials." Research has not yet established whether the use of these vehicles significantly increased the public's political sophistication. Ratings for these outlets, however, do suggest that millions of Americans demanded more than they found in traditional newspaper and television news coverage.

56. See Sunstein, 1993 U Chi Legal F at 26–30 (cited in note 1).

57. See id. at 34–35.

58. See Lichtenberg, ed., *Democracy and the Mass media* (cited in note 44).

59. This is true unless one assumes a Rawlsian original position under which an endogenous and natural distribution of ideas and preferences exists. That notion seems effectively dispatched by Professor Sunstein, who points out that the existing press system relies upon a set of prior government policy decisions regarding private policy rights which themselves may have content-relevant implications. Sunstein, *Democracy and the Problem of Free Speech* (cited in note 44).

60. The essays in Lichtenberg, ed, *Democracy and the Mass Media* (cited in note 44), debate this proposition thoroughly. See especially Owen M. Fiss, *Why the State?* At 136–54; Lee C. Bollinger, *The Rationality of Public Regulation of the Media* at 355–67.

61. See Ithiel de Sola Pool, *Technologies of Freedom* (Belknap Press, 1983). See also Henry Geller, *Mass Communications Policy: Where We Are and Where We Should be Going*, in Lichtenberg, ed, *Democracy and the Mass Media* at 290 (cited in note 44).

62. C. Edwin Baker, *Advertising and a Democratic Press*, 140 U Pa L Rev 2097 (1992).

63. See Lee C. Bollinger, *Freedom of the Press and Public Access: Toward a Theory of Partial Regulation of the Mass Media*, 75 Mich L Rev 1 (1976).

64. Sunstein, *Democracy and the Problem of Free Speech* (cited in note 44).

Negotiating Research: Policy Impact on Research Design

22

Social Science and Social Control

John Dewey
1931

It would require a technical survey, which would be out of place here, to prove that the existing limitations of "social science" are due mainly to unreasoning devotion to physical science as a model, and to a misconception of physical science at that. Without making any such survey, attention may be directly called to one outstanding difference between physical and social facts. The ideal of the knowledge dealing with the former is the elimination of all factors dependent upon distinctively human response. "Fact," physically speaking, is the ultimate residue after human purposes, desires, emotions, ideas and ideals have been systematically excluded. A social "fact," on the other hand, is a concretion in external form of precisely these human factors.

An occurrence is a physical fact only when its constituents and their relations remain the same, irrespective of the human attitude toward them. A species of mosquitoes is the carrier of the germs of malaria, whether we like or dislike malaria. Drainage and oil-spraying to destroy mosquitoes is a social fact because their use depends upon human purpose and desire. A steam locomotive or a dynamo is a physical fact in its structure; it is a social fact when its existence depends upon the desire for rapid and cheap transportation and communication. The machine itself may be understood physically without reference to human aim and motive. But the railway or public-utility system cannot be understood without reference to human purposes and human consequences.

I may illustrate the present practice of slavishly following the technique of physical science and the uselessness of its results by the present zeal for "fact finding." Of course, one cannot think, understand and plan without a basis of fact, and since facts do not lie around in plain view, they have to be discovered. But for the most part, the data which now are so carefully sought and so elaborately scheduled are not social facts at all. For their connection with any system of human purposes and consequences, their bearing as means and as results upon human action, are left out of the picture. At best they are mere physical and external facts. They are unlike the facts of physical science, because the latter are found by methods which make their interrelations and their laws apparent, while the facts of social "fact finding" remain a miscellaneous pile of meaningless items. Since their connections with human wants and their effect on human values are neglected, there is nothing which binds them together into an intelligible whole.

It may be retorted that to connect facts with human desires and their effect upon human values is subjective and moral, and to an extent that makes it impossible to establish any conclusions upon an objective basis: that to attempt inference on this point would land us in a morass of speculative opinion. Suppose, for example, all the facts about the working of the prohibition law and its enforcement were much more completely known than they are; even so, to establish a connection between these facts and the human attitudes lying back of them would be a matter of guess work. As things stand, there is much force in the objection. But if made universal, it would overlook the possibility of another kind of situation.

Wherever purposes are employed deliberately and systematically for the sake of certain desired social results, there it is possible, within limits, to determine the connection between the human factor and the actual occurrence, and thus to get a complete social fact, namely, the actual external occurrence in its human relationships. Prohibition, whether noble or not, is not an experiment in any intelligent scientific sense of the term. For it was undertaken without the effort to obtain the conditions of control which are essential to any experimental determination of fact. The Five Year Plan of Russia, on the other hand, whether noble or the reverse, has many of traits of a social experiment, for it is an attempt to obtain certain specified social results by the use of specified definite measures, exercised under conditions of considerable, if not complete, control.

The point I am making may be summed up by saying that it is a complete error to suppose that efforts at social control depend upon the prior existence of a social science. The reverse is the case. The building up of social science, that is, of a body of knowledge in which facts are ascertained in their significant relations, is dependent upon putting social planning into effect. It is at this point that the misconception about physical science, when it is taken as a model for social knowledge, is important. Physical science did not develop because inquirers piled up a mass of facts about observed phenomena. It came into being when men intentionally experimented, on the basis of ideas and hypotheses, with observed phenomena to modify them and disclose new observations. This process is self-corrective and self-developing. Imperfect and even wrong hypotheses, when *acted upon*, brought to light significant phenomena which made improved ideas and improved experimentations possible. The change from a passive and accumulative attitude into an active and productive one is the secret revealed by the progress of physical inquiry. Men obtained knowledge of natural energies by trying deliberately to control the conditions of their operation. The result was knowledge, and then control on a larger scale by the application of what was learned.

It is a commonplace of logical theory that laws are of the "if-then" type. *If* something occurs, then something else happens; if certain conditions exist, they are accompanied by certain other conditions. Such knowledge alone is knowledge of a fact in any intelligible sense of the word. Although we have to act in order to discover the conditions underlying the "if" in physical matters, yet the material constituting the "if" is there apart from our action; like the movements of sun and earth in an eclipse. But in social phenomena the relation is: "If we *do* something, something else will happen." The objective material constituting the "if" belongs to us, not to something wholly independent of us. We are concerned, not with a bare relation of cause and effect, but with one of means and consequences, that is, of causes deliberately used for the sake of producing certain effects. As far as we intentionally do and make, we shall know; as far as we "know" without making, our so-called knowledge is a miscellany, or at most antiquarian, and hence without relevance to future planning. Only the knowledge which is itself the fruit of a technology can breed further technology.

I want to make the same point with reference to social prediction. Here, too, the assumption is generally made that we must be able to predict before we can plan and control. Here again the reverse is the case. We can predict the occurrence of an eclipse precisely because we cannot control it. If we could control it, we could not predict, except contingently; just as we can predict a collision when we see two trains approaching on the same track—provided that a human being does not foresee the possibility and take measures to avert its happening. The other day I ran across a remark of Alexander Hamilton's to the effect that instead of awaiting an event to know what measures to take, we should take measures to bring the event to pass. And I would add that only then can we genuinely forecast the future in the world of social matters.

Empirical rule-of-thumb practices were the mothers of the arts. But the practices of the arts were in turn the source of science, when once the empirical methods were freed in imagination and used with some degree of freedom of experimentation. There cannot be a science of an art until the art has itself made some advance, and the significant development occurs when men intentionally try to use such art as they have already achieved in order to obtain results which they conceive to be desirable. If we have no social technique at all, it is impossible to bring planning and control into being. If we do have at hand a reasonable amount of technique, then it is by deliberately using what we have that we shall in the end develop a dependable body of social knowledge. If we want foresight, we shall not obtain it by any amount of fact finding so long as we disregard the human aims and desires producing the facts which we find. But if we decide upon what we want socially, what sort of social consequences we wish to occur, and then use whatever means we possess to effect these intended consequences, we shall find the road that leads to foresight. Forethought and planning must come before foresight.

I am not arguing here for the desirability of social planning and control. That is another question. Those who are satisfied with present conditions and who are hopeful of turning them to account for personal profit and power will answer it in the negative. What I am saying is that if we want something to which the name "social science" may be given, there is only one way to go about it, namely, by entering upon the path of social planning and control. Observing, collecting, recording and filing tomes of social phenomena without deliberately trying to do something to bring a desired state of society into existence only encourages a conflict of opinion and dogma in their interpretation. If the social situation out of which these facts emerge is itself confused and chaotic because it expresses socially unregulated purpose and haphazard private intent, the facts themselves will be confused, and we shall add only intellectual confusion to practical disorder. When we deliberately employ whatever skill we possess in order to serve the ends which we desire, we shall begin to attain a measure of at least intellectual order and understanding. And if past history teaches anything, it is that with intellectual order we have the surest possible promise of advancement to practical order.

23

Remarks on Administrative and Critical Communications Research

Paul Felix Lazarsfeld
1941

During the last two decades the media of mass communication, notably radio, print and film, have become some of the best-known and best documented spheres of modern society. Careful studies have revealed the size of the audiences of all major radio programs and the composition of this audience in respect to sex, income, and a few other criteria. The circulations of newspapers and magazines are recorded by specially organized research outfits, and others report currently on which magazine stories and which advertisements are read week by week. Books, radio programs, and movies are tested as to the difficulty of the language they use and as to how adequate they are for the different educational levels of the population. The types of entertainment that different groups of people prefer are being investigated all the time, and many promotional campaigns are tested currently as to their success. A number of important new techniques have been developed in the course of all these research efforts. Modern sampling techniques, for instance, have made great progress because it has been realized that the practical value of a study would be lost if it were conducted among a group of people who are not representative of those sections of the population which the sponsoring agency wants to reach. Interviewing techniques have been greatly refined for similar reasons. The competitive character of much of this work has led to ever better methods of recording facts as to the extent of listening and reading. Where a subject matter doesn't lend itself to simple recording devices, great progress has been made in developing indices for complex attitudes and reactions.[1] Behind the idea of such research is the notion that modern media of communication are tools handled by people or agencies for given purposes. The purpose may be to sell goods, or to raise the intellectual standards of the population, or to secure an understanding of governmental policies, but in all cases, to someone who uses a medium for something, it is the task of research to make the tools better known, and thus to facilitate its use.

As a result, all communication research centers around a standard set of problems. Who are the people exposed to the different media? What are their specific preferences? What are the effects of different methods of presentation? One who uses media of communication is in competition with other agencies whose purposes are different, and thus research must also keep track of what is communicated by others. Finally, communications research has to be aware that the effect of radio, print, or the movie, does not end with the purposive use which is made of it by administrative agencies. If advertisers, for example, feel that radio is an especially powerful selling device, then printed media will receive less money, and research will have to see whether radio brings about a general deterioration of the reading habits of the population.

Studies of this kind are conducted partly by the major publishing organizations and radio networks and partly by academic agencies supported by universities or foundations.[2] Considerable thought has been given during the past years to clarifying the social the political implications of this new branch of social research. Its relationship to the present crisis is very interestingly discussed in a new study by Harold Lasswell.[3] One who has not participated in work of this kind can get a good picture of its atmosphere from a "fable" written by participants in the course of a series of discussions which took place during 1939 and 1940. We quote:

In the interests of concreteness, let us attempt to state the job of research in mass communication in a situation which, though purely hypothetical, serves to illustrate what that job involves.

Let us suppose that government leaders and those responsible for mass communication are in agreement with respect to policy toward alien groups in this country. The public, they believe, should be made aware of the dangers of subversive activities on the part of aliens, but popular antipathy toward aliens in general should be minimized, and, above all, outbreaks of anti-alien sentiment should be avoided. The policy that the channels of mass communication must serve, then, becomes one of increasing public awareness of specific dangers of subversive action, while, at the same time, building tolerance toward aliens in general.*

Suppose that some popular evening radio program, known to attract a considerable portion of the total listening audience, includes an address dealing with the dangers of subversive activities on the part of aliens. The explicit intention of the speaker, of his sponsors, and of the stations which carry the program is simply to further policy outlined above by drawing attention to dangers to which the country should be alive. News dispatches of the next day or two, however, bring reports from various parts of the country of outbreaks of feeling against alien groups. Reports of local utterance in connection with these outbreaks carry allusions to the broadcast address of the evening. As a result, there is at least a strong suspicion that some connection exists between them and what was said on the evening broadcast.

Suppose, too, that those responsible for the original address decide that they are likewise responsible for doing something to repair the damage which they quite innocently caused. This decision takes on new importance as the network involved receives from the Federal Communications Commission a request for the text of the address. Conscientious effort to repair the damage, it is clear, involves learning more of what the damage was. The comment it occasioned in the press makes clear that its effects were felt not through the radio alone, but through reports of the unfortunate address which the newspapers carried, in the local utterances which alluded to it, and even in some widely distributed newsreel reports of the local outbreaks that followed. What people then must be reached if the untoward effects of the broadcast are to be remedied?

What were those effects and precisely what in the broadcast address provoked them? Clearly the broadcast was not alone responsible. Something in what was said evidently combined with the predispositions of the listeners and with the current circumstances—with the force of events, and probably with other widely disseminated communications—to set the stage for what ensued.

Recognizing these questions as basic in any conscientious effort to repair the damage, those responsible set about to get them answered. Each station which carried the address is asked immediately to dispatch to network headquarters all the evidence that can be gathered on the attention it attracted in the area of the station's coverage—newspaper reports of the address itself, editorials and speeches referring to it, reports of the outbreaks that ensued, newsreel treatments of them, etc. Each station too, is asked to assign the best qualified members of its staff to interviewing listeners to determine as best they can what in the address led to the unanticipated outbreaks. Particularly are they urged to have their interviewers talk with individuals who took an active part in the outbreaks in question. Some of the stations, concerned to do their part, enlist the help of competent specialists from nearby universities to study more intensively the predispositions of individuals who were most aroused by the address, and to attempt to discover what other circumstances combined with the address to make them act as they did. The interviewing organization of one of the national polls is also brought into play to study similarly cross-section of the country's population sure to comprise both listeners who were affected and not affected by the broadcast, and some as well whom it did not reach at all, directly or indirectly.

As reports come in from all these inquiries, a new picture of the situation takes shape. To the surprise of the speaker, his sponsors, and the network, what seemed innocent references to the few aliens believed to be engaged in subversive activities were taken by listeners to apply both to aliens generally and to hyphenates from countries thought hostile to American interests and traditions. Some of the individual interviews and the poll reports show an equally surprising attitude of general hostility toward these groups. Some of them specifically allude to what are taken to be racial traits of the group involved, others to specific individuals of the group who are in business competition with the informants. Still others mention seemingly authentic reports of Fifth Column activities in conquered European countries; and a considerable number refer to purported activities of this kind in the United States and South America. Clearly, the stage was set on the evening of the broadcast for what actually happened both by the general psychological predisposition of listeners, and by the force of recent events.

All this, of course, clearly contributed to the unusual attention this particular broadcast received—on the part of the radio audience, through the press dispatches which reported it, in the newsreels, and through the local utterances which ensued. Curiously too, the program in which the address was included on this particular evening had a larger audience than usual. Its rating on that evening, as reported by audience research agencies, jumped substantially from its customary level. To be sure, the inclusion of this particular address had been announced in advance, and by coincidence on this particular evening another popular program ordinarily broadcast at the same time, had gone off the air for the summer. This other program, it was generally assumed, appealed more to less educated listeners, with the apparent result that the audience for this address included, perhaps for the first time, more listeners of lower educational status— a supposition confirmed by a breakdown of audience research figures in terms of socio-economic status and by a check of the ratings of other programs broadcast at the same hour, none of which rose above their usual rating and some of which showed a marked decline.

How to repair the damage done thus becomes more problematical than had at first appeared. Obviously, another address to counteract the one which had caused the damage would not be sufficient. Comparable announcements of it might of course again attract to the program much the same audience as the week before. But, it is pointed out, there is no reason to assume that the predispositions of listeners or the force of circumstances would again lead them to depart from their ordinary listening habits. Furthermore, there is no assurance, for much the same reasons, that a counteracting address would occasion equal attention in the press or in local utterances. Finally, the original speaker is undoubtedly now firmly identified, in the minds of listeners, with the views on alien and hyphenate groups attributed to him as a result of his earlier address. Would another address by him change that identification? What, then, can be done?

In the face of this problem comes the suggestion that outside advice should be had. Unless this broadcast is to go down in record as the beginning of a destructive wave of feeling against all aliens and hyphenates and thus utterly defeat the interest which prompted it, any remedial measures have to be most carefully planned. Who is there who can contribute to a better understanding of what happened, and who to suggest what might be done by way of remedy?

Suppose at this point help is sought from a social psychologist known to have been studying anti-minority feeling. When he is called in, it appears that he has for sometime been recording and analyzing whatever appears in the press, the radio, motion pictures, or in public utterances that seem to have a bearing on the subject. He points out that this is not an isolated episode, but rather, one more in a development which he had for some time been following. Just such anti-minority feeling had been developing in the country over a period of years. The growth of anti-Semitic sentiment in this country had been well recognized, and now the same feelings seemed to be shifting to other scapegoats.

Acccording to his analysis, the recent flow of mass communication had reflected this general trend. The term "Fifth Column," obscurely used in the Spanish Civil War, had had wide currency. In fact, the Allies had missed few opportunities to emphasize the concept, as, for example, in their use of Major Quisling's name. At the same time, reports of Fifth Column activities in the other conquered countries had been coming through, supported in still more recent times by revelations of similar activities in South America. Thus, strong pro-Ally feeling in this country, supported by the growing predisposition to fear and feel hostility toward minority groups, led to the over-generalization of the remarks made in the broadcast address. Such feelings, the specialist might go on to point out, would be less restrained among less educated and less self-conscious groups. Furthermore, these groups in his opinion would be less likely to respond to any intellectual appeal that might be devised to counteract the effect of the earlier talk. This, he advises, must be kept in mind as remedial measures are planned. In fact, he is in doubt as to what any single remedial effort can accomplish. Rather, since the talk in question was no isolated example, remedial effort must take into account all the other factors in current mass communications which tend, as he sees it, to arouse just such anti-minority feeling. To repair the damage, he points out, it is necessary to determine who must be reached, not only in terms of geographical coverage, but in psychological terms as well. His final advice at this stage is therefore to turn to another specialist who has studied both the geographical and psychological composition of the audience reached by various types of mass communication.

This specialist, when called in, readily confirms from his own observations that the program on the night in question reached an audience psychologically different from that it usually attracted. To reach that audience necessitates in his opinion close attention to the listening, reading, movie-going habits of the part of the population affected by the original broadcast. He knows in general the characteristics of each of these audiences and the types of listening, reading, and films which ordinarily attract them. His studies, too, give him some basis for predicting how any given group will respond to a given type of program, though he would need to verify prediction by a careful check on the effects which resulted from the particular address in question. He also knows that the same message conveyed by different media, to reach the audience desired, would have to stress different aspects of the subject which are especially appropriate for the medium in question. If the counteracting measures planned are to be really remedial, he would strongly suggest some pre-testing of the responses which they actually evoke. He would propose, therefore, that any remedial measures should be tried out in advance on a relatively small but typical sample of the population, and that a study of their responses be made as a basis for possible modification before an attempt is made to reach any wider public.

Thus, with the help of these and other specialists, the job begins. Agreed as it is that the possibility of unintended effects must be avoided, the advice of these specialists is followed. There is no need here to attempt to suggest the nature of what is done, but only to indicate how research in mass communication might contribute to the result. With the help of specialists in such research, the audience originally affected is redetermined. Types of radio programs, press releases, and newsreel treatments are worked out, calculated on the basis of the best evidence available to get a new hearing for the subject, adequate to counter the effects of the original address. Undoubtedly an explanation would be prepared for delivery by the original speaker, but other speakers would be enlisted whose position and identification in the public mind are likely to make their parts most widely influential. All materials prepared are pre-tested as had been suggested and at relatively slight expense—indeed, far less expense, proportionately, than merchandisers ordinarily incur in testing the market for new products. Conscientious effort having taken them so far, those responsible agree in wishing now to have some further test of the actual effects of what they have planned by way of remedy. Accordingly, arrangements are made in advance of their campaign to gauge its progress.

A happy ending to this fable can probably take the form of a series of charts which subsequently ease the conscience of all concerned by showing, as their campaign proceeds, a consistent decline in all indices of overt hostility toward the groups against which outbreaks of feeling were directed.

If the fable has a moral, too, that perhaps may come when all concerned, in the relief that follows in their success, philosophize a bit on their experience. The original speaker, the sponsors, and the broadcasters are still convinced of their initial innocence. But they are plagued a bit by certain recollections. One of them remembers, for example, suggesting extra publicity for the broadcast on the ground that the address to be included was particularly timely. Another recalls that the topic of the address was suggested by an acquaintance prominent in an organization which presumably on patriotic grounds had for some time been advocating stricter control of aliens in the country. In the end, their feeling is that however innocent their conscious purposes, they too, as Americans of their time, shared the same predispositions in planning the broadcast, and responded to the force of the same circumstances, as did the listeners to it. It is well, then, that conscious intention should be checked by more objective standards when instrumentalities are used so powerful in their influence as modern mass communication. Somehow the mere fact that they brought objective standards into play seemed to have sharpened their common sense and made them more wary for the future. If similar research had made them warier at the outset, need all this have happened? Need they have run the risk that the inevitable delays in repairing the damage they had caused made its complete repair impossible? Perhaps, they conclude, in media like radio where "instant rejoinder" is often difficult, more trouble should be taken to avoid mistakes like this.

This fable, it is recognized, may seem to exaggerate the importance of research in mass communication. Ordinarily, to be sure, common sense, the high standards of the communications industries, and the controls of legal and administrative regulation have appeared sufficient to assure the use of mass communication in the public interest. Ordinarily, wisdom in that use, it might appear, can be allowed to develop by trial and error and the resulting rules of thumb. A critical situation, like that supposed, admittedly throws into high relief considerations which, though always present, ordinarily seems less urgent. But crisis, as the derivation of the word implies, forces judgment; and a desired solution of the crisis necessitates that judgment shall not be mistaken. The critical situation of our fable, then, rather than exaggerating, perhaps only puts into perspective the consequences of mistaken use of mass communication and the help which research can give in avoiding such mistaken use.

Research of the kind described so far could well be called *administrative research*. It is carried through in the service of some kind of administrative agency of public or private character. Administrative research is subject to objections from two sides. On the one hand, there are the sponsors themselves, some of whom feel that they have not really got their money's worth. One good guess, so the argument goes, is of more practical importance than all the details which might be brought to light by an empirical study. There is, however, a fallacy behind this objection. Although speculation is indispensable for guidance in any kind of empirical work, if honestly carried through it will usually lead to a number of alternative conclusions which cannot all be true at the same time. Which one corresponds to the real situation can be decided only by empirical studies.[4] From another side comes an objection directed against the aims which prevail in the majority of current studies. They solve little problems, generally of a business character, when the same methods could be used to improve the life of the community if only they were applied to forward-looking projects related to the pressing economic and social problems of our time. Robert S. Lynd, in his *Knowledge for What*, has vigorously taken this point of view and has shown many ways whereby research could be made more vital.

Neither of these two arguments doubts that research can and should be done at the service of certain well-defined purposes. But at this point a third argument comes up. The objection is raised that one cannot pursue a single purpose and study the means of its realization isolated from the total historical situation in which such planning and studying goes on. Modern media of communication have become such complex instruments that wherever they are used they do much more to people than those who administer them mean them to do, and they may have a momentum of their own which leaves the administrative agencies much less choice than they believe they have. The idea of *critical research* is posed against the practice of administrative research, requiring that, prior and in addition to whatever special purpose is to be served, the general role of our media of communication in the present social system should be studied. The rest of these remarks are devoted to a formulation of this conception and to a short appraisal of its possible contributions to current communication research.

The idea of critical research has been developed in many studies by Max Horkheimer.[5] It seems to be distinguished from administrative research in two respects: it develops a theory of the prevailing social trends of our times, general trends which yet require consideration in any concrete research problem; and it seems to imply ideas of basic human values according to which all actual or desired effects should be appraised.

As to prevailing trends, everyone will agree that we live in a period of increasing centralization of ownership. Yet, although large economic organizations plan their production to the minutest detail, the distribution of their products is not planned systematically. Their success depends upon the outcome of a competition among a few large units which must rally sizeable proportions of the population as their customers. Thus promotion in every form becomes one of the main forces in contemporary society. The technique of manipulating large masses of people is developed in the business world and from there permeates our whole culture. In the end everything, be it good or bad, is promoted; we are living more and more in an "advertising culture." This whole trend is accentuated still more by the fact that it has to disguise itself. A salesman who has only one line to sell has to explain to each customer why this line suits just his individual purposes. The radio announcer who serves one national advertiser identifies himself to millions of listeners as "your" announcer.

Such an analysis becomes an element of strong concern and solicitude if it is felt that these trends impair basic values in human life. The idea that our times are engulfed by a multitude of promotional patterns is coupled with the feeling that human beings, as a result, behave more and more like pawns upon a chessboard, losing the spontaneity and dignity which is the basic characteristic of the human personality. In order to understand clearly the idea of critical research, one must realize that it is being urged by men who have the idea ever present before them that what we need most is to do and think what we consider true and not to adjust ourselves to the seemingly inescapable.

The theory of a trend toward promotional culture leads to the conclusion that certain tendencies of our time jeopardize basic human values because people are kept from developing their own potentialities to the full. To be fit for the daily competition, we do not spend our leisure time developing a rich range of interests and abilities, but we use it, willingly or unwillingly, to reproduce our working capacity. Thus, not having acquired any criteria of our own, we succumb to and support a system of promotion in all areas of life, which, in turn, puts us in ever-increasing dependence upon such a system; it gives us more and more technical devices and takes away from us any valuable purposes for which they could be used.[6]

Thus the stage is set for the procedures of critical research. A critical student who analyzes modern media of communication will look at radio, motion pictures, the press, and will ask the following kinds of questions: How are these media organized and controlled? How, in their institutional set-up, is the trend toward centralization, standardization and promotional pressure expressed? In what form, however disguised, are they threatening human values? He will feel that the main task of research is to uncover the unintentional (for the most part) and often very subtle ways in which these media contribute to living habits and social attitudes that he considers deplorable.

What are the operations into which critical communication research could be broken down? The answer is not easy and a first attempt might be made by visualizing how a student would be trained to make observations in everyday life and to try to interpret them in terms of their social meaning. You sit in a movie and look at an old newsreel showing fashions of ten years ago. Many people laugh. Why do those things which we admired just a little while ago seem so ridiculous now? Could it be that we avenge ourselves for having submitted to them under general pressure, and now that the pressure in favor of these particular styles has been lifted, we compensate by deriding the idols of yesteryear? At the same time, we submit to the style-promotion of today only to laugh at it a few years from now. Could it be that by laughing at past submission, we gather strength to submit to the present pressure upon us? Thus, what looks to an ordinary observer like a incident in a movie theater, becomes, from this point of view, a symptom of great social significance.

Or you find that a large brewery advertises its beer by showing a man disgustedly throwing aside a newspaper full of European war horrors while the caption says that in times like these the only place to find peace, strength, and courage is at your own fireside drinking beer. What will be the result if symbols referring to such basic human wants as that for peace become falsified into expressions of private comfort and are rendered habitual to millions of magazine readers as merchandising slogans? Why should people settle their social problems by action and sacrifice if they can serve the same ends by drinking a new brand of beer? To the casual observer the advertisement is nothing but a more or less clever sales trick. From the aspect of a more critical analysis, it becomes a dangerous sign of what a promotional culture might end up with.

A next step in trying to explain this approach could be taken by applying it not only to an observation of daily life, but to problems we meet in textbooks current in the social sciences. A text on the family, for example, would not be likely to contain a detailed analysis showing how one of the functions of the family in our society might be that of maintaining the authoritarian structure necessary for our present economic system, that the predominant position of the father might prepare the child to accept the privations he will suffer as an adult, and to do so without questioning their necessity. Applying this to a study of the family in the Depression we might depart from the traditional question of what changes the Depression has brought about in family life. Couldn't it be that the family has influenced the Depression? Interesting research problems would come up: what was the effect of different family constellations upon people's ability to find out-of-the-way jobs, to use initiative in organizations of unemployed, and so on?

Another example could arise from a well-known observation which can be found in every text on social psychology, to the effect that the way we look at the world and react to the problems of the day is determined by our previous experience. The notion of experience is taken as a psychological concept which does not need much further elucidation. But could it not be that what we call "experience" undergoes historical changes? Visualize what experience meant for a man who lived in a rather stable, small community, reading in his newspaper elaborate accounts of events he considered news because they happened a few weeks before, spending many an hour walking through the countryside, experiencing nature as something eternally changeless, and as so rich that years were needed to observe all its details. Today we live in an environment where skyscrapers shoot up and elevateds disappear overnight; where news comes like shock every few hours; where continually new news programs keep us from ever finding out the details of previous news; and where nature is something we drive past in our car, perceiving a few quickly changing flashes which turn the majesty of a mountain range into the impression of a motion picture. Might it not be that we do not build up experiences the way it was possible to do decades ago, and if so wouldn't that have bearing upon all our educational efforts? Studies of smaller American communities have shown that since the turn of the century there has been a steady decrease of efforts in adult education of the old style. Now radio with its Professor Quiz programs brings up new forms of mass education which, in their differences from the old reading and discussion circles, show a striking parallel to the development sketched here.[7]

Omitting a number of details and specifications, the "operation" basic to this approach consists of four steps.

1. A theory about the prevailing trends toward a "promotional culture" is introduced on the basis of general observations. Although efforts are

steadily being made to refine and corroborate this theory it is taken for granted prior to any special study.

2. A special study of any phenomenon consists in determining how it expresses these prevailing trends [introduced in (1)] and in turn contributes to reinforcing them.

3. The consequences of (2) in stamping human personalities in a modern, industrial society are brought to the foreground and scrutinized from the viewpoint of more or less explicit ideas of what endangers and what preserves the dignity, freedom and cultural values of human beings.

4. Remedial possibilities, if any, are considered.

Before we turn to the value which such an approach can have for the specific field of communications research, it is first necessary to meet an objection to the idea of critical research which may be raised against it on its own ground, to wit, that so much of its effort is spent on what might be called "showing up" things, rather than on fact-finding or constructive suggestions. It must be admitted that being constructive is a rather relative concept, and that the question of what are relevant facts cannot be decided only according to established procedures. The situation is somewhat similar to the wave of criticism which started with the reports of the Royal Commission in the British Parliament and with the English social literature of the Dickens type in the first half of the last century. Then, the task was to discover and to denounce the managerial cruelties of the new industrial system: child labor, slum conditions, and so on. Not that all these horrors have now been eliminated, but at least there is enough public consciousness of them so that whenever a student finds similar conditions, for instance among migrant workers or sharecroppers, some steps toward improvement are taken. The trend of public opinion and public administration is toward better social conditions. In cultural matters, a similar development has not yet taken place. The examples given above will be taken by many readers as rather insignificant in a field which is not of great practical importance. It might very well be, however, that we are all so busy finding our place in society according to established standards of success that nothing is more important at this moment than to remind ourselves of basic cultural values which are violated, just as it was of decisive historic importance a hundred years ago to remind the English middle classes that they were overlooking the sacrifices which the new strata of industrial laborers underwent when the modern industrial world was built. As Waller has pointed out,[8] the moral standards of tomorrow are due to the extreme sensitiveness of a small group of intellectual leaders of today. A few decades ago the artist who was destined to be the classic of the succeeding generation was left to starve in his own time. Today we are very eager not to overlook any growing talent, and we have fellowships and many other institutions which try to assist the growth of any seed of artistic development. Why should we not learn also to be more hospitable to criticism and find forms in which more patience can be exercised to wait and, in the end, to see what is constructive and what is not.[9]

And now for the specific contributions which the idea of critical research can make to the student who is engaged in the administrative research side of the problem. As long as there is so little experience in the actual cooperation of critical and administrative research, it is very difficult to be concrete. One way to put it is to point to the strong intellectual stimulation which derives from such joint efforts. There will be hardly a student in empirical research who does not sometimes feel a certain regret or impatience about the vast distance between problems of sampling and probable errors on the one hand, and the significant social problems of our times on the other. Some have hit upon the solution of making their social interests their private avocation, and keeping that separate from their research procedures, hoping that one day in the future the two will again merge. If it were possible in the terms of critical research to formulate an actual research operation which could be integrated with empirical work, the people involved, the problems treated and, in the end, the actual utility of the work would greatly profit.

Such a vitalization of research might well occur in a variety of forms which can only be exemplified and not stated in a systematic way. Quite likely, for instance, more attention will be given to problems of control. If we study the effects of communication, however fine methods we use, we will be able to study only the effects of radio programs or printed material that is actually being distributed. Critical research will be especially interested in such material as never gets access to the channels of mass communication: What ideas and what forms are killed before they ever reach the general public, whether because they would not be interesting enough for large groups, or because they would not pay sufficient returns on the necessary investment, or because no traditional forms of presentation are available?

Once a program is on the air or a magazine is printed, critical research is likely to look at the content in an original way. A number of examples are available in the field of musical programs.[10] Serious music on the radio is not unconditionally accepted as good. The promotion of special conductors, which exaggerates the existing differences and detracts from attention to more important aspects of music, is pointed to as another intrusion of an advertising mentality into an educational sphere. The ceaseless repetition of a comparatively small number of recognized "master works" is derived from the necessity to keep public service programs more in line with commercial fare of the radio. From such an analysis concrete suggestions evolve as to how music programs on the radio should be conducted to make them really serve a more widespread music appreciation. A discussion of the social significance and the probable effect of popular music, to which almost 50 per cent of all radio time is given, is also available and so far represents the most elaborate analysis of a type of mass communication from the point of view of critical social research.[11] Similar studies of printed matter can be made. For instance, what is the significance of the great vogue of biographies during the last decade? A study of their content shows that they all talk in terms of sweeping laws of society, or mankind or the human soul to which every individual is submitted and at the same time point up the unique greatness and importance of the one hero they are treating.[12] The success of this kind of literature among middle class readers is taken as an indication that many of them have lost their bearings in regard to their social problems. These biographies reflect a feeling that we are swept by waves of events over which the ordinary human being has no control and which call for leadership by people with super-human abilities. By such analysis anti-democratic implications are carved out in a literary phenomenon which otherwise would not attract the attention of the social scientist.

On the other end, upon studying the actual effects of communications, larger vistas are opened to someone whose observations are influenced by the critical attitude here discussed. To give only one example: We praise the contribution which radio makes by enlarging so greatly the world of each single individual, and undoubtedly the praise is deserved. But is the matter quite so simple? A farmer might be very well equipped to handle all the problems which his environment brings up, able to distinguish what makes sense and what doesn't, what he should look out for and what is unimportant. Now the radio brings in a new world new problems which don't necessarily grow out of the listener's own life. This world has a character of magic, where things happen and are invisible at the same time; many listeners have no experience of their own which would help them to appraise it. We know that sometimes has very disturbing effects, as witnessed by the attitude of women listeners to daytime serials,[13] by the attitude of millions of letter writers who try to interfere with the world of radio without really believing that their efforts will make any difference. It certainly should be worthwhile not to stop at such incidental observations but to see whether people's attitudes toward reality are not more profoundly changed by radio than we usually find with more superficial observations of their daily habits.

Columbia University's Office of Radio Research has cooperated in this issue of *Studies in Philosophy and Social Science* because it was felt that only a very catholic conception of the task of research can lead to valuable results. If there is any general rule of thumb in intellectual work it should be the advice never to pass over criticism without exhausting all the constructive possibilities which might be implied in another person's pint of view. The present remarks were written for the purpose of clarifying some of the difficulties which were experienced in actually formulating what critical social research consists in and seeing its best place in a scheme of general integration in all efforts. The writer, whose interests and occupational duties are in the field of administrative research, wanted to express his conviction that there is here a type of approach which, if it were included in the general stream of communications research, could contribute much in terms of challenging problems and new concepts useful in the interpretation of known, and in the search for new, data.

Notes

Editor's note: "Aliens" have refers to foreign nationals.

1. For a general orientation to the field see Douglas Waples, *What Reading Does to People*, University of Chicago Press, 1940 and Paul F. Lazarsfeld, *Radio and the Printed Page*, Duell, Sloan and Pearce, 1940. For more current and specific information the *Public Opinion Quarterly*, published by the Princeton University Press, is the best source of articles and bibliography.

2. Among the universities, the University of Chicago Library School and the University of Minnesota Journalism School are especially active in the field of communications research. Organizations doing similar work with foundation funds are the Adult Education Association, the American Film Center, the Columbia University Office of Radio Research, the Library of Congress and the Princeton Public Opinion Research Project. In the magazine field, *Life* and *McCall's* are currently publishing valuable information. Material on radio can best be obtained through the research directors of the Columbia Broadcasting System and the National Broadcasting Company.

3. Harold Lasswell, *Democracy Through Public Opinion*. George Banta Publishing Co. 1941.

4. There is a rather suggestive way to overcome the argument of the futility of empirical research. One might, for instance, tell such an opponent that according to studies which have been done on people who make up their minds during a political campaign as to how to vote are influenced by very different factors than those who have more permanent political affiliations. The opponent will find that immediately understandable and will say that he could have come to this conclusion by using good common sense. It so happens that the opposite is true and that it is possible to predict to a high degree the vote of originally undecided people by means of the same characteristics which describe people with actual party affiliations. There are many other examples by which common sense first can be led to conclusions which then are proved by actual data to be incorrect.

5. Cf. especially "Traditional and Cultural Theory" in the *Zeitschrift fur Socialforschung*, VI (1937), pp. 245–295; "Philosophy and Critical Theory" pp. 625–631. The examples used here in presenting the idea of critical social research were taken from studies done by Dr. T. W. Adorno.

6. It might help to clarify these ideas by comparing them briefly with other trends of thought, such as the consumer movement on the one hand and propaganda analysis on the other. The consumer movement is concerned with concrete wrongs in current advertising and might even denounce all advertising as economically wasteful. For the critical approach, business advertisement is only one of the many promotional forms by which present society is maintained and its cultural rather than its economic implications are discussed. A similar difference appears in comparison with propaganda analysis. The problem is not that people are misled in regard to certain isolated facts, but that they have less and less

opportunity to develop standards of judgment of their own because wherever they turn they are caught by some kind of promotion.

7. Cf. W. Benjamin's study on Baudelaire in this periodical, Vol. VIII (1939–40), p. 50 ff.

8. *The Family*, Dryden Press, 1931.

9. It is quite possible that the radio industry could lead in releasing some of the pressure which, at this time, keeps much social research in conventional forms and cuts it off from expanding into new fields. Already, in the field of politics, the radio industry has proved itself more neutral and more balanced than any other large business institution. The necessity of keeping in touch with the large masses of the population might also make them more amenable to trying methods of research even if, at first, they seem less innocuous. An honest analysis of program contents and program policies might be the first testing ground.

10. See T. W. Adorno, "On a Social Critique of Radio Music," on file at the Office of Radio Research, Columbia University.

11. See T. W. Adorno, "On Popular Music," *Studies in Philosophy and Social Sciences* IX, no. 1 (1941), pp. 17–48.

12. Such an analysis has been carried through by L. Lowenthal of the Institute of Social Research and is now being extended to the many biographies which are currently appearing in American magazines with mass circulation.

13. See the paper of Hertz Herzog, "On Borrowed Experience," *Studies in Philosophy and Social Sciences* IX, no. 1 (1941), pp. 65–95.

24

Researchers at the Federal Trade Commission—Peril and Promise

Ivan L. Preston
1980

Six years ago Wilkie and Gardner [39] assessed the role of marketing research at the Federal Trade Commission, following assignments there as full-time consultants on leave from their universities. This writer is now in that same position, and this article presents observations on that experience.

Wilkie and Gardner wrote of the "underutilization of the skills and insights of researchers in marketing and consumer behavior," and said that FTC policy-makers "appear to be reluctant to incorporate the findings of behavioral science and incapable of understanding inferential research as it bears on their problem." The article presented an agenda of topics which the writers described as mishandled by the FTC staff but capable of correction through researchers' inputs.

Those authors would probably conclude that much of their assessment still applies. It is my purpose, however, to comment on some areas in which FTC staffers have shed their reluctance and in fact have committed themselves thoroughly to research. For example, Brandt and Preston [2] showed that use of consumer surveys and expert testimony to identify deception increased significantly during 1970–73, and a less formal examination shows that the trend has not only continued since 1973 but now approaches maximum possible usage. The same is true in cases involving identification of unfairness and assessment of impact of required corrective messages, affirmative disclosures, and warnings. Generically, the research area involves the meaning of the message, not as literally stated but as conveyed to the mind of the consumer.

In years past the FTC was criticized for looking only at the ad and not at the consumer to identify deception [2]. This probably happened because FTC practice broke with tradition by searching not for deception but for a related characteristic called *capacity to deceive* [28, ch. 9]. Under prior law prosecutors had to prove both actual deception and injury, and also prove that the injury was due to the deception. The FTC, however, was intended by Congress to bring relief to millions of consumers at one time, and obviously there was no way it could prove these points for every case. A further intention was to stop most deception before it happened, which meant that what the commission sought to identify were situations where deception *might* occur.

One problem with using the concept of capacity to deceive was that while the term *deception* encourages one to examine the state of the consumer's mind, the term *capacity to deceive* suggests (however naively) that one need examine only the ad. Thus, the use of this concept, in combination with various legal considerations, led to an early habit of looking only at ads and not at consumers. Even today, the FTC's judges and commissioners assert their legal right to make judgments without consideration of outside evidence such as consumer surveys or testimony from consumer experts [2].

Nonetheless, the situation is much different today. FTC prosecutors as well as defending counsel are introducing research in great quantity, and the judges and commissioners are taking it into account. In the children's rulemaking procedure [7] the FTC staff commissioned nearly forty studies to be entered into the record, obviously expecting that the judge would examine more than just the ads. Clearly, the basis of decisions about advertising impact has been shifted to consumer research.

Bill Wilkie, the first professor to assist the prosecuting staff, gives much credit to Commissioner Mary Gardiner Jones for getting research introduced into advertising cases.[1] Jones first brought Murray Silverman, a Stanford Ph.D. under George Day, to the FTC as one of her assistants, and she and Silverman then arranged to have Wilkie, another of Day's former students, appointed to a staff position for a year in 1972.

Wilkie reports various false starts and uncertain directions as a result of the staff's not understanding his potential role. They did not expect a lot of money to be spent on research, because the totality of their previous research expenditures had been only $800 in partial support of a survey introduced in the Wonder Bread case [21].

Although that modest commitment was the one small step that began a now extensive process, the staff was not at first anxious to repeat it. I was hired in 1972 to testify as to advertising meanings on the basis of theory and expert opinion, and I suggested a survey for further support. Upon being told there was no money I did a cost-free survey using students as subjects, which added to the impact of my testimony on the judge [37, pp. 259–61 and 270–71]. Although the advertiser hired Raymond Bauer of Harvard to criticize my work, the opinion noted that Bauer had done no research of his own on the meaning [37, P. 261]. The judge used the survey as corroborating evidence for his finding of deception.

Wilkie, meanwhile, persuaded the prosecuting staff to make a commitment of $1200 for a survey that helped convince an advertiser to accept a consent settlement [16]. From that time on the research budget was established, and it has grown to approximately a million dollars in the 1979 fiscal year.[2]

Other factors also brought research into FTC cases. In the late 1960s the Educational Foundation of the American Association of Advertising Agencies (A.A.A.A.) had made a series of grants for advertising research. In 1971 the commission sponsored hearings on how advertising works [19] and placed all of that work, as well as that of many other researchers, on the record. Shortly thereafter the FTC staff began choosing academics from this list to appear as expert witnesses. It thus appears that the hearings helped establish both the existence and the respectability of advertising researchers.

Another factor which encouraged research was the campaign for corrective advertising. Although in most cases the commission need argue only a *capacity* to deceive, it can justify the corrective remedy only by proving that deception actually exists and lingers as a memory trace for a substantial time after a claim is discontinued [25]. This prompted the staff to rely heavily on research in the first two important corrective cases [15,21]. As noted earlier, the staff itself spent only $800 for new research, but subpoenaed the companies' own research and also used existing research and theory on learning and memory.

The two cases were failures in that corrective advertising was not obtained, but they were probably the most instrumental of any in establishing research as a basis for evidence of advertising impact. In subsequent cases and rulemaking actions the staff began commissioning much original research, and today it routinely inquires about research needs in the initiation phases of any prosecution.[3]

These developments explain why the FTC has hired more than a dozen professors as advisers for temporary periods. The list includes four—Wilkie, Gardner, Hal Kassarjian, and Keith Hunt—who have served as president of the Association for Consumer Research. In 1979 two professors worked with the prosecuting attorneys, another was a member of the Office of Policy Planning and Evaluation, and one was head of the new Office of Impact Evaluation in the Bureau of Consumer Protection. Numerous other professors and commercial researchers have been used on short-term contracts or consultancies by both the FTC and advertisers.

The bulk of this article will comment on certain results of this extensive utilization of researchers. Although the impact of the experience on the FTC and advertisers will be discussed, it is my personal opinion that the impact of the experience on the researchers is both more important and less thoroughly examined in previous discussions. Thus I will take up that topic fist.

Impact of the FTC and Advertisers on Researchers

To say that the FTC and advertisers impact on researchers is to say that the advocacy process impacts on them. I will attempt to show here that the advocacy role—which, as a participant in legal proceeding, one simply cannot avoid—affects the work of researchers in unfortunate ways. Reseachers are interpreting findings in the direction that favors their side to such an extent that they produce conclusions so contradictory as to be surely unacceptable to the research community as a whole.

The FTC judge in the children's hearings caught this tendency in the following exchange with an FTC witness [13, pp. 959–1036]. Judge Needelman, after listening to the researcher's conclusions, responded, "Perhaps this is academic to you researchers, but when you find something that agrees with you, you always report that, for example, '70 percent of the children studied agree with the hypothesis.' But when you find that only 30 percent of the children agree, you say, 'Well, that's still a very substantial number.' "

The researcher replied, "I always am explicit in presenting what percentage it is, so the reader can weigh the facts for himself." And the judge said, "Well, in your summaries you use more colorful language, as many researchers do." We might conclude that Judge Needel(man) is very aptly named!

I discussed that incident with the researcher, who responded that he feels it is his job not just to present percentages, but to draw conclusions about what they mean. One can agree with his position emotionally, because it is difficult to collect extensive data and then resist interpreting it. One may argue, in fact, that this has become the academic researcher's habit; it is done constantly in our published work. Editors, probably because their pages are brightened by such content, appear not to discourage the habit.

In court, however, the results are different. When that researcher reported his percentages he laid a foundation for doing so (a significant requirement in procedures involving expert witnesses[4]) by describing his personal qualifications and his specific research methodology, so that the percentages he reported reflected the expertise that qualified him to appear. When he tried to testify as to the implications of his data for social policy, however, he went beyond his expertise; that is, he had not laid a foundation which established him as an expert in what the findings mean to society. This is an example of the way researchers may talk out of turn in the courtroom, and one might suppose that the same overextension might be considered unacceptable in the journals as well.

There have been many instances in which researchers on the two sides have drawn models of the consumer that are so different as to suggest they are consumers from different planets. FTC witnesses in the children's rulemaking were absolutely positive that youngsters cannot understand that TV commercials have an underlying selling intent and are created by people who think of kids fundamentally as sales targets. Their opinion was based upon Piaget's theory of child development, which asserts that children below a certain age do not and cannot have certain cognitive abilities [13].

Industry-sponsored researchers were equally positive that children understand selling intent perfectly, and that many children who may not inherently have specific cognitive abilities can be trained to have them [13, p. 4]. There is a similar range of opinion about adults, with FTC witnesses in numerous cases saying in effect that the consumer is stupid and thus needs regulation, while industry witnesses say the consumer is smart and so does not [28, ch. 10].

When the topic of required disclosures arises, the parties change sides. FTC witnesses assert that consumers are smart enough to read disclosures and act appropriately. Industry witnesses conclude the consumer is too stupid to read any disclosures, or if he does he will get the meaning wrong [9, 10, 14].

Differences in stance are also applied to research methods. The head of a research firm testified on behalf of Anacin that tests of TV commercials conducted by ASI are not of value in determining what meanings people get from ads [11, pp. 5494–695]. He described many ways in which ASI's testing environment is not a true home viewing environment, but neglected to note that numerous corporations—among them, Anacin's manufacturer—nonetheless use ASI tests to show what their messages convey to the public. Since in this instance the data were to be used against it, the company chose to represent ASI tests as lacking in value.

Of course, there are reasonable disagreements about research methods, but members of the research community ought not to deny agreement that exists. The witness for one side, for example, says research must always use open-ended questions because structured questions are worthless, while the other side's witness says the opposite [37]. Might it be reasonable to conclude in such instances that someone is quite blatantly and knowingly ignoring various generally accepted understandings?

Until corrections can be applied, there will probably continue to be startling assertions made on the witness stand. One researcher attempted a defense of the .01 level of statistical significance, despite conventional acceptance of the .05 level [11, pp. 4766–851 and 5048–187]. He had wanted to test for differences, but for purposes of advocacy had not wanted to find any. On cross-examination he admitted that a number of the tests which were not significant at .01 were significant at .05.

The same researcher also did a separate set of tests that revealed almost no differences at .01 but also almost none at .05. For this set he declared he had tested at .05, which made it look as though he had tried as hard as possible to find significance but could not. When asked in court to explain why he had used different levels on different tests, he said he did so because his lawyer asked him to. So much for independent expertise!

In another case, a witness who had heard of "primacy" claimed not to be familiar with "recency" [4]. Surely the scholar who has heard of one of these has heard of the other, yet one's advocacy position may be strengthened by recognition of only one.

Another example is the way researchers have been arguing that disclosures of risk will or will not work in ads for over-the-counter antacids [14]. The FTC is considering certain diclosures that are already on product labels—for example, that a product should not be used without a doctor's permission by those who must have low-sodium diets. Industry witnesses stated that TV ads cannot communicate such a warning because it would make the ad's informational content too complex for the typical consumer to process [12, pp. 2624–722 and 2731–808]. TV, they said, following the analysis of Krugman [23, 24], is a low-involvement medium, meaning that people pay little attention and that TV therefore can dependably do nothing more than convey a brand name and some very simple attribute.

Arguably these are misstatements about low involvement. Krugman did not say a low-involvement medium cannot convey information, although it may do so less effectively. Nor did he say that all TV is automatically low-involvement, which the industry witnesses also implied. FTC attorneys might challenge such statements by asking about complex advertising claims which appear to have been successful on TV. McDonald's, for example, with its jingles such as "two all-beef patties, special sauce, lettuce . . . ," etc., have in fact turned complexity into a characteristic that is itself highly involving.

The problem of having opposing sides present opposite pictures of the consumer and of the research process was nicely distilled in a statement made by Fletcher Waller while representing General Mills in the children's rulemaking. Waller quoted what he called Gibson's Rule, which is that for every Ph.D. there is an equal and opposite Ph.D. [13, pp. 603–32].

An unfortunate aspect of this situation is that lawyers see it as acceptable, because it is the framework within which they customarily operate. In every case, there are witnesses lined up on opposite sides. For example, a newsmagazine's feature on psychiatry described how some psychiatrists in the Patty Hearst trial swore she was mentally ill while others said she wasn't [30]. That is not an unusual situation to a lawyer, and in fact they do it themselves. During the children's hearings, Judge Needelman stated to a witness who was an attorney that "every lawyer I meet, on both sides, seems to be absolutely sure about how the Supreme Court will eventually rule on the First Amendment aspects of the children's rule" [13, 4243–87].

Thus, to paraphrase Waller, for every lawyer there is an equal and opposite lawyer, but that does not mean the lawyer is a proper role model for the researcher. A lawyer's job is to take sides, and his defense of the indefensible is no mark of opprobrium; it is the way he is supposed to be. It is much less reasonable to argue that is the way researchers are supposed to be. The point of mentioning the Hearst trial is that the incident was damaging to psychiatry, and surely the same behavior will be equally damaging to advertising and marketing and communication researchers.

Some Beneficial Aspects for Researchers

Meanwhile, there is a way in which participation in legal cases appears beneficial to researchers. It is that the process of cross-examination is an excellent exercise in discipline, more severe than that represented by the criteria of journal editors or dissertation committee members. The latter typically want the candidate to succeed, whereas the cross-examiner wants him to lose. It means that research must in many ways be better for the courtroom.

Sometimes this process can be taken to an unfair extreme. When I first testified, the opposing counsel's opener was to request I be dismissed because my credentials were worthless, the research I'd done was "replete with bias," and I simply had no redeeming social value applicable to the case that he could ascertain [38]. This approach is no longer taken, because the existence of communication researchers has since been granted judicial recognition many times over. An approach that remains popular, however, is to charge that research that isn't perfect (and it never is, after all) must therefore be utterly worthless.

A sample, for instance, because it is not a random selection of the U.S. public, may be represented as not being projectable *at all to* that public [38]. If the researcher has evidence of projectability he can present it and the judge may accept it, but the point is that such argument must be offered explicitly and must withstand scrutiny. In court there is no such thing as assuming that all present are friendly colleagues who will accept a variety of unstated assumptions.

Another aspect of discipline is that one side's research may be bested by that of the other side. In the hearings regarding proposed disclosures about protein supplements, the witness for one side was a researcher who had shown consumers various disclosure statements on cards to determine what meanings were conveyed. The other side's researcher had affixed such statements to bottles that protein supplements actually come in. The latter was judged a superior method, with greater external validity, and more true to life than use of the cards [6; 9, pp. 16–17 and 127–28].

A thesis or journal article will not typically face head-to-head competition that permits only one winner, but that is what happened in the protein supplement rulemaking. Litigation is a stiff level of competition, and it should have a good impact on the quality of research.

Impact of Research on the FTC and Advertisers

On this topic one might first observe that research is an improvement on intuition for getting at the truth. This topic, however, has been discussed before [2], and therefore I would like to concentrate on an aspect of researchers' impact that has not been as closely examined.

The point is that research is essentially pro-FTC, or more broadly, proregulation, proconsumerist. The reason is that research tends to reveal the limitations of the consumer. It shows the extent to which the consumer fails to meet the traditional description of the rational human who has unlimited intellectual and cognitive powers, who always considers all possible information, and who therefore always makes the decision most to his benefit. The failure of the typical consumer to match such a standard provides the rationale for regulation by encouraging the conclusion that many consumers, if left alone, will make decisions that are less than the most beneficial. That is the sense in which we can argue that research is proregulation.

As a person who has exhibited some sympathy toward consumerist and regulatory positions [28], I have performed some introspection in asking myself: What does it mean to me to say I am proregulation? The answer is not that I prefer one group of people or one set of goals over another, but rather that my orientation is simply data-based. It is not ideological; it is simply a research position. Or, put another way, my ideology is that of data.

Such an orientation implies preference for the side supported by the data, be it pro- or antiregulation. This usually means, as observed earlier, a preference for a proregulation position, but there are important exceptions. The outstanding example of data which oppose regulation probably occurred when the FTC was considering outlawing in children's ads the emphasis on premium offers such as the toys that come in cereal boxes [5]. The proposed theory was that kids' interest in the premium would distract them from attention to the product, so that the purchasing influence exercised on parents would lack attention to more central attributes.

Amid these deliberations a study appeared that simply found otherwise [35]. Commercials shown to children were varied so that the premium was featured for ten, fifteen, or twenty of the total thirty seconds. Although the longer presentations interfered with learning about the product, kids who saw the ten-second treatment learned more about it than controls who saw commercials which made no mention of the premium. The premium may have added to the child's motivation to learn about the product. The FTC halted its investigation and issued no rule.

A person committed to data can have no choice but to agree, and if the data always supported industry in that way I would have to be listed as a strong proindustry proponent. But the data typically are *not* that way. See, for example, the FTC's attacks in the 1970s on advertising implications that had not previously been seen as content conveyed to consumers [27]. When I say I am proregulation, therefore, I am simply observing that the picture given of the consumer by research is in my opinion closer to what the FTC says than to what industry says.

This opinion will not go unchallenged, but can rightfully be countered not by the lobbying skills or volume of press releases utilized by industry but only by professional assessments from qualified experts in consumer behavior. Representatives of industry often offer assessments that are not professional, as when a distinguished advertising leader visted the FTC and declared that the American consumer is "the smartest person in the world," and so not in need of government regulatioon [18]. How many times have we heard that claim in advertisers' speeches and writings, and how late it is, in 1980, to be ignoring the facts that refute such a claim.

Although it is now obvious that research may be used against industry, there was a considerable period during which neither industry nor the FTC apparently was aware of that potential. At least one of the research projects sponsored by the A.A.A.A. a decade ago [29] was eventually used against industry in FTC proceedings [37, p. 9].

Nor did the FTC at first recognize the possibilities. When research was first proposed, the prevailing view of commission lawyers was that industry would devote so much more funding than the FTC could muster that the commission would be foolish to conduct its cases on such a basis.[5] Several years passed before they realized that research—in many cases the advertisers' *own* research [e.g., 17, 21]—would primarily favor their position, despite the differential in funding ability.

Today it is evident that the impact of research represents a tough problem for industry. Advertisers may often wish to keep research hidden from view, but the task is difficult in view of FTC subpoena powers that can empty out all the file drawers on Madison Avenue. A solution might be to use research and destroy it immediately, and in fact such a suggestion has been made by Joseph Smith of the Oxtoby-Smith research firm [36].

Smith's remark concerned the verbatim statements collected from subjects about what messages they see in ads. Such verbatims are often found by the FTC to be evidence of deceptive content. What Smith said was that in the future the lifespan of a verbatim was going to be about that of a butterfly in spring; when the FTC came to look, the cupboard would be bare. The remark was undoubtedly made in jest, because researchers probably realize that the existence of a verbatim gap could produce the same impact that a well-known tape gap did. The comment illustrates industry's dilemma, however, in recognizing that research is needed yet can be damaging.

Expectations and Recommendations

This article will conclude with a look at the future, to see what further developments are likely and what steps researchers might take to combat the problems discussed.

Impact of FTC and Advertisers on Researchers

Although desiring an end to tendencies to let advocacy interfere with truth, we should first acknowledge that conflicting views are not always inappropriate. For example, it is arguable that the positions of those who support or refute Piaget are equally valid given today's knowledge of child development, so that early resolution cannot reasonably be demanded. Therefore, we cannot expect full elimination of the "equal and opposite Ph.D." problem, but we can certainly recommend elimination of the many conflicts in which opposing positions are *not* equally valid.

Researchers' professional organizations may be the best vehicles for urging achievement of consensus. Such organizations might conduct debates about what positions to advocate on given topics, then urge members to honor these positions. There are problems with this proposal, of course, including the probability that the organizations cannot exert levels of persuasion or sanctions sufficient to control all of their members, not to mention nonmembers.

Alternatively, changes might be achieved in FTC procedures. One apparent possibility is that a judge might say, "We are not going to have research studies with opposite results in this case. You attorneys must get both sides together, and I will hold you all in contempt unless you develop in thirty days' time one research study you both can accept. That study will be done, and the losing side will not be heard to speak of bias and invalidity."

Probably there is not much hope for such a plan. Conceivably it would produce some Myron Farbers of the research world who would rather go to jail. Further, procedural rules give an advertiser many rights under due process to conduct his defense as he chooses, so that the judge could not stop him from presenting unilaterally conducted research.[6] The chance remains that a judge might persuade parties to cooperate voluntarily, and in fact Wilkie and Hunt once successfully urged such cooperation [16].

It is also conceivable that the FTC might ask its in-house research consultants to assist in issuing advisory guides that approve or disapprove various practices, in hopes of prompting parties to cease disputing these matters. Again, the success of such a plan would depend on the willingness of participants to accept these guides voluntarily.

Probably the best hope for resolution lies in the underlying theory of the advocacy process itself, which holds that the clash of conflicting ideas will lead ultimately to the truth. The word "ultimately" is the key consideration; it means that the process may take a long time. In the short run the lawyers may be badly befuddled, as with the issue of low involvement, because of their lack of familiarity with relevant research.

Yet FTC practice virtually guarantees that such topics will return in subsequent cases, giving the parties a chance to recoup their losses. Typically a lawyer wins a position that lacks merit only because the opposing lawyer fails to reveal properly the merits of his own side. When this failure is corrected, later cases will result in opposite decisions; an excellent example is FTC's success in winning corrective advertising in the Listerine case after a series of prior failures [25].

Of course, the resolution of old conflicts will probably be accompanied by the introduction of new ones. Therefore we cannot predict the end of the types of problems discussed here; we can only recommend steps that may shorten the time required to resolve them.

Impact of Researchers on FTC and Advertisers

Because the impact of research is generally proregulatory, it is surprising that there has been no concerted attempt by industry to reverse or at least dilute such results. There could, for example, be a systematic effort to research the ways in which consumers often do respond rationally, but industry has not yet attempted to make this case.

Industry witnesses in the children's rulemaking hearings [13] have urged that education rather than regulation will solve the problems. There is probably much accuracy in the position, but unless it is researched it must remain an empty claim.

It appears that the advertising industry has not used research adequately to make the points that industry can legitimately make. This is strange when one assumes that industry has far more resources available for the job. Hugstad [20] argued that money will mean victory, but the record of the 1970s suggests that in some cases money could not overcome a superior debating position (as when a company's own research was used against it) and that in other cases the money simply was not spent.

Industry's unfortunate relationship to research is accentuated by the possibility that the FTC may eventually use research to forge various advanced regulatory positions. It might, for example, get into research on puffery claims [26, 32, 33], on claims involving social-psychological or emotional issues [31, 34], or on claims involving pictorial images and other nonverbal messages [1, 22, 38]. To examine these things is to examine what ads imply rather than what they literally state. Although the FTC has attacked many sorts of implications already [27], it has not yet done much work in these areas.

What has kept the commission from attacking puffery is undoubtedly institutional inertia [28] rather than an inability to research what it implies. One can research puffery simply by asking people what a particular claim means and determining whether it implies any factual content. The same is true for emotional claims.

FTC personnel have been heard to say that nonverbal claims cannot be researched.[7] This feeling probably stems from the lawyer's habit of dealing so exclusively in words that pictures may seem out of reach [22]. However, if researchers can use Rorschach inkblot testing, in which a subject reports in words what an abstract image has conveyed, the same can be done with advertisements. Were each consumer to report different words, no conclusion could be drawn. It is arguable, however, that a substantial number of consumers will often agree on the meaning conveyed by nonverbal components of an ad.

To discuss the above types of claims, which comprise virtually the entirety of that advertising which is not yet regulated, is not to imply that all such claims will eventually be found deceptive. It is only to suggest that many of them have not been researched, and that if in the future they are researched, whatever level of deception they convey will then be revealed. This writer's personal feeling is that such an extension of research is likely to reveal many types of deception that the FTC hasn't yet discovered.

This prediction is made because the commission, despite its immense commitment in the 1970s to the above-mentioned types of research, is still far from assimilating the full field of consumer behavior [39]. One may expect that persons such as lawyers, who are highly educated but have not studied research on behavior, are more likely to perceive the typical consumer in terms of what they themselves would do. They would thus conclude that if they themselves disbelieved a claim and were thereby not deceived, the public would do the same and no regulation would be needed.

Those who have studied research on behavior are more likely to attribute to the consumer various instances of cognitive failure, such as the tendency to succumb to wishful thinking or to the power of suggestion. The FTC's grasp of the power of suggestion is, to date, only superficial. This is not to suggest that all suggestion is bad or that the process of persuasion is immoral per se. It is only to observe that from a standpoint of research-based knowledge of human beings, there is much that has not yet been incorporated into the body of facts that the FTC recognizes.

A reasonable prediction, then, is that although industry might do much to counteract the current impact of advertising research, it is likely that research in the future will continue to lend support primarily to the regulatory position.

Notes

1. William L. Wilkie 1979, personal communication.
2. Kenneth Bernhardt 1979, personal communication.
3. Observations made to me by FTC staffers explain how to choose between academic and commercial researchers. Commercial firms are preferable when one

knows exactly what one wants done because they will proceed with the task as requested, whereas professors typically want to change a study to fit their own agenda. However, when original thinking is needed to define the task, an academic researcher is often a better choice, because the commercial firms find that the time spent in analysis is bad for profits. Such firms prefer to offer a standard method which can be used by every client, in order to keep thinking time down and profits up.

4. Wallace Snyder 1979, personal communication.

5. Ibid.

6. Ibid.

7. Ibid.

References

1. Bonoma, Thomas V. and Felder, Leonard C. "Nonverbal Communication in Marketing: Toward a Communicational Analysis." *Journal of Marketing Research*, 14 (May 1977): 169–80.

2. Brandt, Michael T. and Preston, Ivan L. "The Federal Trade Commission's Use of Evidence to Determine Deception." *Journal of Marketing 41* (Jan. 1977): 54–62.

3. Chestnut, Robert W. "Television Advertising and 'Young' Children: Piaget Reconsidered." In *Current Issues and Research in Advertising, 1979*, edited by James H. Leigh and Claude R. Martin, Jr., pp. 5–15. Ann Arbor: The University of Michigan, Graduate School of Business Administration, 1979.

4. Federal Trade. Commission. Transcript of Testimony, Hearing on ITT Continental Baking Co., Dkt. 8860, Washington, D.C. (July 1972): 2612–18.

5. ———. "Proposed Trade Regulation Rule Regarding Premiums in Children's Advertising." *Federal Register*, 39, 134 (July 11, 1974): 25505–10.

6. ———. Transcript of Testimony, Hearing on Proposed Trade Regulation Rule Regarding Advertising and Labeling of Protein Supplements. 16 *Code of Federal Regulations* Part 454, Pub. Rec. No. 215–49, Washington, D.C., 1976: 2751–887, 3100–17.

7. ———. "Proposed Trade Regulation Rule on Children's Television Advertising, Pub. Rec. No. 215-60." *Federal Register 43* (1978): 17967.

8. ———. Report of the Presiding Officer on Proposed Trade Regulation Rule on Food Advertising. 16 *Code of Federal Regulations* Part 437, Pub. Rec. No. 215–40 (Feb. 1978): 69–72.

9. ———. Report of the Presiding Officer on Proposed Trade Regulation Rule Rule Regarding Advertising and Labeling of Protein Supplements. 16 *Code of Federal Regulations* Part 454, Pub. Rec. No. 215–49 (June. 1978).

10. ———. Report of the Presiding officer on Proposed Trade Regulation Rule on Advertising for Over-the-Counter Drugs. 16 *Code of Federal Regulations* Part 450, Pub. Rec. No. 215–51 (Oct. 1978).

11. ———. Transcript of Testimony, Hearing on American Home Products. Dkt. 8918, Washington, D.C. (Feb. 1978).

12. ———. Transcript of Testimony, Rulemaking Hearing on Proposed Trade Regulation Rule on Advertising for Over-the-Counter Antacids. 16 *Code of Federal Regulations* Part 451, Pub. Rec. No. 215–5, Washington, D.C. (Jan. 1979).

13. ———. Transcript of Testimony. Rulemaking Hearing on Proposed Trade Regulation Rule on Children's Television Advertising. 16 *Code of Federal Regulations* Part 461, Pub. Rec. No. 215–56 (Nov. 1979).

14. ———. Report of the Presiding Officer on Proposed Trade Regulation Rule on Advertising for Over-the-Counter Antacids. 16 *Code of Federal Regulations* Part 451, Pub. Rec. No. 215–56 (Nov. 1979).

15. Firestone Tire, litigated order, 81 *FTC Decisions* 398 (1972).

16. Ford Motor, consent order, 84 *FTC Decisions* 729 (1974).

17. Ford Motor, partial order and remand, 87 *FTC Decisions* 756 (1976).

18. Hesse, William R. (Exec. Vice Pres., American Assn. Of Advertising Agencies). Untitled comments to FTC staff, Washington, D.C. (Apr. 30, 1979).

19. Howard, John A., and Hulbert, James. *Advertising and the Public Interest.* Chicago: Crain Communications, 1973.

20. Hugstad, Paul. "Barriers to Further Utilization of Advertising and Marketing Research in Litigation and Public Policy Formation." In *Current Issues and Research in Advertising, 1979*, edited by James H. Keigh and Claude R. Martin, Jr., pp. 65–71. Ann Arbor: The University of Michigan, Graduate School of Business Administration, 1979.

21. ITT Continental Baking, litigated order, 83 *FTC Decisions* 865 (1973).

22. Kramer, Albert. "Marconian Problems, Gutenbergian Remedies: Evaluating the Multiple-Sensory Experience Ad on the Double-Spaced Typewritten Page." *Federal Communications Law Journal* 30 (1977): 35–45.

23. Krugman, Herbert E. "The Impact of Television Advertising: Learning Without Involvement." *Public Opinion Quarterly*, 29 (Fall 1965): 348–56.

24. ———. "The measurement of Advertising Involvement." *Public Opinion Quarterly*, 30 (Winter 1966–67): 583–96.

25. Maddox, Lynda M. and Zanot, Eric J. "Corrective Advertising: Review and Prognosis." In *Current Issues and Research in Advertising 1979*, edited by James H. Leigh and Claude R. Martin, Jr., pp. 53–63. Ann Arbor: The University of Michigan, Graduate School of Business Administration, 1979.

26. Oliver, Richard L. "An Interpretation of the Attitudinal and Behavioral Effects of Puffery." *Journal of Consumer Affairs* 13 (Summer 1979): 8–27.

27. Preston, Ivan L. "The FTC's Handling of Puffery and Other Selling Claims Made 'By Implication.'" *Journal of Business Research*, 5 (June 1977): 155–81.

28. ———. *The Great American Blow-Up: Puffery in Advertising and Selling.* Madison: University of Wisconsin Press, 1975.

29. ———, and Scharbach, Steven E. "Advertising: More than Meets the Eye?" *Journal of Advertising Research*, 11 (June 1971): 19–24.

30. "Psychiatry on the Couch." *Time*, Apr. 2, 1979, pp. 74–77.

31. Reed, O. Lee, Jr., and Coalson, John L., Jr. "Eighteenth-Century Legal Doctrine Meets Twentieth-Century Marketing Techniques: FTC Regulation of Emotionally Conditioning Advertising." *Georgia Law Review*, 11 (Summer 1977): 733–82.

32. Shimp, Terence A. "Do Incomplete Comparisons Mislead?" *Journal of Advertising Research*, 1 (Dec. 1978): 21–27.

33. ———. "Evaluative Verbal Content in Advertising: A Review and Critical Analysis." In *Information Processing Research in Advertising*, edited by Richard A. Harris, forthcoming.

34. ———. "Social Psychological (Mis) Representations in Television Advertising." *Journal of Consumer Affairs*, 13 (Summer 1979): 28–40.

35. ———; Dyer, Robert F. and Divita, Salvatore F. "An Experimental Test of the Harmful Effects of Premium-Oriented Commercials on Children." *Journal of Consumer Research*, 3 (June 1976): 1–11.

36. Smith, Joseph G. "Should We Measure Involuntary Responses?" *Journal of Advertising Research*, 19 (Oct. 1979): 35–39.

37. Sun Oil, litigated order, 84 *FTC Decisions* 247 (1974).

38. Westen, Tracy. "Malfunction in the Marketplace—Advertising 'Versus' Consumer Information." Address at AMA Marketing Educators' Conference, Chicago, Aug. 7, 1978.

39. Wilkie, William L., and Gardner, David M. "The Role of Marketing Research in Public Policy Decision Making." *Journal of Marketing*, 38 (Jan. 1974): 38–47.

25

"Fraught with Such Great Possibilities": The Historical Relationship of Communication Research to Mass Media Regulation

Byron Reeves and James L. Baughman
1983

Social research in the twentieth century has had, at best, an indirect relationship to government policies toward mass communication. Although recent considerations of the FCC, FTC, and Congress have included testimony from selected academics, the crucial political decisions have largely ignored mass communication scholarship. Further, government has been more likely to influence research than research to shape policy. Therefore, the most interesting questions about the interaction of research and policy do not concern the *nature* of, but rather the *constraints*, on the relationship.

The discussion of these constraints revolves around three separate sections: (1) the research on the uses and effects of mass communication; (2) the actors and institutions in the policy-making process; and (3) characteristics of the interaction between research and policy that have and may continue to preclude a productive relationship.

Research on Media Uses and Effects

One of the simplest explanations for the lack of interaction between policy-makers and researchers is that one or both parties were non-existent or inactive, especially during the first half of this century. This explanation would be especially tempting to attribute to mass media researchers. How could research possibly affect policy if appropriate studies did not exist? Many current reviews of effects research support this conclusion by concentrating only on the last fifteen years of research, biasing reviews in favor of television studies, and acknowledging only a handful of important works conducted between the two world wars and before the introduction of television (Cf. Roberts and Bachen, 1972; McLeod and Reeves, 1980; Chaffee, 1977).

Although no comprehensive history of mass communication research has been written, many abbreviated descriptions of the history at least allude to social scientists' studies of media uses and effects through the century's first eight decades. These descriptions suggest that ideas about media impact have progressed from direct (or one-step) effects to indirect (or multi-step) effects. This change was preceded by a "libertarian" view of media and superseded by recent "middle-ground" theories. Authors have different labels for the periods of research, though the specific activities that the terms describe are essentially identical.[1] In fact, agreement about this history is uncanny given the debate that usually governs historical studies about the social sciences. Even scholars who are critical of the "administrative" tone of American media research acknowledge this shift, though they view it less as a theoretical development than as an attempt to direct research toward the interests of media practitioners and to promote the ideology of social democracy (Gitlin, 1981).

Briefly, the conventional history of mass communication research goes as follows: At the turn of the century, libertarianism—here meaning that society was best served by many voices—was firmly in place as an explanation of how people should use information. To participate effectively in the marketplace of ideas, educated individuals must have access to competing ideas. Innate human reason and rationality should result in correct and moral decisions based on uncensored information.[2] But with the great propaganda campaigns associated with World War I which most observers judged highly effective, Harold Lasswell, a professor of political science at the University of Chicago, suggested that people could be easy targets for propaganda. Lasswell (1935) labeled his idea the "hypodermic needle model" of media effects because he assumed that messages have a direct and undifferentiated impact on individuals.[3]

In the 1940s, Lasswell's idea received three comprehensive and sophisticated empirical tests conducted by the sociologist Paul Lazarsfeld and others working in the Bureau of Applied Social Research at Columbia University.[4] These studies questioned the ability of media to effect directly important political decisions and, indeed, found that media had limited persuasive power. What little influence existed, operated through opinion leaders who in turn were able to influence others. This idea about indirect effects was crystallized in the "two-step flow" theory, and it was applied to other areas of media content, most notably fashion, other product choices, and movie attendance (Katz and Lazarsfeld, 1955). This school of inquiry signified a trend toward practical and applied communication research which looked at immediate short-term effects of messages for the benefit of communication administrators in advertising (Martineau, 1957), public relations (Davis and Baran, 1981), and government information campaigns during wartime (Hovland et al., 1940).

The most recent period of media effects research has produced "middle-range" ideas about influence. Joseph Klapper wrote in 1960 that media indirectly effect people through reinforcement rather than change. Media were seen as contributory rather than necessary causes and almost never as necessary and sufficient for audience effects. Researchers began concentrating on the contingent conditions for media effects and variables intervening between media exposure and response (McLeod and Reeves, 1980). Others parted from the notion of passive audiences in favor of ideas about audiences as active participants in the communication process.[5] Interest grew in what people *do with* media rather than with what media *do to* people.[6]

Authors of studies from the most recent era tend to dismiss their predecessors' labors in the 1920s and 1930s with cursory references to "hypodermic needle" models, Lasswell's writing on wartime propaganda, and the reaction of radio listeners in 1938 to the broadcast of Orson Welles' *Invasion from Mars* (Cantril, 1940). A closer look at this period of research shows that there was substantially more policy-relevant research in mass communication than is acknowledged today. Further, those participating in the studies did so with the expectation that their work would help shape a better society, although not always through government action. The cities of Portland, Chicago, and Toledo had by 1920 conducted empirical research on the effects of film on children for the purpose of writing city ordinances regulating local movie houses (Phelan, 1919). Respected academics of the time, including several from the "Chicago school" of sociology conducted studies that explored the negative consequences of film on children. Their conclusions were often voiced as criticism of the film industry, as recommendations for parents, or as prescriptions for government intervention.[7]

The Payne Fund Studies reported in 1932 constitute the most neglected research on film effects.[8] Even by current standards of theory and method, the six volumes of research—conducted by some of the most prominent psychologists, sociologists, and educators of the time—represented a detailed look at the effects of film content on such diverse reactions as sleep patterns, knowledge about foreign cultures, attitudes about violence, and delinquent behavior. Some of the major conclusions of the reports—for example, that the same message would affect children differently depending on the child's age, sex, predispositions, perceptions, and parental influence—are identical to summaries of the most recent studies on children and television (Charters, 1933). Although initiated by critics of the movie industry to lend support for possible regulatory action, the studies were conducted with an air of scientific detachment reminiscent of the 1972 Surgeon General's Report, in which researchers were forbidden to discuss policy in their individual reports. Despite a disinterested tone, summaries of the Payne research were policy-oriented. W. Charters, chairman of the Payne Fund research committee, thought that "the public at present must take, within the limits of censorship, whatever pictures are made" (Charters, 1933, p. 63). He added, however, that the research demonstrated that producers should be expected "to experiment, to invent, to try out, to eliminate, to press persistently until they produce proper solutions to the problem," and that "a research organization is clearly indicated" (Charters, 1933, p. 63). Interestingly, criticism of the Payne Fund studies by Raymond Moley, published five years after the report was released, mentioned the same weaknesses applied to current effects research; that is, that causality is difficult to document, nonmedia information sources (e.g., parents, peers, personal experience) are difficult to eliminate as contributors to the effects, and the conclusions often depend on questionable survey methods (Moley, 1938).

The research on public opinion, propaganda, and promotional campaigns was similarly substantial in this period, both in theory and quantity. Although some recent reviews of this "direct effects" research characterize the logic of the era as heavily shaped by general learning theory and simple stimulus-response models in behaviorist psychology, it is in fact hard to find any evidence that this was the case (Rowland, 1982). Lasswell, who first used the term "hypodermic needle," did assume that messages would have an undifferentiated impact on individuals; however, he based his ideas on Freudian theory about primitive and irrational forces that control the unconscious mind (Lasswell, 1935). He suggested that individuals would be easy targets for propaganda because they would consequently be incapable of resistance or counterargument. By 1932, L. L. Thurston had had a significant effect on the social sciences by popularizing the concept of attitude and introducing a measurement procedure to assess attitudes in a number of different contexts, including studies about newspaper readership (Nafziger, 1930; Gallup, 1930), the effects of promotional campaigns, and the impact of the press on public opinion (Droba, 1931; Annis and Meier, 1934). Thurston was also a contributor to the Payne Fund research and was responsible for many of the survey questionnaires designed to test the influence of film. Many of the other Payne Fund studies also relied on cognitive concepts taken from developmental psychology and, in this sense, these studies resemble the research of today.[9]

All told, the research of this era was also impressive in quantity. In 1931, the Social Science Research Council appointed a Committee on Pressure Groups and Propaganda to compile an annotated bibliography on the "scientific study of propaganda" (Lasswell et al., 1935). The committee collected hundreds of citations and organized them, as perhaps we would today, according to literature on sources of information (e.g., national government, political parties, professional groups, labor groups), channels of information (e.g., educational systems, moving pictures, newspapers, radio, telegraph, books, periodicals), the messages or symbols used (symbols about people, groups, policies, institutions), and the responses to propaganda (e.g., civic activity, health habits, temperance and prohibition, ideas about policies of the government). The introduction to the collection, written by Lasswell, detailed current thinking on theories of propaganda and public opinion; the last section cited methodological advances in the measurement of attitudes and opinions. It is also quite obvious from this collection that social science was expected to serve policy needs. The study of propaganda and the practices of propagandists went one with the other (Lasswell, 1935).

The bulk of research conducted on media effects in the interwar years suggests that current scholars should not be smug either about their field's methodological and theoretical advances or policy implications for governmental regulation. Many of the authors who discuss the history of media research do so for the purpose of showing how much it has progressed. In other words, today's scholars supposedly present more valid conclusions about media effects. Yet this is a misleading summary. The validity of research then—as now—varied. Not only was more research conducted in the 1920s and 1930s than has been acknowledged of late, but the investigators proved in retrospect to be strikingly sophisticated in their labors and social purpose. The authors were not a small band of brothers, offering simple behavioralistic ideas about the process of effects. Some even had well-developed formulations which they expected to be utilized for social betterment (especially if one construed the improvement of broadcasting and government propaganda, rather than mass media regulation per se, as a positive social end).

During the "indirect effects" era of research, attention was concentrated on the practices and needs of industry, largely through the model provided by Lazarsfeld's Bureau of Applied Social Research and the connection with Frank Stanton at CBS. It is clear that Lazarsfeld and others expected their data to have practical applications. And there were major links to practice, as scholars served the growing demands of media administrators for counsel on political and advertising campaigns, and analyses of audience size, demographics, and interests (Lazarsfeld, 1941). Several authors suggest that it was at this point that American researchers abandoned the critical perspectives advocated by European scholars and instead directed research towards the needs of media corporations (Gitlin, 1981; Davis and Baran, 1981).

Misconceptions about this era of research—from 1940 until the introduction of television—could lead to the erroneous conclusion that not much evidence was available for application to policy. Although most of this era's work was hardly hostile to the private sector, there were notable exceptions, even in the volumes, *Radio Research* and *Communications*

Research, edited by Lazarsfeld and Stanton. This other research not only went beyond ideas about a two-step flow, but did not support an overall limited-effects conclusion. For example, in the first volume of the series, Frederick Meine found a direct empirical relationship between children's consumption of newspaper and radio news, and knowledge about current affairs, even controlling for age, sex, and intelligence (Meine, 1941). William Robinson discovered that brand consciousness was greater for radio families and that radio affected even church attendance (Robinson, 1941). The latter two volumes included discussions of song hits shaping sales, wartime propaganda affecting information dissemination and cultural understanding (Peatman, 1944; Siepmann, 1944), and daytime radio serials affecting the social milieu of men and women audiences (Kaufman, 1944).

Other articles in the Lazarsfeld-Stanton volumes warrant a second look, including ones by Rudolf Arnheim (1944) and Herta Herzog (1944) on daytime radio serials and a study by Katherine Wolf and Marjorie Fiske (1949) on children and comics. These studies offer a preview to many of the theoretical concepts discussed as "new" ideas in later television research. The effects of radio serials were thought to depend on "listener gratifications" and the need for vicarious "social participation" (Herzog, 1944, pp. 7, 23). Children received certain "gratifications" from comics as they progressed through three qualitatively different "stages" of sophistication in their ability to read and understand the comics (Wolf and Fiske, 1944, p. 7). "Parental mediation" of media experiences was advocated by almost all mothers, yet few played any role in prohibition (Wolf and Fiske, 1944, p. 37). It is especially worth noting that descriptions of the effects process in these studies were largely psychological. Unlike the sociological basis of ideas about opinion leaders and the multiple steps involved in information dissemination, these studies talked about "psychological identification" with the characters on radio and the psychological differences in children's needs and ability to process information in comics (Arnheim, 1944, pp. 55–57). All told, although most research in the 1940s aided mass communication's administrators, studies did exist that *could* have been used to justify the intervention of mass communication's regulators, especially in relation to child audiences.

With the introduction of television in the 1950s, the amount of media research virtually exploded. Departments of communication formed where none had previously existed, schools of journalism and departments of speech and rhetoric committed themselves to interdisciplinary social research on mass communication, and several important research institutes were either started or grew substantially.[10] New journals that focused on media research (e.g., *Journal of Broadcasting, Journal of Communication*) appeared and research activities in academic associations increased and divisions within the associations became committed sponsors of empirical mass communication research (McLeod and Reeves, 1980, pp. 37–38, 39).

During the 1950s and early 60s, scholars were actively writing definitions of communication and mass communication, proposing models of the communication process, and defending communication research as a behavioral discipline (Shannon and Weaver, 1949; Westley and MacLean, 1957; Berlo, 1960; Miller, 1966). Increasingly, researchers were educated in communication programs and accepted faculty positions in the same programs. Contributors to the research literature began to locate their work not in the traditional areas of psychology and sociology, but in the "new discipline" of communication research. Schramm's observation that communication research was "an oasis in the desert, where many trails cross, and many travelers pass but only a few tarry," was no longer true (Schramm, 1967; Paisley, 1972).

The potential applications of research to government policy offered further legitimization of the area. Although media researchers by this time had experience applying research to the needs of the media's managers, the prospect of participating in government regulation appeared even more hopeful. Robert Merton and Daniel Lerner concluded in 1951 that "the prestige of the social scientist, on a national scale, would seem to be diminished by affiliation with the business community." On the topic of government affiliation, however, they commented that "the distinctive reward of governmental service to the social scientist has been a sharp increase in his power" (Merton and Lerner, 1951).

Researchers have remained optimistic about the potential for their data to relate to policy. And an as yet unpublished analysis of all research done in mass communication reveals that a large number of studies conducted in the last twenty years mention the policies of FCC, FTC, congressional committees, or special considerations by the Surgeon General and presidential commissions (Wartella and Reeves, 1982). Others note possible action by citizens groups, parents, or media practitioners. A few reports actually use the policies, or anticipated policies, as starting points for the design of research; however, most reports relegate policy to the discussion sections of journal articles or to summary chapters in books. This is not to say, however, that researchers refer to specific bills in Congress or case numbers at the FTC or that political orientations are explicit. Jay Blumler noted in a comment about media research reported in an academic journal that "American material seemed virtually unclassifiable in such purposive terms: its social commitments and anchorages were not clearly manifest" (Blumler, 1978). The policy connections are often implicit: determined more obviously by looking at the nature of the questions addressed (and consequently those questions ignored) than by examining the specific links discussed in the reports. That the research is meant to be applied rather than basic, however, seems obvious.

Through all periods of research on the uses and effects of media, therefore, scholars actively studied questions that concerned the public, the communications industries, or government regulators and legislators, and the researchers expected that their efforts could in some form result in social change. They were not, in other words, writing only for themselves, their peers, or scholarly publications.

Regulation of Mass Communication

The preceding comments about studies of mass communication effects summarize thousands of citations generated by hundreds of researchers. Yet, until the 1970s, few regulators of the mass media bothered to integrate communication research into their policy-making deliberations. Although on the national, state, and local level from the beginning of the twentieth century, officials regulating society and business formulated policies with the help of social scientists, broadcasting's overseers were among the last to seek such guidance. Nor did a president see fit to name a communication scholar to one of the seven seats on the Federal Communications Commission.[11] While the FCC itself might ask an engineer or economist for an opinion, almost never did the agency solicit the views of those formally studying the effects of the industry the Commission had been empowered to regulate.

The nonutilization of communication research was ironic given the fate of other disciplines. At the beginning of the twentieth century, first-rank American universities abandoned a view of their knowledge and mission which was best characterized as insular. At such major private urban universities as Columbia and Chicago as well as at such land grant schools as Wisconsin, prominent professors revolted against a rigid and narrow "formalism" in social science and law that had denied the utility or value of knowledge to the state. Such scholars as Charles Van Hise at Wisconsin, John Dewey at Columbia and Charles Merriam at Chicago argued that academics aid in the rationalization and modernization of city, state and national government (White, 1949; Goldman, 1956; Furner, 1975; Karl, 1974).

One impetus for this view was the advent of new forms of urban governance and regulatory authority. During the Progressive Era (1901–14), many cities adopted city manager charters while states and the federal government formed bureaucracies to oversee large and complex industries. The academic "expert," Van Hise and others maintained, could serve these new bodies. And they did. On the state and national level, economists consulted with utility regulators, political scientists fought for nonelected city managers and school boards and other antidemocratic "reforms" and sociologists counseled those new agencies regulating the treatment of factory workers (LaFollette, 1912; McCarthy, 1912; Chambers, 1980; Landis, 1938; Skowronek, 1982).

Historians have only recently recognized that the activities of many academicians during the Progressive era seem less than democratic. Indeed, the university, prominent scholars now argue, was the ivy-covered instrument of a new middle class of professionals anxious to win power from politicians and corporations dominating the state and economy. Many of the "progressive" reforms revealed an antidemocratic, antipluralist bias. "Experts" in the academy and professions sought to oversee a more complex America, but often at the expense of the less educated, and, in many cases, foreign-born, Americans (Hays, 1957 and 1964; Thelen, 1976; Wiebe, 1967; Hobson, 1977).

During the First World War, the guardians of academic knowledge eagerly participated in selling at home and abroad America's role in the conflict. Historians described the past butchery of the Germany military while education professors sought to "Americanize" the newer immigrants. These efforts, eagerly sought by the Wilson Administration, only demonstrated how anxiously historians and others sought to display the "legitimacy" and new "outward look" of their disciplines (Vaughn, 1980; Blakey, 1970; Grattan, 1927; Gruber, 1975).

Academic expertise in government proved less commonplace after the war with the three Republican administrations that followed Wilson's presidency. Virtually none in the Harding and Coolidge cabinets could claim advanced degrees outside of law school. One exception was Secretary of Commerce Herbert Hoover, an engineering graduate of Stanford University. Hoover did solicit the views of experts, and once president in 1929, regularly consulted with academicians (Karl, 1969; President's Research Committee on Social Trends, 1933). Although prominent in radio regulation in the Twenties, Hoover did not, however, engage the new social scientists of the medium. Hoover's Commerce Department issued radio licenses until 1927. But when the secretary assembled several radio conferences beginning in 1922, he invited educators operating radio stations and studying radio physics, not those few examining the possible uses and effects of the medium (Hoover, 1950 and 1922; Herring, 1935).

Interestingly, as Congress determined the future of radio regulation between 1922 and 1927, individual congressmen drew upon a crude theory of communications' effects in creating the Federal Radio Commission (FRC). The Wilson administration's wartime propaganda, perhaps unfairly maligned, had left a bad taste in the mouths of many. Hoover suffered for this mood when he proposed that his department continue to be charged with radio regulation. Congress rebelled and in 1927 created the FRC, independent of him and the president. Several congressmen referred to wartime propaganda, and its supposed easy manipulation of the masses. No single official or administration, they contended, should have power over radio. Broadcast regulation, a Senate committee concluded in May, 1926, "is fraught with such great possibilities that it should not be entrusted to any one man, nor to any administrative department of the government" (U.S. Senate, 1926).[12]

Although modeled after other regulatory bodies that had been designed to rely on academic expertise, the Radio Commission and (after 1934) its successor agency, the FCC, concerned themselves largely with engineering expertise, not that work determining the propaganda potential of American radio. Indeed, the original Radio and Communications Commissioners included many with engineering degrees. Otherwise, former politicians and military men filled vacancies (Lichty, 1961; 1962).

This type of university or professional training related to the narrow mandate Congress gave the Radio and Communications Commissions. The crisis in American broadcasting in the middle 1920s involved interference between stations, not their effects on listeners. Advertising was sparse and political activities over the air infrequent. The problem had mainly been one of licensees broadcasting whenever or wherever (on the spectrum) their moods dictated, or in the cast of Aimee Semple McPherson, the evangelical, when or where God willed her station to operate. The FRC and FCC had to reckon with the then inherent limitations of radio physics to establish who should have a station (Hoover, 1952). The regulatory issue was a technical rather than a behavioral one.

The tendency to name engineers to the FRC and FCC continued into Roosevelt's presidency, even though the new president's appointments to other agencies and departments included an impressive army of economists and political scientists. The President himself consulted regularly with public opinion specialists. Journalists spoke of a "brain trust" at the White House. The New York *Times* commented in May 1933, "Our reigning professors of today are philosophers for whose conduct of public affairs Plato longed."[13]

Few of the bright young men and women drawn to the New Deal wanted to go to the FCC. Congress had invested the agency with the power of allocating frequencies but little else. Section 325 of the Communication Act forbade the censoring of programs. The Commission might insist on general and vague objectives for licensees, but until the 1940s, the broadcasting's overseers only acted against the most offensive operators (See *Columbia Law Review*, 1947; Rosenbloom, 1961; Cox,

1965. Cf. Brinton, 1962). A young Yale law school professor, William O. Douglas, went to the White House in 1939 fearing Roosevelt was about to ask him to chair the FCC, a position Douglas dreaded having to take. Happily for him then and his admirers later, FDR asked him to accept a Supreme Court nomination (Douglas, 1974; Roosevelt, 1938; McIntyre, 1937).

The FCC's rather drab reputation changed at the end of Roosevelt's second term, though academic expertise had little to do with the agency's new look. Again, a crude spectre of propaganda was raised, this time to justify regulating the then two dominant networks, Columbia Broadcasting System (CBS) and the National Broadcasting Company (NBC). FCC Chairman James Lawrence Fly sought to check the networks, who could dictate most of the programming decisions of hundreds of individual affiliate stations. Fly's arguments, however, were grounded not in the work of the social sciences, but the romance of nineteenth century political theory. The two network chief executives, Fly wrote Roosevelt, "can say what more than half of the people may or may not hear" (Fly, 1941. Cf. Hettinger, 1938; Robinson, 1943; Chafee, 1947). In battle with "chain" broadcasters, Fly did not cite expert opinion. Indeed, his agency relied not on legal, economic or behavioral evidence of broadcast oligopoly's harmful effects (Stanton, 1967, pp. 159–60). A few choice quotes from Jefferson about the intrinsic value of many voices sufficed.

If the FCC's concept of research consisted of Bartlett quotes of the third president, the Commission's wards, as already noted, sought more complete evidence. In the late 1930s, CBS began investing substantial sums in mass communication research. Columbia hired a young doctorate in psychology, Frank Stanton, to improve audience measurement. Stanton, in turn, arranged for CBS to fund the work of Paul Lazarsfeld who founded the Bureau of Applied Social Research at Columbia University. Together, Stanton and Lazarsfeld edited three volumes of original research on media effects, programming and institutions (Lazarsfeld and Stanton, 1943; 1944; 1949. Cf. Burns, 1975; Lazarsfeld, 1968; Klapper, 1968; Lindsey, 1962). Much of this and subsequent Bureau work, in turn, belied the older wartime propaganda model of effects. Lazarsfeld's classic study of the mass media's influence in presidential campaigns, *The People's Choice*, published in 1944, suggested that sociological factors and not messages determined voter behavior. The volume was dedicated to Frank Stanton.

Lazarsfeld did briefly try to reach out to the FCC in the middle 1940s. On the initiative of Commissioner Clifford J. Durr, the Commission had prepared to investigate systematically the extent to which broadcast licensees fulfilled their minimal obligations. Lazarsfeld helped the FCC to prepare several case studies, which tended to confirm Durr's own negative sense of industry responsibility. These works also led to the agency's promulgation of the "Blue Book," *The Public Service Responsibility of Broadcast Licensees* (1946), which attempted to dictate "improvements" in programming by mandating more of the less popular or "minority interest" fare.[14]

Durr's utilization of Lazarsfeld's research designs, however, proved to be the exception rather than the rule. Rarely if ever through the 1940s and 1950s did the heirs of James Lawrence Fly refer to this body of literature. (To have done so would have negated the need for active regulation.) Instead, popular writers—and pop sociologists—continued to speak of the pervasive power of the mass media and some accused universities studying the media's effects of being corporate lackeys. "In many of their attempts to work over the fabric of our minds," Vance Packard wrote in 1957, "the professional persuaders are receiving direct help and guidance from respected social scientists."

As tens of millions of American families purchased their first television sets in the 1950s, the study of communication spread to colleges and universities (McLeod and Reeves, 1980, pp. 37–38, 39. Cf. Weaver and Gray, 1980), and those least likely to know of such work included broadcast regulators. The FCC was lead by commissioners who had been trained in law or engineering; many had been state utility regulators.[15] They might know about rates of return but never the two-step flow.

This ignorance probably did not matter. Through most of the 1950s, broadcast regulators were overwhelmed by the task of assigning the first and most lucrative TV channels. Congress had added to the regulators' burdens by imposing in the Administrative Procedure Act of 1946 new and time-consuming procedures (Blachly and Oatman, 1946). The commissioners had enough to read at night. And students of broadcast regulation, many critical of Eisenhower's FCC, continued to analyze the agency in economic and legal, rather than behavioral terms (See, for example, *Law and Contemporary Problems*, 1957; and, Schwartz, 1959; Friendly, 1962).

Briefly in the 1950s, Congress rather than the FCC did seek the opinions of communication researchers. Many American opinion leaders at the time had convinced themselves that America had a new and ominous juvenile delinquency problem. And beginning in 1954, the Senate Judiciary Committee's Juvenile Delinquency Subcommittee inquired into the mass media's relationship to this "crisis." Scholars of the mass media including Lazarsfeld and Eleanor Maccoby of Harvard joined Captain Video and a freelance actor, Ronald Reagan, in testifying. These experts, Chairman Estes Kefauver said in April 1955, "are important in our investigation of this kind" (U.S. Senate, 1955, p. 1).[16]

The witnesses' testimony afforded little consensus. Lazarsfeld insisted that more research was needed and declined to indict the media for antisocial behavior; industry representatives presented a mass of surveys from psychologists denying any link. Maccoby indicated that some children became aggressive after viewing TV series, and, with Lazarsfeld, asked for more time and federal funding to collect data on the problem (U.S. Senate, 1954, p. 4ff, 92–3).

Finally, three witnesses listed instances of violence in comic books and television and insisted that a positive correlation existed tying media violence and adolescent misbehavior. Ralph S. Banay remarked, "TV is a preparatory school for delinquency" while Frederic Wertham launched a virtual one-man crusade which lasted into the 1960s against media violence. Another witness, Dr. Frederick J. Hacker (ABC Radio, 1956) of the Medical Correctional Association, told the committee that

It cannot be stated with any degree of dispassionate scientific accuracy that movies or other mass media cause juvenile delinquency, but innumerable clinical observations prove that they not only describe, but often contribute to or at least shape the content of, criminal activity.[17]

The committee recommended in a 1956 report that more basic research be conducted on the effects of violent programs, and then dropped the mass media from its agenda (ABC Radio, 1956; Mitler and Perian, 1957).

The FCC took little interest in the Senate's inquiry, nor followed its example later in the decade. One commissioner, Frieda Hennock, a liberal New York Democrat, testified and demanded action from the networks.[18] But FCC chairman George McConnaughey disregarded the cries of Wertham and Banay and asked parents to handle the problem. He with others persuaded Eisenhower not to reappoint the noisy Hennock.[19] When the Commission held inquires into network programming, beginning in 1959, of the scores of witnesses brought to Washington, only two were mass communication scholars: Lazarsfeld and Charles Siepmann. The rest consisted of industry executives, artists, advertisers, and such TV stars as Ozzie Nelson and Dick Powell.[20]

Hennock's fate notwithstanding, the Kefauver hearings and subsequent studies (Witty, 1958; Hess and Goldman, 1962; Bailyn, 1962) well conveyed a dichotomy in communication research. Few students of the media took Wertham, Banay or Hacker seriously. Many did respect Lazarsfeld and Maccoby. Yet a gulf separated these two social scientists and their disciplines. Lazarsfeld and his followers stressed the non-effects of the mass media, either directly or by emphasizing the noninformational "uses and gratifications" of media. Others with Maccoby cautiously suggested that some users of mass communication systems might be influenced by the content of their programming. This division continued into the 1960s and confused many a would-be regulator. Discussing the numerous measures of television's effects on children, an FCC bureau chief who, unlike his bosses, wished to police the industry with enthusiasm, told a Wisconsin group, "the so-called experts are not in agreement" (Bryant, 1968).

Perhaps another factor limited the value of communication research into the Sixties to broadcasting's overseers: the very tone or language of those working the field. For every polemical Frederic Wertham, many more scholars couched their public remarks about the mass media's effects in the most indirect or piecemeal fashion. If a Paul Lazarsfeld or Elihu Katz offered grand conclusions, most of their colleagues settled for more modest write-ups, at least that was the perception of regulators. Indeed, a rather exasperated reviewer of communication research trends complained,

While it is necessary to retreat from over-facile generalization unsupported by any significant accumulation of data, there was no need to abjure generalization to the extent found at present in the frequently desiccated and relatively meaningless fragments of data accumulated by empirical statistical research. (Albig, 1957, p. 17)

To the student of media's effects wishing to shape government policy, the challenge came when the FCC enjoyed new life beginning in 1961. The presidency of John F. Kennedy brought a new attitude toward broadcast regulation and the house of intellect, as Kennedy's appointments included numerous holders of advanced degrees. Historian Richard Hofstadter (1961) remarked, "the government swarms with Harvard professors and ex-Rhodes scholars." Kennedy's new FCC chairman, Newton Minow, was interested both in surveying communication research and in vigorously regulating broadcasting. With most major license allocation cases resolved by the time of his appointment, he had relatively more time than his predecessors to concern himself with the content of American television. In May 1961, he shook the industry by dubbing television programming "a vast wasteland" (see Baughman, 1981, ch. 3).

Not long after becoming chairman, Minow read *Television in the Lives of Our Children*, (1961) a study by Wilbur Schramm, Jack Lyle, and Edwin Parker of television's introduction in the home and its effects on the young (see also Minow, 1961; Goldin, 1961). Their findings hardly confirmed the simple and dangerous model that Wertham and others had presented earlier. If anything, the Schramm study contended that television was less a negative force than an unrealized opportunity for educating the young. In their conclusion, the authors commented,

Concerning the cognitive effects of television, the general conclusion is one of disappointment. This is not because television is doing any special harm in this respect, but rather because it isn't realizing its full potential as a carrier of ideas and information. (Schramm, Lyle, and Parker, 1961, p. 173)

Schramm's work unintentionally served to dull the sword Minow planned to unleash at the national networks. Anxious to make his mark as a regulator and concerned with children and the mass media both as a parent and attorney for Encyclopedia Britannica in the 1950s, Minow discovered as FCC head that he did not need to fear TV's influence. He thus took up Schramm's standard of the media as the potential servant rather than the literal enemy of young people. During his chairmanship, which ended in June 1963, Minow spoke of TV as less harmful than possibly beneficial to children. In June 1961, he told a TV interviewer,

Whether or not it [TV violence] causes juvenile delinquency, I really don't know. I am not an expert at that. I do know that it wastes, it seems to me, a great deal of potential which television could bring children in teaching them and stretching their minds. Whether it is actually harmful is something I am not in a position to know. (ABC, 1961, p. 3)

In September, he told an assemblage of TV executives that the medium alone could not be blamed for juvenile delinquency. "But," he asked, "shouldn't television be a major cause of juvenile development?" (Minow, 1964). In a March, 1962 essay, he observed,

I don't think television causes juvenile delinquency. I have been much more impressed by a quiet [sic] paragraph, tucked away in a rather ponderous research report on television and children. That paragraph said that children learn a great deal from TV. (Minow, 1962)

Armed with this concept, Minow and Attorney General Robert F. Kennedy tried to persuade the three networks to run at the same hour, special educational children's programming. Although NBC and CBS agreed, ABC declined and the "children's hour" idea collapsed. The networks did develop between 1962 and 1963 educational programming for children, but were careful not to schedule them—as Minow had requested—simultaneously (See Stanton, 1961 and Syracuse *Herald-Journal*, 1961).

In addition to shaping the FCC chairman's thinking, Schramm and other scholars participated in a new Senate inquiry into juvenile delinquency in 1961. A spate of violent programs increasing between 1958 and 1961 had engendered new interest in TV's ill effects on children and adolescents. In December 1960, FBI Director J. Edgar Hoover had decried the programs' "57 minutes of crime glamorization" and cited bureau cases that had linked crime to TV programs (Miami *Herald*, 4 December 1960). "They tell me TV is a good baby sitter," a mother (Sober, 1961) wrote Minow in June, 1961, "I would just as soon hire Al Capone to babysit."[21] The Judiciary's subcommittee, chaired by Thomas J. Dodd of Connecticut, assembled a great deal of statistical and other

evidence proving that network executives had deliberately infused violence into programming to boost series' ratings. But Schramm, despite
Dodd's badgering, refused to admit that TV contributed significantly to
delinquency.[22]

Although flustered by Schramm's testimony, Dodd did attempt to
encourage further research. Soon after his hearings ended Secretary of
Health, Education and Welfare Abraham Ribicoff agreed to the Senator's
call for additional, empirical work on the effects of television on children. On the invitation of Ribicoff, the three commercial networks and
the National Association of Broadcasters agreed to form a Joint Committee for Research on Television (JCRT). In February 1963, a group of
twenty-five distinguished investigators met to draw up an agenda. The
broadcast underwriters, however, then delayed approving the proposals
based on this agenda. Indeed, the industry's representatives, who dominated the JCRT, made certain to approve only those projects likely to
suggest a cathartic impact on younger consumers while delaying action
on others thought likely to imply otherwise. As a result, the JCRT's
efforts discouraged many potential researchers; JCRT funded two
research studies and one literature review, and had no appreciable impact
on either regulation or the social science of mass communication (U.S.
Senate, 1972, pp. 14–19; Office of the Secretary of Health, Education,
and Welfare, 1962).

While the JCRT played empirical sabotage, Schramm's views still held
sway at the FCC. Minow's successor, E. William Henry, chairman from
1963 to 1966, tended to rely on the work of Schramm and others. Like
Minow, Henry did not join Dodd in arguing that TV harmed Americans
or American youth. Rather, he adhered to a positive standard which
owed something to Schramm's study. Rather than blame television for
the ills of American youth, Henry fought to improve the medium's programming, to enhance the possibilities TV had for enlightening the young
(Henry, 1963; 1964; 1965).

By the late 1960s, however, the FCC again wallowed in lethargy and
indifference to social science's possibilities. Henry departed in frustration
in June 1966, and Presidents Lyndon Johnson and Richard Nixon were
careful to name meek regulatory figures to the agency (U.S. Congress.
Senate. 1976). One extraordinary exception, however, was Nicholas

Johnson (1970; 1971), named by Johnson in mid-1966. Although even more harsh toward TV than Minow or Henry had been, Nicholas Johnson relied on legal and economic arguments reminiscent of James Lawrence Fly's chairmanship. He and most like-minded critics of the media ignored the behavioral possibilities.

Yet the rash of violence in American cities and politics in the late 1960s forced the issue of social science's use by government. And once more, a common sense correlation operated in the minds of many: TV violence had increased just as American urban areas caught fire and a presidential candidate and major civil rights leader were slain. Something had to be done. A New England Republican senator (Cotton, 1986) wrote a member of the American Mothers Committee, "I believe that the television industry has much to answer for in promoting violence." And in early June 1968, aides (Murphy, 1968; McPherson, 1968) to President Johnson implored him to act against TV violence.

On June 10, 1968, Johnson appointed a National Commission on the Causes and Prevention of Violence, chaired by Milton S. Eisenhower, president of Johns Hopkins University and brother of the thirty-fourth president and war hero. Eisenhower's staff, in turn, soon included some fifty academic experts, drawn from sociology, psychology, political science, history, law, and biology, to advise the Commission. And under the auspices of the Eisenhower Commission, a series of directed studies investigated the relationships—economic, historical, and behavioral—between violence and the mass media. Suddenly the government—not just the corporation—had become a major source of research support. The expert on media effects had finally been invited to the lord's supper (Graham and Gunn, 1969).

The Eisenhower Commission's special report, *Mass Media and Violence*, (National Commission on the Causes and Prevention of Violence, 1969), broke little new ground in communication research and none in governmental policy-making. Released in November 1969, *Mass Media and Violence* described much but analyzed little and prescribed not at all. Despite distinguished contributors, the collection proved more disappointing than impressive. Indeed, one scholar likened the volume to so many earlier analyses: "They initiated little new research and produced no continuing instrument for understanding the complex phenomenon being examined" (Action for Children's Television, 1971, p. 74).

Still, the communication scholar feasted again as Senate pressures early in 1969 led to still another governmental inquiry into the mass media's effects. On March 5, 1969, Senator John O. Pastore, chairman of the Commerce Committee's Communication Subcommittee, asked Secretary of Health, Education and Welfare Robert H. Finch to create a Surgeon General's advisory committee on the effects of violent programming. In his letter to Finch, Pastore, citing heretofore contradictory communication research findings, essentially demanded that the Surgeon General once and for all establish the actual effects of violent culture on the masses (U.S. Congress. Senate. 1969; U.S. Congress. Senate. 1971).

Pastore also had an ideal-type of report in mind: the January 1964 Surgeon General's advisory committee analysis of the effects of cigarettes on public health. Surely, Pastore maintained, the connections between violent programming and behavior could be similarly argued. The physical and mental correlations seemed the same to the Senator from Rhode Island (U.S. Congress. Senate. 1969; New York *Times*, 16 May, 1982).

In April 1969, Secretary Finch took up Pastore's call and the Surgeon General began forming his advisory panel. Scholars in communication departments as well as the older social and behavioral sciences began case studies of the mass media's effects. But after three years and $2 million, and despite Senator Pastore's insistence on definitive answers, the committee (consisting of industry and academic representatives) fought over the conclusions of case studies (conducted by academicians) and compromised by obscuring their results. Although most of the researchers agreed that they had demonstrated that the media had effects, those overseeing the investigations divided over the inquiries' implications. As a result, the Surgeon General's report lacked the impact of the smoking panel's survey eight years earlier. The findings thus *seemed* inconclusive and, moreover, were reported as such by much of the national news media. Americans did not discard TV police dramas the way they had half-full packs of Lucky Strikes in 1964. The chance for social and behavioral scientists to inform policy-makers (both the Senate and FCC Chairman Dean Burch had been interested in the Report's assessments) had been lost (U.S. Congress. Senate. 1971; U.S. Congress. Senate. 1974b).

Various explanations have been offered for the outcome of the Surgeon General's March 1972 study. The commercial networks, as has often been observed, enjoyed a veto power over the composition of the committee and wording of the panel's final analysis (See Paisley, 1972; Rowland, 1982, pp. 398–99). (Perhaps too much can be made of this power, however; the tobacco industry had the same rights—and exercised them—during the smoking investigation.[23]) The networks did help to lessen the impact of the reports in two ways. First, as already noted, their representatives on the advisory panel worked to soften or muddle the conclusions in the final report. Second, they discouraged the use of psychologists for conducting the individual case studies. Some of the psychologists deliberately not hired had already established a link between aggressive behavior and violent programming and were not expected to offer results contradicting their earlier labors. Then, too, psychological tests of media effects seemed—especially to the layman—more exacting, more scientific; put differently, they could be likened to the medical evidence that had so damned the cigarette habit. Keeping psychologists off the panel would reduce the probable impact of the final report (U.S. Congress. Senate. 1972, pp. 19–25).

The language of the researchers themselves added to the problem. Case studies tended to be fashioned in the more obtuse style of the social sciences. Precision in the case of many of the individual reports was limited to the tables and charts, not introductory and concluding paragraphs. (It is worth noting that participants proved clear communicators in testifying to Pastore's committee.) Legislators and regulators, most mentally equipped to read law, not psychology, journals, could hardly handle some contributors' weighty discourses replete with telescoped compounds and two-by-two tables. Senator Howard Baker of Tennessee, in an unintended parody, asked the Surgeon General in March 1972,

Are you in a position to say that television provides a substantial modicum of additional aggressive inputs, so it does affect your perception of violence, your evaluation of violence and your likelihood to reenact violence in an antisocial way. (U.S. Congress. Senate. 1972, p. 34)

Adding to the woes of the report's readers was the committee's inability to recommend policies. Secretary Finch had, in charging the panel with the task, insisted that members only conclude from their studies: participants were not to suggest governmental remedies. Finch maintained that HEW had no legal authority over television programming; for his department to promote policies regarding the medium only invited constitutional questions the FCC was best suited to reckon with. His ruling may explain why so many researchers asked only for more research and research support. One committee member, however, commented,

Action, that is public health action, frequently does not wait for that final scientific nail to be driven in. Public health action has to proceed from less than final evidence. (U.S. Congress. Senate. 1972, pp. 36, 38, 76)

One senator remarked in exasperation,

If, in fact, the government is going to select a committee and if, in fact, we are going to spend $2 million of the people's money of this country and not come up with recommendations, even if they are recommendations that we sit down with the networks and try to work out a system, are we really doing our job. (U.S. Congress. Senate. 1972, p. 37)

The news media, not surprisingly, shared the senators' confusion and offered concerned citizens wildly conflicting interpretations of the Surgeon General's report (See Cater and Strickland, 1975; U.S. Congress. Senate. 1972, pp. 27, 69, 147).

What is often not appreciated is the extent to which the *mere interest* of the government in the effects of mass media can alter the the behavior of mass communicators. Minow's very presence on the FCC probably caused some television producers and network executives to change some of their practices regarding TV violence and children's programming. Seven years later, TV producers lessened the gunplay of their series as the government again interested itself in the possible relationships between video misbehavior and mass violence (See Cantor, 1971; *Variety*, 11 June 1968; Clark and Blankenberg, 1972).

As the surgeon General and Eisenhower commission experts labored, still another party became involved in the academic minefield of mass media effects research. Action for Children's Television (ACT), an alliance of upper-middle-class Bostonians, petitioned the FCC in

February 1970 to regulate advertising designed for children and the excessive commercialization of programming itself. Although commissioners of various ideological stripes shared some of ACT's concern over children's television, the FCC's moderate-to-conservative majority refused to accept ACT's more extreme recommendations or to encourage those experts testifying in the agency's proceedings. The FCC conducted major regulatory initiatives in the area of children's programming without much attention to the labors of media effects specialists. Rather, the FCC commissioned economic rather than behavioral inquiries into the mass media (Melody, 1973; Cole and Oettinger, 1978; Cowan, 1979).

The FCC's distance from ACT led the Boston-based group to another part of Washington, the offices of the Federal Trade Commission (FTC). In November 1972, the ACT petitioned the Trade Commission to police advertising directed toward young children. Initially, the ACT's arguments consisted of common-sense correlations, if not diatribes, about the ill effects of mass communications directed toward children.[24] But as the Federal Trade Commission pursued the ACT's agenda, Commission staff members sought out expert knowledge and, indeed, experts were soon to be found on the agency staff itself.

The greater receptivity at the FTC (when compared to the FCC) can be explained by a number of factors. First, the former agency had long been concerned (and legally obliged to be) about advertising and children (U.S. Congress. Senate. 1974a; *FTC v. Keppel*, (1934). Then, too, the agency's powers had expanded as a result of favorable court decisions and congressional legislation (See Congressional Quarterly, 1974, pp. 598, 611, 612; New York *Times*, 4 April 1982). Even those on the FTC staff like Gerald Thain, who had been trained in the law, embraced the social and behavioral sciences as part of their larger regulatory mission. In October 1970, Thain, assistant director of the FTC's Food and Drug Advertising division, told ACT:

In special cases, and I think this includes attempts to set down standards of deception to children, the FTC may well need the aid of experts in building an effective regulatory policy—experts in social psychology, child psychology, broadcasting techniques, and related specialties and disciplines. I invite such people to contact me or the Commission staff and make their views known to those of use who are concerned with this problem. I don't think you need to wait for a formal invitation. Your initiative in contacting us would help us to do something effective in those areas that need your action. (Action for Children's Television, 1971, p. 45; see also U.S. Congress. Senate. 1974a)

The notion that academic knowledge of communication equaled the public interest thus became commonplace at the Trade Commission's headquarters. Studies of expert witnesses used between the 1950s and 1970s plainly showed that Thain sincerely meant his invitation. And by the middle and late Seventies, even the legal arguments over the regulation of advertising for children included references to social and behavioral research. The communication researcher was less the infrequent visitor at agency proceedings than the active participant (See Thain, 1976; Lees, 1978; Wattwood, 1978; New York *Times*, 17 April 1977, 8 August 1978, 5 March 1979; Brant and Preston, 1977; Preston, 1982).

It had taken a long time, however, for those who studied the media and their effects to become footnotes in legal periodicals. In contrast, the first Supreme Court brief to utilize sociological knowledge had been filed in 1908 (*Muller v. Oregon*, 1908. Cf. Commager, 1950, ch. 18). As already noted, during the Progressive and New Deal eras, the academic expert had been a frequent visitor to the citadels of powers. With the Employment Act of 1946, Congress created the Council of Economic Advisers, all but two members of which, through 1974, had held professional rank prior to joining the council (Seidman, 1975). In the 1960s, ten years before the children's commercials issue, sociologists had been advising the Johnson administration on such issues as school desegregation and antipoverty. Of course, their arguments had often been controversial (i.e., the Coleman and Moynihan Reports; see Feuer, 1967; Rainwater and Yancey, 1967; Coleman, 1981; Miller, 1980). But that had not stopped the flow of information from the universities to the District of Columbia.

The Interaction of Research and Policy

Why has it taken so long for communication scholarship to influence public policy? One conclusion is that until recently the two communities had been operating out of sync. In the 1920s and 1930s, even though effects were found in several areas, regulators had not even sorted out the technical problems with the "American" system of broadcasting, let alone questions about social impact. During the 1940s, the regulators had moved from technical to legal and economic issues, but even if they had gone looking for social research, they would have found studies geared to communication administrators, declarations of "limited effects," or research so obscure that it was politically uninformative.

Not until recently has research served mutual needs. Media researchers have gained in legitimacy and, indeed, importance, and regulators have gained a sympathetic support group armed with "the facts." Researchers could impress administrative law judges and help to win cases. And government officials impressed colleagues back at the university that they had money for research support or they indirectly encouraged other sources to chip in for the good of future media policy.

Mutual interests are reflected in changing research agendas. Studies related to each major policy consideration of the last two decades existed both before and shortly after the specific policy debates; however, it is also true that the largest quantity of work, and the most influential studies, appeared before any hearings were held. Studies of media and violence dominated the literature on children and television at the time of the Surgeon General's report and the subsequent Congressional hearings. Yet since 1975, there have been fewer studies about media violence than would have been predicted given the number of questions left unanswered. A similar fate has befallen children's advertising research. Immediately before and during the FTC's hearings on Saturday morning cereal ads, advertising studies were numerous. After the hearings and the termination of the case, the question seemed less important and similar research will probably continue to evaporate.

Several other explanations for the constrained policy-research relationship could be offered. Communication has been relatively slow to develop as an academic area when compared to economics, psychology, sociology, or political science. Then, too, regulators have tended to have not only legal educations, but fairly narrow ones at that. Only recently have most law schools introduced social sciences into their curricula. Also, most government officials came from eastern or District of Columbia-based universities. Few hailed from those midwestern and western universities that exposed curious undergraduates to a new and dynamic area of inquiry.[25]

Finally, media research has often appeared to be non-cumulative, inconclusive, and contradictory. The first two of these problems may have resulted from a poor sense of the history of the research and a self-conscious desire to move on to "hot" questions before older ones were answered. The last problem is in part an accurate statement about the research; there have been disagreements. Yet this condition exists in all sciences and may be more of a stimulus to quality than a source of disabling competition.

The problem of contradictions within the field is more serious in media research, however, because everyone has experience with media and, therefore, feels confident enough to comment critically on survey questionnaires and experimental designs. Congressmen in media hearings, for example, have been anxious to compare research results with the media behavior in their own families; TV violence and sex horrified those legislators occasionally watching television. Then, too, media research has been publicly evaluated not only because it was interesting and pertinent, but also because, relative to other disciplines, it was easy to read and understand. Even when researchers are in agreement, less important differences, which many lay observers are capable of evaluating, often cloud summary conclusions. And when the debate over regulation is reduced to the interpretation of a single zero-order correlation, the major policy issues are easily forgotten. Perhaps the status of media research would be increased if, as in the case of medical testimony on cigarette advertising, the research contribution was so technical that regulators were forced to accept conclusions at face value.

In conclusion, it is important to note that the historical failures of this interaction are not sufficient justification to conclude that the research was awful or policy ill-informed. Good research is not necessarily that which helps regulators do a good job, just as good regulation in many cases would not benefit from social research. In fact, there are people on both sides who advocate that the relationship should not exist, or if it does, an antagonism should prevail. James Carey, in a comment on a BBC report which suggested greater cooperation between media organizations and researchers, noticed that a "silent embrace" has been growing up between the two communities which has not and will not produce any benefits for scholarship. He added the following:

> In fact, I think a better case can be made that scholarship, like many of the arts, flourishes when it stands in determined opposition to the established order. If you are in opposition, you have to work very much harder to get a hearing at all and that extra effort makes the critical difference . . . Were this relationship successful it would rob society of one useful role scholars can perform: the statement of problems, issues, and solutions in terms that are outside and opposed to the established center of power and authority. That scholars have been badly corrupted on this matter is no argument to extend the corruption. (Carey, 1978, pp. 116–17)

There is little doubt that several current government officials are also pessimistic about research and policy, though for quite different reasons than Carey mentioned. A large ideological circle of opinion leaders[26]— and now the Reagan administration—have determined that the marketplace, and not the government, should rule the airwaves. They are suspicious of a liberal bias in the social sciences and of the ability of these "soft" disciplines to establish rigid "laws" that government officials need only know to make better policy (See, for example, Goodman, 1977; Wilson, 1981). Their concerns recall Harold Laski's warning to his fellow Labourites in England in 1931: "The expert," he wrote, "should be on tap, not on top . . . Government by experts would, however ardent their original zeal for the public welfare, mean after a time government in the interest of experts" (Laski, 1931, pp. 13–14).[27]

Many of these concerns reflect a misunderstanding about the possibilities of utilizing data. There is an implicit assumption—shared by many academics—that somehow data will leap out of statistical tables and present the finder with the "right" policy solution. This is simply not the case. Consider, for example, the finding that 37 percent of the mother-child discussions about the purchase of sugared cereal involve verbal abusive conflict caused by television (Reeves and Atkin, 1979). Further, suppose that the conclusion is methodologically and statistically error-free. There is no way this information could be applied to an FTC policy without mixing the data with values. Is 37 percent a lot? Should the federal government regulate family conflict? Are the advertisers legally protected under the First Amendment anyway? Would the economic hardships imposed on broadcasters cause further problems for television? If the criterion concern shifted to tooth decay, unfair treatment of children, or even, as in the case of the cigarette commercials, cancer, the values imposed on the policy would likely change. Although it would be hard to imagine proposing a policy that was not based on objective information, it is important to note that values dictate the importance of a proposal, not statistics or research methods per se.

This discussion has not been intended to diminish the contributions already made by academics, irrespective of the origin of their research questions. Examples of research-based applications include suggestions for restructuring election campaigns (Blumler, 1977), and policies for televised advertising for children (FCC, 1981). A more liberal definition of policy would include other applications such as education programs about critical viewing skills (Roberts et al., 1980) and, of course, applications in the communications industry.[28] It is difficult, however, to point out specific lines in the regulatory literature that match one-to-one with the suggestions of a social scientist. Some positive benefit accrues, even if only the acknowledgement that questions about social impact are reasonable.

Notes

1. Numerous reviews of research history exist in the literature. See Davis and Baran, 1981; Weis, 1969; DeFleur and Ball-Rokeach, 1975; Comstock et al., 1978; Rogers, 1973.

2. For a full discussion of the development of "libertarian" thought, see Rivers, Peterson, and Jensen, 1971.

3. Early twentieth century European students of public opinion were less sanguine about the rationality of the masses. See Fleming, 1967. This work in turn began to influence some American intellectuals just prior to the Great War. See May 1959.

4. The three studies are reported in Lazarsfeld et al., 1944 and Katz and Lazarsfeld, 1955. The data reported in *Personal Influence* were collected in 1945.

5. One of the fundamental assumptions of functional and of uses and gratifications research is that audiences are actively processing information. For reviews of this research see Katz et al., 1974 and McLeod and Becker, 1982.

6. This perspective was also part of the uses and gratifications approach discussed in Katz, Blumer, and Gurevitch. This shift in emphasis is particularly relevant to the literature on children and television. See Wartella (1979) and Collins (1981).

7. Of the many studies conducted in sociology at the University of Chicago were the graduate student thesis projects of Halley (1929) and Hauser (1933). There were approximately fifteen other similar projects. In the late 1920s and the early 1930s, Herbert Blumer conducted two of the Payne Fund studies reported in 1933. They were *Movies and Conduct* (1933) and *Movies, Delinquency and Crime* (1933). The latter study was conducted with Philip Hauser.

8. There were 12 separate studies conducted under the Payne Fund project. For a summary of each report see Charters (1933).

9. The two studies in the Payne Fund series that most heavily relied on cognitive concepts were Holaday and Stoddard (1933) and Peterson and Turston (1933).

10. No specific history of the development of communication programs exists. A PhD program in mass communication was first established at the University of Minnesota in 1950. Others soon followed at Wisconsin, Michigan State, Illinois, North Carolina, and Stanford. The first research institutes in communication were established at Illinois and Stanford. Other institutes at Columbia and Chicago had already been operating but did not exclusively deal with media.

11. According to a 1975 measure, even the FCC's twenty-two advisory committees included only a few academics. See U.S. Congress. Senate. 1977.

12. See also *Congressional Record* (1926, pp. 557–558); Buffalo *Evening News*, (8 March 1927); New York *Times*, (21 March 1926); Rosen, (1980).

13. See also Kirkendall (1962); New York *Herald Tribune*, 16 October 1933; *Independent Journal* 2 (16 October 1933); Kent, (1933). Cantril (1967) and Steele (1974) discuss FDR's work with pollsters.

14. In his memoir, Lazarsfeld incorrectly identifies Durr as FCC chairman, and he slightly misdates the time of the Blue Book inquiry. See also Siepmann (1946; 1950) and Peterson (1973).

15. See Lichty (1961–62, pp. 33–34) and Comstock et al. (1968, p. 457). Communication and speech instructors did occasionally angle to obtain a seat on the FCC. In March 1958, for example, Lee Sherman Dreyfus of Wayne State's Speech Department unsuccessfully sought an FCC vacancy. See Ellery (1958).

16. See also U.S. Congress. Senate. (1954; 1955); Congressional Quarterly (1955); Goodman (1957); Toffler (1955).

17. See U.S. Congress. Senate. (1955, p. 83; 1955, pp. 49ff); Wertham (1954; 1960); Wylie (1955).

18. Hennock proposed not renewing the licenses of those found airing a large amount of violent fare. See her statement to the committee (Hennock, 1955). See also Hennock, (1955b) and Conklin (1955).

19. See Willis (1955); Gray (1958). McConnaughey's views on the media and children are found in his address, "Educational Broadcasting."

20. See Docket 12782 in U.S. Senate (1977, Vol. IV; 1977, Vol. III, pp. 597ff, 627ff) and *Television Magazine* (1960, pp. 48, 107).

21. Cf. Clark and Blankenberg (1978); Mathes (1961); Prince (1959); Cort (1959); Cousins (1959); Kern (1961).

22. See U.S. Congress. Senate. (1961–62); Dodd (1961). On Dodd's questionable conduct of these hearings, see Boyd (1968) and Levy (1964).

23. See Cater and Strickland (1975, p. 75, ch. 8 and *passim*); U.S. Congress. Senate. (1972, pp. 27, 69, 149).

24. Compare ACT presentations at U.S. Senate Commerce Committee (1970) with U.S. Congress. Senate. (1974a).

25. See Stanley et al., (1967). During both Eisenhower's and Kennedy's presidencies, just over 20 percent of all appointed officials attended one of three schools—Harvard, Yale, or Princeton.

26. See Bazelon, 1978; Goldberg and Couzens, 1978; Brotman, 1978; Foote and Mnookin, 1980; New York *Times*, 3 April 1981, 25 July 1982; Chicago *Tribune*, 11 April 1981; Washington *Post*, 27 June 1981; *Variety*, 30 September 1981, pp. 1, 108, 13 January 1982, pp. 143–45, 180, 182).

27. See also Hughes (1962); Krauthammer (1981).

28. Numerous studies fall into this category and cover practices of broadcasters, newspaper editors, audience analysts, advertising and public relations practitioners, entertainment producers, and others. For a review of applications of research in these areas see Chaffee and Petrick (1975).

References

Action for Children's Television. (1971). "Action for Children's Television." New York: Avon.

Albig, W. (1957). Two decades of opinion study. *Public Opinion Quarterly 21* (Spring), 17.

ABC (1961). Transcript of "Issues and Answers."(June 18) 3. Copy in Minow MSS., Box 46, State Historical Society of Wisconsin.

ABC Radio. (1956). Transcript of "Edward P. Morgan and the News," (April 6). Copy in Alexander H. Wiley MSS., Series 4, Box 11, State Historical Society of Wisconsin.

Annis, A. D., and Meier, N. C. (1934). Induction of opinion suggested by means of planted content. *Journal of Social Psychology 5*, 68–81.

Arngeim, R. (1944). The world of the daytime serial. *In* P. Lazarsfeld and F. Stanton (Eds.), "Radio Research 1942–43." New York: Duell, Sloane, Pearce.

Bailyn, L. (1962). The uses of television. *Journal of Social Issues 18*, 1–61.

Baughman, J. L. (1981). "Warriors in the Wasteland: The Federal Communications Commission and American Television." Unpublished dissertation, Columbia University.

Bazelon, D. (1978). The first amendment and the 'new media'—new directions in regulating telecommunications. *Federal Communications Law Journal 31* (Spring), 201–231.

Berlo, D. K. (1960). "The Process of Communication." New York: Holt, Rinehart, and Winston.

Blachly, F. P., and Oatman, M. E. (1946). Sabotage of the administrative process. *Public Administration Review 6*, 213–27.

Blakey, G. T. (1970). "Historians on the Home Front: American Propagandists for the Great War." Lexington, KY: University Press of Kentucky.

Blumer, H. (1933a). "Movies and Conduct." New York: MacMillan.

Blumer, H. (1933a). "Movies, Deliquency, and Crime." New York: MacMillan.

Blumler, J. G. (1977). "The Intervention of Television in British Politics." Essay submitted to the Annan Committee. London, England. (Appendix E. Cmnd. 6753-1, HMSO).

Blumler, J. G. (1978). Purposes of mass communication research: A transatlantic perspective. *Journalism Quarterly 55*, 219–230.

Boyd, J. (1968). "Above the Law: The Rise and Fall of Senator Thomas J. Dodd." pp. 188–93, New York: New American Library.

Brant, M. T., and Preston, I. L. (1977). The federal trade commission's use of evidence to determine deception. *Journal of Marketing* (January), 54–62.

Brinton, A. W. "The Regulation of Broadcasting by the FCC: A Case Study in Regulation by Independent Commission." Unpublished dissertation, Harvard University.

Brotman, S. N. (1978). Judge David Bazelon: Making the first amendment work. *Federal Communications Law Journal 33* (Winter), 39–34.

Bryant, A. P. (1968). Address, 27 April 1962. *In* H. J. Skornia and J. W. Kitson (Eds.), "Problems and Controversies in Television and Radio," p. 272, Palo Alto, CA: Pacific Books.

Buffalo *Evening News*. 8 March 1927. Clipping in Hoover MSS., Box 490, Hoover Presidential Library, Stanford University.

Burns, J. S. (1975). "The Awkward Embrace: The Creative Artist and the Institution in America." pp. 13–14; 110–113, New York: Knopf.

Cantor, M. (1971). "The Hollywood TV Producer." New York: Basic Books.

Cantril, H. (1940). "The Invasion from Mars: A Study in the Psychology of Panic." Princeton, NJ: Princeton University Press.

Cantril, H. (1967). "The Hidden Dimension: Experiences in Policy Research." New Brunswick, NJ: Rutgers University Press.

Carey, J. W. (1978). The ambiguity of policy research. *Journal of Communication 28* (Spring), 116–17.

Cater, D. and Strickland, S. (1975). "TV Violence and the Child: The Evolution and Fate of the Surgeon General's Report." New York: Russell Sage Foundation.

Chafee, Z. (1947). "Government and Mass Communications." 2 vols. Chicago, IL: University of Chicago Press.

Chaffee, S. H., and Petrick, M. (1975). "Using the Mass Media." New York: Prentice-Hall.

Chaffee, S. H. (1977). Mass media effects: new research perspectives. *In* D. Lerner and L. M. Nelson (Eds.), "Communication Research—A Half-Century Appraisal," pp. 210–214, Honolulu, HI: University Press of Hawaii.

Chambers, J. W. II. (1980). "The Tyranny of Change: America in the Progressive Era." New York: St. Martins.

Charters, W. W. (1933). "Motion Pictures and Youth." New York: MacMillan.

Chicago *Tribune*. 11 April 1981, n.p.

Clark, D. G., and Blankenburg, W. B. (1972). Trends in violent content in selected mass media, *In* G. A. Comstock and E. Rubinstein (Eds.), "Television and Social Behavior," 6 Vols. Rockville, MD: National Institute of Mental Health.

Cole, B., and Oettinger, A. (1978). "Reluctant Regulators: the FCC and the Broadcast Audience." Reading, MA: Addison-Wesley.

Coleman, J. (1981). Public schools, private schools, and the public interest. *The Public Interest* No. 64 (Summer).

Collins, A. (1981). Recent advances in research on cognitive processing and television viewing. *Journal of Broadcasting 25*, 327–34.

Columbia Law Review 47 (September 1947), 1045.

Conklin, E. G. (1955). Letter to Frieda Hennock. 12 April 1955. Hennock MSS., Schlesinger Library, Radcliffe College. Box 2–29.

Commager, H. S. (1950). "The American Mind." New Haven, CT: Yale University Press.

Comstock, G. A., Chaffee, S. H. Katzman, N., McCoombs, M., and Roberts, D. (1978). "Television and Human Behavior." New York: Columbia University Press.

Comstock, G. A. and Rubinstein, E. (Eds.). (1972). "Television and Social Behavior." 6 Vols. Rockville, MD: National Institute of Mental Health.

Congressional Record. (1926). Vol. 67, pt. 5, 69th Congress, 1st session. Washington, DC: Government Printing Office.

Congressional Quarterly. (1955). "Congressional Quarterly Almanac 1954." Washington, DC: Congressional Quarterly, Inc.

Congressional Quarterly. (1974). "Congressional Quarterly Almanac 1973." Washington, DC: Congressional Quarterly, Inc.

Cort, D. (1959). Arms and the man. *Nation 188* (May 23), 475–77.

Cotton, N. (1968). Letter to Dorothy Lewis, 13 August 1968. Cotton MSS., Box 100, University of New Hampshire.

Cousins, N. (1959). The real fraud. *Saturday Review, 43* (November 21), 27.

Cowan, G. (1979). "See No Evil: the Backstage Battle Over Sex and Violence on Television." New York: Simon and Schuster.

Cox, K. A. (1965). The FCC, the Constitution, and religious programming. *George Washington Law Review 34* (December), 196–218.

Davis, D. K., and Baran, S. (1981). "Mass Communication and Everyday Life." Belmont, MA: Wadsworth Publishers.

Defleur, M., and Ball-Rokeach, S. (1975). "Theories of Mass Communication." 3rd ed., New York: Longman.

Dodd, T. (1961). Letter to Alexander H. Wiley, 2 June 1961. Alexander H. Wiley MSS., Series 4, Box 12. State Historical Society of Wisconsin.

Douglas, W. O. (1974). "Go East, Young Man: The Early Years." New York: Random House.

Droba, D. (1931). Methods used in measuring public opinion. *American Journal of Sociology 37*, 410–23.

Ellery, J. B. (1958). Letter to Sherman Adams, 7 March 1958. Eisenhower MSS., General Files 41–A. Box 381.

Federal Communications Commission. (1981). Children's television programming and advertising practices, proposed rules. *Federal Register 45* (January 6), 1976–1986.

FTC v. Keppel 291 U.S. 304 (1934).

Feuer, L. (1967). The elite of the alienated. *New York Times Magazine* (March 26), pp. 22–23.

Fleming, D. (1967). Attitude: The history of a concept. *Perspectives in American History 1*, 285–365.

Fly, J. L. (1941). Letter to Franklin D. Roosevelt, 5 May 1941. Roosevelt MSS., President's Secretary File, Box 149, Roosevelt Library.

Foote, S. B., and Mnookin, R. H. (1980). The "Kid Vid" crusade. *The Public Interest* No. 61 (Fall), 90–105.

Friendly, H. J. (1962). "The Federal Administrative Agencies." Cambridge, MA: Harvard University Press.

Furner, M. O. (1975). "Advocacy and Objectivity: A Crisis in the Professionalization of American Social Science." Lexington, KY: University Press of Kentucky.

Gallup, G. (1930). A scientific method for determining reader interest. *Journalism Quarterly 7*, 1–13.

Gitlin, T. (1981). Media sociology: The dominant paradigm. *In* G. C. Wilhoit and M. deBock (Eds.), "Mass Communication Review." Vol. 2, pp. 73–122, Beverly Hills, CA: Sage Publications.

Goldberg, H., and Couzens, M. (1978). 'Peculiar characteristics': An analysis of the first amendment implications of broadcast regulation. *Federal Communications Law Journal 31* (Winter).

Goldin, H. (1961). Letter to Minow, 24 April 1961. Minow MSS., Box 8, State Historical Society of Wisconsin.

Goldman, E. (1956). "Rendevous With Destiny: A History of Modern American Reform." rev. ed., New York: Knopf.

Goodman, W. (1957). "The Clowns of Commerce." New York: Sagamore.

Goodman, W. (1977). The invasion of the experts. New York *Times* (April 17), n. p.

Graham, H. D., and Gurr, T. R. (1969). "Violence in America." New York: New American Library.

Grattan, C. H. (1927). The historians cut loose. *American Mercury 11* (August), 414–30.

Gray, R. (1958). Letter to Sherman Adams, 12 February 1958. Eisenhower MSS., Official File 16, Box 188.

Gruber, C. S. (1975). "Mars and Minerva: World War I and the Uses of Higher Learning in America." Baton Rouge, LA: Louisiana State University Press.

Halley, L. K. (1929). "A Study of Motion Pictures in Chicago as a Medium of Communication." Masters thesis, University of Chicago.

Hauser, P. M. (1933). "Motion Pictures in Penal and Correctional Institutions: A Study of the Reactions of Prisoners to Movies.: Masters thesis. University of Chicago.

Hays, S. P. (1957). "Response to Industrialism, 1877–1912." Chicago, IL: University of Chicago Press.

Hays, S. P. (1964). The politics of reform in municipal government in the progressive era. *Pacific Northwest Quarterly 55* (October), 161.

Hennock, F. (1955a). Address, 3 May 1955. Hennock MSS., Schlesinger Library, Radcliffe College, Box 8–136.

Hennock, F. (1955b). Statement to Senate Judiciary Committee. Sub-Committee on Juvenile Deliquency, 6 April 1955. Hennock MSS., Schlesinger Library, Radcliffe College, Box 8–136.

Henry, E. J. (1936). Letter to Schramm, 4 September 1963. Henry MSS., Box 21. State Historical Society of Wisconsin.

Henry, E. J. (1964). Address, 7 December 1964. p. 5. Henry MSS., Box 77, State Historical Society of Wisconsin.

Henry, E. J. (1965). Educational TV is still just a promise. *American Education 1* (February), 27–28.

Herring, E. P. (1935). Politics and radio regulation. *Harvard Business Review 13* (January), 167–178.

Herzog, H. (1944). What do we really know about daytime serial listeners. *In* P. Lazarsfeld and F. Stanton (Eds.), "Radio Research 1942–1943," New York: Duell, Sloane, Pearce.

Hess, R. D., and Goldman, H. (1962). Parent's view of the effects of television on children. *Child Development 33*, 411–26.

Hettinger, H. S. (1938). The economic fact in radio regulation. *Air Law Review 9* (April).

Hobson, W. K. (1977). Professionals, progressives and bureaucratization: A reassessment. *Historian 39* (August), 639–658.

Hofstader, R. (1961). A note on intellect and power. *American Scholar 30* (Autumn).

Holaday, P. W., and Stoddard, G. D. (1933). "Getting Ideas from the Movies." New York: MacMillan.

Hoover, H. (1922). Statement to first national radio conference, 27 February 1922. Radio File, Hoover MSS., Stanford University.

Hoover, H. (1950). "The Reminiscences of Herbert Hoover." Oral History Research Office. Columbia University. pp. 1–17.

Hoover, H. (1952). "The Memoirs of Herbert Hoover: The Cabinet and the Presidency, 1920–1933." New York: Macmillan.

Hovland, C., Lumsdaine, A. A., and Sheffield, F. D. (1949). "Experiments in Mass Communication." Princeton, NJ: Princeton University Press.

Hughes, H. S. (1962). "An Approach to Peace." New York: Antheneum.

Independent Journal. (1933). 2 (October 16), 4.

Johnson, N. (1970). "How to Talk Back to Your Television Set." Boston, MA: Atlantic/Little, Brown.

Johnson, N. (1971). A new fidelity to the regulatory ideal. *Georgetown Law Journal 59* (March), 869–908.

Karl, B. D. (1974). "Charles E. Merriam and the Science of Politics." Chicago, IL: University of Chicago Press.

Karl, B. D. (1969). Presidential planning and social science research: Mr. Hoover's experts. *Perspectives in American History 3*, 347–409.

Katz, E., et al. (1974). Utilization of mass communication by the individual. *In* J. G. Blumler and E. Katz (Eds.), "The Uses of Mass Communications," Beverly Hills, CA: Sage Publications.

Katz, E., and Lazarsfeld, P. (1955). "Personal Influence." New York: Free Press.

Kaufman, H. J. (1944). The appeal of specific daytime serials. *In* P. Lazarsfeld and F. Stanton (Eds.), "Radio Research 1942–1943," pp. 86–110, New York: Duell, Sloane, Pearce.

Kent, F. (1933). Baltimore *Sun*, (December 6).

Kern, J. (1961). TV: Too violent? *Chicago American Leisure Magazine*, (October). Copy in Minow MSS., Box 24, State Historical Society of Wisconsin.

Kirkendall, R. S. (1962). Franklin D. Roosevelt and the service intellectual. *Mississippi Valley Historical Review 49* (January), 456–71.

Klapper, J. (1960). "The Effects of Mass Communication." New York: Free Press.

Klapper, J. (1968). Testimony, National Commission on the Causes and Prevention of Violence, "Proceedings" pp. 1344, 1392, 16 October 1968. Copy in Roman Hruska MSS., Box 89, Nebraska Historical Society.

Krauthammer, C. (1981). Science ex machina. *The New Republic 184*, (June 6), 19–25.

La Follete, R. M. (1912). "Autobiography." Madison, WI: La Follete Co.

Landis, J. B. (1938). "The Administrative Process." New Haven, CT: Yale University Press.

Laski, H. J. (1931). The limitations on the expert. *Fabian Tract* No. 235, 13–14.

Lasswell, H. D. (1935a). "World Politics and Personal Insecurity: A Contribution to Political Psychiatry." New York: McGraw-Hill.

Lasswell, H. D., Casey, R. D., and Smith, B. L. (1935). "Propaganda and Promotional Activities: An Annotated Bibliography." Minneapolis, MN: University of Minnesota Press.

Law and Contemporary Problems. (1958). *23* (Winter), n.p.

Law and Contemporary Problems. (1957). *23* (Autumn), n.p.

Lazarsfeld, P., and Stanton, F. (Eds.). (1943). "Radio Research 1941–1942," New York: Duell, Sloane, Pearce.

Lazarsfeld, P., and Stanton, F. (Eds.). (1944). "Radio Research 1943–1944," New York: Duell, Sloane, Pearce.

Lazarsfeld, P., and Stanton, F. (Eds.). (1949). "Communication Research 1948–1949," New York: Harper.

Lazarsfeld, P. (1968). An episode in the history of social research: A memoir. *Perspectives in American History 2.*

Lazarsfeld, P., Berelson, B., and Gaudet, H. (1944). "The People's Choice." New York: Duell, Sloane, Pearce.

Lees, G. E. (1978). Unsafe for little cars? The regulation of broadcast advertising to children. *UCLA Law Review 25* (June), 1131–86.

Levy, D. (1964). "The Chameleons." New York: Dodd, Mead.

Lichty, L. (1962). The impact of FRC and FCC commissioners' backgrounds on the regulation of broadcasting. *Journal of Broadcasting 6*, 97–110.

Lichty, L. W. (1961–62). Members of the Federal Radio Commission and Federal Communications Commission, 1927–1961. *Journal of Broadcasting* 6 (Winter).

Lichty, L. W. (1961). An analysis of the FCC membership. *Public Utilities Fortnightly* 68, 828–33.

Lindesy, O. R. (1962). A behavioral measure of television viewing. Journal of Advertising Research 2 (September), 2.

McCarthy, C. (1912). "The Wisconsin Idea." New York: MacMillan.

McConnaughey, G. (1954). Address, "Educational Broadcasting," 28 October 1954. Copy in Hennock MSS., Schlestinger Library, Radcliffe College, Box 15–146.

McIntyre, M. (1937). Letter to Wetmore Hodges, 23 July 1937. Roosevelt MSS., White House Central Files, Box 1059 #2.

McLeod, J. M., and Becker, L. (1982). The uses and gratifications approach to political communications research. *In* D. Nimmo and K. Sanders (Eds.), "Handbook of Political Communication." Beverly Hills, CA: Sage Publications.

McLeod, J. M., and Reeves, B. (1980). On the nature of mass media effects. *In* S. B. Withey and R. P. Abeles (Eds.), "Television and Social Behavior: Beyond Violence and Children," pp. 17–54, New York: Laurence Erlbaum Associates.

McPherson, H. C. (1986). Letter to Lyndon B. Johnson, 7 June 1968. Johnson MSS., Group UT-1, Johnson Library.

Martineau, P. (1957). "Motivation in Advertising: Motives That Make People Buy." New York: McGraw–Hill.

Mathes, Mrs. W. L. (1961). Letter to Andrew Schoeppel, 17 March 1961. Schoeppel MSS., Kansas Historical Society.

May, H. F. (1959). "The End of Innocence." New York: Knopf.

Meine, F. J. (1941). Radio and the press among young people. *In* P. F. Lazarsfeld and F. N. Stanton (Eds.), "Radio Research 1941," New York: Duell, Sloane, and Pearce.

Melody, W. (1973). "Children's Television: The Economics of Exploitation," pp. 87–97. New Haven, CN: Yale University Press.

Merton, R. K., and Lerner, D. (1951). Social scientists and research policy. *In* D. Lerner and H. Lasswell (Eds.), "The Policy Sciences," Stanford, CA: Stanford University Press.

Miller, G. R. (1966). "Speech Communication: A Behavioral Approach." Indianapolis, IN: Bobbs-Merrill.

Miller, H. L.(1980). Hard realities and soft social science. *The Public Interest* No. 59 (Summer), 67–82.

Minow, N. (1961). Letter to Jessie Tufts Jackson, 12 April 1961. Minow MSS., Box 8, State Historical Society of Wisconsin.

Minow, N. (1962). Draft article for *This Week* (c. March). Minow MSS., Box 43, State Historical Society of Wisconsin.

Minow, N. (1964). "Equal Time: The Private Broadcaster and the Public Interest." New York: Atheneum.

Mitler, E. A., and Perian, C. L. (1957). Memorandum to Thomas C. Hennings, Jr., 14 February 1957. Copy in Alexander H. Wiley MSS., Series 4, Box 11, State Historical Society of Wisconsin.

Moley, R. (1938). "Are We Movie Made." New York: Macy-Masius.

Muller v. Oregon 208 U.S. 412 (1908).

Murphy, C. S. (1968). Letter to Lyndon B. Johnson, 7 June 1968. Johnson MSS., Group UT-1, Johnson Library.

Nafziger, R. O. (1930). A reader interest survey of Madison, Wisconsin. *Journalism Quarterly* 7, 128–141.

National Commission on the Causes and Prevention of Violence. (1969). "Mass Media and Violence." Washington, DC: Government Printing Office.

New York *Herald Tribune*, 16 October 1933. n.p.

New York *Times*. 16 May 1982. n.p.

New York *Times*. 25 July 1982. n.p.

New York *Times*. 4 April 1982. n.p.

New York *Times*. 3 April 1981. n.p.

New York *Times*. 5 March 1979. n.p.

New York *Times*. 8 August 1978. n.p.

New York *Times*. 17 April 1977. n.p.

New York *Times*. 21 March 1926, clipping in Hoover MSS., Box 490, Hoover Presidential Library, Stanford University.

Office of the Secretary of Health, Education, and Welfare. (1962). Press release (July 9). Copy in Minow MSS., Box 8, State Historical Society of Wisconsin.

Packard, V. (1957). "The Hidden Persuaders." New York: Pocket Books, paperback edition.

Paisley, M. B. (1972). "Social Policy Research and the Realities of the System: Violence Done to TV Research." Unpublished paper, Institute for Communication Research. Stanford University, March.

Paisley, W. (1972). "Communication Research as a Behavioral Discipline." Unpublished manuscript, Stanford University.

Peatman, J. G. (1944). Radio and popular music. *In* P. Lazarsfeld and F. N. Stanton (Eds.), "Radio Research 1942–1943," pp. 335–396. New York: Duell, Sloane, Pearce.

Peterson, G. E. (1973). "President Harry S. Truman and the Independent Commissions, 1945–1952." Unpublished dissertation, University of Maryland.

Peterson, R. C., and Thurston, L. L. (1933). "Motion Pictures and the Social Attitudes of Children." New York: MacMillan.

Phelan, J. J. (1919). "Motion Pictures in a Typical City." Toledo, OH: Little Book Press.

President's Research Committee on Social Trends. (1933). "Recent Social Trends in the United States." 2 Vols. New York: McGraw-Hill.

Preston, I. L. (1982). Researchers and the Federal Trade Commission—peril and promise. "Current Issues and Research in Advertising," pp. 2–4. Ann Arbor, MI: Graduate School of Business Administration, University of Michigan.

Prince, W. L. (1959). Letter to Norris Cotton, 16 December 1959. Cotton MSS., Box 45, University of New Hampshire.

Rainwater, L., and Yancey, W. L. (1967). "The Moynihan Report and the Politics of Controversy." Cambridge, MA: MIT Press.

Reeves, B., and Atkin, C. (1979). "The Effects of Saturday Morning Television Advertising on Mother-Child Interactions in the Grocery Store." (Paper presented at Association for Education in Journalism, Houston, Texas).

Rivers, W., Peterson, T., and Jensen, J. W. (1971). "The Mass Media in Modern Society." 2nd ed., New York: Holt, Rinehart, and Winston.

Roberts, D., and Bachen, C. (1981). Mass communications effects. *In* "Annual Review of Psychology," *32.*

Roberts, D. F., Christenson, P., Gibson, W. A., Mooser, L., Goldberg, M. E. (1980). Developing discriminating consumers. *Journal of Communication 30,* 94–105.

Robinson, T. P. (1943). "Radio Networks and the Federal Government." New York: Columbia University Press.

Robinson, W. S. (1941). Radio comes to the farmer. *In* P. F. Lazarsfeld and F. N. Stanton (Eds.), "Radio Research 1941," pp. 224–72, New York: Sloan and Pearce.

Rogers, E. (1973). Mass media and interpersonal communication. *In* I. de Sola Pool and W. Schramm (Eds.), "Handbook of Communication," pp. 290–312, Chicago, IL: Rand McNally.

Roosevelt, F. D. (1938). Letter to Norman Case, 30 June 1938. Roosevelt MSS., White House Central Files, Box 1059 #2.

Rosen, P. (1980). "The Modern Stentors: Radio Broadcasters and Federal Government." Westport, CT: Greenwood Press.

Rosenblum, J. (1961). Authority of the Federal Communications Commission. *In* J. E. Coons (Ed.), "Freedom and Responsibility in Broadcasting," pp. 96–170. Evanston, IL: Northwestern University Press.

Rothschild, R. K. (1961). Letter to Alexander H. Wiley, 17 June 1961. Alexander H. Wiley MSS., Series 4, Box 12. State Historical Society of Wisconsin.

Rowland, W. D., Jr. (1982). The symbolic uses of effects: Notes on the television violence inquiries and the legitimation of mass communication research. *In* M.

Burgoon (Ed.), "Communication Yearbook 5," pp. 385–404. New Brunswick, NJ: Transaction Books.

Schramm, W. (1967). "Human Communication as a Field of Behavioral Science." Unpublished manuscript, Stanford University.

Schramm, W., Lyle, J., and Parker, E. (1961). "Television in the Lives of Our Children." Stanford, CA: Stanford University Press.

Schwartz, B. (1959). Comparative television and the chancellor's foot. *Georgetown Law Journal 47* (Summer), 655–99.

Seidman, H. (1975). "Politics, Position, and Power: The Dynamics of Federal Organization," 2nd ed. New York: Oxford University Press.

Shannon, C., and Weaver, W. (1949). "Mathematical Theory of Human Communication." Urbana, IL: University of Illinois Press.

Slepmann, C. A. (1944). American radio in wartime. *In* P. Lazarsfeld and F. N. Stanton (Eds.), "Radio Research 1942–1943," pp. 110–50. New York: Durell, Sloane, Pearce.

Slepmann, C. A. (1946). "Radio's Second Chance." Boston, MA: Little, Brown.

Slepmann, C. A. (1950). "Radio, Television, and Society." New York: Oxford University Press.

Skowronek, S. (1982). "Building a New American State: The Expansion of National Administrative Capacities, 1877–1920," pp. 160–61, 165, 286. Cambridge, MA: Cambridge University Press.

Sober, T. Mrs. (1961). Letter to Newton Minow, 24 June 1961. FCC MSS., General Services Administration, Box 243, Invoice No. 63A83.

Stanley, D. et al. (1967). "Men Who Govern." Washington, DC: Brookings Institution.

Stanton, F. (1967–68). "The Reminiscences of Frank Stanton," pp. 159–60. Oral History Research office. Columbia University.

Stanton, F. (1961). Letter to Minow, 22 August 1961. Minow MSS., Box 41, State Historical Society of Wisconsin.

Steele, R. W. (1974). The pulse of the people: Franklin D. Roosevelt and the gauging of public opinion. *Journal of Contemporary History 9* (October), 195–216.

Syracuse *Herald-Journal*. 25 September 1961. n.p.

Thain, G. (1976). Suffer the hucksters to come unto the little children? *Boston University Law Review 56* (July), 65–84.

Thelen, D. P. (1976). "Robert M. La Follette and the Insurgent Spirit," pp. 113–18. Boston, MA: Little, Brown.

Toffler, A. (1955). Crime in your parlor. *Nation 181* (15 October), 323–24.

U.S. Congress. Senate. (1977). Committee on Government Affairs. "Study on Federal Regulation, vol. 3: Public Participation in Regulatory Agency Proceedings, pp. 151, 152. Doc. No. 95–71. 95th Congress. 1st session.

U.S. Congress. Senate. (1976). Committee on Commerce. "Appointments to the Regulatory Agencies: The Federal Communications Commission and the Federal Trade Commission (1949–1974), Chs. 16, 18 and Pt. IV. Committee report. 94th Congress. 2nd session.

U.S. Congress. Senate. (1974a). Committee on Commerce. "Federal Trade Commission Oversights," hearings. 93rd Congress. 2nd session.

U.S. Congress. Senate. (1974b). Committee on Commerce. "Violence on Television," pp. 15–16. Hearings. 93rd Congress. 2nd session.

U.S. Congress. Senate. (1972). Committee on Commerce. "Surgeon General's Report by the Scientific Advisory Committee on Television and Social Behavior," pp. 14–19. Hearings. 92nd Congress. 2nd session.

U.S. Congress. Senate. (1971). Committee on Commerce. "Scientific Advisory Committee on TV and Social Behavior," pp. 1–2, 7–11. Hearings. 92nd Congress. 1st session.

U.S. Congress. Senate. (1970). Committee on Commerce. "Dry Cereals." Hearings. 91st Congress. 2nd session.

U.S. Congress. Senate. (1969). Committee on Commerce. "Federal Communications Policy-makers and Television Programming," pp. 337–38. Hearings. 91st Congress. 1st session.

U.S. Congress. Senate. (1961–62). Judiciary Committee. Subcommittee on Juvenile Delinquency. "Effects on Young People of Violence and Crime," hearings, pp. 1770–773. 87th Congress. 1st session.

U.S. Congress. Senate. (1955a). Judiciary Committee. Subcommittee on Juvenile Delinquency. "Juvenile Delinquency (Comic Books)," hearings. 84th Congress. 1st session.

U.S. Congress. Senate. (1955b). Judiciary Committee. Subcommittee on Juvenile Delinquency. "Juvenile Delinquency (Motion Pictures)," hearings. 84th Congress. 1st session.

U.S. Congress. Senate. (1955c). Judiciary Committee. Subcommittee on Juvenile Delinquency. "Juvenile Delinquency (Television Programs)," p. 1, hearings. 84th Congress. 1st session.

U.S. Congress. Senate. (1954). Judiciary Committee. Subcommittee on Juvenile Delinquency. "Juvenile Delinquency (Television Programs)," hearings. 83rd Congress. 1st session.

U.S. Congress. Senate. (1926). Interstate and Foreign Commerce Committee. "Regulation of Radio Transmission." Report No. 772. 69th Congress. 1st session.

Variety. 13 January 1982, 143–45; 180; 182.

Variety. 30 September 1981, pp. 1, 108.

Variety. 11 June 1968, pp. 1, 11. Clipping in Norman Jewison MSS., Box 17, State Historical Society of Wisconsin.

Vaughn, S. L. (1980). "'Holding Fast the Inner Lines': Democracy, Nationalism, and the Committee on Public Information." Chapel Hill, NC: University of North Carolina Press.

Wartella, E. (1979). The developmental perspective. *In* E. Wartella (Ed.), "Children Communicating: Media and the Development of Thought, Speech, and Understanding," ch. 1. Beverly Hills, CA: Sage Publications.

Wartella, E. and Reeves, B. (1982). "Research on Media and Youth: The American Experience in Historical Perspective." (Paper presented at the International Association of Mass Communication Research, Paris, France.)

Washington *Post.* 27 June 1981. n.p.

Wattwood, R. (1978). FTC regulation of TV advertising to children—they deserve a break today. *University of Florida Law Review 30* (Fall), 946–78.

Weaver, D. H., and Gray, R. G. (1980). Journalism and mass communication research in the United States: Past, present, and future. *In* G. C. Wilhoit (Ed.), "Mass Communication Review Yearbook 1980," Vol. 1, ch. 6.

Weis, W. (1969). Effects of mass communication. *In* G. Lindsey and E. Aronson (Eds.), "The Handbook of Social Psychology," Vol. 5. New York: Addison-Wesley.

Wertham, F. (1954). "Seduction of the Innocent." New York: Rinehart.

Wertham, F. (1960). How movie and tv violence affects children. *Ladies Home Journal 77*, (February), 58–59.

Westley, B. F., and Maclean, M. (1957). A conceptual model for communication research. *Journalism Quarterly 34*, 31–38.

White, M. (1949). "Social Thought in America: The Revolt Against Formalism." New York: Viking.

Wiebe, R. H. (1967). "The Search for Order, 1877–1920." New York: Hill and Wang.

Willis, C., Jr. (1955). Letter to Spessard Holland, 25 April 1955. Eisenhower MSS., Official File 41–A, Box 383.

Wilson, J. Q. (1981). 'Policy Intellectuals' and public policy. *The Public Interest* No. 64 (Summer), 31–46.

Witty, P. (1958). Some results of eight yearly studies of television. *School and Society 87*, 287–89.

Wolf, K. M., and Fiske, M. (1949). The children talk about comics. *In* P. Lazarsfeld and F. Stanton (Eds.), "Communications Research 1948–1949," pp. 3–46. New York: Harper.

Wylie, M. (1955). "Clear Channels: Television and the American People." New York: Funk & Wagnalls.

IV

Conclusions

26

Enduring Tensions and Lessons Learned

Sandra Braman
2002

However agonizing current dilemmas may be, they are not new. Rather, the same kinds of problems recur over and over again. They fall into two categories: some result from essentially unresolvable issues, while others are resolvable on the basis of lessons learned from past experience. Distinguishing between the two is a first step in addressing several deep contradictions:

• Because the U.S. government has spent massive amounts of funds on the development of information technologies but almost nothing on understanding their uses and effects, policy-makers are crippled when it comes to making policy for the information infrastructure.

• Because universities narrowly define the categories of work to be considered for promotion and tenure—despite the long-standing legal position that the fundamental function of universities is to provide a variety of forms of service to society—researchers interested in providing public service find doing so is often self-destructive in career terms.

• Because the literature on policy-making restricts itself to the formal processes of what is now referred to as legacy law and training in how to think about policy is so thin, communication researchers wishing to engage with the policy world often do so precisely at the moments when they are least likely to be effective.

• For those who study information, communication, and culture the field as a whole faces the dilemma that precisely when its insights are most needed those who know the most are barely in the conversation at all.

All of this matters not because the discipline "must survive," or because it serves the personal goals of particular individuals, but because it is a matter of national capacity—our ability as a society to make it possible to craft a world in which we would like to live.

Enduring Tensions

Enduring tensions arise when individuals must make choices in circumstances characterized by multiple but often mutually exclusive goals, guiding principles, rights, and responsibilities. They appear in the course of defining relationships between researchers and policy-maker, the design of research questions, and the structuring of decision-making processes.

Relationships

Researchers who seek input into policy-making processes face issues raised by their relationships with policy-makers, with their employing institutions, and with themselves.

Between Researcher and Policy-maker   The inevitably political aspect of policy work yields a spectrum of possible relationships between researcher and policy-maker. In the easiest situation, a researcher may be in complete agreement with the goals of a policy-maker. Often, however, researchers are interested in expanding the range of policy alternatives under consideration or in effecting a specific change in policy. When either of these is the case, the researcher will need to protect his or her autonomy in the conduct of research and interpretation of its results—and must be able to separate both from negotiations over creating and implementing specific policies. Keeping the scholarly and political tasks separate will increase the utility and efficacy of each.

To do so does not require taking the position that research is neutral. As within the exclusively scholarly context, research is still strongest when the biases and assumptions of researchers are acknowledged, the weaknesses and limitations of the chosen research method are explained, and the nature of the Hawthorne effect, if any—the impact of the research itself upon the subject studied—is identified. It does, however, require acknowledging that the translation of research results into policy requires normative and political arguments as well as information. Data may reveal the shape of a policy problem but cannot determine, on its own, which out of what is always a multitude of possible policy responses is best under a given set of empirical and political conditions.

The manner with which work that is critical or urges policy-makers to take alternative choices is presented makes a big difference to the reception of those ideas. Framing critical arguments within the language of the dominant policy-making discourse is likely to be more successful than demanding that policy-makers attend to a discourse framed in language unfamiliar to them and untranslatable into terms that are. Those who argue that communication policy has been unable to deal fully with questions of equity and civil liberties because it relies solely upon quantitative data have a responsibility to act upon the alternatives:

1. find ways of quantifying concepts historically treated as unquantifiable so that they may be incorporated into existing decision-making processes;

2. develop ways of adapting decision-making processes currently in use so that they can identify moments when other types of inputs are required and kick decisions that require this into another decision loop; and/or

3. develop new modes of decision making that can incorporate consideration of both quantitative and qualitative kinds of data, an approach more possible with today's information technologies than it has been historically.

Trust between policy-maker and researcher is clearly important in creating a situation in which even critical arguments or requests for change are being made. As a result, personal relationships with policy-makers are important for researchers who would like to have some impact. Demonstrating a willingness to go to where policy-makers are— to travel to Washington, take part in conversations exploring policy issues, respond to calls for policy input, meet with staffers with communications policy responsibilities, etc.—as well as demanding that those in the policy world "come over" to academia, can also make a big difference.

Relationships between communication researchers and policy-makers can also be structured in multiple ways. Some believe that the researcher who works as an insider—as a staffer—is likely to be most successful. Skeptics suggest that the impact of advocates may be limited because they are seen as non-representative voices from outside the policy process, while enthusiasts claim advocates play an invaluable role because they ensure that a diversity of viewpoints is expressed and because they offer at least some lobbying counterweight to the perspectives based in the corporate world. The role that can be played by training those who will ultimately become policy-makers and can serve as bridges between the worlds of research and decision-making should also not be undervalued; curricular issues within higher education should be considered one of the ways by which research is brought into policy-makers' hands.

Some researchers operate like clinicians, treating policy-makers like clients who need help either because they are deficient or because they are facing pressures with which they cannot cope. Others take the identity of strategist, treating the policy-maker as a client who is simultaneously a colleague with whom the researcher seeks to collaborate in the effort to merge practical knowledge with more systematic modes of analysis. Or the researcher may treat a policy-maker client or sponsor as an "alter," because in the policy world a client individual or institution may at another point in time become a set of resources or the environment within which the researcher must operate. This last notion enriches the concept of the "revolving door" through which individuals move from academia to government and back by emphasizing that researchers are also citizens.

There will of course always be those who believe that to engage at all with policy-makers or policy questions is to be coopted. A researcher's choice to maintain a distance from all governmental concerns, however, provides no guarantee that his or her work once published will not be used by policy-makers. Results of research may even be used to policy ends quite other than those desired by the researcher. Inaction by researchers, whether deliberate or through lack of consensus, has the effect of providing support for the status quo.

Between Researcher and Employer   Though job responsibilities for American academics are ritually described as "research, teaching, and service," it is widely known that research publication has long been considered far more important than the other two for promotion and tenure purposes, and in recent years "receiving outside funds" has become the unspoken item added to the front of the list. While research reports aimed at policy-makers and other types of engagements with policy-making processes can be intensely time-consuming and intellectually rigorous, such activities are usually relegated to the relatively low-ranking category of "service."

The same kind of research can result in either a policy intervention or publication (or both), but the two types of work products are quite different as genres. This is not only a question of narrative form; publication in the kind of refereed scholarly journals of the type required for promotion and tenure in universities not only in the United States but increasingly around the world require achievement of generalizations, while policy analysis and solutions are always and inevitably particular and unique to the circumstances. There may even be a difference in the types of questions asked.

Thus communication researchers interested in contributing to policy-making processes must often choose between attending to policy-related research questions and audiences and their own professional survival. Those who receive outside funding for policy-related work may find themselves somewhat more protected professionally for economic reasons, but the genuinely critical work so important to healthy policy-making processes is less likely to receive funding than that which directly serves existing corporate or other institutional interests. Those engaged in useful policy analysis that does serve existing institutional needs face an additional complication—when the then-chief economist of the FCC issued a call for researcher input in the mid-1990s he acknowledged that anyone capable of actually addressing the questions to which the agency sought answers was likely already to be in the employ of the industries being regulated for sums of money so substantial that he or she would be unlikely to turn attention to pro bono work.

In a world as driven by personal reputation and interpersonal competition as academia, a response from the policy world to the ideas and data of researchers can lead to hubris. Remaining in contact with the academic environment may provide a useful grounding when excitement about being close to those in power may tempt individuals into unsound or inappropriate work.

Between the Researcher and the Self   A researcher interested in policy-related matters must undergo a series of negotiations not only with the policy institutions of interest but also with him or herself. Those struggles include the need to acknowledge the gap between an ideal world in which one might believe and the political realities of the real world; difficulties encountered with colleagues who may treat policy-related work with scorn or not take it seriously; identity questions raised by the addition of new roles to those of scholar, researcher, and teacher; and the simple pragmatic problem that however theory- and research-rich it is, often policy work does not count in academic promotion and tenure processes. These, too, are political issues—one may find one's work used by decision makers with whose politics you are uncomfortable, have to live with failures of policies promoted by one's work, or be forced to choose between a research program driven by one's theoretical position as opposed to one's political choices.

Research Questions

The horizon against which policy problems are defined, the need for research questions dealing with decision-making processes and the effects of the implementation of policy to be cast in terms that are empirically valid, the degree to which their analysis focuses on generalizable as opposed to unique features, the extent to which research questions are critical in nature, and the desirability of consensus are dimensions of question definition that can affect the utility of communication research to policy-makers.

The Horizon   The difference in the rhythm of the processes with which researchers and policy-makers are engaged creates another enduring tension: Policy-makers generally work on a very short time horizon and need immediate answers to pressing questions, while those involved in research rely upon time-intensive habits of conceptual development and exhaustive research projects that are often of greatest value when longitudinal. Waiting upon scholarly publication cycles for public presentation of work additionally adds potentially years to the process, though there are multiple ways work can effectively come to the attention of policy-makers before it reaches official publication: manuscripts can be sent to staffers and policy-makers, *amicus curiae* briefs can be filed in court cases, and, today, electronic modes of publication can disseminate findings in the form of working papers and reports long before results reach more formal print forms.

Even such techniques, however, cannot address the problem of taking into account the needs of future generations. Environmental problems have drawn attention to the fact that while it may be possible to get the consent of the governed from those currently living, it is not possible to get policy agreement from those yet unborn. Yet the path dependency of decisions about information infrastructure and its uses means that some method of taking the future into account is necessary. In some policy issue areas there is experimentation with techniques for "discounting the future" and otherwise incorporating long-range impacts into contemporary decision making, and the same needs to be done in the area of policy dealing with information, communication, and culture. This problem is exacerbated by technological change. Policy analysts working in the contemporary environment must deal both with what even the FCC is now referring to as "legacy law"—law and regulation designed for a technological world of media distinguishable for legal treatment that no longer exists—as well as with emergent infrastructural, social, and legal realities.

The Validity of Research Questions The formal policy-making processes to which most communication policy research refers are not the only processes of importance to the real world of how decisions are made and the ways in which they are implemented. Informal negotiations, variables that intervene in the ways in which policies are put into place on the ground, and the intersections among the multiple types of social systems that convene on the policy process should all be subjects of research. Increasingly policy-making is only one among the many structural forces shaping the communications environment. Thus other factors, such as the structural influence of software and infrastructure system design, need attention as well.

The Global and the Local   While policy analysts tend to look for what can be generalized across cases, actual instances of policy-making will always be unique and thus will not be susceptible to a fixed set of analytical rules. Every social process and phenomenon, that is, occurs at a unique conjuncture of numerous causal forces. Policy decisions, too, arise at the intersection of multiple different games, only some of which explicitly involve the policy-making process itself. Neither policy processes nor their solutions are necessarily applicable across environments. Even the elements of the policy world may take on different roles as they move from context to context. In South Africa in the late 1990s, for example, structuring regulatory agencies became a form of discourse, discourse a form of policy tool, policy tools a form of cultural expression, and culture the data upon which regulation was to be based. The implication for communication researchers interested in having an influence on policy processes is that analysis must be responsive to the the particularities of specific situations—though an overemphasis on the particular can also be dangerous.

Administrative versus Critical   Though many argue that there is an enduring tension between critical research and policy research, others take the position that policy research at its best *is* critical research, applied. Certainly there have been cases when criticism of specific policies or policy-making processes and institutions has been welcomed; indeed, at times those inside decision making organizations try to elicit critical input in order to stimulate or affect specific internal processes. Those who believe that the most valuable role of communication research for policy-makers is putting new ideas on the table are suggesting that critical work is not only inevitable but intrinsic to the process. For this to be successful, however, one must attend to matters of presentation, the nature of the relationship between researcher and policy-maker, and the question of trust. Thus the enduring tension here is not between the types of research but, rather, between the content of the ideas presented and the mode and manner of presentation. There is always the danger that the messenger may be shot.

Innovation versus Consensus   Of the various roles researchers can play in policy-making processes, clearly one of the most effective is expanding the range of potential policy choices by putting new ideas on the table. At the same time, policy-makers are uncomfortable when there is a lack of consensus among researchers—or use such disagreement to turn the results of research to their own political ends. Of course ideas that are new at one point in time can become the subjects of consensus at another, but this enduring tension intersects with that between short and long time horizons to make identification of specific tactics for researchers non-obvious.

Process
The distinction between research and policy is an enduring tension for communication researchers because of the temptation to insert one's personal policy preferences into the presentation of research data or, in some, the belief that the policy implications of one's data are obvious and inevitable. Coping with this tension can include foregrounding the normative assumptions in one's research as well as the ways in which conducting research on a policy problem can constitute an intervention in itself. The Canadian-based nongovernmental organization (ngo) International Development Research Centre (IDRC) provides a model of the latter by incorporating the Hawthorne effect explicitly into the design of its research projects on communication policy-related issues across the developing world. Dolf Zillman's recommendation that the process of bringing research into policy-making processes be carefully broken down into the separate stages of problem definition, synthesis of research, identification of alternative policy responses, and making a policy decision is another way of responding to this problem.

Almost all communication policy research aims at legislation once proposed or put in place—precisely the points at which it is least likely to have impact. While it may be easiest to see the target at this stage, those who want to have effect need to enter the process both much earlier (when the range of possible policy alternatives is being determined) and much later (when the effects of the implementation of policies are being evaluated).

Lessons Learned

Certain lessons for researchers and policy-makers can be garnered from the experience of others.

Assume That Ideas Matter

Oddly, academics often underestimate the weight of ideas. It is only in the last dozen years that social scientists have begun to incorporate ideas into their analyses of social processes. While the realistic set of policy options may be narrow, the policy process itself is a voracious consumer of ideas. Ideas fulfill multiple roles—they illuminate, they legitimate, and they are critical to keeping debate alive. One of the most important functions for academics is theoretical, for theoretical innovation provides conceptual frameworks that in turn suggest new policy options. This function is particularly important during a period in which the very nature of the information infrastructure is undergoing such radical change.

Of course this can be taken too far. Ideas may be taken up for short-lived political purposes or rhetorical effect. The actual animating logics of policy-makers may be spurious or even counter-indicative. Concepts and belief structures that shape policy-making may not be explicit, so that one of the jobs for researchers should be to bring them into the light.

The "weak Baconian"[1] position acknowledges that knowledge may be power, but it is not a 1:1 relationship. The lesson for communication researchers is that while specific ideas may not always win, they do matter. Generating ideas is thus fundamental to the metabolism of the policy-making process; to do so is to serve as a public intellectual. The greatest benefit from those who choose to play the role of public intellectual may be not in answering questions but in clarifying the questions to be asked.

Policy Analysis Demands Theory Development

While existing theory can usefully be applied in the course of policy analysis, the conceptual task does not stop there. As with any other engagement with the empirical world, policy analysis should serve to refine theory and move it forward. Unlike research data generated in the controlled conditions of laboratories or via a restriction of variables examined in a natural setting, the study of policy problems requires accepting multicausal explanations of events and processes that unfold in complex environments involving a myriad of variables. One of the ways, therefore, that addressing policy problems may create a "happy moment" in the development of the field is that it forces the evolution of theory complex enough to map validly onto the world we experience, demands the development of meso-level theory linking abstractions with the ground, requires linkage of theories that apply to different levels of analysis, insists that longitudinal analyses be undertaken, and must start with fundamental questions involving the nature of society and communication within it.

Treat Policy-making as a Coalition Process

Though researchers are generally accustomed to working alone or only with other researchers, policy-making involves a coalition among social scientists and many other kinds of actors. As a result, success in the world of policy requires negotiating skills additional to those required for scholarship. Responding to critiques of research with anger or withdrawal, for example, may work in the scholarly world but is completely dysfunctional in the policy environment.

The coalition nature of the process is one explanation for the unpredictable or limited impact of research results. Though in the minds of academics data may be determinative, in the political world they are only one among many inputs into decision-making processes that are themselves not linear in nature. The complexity of these processes, then, has research as well as behavioral implications. The notion of the policy world as an ecology of games is one way of responding to this situation conceptually and methodologically. Appreciation of the tacit knowledge of working policy-makers is another. Onoing relationships between researchers and policy-makers are a third feature of the coalition nature of the process. Policy research reports are in fact often superfluous in themselves, having been designed into the process as a means of legitimating systematic interactions between researchers and policy-makers. Acknowledging that policy-making is a coalition venture can also open up opportunities for academics, who otherwise find they may have only limited access to pertinent data.

Particularly in issue areas in which circumstances are as rapidly changing as they are in the area of the building, regulation, and use of the global information infrastructure, a great deal of the critical policy thinking and decision making takes place orally during face-to-face meetings at seminars, colloquia, and other venues for public discussion. The slow pace of academic publishing means that even when refereed journal articles or books are on-point for specific problems, they may arrive on the scene long after pertinent decisions have been made. For this reason, too, participating in oral conversation is important. Doing so also contributes to the building of the personal relationships with policy-makers that goes far in developing the kind of trust and credibility required for one's work to be taken into account in the course of policy-making.

Beware of Overgeneralization

Overgeneralization of research findings—whether across time periods, societies, or situations—is one of the greatest weaknesses of communication research as applied to policy problems. Though research results are often presented as if they are independent of their social parameters, it is now understood that any specific social process or phenomenon occurs at an always-unique confluence of multiple different causal forces. To enhance the usefulness of research results for policy-makers, academics must thus:

1. clarify the conditions under which those results obtain;
2. resist ahistorical interpretations of data;
3. distinguish between short-lived phenomena and long-term trends;
4. acknowledge the limitations of findings; and
5. be willing to reexamine policy conclusions when new research appears.

Working in interdisciplinary teams—another form of coalition effort—can help avoid the monocausal explanations of complex situations so tempting to researchers whose research streams are based in single theories.

Theory and concepts, too, can be essentially overgeneralized. Even notions such as secrecy are far from static over time and across cultures, the result of dynamic ongoing negotiations responsive both to social processes and technological change.

Build a Coherent Research Agenda

The fragmented nature of too many scholarly research agendas seriously handicaps the academic community vis-à-vis the systematic and comprehensive efforts of the corporate world. Across researchers this contributes to a perception on the part of policy-makers that communications as a field lacks a consensus and has failed to deal with many of the issues of primary concern. At the individual level, fragmentation of research agendas undermines efforts to build enduring relationships both with policy-makers and with those who fund policy research. Sustained attention to specific problems over time is critical to building credibility and developing a reputation for subject-specific expertise.

A related characteristic of research programs is endurance. The policy-making openness to research changes over time as ideas first seen as radical or irrelevant may move to the center of discussion a few years later. One of the values of publication is that it keeps information and ideas available over long periods. On the personal level, too, researchers should not be discouraged if first attempts to influence decision making fail; rather, the effort should be conceived of as decades-long. Coherence does not mean oversimple—it means focused.

Respond to Actual Policy Problems

Working politicians and policy-makers are not concerned with theory, however sexy—they are concerned with solving problems. This reality has several implications for communication researchers interested in having some impact in the policy world. Communication researchers for much of the twentieth century have pursued questions very different from those addressed by policy-makers. While First Amendment scholarship focuses on the production of ideas, policy-makers also must address the distribution and use of information as pressing political problems. Audience research has gripped much of the communication research community over the course of the decades during which the pressing policy issue was design of the architecture of the information infrastructure. In both of these exemplar cases there is a relationship between the questions pursued by each but those connections must be explicitly drawn and this is almost never done. While of course any research must be informed by theory and theory will always be the source of any ideas of value to policy-makers, defining a research agenda that is solely driven by theoretical questions may well not yield results of value to policy-makers without additional effort on the part of researchers. Taking an alternative approach need not necessarily require selling out by emptying analyses of a grounding in social theory. Rather, it may be a simple matter of working with presentation modes to ensure that theoretical work and research intersect with the ongoing discourse among policy-makers.

Even when a desired law or regulation is put into place, there is no guarantee that it will be fully or appropriately implemented. On the policy-making side there may be a shortage of funds, lack of nerve, absence of political sponsorship or acceptance by necessary collaborators, or a lack of effective method. The media or other industries to which policies apply may not live up to their commitments. Too, policies once implemented may have effects quite other than those intended. Therefore researchers who are interested in influencing the structure of society and the nature of social processes through the avenue of policy should include evaluation of the effects of the implementation of policies in their research agendas. Without this additional step all other efforts may be for nought.

It is often difficult for policy-makers to link the results of research or ideas with which they are presented to specific decisions they need to make. Researchers can address this problem by making explicit the relationship between their research results and legislation or regulatory decisions facing policy-makers. Linking research to specific pieces of legislation makes it much easier for policy-makers to locate the information and understand its pertinence. When there are no specific pieces of legislation on the table to which research results or theoretical developments apply, it is still valuable for researchers to detail the policy implications of their work. Often policy-makers otherwise simply cannot see the utility of the information that is offered to them.

Adapt Presentation to Audience
Very few policy-makers will have the skills necessary to understand either ideas or data presented in academic terms. The fact that decisions already in place may have been based on intensive empirical investigations is often unknown to contemporary policy-makers. Researchers who seek policy use of their findings, therefore, must repackage their information in forms accessible and usable to policy-makers. Synthesizing complex findings into easily grasped conclusive statements is critical for success, as is contextualizing findings in terms familiar to the policy-making world. Researchers who are able—and willing—to be explicit about the values informing their work and the assumptions embedded within it are also likely to increase their effectiveness with policy-makers.

The arguments built upon research results, too, must be comprehensible to the layperson. Policy-makers will not be attuned to subtleties of theoretical position or to arguments internal to the social sciences over the relative value of various research methods. Rather, the quality of the argument presented will be determinative of their responses. It is worth taking into account during design of presentations that the results of research are often of more interest to those in mid-level decision-making positions than to those at the top. Another danger that attention to the manner of presentation can help avoid is what Wartella describes as "ghettoization" of findings, the application of ideas and research results to single issues when they have more general applicability. Higher education curricula intended to train communication researchers for involvement in the world of policy should incorporate courses that train students in a range of policy research genres that go beyond scholarly journal articles to include executive summaries, reports, press releases, media briefings, and other techniques designed to reach the wide variety of audiences of importance.

The fora for presentation of research results are also important. Contributing to oral debate has already been mentioned. Editorial pieces in newspapers and magazines, letters to the editor, articles for elite but non-academic intellectual magazines, and books written for a trade rather than academic audience are all ways of bringing scholarly ideas and the results of research in front of working policy-makers. For all of these venues, academics must be clear about just which public is being addressed, and adapt language, syntax, and modes of argument as appropriate. The public at large needs a different type of presentation than do working policy-makers, technical specialists, or the cultural and socioeconomic elites who influence policy-makers.

Clarify the Researcher's Role

There are a number of different roles a researcher can play in the policy-making process, from advocate to staffer to expert witness. Not all of what an academic will do in a policy process is necessarily research itself. One may also be called upon to summarize positions of parties, propose alternative policies, assess potential impacts of policies, or simply educate decision makers. Being clear about just what the role is what function is to be filled will enhance a researcher's chances of success in the policy world. A number of the pieces included in this collection identify cases in which researchers were less effective than they might have been because of confusion regarding roles.

Research brokers—insiders in government open to new ideas and willing to bring them into policy-making processes—are one of the most important but least understood and often nonexistent links of the chain of connections needed if research is to effectively influence policy. Brokers may be politicians who are unusually forward-looking or staffers with advanced academic training (often under those whose ideas they subsequently bring into government). Brokers are key to success because they have daily access to decision-making processes, like the industries being regulated but unlike academics brought in upon occasion for expert advice. What it takes to successfully establish such a function will differ, of course, from society to society; it is easier where the population is smaller and the number of hierarchical layers between elites and the general population is lower. The lesson here, though, is the formation of task-specific institutions designed to bring the research and policy communities together can be valuable.

It would be useful were policy-makers to become better equipped to understand and use the results of research. Legal realists early in the twentieth century began to argue that those involved in making, interpreting, and implementing the law ought to pay more attention to the results of empirical research and the thinking of social scientists. As early as the 1940s the suggestion was made that traditional legal education should either be replaced by or be enriched with training in social science research techniques, and the suggestion of enriching law school curricula this way remains on the table today. Many policy-makers work their way into political activity from other educational backgrounds as well, so all teaching in the area of information, communication, and culture may serve as inputs into later policy-making processes via its impact on students.

Become Involved in Institutional Design
This book has not attended to issues raised by policy-making processes as organizational forms or by their communicative aspects, but tinkering with the design of policy-making processes and institutions themselves is among the techniques available for bringing the research and policy communities closer together. The study of policy-making as organizational and communicative forms is likely to yield additional useful insights as to how to do this most successfully. To further this end, researchers ought to be involved in processes of design and review of policy institutions.

One way in which the use of new information technologies can make it easier for communication researchers to influence policy is through establishment of widely available and easily accessible databases of existing research and the formation of national and international research networks. Computerized databases and nongovernmental organizations (NGOs) that include the liaison function in their mission statements have begun to perform some of these functions over the past couple of decades. Recent breakthroughs in the design of knowledge management software should increase capabilities of this kind in future.

Notes

1. Thanks to Andrew Blau for articulating the "weak Baconian" position.

Contributors

James L. Baughman, Professor of Journalism and Mass Communication, University of Wisconsin–Madison, is a historian of American journalism and broadcasting. *The Republic of Mass Culture: Journalism, Filmmaking, and Broadcasting in America since 1941* (Johns Hopkins University Press, 1997) is now in its second edition. His work in the area of policy analysis includes *Television's Guardians: The FCC and the Politics of Programming, 1948–1967* (University of Tennessee Press, 1985).

Sandra Braman, Professor of Communication and Director of Digital Arts, University of Wisconsin–Milwaukee, conducts research on the macro-level effects of the use of new information technologies and their policy implications. Current work includes *Change of State: An Introduction to Information Policy* (MIT Press, forthcoming) and the edited volumes *The Emergent Global Information Policy Regime* (Palgrave Macmillan, 2003) and *The Meta-Technologies of Information: Biotechnology and Communication* (Erlbaum, forthcoming).

William Buxton's research agenda focuses on the history of sociology and relations between sociologists and the nation-state. Recent work includes *Harold Innis in the New Century* (with Charles Acland, McGill-Queen's University Press, 2000).

James W. Carey, Professor of Journalism, Columbia University, is one of the best exemplars of his own argument that the most valuable task of academics seeking to influence policy is developing theories of communication in society. His work has long focused on the implications of communication for the polity, most fully presented in *Communication as Culture: Essays on Media and Society* (Unwin Hyman, 1989).

John Dewey (1859–1952) was a prolific scholar who published his most influential work while on the faculties of the University of Chicago and Columbia University. His work on communication, which he saw as a fundamental concept because it is the process by which both the public and the community are formed out of individuals, has shaped U.S. communications research and thought regarding the functions of the media. Books of import to those concerned about the policy implications of communication include *How We Think* (1910/1933) and *The Public and Its Problems* (1927).

Robert Entman, Professor of Communication, North Carolina State University, does research on the relationships between the media and politics. On the academic side his work includes *Democracy without Citizens: Media and the Decay of American Politics* (Oxford University Press, 1989) and *The Black Image in the White Mind* (with Andrew Rojecki, University of Chicago Press, 2000). Entman's contributions on the policy side include his work as senior author of *Mass Media and Reconciliation*, a report for the Clinton administration's Initiative on Race, and reports for the Commission on Radio and Television Policy and the U.S. House of Representatives Subcommittee on Telecommunications.

Cecilie Gaziano, President, Research Solutions Inc., Minneapolis, does research on media effects that have political implications, including the knowledge gap, the impact of chain newspapers on politics, and the problem of journalistic credibility. Recent work with policy relevance includes "Forecast 2000: Widening Knowledge Gaps" in *Journalism and Mass Communication Quarterly* (1997) and "Chain Newspaper Homogeneity and Presidential Endorsements, 1971–1988" in *Journalism Quarterly* (1989).

Elihu Katz, Distinguished Trustee Professor of Communication, University of Pennsylvania, and Professor Emeritus of Communication, Hebrew University, is a sociologist whose work has focused on the communication issues of the nature of persuasion, the role of media events, interactions between communication and leisure, and cross-cultural differences in the ways in which meaning is made out of media content. Books include *The Export of Meaning* (with Tamar Liebes, 1990), *Media Events* (with Daniel Dayan, 1992), and the edited volume *Canonical Texts in Media Research* (with Tamar Liebes, John Durham Peters, and Avril Orloff, 2002).

Donald Lamberton is an economist who has played a key role in creating the subfield of the economics of information out of formerly disparate strands of work on informational issues. He has also contributed significantly to understanding the implications of communication technologies in the developing world. Lamberton's books include the edited volume *The Economics of Communication and Information* (Edward Elgar, 1996), *Beyond Competition: The Future of Telecommunications* (Elsevier, 1995), and *Communication Economics and Development* (with Meheroo Jusawalla, Elsevier Science, 1982).

Harold Lasswell (1902–1978) was a psychologist who conducted research on the psychological impact of the media on politics. His dissertation, *Propaganda Technique in World War I* (1927) provided the foundation for the study of propaganda. Other works important to policy analysis include *Politics: Who Gets What, When, and How* (1936), *Decision Process: Seven Categories of Functions* (1956), and *Political Communication: The Public Language* (1969).

Paul Felix Lazarsfeld (1901–1976) was a sociologist who played a large role in developing quantitative social science research methods and applying them to the study of communication. He founded the Bureau of Applied Social Research at Columbia University. His own work focused on the effects of communication on politics. Important books include *The People's Choice* (with Bernard Berelson and Hazel Gaudet, 1944) and *Radio Listening in America* (with Robert K. Merton).

Don R. LeDuc, Professor Emeritus of Journalism and Mass Communication, University of Wisconsin–Milwaukee, is coauthor of a textbook on communication law (*Law of Mass Communications*, with Dwight L.

Teeter, Jr. and Bill Loving, Foundation Press, 2001). He has examined the policy treatment of cable television in depth (*Cable Television and the FCC*, Temple University Press, 1974).

Daniel Linz, Professor of Communication and Director of the Law and Society Program at the University of California–Santa Barbara, conducts research on communication and the law, the psychological effects of the media, and interactions between the two.

Bruce M. Owen, Gordon Cain Senior Fellow, Institute for Economic Policy Analysis, Stanford University, and Director, Economists Incorporated, was one of the first economists to study the relationships between the mass media and the telecommunications network. He is best known for his work on the economics of television, including *The Internet Challenge to Television* (Harvard University Press, 1999) and *Video Economics* (with Steven S. Wildman, Harvard University Press, 1992).

Bryant Paul is doing research at the intersection of social and psychological effects of sexually explicit material in the media and communication and the law. He is an assistant professor at Indiana University–Bloomington.

Ivan L. Preston, Professor Emeritus of Journalism and Mass Communication, University of Wisconsin–Madison, conducted research on media effects, deceptiveness in advertising, and advertising regulation. His work includes *The Great American Blow-up: Puffery in Advertising and Selling* (University of Wisconsin Press, 1996) and *The Tangled Web They Weave: Truth, Falsity, and Advertisers* (University of Wisconsin Press, 1994).

Byron Reeves, Paul C. Edwards Professor of Communication, Stanford University, conducts media effects research and analyzes the history of communication research and theory. Recent work with direct policy relevance includes *The Media Equation: How People Treat Computers, Television, and New Media like Real People and Places* (with Clifford Nass, Cambridge University Press, 1996).

Willard D. Rowland, Jr., Professor of Journalism, University of Colorado–Boulder, has served on both sides of the policy/research fence. Before entering academia, he served as director of research and long-range planning for the Public Broadcasting Service. As a scholar, he has examined the nature of the policy-making process, and the implications of communication research for policy. His 1983 book, *The Politics of TV Violence: Policy Uses of Communication Research* (Sage), stands alone in the thoroughness of its analysis of policy uses of research.

Bradley J. Shafer is a partner with Shafer and Associates in Lansing, Michigan. He is also a member of the First Amendment Lawyers Association.

Christopher Simpson, Associate Professor of Journalism, American University, is an investigative journalist and scholar. Recent work includes *Universities and Empire: Money and Politics in the Social Sciences during the Cold War* (The New Press, 1999) and *Presidential Directives: National Security during the Reagan–Bush Years: The Declassified History of the U.S. Political and Military Policy, 1981–1991* (Westview Press, 1995).

Alan G. Stavitsky, Associate Dean and Professor of Journalism, University of Oregon, does research on policy issues raised by U.S. public radio, including changing definitions of the concept of localism, minority preference policies, and factors affecting news in the public radio environment. Recent work includes "Theory into Practice: By the Numbers—The Use of Ratings Data in Academic Research" in *Journal of Broadcasting & Electronic Media* (2000).

Ellen Wartella is Dean of the College of Communication at the University of Texas–Austin. She is an expert on the effects of television and new media on children as well as on the history of mass communication theory and research. Wartella is active as a public intellectual, speaking publicly, sitting on boards of directors, and translating research for the policy arena. One recent effort by Wartella to bridge the research and policy worlds was a report on the effects of new media on children for the Markle Foundation.

Fred W. Weingarten is the Director of the Office for Information Technology Policy of the American Library Association.

Woodrow Wilson (1856–1924) was a scholar of public administration as well as the twenty-eighth president of the United States.

Dolf Zillmann, Professor Emeritus of the University of Alabama, conducted experimental research on behavioral and cognitive effects, of violence, humor, and exemplification. His books include *Exemplification in Communication* (Erlbaum, 2000) and *Connections between Sexuality and Aggression* (Erlbaum, 1998).

Index